The Illustrated Children's DICTIONARY

EDITOR IN CHIEF: **Laurence Urdang**

LONGMEADOW PRESS

Introduction

This dictionary has been planned to help children from the age at which they are established readers until they are old enough to make full use of adult dictionaries. The vocabulary is that of students in their third or fourth to seventh or eighth grade.

To use a dictionary at all, children must have a basic recognition vocabulary. Therefore many words that appear in first reading books have been omitted, as have many simple three- and four-letter words, which children know and find easy to understand, read, and spell. Thus, the book does not contain a full vocabulary of all children in the age range.

Instead, it is designed to help children to read, to understand unfamiliar words, and to develop and increase their vocabulary and confidence in using words. Its purpose is to support them in their efforts to write letters, stories, and accounts of events with increased imagination, understanding, and accuracy. The entries have been selected to reflect the language met in school and in everyday life; the meanings reflect current general usage.

The dictionary should also be used to help children with their spelling: particular care has been taken to include difficult spellings and derivatives. For instance, many children can spell *begin*, but has *beginning* one *n* or two?

Finally, the book has been designed to resemble adult dictionaries in style and format. We hope that it will help to teach children to use dictionaries correctly and encourage them to consult dictionaries regularly, thus forming a habit that will be rewarding throughout a lifetime.

Compiled by Laurence Urdang Associates Ltd., Aylesbury

Contributors:

John Daintith
Alan Isaacs
Patrick Hanks
Sarah Mitchell
Stephanie Pain
Della Summers
Carolyn Herzog
Jennifer Speake
William Gould
Elizabeth Martin
Judith Scott
Catherine Limm

Design: Logos Design, Windsor

Illustrators: Terry Allen Designs Ltd/Roger Courthold, Nick Skelton, Bob Stoneman; Barbosa, Patricia Capon, Roy Castle, Nigel Chamberlain, T. Crosby Smith, Karen Daws, Viv Donkin, Ian Garrard, Tony Gibbons, Donald Harley, Tim Hayward, Richard Hook, Mike Jaroszko, John Keay, Pavel Kostal, Jack Kunz, John Marshall, Donald Myall, David Nockels, Osborne/Marks, Stanley Paine, Gillian Platt, John Rignall, Ian Robertson, Sarson/Bryan, Doug Sheldrake, Michael Strand, Joan Thompson, George Thompson, David Warner, Phil Weare, Roy Wiltshire, Douglas Woodall.

This edition published for Waldenbooks in 1984 by Cathay Books Limited
59 Grosvenor Street
London W1

ISBN 0 681 30376 X

Printed in Portugal by Gris Impressores, S.A.R.L.
D.L. 3845/84

How to use this book

This dictionary contains a list of words together with their meanings and other information. A word, together with all its information, is called an *entry*. Below, you can find some typical dictionary entries with the kind of information given.

headword (entryword)	**a·corn** ('ākôrn) *n.* the fruit of the oak tree, consisting of a smooth nut in a woody cup.
pronunciation	**junk¹** (jungk) *n.* rubbish; something worthless or useless: *that car is complete junk.*
	junk² (jungk) *n.* a Chinese boat with large sails.
definition	**i·vor·y** ('īvərē) *n.* 1. the hard white bony substance of elephants' and walruses' tusks, used for making ornaments and piano keys. 2. a pale cream color.
parts of speech	**jail** (jāl) *n.* a prison. —*vb.* to put in jail; imprison.
example sentence	**tang** (tang) *n.* a strong taste or smell: *the wind had the salt tang of the sea.*
cross reference	**beech** (bēch) *n.* 1. a DECIDUOUS tree with a smooth hard bark, shiny oval leaves, and small edible nuts. 2. the wood of this tree.

acorn

The headword The main words entered in the dictionary are called *headwords*. These are printed in large heavy type. The headword shows you how to spell the word. Sometimes the same spelling is given twice and numbers are added: **junk¹** (rubbish) and **junk²** (a Chinese boat) are different words with widely different meanings, although they have the same spelling. Sometimes there is more than one way of spelling a word: **Gyp·sy** and **Gip·sy** are different spellings of the same word. In this dictionary we put the more common spelling first, but both are correct. The dots in the headword (and other forms of the word) show how the word is divided into syllables (see page v).

The pronunciation This comes after the headword and is placed in brackets. It tells you how to say (pronounce) the word, using some special symbols. Each symbol represents one – only one – English sound. These are explained on page v.

The part of speech Words are classified into a few groups depending on how they are used in a sentence. These are called parts of speech. An abbreviation, printed in italic type, shows the part of speech of each word. Note that some words have more than one part of speech: **jail**, for example, is both a noun (*n.*) and a verb (*vb.*). Abbreviations used for parts of speech are:

noun	*n.*	pronoun	*pron.*
verb	*vb.*	preposition	*prep.*
adjective	*adj.*	interjection	*interj.*
adverb	*adv.*	conjunction	*conj.*

To find out more about these, look up the entries for noun, verb, and so on, in the dictionary.

plural

oc·to·pus ('oktəpəs) *n.,pl.* oc·to·pus·es. a sea creature, ranging from 6 inches to 32 feet in length, with a soft rounded body and eight arms bearing rows of suckers.

comparative (prettier)
superlative (prettiest)

run-on

pret·ty ('pritē) *adj.* pret·ti·er, pret·ti·est. pleasing to the eye or ear. —*adv.* quite: *it hit him pretty hard.* — 'pret·ti·ness *n.*

sub-entry

i·tem ('itəm) *n.* 1. one article from a list, collection, etc: *one item is missing*. 2. a short piece of information or news, esp. in a newspaper. 'i·tem·ize *vb.* i·tem·iz·ing, i·tem·ized. to make a list of items.

present participle (sowing)
past tense (sowed)
past participle (sown)

sow[1] (sō) *vb.* sowing, sowed, sown. to plant (seeds).

octopus

The definition This is the part of the entry that describes what the word means. Note that many words have more than one meaning; **ivory**, for example, can be the material from elephants' tusks or the color of elephants' tusks. Some definitions have an example sentence in *italic* type to help you understand the meaning or to show how the word is used. Words in capital letters, such as DECIDUOUS in the entry for **beech**, are cross-references: they direct you to other words where you can get more information.

Plural nouns Sometimes the plural of a noun is written after the part of speech label to show its spelling: **octopuses**, for example, is the plural of **octopus**. This is only done when the plural spelling is unusual or difficult. Most English nouns form plurals by adding the letter -s (dogs, cats, etc.) or by adding -es (brushes, matches, passes, etc.)

Adjectives The spelling of adjectives can be changed when the adjective is used in comparing two or more nouns. Thus, one can say *this picture is prettier than that one* or *this is the prettier of the two pictures*. **Prettier** is called the *comparative* form of the adjective *pretty*. It is used when speaking of two objects. When three or more pictures are involved one can say *this picture is the prettiest*. **Prettiest** (meaning 'most pretty') is the *superlative* form of the adjective *pretty*. Comparatives and superlatives are only shown when they are difficult or unusual. Most words simply add -er and -est (hard, harder, hardest; strong, stronger, strongest).

Verbs Several forms of verbs are also given in this dictionary. The first form, ending in -ing, is the *present participle*. Thus, **playing** is the present participle of **play**. It is used with the verb *to be* to form different tenses of the verb, as in *I am playing next year* or in *he was sowing seeds yesterday*. The present participle can also be used as a noun, as in *sowing takes place in the Spring*. The second form of the verb gives the *past tense* and *past participle*. The past tense is used in sentences such as *I played last year*. The *past participle* is the word used with the verb *to have* forming sentences such as *he has played*. It is also used with the verb *to be* to form passive sentences. For instance, **kicked**, the past participle of **kick**, is used in *the ball was kicked by the boy*. The past participle is also used as an adjective, as in *a kicked ball*.

Some verbs have a past tense that is different from the past participle. In these cases the past participle is given last. Thus, **sowed** is the past tense of **sow** (*I sowed the seeds*) and **sown** is the past participle (*I have sown the seeds*).

Forms of the verb other than the base form are shown only when they are difficult to spell. Otherwise *-ing* and *-ed* are simply added to the verb (*walk, walking, walked; add, adding, added*; etc.).

Sub-entries These are words or phrases formed from the main entry and given their own definition: **itemize**, for example, is a sub-entry for the main headword **item**. The mark (') in **'i·tem·ize** is called a *stress mark* (see page v).

Run-ons Many words are formed by adding common endings (suffixes) to the main word, and their meanings should be clear without any explanation. These are called *run-on entries*. Some common endings used in this book are:

-ness forms nouns from adjectives: prettiness – the state of being pretty.

-ly forms adverbs from adjectives: happily – in a happy way.

-ation forms nouns from verbs: separation – the act of separating or anything that has been separated.

-ful forms adjectives from nouns: scornful – full of scorn; having scorn.

Pronunciation

The pronunciation of a word is the way it is said. In this dictionary a pronunciation is written in brackets after each headword. If you look at these you will see that some unfamiliar symbols are used. The purpose of these unfamiliar symbols is to ensure that each symbol represents one – and only one – English speech sound. Letters that represent more than one sound are not used in the pronunciation guide. So we do not use *c*, because it could mean either *s* or *k*.

You may have noticed that the same letter is often given a different sound in spelling different words: the *a* in *cat*, *rate* and *farm* is sounded differently. These differences are shown by putting marks (accents) above the letters, as in ā and â.

Another feature of the pronunciation guide is that sometimes two letters are joined together as in c̮h or s̮h. This shows that the letters form one sound, as in *chin* and *shoe*.

The symbol ə (an e upside down) is used in many pronunciations. It represents an indistinct sound – for example the 'a' in ago, the 'o' in *lemon* and the 'e' in *agent* all have the same sound. The symbol is called *schwa*.

Finally, some pronunciations contain a mark (′) to show where the stress (or weight) is put in saying the word. Most words are pronounced in parts (syllables). The word *retire* has two syllables *re·tire* and the mark comes before the stressed syllable ri′tīər shows that the second part of the word is pronounced a little louder: reTIRE.

The table below shows all the different sound symbols used in this dictionary with examples for words in which the sound occurs.

VOWELS		CONSONANTS	
a	*cat*	b	*bat*
ā	*rate*	c̮h	*chin*
â	*farm*	d	*dog*
e	*get*	d̮h	*then*
ē	*keep*	f	*fog*
i	*tin*	g	*get*
ī	*ice*	h	*how*
o	*jog*	j	*joy*
ō	*go*	k	*keep*
ô	*saw*	l	*like*
oi	*boy*	m	*my*
ou	*out*	n	*no*
o͞o	*too*	n͡g	*sing*
o͝o	*look*	p	*put*
u	*hush*	r	*race*
û	*hurt*	s	*sign*
ə	*ago, agent, sanity, lemon, circus*	s̮h	*shoe*
		t	*top*
		t̮h	*thin*
		v	*very*
		w	*wag*
		y	*yell*
		z	*zoo*
		z̮h	*measure*

ab·a·cus ('abəkəs) *n.* a device used for calculating, consisting of a frame in which parallel wires or rods are set with beads or counters that are pushed along them to indicate the quantities.

a·ban·don (ə'bandən) *vb.* to give up or leave behind; surrender, desert, or forsake: *the crew abandoned the sinking ship.* **abandon oneself to** to yield completely to; give way to: *she abandoned herself to grief when her puppy died.*

ab·bey ('abē) *n.* 1. a group of buildings housing a community of monks or nuns. 2. the church belonging to or formerly belonging to such a community.

abbey

ab·bot ('abət) *n.* a man who is the head of a community of monks. See MONASTERY.

ab·bre·vi·ate (ə'brēvēāt) *vb.* **ab·bre·vi·at·ing, ab·bre·vi·at·ed.** to shorten for convenience: *he abbreviated his speech as time was short.* **ab·bre·vi'a·tion** *n.* 1. a shortened form of a word, phrase, or title: *Mr. is an abbreviation for mister.* 2. the act or an instance of abbreviating.

ab·di·cate ('abdəkāt) *vb.* **ab·di·cat·ing, ab·di·cat·ed.** to give up a position of authority to another, esp. voluntarily. **—ab·di'ca·tion** *n.*

aborigine

ab·do·men ('abdəmən) *n.* 1. the lower part of the human body, between the chest and the hips; belly. 2. (in insects, crabs, etc.) the rear part of the body. **—ab·dom·i·nal** (ab'dominəl) *adj.*

a·ble ('ābəl) *adj.* **a·bler, a·blest.** 1. having the talent or opportunity to do something: *I am able to speak French fluently.* 2. generally capable; competent: *he is an able teacher and respected by his pupils.* **a'bil·i·ty** (ə'bilitē) *n.,pl.* **a·bil·i·ties.** talent or skill: *she has the ability to be a great singer.* **'a·bly** *adv.* competently.

ab·nor·mal (ab'nôrməl) *adj.* not normal; strange; unusual; unnatural. **—ab·nor'mal·i·ty** *n.,pl.* **ab·nor·mal·i·ties. —ab'nor·mal·ly** *adv.*

a·board (ə'bôrd) *prep., adv.* on (a boat, train, or airplane): *the passengers came aboard.*

a·bol·ish (ə'bolish) *vb.* to ban or do away with: *he believes that prisons should be abolished.* **ab·o·li·tion** (abə'lishən) *n.* the act or an instance of abolishing; (often used of the ending of slavery) a formal ban.

ab·o·rig·i·ne (abə'rijinē) *n.* 1. one belonging to the original or native race of a country. 2. **Aborigine** a member of the race that originally inhabited Australia. **—ab·o'rig·i·nal** *adj.*

a·bra·sion (ə'brāzhən) *n.* 1. the process of rubbing or scraping. 2. a graze or scratch. **a'bra·sive** *adj.* 1. irritating; harsh: *he has an abrasive personality.* 2. producing roughness, e.g. on a surface. *n.* a gritty substance for cleaning, grinding, or polishing.

a·broad (ə'brôd) *adv.* 1. in or to a country other than one's own: *we went abroad last summer to France.* 2. roaming about; at large: *the lions that escaped from the zoo are still abroad.*

ab·rupt (ə'brupt) *adj.* 1. sudden, sharp, or unexpected: *the blackout accidentally gave the TV program an abrupt ending.* 2. rude; bad-mannered: *his manner was abrupt and she was offended.* **—ab'rupt·ly** *adv.* **—ab'rupt·ness** *n.*

ab·sent ('absənt) *adj.* 1. not present; away. 2. lacking. **absent oneself** (ab'sent) to stay away deliberately: *he absented himself from school to watch football.* **'ab·sence** *n.* a period or state of being away.

ab·so·lute ('absəloot) *adj.* 1. complete; total: *an absolute failure; absolute freedom.* 2. unlimited; unconditional: *the dictator had absolute power over his people.* **—ab·so·lute·ly** (absə'lootlē, 'absəlootlē) *adv.*

ab·sorb (ab'sôrb, ab'zôrb) *vb.* 1. to soak up: *this material will absorb* *moisture.* 2. to take in; understand: *she was able to absorb the lesson easily.* 3. to engage (one's whole attention): *the game absorbed him for three hours.* —**ab'sorb·ent** *adj.*

ab·surd (ab'sûrd, ab'zûrd) *adj.* ridiculous, laughable, or silly. —**ab'surd·i·ty** *n.,pl.* **ab·surd·i·ties.** —**ab'surd·ly** *adv.*

a·bun·dant (ə'bundənt) *adj.* plentiful; ample; lavish: *we have an abundant supply of food for the party.* —**a'bun·dance** *n.* —**a'bun·dant·ly** *adv.*

a·buse *vb.* (ə'byo͞oz) **a·bus·ing, a·bused.** 1. to make the wrong use of: *he abused his position as leader by giving favors to his friends.* 2. to speak rudely to or insult (someone). —*n.* (ə'byo͞os) 1. misuse or ill treatment: *the dog had suffered much abuse from its cruel owners.* 2. insulting language or behavior. —**a'bu·sive** *adj.*

ac·a·dem·ic (akə'demik) *adj.* 1. of or relating to a school, college, or university: *the academic year.* 2. theoretical; not concerned with practical matters. —*n.* a university teacher or research student. —**ac·a'dem·i·cal·ly** *adv.*

ac·cel·er·ate (ak'selərāt) *vb.* **ac·cel·er·at·ing, ac·cel·er·at·ed.** to move or cause to move faster or happen sooner; to speed up. **ac'cel·er·a·tor** *n.* the pedal, or other control used for changing the speed of an engine, esp. that of a car. —**ac·cel·er'a·tion** *n.*

ac·cent *n.* ('aksent) 1. a way of pronouncing words or speaking that indicates the speaker's nationality, region, etc.: *a Brooklyn accent.* 2. the stress put on one SYLLABLE of a spoken word, e.g. *umbrella* has the accent on the middle syllable. 3. a printed mark indicating a stressed syllable or musical note or (in some foreign languages) a particular way of pronouncing a VOWEL.

ac·cept (ak'sept) *vb.* 1. to take something that is offered: *she accepted the flowers gratefully.* 2. to agree or admit: *I accept that I was wrong.* **ac'cept·a·ble** *adj.* worth accepting; satisfactory. —**ac'cept·ance** *n.*

ac·cess ('akses) *n.* 1. the way in; approach: *the only access to the house was up a steep hill.* 2. the opportunity or ability to approach or use: *pianists need to have access to a good piano.* —**ac'ces·si·ble** *adj.*

ac·ces·so·ry (ak'sesərē) *n.,pl.* **ac·ces·so·ries.** 1. an object or article used or worn in addition to something else: *the accessories matching her dress were her handbag and shoes.* 2. (law) a person guilty of helping in a crime: *he was an accessory to murder.*

ac·ci·dent ('aksidənt) 1. an event that is unexpected or outside one's control; an unpleasant event, e.g. a fall or car crash. 2. a chance occurrence: *we met quite by accident.* **ac·ci'den·tal** *adj.* my mistake, or unimportant. —**ac·ci'den·tal·ly** *adv.*

ac·claim (ə'klām) *vb.* to meet with loud or enthusiastic approval; hail or applaud: *the astronauts were acclaimed as heroes.* —*n.* (also **'ac·cla·ma·tion**) (akla'māshən) enthusiastic approval; applause.

ac·com·mo·date (ə'komədāt) *vb.* **ac·com·mo·dat·ing, ac·com·mo·dat·ed.** 1. to house or provide room for: *this hall can accommodate a thousand people.* 2. to adapt to the needs or desires of: *this restaurant is unable to accommodate my tastes.* **ac·com·mo'da·tion** *n.* a place to live or stay in; lodgings.

ac·com·pa·ny (ə'kumpənē) *vb.* **ac·com·pa·ny·ing, ac·com·pa·nied.** to go along with or attend. **ac'com·pa·ni·ment** *n.* the musical support given to a soloist by another instrument.

accordion

ac·cor·di·on (ə'kôrdēən) *n.* a portable musical instrument that works by means of bellows and a keyboard.

ac·count (ə'kount) *n.* 1. a report or description of an event: *the critic gave an enthusiastic account of the play.* 2. a recorded count: *keep an account of all you spend.* 3. a statement of money owing; bill. 4. a banking arrangement by which money can be paid in or drawn out. 5. **ac·counts** (*pl.*) written records of money received and paid. **account for** to explain or answer for: *he could not account for his sudden fear.* **ac'count·ant** *n.* a person whose job is to keep or inspect business accounts.

ac·cu·mu·late (ə'kyo͞omyəlāt) *vb.* **ac·cu·mu·lat·ing, ac·cu·mu·lat·ed.** to pile up or collect: *over the years he accumulated an enormous fortune.* —**ac·cu·mu'la·tion** *n.*

ac·cu·rate ('akyərit) *adj.* 1. containing no mistakes; correct or right: *accurate typing.* 2. precise or exact: *the witness gave an accurate description of the robber.* —**'ac·cu·ra·cy** *n.* —**'ac·cu·rate·ly** *adv.*

ac·cuse (ə'kyo͞oz) *vb.* **ac·cus·ing, ac·cused.** to charge (someone) with doing wrong; blame: *she accused him of stealing her handbag.* —**ac·cu·sa·tion** *n.*

ac·cus·tom (ə'kustəm) *vb.* to make (someone) used to something; adapt: *he was accustomed to a hard life.*

ache (āk) *n.* a prolonged dull pain. —*vb.* **ach·ing, ached.** to feel or produce an ache.

a·chieve (ə'chēv) *vb.* **a·chiev·ing, a·chieved.** 1. to carry out successfully; accomplish: *she achieved top marks in English.* 2. to acquire, often with effort: *achieving success in life is rarely easy.* —**a'chieve·ment** *n.*

ac·id ('asid) *n.* a chemical containing hydrogen that forms salts with metals and alkalis and turns LITMUS paper red. It is often very sour and corrosive. —*adj.* 1. tasting sour or sharp. 2. biting; sarcastic: *his acid remarks hurt her feelings.* —**a·cid·i·ty** (ə'siditē) *n.*

ac·knowl·edge (ak'nolij) *vb.* **ac·knowl·edg·ing, ac·knowl·edged.** 1. to admit to be true, worthy, or valid; concede: *I had to acknowledge that he was a better swimmer than I was.* 2. to indicate that one has received something: *to acknowledge a letter.* 3. to indicate thanks or appreciation: *the actor acknowledged the applause by bowing several times.* 4. to show that one has noticed or recognized (somebody): *he acknowledged me with a smile.* —**ac'knowl·edg·ment** or **ac'knowl·edge·ment** *n.*

acorn

a·corn ('ākôrn) *n.* the fruit of the oak tree, consisting of a smooth nut in a woody cup.

ac·quaint (ə'kwānt) *vb.* (+ *with*) to make known or familiar to: *I will acquaint you with the facts.* **ac'quaint·ance** *n.* 1. a person one knows but who is not a close friend. 2. knowledge or familiarity: *his acquaintance with French is slight.*

ac·quire (ə'kwīər) *vb.* **ac·quir·ing, ac·quired.** to obtain or gain.

ac·quit (ə'kwit) *vb.* **ac·quit·ting, ac·quit·ted.** to declare (a person) not guilty of a charge. **acquit oneself** to play one's part: *in spite of the heat the team members acquitted themselves well.* —**ac'quit·tal** *n.*

a·cre ('ākər) *n.* a measure of land covering 4840 square yards or 43 560 square feet (about 4000 square meters).

ac·ro·bat ('akrəbat) *n.* a person who performs skillful gymnastic tricks. —**ac·ro'bat·ic** *adj.* —**ac·ro'bat·ics** *pl.n.*

ac·tion ('akshən) *n.* 1. the process of acting or doing or the state of being active. 2. something that is done; a deed; act: *I don't approve of his stupid action.* 3. a gesture or movement of the body. 4. the mechanism of a machine, clock, gun, etc. 5. a battle; fighting: *the main action of the war was a battle on the border.* 6. a legal case or proceeding. 7. the events in a play, movie, novel, etc.: *the action takes place in New York.*

ac·tive ('aktiv) *adj.* 1. energetic; busy; lively. 2. in operation; working: *an active volcano is dangerous.* 3. (grammar) indicating that the subject of a verb is doing something or performing an action, e.g. *painted* in the sentence *John painted the picture* is an active verb. Compare PASSIVE. **ac'tiv·i·ty** *n.,pl.* **ac·tiv·i·ties.** 1. movement; liveliness: *there was a lot of activity in the main hall.* 2. something that one does; an interest: *outside activities need not interfere with school work.* —**'ac·tive·ly** *adv.*

ac·tu·al ('akchōōəl) *adj.* existing or real: *what are the actual facts of this case?* —**ac·tu'al·i·ty** *n.* —**'ac·tu·al·ly** *adv.*

a·cute (ə'kyōōt) *adj.* 1. severe or intense: *acute embarrassment.* 2. of grave importance; extremely serious: *an acute shortage of water.* 3. (of the senses) keen or sharp: *she had such acute hearing that she heard the noise long before we did.* 4. (of an illness or disease) quickly and suddenly reaching a crisis: *acute appendicitis.* Compare CHRONIC. **acute angle** an angle of less than 90°. See ANGLE. —**a'cute·ly** *adv.* —**a'cute·ness** *n.*

a·dapt (ə'dapt) *vb.* 1. to adjust to new conditions or circumstances: *when they moved to Alaska they had to adapt to a new climate.* 2. to change or alter for a specific purpose: *the author adapted his novel for the stage.* **a'dapt·er** *n.* a device used to alter a piece of machinery, apparatus, etc., so that it can be used for a different purpose. —**a'dapt·a·ble** *adj.* **ad·ap·ta·tion** (adəp'tāshən) *n.* 1. the act or state of being adapted. 2. something produced by adapting.

ad·der ('adər) *n.* 1. a small poisonous snake found mainly in Europe and Asia; viper. 2. a small harmless North American snake resembling the viper.

adder

ad·dress (ə'dres, 'adres) *n.* 1. the details of the exact location of a house, office, etc. 2. a public speech: *a Presidential address to the nation.* —*vb.* 1. to write an address (def. 1) on a letter, parcel, etc. 2. to speak directly to: *he addressed the whole school.*

ad·e·quate ('adikwit) *adj.* just enough for one's needs; sufficient: *the settlers had an adequate supply of food to last them through the winter.* —**'ad·e·qua·cy** *n.* —**'ad·e·quate·ly** *adv.*

ad·here (ad'hēr) *vb.* **ad·her·ing, ad·hered.** 1. to stick to something: *the mud adhered to my boots.* 2. to support: *I adhere to the principle of free speech.* **ad'her·ent** *n.* a supporter.

ad·he·sion (ad'hēzhən) the process of sticking or adhering to something. **ad'he·sive** *adj.* 1. sticky. 2. able to stick to something. *n.* a substance used for sticking things together; glue.

ad·ja·cent (ə'jāsənt) *adj.* next to; close to: *a house adjacent to a hospital.*

ad·jec·tive ('ajiktiv) *n.* a word used to describe or modify a noun, e.g. *red* in a *red* ball or *small* in a *small* house. —**ad·jec·ti·val** (ajik'tīvəl) *adj.*

ad·just (ə'just) *vb.* 1. to alter or regulate: *if you adjust the controls the machine will work faster.* 2. to change or modify one's behavior; adapt: *they adjusted to a new life in Australia.* —**ad'just·a·ble** *adj.* —**ad'just·ment** *n.*

ad·min·is·ter (ad'ministər) *vb.* 1. to manage or control: *a large staff administers the college.* 2. to hand out or dispense: *the court administers justice.* **ad·min·is'tra·tion** *n.* 1. the act of administering. 2. a government or management: *the present administration has lasted almost six years.* —**ad'min·is·tra·tive** *adj.* —**ad'min·is·tra·tor** *n.*

ad·mi·ra·ble ('admərəbəl) *adj.* worthy of admiration: *an admirable achievement.* —**'ad·mi·ra·bly** *adv.*

ad·mire (ad'mīər) *vb.* **ad·mir·ing, ad·mired.** to regard with respect or praise; appreciate or value: *she admires beautiful things.* **ad·mi·ra·tion** (admə'rāshən) *n.* a feeling of approving pleasure or wonder. See also ADMIRABLE. —**ad'mir·er** *n.*

ad·mis·sion (ad'mishən) *n.* 1. (also **ad·mit·tance**) the power, right, or permission to enter a place. 2. an acknowledgment or confession: *an admission of guilt.*

admit (ad'mit) *vb.* **ad·mit·ting, ad·mit·ted.** 1. to permit entry or access: *the doorman has instructions to admit them both.* 2. to acknowledge or agree, often reluctantly, that something is true or right: *I admit that he is friendly, but I don't like him very much.* 3. to accept responsibility for something: *he was forced to admit his error.* —**ad'mit·ted·ly** *adv.*

ad·o·les·cent (adə'lesənt) *n.* a person who is no longer a child but not yet an adult. —*adj.* 1. growing from childhood to maturity. 2. of or relating to this period: *an adolescent interest in ships led to his joining the Navy.* —**ad·o'les·cence** *n.*

a·dopt (ə'dopt) *vb.* 1. to take legal responsibility for bringing up a child and acting as its parent. 2. to take up (a new idea, plan, fashion, etc.): *the committee voted to adopt the policy suggested.* —**a'dop·tion** *n.*

a·dore (ə'dôr) *vb.* **a·dor·ing, a·dored.** 1. to love with extreme devotion. 2. to have a great liking for: *the miser so adores money that he cannot bear to part with it.* —**a'dor·a·ble** *adj.* —**ad·o·ra·tion** (adə'rāshən) *n.*

a·dult (ə'dult, 'adult) *n.* one who has grown up and reached maturity. —*adj.* mature; fully grown. —**a'dult·hood** *n.*

ad·vance (ad'vans) *vb.* **ad·vanc·ing, ad·vanced.** 1. to move forward; progress: *the general commanded the army to advance across the bridge.* 2. to help the progress of; encourage: *the agreement did much to advance peace.* 3. to make a loan to: *my father advanced me five dollars.* —*n.* 1. a forward progression. 2. a loan or payment. 3. **ad·vanc·es** (*pl.*) gestures or overtures, often of friendship. —**ad'vance·ment** *n.*

ad·van·tage (ad'vantij) *n.* 1. a benefit or privilege: *he had the advantage of wealth.* 2. superiority over another: *the strong have an advantage over the weak.* —**ad·van·ta·geous** (advən'tājəs) *adj.*

ad·ven·ture (ad'venchər) *n.* an exciting, often dangerous, undertaking or experience. **ad'ven·tur·ous** *adj.* bold, daring, or courageous.

ad·verb ('advûrb) *n.* a word used to modify a verb or adjective, usu. expressing a relation of time, place, manner, degree, etc., e.g. *quickly, happily.* —**ad'ver·bi·al** *adj.*

ad·verse (ad'vûrs, 'advûrs) *adj.* acting against something; unfavorable: *fog and ice created such adverse weather conditions that the airplane could not take off.*

ad·ver·tise ('advərtīz) *vb.* **ad·ver·tis·ing, ad·ver·tised.** to give publicity to (something); make widely or well known. **ad·ver·tise·ment** (advər'tīzmənt, ad'vûrtizmənt) *n.* a public announcement on television, on billboards, in newspapers or magazines, etc., designed to attract notice or to promote the sale of goods. —**'ad·ver·tis·er** *n.*

ad·vice (ad'vīs) *n.* guidance or opinion that helps one to solve a problem, decide on a course of action, etc.: *my teacher gave me a lot of advice about careers.*

ad·vise (ad'vīz) *vb.* **ad·vis·ing, ad·vised.** 1. to counsel or give advice. 2. to notify. **ad'vis·a·ble** *adj.* wise; to be recommended. —**ad'vis·er** *n.*

aerosol

aer·o·sol ('eərəsôl) *n.* 1. a mixture of very fine particles suspended in a gas. 2. (also **aerosol bomb, aerosol container,** etc.) a push-button container in which a liquid is kept under pressure, to be released in the form of a spray.

af·fair (ə'feər) *n.* 1. an event or concern: *when I tried to help, he told me that it was his own affair.* 2. a romantic relationship, esp. one carried on outside marriage: *a secret love affair.* 3. **af·fairs** (*pl.*) general business matters.

af·fect[1] (ə'fekt) *vb.* to cause a change; influence: *the weather will affect the success of the parade.*

af·fect[2] (ə'fekt) *vb.* to assume or pretend (an attitude, emotion, etc.): *though she already knew what her birthday present was, she affected surprise.* **af·fec·ta·tion** (afek'tāshən) *n.* an artificial or pretended mannerism: *his French accent is just an affectation since he was raised in Brooklyn.*

af·fec·tion (ə'fekshən) *n.* a friendly, warm, or loving feeling; fondness; love. —**af'fec·tion·ate** *adj.* —**af'fec·tion·ate·ly** *adv.*

af·flu·ent ('aflōōənt) *adj.* having great wealth. —**'af·flu·ence** *n.*

af·ford (ə'fôrd) *vb.* 1. to have enough money or time for something: *we can't afford a new car.* 2. to be prepared or able to do something risky or potentially harmful: *the politician could not afford to do anything that would damage his reputation.*

a·fraid (ə'frād) *adj.* 1. frightened; scared; filled with fear or anxiety: *are you afraid of spiders?* 2. sorry; regretful: *I am afraid I can't help you.*

a·gent ('ājənt) *n.* 1. a person who acts on behalf of his firm or other people, usu. offering a special service: *a travel agent.* 2. a force or influence that produces a change: *bleach is a chemical agent that whitens clothes.* **'a·gen·cy** *n.,pl.* **a·gen·cies.** 1. a business employing agents who act on a client's behalf: *a detective agency.* 2. influence or use: *he gained his position through the agency of friends.*

ag·gra·vate ('agrəvāt) *vb.* **ag·gra·vat·ing, ag·gra·vat·ed.** 1. to make worse: *conditions on the crowded roads were aggravated by the snow.* 2. to annoy or irritate: —**ag·gra'va·tion** *n.*

ag·ile ('ajəl) *adj.* quick-moving or active; deft or nimble: *he had an agile mind and solved the problems faster than anyone else.* —**'ag·ile·ly** *adv.* —**a'gil·i·ty** *n.*

ag·i·tate ('agitāt) *vb.* **ag·i·tat·ing, ag·i·tat·ed.** 1. to disturb or worry: *she became agitated when her son did not return from school.* 2. to stir or shake up (a liquid, etc.). **'ag·i·ta·tor** *n.* a person who encourages others to protest, go on strike, rebel, etc. —**ag·i'ta·tion** *n.*

ag·o·ny ('agənē) *n.,pl.* **ag·o·nies.** intense pain or suffering of the body or mind.

a·gree (ə'grē) *vb.* **a·gree·ing, a·greed.** 1. to feel the same way as another about something; share the same opinion: *I agree with you.* 2. to consent to; approve: *the committee agreed to our plans.* 3. to be consistent; correspond: *they claim that they both saw the accident but their stories don't agree.* **a'gree·a·ble** *adj.* pleasant or amiable: *an agreeable evening.* —**a'gree·a·bly** *adv.* —**a'gree·ment** *n.*

ag·ri·cul·ture ('agrikulchər) *n.* the practice or study of farming. —**ag·ri'cul·tur·al** *adj.*

aid (ād) *vb.* to help or assist; support. —*n.* help or assistance; support: *the country asked for foreign aid after the earthquake.*

air (eər) *n.* 1. the invisible mixture of gases that surrounds the earth. It consists of oxygen and nitrogen, with smaller amounts of other gases. 2. a small movement of the air; a light breeze. 3. the appearance or character of a person or thing: *he had an air of confidence.* 4. a tune or melody. 5. **airs** (*pl.*) affected or snobbish behavior: *he puts on airs.* —*vb.* 1. to make (a room, hall, etc.) open to the air to make it cooler or fresher. 2. to expose (sheets, clothes, etc.) to the air in order to remove all traces of dampness; freshen. 3. to make known or publicize: *you can all air your views at the public meeting.*

air·craft ('eərkraft) *n.,pl.* **air·craft.** any machine capable of flight in the air, including balloons, helicopters, gliders, and airplanes. **aircraft carrier** a large warship with a flat deck designed for the take-off and landing of airplanes.

air·field ('eərfēld) *n.* a place at which aircraft can take off and land, usu. with hard runways.

air·plane ('eərplān) *n.* (often shortened to **plane**) a propeller-driven or jet-driven heavier-than-air craft.

air·port ('eəpôrt) *n.* 1. a place with runways, hangars, workshops, buildings, etc., for airplanes and for receiving and dispatching passengers and freight by air.

aisle (īl) *n.* 1. the way leading down the center of a church to the altar. 2. a passageway separating rows of seats in a theater, movie theater, etc.

a·larm (ə'lârm) *n.* 1. a sound or sign made to warn others of approaching danger. 2. a sudden fear or anxiety. —*vb.* to give a warning to or arouse a feeling of approaching danger: *her threats alarmed me.*

al·bi·no (al'bīnō) *n.,pl.* **al·bi·nos.** a person or animal born with white skin and hair and pink eyes.

al·bum ('albəm) *n.* 1. a book of blank pages used for displaying photographs, stamps, autographs, etc. 2. a phonograph record or a collection of items on one record.

albino

al·co·hol ('alkəhôl) *n.* a colorless liquid that forms the intoxicating content in drinks such as wine, beer, and whiskey. **al·co'hol·ic** *adj.* of or containing alcohol. *n.* a person who regularly drinks alcohol so heavily that his health suffers; one addicted to alcohol. —**'al·co·hol·ism** *n.*

al·cove ('alkōv) *n.* a space or recess set back in the wall of a room, sometimes containing a bed, a seat, or shelves.

a·lert (ə'lûrt) *adj.* 1. watchful; wary; ready for action: *a good soldier remains alert at all times.* 2. lively; wide awake; responsive. —*vb.* to order to stand ready; to make aware: *the alarm alerted the police.*

al·gae ('aljē) *pl.n., sing.* **al·ga** ('algə). a group of moisture-loving plants that includes pond scum and most seaweeds.

airplanes

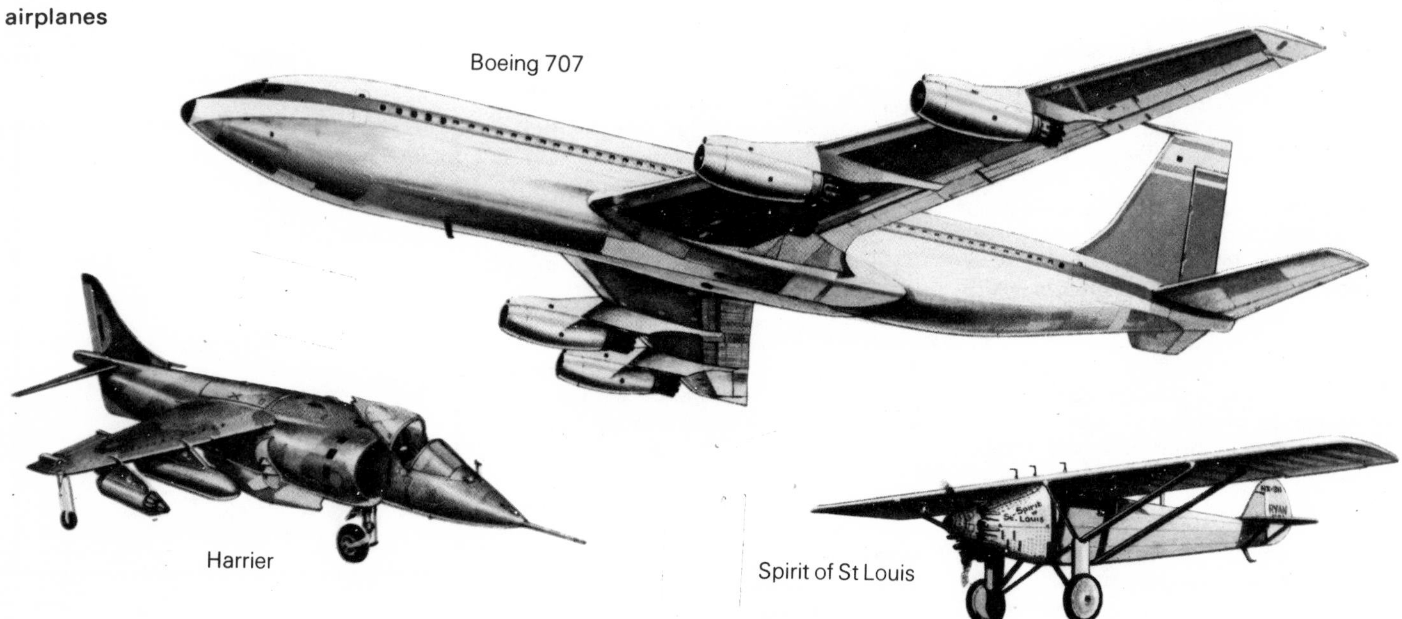

Boeing 707

Harrier

Spirit of St Louis

alligator

al·ge·bra ('aljibrə) *n.* a branch of mathematics that uses letters or symbols in place of numbers in order to simplify complex calculations. —**al·ge·bra·ic** (aljə'brāik) *adj.*

a·li·en ('ālēən) *adj.* 1. foreign. 2. unnatural; contrary to: *violence is alien to her nature.* —*n.* a foreigner, usu. one living in a country not his own. '**a·li·en·ate** *vb.* **a·li·en·at·ing, a·li·en·at·ed.** to lose the affection or interest of: *by her bad behavior Anne alienated nearly all her friends.* —**a·li·en'a·tion** *n.*

a·light[1] (ə'līt) *adj.* 1. on fire. 2. bright; gleaming: *his face was alight with happiness.*

a·light[2] (ə'līt) *vb.* **a·light·ing, a·light·ed** *or* **a·lit.** 1. to get down from a bus, train, etc. 2. (of winged creatures or anything airborne) to settle or take up a perch: *the sparrow alighted on the branch.*

al·ka·li ('alkəlī) *n.,pl.* **al·ka·lis** *or* **al·ka·lies.** a chemical, like soda or ammonia, that forms salts with acids and turns LITMUS paper blue. —'**al·ka·line** *adj.*

al·lege (ə'lej) *vb.* **al·leg·ing, al·leged.** 1. to assert or declare (something) without proof: *he alleges he is a fine swimmer but I've never seen him in the water.* —**al·le·ga·tion** (alə'gāshən) *n.* an unsupported assertion.

al·le·giance (ə'lējəns) *n.* the loyalty and service given to a ruler, leader, country etc.: *they pledged their allegiance to America.*

al·li·ance (ə'līəns) *n.* 1. a friendly union of countries, families, or other groups. 2. an agreement (usu. between nations) to work together for a joint aim.

al·li·ga·tor ('aləgātər) *n.* a large fish-eating REPTILE having very long jaws with a large number of teeth. It lives in some lakes, swamps, and rivers of subtropical America and China.

al·lo·cate ('aləkāt) *vb.* **al·lo·cat·ing, al·lo·cat·ed.** to set aside (money, time, etc.) for a specific purpose; arrange as a person's share: *the judges allocated prizes to the three top sportsmen of the year.* —**al·lo'ca·tion** *n.*

al·lot (ə'lot) *vb.* **al·lot·ting, al·lot·ted.** to deal out, distribute, or assign: *the teacher allotted us three hours of homework a week.*

al·low (ə'lou) *vb.* 1. to permit. 2. to arrange to give (money, time, etc.): *they allowed us 5 dollars toward expenses.* 3. to leave time or room for: *I allowed myself ten minutes to get to the station.* **al'low·ance** *n.* a fixed sum of money given regularly for a special purpose: *a monthly clothes allowance.*

al·ly *vb.* (ə'lī) **al·ly·ing, al·lied.** to unite or work together for a common purpose often by means of a treaty or agreement. **allied to** connected with or related to. —*n.* ('alī), *pl.* **al·lies.** a country, person or group that unites with others, esp. against a common enemy; friend.

al·mond ('âmənd, 'amənd) *n.* the edible nut found inside the stone of the fruit of the sweet almond tree. When ground, almonds form the main ingredient of MARZIPAN.

al·pha·bet ('alfəbet) *n.* the set of letters, usu. in a certain order, used in a language. '**al·pha·bet·ize** *vb.* **al·pha·bet·iz·ing, al·pha·bet·ized.** to arrange (names, words, etc.) so that the first letters have the same order as the alphabet: *the words in a dictionary are alphabetized.* —**al·pha'bet·i·cal** *adj.*

al·read·y (ôl'redē) *adv.* 1. by a certain time: *I have already eaten.* 2. so soon: *is it lunchtime already?*

al·tar ('ôltər) *n.* 1. the table found in the east end of Christian churches at which Holy Communion is celebrated. 2. a raised flat-topped structure such as a table or large rock on which offerings of wine, food, etc., and sometimes sacrifices of animals are made to a god.

al·ter ('ôltər) *vb.* to change; to make or become different: *his watch was fast so he altered it to the correct time.* —**al·ter'a·tion** *n.*

al·ter·nate *vb.* ('ôltərnāt) **al·ter·nat·ing, al·ter·nat·ed.** to vary with something or between two choices: *she alternated between crying and laughing.* —*adj.* ('ôltərnit) every other: *they go to Chicago on alternate weekends.* **al·ter·na·tive** (ôl'tûrnətiv) *adj.* another possibility; different: *an alternative method. n.* a choice: *you have no alternative but to come tomorrow.*

al·though (ôl'thō) *conj.* even though; in spite of the fact that: *Tom was not given the prize, although he deserved it.*

al·ti·tude ('altitood, 'altityood) *n.* height above sea-level: *pilots use breathing apparatus at high altitudes.*

al·to·geth·er (ôltə'gedhər) *adv.* entirely; completely: *you missed the point of the lecture altogether.*

alphabet: Roman (top); Greek (center); Hebrew (bottom).

a·lu·mi·num (ə'loōminəm) *n.* a strong lightweight silver-white metal made chiefly from the mineral bauxite and often used for making aircraft parts, technical instruments, kitchen equipment, etc. Chemical symbol: Al.

am·a·teur ('amәchoŏr, 'amәtûr) *n.* a person who does something (esp. sport, acting, or playing a musical instrument) in his spare time, out of interest rather than for money.

a·maze (ә'māz) *vb.* **a·maz·ing, a·mazed.** to astonish, bewilder, or surprise greatly: *the magician amazed us by making himself invisible.* —**a'maze·ment** *n.*

am·bas·sa·dor (am'basәdәr) *n.* a minister sent to represent his country in a foreign land.

am·ber ('ambәr) *n.* a hard brownish-yellow substance formed from resin produced by certain trees millions of years ago. It is used for decoration and jewelry. —*adj.* of the color of amber.

am·big·u·ous (am'bigyoōәs) *adj.* having more than one possible meaning, e.g. "blue man's bicycle for sale" is ambiguous. (Does it mean a blue man or a blue bicycle?) **am·bi·gu·i·ty** (ambi'gyoōitē) *n.,pl.* **am·bi·gu·i·ties.** anything that is ambiguous.

am·bi·tion (am'bishәn) *n.* a strong desire for success, power, or fame, esp. in a job or any competitive activity: *her ambition is to be the first woman president.* —**am'bi·tious** *adj.*

am·bu·lance ('ambyәlәns) *n.* a vehicle designed to carry sick or injured people to hospital.

am·bush ('amboŏsh) *n.* a trap in which a force lies in wait to make an unexpected attack. —*vb.* to attack by surprise.

a·men·i·ty (ә'menәatē, ә'mēnәtē) *n.,pl.* **a·men·i·ties.** something in a place that makes life easy or convenient, e.g. good shops or a frequent bus service.

am·e·thyst ('amithist) *n.* a clear purple form of a mineral called quartz, used as a precious stone.

a·mi·a·ble ('āmēәbәl) *adj.* friendly, affectionate, or likable: *my father was an amiable man who never lost his temper.*

am·mo·ni·a (ә'mōnyә) *n.* 1. a strong-smelling colorless gas made up of nitrogen and hydrogen and used in the manufacture of fertilizers. 2. a household cleaning liquid made up of ammonia and water.

am·mu·ni·tion (amyә'nishәn) *n.* materials such as gunpowder, bullets, shells, grenades, bombs, and rockets, that are used in a military attack.

am·nes·ty ('amnistē) *n.,pl.* **am·nes·ties.** a general pardon granted for crimes, esp. to political offenders: *the rebel leader was released from prison when the new government granted an amnesty.*

a·mount (ә'mount) *n.* quantity; sum; full value: *he only paid half the amount that he owed me.* —*vb.* (+ *to*) to add up to or equal: *so far the fund amounts to twenty dollars.*

am·phib·i·an (am'fibēәn) *n.* 1. an animal able to live both on land and in water. 2. a tank or other vehicle adapted to travel on land and in water. —**am'phib·i·ous** *adj.*

am·phi·the·a·ter ('amfithēәtәr) *n.* a round or oval open area or building in which seats are arranged in tiers around and above a central stage or arena, used for plays, games, etc., esp. in classical times.

am·ple ('ampәl) *adj.* 1. large or spacious: *the house has two ample living rooms.* 2. more than enough: *two cakes will be ample for me.*

am·pli·fy ('amplәfī) *vb.* **am·pli·fy·ing, am·pli·fied.** 1. to enlarge or expand (a statement, description, etc.): *you will have to amplify your explanation before I can understand it.* 2. to make louder. **'am·pli·fi·er** *n.* a piece of electrical equipment used to increase the sound volume of record players, musical instruments, etc.

am·pu·tate ('ampyoōtāt) *vb.* **am·pu·tat·ing, am·pu·tat·ed.** to cut off (a hand, arm, leg, etc.) usu. by means of a surgical operation. —**am·pu'ta·tion** *n.*

a·muse (ә'myoōz) *vb.* **a·mus·ing, a·mused.** 1. to be humorous; make (a person) smile or laugh. 2. to entertain or occupy pleasantly: *we managed to amuse ourselves while waiting for him.* —**a'muse·ment** *n.*

an·a·lyze ('anәlīz) *vb.* **an·a·lyz·ing, an·a·lyzed.** 1. to examine or separate (something) into its parts in order to learn what it is made up of: *the chemist analyzed the drink to see if it contained poison.* 2. to study all the details of (something): *having analyzed the situation I can see no easy solution.* **a·nal·y·sis** (ә'nalisis) *n.,pl.* **a·nal·y·ses** (ә'nalisēz). the act or result of analyzing something.

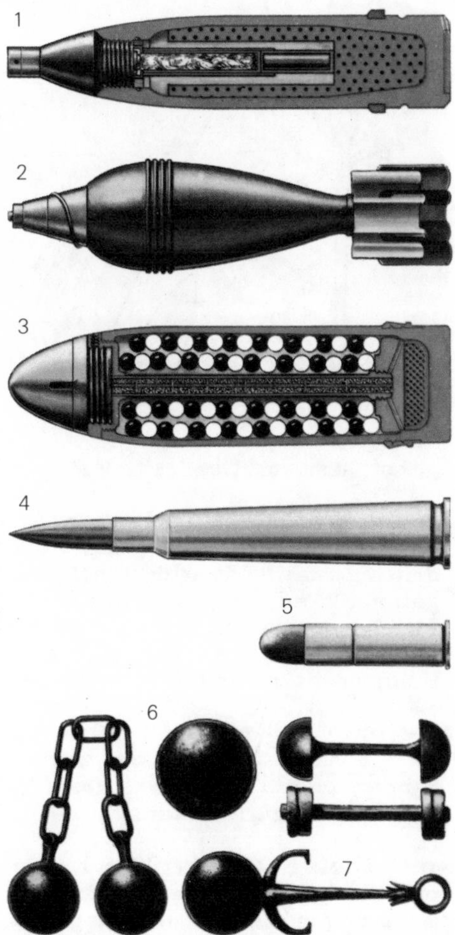

ammunition: 1 high explosive shell; 2 light mortar; 3 shrapnel shell; 4 high velocity rifle bullet; 5 revolver cartridge; 6 cannonball; 7 assortment of chain and bar shot.

an·ar·chy ('anәrkē) *n.* a state of society without any law or government. **an·ar·chist** ('anәrkist) *n.* a person who does not believe in government.

a·nat·o·my (ә'natәmē) *n.,pl.* **a·nat·o·mies.** 1. the study of the structure of the body. 2. the structure of the human body or an animal or plant. —**an·a·tom·i·cal** (anә'tomikәl) *adj.* —**a'nat·o·mist** *n.*

an·ces·tor ('ansestәr) *n.* a person from whom one is descended, esp. a long-dead relative. —**an'ces·tral** *adj.* —**'an·ces·try** *n.,pl.* **an·ces·tries.**

anchor: 1 admiralty type; 2 stockless.

an·chor ('an͡gkər) *n.* 1. a heavy metal object that prevents a ship from drifting away by securing it to the sea bottom. 2. anything that ties down, fastens, or gives security. —*vb.* 1. to lower the anchor of (a ship, etc.). 2. to tie up or make secure.

an·cient ('ānshənt) *adj.* 1. belonging to the earliest times: *the Roman Empire existed in ancient times.* 2. very old: *an ancient man.*

an·es·thet·ic (anis'thetik) *n.* a drug or other agent used to put a person to sleep or produce loss of feeling in a part of his body. It is used during surgical operations. **an·es·the·tize** (ə'nesthətīz) *vb.* **an·es·the·tiz·ing, an·es·the·tized.** to treat (a person or part of the body) with an anesthetic. —**a'nes·the·tist** *n.*

an·gel ('ānjəl) *n.* 1. (in the Christian and other religions) an immortal being acting as an attendant to God and a messenger between God and man, usu. represented in pictures as having human form and wings. 2. anyone thought of as being particularly kind and good. —**an·gel·ic** (an'jelik) *adj.*

an·ger ('an͡ggər) *n.* a feeling of fury or resentment caused by a real or imagined wrong. —*vb.* to make angry; enrage.

an·gle[1] ('an͡ggəl) *n.* 1. a measure of the space between two straight lines extending from a common point. 2. the shape of a projecting corner. 3. a way of looking at things; viewpoint. —*vb.* **an·gling, an·gled.** to point, divert, or propel at an angle: *the tennis-player angled the ball.*

an·gle[2] ('an͡ggəl) *vb.* **an·gling, an·gled.** 1. to fish with a rod and line. 2. (+ *for*) to invite or try for by sly or clever means: *he was angling for a compliment by mentioning his new clothes.* —'**an·gler** *n.*

An·gli·can ('an͡gglikən) *adj.* belonging to the Church of England. —*n.* a member of the Church of England.

an·gu·lar ('an͡ggyələr) *adj.* 1. having or displaying angles or sharp edges. 2. bony; thin: *an angular face.* 3. acting or moving awkwardly; stiff.

an·i·mal ('anəməl) *n.* any living thing that is not a plant. —*adj.* relating to or concerned with animals: *animal behavior; animal fats.*

an·i·mate *vb.* ('anəmāt) **an·i·mat·ing, an·i·mat·ed.** 1. to give life to (something); make alive. 2. to make lively. —*adj.* ('anəmit) alive; living: *plants are animate objects.* **an·i·mat·ed** *adj.* ('anəmātid) 1. full of life; lively. 2. appearing to be alive or moving: *an animated cartoon.*

an·kle ('an͡gkəl) *n.* the part of a person's leg between the foot and the shin.

an·nex *vb.* (ə'neks) 1. to join or add something to something larger or more important; unite. 2. to take political control or possession of (territory, another country, etc.): *the powerful country annexed a neighboring state.* —*n.* ('aneks) something that is added or joined, esp. a small building to a larger one: *a hotel annex.*

an·ni·hi·late (ə'nīəlāt) *vb.* **an·ni·hi·lat·ing, an·ni·hi·lat·ed.** 1. to destroy completely; obliterate: *the town was annihilated by enemy bombs.* 2. (informal) to defeat soundly: *the visiting hockey team annihilated the opposition.*

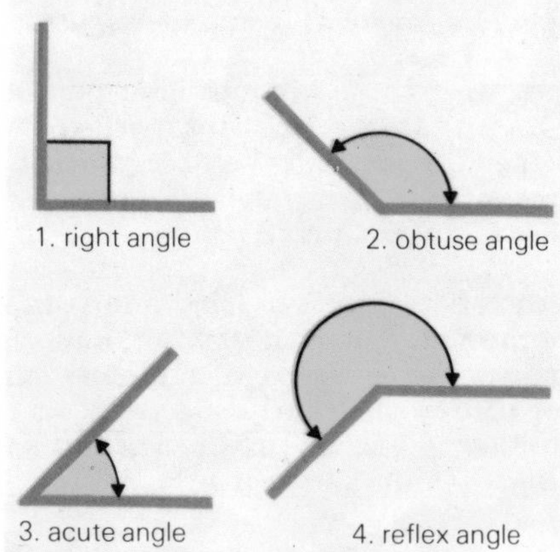

angle

an·ni·ver·sa·ry (anə'vûrsərē) *n.,pl.* **an·ni·ver·sa·ries.** a special day that marks an event, like a wedding, that took place on that date in some previous year.

an·nounce (ə'nouns) *vb.* **an·nounc·ing, an·nounced.** 1. to tell of publicly; proclaim: *the hostess announced that dinner would be late.* 2. to make known the arrival or presence of: *the doorman announced the guests as they came in.* **an'nounc·er** *n.* someone who announces something, esp. on radio or television. —**an'nounce·ment** *n.*

an·noy (ə'noi) *vb.* to irritate, bother, disturb, or cause trouble: *the noise from the street annoyed the people in the office.* —**an'noy·ance** *n.*

an·nu·al ('anyōōəl) *adj.* 1. concerning or relating to a year: *annual income.* 2. occurring or recurring every year; yearly: *an annual vacation.* 3. (of a plant) living for only one year or growing season. —*n.* 1. a plant living for only one year or growing season. 2. a yearly publication. —'**an·nu·al·ly** *adv.*

a·noint (ə'noint) *vb.* to put oil on, esp. as part of a ceremony.

a·non·y·mous (ə'nonəməs) *adj.* 1. an unknown or unnamed author or source; coming from such a source: *an anonymous gift.* 2. undistinguished or unremarkable; lacking individuality: *the stranger was completely lost in the anonymous streets.* —**an·o·nym·i·ty** (anə'nimitē) *n.* —**a'non·y·mous·ly** *adv.*

an·swer ('ansər) *n.* 1. a reply to a question, suggestion, etc.; response: *he knew all the answers to the examination questions.* 2. to be like; fit: *the suspect answered the description of the wanted man.* —*vb.* make an answer to (a person or question). '**an·swer·a·ble** *adj.* (+ *for*) responsible: *the teacher was answerable for the behavior of his pupils on the school outing.*

ant (ant) *n.* any of several kinds of small insect that live in complex social groups.

ant·arc·tic (ant'ârktik) *adj.* (sometimes **Antarctic**) of or relating to the cold region of the earth surrounding the South Pole. **Ant'arc·ti·ca** *or* **the Antarctic** *n.* the snow-covered continent in which the South Pole lies. Compare ARCTIC.

an·te·lope ('antəlōp) *n.* one of a large and varied family of hoofed MAMMALs that have horns on their heads, and are found mainly in Africa and Asia.

an·ten·na (an'tena) *n.* 1. (*pl.* **an·ten·nae** (an'tenē)) one of two long thin feelers on an insect's head. 2. (*pl.* **an·ten·nas**) a metal conductor, usu. a rod or wire, by means of which radio and television signals can be transmitted or received. Sometimes called an **aerial.**

an·them ('anthəm) *n.* a song or hymn, usu. expressing a particular sentiment such as praise, patriotism, etc.

an·thol·o·gy (an'tholəjē) *n.,pl.* **an·thol·o·gies.** a collection of poems, stories, etc., often reflecting a particular theme: *an anthology of detective stories.*

an·ti·freeze ('antifrēz) *n.* a liquid with a low freezing point added to the radiator of a motor vehicle to prevent the water from freezing in very cold weather.

an·tique (an'tēk) *adj.* 1. of or belonging to the distant past; ancient. 2. (of an article, work of art, piece of furniture, etc.) of a period relatively much earlier than the present, esp. more than a hundred years old. —*n.* an article, work of art, piece of furniture, etc., from an earlier period than the present.

an·ti·sep·tic (anti'septik) *n.* a substance used to sterilize wounds, etc., by destroying the tiny organisms that cause infection. —*adj.* preventing infection.

ant·ler ('antlər) *n.* one of the bony growths, usu. having branches, on the head of a male deer. Antlers are cast off and grown again every year.

an·vil ('anvil) *n.* 1. an iron block on which metals can be beaten into various shapes. 2. one of the three small bones in the middle ear that transmit sounds to the inner ear. See EAR.

anx·i·e·ty (ang'zīitē) *n.,pl.* **anx·i·e·ties.** uneasiness or worry; great apprehension. —**anx·ious** ('angkshəs) *adj.* —'**anx·ious·ly** *adv.*

a·part·ment (ə'pârtmənt) *n.* a residence consisting of a self-contained set of rooms within a house.

a·pex ('āpeks) *n.* the top, tip, summit, or highest point of something: *the apex of a triangle.*

a·pol·o·gy (ə'poləjē) *n.,pl.* **a·pol·o·gies.** an admission of blame and expression of regret offered for some error, injury, offense, etc.: *he gave me an apology for his rudeness.* **a'pol·o·gize** *vb.* **a·pol·o·giz·ing, a·pol·o·gized.** to express an apology to someone. —**a·pol·o·get·ic** (əpolə'jetik) *adj.*

a·pos·tle (ə'posəl) *n.* one of the original followers of Jesus Christ who spread His teaching throughout the ancient world; disciple.

ap·pa·rat·us (apə'ratəs, apə'rātəs) *n.,pl.* **ap·pa·rat·us** *or* **ap·pa·rat·us·es.** a collection of instruments, tools, or other equipment used for a specific purpose, e.g. in a scientific experiment: *the photographer's apparatus.*

ap·par·ent (ə'parənt) *adj.* 1. capable of being clearly seen; visible. 2. capable of being easily understood; evident; obvious. 3. seeming; according to appearances: *he showed apparent distress at the news.*

ap·peal (ə'pēl) *n.* 1. an earnest request for help, mercy, etc.: ***she made an emotional appeal for donations to help the fire victims.*** 2. an application to an impartial source to support a statement, settle an argument, etc. 3. (law) an application to a higher court to look again at the decision of a lower court. 4. attraction; interest: ***this party has lost its appeal since the food has run out.*** —*vb.* 1. to make an appeal for help or mercy or about a problem, argument, or decision. 2. (law) to make an appeal to a higher court. 3. to attract, be of interest, etc.: ***the idea appeals to me.***

ap·pear (ə'pēr) *vb.* 1. to become visible; come into sight: ***she appeared in the distance.*** 2. to give an impression; seem: ***he appeared to be unwell.*** 3. to be apparent or obvious: ***it appears that we have missed the last bus.*** 4. to make an appearance in public: ***his new novel will appear in the spring.*** 5. to come into existence: ***legs appear in the tadpole when it is several weeks old.*** —**ap'pear·ance** *n.*

ap·pen·dix (ə'pendiks) *n.,pl.* **ap·pen·dix·es** *or* **ap·pen·di·ces** (ə'pendisēz). 1. extra material at the end of a book or similar publication giving additional information, etc. 2. a narrow tubelike part of the digestive system. **ap·pen·di·ci·tis** (əpendi'sītis) *n.* a disease caused by inflammation of the appendix.

ap·pe·tite ('apitīt) *n.* the desire for something to satisfy one's bodily needs, esp. for food and drink: ***the strenuous exercise gave her an enormous appetite.***

ap·plaud (ə'plôd) *vb.* 1. to express approval, appreciation, or praise of someone, esp. by clapping the hands together. 2. to approve of or welcome: ***they all applauded his decision.*** —**ap'plause** *n.*

ap·ply (ə'plī) *vb.* **ap·ply·ing, ap·plied.** 1. to request something; offer oneself for consideration for a job, favor etc.: ***he applied for a raise in pay.*** 2. to be relevant or of use to a particular thing: ***the rules do not apply to this game.*** 3. to put something on top of something else; cover or bring into contact with: ***they applied a new coat of paint.*** 4. to devote (something) to a particular use: ***he applied his scientific knowledge to the problem.*** 5. to devote oneself diligently: ***he applied himself to his work.*** **ap·pli·cant** ('aplikənt) *n.* someone who applies for a job, etc. **ap·pli·ça·ble** ('apləkəbəl, ə'plikəbəl) *adj.* relevant; connected with. —**ap·pli'ca·tion** *n.*

ap·point (ə'point) *vb.* 1. to select, nominate, or designate: ***he was appointed chairman.*** 2. to fix or determine, esp. by agreement: ***they appointed next Thursday as the time for their meeting.*** **ap'point·ment** *n.* an appointed time or position.

ap·pre·ci·ate (ə'prēshēāt) *vb.* **ap·pre·ci·at·ing, ap·pre·ci·at·ed.** 1. to value or regard highly; esteem: ***he appreciated their kindness.*** 2. to be aware or conscious of: ***they appreciated the difficulty of the task ahead.*** 3. to increase in value: ***the ring cost 500 dollars but it will appreciate when the price of gold goes up.*** —**ap·pre·ci'a·tion** *n.*

ap·pren·tice (ə'prentis) *n.* 1. a person who is learning a trade or craft, usu. receiving quite low wages in return for instruction from his employer: ***a carpenter's apprentice.*** 2. any beginner in a craft, skill, or profession. —**ap'pren·tice·ship** *n.*

ap·proach (ə'prōch) *vb.* 1. to come nearer or near to: ***they approached the house.*** 2. to make a proposal or advance to (someone): ***he approached the sergeant with his plan.*** —*n.* 1. the act of coming near: ***their approach was very noisy.*** 2. the means of access to a place, such as a road: ***the approach to the house was up a hill.*** 3. the act or method of making contact with or presenting a proposal to someone or of dealing with a problem: ***her approach to the job was original.***

ap·pro·pri·ate *adj.* (ə'prōprēit) suitable or fitting: ***his closing remarks seemed to be very appropriate.*** —*vb.* (ə'proprēāt) **ap·pro·pri·at·ing, ap·pro·pri·at·ed.** 1. to set aside, esp. for a particular purpose: ***the university appropriated funds for the new building.*** 2. to take over for oneself: ***he appropriated the baseball bat and would let no one else use it.***

ap·prove (ə'proōv) *vb.* **ap·prov·ing, ap·proved.** to agree to; officially confirm: ***the committee approved the plans to build a new road.*** **approve of** to regard favorably; think well of: ***he approved of her new dress.*** **ap'prov·al** *n.* the act of approving or agreeing.

ap·prox·i·mate *adj.* (ə'proksəmit) 1. nearly exact: ***the approximate time.*** 2. almost or very nearly the same as: ***he sketched an approximate circle.*** 3. rough or inaccurate: ***an approximate total.*** —*vb.* (ə'proksəmāt) **ap·prox·i·mat·ing, ap·prox·i·mat·ed.** 1. to estimate; guess at: ***we have approximated a solution to the problem.*** 2. to approach or come near to in quality, amount, style, etc.: ***his painting approximates that of Picasso.*** —**ap'prox·i·mate·ly** *adv.* —**ap·prox·i'ma·tion** *n.*

ap·ri·cot ('aprikot, 'āprikot) *n.* a soft-skinned orange-colored fruit rather like a peach and related to the plum. —*adj.* of the color of the apricot.

aq·ua·lung ('akwəlung) *n.* a device used by underwater swimmers consisting of cylinders of compressed air connected to a face mask.

a·quat·ic (ə'kwatik, ə'kwotik) *adj.* living in or connected with water: ***aquatic sports.***

aq·ue·duct ('akwidukt) *n.* a channel or canal made for carrying water, often over a bridge across a valley.

aqueduct

arc (ârk) *n.* 1. part of the circumference of a circle or of some other curved line. See GEOMETRY. 2. anything bow-shaped.

arch (ârch) *n.* 1. a curved structure, often over an entrance or sometimes supporting a bridge, and generally made of stone or brick. 2. (also **arch·way**) a passageway or entrance with a curved roof. 3. the curved part of the sole of the foot between the ball and the heel. 4. anything that is curved like an arch. —*vb.* to form an arched shape: *the angry cat arched its back.*

ar·chae·ol·o·gy (ârkē'oləjē) *n.* the study of ancient times based on the evidence of relics and remains. —**ar·chae·o·log·i·cal** (ârkēə'lojikəl) *adj.* —**ar·chae'ol·o·gist** *n.*

arch·bish·op (ârch'bishəp) *n.* a bishop of the highest rank with authority over other bishops.

arch·er ('ârchər) *n.* a person who shoots with a bow and arrows, now usu. in sport but formerly in battle. **'ar·cher·y** *n.* the art and practice of shooting with a bow and arrows.

ar·chi·tect ('ârkitekt) *n.* a person who plans and designs buildings. **'ar·chi·tec·ture** *n.* 1. the art of planning and designing buildings. 2. the style of building. —**ar·chi'tec·tur·al** *adj.*

arc·tic ('ârktik) *adj.* 1. (sometimes **Arctic**) of or relating to the cold region of the earth surrounding the North Pole. 2. extremely cold. **the Arctic** the area of ice-covered seas and islands in which the North Pole is situated. Compare ANTARCTIC.

ar·e·a ('eərēə) *n.* 1. a region or district: *a country area.* 2. any space: *a shopping area.* 3. the general scope of a subject, field of study, or activity: *his interest was in the area of drama.* 4. the size of the surface of a square, circle, etc.

a·re·na (ə'rēnə) *n.* 1. the central circular or oval area in a Roman AMPHITHEATER or a modern sports stadium. 2. any area where action takes place: *the political arena.*

ar·gue ('ârgyōō) *vb.* **ar·gu·ing, ar·gued.** 1. to disagree or quarrel with someone. 2. to discuss or put forward (a matter, etc.) with someone. —**'ar·gu·ment** —**ar·gu'men·ta·tive** *adj.*

ar·id ('arid) *adj.* 1. (of land) dry; parched; infertile or barren. 2. dull and uninteresting; fruitless. —**a·rid·i·ty** (ə'riditē) *or* **'ar·id·ness** *n.*

ar·mor ('ârmər) *n.* 1. protective covering, usu. made of metal and formerly worn to shield the body in battle. 2. heavy metal plates used to protect tanks, warships, etc.

ar·my ('ârmē) *n.,pl.* **ar·mies.** 1. a nation's military force specially trained for war. 2. a huge throng: *an army of locusts destroyed the crops.*

ar·range (ə'rānj) *vb.* **ar·rang·ing, ar·ranged.** 1. to put in order: *please arrange these flowers.* 2. to organize, fix, or plan: *I will arrange a trip to the zoo.* 3. to adapt a musical composition for different instruments or voices. —**ar'range·ment** *n.*

ar·rest (ə'rest) *vb.* 1. to seize (a suspected criminal) by warrant or other authority; take into custody. 2. to stop or check (movement, a process, etc.): *the doctor was able to arrest the bleeding immediately.* 3. to capture and hold (a person's attention, etc.). —*n.* the act of arresting.

ar·rive (ə'rīv) *vb.* **ar·riv·ing, ar·rived.** 1. to come to be present at a place or point in time; come to; reach: *after a hard climb we arrived at the top of the hill.* 2. (of a time) to be or come: *the day of the wedding arrived at last.* **ar'riv·al** *n.* 1. the act of arriving. 2. a person or thing that arrives.

ar·se·nic ('ârsənik) *n.* a chemical element, grayish-white in color, that is used in rat poisons, medicines, etc. Chemical symbol: As.

ar·ter·y ('ârtərē) *n.,pl.* **ar·ter·ies.** 1. a vessel in the body that carries blood away from the heart. 2. the main channel in a series of smaller ones as in a road or drainage system. —**ar·te·ri·al** (âr'tērēəl) *adj.*

art·ful ('ârtfəl) *adj.* 1. crafty; cunning: *the artful fox stole all the chickens.* 2. skillful or ingenious. —**'art·ful·ly** *adv.* —**'art·ful·ness** *n.*

ar·ti·cle ('ârtikəl) *n.* 1. a piece of writing on a specific topic, esp. in a newspaper or magazine. 2. any individual object: *an article of furniture.* 3. (in some languages) a word that precedes and signifies a noun, as in English, 'the' (definite article) and 'a' or 'an' (indefinite article).

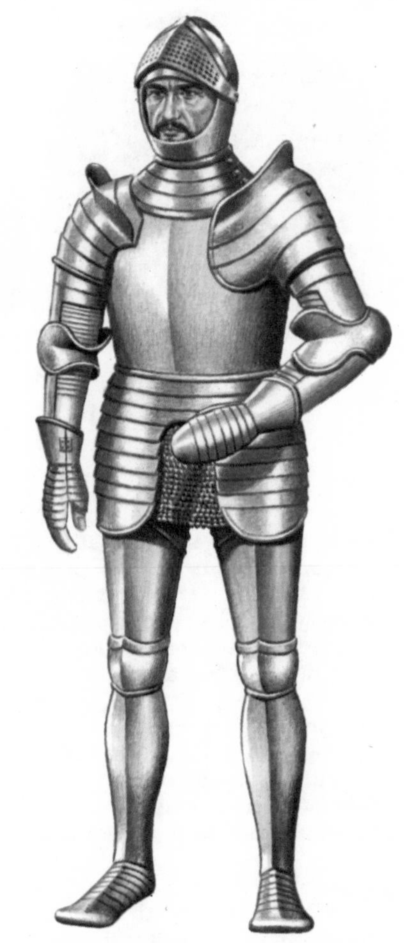

armor

ar·ti·fi·cial (ârti'fishəl) *adj.* 1. not made or occurring in nature; not natural. 2. not sincere; false. —**ar·ti'fi·cial·ly** *adv.*

ar·til·ler·y (âr'tilərē) *n.* 1. large guns, cannons, and similar military weapons considered collectively. 2. the troops or the branch of an army responsible for such weapons.

art·ist ('ârtist) *n.* 1. a painter or sculptor. 2. a stage performer, such as a singer, musician, actor, etc. —**ar'tis·tic** *adj.* —**ar'tis·ti·cal·ly** *adv.*

as·cend (ə'send) *vb.* 1. to move upward; climb. 2. to reach a higher position: *he ascended through the company and became the managing director.* **as'cent** *n.* 1. the act of going up. 2. a way up. —**as'cen·sion** *n.*

ash[1] (ash) *n.* 1. the fine powder or other material that is left after something has been burned. 2. the powdery lava emitted by an erupting volcano. **'ash·en** *adj.* pale, e.g. because of grief: *his face was ashen after he had heard the terrible news.*

ash

ash² (ash) *n.* 1. a DECIDUOUS tree common in Europe, North America, and parts of Asia, that bears black velvety buds in early spring, and has a tough gray-brown bark. 2. the wood of this tree used as timber.

a·shamed (ə'shāmd) *adj.* 1. feeling shame, guilt, or embarrassment. 2. unwilling to do something through fear of disapproval: *he was ashamed to admit that he had lost his money.*

as·par·a·gus (ə'sparəgəs) *n.* a vegetable consisting of the young tender shoots (spears) of a plant of the lily family.

as·phalt ('asfôlt) *n.* a substance made partly from earth minerals and partly from industrial materials, used to cover roads. —*vb.* to cover (a road) with asphalt.

as·pi·rin ('asprin) *n.* a chemical substance usu. taken in white tablet form for the relief of headache, toothache, rheumatism, and other pains.

as·sas·si·nate (ə'sasināt) *vb.* **as·sas·si·nat·ing, as·sas·si·nat·ed.** to kill a person of prominence, esp. for political or religious reasons. **as'sas·sin** *n.* a person who assassinates someone. —**as·sas·si'na·tion** *n.*

as·sault (ə'sôlt) *n.* the act of attacking violently. —*vb.* to attack with violence.

as·sem·ble (ə'sembəl) *vb.* **as·sem·bling, as·sem·bled.** 1. to bring or gather together in one place: *the whole school assembled to listen to the principal.* 2. to fit together the different parts of (a machine, model, etc.). **as'sem·bly** *n.,pl.* **as·sem·blies.** a collection of people or things that have been assembled. **assembly line** (in a factory) an arrangement of machines and workers each performing separate tasks in the production of a particular article.

as·sess (ə'ses) *vb.* 1. to estimate (the value of income, property, etc.), e.g. for taxation or insurance purposes. 2. to determine the amount of (a fine, tax, etc.): *damages were assessed at 5000 dollars.* 3. to judge or evaluate: *the examiners assessed the student's project work.* —**as'sess·ment** *n.* —**as'ses·sor** *n.*

as·sist (ə'sist) *vb.* to help or aid (someone) to do something. —**as'sis·tance** *n.* —**as'sis·tant** *n.*

as·so·ci·ate *vb.* (ə'sōshēāt, ə'sōsēāt) **as·so·ci·at·ing, as·so·ci·at·ed.** 1. to connect or relate in thought: *we associate war with suffering.* 2. to join as a friend, partner, etc.; keep company: *she only associates with the rich.* —*n.* (ə'sōshēit, ə'sōsēit) a friend or colleague. —*adj.* (ə'sōshēit, ə'sōsēit) 1. joined or related for companionship, business, etc.: *an associate partner.* 2. not possessing full rights or privileges: *an associate member.* **as·so·ci'a·tion** *n.* 1. the act of associating. 2. companionship. 3. a group of people joined together for some common purpose; organization; society: *a tenants' association.* —**as'so·ci·a·tive** *adj.*

as·sume (ə'sōōm) *vb.* **as·sum·ing, as·sumed.** 1. to take for granted without being positive; presume; suppose: *I assumed he was coming although I had not heard from him.* 2. to take on (a new role, task, etc.): *she assumed leadership of the group.* —**as·sump·tion** (ə'sumpshən) *n.*

as·sure (ə'shoor) *vb.* **as·sur·ing, as·sured.** 1. to declare positively in order to be believed: *they assured us that the bridge was safe.* 2. to ensure; make certain; guarantee: *his excellent performance assures him a place in the team.* **as'sured** *adj.* 1. made certain; guaranteed. 2. self-confident. **as'sur·ance** *n.* 1. a positive statement giving confidence, encouragement, etc. 2. self-confidence; trust.

as·ton·ish (ə'stonish) *vb.* to amaze; surprise greatly: *we were astonished that the little girl could run so fast.* **as'ton·ish·ment** *n.* amazement.

as·tro·naut ('astrənôt) *n.* a person who pilots, navigates, or is a member of the crew of a spacecraft. **as·tro'naut·ics** *n.* the science or study connected with the principles and techniques of space flight.

as·tron·o·my (ə'stronəmē) *n.* the scientific study of the sun, moon, planets, and stars. —**as'tron·o·mer** *n.* **as·tro·nom·i·cal** (astrə'nomikəl) *adj.* 1. connected with or used in astronomy: *an astronomical telescope.* 2. very large; great or considerable: *the expense was astronomical.*

ath·lete ('athlēt) *n.* a person trained and skillful in contests of strength, speed, endurance, etc., esp. in sports events, e.g. running. **ath·let·ic** (ath'letik) *adj.* 1. of or relating to an athlete or athletics. 2. strong, well-built, or agile. **ath'let·ics** *n.* a branch of sport consisting of track and field events such as running, jumping, and throwing.

at·mos·phere ('atməsfēr) *n.* 1. the layer of gas that surrounds the earth, consisting mainly of nitrogen and oxygen; the AIR. 2. the particular nature or quality of the air in an enclosed space: *a smoky atmosphere.* 3. the effect created by one's surroundings: *a calm atmosphere.* —**at·mos·pher·ic** (atməs'ferik) *or* **at·mos'pher·i·cal** *adj.*

at·om ('atəm) *n.* one of the tiny particles of which all matter is formed. Every atom consists of a NUCLEUS (def. 1) and its surrounding particles. **atom bomb** (also **atomic bomb**) a very powerful bomb whose force is created by the splitting of atoms. —**a·tom·ic** (ə'tomik) *adj.*

a·tro·cious (ə'trōshəs) *adj.* 1. very cruel or brutal; wicked; evil: *an atrocious crime had been committed.* 2. (informal) bad; awful: *we had an atrocious time.* **a·troc·i·ty** (ə'trositē) *n.,pl.* **a·troc·i·ties.** a brutal or cruel act.

at·tach (ə'tach) *vb.* 1. to connect or fasten; join; fix: *he attached a new TV antenna to the roof.* 2. to assign or ascribe: *we don't attach much importance to trivial events.* **attached to** 1. personally involved with or fond of: *the sisters were very attached to each other.* 2. appointed to a specific task or role: *he is at present attached to the British embassy in Washington.* —**at'tach·ment** *n.*

at·tack (ə'tak) *vb.* 1. to make a hostile and violent move against someone: *the enemy attacked unexpectedly.* 2. to criticize fiercely or harshly: *his statements were attacked by the press.* —*n.* 1. a hostile violent move: *an enemy attack.* 2. strong criticism. 3. a sudden violent spell of illness, pain, etc.: *an attack of asthma.*

at·tain (ə'tān) *vb.* 1. to reach: *Bill has attained the age of 90.* 2. to accomplish: *the scientist attained fame while he was alive.*

at·tempt (ə'tempt) *vb.* to try; to make an effort (to do something). —*n.* an effort or try.

at·tend (ə'tend) *vb.* 1. to be present at (a meeting, school, etc.): *I attend classes three times a week.* 2. to care for or to wait on: *the nurse attended the sick man.* **attend to** 1. to listen to; pay attention. 2. to deal with; look after or manage: *we attend to 50 complaints a week.* **at'tend·ant** *n.* a person who looks after someone or something: *a garage attendant.* —**at'tend·ance** *n.*

at·ten·tion (ə'tenshən) *n.* 1. the concentration of one's mind on something or someone: *may I have your attention please!* 2. notice: *the strange noise attracted his attention.* 3. care or treatment; service: *this patient requires special attention.* —*interj.* 1. a military command to stand upright with the arms at the sides, heels together, and the head facing forward. 2. a warning or request to watch closely, listen carefully, etc. **at'ten·tive** *adj.* paying attention; careful.

at·ti·tude ('atitōōd, 'atityōōd) *n.* a particular belief, opinion, feeling, or type of behavior toward someone or something: *her attitude toward him was one of curiosity.*

at·tract (ə'trakt) *vb.* 1. to draw or cause to draw closer; pull nearer: *a magnet attracts iron.* 2. to arouse the interest or claim the attention of: *her beautiful smile attracted him.* —**at'trac·tion** *n.* —**at'trac·tive** *adj.*

au·burn ('ôbərn) *adj.* (esp. of hair) of a reddish-brown color.

auc·tion ('ôkshən) *n.* a public sale in which animals, houses, furniture, etc., are sold to the person who offers the most money. —*vb.* to sell by auction. **auc·tion'eer** *n.* a person who conducts an auction and accepts offers (bids) for items being sold.

au·di·ence ('ôdēəns) *n.* listeners; spectators in an auditorium, theater, etc.

aug·ment (ôg'ment) *vb.* to enlarge or increase, esp. by the addition of something: *he augmented his income by working nights.*

au·then·tic (ô'thentik) *adj.* true or valid; genuine or real: *the painting was not an authentic Picasso but a forgery.* —**au'then·ti·cal·ly** *adv.* —**au·then·tic·i·ty** (ôthen'tisitē) *n.*

au·thor ('ôthər) *n.* 1. a person who writes books, articles, etc., that are published. 2. the originator or creator (of a plan, scheme, etc.).

au·thor·i·ty (ə'thôritē) *n.,pl.* **au·thor·i·ties.** 1. the power or right to control, judge, or demand obedience. 2. sometimes **authorities** (*pl.*) a person or group, such as the government, police, etc., with such power. 3. an expert: *he is an authority on antiques.* **au·thor·ize** ('ôthərīz) *vb.* **au·thor·iz·ing, au·thor·ized.** to give (someone) power or authority; sanction: *the manager was authorized to sign the company's checks.* —**au·thor·i'za·tion** *n.*

au·to·graph ('ôtəgraf) *n.* a signature (esp. of a famous person) written in his own handwriting. —*vb.* to sign one's name: *the author autographed his latest book.*

au·to·mat·ic (ôtə'matik) *adj.* 1. (of a machine) able to operate independently; self-regulating: *an automatic dishwasher.* 2. occurring as a matter of routine, without conscious effort or thought: *blinking is an automatic action.* —*n.* a firearm capable of reloading itself and firing repeatedly when the trigger is pulled. **au·to·ma·tion** (ôtə'māshən) *n.* the use of automatic machinery in industry to speed up production and cut down on manpower, labor costs, etc. —**au·to'mat·i·cal·ly** *adv.*

au·tumn ('ôtəm) *n.* the season following summer; fall. —*adj.* (also **au·tum·nal** (ô'tumnəl)) of or occurring in the autumn.

a·vail·a·ble (ə'vāləbəl) *adj.* able to be obtained or used.

av·o·ca·do (avə'kâdo) *n.,pl.* **av·o·ca·dos.** (also **avocado pear**) a tough-skinned pear-shaped tropical fruit.

avocado

a·void (ə'void) *vb.* to keep or turn away from someone or something: *she avoided the puddle by walking around it.* —**a'void·ance** *n.*

a·ward (ə'wôrd) *n.* something given as a token of honor; prize: *he valued his sports awards very highly.* —*vb.* to give (a prize, money, etc.): *the judges awarded him first prize.*

awe (ô) *n.* a sense of deep respect, fear, or wonder: *we were filled with awe at the beautiful cathedral.* —*vb.* **aw·ing, awed.** to fill with awe. **'awe·some** *adj.* causing or filling with awe: *the eruption of the volcano was an awesome sight.*

awk·ward ('ôkwərd) *adj.* 1. clumsy; unskillful; not elegant: *her broken arm made her movements awkward.* 2. badly designed: *an awkward shape.* 3. embarrassing or inconvenient: *no-one knew what to say and there was an awkward silence.* 4. hard to deal with; difficult: *an awkward customer.* —**'awk·ward·ly** *adv.* —**'awk·ward·ness** *n.*

ax (aks) *n.* a sharp-bladed tool with a long wooden handle, usu. used for chopping wood. See TOOL.

ax·le ('aksəl) *n.* the rod or bar on which a wheel turns.

B

ba·boon (ba'bo͞on) *n.* a large short-tailed monkey with a doglike face and large sharp teeth, found in various parts of Africa.

bach·e·lor ('bachələr) *n.* 1. an unmarried man. 2. a person who has taken his first degree at a college or university: *Bachelor of Science.*

back·bone ('bakbōn) *n.* 1. the spine. 2. moral strength; courage: *a coward is a person with no backbone.*

back·fire ('bakfīər) *vb.* **back·fir·ing, back·fired.** 1. (of a car engine) to produce an explosion of unburned fuel in the exhaust pipe. 2. (of a plan) to fail and cause harm to those who made it up: *the criminals were caught when their plans backfired.*

back·ground ('bakground) *n.* 1. that part of a scene that is furthest away from the observer. Compare FOREGROUND. 2. a person's past experience, family history, education, etc.: *she comes from a musical background.* 3. information that adds to one's understanding of a situation; context. **in the background** out of direct view; not prominent.

back·log ('baklôg, 'baklog) *n.* an accumulation (of work not yet done, unpaid debts, etc.).

back·ward ('bakwərd) *adj.* 1. moving or directed towards the back: *a backward glance.* 2. slow to learn: *a backward child.* 3. (of a nation) undeveloped; uncivilized. 4. shy or reluctant. **'back·ward** *or* **'back·wards** *adv.* 1. toward the back. 2. in reverse. 3. with the back end foremost. 4. into the past.

bagpipes

ba·con ('bākən) *n.* the meat of a pig, taken from its back and sides and salted and smoked.

bac·te·ri·a (bak'tērēə) *pl.n.* the tiny organisms belonging to the plant kingdom that cause decay and certain diseases. They also help to produce alcohol from grain or grapes in making beer or wine. —**bac'te·ri·al** *adj.*

bade (bād) *or* **bad** (bad) *vb.* the past tense of BID (vb. defs. 4 – 6).

badg·er ('bajər) *n.* a dark gray burrowing animal related to the weasel, with a white striped head and back, found in Europe, Asia, and North America. —*vb.* to pester; keep on at: *the children badgered him to tell them a story.*

bad·min·ton ('badmintən) *n.* a game similar to tennis but played on a shorter court, with a higher net and a shuttlecock instead of a ball.

baf·fle ('bafəl) *vb.* **baf·fling, baf·fled.** to bewilder; make (a person) feel puzzled and at a loss: *she was baffled by the corridors leading off in all directions.* —**'baf·fle·ment** *n.*

bag·pipes ('bagpīps) *pl.n.* a musical instrument in which sound is produced by reed pipes, played by means of air from a bag inflated by the player's mouth or by bellows held under the arm.

bail[1] (bāl) *n.* a sum of money paid by or on behalf of a person accused of a crime, which allows him to leave prison. The money is forfeited if the person fails to appear at his trial. —*vb.* (+ *out*) 1. to secure (a person's) release from custody by paying bail. 2. to rescue (someone) from an awkward or dangerous situation: *Peter bailed his friend out of trouble by lending him some money.*

bail[2] (bāl) *vb.* (often + *out*) 1. to scoop (water) out of a boat. 2. to parachute out of an aircraft in an emergency. 3. to abandon at the last minute: *just as the plans were completed, he bailed out of the project.* —*n.* (also **bail·er**) a scoop used for bailing (def. 1.)

bait (bāt) *n.* 1. food or imitation food used to attract and catch fish or animals. 2. anything that attracts or tempts a person toward something. —*vb.* 1. to put bait on or in. 2. to tease and enrage: *the children baited the boy by calling him names.*

bal·ance ('baləns) *n.* 1. a device for weighing things, usu. having two dishes or pans hung from each end of a bar or beam supported at its exact center. 2. the ability to stand upright; equilibrium: *it's easy to lose your balance on skates.* 3. a state in which differences have been evened out or all aspects agree and harmonize: *the right balance of high and low voices is important in forming a choir.* 4. the amount left over or due when money paid has been subtracted from money owing; remainder: *give me half now and you can pay the balance next week.* 5. the remainder of anything. 6. the part of a clock or watch that

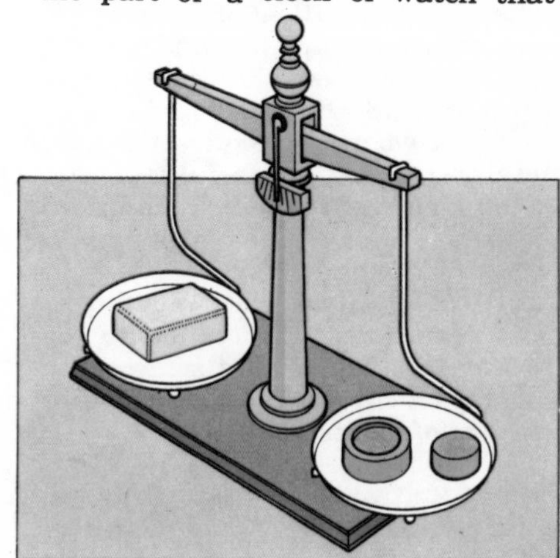

balance

controls its speed. —*vb.* **bal·anc·ing, bal·anced.** 1. to place or keep or be placed or kept in a state of balance: *sea lions balance balls on their noses.* 2. to even up; achieve a balance. **'bal·anced** *or* **well-'bal·anced** *adj.* even-tempered and in good mental health.

bamboo

bal·co·ny ('balkənē) *n.,pl.* **bal·co·nies.** 1. a narrow railed or walled platform built out from an upper floor of a building. 2. the seats in the upperfloor in a theater, auditorium etc.

bald (bôld) *adj.* 1. having no hair on the head. 2. lacking natural fur, feathers, leaves, etc.; bare. 3. without detail or disguise: *Ted gave a bald statement to outline his argument.* —**'bald·ly** *adv.* —**'bald·ness** *n.*

bale (bāl) *n.* 1. a large bundle of goods, esp. hay, wool, cotton, etc., packed for transportation. —*vb.* **bal·ing, baled.** to make into bales.

bale·ful ('bālfəl) *adj.* with evil intentions; harmful: *the neighbor gave us a baleful look when our ball broke his greenhouse window.* —**'bale·ful·ly** *adv.* —**'bale·ful·ness** *n.*

bal·lad ('baləd) *n.* 1. a simple poem that tells a story, usu. in a number of short verses. 2. a romantic song.

bal·let (ba'lā, 'balā) *n.* 1. a formal type of dancing in which intricate steps, movements, and mime are used, often telling a story. 2. an entertainment or a piece of music written for such dancing.

bal·loon (bə'lo͞on) *n.* 1. a rubber bag that may be blown up with air or other gas and used as a child's toy. 2. a gas-filled inflatable bag used for carrying a container of cargo or passengers through the atmosphere. —*vb.* 1. to swell or cause to swell like a balloon: *her skirt ballooned as the wind caught at it.* 2. to travel by balloon.

bal·lot ('balət) *n.* 1. the card, sheet, or ticket used for voting. 2. a method of secret voting in which cards, etc., are put into a box (**ballot box**) and are counted later. —*vb.* to vote by means of a ballot.

bam·boo (bam'bo͞o) *n.* a tall grass that grows mainly in tropical regions, having stems used to make furniture, baskets, paper, etc.

ba·na·na (bə'nanə) *n.* 1. a long bow-shaped fruit having a yellow, red, or green skin surrounding a soft pulpy flesh. 2. the broad-leaved tree on which bananas grow.

band[1] (band) *n.* 1. a strip of material (metal, rubber, etc.) used as a trimming, binding, or decoration. 2. a colored stripe. —*vb.* to put or place a band on something.

band[2] (band) *n.* 1. a group of people doing something together: *a band of actors.* 2. a number of musicians who play music for marching, dancing, or for outdoor entertainment. —*vb.* (often + *together*) to unite in a band.

band·age ('bandij) *n.* a strip of material used to cover and protect a wound. —*vb.* **band·ag·ing, band·aged.** to put a bandage on a wound.

ban·dit ('bandit) *n., pl.* **ban·dits** *or* **ban·dit·ti** (ban'ditē). an outlaw; robber.

ban·ish ('banish) *vb.* 1. to expel (a person) from a country; drive into exile. 2. to send off; dismiss from one's mind. —**'ban·ish·ment** *n.*

ban·jo ('banjō) *n.,pl.* **ban·jos.** a musical instrument like a guitar, used mainly in jazz or folk music and having a long neck, a round body, and a set of strings played by plucking.

banjo

bank·rupt ('bangkrupt) *n.* a person unable to pay his debts whose remaining money and possessions are legally removed so that they can be shared out fairly among his creditors. —*vb.* to make (someone) bankrupt. —*adj.* 1. declared or found to be a bankrupt; 2. (of a business) failed or collapsed. 3. completely empty; devoid: *the play was bankrupt of ideas.* —**'bank·rupt·cy** *n.,pl.* **'bank·rupt·cies.**

ban·ner ('banər) *n.* 1. a flag often bearing a slogan carried between two poles on a march or at a rally, sports event, etc. 2. a flag bearing a pattern, coat of arms, etc., carried on a single pole; standard.

ban·quet ('bangkwit) *n.* a large, often formal, feast. —*vb.* to be at or have a banquet.

bap·tism ('baptizəm) *n.* (in the Christian Church) a ceremony in which a person is christened and sprinkled with or plunged into water so that he may be cleansed of sin and thus admitted into the church. **bap·tize** (bap'tīz, 'baptīz) *vb.* **bap·tiz·ing, bap·tized.** to perform a baptism on (someone); to christen and give a name to.

bar·bar·i·an (bâr'beərēən) *n.* an uncivilized or primitive person. —*adj.* rough and uncultured: *barbarian manners.* **bar·bar·ic** (bâr'barik) *adj.* 1. of or like a barbarian. 2. crude or vulgar in style, taste, etc. —**bar·ba·rism** ('bârbərizəm) *n.*

bar·bar·i·ty (bâr'baritē) *n.,pl.* **bar·bar·i·ties.** a brutal and savage act or practice; cruelty: *the barbarity of torture.* **bar·bar·ous** ('bârbərəs) *adj.* 1. savagely cruel or brutal; atrocious. 2. (of language) nonstandard; unrefined: *a barbarous form of English.*

bar·be·cue ('bârbəkyōō) *n.* 1. a meal usu. consisting of meat roasted over a charcoal grill and generally eaten out of doors. 2. an iron frame or grill over which barbecues are prepared. —*vb.* **bar·be·cu·ing, bar·be·cued.** 1. to roast over a charcoal grill. 2. to prepare food with a highly seasoned sauce.

bar·ber ('bârbər) *n.* a person whose job it is to cut men's hair and shave or trim their beards.

bare (beər) *adj.* 1. naked; uncovered: *he took off his shoes and socks and walked in bare feet.* 2. lacking equipment, decoration, furnishings, etc.: *the room was almost bare of furniture.* 3. scanty; mere: *a bare handful of people.* **lay bare** to expose (a secret, etc.). —*vb.* **bar·ing, bared.** to uncover; reveal. **'bare·ly** *adv.* 1. nakedly; thinly; sparsely. 2. hardly; scarcely; only just: *there was barely enough to feed us all.* —**'bare·ness** *n.*

bar·gain ('bârgən) *n.* 1. an agreement between two or more sides, often made according to certain conditions: *the bargain was that she would do the shopping if he would do the cooking.* 2. a surprisingly cheap purchase; a good buy: *the old chair was a real bargain.* —*vb.* (usu. + *with*) to discuss in order to make a bargain; negotiate. **bargain for** to expect or anticipate; be prepared for: *the tickets cost more than we bargained for.*

barge (bârj) *n.* a low flat boat used on inland waterways for transporting goods. —*vb.* **barg·ing, barged.** (+ *about, in, into,* etc.) to move clumsily or rudely: *Charles barged into the chair and knocked it over in his hurry.*

bark[1] (bârk) *n.* 1. the loud abrupt cry made by dogs, foxes, seals, etc. 2. a sudden shout similar to a dog's: *he gave a bark of contempt.* —*vb.* to utter or make a bark.

bark[2] (bârk) *n.* the woody outer covering of a tree trunk and branches. —*vb.* to scrape (one's skin); graze badly.

bark·er ('barkər) *n.* a person who works at a fair, sideshow, carnival etc., and calls loudly to passers-by to come in and see the show.

bar·ley ('bârlē) *n.* a grain-producing grass similar to wheat but with long feathery whiskers, used for food and in making beer and whiskey.

ba·rom·e·ter (bə'romitər) *n.* an instrument for measuring atmospheric pressure. It is used to show changing weather conditions. —**bar·o·met·ric** (barə'metrik) *adj.*

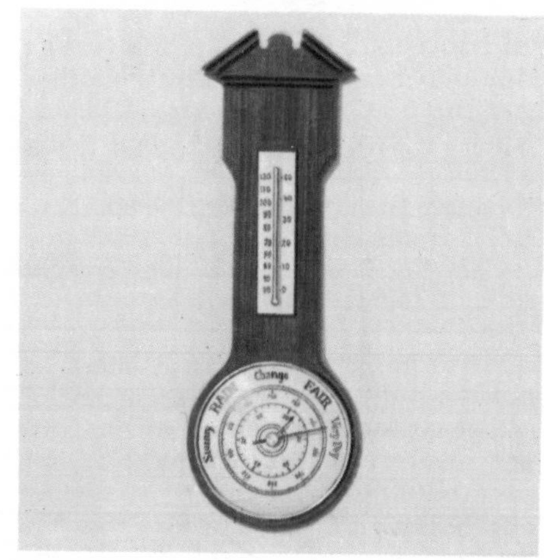

barometer

bar·on ('barən) *n.* a nobleman of some European countries, belonging to the lowest rank of the peerage.

bar·racks ('barəks) *pl.n.* buildings for housing soldiers, often at an army camp.

bar·rel ('barəl) *n.* 1. a cylinder-like container with bulging sides often made of wooden slats bound with hoops. 2. the tubular metal part of a gun through which a bullet is fired.

bar·ren ('barən) *adj.* 1. (of land) unable to produce crops; infertile or arid: *the long drought made the fields barren. 2. unable to bear offspring. 3. useless; unprofitable: a barren task.* —**'bar·ren·ness** *n.*

bar·ri·cade ('barəkād) *n.* a temporary makeshift barrier set up to block a street or passageway. —*vb.* **bar·ri·cad·ing, bar·ri·cad·ed.** to obstruct in order to prevent access; block: *they barricaded the door to keep the soldiers out.*

bar·ri·er ('barēər) *n.* 1. an obstacle such as a fence, wall, or gate, erected to prevent or control access and often used to mark a boundary. 2. anything that prevents communication or progress: *a language barrier.*

bar·row[1] ('barō) *n.* a small handcart, esp. with one or two wheels, used for carrying loads.

bar·row[2] ('barō) *n.* a large mound of earth raised over a burial ground or grave in ancient times.

base[1] (bās) *n.* 1. the bottom, foundation, or support of something: *grass grew around the base of the pillar.* 2. (also **ba·sis**) the main ingredient or part of a mixture: *some paints have an oil base.* 3. a center of operations for the army, navy, air force, business company, etc.: *a rocket base.* 4. BASIS (def.1.). 5. one of the positions on a baseball diamond. See BASEBALL. —*vb.* **bas·ing, based.** 1. to set up or establish a base. 2. to place or be placed in a military base. 3. to take as a basis or starting point: *she based her novel on her experiences in Africa.*

base[2] (bās) *adj.* low or mean; vile: *Judas was a base traitor.*

base·ball ('bāsbôl) *n.* a game played by two teams of nine players each on a field with four bases arranged in a diamond pattern. After hitting the pitched ball with a bat, the batter attempts to run around the field and touch each base to score a run.

base·ment ('bāsmənt) *n.* the lowest story of a building, usu. below ground level.

bash·ful ('bashfəl) *adj.* shy; hesitant; over-modest: *Maria gave the teacher a bashful look when he praised her work.* —**'bash·ful·ly** *adv.*

ba·sic ('bāsik) *adj.* forming a basis or starting-point; fundamental or essential: *the basic cause of revolution is discontent.* —**'bas·i·cal·ly** *adv.*

ba·sis ('bāsis) *n.,pl.* **bas·es** ('bāsēz). 1. (also **base**) the foundation or principle on which something rests or can be developed: *their common interests gave them a firm basis for friendship.* 2. BASE[1] (n. def. 2).

bask (bask) *vb.* 1. to lie or laze in comfortable warmth. 2. to revel or take delight in: *the winner basked in the thunderous applause.*

bas·ket·ball (bas'kitbôl) *n.* 1. a team sport played on a court with a basket set at each end, the object being for each side of five players to toss the ball through the opponents basket as often as possible. 2. the ball that is used in this game.

bass[1] (bās) *n.* 1. the lowest male singing voice. 2. a singer having such a voice, or a musical instrument having a low, deep tone. —*adj.* 1. written for or sung by a bass. 2. lowest in sound in a class of musical instruments: *a bass guitar.*

bass[2] (bas) *n.* a sea or freshwater fish with large spiny fins.

bas·soon (bə'so͞on) *n.* a musical wind instrument belonging to the oboe class, of which it is the largest member and the lowest in pitch.

baste (bāst) *vb.* **bast·ing, bast·ed.** to moisten (meat) with butter, fat, etc., during cooking.

bat[1] (bat) *n.* a heavy wooden stick with a handle, used for striking a ball in games like baseball. —*vb.* **bat·ting, bat·ted.** to hit (a ball) with a bat. —'**bat·ter** *n.*

bat[2] (bat) *n.* a small mouselike flying animal with wings of thin skin stretched over very long finger bones.

batch (bach) *n.* 1. a quantity of bread, cakes, biscuits, etc., that have been prepared and baked at the same time. 2. a group of people or things taken as a set: *a batch of exam papers.*

bat·on (bə'ton) *n.* 1. a short stick used by a conductor to direct an orchestra. 2. a rod carried or twirled by a drum major or majorette. 3. a short stick passed between runners in a RELAY race. 4. a short rod carried by an army or other officer as a symbol of his rank.

bat·ter[1] ('batər) *vb.* to beat savagely and repeatedly: *the firemen battered down the door to rescue the trapped people.*

bat·ter[2] ('batər) *n.* flour, milk, and eggs beaten together to form a mixture for pancakes, puddings, a coating for fish, etc.

bat·ter·y ('batərē) *n.,pl.* **bat·ter·ies.** 1. a device consisting of electric CELLs (def 3.) joined together to produce an electrical voltage. 2. a number of heavy guns firing from one place, or the men in charge of them; artillery. 3. a large impressive set or series of anything: *she faced a battery of cameras at the press conference.* 4. the action, result, or crime of battering or beating.

bat·tle ('batəl) *n.* 1. a violent fight or contest between enemies, esp. one using trained military forces. 2. any struggle: *a battle for higher wages.* —*vb.* **bat·tling, bat·tled.** 1. to fight fiercely: *they battled for control of the river.* 2. to struggle bravely; strive. '**bat·tle·ship** *n.* a warship armed with heavy guns.

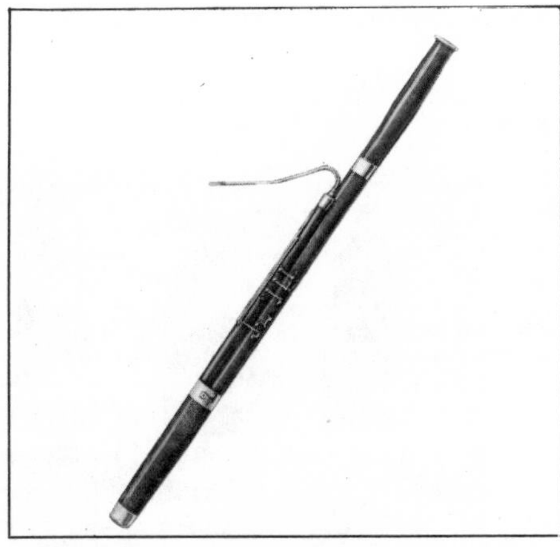

bassoon

bay[1] (bā) *n.* a wide curved inlet of the sea or a lake.

bay[2] (bā) *n.* 1. an opening or recess in a wall or between two columns; a compartment. 2. a special area set aside for parking or the loading and unloading of goods. **bay window** a window projecting out from a wall so forming a recess inside.

bay[3] (bā) *vb.* (esp. of a hound picking up a scent) to bark deeply and repeatedly. —*n.* a continuous barking sound. **at bay** (esp. of a hunted animal) cornered and forced to turn and face the attacker. **hold** *or* **keep at bay** to keep at a distance; ward off.

bay[4] (bā) *n.* a type of LAUREL whose pointed oval leaves are used to flavor food and were in ancient times woven into crowns for heroes.

bay[5] (bā) *adj.* (of horses) of a reddish-brown color. —*n.* a reddish-brown horse with a black mane and tail.

bay·o·net ('bāənet) *n.* a short steel blade fixed to the muzzle of a rifle.

beach (bēch) *n.* a stretch of sand lying beside the sea and forming part of the shore. —*vb.* to run or pull (a ship or boat) onto the beach.

bea·con ('bēkən) *n.* 1. a hill-top or a fire lit on it to serve as a signal or warning. 2. a lighthouse or anything with a flashing light that warns of a danger at sea.

bea·gle ('bēgəl) *n.* a small dog of the hound family, originally bred for hunting. It has a smooth coat with tan, white, and often black markings, drooping ears, and fairly short legs.

beak (bēk) *n.* the nose and mouth of a bird; bill.

beam (bēm) *n.* 1. a long horizontal piece of wood, metal, concrete, etc., used to bear the weight of the roof or floor of a building. 2. a ray of light, radio waves, etc. 3. the widest part of a ship. 4. a broad smile. —*vb.* 1. to send out (rays of light or radio waves). 2. to smile radiantly.

bean (bēn) *n.* 1. any of several plants eaten as vegetables and having long seed-containing pods, e.g. string bean. 2. the seed itself or any seed whose shape is similar, e.g. coffee bean.

bear[1] (beər) *vb.* **bear·ing, bore, borne** *or* (def. 4) **born.** 1. to carry or support; hold up: *the tallest man had to bear most of the weight.* 2. to have, show, or display: *the letter bore his signature.* 3. to tolerate or endure: *I could not bear to see her cry.* 4. to give birth to: *she is too young to bear a child.* 5. (of plants) to produce or yield: *the holly tree bears red berries.* '**bear·a·ble** *adj.* tolerable; endurable. —'**bear·er** *n.*

bear[2] (beər) *n.* a large thick-furred animal, found in parts of Europe, Asia, and America, that lives on both vegetation and meat.

beard (bērd) *n.* 1. the hair growing on a man's face and chin. 2. anything resembling a beard, like the tuft of hairs on a goat's jaw.

beast (bēst) *n.* 1. an animal other than man. 2. (informal) a nasty or cruel person. —**beast·ly** *adj.* **beast·li·er, beast·li·est.**

beau·ty ('byo͞otē) *n.,pl.,* **beau·ties.** 1. the quality of being very pleasing to the senses, esp. to the eyes: *they admired the beauty of the scenery.* 2. a person or thing that possesses this quality: *that new airplane is a beauty.* —'**beau·ti·ful** *adj.* —'**beau·ti·ful·ly** *adv.*

bea·ver ('bēvər) *n.* a river animal of the rat family with webbed hind feet, a broad tail, and long sharp teeth, which it uses to cut down trees to build dams around its den. It lives mainly in North America.

beck·on ('bekən) *vb.* to summon with a gesture of the hand or head: *Beth beckoned her friend across the room to come over and talk.*

bee (bē) *n.* 1. a stinging insect with a thick hairy body. Honey bees build HONEYCOMBs out of BEESWAX and feed on NECTAR (from which they make honey) and pollen. 2. a meeting for work or pleasure; a contest: *a spelling bee.*

beech (bēch) *n.* 1. a DECIDUOUS tree with a smooth hard bark, shiny oval leaves, and small edible nuts. 2. the wood of this tree.

beef (bēf) *n.* 1. the meat of the ox, bull, or cow. 2. (informal) a complaint. —*vb.* (informal) to complain: *she beefed about doing her homework.* **'beef·y** *adj.* **beef·i·er, beef·i·est.** 1. containing or tasting like beef. 2. strong; muscular. —**'beef·i·ness** *n.*

bee·hive ('bēhīv) *n.* See HIVE.

beer (bēr) *n.* an alcoholic drink usu. made from barley, yeast, and hops.

bees·wax ('bēzwaks) *n.* wax made by honey bees, from which polishes, candles, etc. are made.

beet (bēt) *n.* 1. (also **sugar beet**) a small plant whose white carrot-shaped root provides sugar. 2. a similar plant whose red root is eaten as a vegetable. 3. the root of a beet plant.

bee·tle ('bētəl) *n.* 1. a type of insect with hard wing-covers. 2. any other insect resembling this, e.g. the cockroach.

beg (beg) *vb.* **beg·ging, begged.** 1. to ask people for money. 2. to ask (someone) for something or to do something, esp. with great emotion or feeling: *he begged her to forgive him.* 3. (of a dog) to sit on its haunches with its front paws raised. **'beg·gar** *n.* 1. a person who begs for money. 2. (informal) a worthless person.

be·have (bi'hāv) *vb.* **be·hav·ing, be·haved.** 1. to act or conduct oneself: *you are behaving like a baby.* 2. to act properly or correctly: *if you do not behave I shall be furious.* 3. to respond or react: *how does the fish behave if you throw it food?* **be'hav·ior** *n.* conduct or response.

beige (bāzh) *n.* a light creamy brown color. —*adj.* having this color.

bel·fry ('belfrē) *n.,pl.* **bel·fries.** 1. a bell-tower. 2. the part of a tower or a church steeple in which the bells are hung.

belfry

be·lief (bi'lēf) *n.* 1. a feeling that something is real, right, or true; conviction: *it is my belief that honesty is the best policy.* 2. trust or confidence: *I have great belief in his ability as a lawyer.* 3. a religious doctrine or faith: *the Christian belief.*

be·lieve (bi'lēv) *vb.* **be·liev·ing, be·lieved.** 1. to feel certain or be convinced of (the reality, rightness, or truth of something): *I believe in equality.* 2. to have trust or confidence in (someone or something): *I believe in your talent.* 3. to suppose: *I believe you know Mrs. Robinson.* **make believe** to imagine or pretend. **'make-be·lieve** *n.* pretense.

bell (bel) *n.* 1. a hollow metal cup-shaped instrument, which is struck by a clapper or hammer to make a ringing sound. 2. anything bell-shaped, e.g. a bluebell, etc.

bel·lig·er·ent (bə'lijərənt) *adj.* 1. hostile; eager to fight: *Bobby is very belligerent and so is always getting into fights.* 2. engaged in fighting; at war: *the belligerent nations increased their production of arms.* —*n.* a person or nation engaged in fighting. —**bel'lig·er·ent·ly** *adv.* —**bel·lig·er·ence** (bə'lijərəns) *n.*

bel·low ('belō) *vb.* 1. to roar like a bull. 2. to shout in a loud deep voice. —*n.* an angry roaring noise.

bel·lows ('belōz) *pl.n.* a mechanical device for producing a strong blast of air for a fire or furnace or certain musical instruments such as the organ, bagpipes, etc.

bel·ly ('belē) *n.,pl.* **bel·lies.** 1. (informal) the lower abdomen, stomach, or womb. 2. the bulging interior of a ship or the undercarriage of an aircraft. —*vb.* **bel·ly·ing, bel·lied.** to bulge out or swell: *we could see the yacht's sails bellying out as it left the harbor.*

belt (belt) *n.* 1. a strip of leather or other material worn around the waist. 2. a geographical region, esp. one with distinctive characteristics: *cotton belt.* **con·vey·or belt** a long continuous strip of rubber or other material that is kept moving by means of wheels or rollers and used in factories, etc., for carrying goods. —*vb.* 1. to fasten with a belt. 2. to beat with a belt; hit or strike.

bench (bench) *n.* 1. a seat usually wooden, long enough for several people, and often found in parks and other public places. 2. a work-table used by carpenters, mechanics, etc. **the Bench** (in a law court) a judge's seat, the judge himself, or judges, magistrates, etc., collectively. **'bench·mark** *n.* a surveyor's mark on a rock or post, used as a reference point from which to measure distances or heights.

bend (bend) *vb.* **bend·ing, bent.** 1. to force or be forced into a curved, angular, or other shape: *the circus strong man bent the iron bar into a hoop.* 2. to turn in a certain direction: *the road bends to the left.* 3. to apply one's energies to something: *we bent to the task of moving the log.* —*n.* 1. a curve: *a bend in the road.* 2. the act of bending or state of being bent.

ben·e·fit ('benəfit) *n.* 1. something that acts as an advantage, does good, or gives pleasure: *he sang for the benefit of his friends.* 2. money paid by an insurance company, government agency or some other institution, for example, to the old, sick or disabled. 3. a performance of a play, match, etc., the revenue of which is given to charity or to one particular cause. —*vb.* 1. to do good. 2. to gain or profit from. **ben·e·fi·cial** (benə'fishəl) *adj.* acting to someone's good: *the climate was beneficial for her health.*

bent (bent) *vb.* the past tense and past participle of BEND. —*adj.* curved or crooked: *the nail was bent and could not be used.* **bent on** determined: *Louis was bent on buying a new car.* —*n.* a natural ability or interest: *Jane's parents discovered that she had a musical bent.*

beret

ber·et (bə'rā, 'berā) *n.* a flat round cap, usu. made of woolen material.

ber·ry ('berē) *n.,pl.* **ber·ries.** a small juicy fruit, usu. with seeds or pips.

berth (bûrth) *n.* 1. a place in a dock where a ship is anchored. 2. a sleeping-place in a train, ship, etc. —*vb.* (of a ship) to dock.

be·siege (bi'sēj) *vb.* **be·sieg·ing, be·sieged.** 1. to lay SIEGE to (a town, city, etc.): *the enemy besieged the town for a year before it surrendered.* 2. to crowd around (someone), esp. to ask numerous questions, make demands, etc.: *reporters besieged the politician.*

bet (bet) *vb.* **bet·ting, bet.** 1. to make an agreement to risk money by guessing the outcome of an event: *Tim bet Jane that he could swim further underwater than she could.* 2. (informal) to be certain: *I bet he will forget to come.* —*n.* 1. the agreement to risk money on an uncertain event. 2. the money risked.

be·tray (bi'trā) *vb.* 1. to act against one's country, a friend, etc., by assisting an enemy. 2. to act disloyally by giving away a secret, breaking a promise, etc. 3. to reveal unintentionally: *her clenched fists betrayed her anger.* —**be'tray·al** *n.* —**be'tray·er** *n.*

be·wil·der (bi'wildər) *vb.* to perplex, confuse, or puzzle: *the problem bewildered her.* —**be'wil·der·ment** *n.*

be·yond (bē'ond) *prep.* 1. on the far side of: *you can see the hills beyond the river.* 2. outside the limits, scope, or range of; out of reach of: *that idea is beyond my understanding.* —*adv.* further away: *they traveled over the mountains and beyond.*

bi·an·nu·al (bī'anyōōəl) *adj.* happening or occurring twice a year; half-yearly. —**bi'an·nu·al·ly** *adv.*

bi·as ('bīəs) *n.* 1. a tendency or leaning: *he had a bias towards mathematics and wanted to be an accountant.* 2. a prejudice: *the old woman had a bias against students.* 3. a slanted line cut across the weave of a fabric. —*vb.* **bi·as·ing, bi·ased.** to prejudice or influence.

bi·cy·cle ('bīsikəl) *n.* a pedal-operated vehicle having two wheels, one in front of the other, a saddle-like seat for the rider and handlebars for steering it.

bid (bid) *vb.* **bid·ding, bid** (for defs. 1–2); **bid·ding, bade** *or* **bad, bid·den** (for defs. 3–4). 1. to offer to buy something at a certain price, esp. at an auction: *the man bid $5000 for the painting.* 2. to state one's price for doing a job. 3. to command: *do as he bids.* 4. to say as a greeting: *I bid you goodnight.* —*n.* the act of bidding; an offer. —'**bid·der** *n.*

bi·en·ni·al (bī'enēəl) *adj.* 1. lasting for two years: *a wallflower is a biennial plant.* 2. happening once every two years. —*n.* a plant with a two-year life cycle, flowering and producing seeds or fruit in the second year. Compare ANNUAL and PERENNIAL. —**bi'en·ni·al·ly** *adv.*

bi·ki·ni (bi'kēnē) *n.* a brief two-piece swimsuit worn by women.

bill[1] (bil) *n.* 1. a list of costs or charges presented to a person for the goods or services he has received. 2. a draft of a proposed new law put before a legislative body for debate. 3. a poster or public notice advertising some product or event.

bill[2] (bil) *n.* the beak of a bird.

bil·liards ('bilyərdz) *n.* any of various games played with long tapered poles (**billiard cues**) and balls (**billiard balls**), on a rectangular table (**billiard table**) often with six side-pockets.

bind (bīnd) *vb.* **bind·ing, bound.** 1. to fix firmly by tying round with string, rope, etc. 2. to unite legally or morally; tie or put under an obligation: *marriage binds two people together.* 3. to put a border on (the edge of something), esp. to prevent fraying. 4. to stitch or glue together (one edge of several pages and covers) to form a book. '**bind·er** *n.* 1. a man or machine that binds books. 2. a loose cover for holding and protecting sheets of paper, magazines, etc. '**bind·ing** *n.* 1. the outside covers of a book. 2. a strip of material used to bind the edge of something.

bi·noc·u·lars (bə'nokyələrz) *pl.n.* an optical instrument for making distant objects seem larger and nearer, containing a system of LENSes for magnifying the image.

binoculars

bi·og·ra·phy (bī'ogrəfē) *n.,pl.* **bi·og·ra·phies.** the story of a (real) person's life written by someone else. —**bi'og·ra·pher** *n.* —**bi·o·graph·i·cal** (bīə'grafikəl) *adj.*

bi·ol·o·gy (bī'oləjē) *n.* the science and study of the function, structure, and development of animals and plants. —**bi·o·log·i·cal** (bīə'lojikəl) *adj.* —**bi·o'log·i·cal·ly** *adv.* **bi'ol·o·gist** *n.* a person who studies or specializes in biology.

birch (bûrch) *n.* a tree that grows in cool climates, the commonest variety being the silver birch, which has a silver and black patched bark.

birth (bûrth) *n.* 1. a baby's coming into the world. 2. the beginning of something: *the birth of the society was celebrated with a party.*

bis·cuit ('biskit) *n.* a small light piece of bread, usu. made with baking powder or soda.

bish·op ('bishəp) *n.* 1. a person of high rank in the Christian Church, in charge of all clerical matters in his area (diocese or **bish·op·ric**) and with authority to ordain priests. 2. a chess piece that can move diagonally on the board.

bison

bi·son ('bīsən) *n.,pl.* **bi·son.** a large grazing animal, related to the ox that lives in herds in North America. See also BUFFALO.

bit[1] (bit) *n.* 1. a small piece or amount of something: *he dropped a bit of paper* 2. a short time; moment: *they had to wait for a bit.* 3. (informal) twelve and a half cents.

bit[2] (bit) *n.* 1. the thin metal bar of a BRIDLE that is put in a horse's mouth. 2. a sharp-pointed boring tool fixed to the end of a drill or brace. See TOOL.

bit[3] (bit) *vb.* the past tense of BITE.

bite (bīt) *vb.* **bit·ing, bit, bit·ten.** 1. to take hold of or cut into with the teeth (or mouthparts in insects) as in eating or as a means of attack: *the dog bit me on the leg.* 2. to eat into; corrode: *acid bites into metals.* 3. to sink or cut into: *the wire bit into the soft wood.* 4. (esp. of fish) to take a baited hook. —*n.* 1. an instance or the act of biting. 2. a wound caused by biting. 3. a piece or amount that has been bitten off. 4. a sharp stinging sensation: *the bite of the wind.* 5. food: *a bite to eat.* '**bit·ing** *adj.* 1. causing a stinging pain: *a biting wind.* 2. sarcastic or hurtful: *a biting remark.*

bit·ter ('bitər) *adj.* 1. sour and sharp-tasting: *fresh lemon juice tastes bitter.* 2. painful; causing suffering or distress: *a bitter experience.* 3. intensely hostile: *bitter enemies.* 4. biting: *a bitter wind.* 5. resentful through suffering: *the housewives became very bitter about rising prices.* —'**bit·ter·ly** *adv.* —'**bit·ter·ness** *n.*

black·ber·ry ('blakberē) *n.,pl.* **black·ber·ries.** 1. a purplish-black edible berry. 2. the thorny bush on which these berries grow.

black·bird ('blakbûrd) *n.* 1. a European songbird, related to the thrush, with black plumage and a yellow bill. 2. any of various American birds that are black or dark in color.

black·mail ('blakmāl) *vb.* to obtain money or favors (from someone), by threatening to disclose a secret, reveal a past crime, etc. —*n.* 1. the act of blackmailing. 2 the payment obtained from such a practice. —'**black·mail·er** *n.*

black·out ('blakout) *n.* 1. temporary loss of consciousness: *he suffered a blackout and could remember nothing that happened.* 2. an electricity failure; power cut.

blad·der ('bladər) *n.* the expanding bag in which URINE collects in human and animal bodies.

blade (blād) *n.* 1. the narrow leaf of grass, corn, etc. 2. the flat cutting part of a sword, knife, ax, etc. 3. the wide flat part of an oar, propeller, etc. 4. a sword.

blame (blām) *vb.* **blam·ing, blamed.** to attach guilt or responsibility to (a person or thing) for (a crime, etc.): *they blamed the weather for the poor attendance at the ball game.* —*n.* responsibility for a fault, etc.

blank (blangk) *adj.* 1. not written on; unmarked: *a blank page.* 2. expressionless; empty of understanding, emotion, or interest: *he looked blank when I told him my name.* 3. absolute; utter: *blank despair overwhelmed him.* **blank verse** non-rhyming verse. —*n.* 1. a space to be filled in, e.g. on a form. 2. a state of emptiness: *my mind was a blank.* 3. a cartridge without a bullet. —'**blank·ly** *adv.* —'**blank·ness** *n.*

blast (blast) *n.* 1. a gust or sudden rush of wind, air, etc. 2. an explosion: *a blast of gunfire.* 3. a blare of trumpets, horns, etc. —*vb.* 1. to break (something) or make a hole by setting off an explosion: *thieves had blasted the safe open.* 2. (+ *off*) (of a rocket or spacecraft) to take off; launch.

blaze[1] (blāz) *n.* 1. a burst or glow of bright flames or light. 2. a rush or outburst: *we finished the decorating in a blaze of activity.* —*vb.* **blaz·ing, blazed.** 1. to flare or light up suddenly; burn, glow, or shine brightly. 2. to flare up with emotion: *she was blazing with rage.*

blaze[2] (blāz) *n.* 1. a white mark on the face of a horse or cow. 2. a white mark chipped or painted on a tree trunk. —*vb.* **blaz·ing, blazed.** (usu. in **blaze a trail**) 1. to mark (a trail) by cutting blazes on trees. 2. to show the way or be a pioneer: *early spacemen blazed the trail to the moon.*

blaze

bleach (blēch) *vb.* to remove color by the action of sunlight, chemicals, etc. —*n.* any substance that bleaches.

bleak (blēk) *adj.* 1. desolate, cold, or bare: *a bleak landscape.* 2. dreary; dull; unpromising: *a bleak future* —'**bleak·ly** *adv.* —'**bleak·ness** *n.*

blem·ish ('blemish) *vb.* to spoil or damage; mar: *the scandal blemished his reputation.* —*n.* 1. a mark, esp. on the skin, that damages or spoils the look of something. 2. a fault, flaw, or defect: *laziness was a blemish in her character.*

blend (blend) *vb.* 1. to mix thoroughly: *the ingredients for the sauce were blended together.* 2. to merge: *chameleons change color to blend into the background.* —*n.* a mixture.

bless (bles) *vb.* 1. to wish heavenly happiness (on a person) by praying. 2. to make holy; consecrate. 3. to feel grateful to: *I blessed my wife for remembering the theater tickets.* **bless·ed** ('blesid) *adj.* 1. having been blessed; holy. 2. welcome: *after constant quarreling blessed peace reigned at last.* '**bless·ing** *n.* 1. the giving of a prayer for God's favor. 2. anything bringing happiness; benefit: *television is a blessing for elderly people.* 3. approval: *the mayor gave his blessing to the tree-planting program.*

blew (blo͞o) *vb.* the past tense of BLOW[1].

blight (blīt) *n.* 1. a disease, fungus, or insect that attacks and destroys plants. 2. anything that has an unpleasant or destructive effect. —*vb.* to affect with or cause a blight.

blind (blīnd) *adj.* 1. unable to see. 2. hidden: *they could not see the car coming out of the blind entrance.* 3. heedless; not noticing: *she was blind to his faults.* 4. reckless; not thinking of the consequences: *blind panic seized him and he ran.* —*n.* a window shade, esp. one that rolls up. —*vb.* 1. to make blind. 2. to mislead: *his confident talk blinded us.* '**blind·fold** *vb.* to cover (a person's eyes) with a handkerchief, scarf, mask, etc. *n.* such a mask.

blink (blingk) *vb.* 1. to close and open the eyes quickly. 2. (of lights) to go on and off rapidly.

bliss (blis) *n.* perfect happiness. —'**bliss·ful** *adj.* —'**bliss·ful·ly** *adv.*

blis·ter ('blistər) *n.* 1. a small fluid-filled swelling on the skin caused by a burn, rubbing, etc. 2. a small air pocket on a coat of paint, etc. —*vb.* to cause or come out in a blister. '**blis·ter·ing** *adj.* 1. causing a blister. 2. scorching; extremely hot.

blitz (blits) *n.* 1. an intensive attack on something. *the townspeople decided to have a blitz on litter.* 2. a sudden attack from the air; an air raid. **the Blitz** the series of intensive German air raids on Britain in 1940.

bliz·zard ('blizərd) *n.* an extensive and heavy snowfall accompanied by strong winds, poor visibility, and huge deep drifts.

bloat (blōt) *vb.* to swell up; inflate: *the huge meal bloated his stomach.*

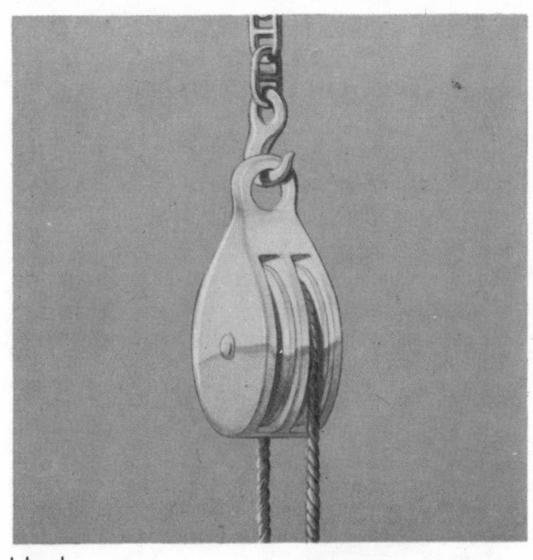
block

block (blok) *n.* 1. a solid, usu. rectangular piece of concrete, wood, stone, etc., esp. when used in building. 2. a number of buildings totally surrounded by streets: *the store is two blocks down that street.* 3. a group of seats in a theater. 4. a device with pulleys for lifting heavy weights. 5. (also **block·age**) something that stops progress, flow, movement, etc.: *a block in the pipe.* —*vb.* to prevent or stop with a barrier: *ignorance blocks progress.*

block·ade (blo'kād) *n.* the prevention, by enemy forces, of supplies getting in or out of a town, port, etc. —*vb.* **block·ad·ing, block·ad·ed.** to conduct a blockade on (a town, port, etc.).

blond (blond) *adj.* 1. (of hair) golden or fair. 2. having golden or fair hair. **blonde** *n.* a woman with blond hair.

blood (blud) *n.* 1. the red liquid that is pumped through the body by the heart. See also CORPUSCLE. 2. descent or breeding: *she is of royal blood.* '**blood·y** *adj.* **blood·i·er, blood·i·est.** covered or stained with blood.

blood·shed ('bludshed) *n.* the spilling of blood by violent means.

bloom (blo͞om) *n.* 1. a flower head; blossom. 2. a fresh or healthy glow: *the bloom of her cheek.* 3. a state or condition of health or vigor: *the bloom of youth.* —*vb.* 1. to come into flower; blossom. 2. to glow with health, beauty, etc.; appear bright and fresh: *Rita bloomed with health after a morning run.*

blos·som ('blosəm) *n.* a flower, or a mass of flowers, esp. of a fruit tree: *apple blossom.* —vb. 1. to produce blossom; bloom: *cherry trees blossom in spring.* 2. to grow beautiful or attractive: *Lucy blossomed into a woman when she was eighteen.* 3. to reveal one's full talent or aptitude; flourish: *he blossomed as an artist.*

blot (blot) *n.* 1. a mark or stain, esp. of a liquid: *an ink blot.* 2. fault; disgrace. —*vb.* **blot·ting, blot·ted.** 1. to make an ink stain, spot, or mark (on something). 2. to stain or spoil: *his career was blotted by the scandal.* 3. to dab (ink, etc.) with absorbent paper (**blotting paper**) in order to dry it. 4. (+ *out*) to shut out or wipe out; obliterate: *the clouds were blotting out the sun.*

blow[1] (blō) *vb.* **blow·ing, blew, blown.** 1. (of the wind or air) to be in motion; move or flow. 2. to move or to be carried along by or as if by the force of the wind: *the leaves were blown away.* 3. to send out a rush of air esp. from the mouth: *blow out the candles.* 4. (of a tire, fuse, etc.) to stop functioning suddenly; fail or perish. **blow up** 1. to inflate a balloon, tire, etc. 2. to explode or cause an explosion. 3. (informal) to lose one's temper. 4. to enlarge a photograph. —*n.* the act or an instance of blowing.

blow[2] (blō) *n.* 1. a hit with the fist, a weapon, etc.: *he knocked his opponent out with a single blow.* 2. a shock or setback; severe disappointment: *his exam failure was a severe blow to his career hopes.*

blub·ber ('blubər) *n.* the fatty layer between the skin and muscle of a whale, seal, or similar animal from which oil is made. —*vb.* (informal) to cry noisily.

bluff (bluf) *vb.* to pretend confidently; mislead or deceive by behaving or acting boldly: *he bluffed his way out of the situation.* —*n.* the act or an instance of bluffing.

blun·der ('blundər) *n.* a stupid or careless mistake, esp. an embarrassing one. —*vb.* 1. to make a blunder. 2. to stumble or wander about carelessly.

blunt (blunt) *adj.* 1. not sharp; having a dull or rough edge: *the blunt knife would not cut the bread.* 2. forthright or outspoken: *he complained to the manager in a blunt manner.* —*vb.* 1. to make something blunt; dull: *he blunted the knife trying to saw through wood* 2. to weaken or diminish the strength or force of (something): *smoking blunted her sense of taste.* —'**blunt·ly** *adv.* —'**blunt·ness** *n.*

blur (blûr) *n.* 1. something hazy, ill-defined, or indistinct: *the distant figure on the horizon was a blur.* 2. a smear or smudge. —*vb.* **blur·ring, blurred.** 1. to make or become hazy or indistinct: *the strong sun blurred his vision.* 2. to smear or smudge. 3. to confuse or disguise: *he deliberately blurred the facts.*

blush (blush) *vb.* to glow pink or red, esp. on the face through embarrassment, surprise, etc. —*n.* 1. a pink glow, esp. on the face. 2. a rosy color.

boar (bôr) *n.* a male pig.

board (bôrd) *n.* 1. a flat piece of hard material such as wood. 2. such a flat slab of wood, or other material used for a particular purpose: *an ironing board.* 3. any group of people who officially direct, control, or supervise something: *a board of directors.* —*vb.* 1. to climb onto or enter a ship, aircraft, train, etc. 2. (often + *up*) to cover or enclose with boards: *he boarded up the window.* 3. to offer or receive accommodation, meals, etc., in return for payment; lodge.

boast (bōst) *vb.* 1. to speak with excessive vanity or pride, esp. about oneself; brag. 2. to have the distinction of possessing: *this house boasts a large garden.* —*n.* an act or instance of boasting. —'**boast·ful** *adj.*

bod·y ('bodē) *n.,pl.* **bod·ies.** 1. the physical structure of a person or animal: *the human body.* 2. a corpse. 3. that part of a person or animal excluding the head, arms, and legs; trunk or torso. 4. a group of people taken collectively: *the student body.* 5. the main or major part of something: *the body of the truck was painted red.* 6. a mass: *a body of water.* 7. substance or strength; dense consistency: *the vegetables gave the stew more body.* '**bod·i·ly** *adj.* of or relating to the body: *his bodily needs were food and water. adv.* as a whole; completely and physically: *he was removed bodily from the hall.*

bog (bog) *n.* a damp soggy area of ground; marsh. —*vb.* **bog·ging, bogged.** (usu. + *down*) 1. to sink in or as if in a bog: *bogged down in the mud.* 2. (informal) to be unable to make progress in some activity: *bogged down with work.*

boil[1] (boil) *vb.* 1. to change from a liquid to a gaseous state when heated; bubble and produce steam. 2. to cook by boiling. 3. to become hot and red with emotion, esp. anger: *boil with rage.* '**boil·er** *n.* any vessel or large container used for boiling or heating water, etc.

boil[2] (boil) *n.* an inflamed pus-filled sore or swelling of the skin.

bold (bōld) *adj.* 1. brave, daring, or courageous; fearless: *a bold explorer.* 2. strong and firm: *bold handwriting.* —'**bold·ly** *adv.* —'**bold·ness** *n.*

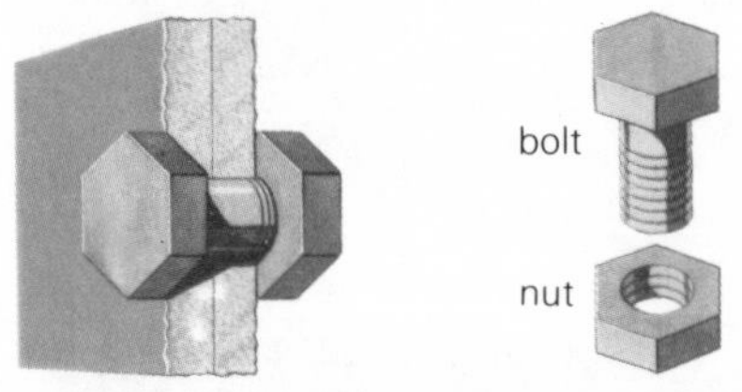

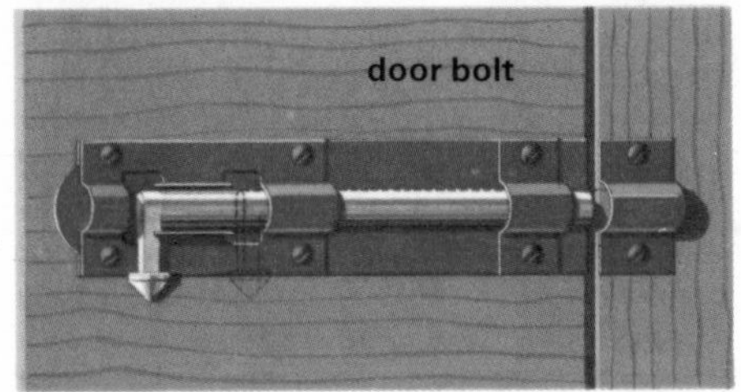

bolt

bolt (bōlt) *n.* 1. a movable bar, usu. of metal, that slides into a socket to fasten a door, gate, etc. 2. any strong metal pin with a THREAD (def. 3) at one end and a head at the other that may be tightened with a wrench to hold or secure parts of machines, etc. 3. a sudden dash or run. —*vb.* 1. to fasten with a bolt: *the machine is bolted to the floor.* 2. to run away in great haste; dash off. 3. to swallow (food) hurriedly.

bomb (bom) *n.* a weapon consisting of a metal container packed with explosive. —*vb.* to attack with bombs. '**bomb·er** *n.* 1. a person who uses bombs. 2. an aircraft used for dropping bombs.

bom·bard (bom'bârd) *vb.* 1. to use prolonged artillery fire against (an enemy position). 2. to assail continually with questions or remarks: *he bombarded us with questions about our holidays.* —**bom'bard·ment** *n.*

bond (bond) *n.* 1. usu. **bonds** (*pl.*) chains or imprisonment. 2. something that joins or unites: *a strong bond of friendship between two people.* 3. a written promise, esp. concerning money, that must be kept by law. 4. a special paper issued by the government or a business promising to repay borrowed money at an agreed date.

bone (bōn) *n.* 1. the hard material that makes up the skeleton in animals. 2. a part of this skeleton. —*vb.* **bon·ing, boned.** to remove the bones from meat or fish.

boom·er·ang ('boōmərang) *n.* a curved flat throwing stick used esp. by Australian ABORIGINEs for hunting animals. If it misses its target it returns to the thrower.

boost (boōst) *vb.* 1. to lift by pushing from underneath. 2. to increase; raise: *the athlete's win boosted his confidence.* —*n.* a push forward. '**boost·er** *n.* 1. rocket used for launching a satellite or spacecraft. 2. an injection given to help keep up the strength of a vaccine injected at an earlier date.

bor·der ('bôrdər) *n.* 1. an edge or margin. 2. a frontier or boundary: *guards patrolled the border.* —*vb.* 1. to be next to: *my land borders on farmland.* 2. to be on the brink of; approach: *his jealousy bordered on madness.*

bore[1] (bôr) *vb.* **bor·ing, bored.** 1. to make a hole in: *termites bore into wooden frames of houses.* 2. to drill: *the desert is being bored for oil.* —*n.* the inside diameter of a tube, etc.

bore[2] (bôr) *vb.* **bor·ing, bored.** to make someone weary by being dull and tedious. —*n.* 1. a person who bores others by dull talk. 2. anything dull and tedious. —'**bore·dom** *n.*

bore[3] (bôr) *vb.* the past tense of BEAR[1].

born (bôrn) *vb.* the past participle of BEAR[1] (def. 4).

borne (bôrn) *vb.* the past participle of BEAR[1] (defs. 1 – 3, 5).

bor·row ('borō) *vb.* 1. to take on loan. 2. to use (another's ideas, words, etc.): *Mike borrowed the idea for his project from Tom.* —'**bor·row·er** *n.*

bos·om ('boōzəm) *n.* 1. the human breast: *he clasped his daughter to his bosom.* 2. the female breasts. 3. the very heart or center of a person or thing: *Mandy felt secure in the bosom of her family.*

boss[1] (bôs) *n.* an employer, manager, foreman, superior, or person in charge. —*vb.* 1. to order about. 2. to supervise; be in charge. '**boss·y** *adj.* **boss·i·er, boss·i·est.** enjoying ordering others about.

boss² (bôs) *n.* a stud, or raised knob-like ornament or part, e.g. one concealing a joint in certain types of ceiling.

bot·a·ny ('botənē) *n.* the study of plants. —**bo·tan·i·cal** (bə'tanikəl) *adj.* —'**bot·a·nist** *n.*

both·er ('bodhər) *vb.* 1. to annoy: *don't bother me while I'm working.* 2. to take trouble or make an effort: *don't bother to get up.* —*n.* 1. fuss or annoyance. 2. trouble or extra effort.

bough (bou) *n.* a tree branch.

boul·der ('bōldər) *n.* a large rounded or smooth rock.

bounce (bouns) *vb.* **bounc·ing, bounced.** 1. to rebound or cause to rebound: *the ball bounced along the ground.* 2. to jump, move, or spring up and down, —*n.* 1. a rebound, spring, or lift. 2. vigor; energy: *Bob was full of bounce at the start of the game.*

bound¹ (bound) *vb.* the past tense and past participle of BIND. —*adj.* certain: *it's bound to rain soon.*

bound² (bound) *vb.* to leap or spring (along). —*n.* a leap or jump.

bound·a·ry ('boundərē) *n.,pl.* **bound·a·ries.** the extreme edge or limit of something; a frontier: *the Rio Grande forms a boundary between Texas and Mexico.*

bou·quet (bōō'kā) *n.* 1. a bunch of flowers. 2. the quality of wine judged from its scent.

bou·tique (bōō'tēk) *n.* a shop, esp. one selling clothes.

bow¹ (bou) *vb.* 1. to nod the head or bend forward from the waist as a sign of reverence or acknowledgment: *the subjects bowed to the queen.* 2. to bend forward: *he bowed his head in shame.* 3. to give way or yield: *I will not bow to your demands.* —*n.* a bending of the head or body, usu. as a mark of respect.

bow² (bō) *n.* 1. a weapon made of flexible wood or metal drawn into a curve by a string stretched between the ends which is pulled taut and then released to shoot arrows. 2. a curve or bend: *this wall has a slight bow in it.* 3. a stick with horsehair strung from end to end, used in playing the violin and similar stringed instruments. 4. a knot with two loops which pulls out easily, or any decorative looped knot or tie.

bow³ (bou) *n.* sometimes **bows** (*pl.*) the forward end of a boat. Compare STERN².

bow·els ('bouəlz) *pl.n.* 1. sometimes **bowel** (*sing.*) the long tubelike organs in the body in which food is absorbed into the blood and waste material is collected before discharge. 2. the deepest part of anything.

bowl¹ (bōl) *n.* 1. a round deep-sided dish. 2. something in the shape of a bowl, e.g. a sports arena.

bowl² (bōl) *n.* 1. a heavy round ball used in games such as tenpins. —*vb.* to take one's turn in rolling a bowl. **ten·pin bowl·ing** an indoor game played with large balls which are rolled down a hardwood alley to knock down as many as as possible of the ten pins set up at the other end. **bowls** *n.* a game in which bowls are rolled across a level grass pitch (**bowl·ing green**).

Braille

box¹ (boks) *n.* 1. a flat-bottomed container, often with a lid, and made of wood, metal, cardboard, etc. 2. an enclosed private set of seats in a theater. **box office** the ticket office of a theater, stadium, etc.

box² (boks) *vb.* 1. to fight with the fists. 2. to hit, esp. on the ears. —*n.* a blow or hit. '**box·er** *n.* 1. a person who competes in boxing as a sport. 2. a breed of dog with short smooth brown hair and a flattened face. '**box·ing** *n.* a sport in which two people wearing padded gloves fight in a roped-off arena (**boxing ring**).

box³ (boks) *n.* an evergreen shrub often used for garden hedges.

boy·cott ('boikot) *vb.* to refuse to handle (goods) or deal with (a person, country, etc.) on moral or political grounds. —*n.* the act or practice of boycotting.

brace (brās) *n.* 1. something that grips or holds firm; clamp. 2. a piece of iron or timber used to strengthen a building. 3. (esp. of game-birds) a pair or couple. —*vb.* **brac·ing, braced.** 1. to give support to; strengthen. 2. to prepare oneself; get ready to face: *we braced ourselves for a hard day.*

brace·let ('brāslit) *n.* a decorative band, chain, etc., worn on the wrist.

brack·et ('brakit) *n.* 1. a support for a shelf, lamp, etc., usu. fixed to a wall. 2. one of a pair of punctuation marks, in the form of square parentheses, used to enclose information. 3. a grouping or scale: *the middle income bracket.* —*vb.* 1. to put into brackets. 2. to group together.

brag (brag) *vb.* **brag·ging, bragged.** to boast: *he bragged about the huge fish he caught.*

Braille (brāl) *n.* a type of printing for the blind, consisting of patterns of raised dots that can be read by touch.

brain (brān) *n.* 1. the soft mass of gray and white matter inside the skull of man and the higher animals. It is the center of the nervous system, controlling thought, memory, bodily actions, etc. 2. also **brains** (*pl.*) intelligence or intellectual power: *he has a superb brain.* '**brain·y** *adj.* **brain·i·er, brain·i·est.** intelligent or clever.

brain·wash·ing ('brānwoshing) *n.* a method of gaining control of a person's mind to make him believe what one wants, sometimes achieved by the use of drugs or torture.

brake (brāk) *n.* a device for slowing down or stopping a vehicle or other moving mechanism, usu. by pressure against some part of the wheels. —*vb.* **brak·ing, braked.** to stop (a vehicle) by applying the brake.

bram·ble ('brambəl) *n.* a form of prickly bush; the class of plant to which the blackberry belongs.

branch (branch) *n.* 1. a part of a tree or other plant that comes from the main body of the plant. 2. a subdivision or extension of something: *a branch of a bank.* —*vb.* 1. (often + *off*) to turn or lead off in a different direction: *the road branched off the main highway.* 2. (+ *out*) to extend one's activities: *the store branched out and began to sell new lines.*

brand (brand) *n.* 1. a tradename on manufactured goods, foodstuffs, etc.: *she bought the best brand of butter.* 2. a mark on an animal showing ownership, often made with a hot iron (**brand·ing iron**). —*vb.* 1. to mark with a brand. 2. to identify or mark as bad or disgraceful: *his crime branded him forever.*

brand·y ('brandē) *n.,pl.* **brand·ies.** a strong alcoholic drink, made by distilling the juice of grapes or other fruit.

brass (bras) *n.* 1. a strong yellowish metal made from copper and zinc. 2. any article made of brass. 3. a collective term for musical instruments like the trumpet, trombone, French horn, etc., which are usu. made of brass. —'**brass·y.** *adj.* **brass·i·er, brass·i·est.**

breach (brēch) *n.* 1. a gap made in a wall, dam, or other structure. 2. the breaking of a promise, law, etc.; violation or infringement. —*vb.* to make a breach in something.

breadth (bredth) *n.* 1. width; broadness; the distance from one side of something to the other. 2. fullness of extent, scope, or range: *he shows great breadth of knowledge.*

break (brāk) *vb.* **break·ing, broke, bro·ken.** 1. to come or cause to come to pieces; damage: *the glass broke when dropped on the floor.* 2. to discontinue: *it was difficult to break the habit.* 3. to force a way: *thieves have broken into the bank.* 4. to appear suddenly: *dawn is breaking.* **break down** to fail to work. —*n.* an action or instance of breaking. '**break·down** *n.* a failure to work.

breast (brest) *n.* 1. the front of the body from the neck to the abdomen; chest. 2. the organ producing milk in women and some female animals.

breath (breth) *n.* 1. the air taken in or let out of the lungs. 2. a single intake of air: *he took a deep breath.* 3. a light movement of air: *a breath of wind.* 4. a faint trace or hint: *a breath of excitement.* —'**breath·less** *adj.*

breathe (brēdh) *vb.* **breath·ing, breathed.** 1. to take in and let out air. 2. to utter very quietly: *she breathed a warning in his ear.*

breed (brēd) *vb.* **breed·ing, bred.** 1. to produce (offspring): *some animals do not breed in captivity.* 2. to mate and rear animals, usu. with careful attention to parentage, in order to produce good stock. 3. to cause or produce: *familiarity breeds contempt.* —*n.* a type or strain of animal: *a breed of cattle.* '**breed·ing** *n.* good manners and fine taste as produced by family influence and training; elegance. —'**breed·er** *n.*

breeze (brēz) *n.* a gentle wind. **breeze in** *or* **out** (informal) to come in or out in a relaxed and high-spirited way. '**breez·y** *adj.* **breez·i·er, breez·i·est.** 1. windy, in a pleasant way. 2. casual and good-humored: *Charles' breezy manner put people at ease.*

brew (broo) *vb.* 1. to make (beer, etc.) by fermenting liquid from boiling hops together with yeast, malt, and sugar. 2. to make (tea, coffee, etc.). 3. (esp. of something unpleasant) to be forming or about to happen: *a storm was brewing.* —*n.* any liquid that has been brewed. '**brew·er·y** *n.,pl.* **brew·er·ies.** a place where beer is made. —'**brew·er** *n.*

bribe (brīb) *n.* a present of money or something of value given to a person in order to gain information, favors, etc., illegally or dishonestly. —*vb.* **brib·ing, bribed.** to offer or give a bribe: *the criminal tried to bribe the police to release him.*

brick (brik) *n.* 1. a rectangular block made of fired or sunbaked clay, used in building. 2. anything similar to this in shape. —*vb.* (+ *up*) to seal or enclose with bricks: *they bricked up the windows of the deserted house.*

bride (brīd) *n.* a woman just married or about to be married. '**bride·groom** (often shortened to **groom**) *n.* a man just married or about to be married. —'**brid·al** *adj.*

bridge (brij) *n.* 1. a structure built over a river, valley, road, etc., to allow the passage of people and traffic. 2. the upper part of the nose. 3. the raised part of a ship where the officer on watch is stationed. 4. a raised strip of wood on the body of a violin, cello, etc., over which the strings pass. —*vb.* **bridg·ing, bridged.** to span; cross with or as if with a bridge.

bridges

1

2

3

4

bridge: 1 arch bridge; 2 girder bridge; 3 cantilever bridge; 4 suspension bridge.

bri·dle ('brīdəl) *n.* a leather head-harness for a horse, including the REINs and a BIT[2]. —*vb.* **bri·dling, bri·dled.** 1. to put a bridle onto a horse. 2. to hold back, control, or restrain (one's feelings): *he bridled his anger.* 3. to lift the head and draw in the chin as an expression of scorn, resentment, etc.: *she bridled at his sarcastic remark.* '**bri·dle·path** *n.* a path suitable for horses.

brief (brēf) *adj.* short: *there was a brief interval between the programs.* —*n.* 1. (law) details concerning one side of a case given or offered to a lawyer on behalf of his client. 2. a list of instructions or the outline of a plan to be acted upon: *he was given a brief of the project before beginning the work.* 3. **briefs** (*pl.*) very short tight-fitting underpants. —*vb.* to instruct or inform: *the manager briefed him about the job.* '**brief·case** *n.* a flat case usu. made of plastic or leather, used for carrying papers. **brief·ing** *n.* advice or instructions given in advance.

bri·gade (bri'gād) *n.* 1. a subdivision of an army, commanded by a brigadier, usu. made up of an infantry battalion, armor, and artillery. 2. any organized band or work-force: *a fire brigade.*

bright (brīt) *adj.* 1. giving off much light: *a bright star.* 2. (of colors) vivid: *bright blue.* 3. lively and intelligent; clever. '**bright·en** *vb.* to make or become bright or brighter. —'**bright·ly** *adv.* —'**bright·ness** *n.*

bril·liant ('brilyənt) *adj.* 1. extremely bright: *brilliant sunshine.* 2. highly intelligent: *a brilliant student.* 3. outstanding: *a brilliant performance.* —'**bril·liance** *n.* —'**bril·liant·ly** *adv.*

brim (brim) *n.* 1. the projecting edge of a hat. 2. the topmost edge of a cup or bowl. —*vb.* **brim·ming, brimmed.** to be full up to the brim with something; overflow.

brink (bri<u>n</u>gk) *n.* 1. the edge of something, usu. of a steep place and often over water. 2. the moment before a change of mood or events; verge: *on the brink of tears.*

brisk (brisk) *adj.* 1. with a quick smart movement: *a brisk trot.* 2. (of weather) healthy; cool and bracing. —'**brisk·ly** *adv.* —'**brisk·ness** *n.*

bris·tle ('brisəl) *n.* 1. a stiff short hair, esp. of an animal such as the pig. 2. anything resembling this, esp. as part of a toothbrush, hairbrush, etc. —*vb.* **bris·tling, bris·tled.** 1. (of the hair, bristles, etc.) to stand on end, often in anger or fear. 2. to show a hostile reaction: *John bristled when I suggested he might be wrong.* 3. (+ *with*) to be full of (difficulties, etc.); teem with: *the plan bristled with dangers.*

brit·tle ('britəl) *adj.* (of glass, ice, bones, etc.) easily snapped or broken. —'**brit·tle·ness** *n.*

broad (brôd) *adj.* 1. wide: *a broad river.* 2. extensive: *a broad range of goods.* 3. (of opinions, views, attitudes, etc.) tolerant; liberal: *a broad mind.* 4. clear or obvious: *a broad hint.* '**broad·en** *vb.* to make or become broader. —'**broad·ness** *n.* See also BREADTH.

broad·cast ('brôdkast) *vb.* **broad·cast·ing, broad·cast** *or* **broad·cast·ed.** 1. to transmit by television or radio. 2. to make widely known: *it was broadcast around the neighborhood that there would be a party.* —*n.* an instance or the action of broadcasting.

broc·co·li ('brokəlē) *n.* a vegetable related to the cabbage with green or purple edible flowerheads.

bro·chure (brō'sh<u>oo</u>r) *n.* a printed booklet or pamphlet containing information or advertisements for a product, service, etc.

broil (broil) *vb.* to cook meat, fish etc., on a metal grid directly under or over a source of heat. —'**broil·er** *n.*

bronze (bronz) *n.* 1. a shiny reddish metal made of copper and tin. 2. a work of art made of bronze. —*adj.* made from or having the color of bronze. —*vb.* **bronz·ing, bronzed.** to cover with or become the color of bronze. **bronzed** *adj.* suntanned.

brooch (brōch, brōōch) *n.* a piece of jewelry fixed onto clothing by a pin or clasp.

brood (brōōd) *n.* 1. the offspring of egg-producing animals, esp. birds. 2. (informal or humorous) the children in one's family. —*vb.* 1. (of a bird) to sit on eggs until they are hatched. 2. to think about something in a gloomy, bad-tempered way; sulk: *William brooded about the scolding he was given.* '**brood·y** *adj.* **brood·i·er, brood·i·est.** 1. (esp. of hens) tending to brood. 2. moody or sulky.

brow (brou) *n.* 1. the top or edge of a hill or cliff. 2. the forehead. 3. an eyebrow.

browse (brouz) *vb.* **brows·ing, browsed.** 1. to look through (books, shelves, etc.) in a leisurely and random way. 2. (of goats, deer, etc.) to feed off leaves, shoots, and other vegetation. —'**brows·er** *n.*

bruise (brōōz) *n.* an injury in which the skin is discolored but not broken. —*vb.* **bruis·ing, bruised.** to suffer or cause to suffer a bruise.

bru·nette (brōō'net) *adj.* 1. (of hair) dark brown in color. 2. having hair of this color. —*n.* a woman with brunette hair.

bru·tal ('brōōtəl) *adj.* cruel and savage. —**bru·tal·i·ty** (brōō'talitē) *n.,pl.* **bru·tal·i·ties.**

brute (brōōt) *n.* 1. a beast. 2. a cruel or physically violent person. 3. anything that causes trouble or is difficult to handle: *a brute of a car.* —*adj.* purely physical: *brute force.* —'**brut·ish** *adj.*

bub·ble ('bubəl) *n.* a sphere of gas present in a liquid or found free with a thin liquid covering around it. —*vb.* **bub·bling, bub·bled.** 1. to produce bubbles. 2. to make the sound of bubbles rising and bursting; gurgle. 3. (of a person) to show happiness; sparkle.

buck·le ('bukəl) *n.* a fastener made of metal, plastic, etc., with a spike attached to it, which passes through a hole in a belt, strip of material, etc. —*vb.* **buck·ling, buck·led.** 1. to fasten with a buckle. 2. to crumple, collapse, or warp under pressure, heat, etc.

bud (bud) *n.* the small swelling on a branch or stalk that will grow into a flower, leaf, or new branch. —*vb.* **bud·ding, bud·ded.** to put out buds; begin growing.

budg·et ('bujit) *n.* a financial statement or plan predicting or estimating how the money one earns or obtains is to be used or controlled. —*vb.* to make a budget.

buf·fa·lo ('bufəlō) *n.,pl.* **buf·fa·loes** *or* **buf·fa·lo.** a large plant-eating animal with heavy curved horns. It is related to the ox, and is found mainly in India (water buffalo) and Africa (Cape buffalo). The North American BISON is also sometimes called a buffalo.

buf·fet[1] ('bufit) *n.* a blow. —*vb.* to strike repeatedly; knock about: ***big waves buffeted the boat.***

buf·fet[2] (bə'fā, bo͞o'fā) *n.* 1. (at a wedding, party, etc.) refreshments set out on a bar or table for guests to help themselves. 2. a piece of dining-room furniture used for serving food.

bug (bug) *n.* 1. any insect, esp. a flea or something similar. 2. (informal) a microbe, esp. one that can cause disease. 3. a concealed microphone or other device used to pick up conversations secretly. —*vb.* **bug·ging, bugged.** 1. (slang) to pester or annoy persistently. 2. to conceal a microphone or tape-recorder in a room, telephone, etc., to spy on people.

bu·gle ('byo͞ogəl) *n.* a brass musical instrument used for military signals and fanfares. —*vb.* **bu·gling, bu·gled.** to sound a bugle.

bugle

build (bild) *vb.* **build·ing, built.** to construct; make something, e.g. a house, from an assortment of parts or materials.

bulb (bulb) *n.* 1. the swollen underground part of such plants as onions, daffodils, tulips, etc., that stores nourishment for new growth. 2. anything shaped like a bulb, e.g. an electric light bulb. —'**bulb·ous** *adj.*

bulge (bulj) *n.* a swelling or lump. —*vb.* **bulg·ing, bulged.** to stick out.

bulk (bulk) *n.* 1. greatness of volume, size, or weight. 2. the main part: ***the bulk of the work was completed today.*** —'**bulk·y** *adj.* **bulk·i·er, bulk·i·est.**

bull (bo͝ol) *n.* 1. the male of cattle, buffalo, etc., and of certain other animals, e.g. the elephant or seal.

bulldozer

bull·doz·er ('bo͝oldōzər) *n.* a large heavy tractor used for clearing land, knocking down buildings, etc. '**bull·doze** *vb.* **bull·doz·ing, bull·dozed.** 1. to clear and level (land, etc.) using a bulldozer. 2. to get one's own way by using threats or violence; bully: ***Ken bulldozed his way into the job.***

bul·let ('bo͝olit) *n.* a small metal pellet that is part of a CARTRIDGE and is the projectile shot from a firearm.

bul·ly ('bo͝olē) *n.,pl.* **bul·lies.** a person who uses force to frighten someone weaker than himself. —*vb.* **bul·ly·ing, bul·lied.** to frighten or intimidate (a weaker person): ***he bullied his little sister.***

bump (bump) *vb.* 1. to hit sharply: ***he bumped his head on the low ceiling.*** 2. to move with a series of bumps: ***the car bumped along the track.*** **bump into** 1. to knock into or collide with. 2. to meet someone by chance: ***I bumped into Jane on my way to Simon's party.*** —*n.* 1. a blow or dull thump caused by a collision. 2. a lump or swelling on the surface of something. ***a bump in the road.*** 3. a sudden jolt. —'**bump·y** *adj.* **bump·i·er, bump·i·est.**

bump·er ('bumpər) *n.* a bar at the back and front of motor vehicles, that is designed to weaken the force of a collision. —*adj.* unusually large: ***because of the fine summer, we had a bumper crop of apples,***

bunch (bunch) *n.* 1. a cluster of fruit, small collection of flowers, etc. 2. a group of things or people gathered together: ***a bunch of children played in the street.*** —*vb.* to gather together in a group: ***the papers were bunched together in a file, and we had difficulty in sorting them out.***

bun·dle ('bundəl) *n.* a collection of things held loosely together: ***a bundle of firewood.*** —*vb.* **bun·dling, bun·dled.** 1. to put together into a bundle. 2. to throw (something) untidily into something else: ***he bundled his clothes into a suitcase.*** 3. to go or send (someone) off hurriedly and without ceremony: ***we bundled him off to the meeting.***

bun·ga·low ('bunggəlō) *n.* a single-storied house.

bun·ion ('bunyən) *n.* an inflamed swelling of a joint of the foot, usu. on the big toe.

bunk (bungk) *n.* 1. a sleeping-berth on a boat. 2. one of a pair of narrow beds often attached to a wall and placed one above the other.

bu·oy ('bo͞oē, boi) *n.* 1. an anchored float, usu. colored and sometimes bearing a colored light, used to mark rocks or other hazards or to indicate a channel. 2. a life preserver. —*vb.* 1. to mark with a buoy. 2. (+ *up*) to keep afloat or keep up.

buoy

buoy·ant ('boiənt) *adj.* 1. able to float or (of liquids) capable of supporting a floating object. 2. cheerful or lively: *Roy's buoyant personality made him very popular.* —'**buoy·an·cy** *n.* —'**buoy·ant·ly** *adv.*

bur·den ('bûrdən) *n.* 1. a heavy load. 2. a responsibility, task, duty, emotion, etc., that is difficult to bear: *the new job was a burden to him.* —*vb.* to place a load or burden on someone or something: *he burdened me with his worries.* —'**bur·den·some** *adj.*

bu·reau ('byŏŏrō) *n.,pl.* **bu·reaux** *or* **bu·reaus** ('byŏŏrōz). 1. a writing desk with drawers. 2. an office, agency, or government department concerned with specific activity.

bur·glar ('bûrglər) *n.* a person who breaks into and steals from a house, shop, etc. '**bur·gla·ry** *n.,pl.* **bur·gla·ries.** the crime or act of breaking into a building in order to steal. **bur·glar·ize** *vb.* **bur·glar·iz·ing bur·glar·ized.** to commit burglary.

bur·i·al ('berēəl) the action or an instance of burying something, esp. a dead body at a funeral.

burn (bûrn) *vb.* **burn·ing, burned** *or* **burnt.** 1. to destroy or injure with heat, fire, etc. 2. to catch or be on fire; be destroyed or changed by fire. 3. to produce or suffer a stinging feeling on the skin because or as if because of heat. 4. to be strongly affected by anger, passion, etc.: *he burned with rage.* —*n.* 1. an injury on the skin, etc., produced by heat. 2. a short burst from the engines of a spacecraft.

bur·row ('burō) *n.* a hole or underground tunnel made by rabbits, moles, etc. —*vb.* to dig or tunnel underground.

burst (bûrst) *vb.* **burst·ing, burst.** 1. to break open suddenly due to pressure or force: *the severe frost caused the pipes to burst.* 2. to do something suddenly and forcefully: *the wood burst into flames.* —*n.* a sudden outbreak: *a burst of applause.*

bur·y ('berē) *vb.* **bur·y·ing, bur·ied.** 1. to place (a dead person's body) in a grave at a funeral ceremony. 2. to place or hide something, esp. under the earth. See also BURIAL.

bush (bŏŏsh) *n.* a small woody plant. **the Bush** the large thinly populated uncultivated areas of tountryside, esp. in Australia and Africa. '**bush·y** *adj.* **bush·i·er, bush·i·est.** 1. covered with bushes. 2. growing thickly: *a bushy tail.*

busi·ness ('biznis) *n.* 1. commerce or trade: *business was poor in January.* 2. a firm or organization: *he owned a retail business.* 3. affair or concern: *it is not my business to interfere.*

bust (bust) *n.* 1. the part of the body including the head, neck, and shoulders, often represented in a sculpture. 2. a woman's chest.

bus·tle ('busəl) *vb.* **bus·tling, bus·tled.** to hurry; behave or move about in a brisk or energetic way. —*n.* the action or an instance of bustling.

bus·y ('bizē) *adj.* **bus·i·er, bus·i·est.** occupied with a large number of jobs or duties. —*vb.* **bus·y·ing, bus·ied.** to keep someone busy or occupied.

butch·er ('bŏŏchər) *n.* 1. a person who slaughters animals or prepares and sells meat. —*vb.* 1. to slaughter animals. 2. to murder savagely and brutally. —'**butch·er·y** *n.*

but·ler ('butlər) *n.* a male servant, esp. the head servant in a big house.

butt[1] (but) *n.* 1. the thicker or blunter end of something: *the butt of a rifle.* 2. the part of a cigarette or cigar left after most of it has been smoked. 3. a person who is an object of mockery, scorn, sarcasm, etc.: *the fat girl was the butt of the children's teasing.*

butt[2] (but) *vb.* 1. to push or ram with the head or horns. 2. (+ *in*) (informal) to interrupt or push one's way in: *Arnold butted into the conversation.*

butte (byŏŏt) *n.* a geographical feature resembling a mountain with the top cut off, usu. rising from a relatively flat plain, as in the western U.S.

but·ter ('butər) *n.* a soft fatty yellow foodstuff made from milk or cream. —*vb.* to spread butter on something.

but·ter·fly ('butərflī) *n.,pl.* **but·ter·flies.** 1. an INSECT often with large brightly-colored wings. 2. a stroke in swimming in which both arms are thrust through the water beneath the swimmer and brought forward above the water together.

but·tock ('butək) *n.* either of the fleshy parts of the body at the back and lower end of the TRUNK (def. 2).

but·ton ('butən) *n.* 1. a small object on a jacket, shirt, dress, etc., that may be passed through a hole (**but·ton·hole**) to fasten the garment. 2. a small knob or disk that is pressed with the finger to operate an electrical device. —*vb.* (often + *up*) to fasten (a jacket, etc.) with a button.

but·tress ('butris) *n.* a structure built up against the outside wall of large buildings to support them. —*vb.* to support with or as with a buttress.

buttress

buy (bī) *vb.* **buy·ing, bought.** to give money or other payment in exchange for: *buy some ice cream.* —*n.* something bought; a bargain: *a good buy.* '**buy·er** *n.* a person who buys, esp. one who buys stock for a large store.

buzz (buz) *n.* a low continuous vibrating humming sound, as of wasps, bees, machinery, etc. —*vb.* to make such a sound. '**buzz·er** *n.* a device like an electric bell that makes a harsh buzzing sound.

by·pass ('bīpas) *n.* a road built to avoid a town center. —*vb.* to go round or make a detour.

C

cab·bage ('kabij) *n.* a green vegetable with large overlapping outer leaves and round center.

cab·in ('kabin) *n.* 1. a simple hut or small house built of wood or other materials. 2. a living compartment on board ship. 3. (in an aircraft) the area occupied by the crew and passengers. **cabin cruiser** a motorboat with living accommodation.

cab·i·net ('kabinit) *n.* a cupboard with drawers or shelves and often glass-fronted, usu. used for storing and displaying glass, china, ornaments, etc. **the Cabinet** (in the U.S.) the heads of 13 governmental departments selected by the President with the approval of the Senate. It advises the President on governmental matters and meets privately to discuss administration, make policies, etc.

ca·ble ('kābəl) *n.* 1. a strong braided or twisted rope of wire, etc. 2. a wire or line, carried overhead, underground, or under the sea, along which telephone or telegraph messages or electrical power may be sent. 3. a telegram transmitted by cable. —*vb.* **ca·bling, ca·bled.** to send a telegram by cable.

cac·tus ('kaktəs) *n.,pl.* **cac·ti** ('kaktī) *or* **cac·tus·es.** a fleshy plant, often covered in spiny prickles, that grows in very dry areas, being able to store its moisture for long periods.

cactus

ca·det (kə'det) *n.* a student training to be an officer in the U.S. Army at a military academy.

ca·fé *or* **ca·fe** (kə'fā) *n.* a small restaurant or bar.

caf·e·te·ri·a (kafi'tērēə) *n.* a self-service restaurant.

cage (kāj) *n.* 1. a framework of wood, wire, iron bars, etc., used for keeping animals or birds in captivity. 2. (in a mine) an elevator. 3. anything like a cage; anything that imprisons. —*vb.* **cag·ing, caged.** to place or keep in a cage.

cal·en·dar ('kaləndər) *n.* a chart of the months, weeks, and days of a particular year.

calf[1] (kaf) *n.,pl.* **calves** (kavz). 1. the young of a cow. 2. the young of other mammals, such as elephants, deer, seals, and whales.

calf[2] (kaf) *n.,pl.* **calves** (kavz). the fleshy part of the back of the leg below the knee.

cal·o·rie *or* **cal·o·ry** ('kalərē) *n.,pl.* **cal·o·ries.** 1. a unit of heat; the amount of heat needed to raise one gram of water through one degree Celsius. 2. **Calorie** *or* **large calorie** 1000 calories; the unit for measuring energy produced by food. —**cal·o'rif·ic** *adj.*

calve (kav) *vb.* **calv·ing, calved.** to give birth to a calf or calves.

calves (kavz) *n.* the plural of CALF[1] and CALF[2].

cam·el ('kaməl) *n.* a large long-necked, heavy-footed, plant-eating animal with either one hump (Arabian camel *or* dromedary) or two (Bactrian camel), found mainly in the desert areas of the Middle East and Asia, and used mainly for carrying loads over long distances.

cam·e·ra ('kamərə) *n.* an apparatus for taking photographs, consisting of a sealed box containing light-sensitive film and a shutter which opens very briefly to admit light through a LENS, thus producing an image on the film. **TV Camera** a device in which the television picture is formed before being broadcast. **movie camera** a camera that takes moving pictures produced on a moving strip of film. **'cam·e·ra·man** *n.,pl.* **cam·e·ra·men.** a man who operates a movie or television camera.

cam·ou·flage ('kaməflâzh) *n.* 1. the natural coloring or patterning of an animal that allows it to blend easily with its surroundings, thus hiding it from enemies. 2. (military) the disguising of buildings, vehicles, weapons, etc., to make them hard to see: *the color of the army's trucks served as a camouflage during the drive through the forest.* —*vb.* **cam·ou·flag·ing, cam·ou·flaged.** to disguise something so that it is not easily seen: *a tiger's stripes camouflage it when it hunts in tall grass.*

camouflage

camp (kamp) *n.* 1. the tents or temporary housing used by vacationers, an army, etc. 2. the area where the tents, etc., are placed. **summer camp** a recreational facility accommodating children or adults for extended visits and equipped to offer a wide variety of sports activities. —*vb.* 1. to set up a camp or pitch one's tent at a camp. 2. (+ *out*) to sleep outside, usu. in a tent.

cam·paign (kam'pān) *n.* 1. a series of battles or planned military operations. 2. a lengthy and organized effort: *a campaign against litter.* —*vb.* to seek public support for (a cause, political candidate, etc.): *the canditates for governor campaigned in all the major towns in the state.* —**cam'paign·er** *n.*

ca·nal (kə'nal) *n.* an artificial inland waterway used for transporting goods, for travel, or for irrigation.

ca·nar·y (kə'neərē) *n.,pl.* **ca·nar·ies.** a bright yellow songbird popular as a pet.

can·cel ('kansəl) *vb.* 1. to notify or state that something previously arranged will not be done, not take place, or is no longer required: *we canceled our trip to France.* 2. to cross out or mark in some way (a ticket, check, postage stamp, etc.) to show that it cannot be reissued or used again. 3. (+ *out*) to prevent or destroy (something) by being equal or opposite to: *his handsomeness was canceled out by his rudeness.*

can·cer ('kansər) *n.* a disease in which cells grow abnormally on the skin or to form a tumor or swelling in an organ. —'**can·cer·ous** *adj.*

can·did ('kandid) *adj.* frank, open, and honest; not afraid to tell the truth; outspoken: *he admitted in his candid way that he detested the play.* '**can·dor** ('kandər) *n.* frankness; honesty. —'**can·did·ly** *adv.*

can·di·date ('kandidāt) *n.* a person applying for a position or job, taking an examination, running for election, etc.

can·dle ('kandəl) *n.* a long stick of wax, tallow, etc., containing a wick that draws up melted wax, which burns slowly to provide light.

cane (kān) *n.* 1. the hollow woody stem of certain plants, e.g. bamboo, sugar cane, raspberry plants, etc. 2. a piece of cane used as a walking stick, for beating as a punishment, etc. —*vb.* **can·ing, caned.** to beat with a cane.

canoe

can·ni·bal ('kanibəl) *n.* an animal that eats its own species, esp. a man-eating human. —'**can·ni·bal·ism** *n.* —**can·ni·ba'list·ic** *adj.*

can·non ('kanən) *n.,pl.* **can·nons** *or* **can·non.** 1. a large gun mounted on a cart and having a barrel suitable for firing heavy missiles. 2. a large automatic aircraft gun which fires explosive shells.

ca·noe (kə'nōō) *n.* a long narrow open boat propelled by paddles. —*vb.* **ca·noe·ing, ca·noed.** to paddle a canoe.

can·on ('kanən) *n.* 1. a law or set of laws laid down by a church. 2. a standard by which something is judged: *the canon of good manners should be followed by everyone.* 3. those books of the Bible or of a particular writer that are considered to be genuine. 4. a list of saints recognized by a church. 5. a musical composition in which all the parts overlap while having the same melody throughout. 6. a church official.

can·o·py ('kanəpē) *n.,pl.* **can·o·pies.** 1. a covering, supported above a throne, entrance, or bed. 2. any shelter or protective cover. 3. the umbrella-shaped sail of a PARACHUTE.

can·teen (kan'tēn) *n.* 1. a self-service restaurant attached to factories, schools, etc. 2. a water container for carrying on a long journey.

can·ter ('kantər) *n.* the running pace of a horse slower and more relaxed than a gallop but faster than a trot. —*vb.* to move at a canter: *the riders cantered across the fields.*

can·vas ('kanvəs) *n.* 1. a rough strong cloth used according to thickness for sails, tents, shoes, the base for oil paintings, etc. 2. an oil painting.

can·vass ('kanvəs) *vb.* 1. to seek support or favors, esp. votes at an election. 2. to find out what support there is for a party, issue, etc., by talking to people: *he canvassed opinion in the neighborhood.* '**can·vass·er** *n.* one who canvasses, esp. for a political party.

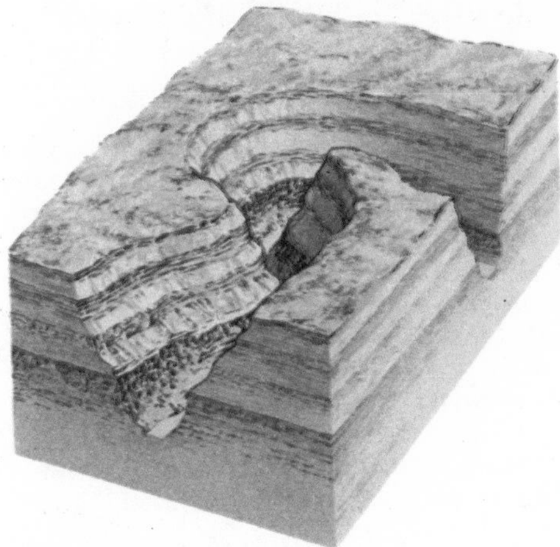

canyon

can·yon ('kanyən) *n.* a deep steep-sided valley often with a stream flowing through it.

ca·pa·ble ('kāpəbəl) *adj.* competent; having ability: *Sam is capable of making a table.* **ca·pa'bil·i·ty** *n.,pl.* **ca·pa·bil·i·ties.** 1. the quality of being capable. 2. an advantage.

cape[1] (kāp) *n.* a narrow pointed stretch of land jutting out into the sea or other body of water.

cape[2] (kāp) *n.* a loose-fitting outer garment that has no sleeves and is worn over the shoulders.

cap·i·tal ('kapitəl) *n.* 1. a city where the seat of government is situated: *Rome is the capital of Italy.* 2. the money needed for starting a company, etc., or investing in it in order to help it to grow. 3. (architecture) the top of a pillar. 4. a capital letter. *—adj.* 1. most important; chief: *London is England's capital city.* 2. relating to financial capital: *capital investment.* 3. punishable by death: *murder is still a capital crime in some countries.* 4. indicating the large form of a letter of the alphabet used at the beginning of sentences, proper names, etc. **'cap·i·tal·ism** *n.* a social and economic system based on the privately owned (rather than state-owned) commercial companies kept in existence by private investments and paying out part of their profits to the investors. **—capitalist** *n., adj.*

cap·size ('kapsīz, kap'sīz) *vb.* **cap·siz·ing, cap·sized.** 1. (of a boat) to overturn in water. 2. to overturn (a boat) in water: *the strong wind capsized the yacht.*

cap·sule ('kapsəl) *n.* 1. a small protective container holding a dose of medicine. 2. a section of a spacecraft containing the crew or vital machinery.

cap·tain ('kaptin) *n.* 1. the leader of an organized group of people, such as a sports team or a ship's crew. 2. a rank in the Army, Air Force, and Marine Corps between lieutenant and major. *—vb.* to lead: *Don captained the chess team.*

cap·tion ('kapshən) *n.* 1. a heading of a picture in a newspaper, etc. 2. a title or other wording shown on the screen during a film or T.V. program.

cap·tive ('kaptiv) *n.* a person who has been taken prisoner. *—adj.* having been captured: *the captive soldiers were chained to the wall.* **cap'tiv·i·ty** *n.* the state of being held (as a) captive: *the injured fox was kept in captivity until it was well.*

cap·ture ('kapchər) *vb.* **cap·tur·ing, cap·tured.** to seize, take possession of, or take prisoner: *the wanted criminals were captured by the police after a car chase.* *—n.* the action or an instance of capturing: *the capture of the rare animal excited the zoo.*

car·bo·hy·drate ('kârbō'hīdrāt) *n.* any of a large number of chemicals that make up plants and are important in the food of man and animals.

car·bon ('kârbən) *n.* an element found as charcoal, graphite, diamond, and soot, present in coal and all living things. Chemical symbol: C.

care (keər) *n.* 1. concern; consideration; serious thought: *he handled the box with care.* 2. guardianship; protection; love: *Ron left the parcel in his neighbor's care.* 3. worry; anxiety: *the cares of looking after them all made her ill.* *—vb.* **car·ing, cared.** 1. (+ *for*) to look after; show concern or love for: *neighbors cared for the little girl when her family was away.* 2. (usu. + *about*) to mind; be concerned: *I don't care what you think.* **'care·ful** *adj.* paying thoughtful attention to what one is doing, using, etc.: *Alice was careful when she used the best glasses.* **'care·ful·ly** *adv.* with care. **'care·less** *adj.* 1. not paying proper attention to what one is doing; thoughtless. 2. lacking a sense of concern, love, or morality: *he was careless of her feelings.* —**'care·less·ly** *adv.*

ca·reer (kə'rēr) *n.* 1. a job of work with opportunities for promotion to senior positions. 2. a headlong rush. *—vb.* to rush madly and uncontrollably: *Fred careered along the road in his hurry to get home.*

car·go ('kârgō) *n.,pl.* **car·goes.** the goods carried in the hold of a ship.

car·ni·val ('kârnəvəl) *n.* 1. a festive procession or fair, esp. one set up during a public holiday for organized enjoyment. 2. noisy celebration or rejoicing. 3. the period of such activities, esp. in some countries the short period before Lent.

car·niv·o·rous (kâr'nivərəs) *adj.* of animals (and some plants) that feed on meat.

carp (kârp) *n.* a large freshwater fish caught for food.

car·pen·ter ('kârpintər) *n.* a man skilled in working with wood and making wooden articles, furniture, etc. —**'car·pen·try** *n.*

car·riage ('karij) *n.* 1. a wheeled passenger-carrying vehicle pulled by horses. 2. the way a person moves or carries his body: *the soldier had an upright carriage.*

car·rot ('karət) *n.* 1. a plant with an orange-colored root 2. the root of this plant, eaten as a vegetable.

car·toon (kâr'tōōn) *n.* 1. a drawing showing a humorous scene, or a series of drawings telling a story in a newspaper or magazine. 2. a movie, usu. short, made up of moving cartoon pictures. 3. the drawing of a design to be used for a painting or a tapestry.

car·tridge ('kârtrij) *n.* 1. a thick paper case holding exactly the right amount of gunpowder for firing a shotgun. 2. a metal case containing an explosive powder which, when struck, fires a bullet from a firearm. 3. (in certain types of pen) a replaceable plastic container for the ink.

carve (kârv) *vb.* **carv·ing, carved.** 1. to cut into or shape by cutting (wood, stone, etc.): *he carved a statue out of marble.* 2. to cut up (a roast or other meat) for serving.

case[1] (kās) *n.* 1. an instance or example of something: *the broken toy was a case of bad workmanship.* 2. the facts of a situation: *if that's the case we'll go home.* 3. a legal action or the argument put forward by one of the parties in it. 4. (in some languages) the form of a noun or adjective which changes according to its grammatical function in a sentence.

case[2] (kās) *n.* 1. a box, chest, bag, etc., for holding or carrying things, esp. clothes, papers, etc. 2. any sort of container, esp. a protective one: *a watch case.* *—vb.* **cas·ing, cased.** 1. to cover with or enclose in a case. 2. (slang) to examine or keep watch on (a building), esp. so as to find out how to break into or steal from it: *the criminal cased the bank.*

cash (kash) *n.* money in the form of coins and notes that can be used immediately. **petty cash** a small amount of money kept by a company for ordinary expenses, e.g. for buying postage stamps, etc. *—vb.* to change (a check, etc.) into currency: *he cashed a check at the bank.*

cas·se·role ('kasərōl) *n.* 1. a stewpot with a lid for use in an oven or on direct heat. 2. a stew of meat, gravy, and vegetables that has been cooked in a casserole: *she cooked a delicious casserole.*

cas·sette (kə'set) *n.* a small flat case containing a tape for a tape-recorder or a film for a camera.

cats

bobcat

jaguar

tiger

Calico cat

Siamese cat

lion

Blue Persian cat

cast (kast) *vb.* **cast·ing, cast.** 1. to throw: *Andy cast his clothes onto the floor.* 2. to send out (a look, glance, etc.) at someone or something or in a certain direction: *could you cast a look at my essay? 3. to cause (light, a shadow, etc.) to fall upon something: he cast a shadow on the wall in the moonlight.* 4. (+ *about*) to search in one's mind: *he cast about for an excuse for being late.* 5. to make from a mold: *he cast the statue in bronze.* 6. to assign parts to actors in a play. 7. (+ *on*) to start a row of stitches in knitting. 8. (+ *off*) to finish off knitting stitches to form an edge. 9. (+ *off*) to untie (a boat) at the start of a voyage. —*n.* 1. the action of casting; a throw, esp. of a fishing line. 2. a list or group of characters in, or actors needed for, a play. 3. a model of something made from a mold. 4. (also **plaster cast**) a casing made from plaster of Paris and put on a broken limb while it is healing. 5. (also **worm cast**) the heap of earth brought up to the surface by a worm.

cas·ta·net (kastə'net) *n.* either one of a pair of shaped pieces of wood or ivory held in one hand and rhythmically clicked together. They are used esp. in Spanish dancing and music.

cast·a·way ('kastəwā) *n.* someone who has been abandoned, esp. on a desert island.

caste (kâst) *n.* one of the divisions of Hindu society in India to which a person belongs as a result of his being born into a family within that particular division.

castanet

cas·u·al ('kazhōōəl) *adj.* 1. not especially arranged or organized; happening by chance: *we paid a casual visit to our neighbors without warning them first.* 2. informal; relaxed: *I wear casual clothes on weekends.* —**'cas·u·al·ly** *adv.*

cas·u·al·ty ('kazhōōəltē) *n.,pl.* **cas·u·al·ties.** 1. an unlucky accident, usu. serious or fatal. 2. (military) any man lost because of death, injury, etc. 3. any person or thing killed, injured, or damaged purely by accident: *the hospital took in several casualties after the crash.*

cat (kat) *n.* any one of the family of flesh-eating MAMMALs that ranges in size from the cats that are kept as pets to tigers, lions, and jaguars, etc.

cat·a·log *or* **cat·a·logue** ('katəlog) *n.* a list that is arranged in alphabetical or some other order, usu. with a short description of the listed items. —*vb.* **cat·a·log·ing, cat·a·loged** *or* **cat·a·logu·ing, cat·a·logued.** to make a catalog or enter (something) into a catalog: *we must catalog all the books in the library.*

ca·tarrh (kə'târ) *n.* the thick discharge produced by the tissues in the nose, throat, etc., when they are painfully inflamed, e.g. by a cold.

catch (kach) *vb.* **catch·ing, caught.** 1. to lay hold of; seize or capture. 2. to stop and hold with the hand: *to catch a ball.* 3. to reach and board (a bus, train, etc.). 4. to be affected by (an infectious illness): *he caught a cold.* 5. (often + *up* or *up with*) to come near to or overtake (something): *the horse made a bad start, but caught up with the others halfway through the race.* 6. (+ *on*) to become popular: *the craze for skateboarding caught on quickly.* 7. (+ *on*) to understand or realize: *Mandy caught on to what her friend was trying to explain.* —*n.* 1. the action of catching or seizing; a capture. 2. something caught, esp. fish. 3. a fastener: *a catch on a window.* 4. a trick; drawback: *this is a genuine offer and there's no catch.* **'catch·y** *adj.* **catch·i·er, catch·i·est.** pleasant and easily learnt: *a catchy melody.*

cat·er·pil·lar ('katərpilər) *n.* 1. the plump worm-like LARVA of a moth or butterfly. It feeds on leaves and other vegetation. 2. a special vehicle for traveling over rough or snow-covered ground and having wheels that move inside an endless belt (**caterpillar track**).

caterpillar

ca·the·dral (kə'thēdrəl) *n.* the chief church of a diocese.

cat·tle ('katəl) *pl.n.* 1. animals such as cows, oxen, buffaloes, etc. 2. the domestic cows and bulls used for milk and meat.

caught (kôt) *vb.* the past tense and past participle of CATCH.

caul·i·flow·er ('kôlēflouər, 'kolēflouər) *n.* a plant of the cabbage family with a large hard compact white flowerhead that is widely eaten as a vegetable.

cau·tion ('kôshən) *n.* 1. care taken to avoid danger: *the children used caution when crossing the highway.* 2. a warning or reprimand. —*vb.* to warn (a person) to be sensible, careful, etc.: *the doctor cautioned him to look after his health.* **'cau·tious** *adj.* 1. prudent; careful. 2. timid; unadventurous. —**'cau·tious·ly** *adv.*

cav·al·ry ('kavəlrē) *n.* the part of an army that fights on horseback; horse soldiers.

cease (sēs) *vb.* **ceas·ing, ceased.** to stop or come to an end: *fighting ceased completely.* **'cease·less** *adj.* continuous: *the neighbors complained about the ceaseless noise from the radio.*

ce·dar ('sēdə) *n.* a large spreading cone-bearing evergreen tree with tough sweet-smelling reddish wood. See CONIFER.

ceil·ing ('sēling) *n.* 1. the overhead surface of a room. 2. the highest possible limit: *in Britain, most goods have a price ceiling.*

cel·e·brate ('seləbrāt) *vb.* **cel·e·brat·ing, cel·e·brat·ed.** to mark a special occasion, esp. with a ceremony, party, etc.: *we usually celebrate Christmas at home.* **'cel·e·brat·ed** *adj.* famous: *Beethoven is a celebrated composer.* —**cel·e'bra·tion** *n.*

ce·leb·ri·ty (sə'lebritē) *n.,pl.* **ce·leb·ri·ties.** a person well known to the public for achievements in entertainment, sport, arts, etc.

cel·er·y ('selərē) *n.* a vegetable with long white stalks, which are eaten raw or cooked.

ce·les·tial (si'leschəl) *adj.* appearing in or connected with heaven or the heavens: *a star is a celestial object.*

cell (sel) *n.* 1. a small, barely furnished room in a prison, monastery, etc. 2. the smallest unit of living matter capable of producing energy and reproducing itself, out of which all plants and animals are formed. 3. apparatus for producing electricity by chemical action, e.g. in a battery.

cel·lar ('selər) *n.* a windowless room below ground level often used for storage.

cel·lo ('chelō) *n.,pl.* **cel·los.** a musical instrument of the violin family, pitched lower than the viola and higher than the double bass. Also called **vi·o·lon·cel·lo** (vīəlin'chelō). —**'cel·list** *n.*

Cel·si·us ('selsiəs) *adj.* of a temperature scale extending from the freezing point of water (0°) to its boiling point (100°). Also called **cen·ti·grade.**

ce·ment (si'ment) *n.* 1. a mixture of burnt and powdered limestone and clay that sets hard when combined with water, used as a building material. 2. any glue that sticks by setting hard. 3. a soft plastic material that sets hard to fill cavities in teeth. —*vb.* 1. to cover or join together with cement. 2. to unite and confirm: *the vacation cemented their friendship.*

cem·e·ter·y ('semiterē) *n.,pl.* **cem·e·ter·ies.** an area of land that is used for burying the dead.

cen·sor ('sensər) *n.* a person responsible for examining letters, plays, newspapers, films, etc., in order to remove from them anything he considers to be immoral, obscene, or secret. —*vb.* to act as a censor. **cen·so·ri·ous** (sen'sôrēəs) *adj.* tending to find fault; smugly disapproving. —**'cen·sor·ship** *n.*

cen·sus ('sensəs) *n.,pl.* **cen·sus·es.** an official population count that sometimes includes details of housing, etc.

cent (sent) *n.* a small unit of currency in the U.S. and certain other countries; the 100th part of a DOLLAR.

cen·ten·ni·al (sen'tenēəl) *n.* the hundredth anniversary of an event. —*adj.* relating to a hundred year period or a hundredth anniversary: *centennial celebrations.*

cen·ter ('sentər) *n.* 1. the middle. 2. the middle point, esp. of a circle or sphere. 3. a place where certain activities are concentrated: *a shopping center.* 4. a person or thing receiving a great deal of interest, attention, etc: *Joanne was the center of attention at the dance.* 5. a player in some team games who occupies the middle position. **center of gravity** the point at which an object will balance when supported. —*vb.* 1. to place in the center. 2. to concentrate upon: *all efforts were centered on rescuing people from the flood.* —*adj.* 1. of or placed at the center. 2. (of a

cello

political party or opinion) moderate. '**cen·tral** *adj.* 1. at the center: *the central figure in the photograph.* 2. main or principal: *our central office is in New York.* 3. basic; most important: *the points he raised at the end were not connected with the central issue of his speech.*

cen·ti·grade ('sentigrād) *adj.* See CELSIUS.

cen·ti·me·ter ('sentəmētər) *n.* a unit of measure equal to one hundredth of a meter (0.3937) inches).

cen·ti·pede ('sentəpēd) *n.* a small creature with a long body and many legs. See INVERTEBRATE.

cen·tu·ry ('senchərē) *n.,pl.* **cen·tu·ries.** 1. a period of one hundred years. 2. (in ancient Rome) an army company consisting originally of a hundred men and commanded by an officer called a **cen·tu·ri·on.**

ce·re·al ('sērēəl) *n.* 1. a grass such as wheat, barley, rye, oats, etc., that produces grains or seeds used for food. 2. a breakfast food containing wheat, etc.

cer·e·mo·ny ('serəmōnē) *n.,pl.* **cer·e·mo·nies.** 1. a solemn act or ritual that follows a set pattern: *a wedding ceremony.* 2. formal behaviour; pomp: *the visiting minister was greeted with much ceremony.* **cer·e'mo·ni·al** *adj.* formal; used in ceremonies: *ceremonial robes.* —**cer·e'mo·ni·al·ly** *adv.* —**cer·e'mo·ni·ous** *adj.* —**cer·e'mo·ni·ous·ly** *adv.*

cer·tain ('sûrtən) *adj.* 1. particular; fixed: *the sun rises at a certain time.* 2. without any possible doubt: *it was certain that Mel would win the race.* 3. moderate: *we had a certain amount of snow.* '**cer·tain·ly** *adv.* 1. without doubt: *it was certainly a cold day.* 2. indeed: *may I have a cake? certainly.* —'**cer·tain·ty** *n.,pl.* **cer·tain·ties.**

cer·tif·i·cate (sûr'tifəkit) *n.* a written statement giving proof of some fact or achievement: *a birth certificate states when and where one was born.*

cer·ti·fy ('sûrtəfī) *vb.* **cer·ti·fy·ing, cer·ti·fied.** 1. to declare as certain: *the man certified that he had not driven the car for a week.* 2. to declare in writing or by means of a certificate: *he was the certified owner of the car.* 3. to declare, officially, (a person) to be insane.

chain (chān) *n.* 1. a length of connected links usu. of metal. 2. a series of connected things: *a chain of grocery stores; a chain of events.* 3. a unit of distance equal to 22 yards. 4. **chains** (*pl.*) imprisoning or restraining bands: *the prisoners were kept in chains.* **chain mail** flexible armor made of small metal links. **chain reaction** a series of events, each set off by the one before it. —*vb.* to fasten, connect, or imprison with a chain: *the dog was chained to the kennel.*

chalk (chôk) *n.* 1. soft white limestone rock found in cliffs, hills, etc. 2. a drawing or writing crayon made of chalk. —*vb.* 1. to write, mark, or cover with chalk: *he chalked a circle on the board.* 2. (+ *up*) to earn or reach: *Harry chalked up a very high score.* —'**chalk·y** *adj.* **chalk·i·er, chalk·i·est.**

chal·lenge ('chalinj) *vb.* **chal·leng·ing, chal·lenged.** 1. to invite, demand, or dare (a person) to take part (in a duel, argument, contest, etc.): *Tom challenged his brother to a race.* 2. to question: *I challenged his right to be present.* —*n.* 1. the act of challenging. 2. any task, scheme, etc., in which a person can prove his skill, energy, imagination, etc.: *the problem was a challenge to him.*

cha·me·le·on (kə'mēlēən) *n.* 1. a small lizard with an ability to change its skin color to match its background. 2. a person who changes his behavior and attitudes to match those of his companions.

cham·ois ('shamē, 'shamwâ) *n., pl.* **cham·ois** ('shamēz, 'shamwâz). a small goatlike deer living in mountainous areas of Europe and Russia. **cham·ois, cham·my,** *or* **sham·my leather** (all pronounced 'shamē) leather treated with special oil to make it flexible, originally obtained from the chamois. It is often used for cleaning windows.

cham·pagne (sham'pān) *n.* a sparkling French white wine.

cham·pi·on ('champēən) *n.* 1. a proved competition or contest winner. 2. an active supporter of a cause or person: *Sarah was a champion of wildlife preservation.* —*vb.* to support (a cause, issue, person, etc.). '**cham·pi·on·ship** *n.* 1. the position of being a champion. 2. a series of contests to find an overall champion. 3. support.

chan·de·lier (shandə'lēr) *n.* a light fixture usu. made of glass, hung from the ceiling, with a number of branches to carry several lights.

chan·nel ('chanəl) *n.* 1. a long narrow stretch of water; strait. 2. a course or route along which water flows. 3. a path by which news or information is passed or communicated. 4. usu. **chan·nels** (*pl.*) procedures for doing something: *he applied for permission through the usual channels.* 5. the wavelength or set of wavelengths used by a television company for its broadcasts. —*vb.* to send through or as if through a channel: *the canal channeled water from the river to the lake.*

chant (chant) *n.* a rhythmic repetition of words by shouting or singing. —*vb.* to sing a chant: *the monks chanted prayers for hours at a time.*

cha·os ('kāos) 1. a state of utter confusion: *the room was in chaos after the party.* 2. the huge disordered jumble of matter from which, according to some religions, the universe was formed. —**cha'ot·ic** *adj.*

chap·el ('chapəl) *n.* 1. a place for Christian worship attached to a school, university, etc. 2. a place of worship for Protestants outside the established church: *a Methodist chapel.* 3. a small area or room, e.g. in a church, set aside for private worship. See also CHURCH.

chap·ter ('chaptər) *n.* 1. a section of a book. 2. the members or organizers of a religious organization, society, etc.

char·ac·ter ('kariktər) *n.* 1. the collection of qualities that make one person or thing different from another: *the character of a room* *changes when it is painted.* 2. moral or spiritual strength: *the preacher was a man of character.* 3. a person: *he was an amusing character.* 4. a person in a story, play, etc. 5. any alphabetical symbol. **char·ac·ter'is·tic** *n.* a particular quality or feature: *the second-hand car had several unpleasant characteristics. adj.* typical: *the present was characteristic of his kind nature.* '**char·ac·ter·ize** *vb.* **char·ac·ter·iz·ing, char·ac·ter·ized.** to give a special quality to; distinguish; show the nature of: *the area is characterized by high mountains and deep valleys.*

char·coal ('chârkōl) *n.* 1. the black substance, consisting of pure CARBON, that is produced by the incomplete burning of wood or other living matter. 2. a drawing made with charcoal.

charge (chârj) *vb.* **charg·ing, charged.** 1. to attack with a forward rush. 2. to demand or require money in return for goods or services: *the restaurant charged ten dollars for a meal.* 3. (+ *with*) to accuse (someone) of something: *he was charged with robbery.* 4. to fill with electricity: *to charge a battery.* 5. (+ *with*) to place a duty, responsibility, etc., upon someone. 6. to note down (something) to be paid for later: *charge it to my account.* —*n.* 1. a forward-rushing attack: *the bull made a charge towards the gate.* 2. (esp. of services rather than goods) the money to be paid; price: *there is a charge of one dollar for each item.* 3. an accusation or criticism: *a charge of stupidity.* 4. control or guardianship: *I'm in charge here.* 5. the amount of explosive to be set off at one blast. 6. the amount of electricity or energy in something.

char·i·ty ('charitē) *n.,pl.* **char·i·ties.** 1. generosity and kindness toward others, esp. the poor. 2. an organization providing money, often given to it by the public, to finance projects for relieving poverty, etc.

charm (chârm) *n.* 1. a quality of character that makes a person or place attractive: *that area of Italy is full of charm.* 2. an object, phrase, etc., supposedly having magic powers or bringing good luck: *he kept a lucky charm in his pocket during the exam.* —*vb.* 1. to please; attract. 2. to work magic upon (someone). '**charm·ing** *adj.* pleasant; attractive: *her charming manners made her very popular.*

chart (chârt) *n.* 1. a drawing, table, or graph giving information on something. 2. a map, esp. of a sea area. —*vb.* to make a chart of or plan out, as on a chart.

char·ter ('chârtər) *n.* an official paper granting someone certain special rights. —*vb.* 1. to give a charter. 2. to hire (a bus, aircraft, etc.) for a special purpose.

chauf·feur ('shōfər, shō'fûr) *n.* a person hired to drive a private car.

cheap (chēp) *adj.* 1. costing little money. 2. poor in quality or value: *the cheap dress fell apart.* 3. unkind; lacking tact: *a cheap joke.* '**cheap·en** *vb.* to make cheap: *the quality of her bag was cheapened by its broken clasp.*

cheetah

cheat (chēt) *vb.* to trick (someone); act dishonestly, esp. regarding money, the rules of a game, etc.: *he cheated his sister into giving him the money she had won at cards.* —*n.* a person who cheats.

check (chek) *vb.* 1. to stop or restrain: *the spread of the fire was checked by the firemen.* 2. to make sure about the correctness of (a fact, etc.). 3. (chess) to threaten one's opponent's king. —*n.* 1. a written order from a customer to his bank to pay a certain sum of money from his account to a person or company designated. 2. the action or an instance of checking; a restraint, investigation, etc. 3. a pattern of squares, as on cloth. 4. the threat to a king at chess. —*adj.* patterned in squares. '**check·book** *n.* a book of blank checks supplied by a bank to its customers. '**check·mate** *n.* (chess) the final threat to an opponent's king, from which there is no escape. '**check·out** *n.* the place in a supermarket where one pays for things bought.

check·ers ('chekərz) *n. sing.* or *pl.* a board game in which each of two players tries to capture his opponent's pieces. '**check·er** *n.* one of the pieces in the game of checkers. '**check·er·board** *n.* the board on which checkers, chess, and other games are played consisting of a pattern of 64 squares of alternating colors. *adj.* in a pattern resembling that of a checkerboard; of regularly alternating colors.

cheek (chēk) *n.* the side of the face between the eye and the jaw.

cheer (chēr) *n.* 1. a state of pleasant comfort; happiness or gladness. 2. a shout of joy, approval, encouragement, etc. —*vb.* 1. to comfort or encourage. 2. to give a shout of joy, approval, encouragement, etc. —'**cheer·ful** *adj.* —'**cheer·ful·ly** *adv.* —'**cheer·ful·ness** *n.*

cheese (chēz) *n.* a food made from the solid fatty part of milk.

chee·tah ('chētə) *n.* an animal belonging to the cat family and having a spotted coat and long legs. It is found in parts of Asia and Africa and is famous for its great speed.

chef (shef) *n.* the head cook in a restaurant.

chem·i·cal ('kemikəl) *adj.* concerning or connected with the science or processes of chemistry. —*n.* a substance made by or used in chemistry. —'**chem·i·cal·ly** *adv.*

chem·ist ('kemist) *n.* an expert in the science of chemistry. '**chem·is·try** *n.* the science concerned with the elements and compounds that make up different substances and their properties, reactions, and effects.

cher·ry ('cherē) *n.,pl.* **cher·ries.** 1. a type of tree with decorative blossom growing in temperate regions. 2. the small round red or yellow fruit of this tree. —*adj.* bright red.

chess (ches) *n.* a game played by two people, each moving 16 pieces (**chessmen**) on a board having 64 alternating squares of black and another color (**chessboard**).

chest (chest) *n.* 1. the upper front part of the human body. 2. a large wooden box used for storage, etc. **chest of drawers** a piece of furniture with several drawers used for storing linen, clothes, etc.

chest·nut ('c̮hesnut) *n.* 1. the smooth shiny edible brown nut of the sweet chestnut tree, that grows inside a prickly green case. 2. the inedible nut of the horse chestnut tree. 3. a horse of a reddish-brown color. 4. an old and well-worn joke, question, etc. —*adj.* of a rich reddish-brown color: *chestnut hair.*

chew (c̮hōō) *vb.* 1. to crush or grind between the teeth. 2. (+ *up*) to destroy or ruin (something) as if by chewing; mangle: *the machine chewed up my ticket.* —*n.* the action or an instance of chewing.

chic (s̮hēk) *adj.* stylish, smart, or fashionable; graceful, attractive, and tasteful: *her mother keeps up with the latest fashions and always looks very chic.*

chick·en ('c̮hikin) *n.* 1. a domesticated bird whose flesh and eggs are used as food. 2. (slang) a coward. —*adj.* (slang) cowardly.

chide (chīd) *vb.* to scold mildly; express disapproval: *the teacher chided him for forgetting his books.*

chestnut

chimpanzee

chief (c̮hēf) *n.* the head or leader of a group, society, tribe, etc. —*adj.* main; most important. —**chief·ly** *adv.*

chil·blain ('c̮hilblān) *n.* usu. **chil·b-lains** (*pl.*) one of a number of sore and itchy swellings generally found on the hands and feet and caused by intense cold or bad circulation of the blood.

chill (c̮hil) *n.* 1. a sharp or sudden feeling of coldness: *a chill in the air.* 2. a feverish cold. —*vb.* to make or become cold or colder: *the orange juice was chilled.* '**chil·ly** *adj.* **chil·li·er, chil·li·est.** 1. rather cold. 2. unwelcoming, unfriendly: *a chilly reception.* —'**chil·li·ness** *n.*

chime (c̮hīm) *n.* the sound produced by a striking bell or clock. —*vb.* **chim·ing, chimed.** 1. to ring out like a bell. 2. (+ *in*) to interrupt or break into a conversation: *when the argument began, everyone chimed in at once.*

chim·ney ('c̮himnē) *n.* an open hollow pillarlike structure built above a fireplace, furnace, etc., to allow smoke, gases, etc. to escape. **chimney sweep** a person who cleans the soot from chimneys.

chim·pan·zee (c̮himpan'zē, c̮him'panzē) *n.* a small highly intelligent African ape smaller than a gorilla that lives in trees.

chin (c̮hin) *n.* the part of the face below the mouth.

chi·na ('c̮hīnə) *n.* 1. very fine fragile earthenware pottery first made in China. 2. plates, cups, etc., collectively: *her parents gave her a very attractive set of china as a wedding present.* —*adj.* made of china.

chin·chil·la (c̮hin'chilə) *n.* 1. a South American animal that looks like a squirrel. 2. the thick soft pale gray fur of this animal, which is highly valued for making coats, etc.

chink[1] (c̮hiñgk) *n.* a narrow crack or slit, esp. one with light showing through it.

chink[2] (c̮hiñgk) *vb.* to make a sound like that of coins or glasses struck together. —*n.* a chinking sound.

chip (c̮hip) *n.* 1. a small piece or splinter of wood, stone, china, etc., that has been broken or cut off. 2. a crack or mark on a piece of crockery, glass, etc., caused by chipping. 3. **potato chip** a paper-thin slice of potato that has been deep-fried and usu. seasoned. 4. a counter or token used in gambling. —*vb.* **chip·ping, chipped.** 1. to remove chips from an object: *the sculptor chipped at the stone with a chisel.* 2. to be chipped or broken: *be careful of that china because it will chip if you treat it roughly.* 3. (+ *in*) (informal) to give or contribute money to a fund, outing, etc.: *when the waiter brought the check, we all chipped in.*

chip·munk ('c̮hipmuñgk) *n.* a North American animal related to the squirrel. It has brown or gray fur with stripes on the back.

chis·el ('c̮hizəl) *n.* a long metal TOOL having a blade that is sharp at the end, used for shaping wood, stone, or metal. —*vb.* to shape or cut with a chisel.

chiv·al·ry ('s̮hivəlrē) *n.* the qualities of honor, courage, kindness, etc., such as knights in the Middle Ages were expected to have. —'**chiv·al·rous** *adj.*

choice (chois) *n.* 1. the action or an instance of choosing: *a difficult choice.* 2. the thing chosen: *her final choice.* 3. the range or variety available: *a wide choice of dresses.* —*adj.* **choic·er, choic·est.** excellent: *a choice cut of meat.*

choir (kwīər) *n.* a group of singers, esp. one that takes part in the services at a church; chorus.

choke (chōk) *vb.* **chok·ing, choked.** 1. to block or prevent air from entering the windpipe of (a person): *the collar of his new shirt was so tight that it choked him.* 2. to be unable to breathe or swallow; suffocate: *he choked on a fish bone.* 3. to obstruct a passage, etc.: *weeds choked the drains.* —*n.* a device in a gasoline engine that regulates the amount of air taken into the engine.

choose (chōōz) *vb.* **choos·ing, chose, cho·sen.** 1. to select: *I chose a dress for the party.* 2. to decide (on something): *I chose to disobey him.* '**choos·y** *adj.* **choos·i·er, choos·i·est.** (informal) very fussy.

chop (chop) *vb.* **chop·ping, chopped.** 1. to cut with a heavy blow, as with an ax: *we chopped the wood for the fire.* 2. to cut up into small pieces: *chop the parsley finely.* —*n.* 1. a short sharp cut or blow. 2. a piece of pork, lamb, or veal containing part of a rib-bone. '**chop·per** *n.* 1. a heavy ax with a large flat blade. 2. (informal) a helicopter.

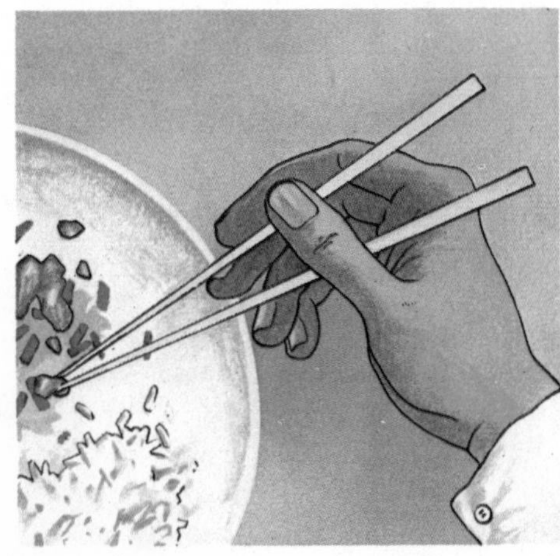

chopstick

chop·stick ('chopstik) *n.* one of two small wooden, plastic, or ivory sticks, both held in one hand and used by Oriental people for eating food.

cho·ral ('kôrəl) *adj.* 1. connected with, or relating to, a choir or chorus. 2. written, composed, or adapted for, or sung by a choir, or chorus: *choral music.*

chord (kôrd) *n.* 1. a combination of three or more musical sounds played or sung together. 2. a straight line passing through two points on a circle or curve.

chore (chôr) *n.* 1. a necessary but usu. dull or boring task. 2. an odd job.

cho·rus ('kôrəs) *n.,pl.* **cho·rus·es.** 1. a company of singers or dancers, esp. those who support the soloists in an opera, ballet, etc. 2. a choir. 3. a section of a song that is usu. repeated at the end of each verse.

chose (chōz) *vb.* the past tense of CHOOSE.

cho·sen ('chōzən) *vb.* the past participle of CHOOSE.

chris·ten ('krisən) *vb.* 1. (in the Christian Church) to baptize and give a name to (someone).

Chris·tian ('krischən) *n.* a person who believes in and follows the teachings of Jesus Christ. —*adj.* of or relating to Christianity. **Chris·ti·an·i·ty** (krischē'anitē) *n.* the Christian faith based on the teachings of Jesus Christ.

Christ·mas (kris'məs) *n.* the annual commemoration of the birth of Jesus on December 25th, which is a holiday in many countries.

chron·ic ('kronik) *adj.* 1. (of a disease, illness, etc.) long-lasting and continuous. 2. (informal) continuing: *a chronic housing shortage.* —'**chron·i·cal·ly** *adv.*

chron·i·cle ('kronikəl) *n.* often **chronicles** (*pl.*) a list or description of past events, usu. arranged in order of time. —*vb.* **chron·i·cling, chron·i·cled.** to record in a chronicle.

chro·nol·o·gy (krə'noləjē) *n.,pl.* **chro·nol·o·gies.** 1. the study or arrangement of events with respect to the sequence in which they happen. 2. a list of events arranged in the order in which they occurred. —**chron·o·log·i·cal** (kronə'lojikəl) *adj.* —**chron·o'log·i·cal·ly** *adv.* —**chro'nol·o·gist** *n.*

chrys·a·lis ('krisəlis) *n.* the PUPA of a moth or butterfly.

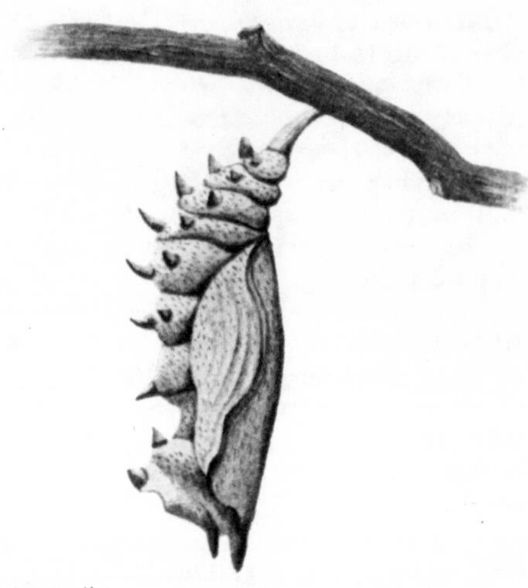

chrysalis

chry·san·the·mum (kri'santhəməm) *n.* one of a family of garden plants that flower in the fall, usu. with large showy blooms.

chuck·le ('chukəl) *vb.* **chuck·ling, chuck·led.** to laugh quietly to oneself in a gently cheerful way. —*n.* a quiet laugh.

chunk (chungk) *n.* a large thick piece or slice: *a chunk of meat.* '**chunk·y** *adj.* **chunk·i·er, chunk·i·est.** 1. in a chunk or chunks. 2. somewhat short and squat in stature.

church (chûrch) *n.* (often **Church**) 1. a building used for Christian or other religious services. 2. a particular group of Christians following its own interpretation of Christ's teachings: *the Methodist Church.* 3. all clergymen considered as a single group. 4. the career of a clergyman: *Charles decided at an early age to go into the church.* '**church·yard** *n.* a burial ground surrounding a church.

churn (chûrn) *n.* the container in which milk or cream is stirred or beaten to make butter. —*vb.* (often + *up*) to shake or beat violently; stir up: *the horses' hoofs churned up the mud.*

ci·der ('sīdər) *n.* a liquid or drink made from the juice of apples. **hard cider** cider that has fermented, making it alcoholic. **Sweet cider** unfermented cider.

cin·e·ma ('sinəmə) *n.* the craft of making MOTION PICTUREs.

cir·cle ('sûrkəl) *n.* 1. a closed curved line all points of which are the same distance away from the CENTER; a ring. See GEOMETRY. 2. a group of people with the same interests.

—*vb.* **cir·cling, cir·cled.** 1. to surround with a ring: *the hunters circled the animal before attacking.* 2. to move in a circle: *the kitten nervously circled the sleeping dog; the aircraft circled over the town.*

cir·cuit ('sûrkit) *n.* 1. the route or way around a course or area that has been marked out; lap: *any runners that did not follow the circuit were knocked out of the race.* 2. the path taken by an electric current. 3. a number of places, e.g. theaters or law courts, that are linked in some way; chain.

cir·cu·lar ('sûrkyələr) *adj.* 1. in the shape of a circle or ring; round: *a circular table.* 2. tending to bring one back to the original starting point: *a circular argument.* **circular saw** an electrically powered saw that is disk-shaped with a sharp-toothed edge. —*n.* a printed letter, notice, advertisement, etc., distributed to a number of people.

cir·cum·fer·ence (sər'kumfərəns) *n.* 1. the boundary line of a circle or circular area; perimeter. 2. the length of this line. See GEOMETRY.

cir·cum·stanc·es ('sûrkəmstansiz) *pl.n.* the conditions or facts connected with a person, event, etc.: *what were the circumstances of the accident?*

cir·cus ('sûrkəs) *n.,pl.* **cir·cus·es.** 1. a traveling show with performing animals, acrobats, clowns, etc. 2. a central arena as in a Roman amphitheater.

cis·tern ('sistərn) *n.* a water tank.

cit·a·del ('sitədəl) *n.* a strongly fortified place, esp., in former times, for keeping inhabitants of a nearby town under control.

cit·i·zen ('sitizən) *n.* a person who enjoys the rights or privileges of a particular city, town, or country: *an American citizen.*—'**cit·i·zen·ship** *n.*

cit·rus ('sitrəs) *n.* a family of trees, consisting of the orange, lemon, grapefruit, etc., cultivated in warm climates. —*adj.* of or relating to such trees or their fruit.

cit·y ('sitē) *n.,pl.* **cit·ies.** a large settlement where many people work and live.

civ·ic ('sivik) *adj.* of or relating to the affairs of a city or citizenship: *civic pride.*

civ·il ('sivəl) *adj.* 1. of or relating to the state, cities, citizens, etc., esp. as distinguished from the Church or the army, navy, or air force. 2. courteous or polite: *he was very annoyed but still gave civil replies to the questions.* **civil war** a war between members or parties of the same state or country.

ci·vil·ian (si'vilyən) *n.* a person who is not in the armed forces. —*adj.* of or relating to a person or life outside the armed forces: *civilian clothes.*

civ·i·lize ('sivəlīz) *vb.* **civ·i·liz·ing, civ·i·lized.** to bring (a people or nation) out of a primitive or savage condition by the introduction of education, law, government, trade, etc. **civ·i·li'za·tion** *n.* 1. the act or process of civilizing a people or nation. 2. a society, nation, or empire having a highly developed cultural, social, economic, and political structure: *Aztec civilization; ancient Roman civilization.* '**civ·i·lized** *adj.* 1. having been civilized. 2. well-bred or polite.

claim (klām) *vb.* 1. to demand or take possession of (something) as one's right: *he claimed the umbrella from the lost-and-found office.* 2. to insist that something is true: *he claims to be 100 years old.* —*n.* 1. a demand or the thing claimed. 2. an area of unused land marked out by a settler or miner for future use. '**claim·ant** *n.* one who claims something, esp. land or a title.

clamp (klamp) *n.* a tool or device that can be tightened to grip, or hold something together. —*vb.* to grip or hold (something) in or as if in a clamp.

clarinet

clar·i·net (klarə'net) *n.* a musical instrument of the woodwind family in which a reed set in the mouthpiece is made to vibrate the air in a tube. —**clar·i'net·ist** *or* **clar·i'net·tist** *n.*

clash (klash) *vb.* 1. to bang two or more things together or collide, making a loud harsh metallic sound: *their swords clashed.* 2. to disagree very strongly; conflict: *these two colors clash violently.* 3. (of events) to coincide: *we couldn't study both subjects because they clashed on the timetable.* —*n.* the action, the sound, or an instance of clashing.

clasp (klasp) *n.* 1. a small fastening, such as a hook, pin, or buckle, generally made of metal and often used in jewelry. 2. a firm handshake or grip. —*vb.* to grasp or hold (something) tightly.

class (klas) *n.* 1. a group or set of people, animals, plants, objects, words, etc., having qualities or characteristics in common: *mammals form a class of the animal kingdom.* 2. a category or grade: *first class.* 3. a group of students who take the same course, or who graduate together. 4. (informal) excellence; fine style or quality: *this chess-player has great class.* —*vb.* to place in or regard as belonging to a particular class or group.

clas·sic ('klasik) *adj.* (also **clas·si·cal**) 1. (esp. of art or literature) of the very highest or finest class or standard. 2. (of well-established practices or traditions) serving as a model or guide: *a classic example.* 3. relating to or typical of ancient Greek or Roman culture or art: *the classic style of architecture.* —*n.* 1. a work of art, book, piece of music, etc., that has been regarded as one of the best of its kind: *his book on butterflies is a classic.* 2. an ancient Greek or Roman writer or book.

clas·si·cal ('klasikəl) *adj.* 1. (of a work of art, music, etc.) based on traditional forms; balanced and restrained; (often opposed to popular) serious: *classical music.* 2. (also **classic**) of or in accordance with ancient Greek or Roman style in art, literature, architecture, etc.

clas·si·fy ('klasəfī) *vb.* **clas·si·fy·ing, clas·si·fied.** to put in order; sort or arrange into classes or groups: *we classify the books according to their subjects.* —**clas·si·fi'ca·tion** *n.*

clause (klôz) *n.* 1. a sentence or part of a sentence containing a subject and a verb as in *here is the house* (main clause) *where Joan lived last year* (subordinate clause). 2. a single paragraph in a legal document.

claw (klô) *n.* one of the sharp curved nails on the feet of birds and certain animals. —*vb.* to scratch, tear, or pull at (something) with nails or claws: *the cat clawed at the furniture.*

clay (klā) *n.* a heavy, smooth type of earth or mud that holds together when wet and hardens when baked, used for making pots, bricks, etc.

clench (klench) *vb.* to close (one's fists or teeth) very tightly.

cler·gy ('klûrjē) *n.* ministers, bishops, etc., considered collectively or as a special group. **'cler·gy·man** *n.,pl.* **cler·gy·men.** a member of the clergy.

clerk (klûrk) *n.* 1. an office or shop employee who deals with records, papers, and documents. 2. usu. **court clerk** *or* **clerk of the court** a person who keeps the records, etc., at a law court. 3. someone who sells things or helps customers in a store.

cliff (klif) *n.* a steep rocky face, esp. a high one.

cli·mate ('klīmit) *n.* 1. the general weather conditions of a region. 2. a general set of circumstances, attitudes, or opinions: *the political climate.* —**cli·mat·ic** (klī'matik) *adj.*

cli·max ('klīmaks) *n.* a point of greatest excitement, intensity, etc.: *the music rose to its climax.* —**cli'mac·tic** *adj.*

climb (klīm) *vb.* to go up; ascend: *he climbed the tree.* —*n.* 1. the act or an instance of climbing. 2. a slope: *the hill was a steep climb.* **'climb·er** *n.* a person who climbs mountains, cliffs, etc., for sport.

cling (kling) *vb.* **cling·ing, clung.** 1. to hold on tightly: *the monkey clung to his trainer's coat.* 2. to stay with: *the smell of curry clung to him all day.* 3. (of thin clothes, etc.) to fit closely, showing the shape of the body.

clinic ('klinik) *n.* a place that people visit to receive medical or dental treatment. **'clin·i·cal** *adj.* 1. clean and hygienic. 2. excessively clean and bare: *the tidy living-room had an unfriendly, clinical atmosphere.*

clip (klip) *vb.* **clip·ping, clipped.** 1. to trim or shorten: *she clipped the hedge.* 2. to cut items from a newspaper, magazine, etc. 3. to fasten tightly: *he clipped the papers together.* 4. to hit or strike: *she clipped him on the chin.* —*n.* an object used for fastening things together, esp. papers or women's hair. **clip·pers** *pl.n.* a tool for cutting hair, grass, claws, etc.

cloak (klōk) *n.* a long outer garment worn wrapped round the shoulders, for outdoor use. —*vb.* to hide or cover with or as if with a cloak. **'cloak·room** *n.* a place where coats, umbrellas, etc., are left.

clock

clock (klok) *n.* an instrument for measuring time. **'clock·wise** *adv.* circling in the direction in which the hands of a clock turn: *most screws are tightened by turning them clockwise.* *adj.* characterized by moving in this direction: *the apparent clockwise motion of the moon when viewed from above the North Pole.* Compare COUNTERCLOCKWISE. **clock·work** ('klokwûrk) *n.* 1. the mechanism of a clock. 2. something that can be characterized as repetitive, regular, or precise; a routine: *every day she went to work and returned home at the same time, like clockwork.*

clog (klog) *n.* 1. a shoe with a thick sole and no back. 2. a wooden shoe traditionally worn in Holland. —*vb.* **clog·ging, clogged.** to block up: *the drain was clogged with dead leaves.*

clois·ter ('kloistər) *n.* a covered place for walking along the side of a building, often built around courtyards of monasteries.

cloth (klôth) *n.* 1. material or fabric. 2. a piece of material serving any of several purposes, e.g. cleaning or covering.

clothe (klōdh) *vb.* **cloth·ing, clothed.** 1. to provide with clothes; dress. 2. to cover: *he clothed his real feelings in polite words.*

cloud (kloud) *n.* 1. a visible mass of water vapor in the form of tiny droplets or ice crystals in the sky. 2. a mass of dust, smoke, etc. 3. a cause of gloom, darkness, or disgrace: *he was suspected of stealing from his employer and left under a cloud.* —*vb.* 1. (+ *over*) to become full of clouds. 2. to make dark or gloomy: *the atmosphere clouded after they had a row.* —**'cloud·y** *adj.* **cloud·i·er, cloud·i·est.**

clown (kloun) *n.* 1. a person who entertains by playing the fool (often wearing funny clothes and make-up), e.g. in a circus. 2. an ignorant person who acts foolishly. —*vb.* to act like a clown: *Philip clowned around for the amusement of his friends.*

club (klub) *n.* 1. a heavy stick used as a weapon. 2. a stick used in games such as golf to hit the ball. 3. an association or group of people with a common interest, and often rules of membership. —*vb.* **club·bing, clubbed.** to hit with a club.

clue (kloo) *n.* a hint or suggestion leading to the solution of a problem: *the detective found a clue to the burglar's identity.*

clump (klump) *n.* 1. a cluster or group, e.g. of bushes, trees, etc. 2. a mass of anything: *the dog had clumps of earth attached to its fur.* —*vb.* to tread loudly and heavily: *the elephant clumped through the jungle.*

clum·sy ('klumzē) *adj.* **clum·si·er, clum·si·est.** awkward; lacking in gracefulness.

clung (klung) *vb.* the past tense and past participle of CLING.

clus·ter ('klustər) *n.* a group of closely associated things; bunch: *a cluster of daffodils grew under the tree.* —*vb.* to gather or be gathered into a cluster.

clutch (kluch) *vb.* (often + *at*) to catch hold of (something) tightly: *the man in the water clutched at the rope thrown to him.* —*n.* 1. often **clutch·es** (*pl.*) power or influence: *in the clutches of the enemy.* 2. a grip or grasp.

coach (kōch) *n.* 1. (sometimes **stage·coach**) a passenger vehicle drawn by several horses. 2. a bus. 3. a railroad car for passengers. 4. one who gives individual teaching, or who trains an athletics team. —*vb.* to teach or train.

coal (kōl) *n.* a hard, usu. black mineral composed mainly of carbon and formed under heat and pressure from plants that decayed millions of years ago. It is used as a fuel.

coarse (kôrs) *adj.* 1. (of cloth, etc.) rough. 2. having or showing a lack of good manners, etc.: *coarse behavior.* **'coars·en** *vb.* to make or become coarse or coarser.

coast (kōst) *n.* the part of a land or island that meets the sea; shore. —*vb.* 1. to move or work in a relaxed way: *Fred coasted along at work, doing just enough to get by.* 2. (of a vehicle) to be driven without motive power.

coax (kōks) *vb.* to persuade by flattery or kindness: *Marion coaxed her brother to take her to the dance.*

co·bra ('kōbrə) *n.* a highly poisonous African and Asian snake of the type kept by snake charmers.

cob·web ('kobweb) *n.* the web spun by a spider to capture small insects for food.

cock (kok) *n.* 1. a male chicken. 2. a male bird of any species. 3. (also **stop·cock**) a device for regulating the flow of liquid, esp. water. —*vb.* 1. to set (one's hat, head) at a slanting angle. 2. to raise the hammer of a pistol or rifle, ready for firing.

cock·tail ('koktāl) *n.* a short drink, usu. mixed from several alcoholic ingredients.

co·coa ('kōkō) *n.* 1. a kind of chocolate powder made from the crushed beans of a cacao tree. 2. the drink made from this powder.

co·co·nut ('kōkənut) *n.* the large round fruit of a tall tropical tree (**coconut palm**), that has a very hard hairy shell, an inner lining of soft sweet white flesh, and a whitish sweet juice (**coconut milk**).

co·coon (kə'ko͞on) *n.* the silky ball spun around itself by a silkworm or other insect, in which it grows into a winged adult.

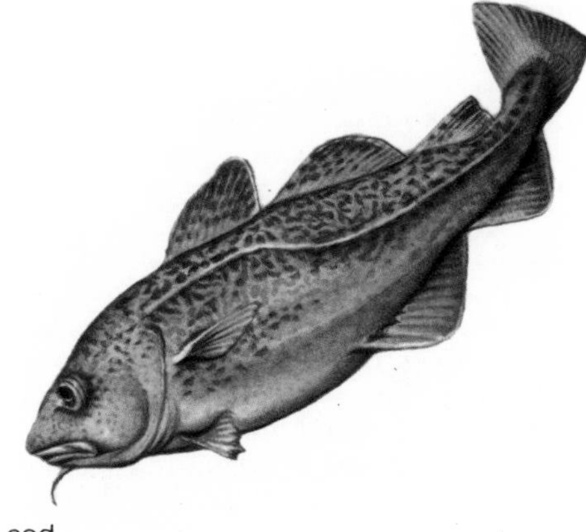

cod

cod (kod) *n.,pl.* **cod.** a large sea-fish of the northern Atlantic, important as food. **cod·liver oil** an oil obtained from cod and used as a source of vitamin A.

code (kōd) *n.* 1. a system for transmitting messages briefly or secretly: *Morse code.* 2. an organized system of rules governing behavior, etc.: *medieval knights lived by the code of chivalry.*

cof·fee ('kôfē, 'kofē) *n.* 1. a drink made from roasted and ground coffee beans. 2. the tropical tree that produces these beans.

cof·fin ('kôfin, 'kofin) *n.* a long wooden or metal chest in which a dead body is laid for burial.

cog (kog, kôg) *n.* any of several teeth on the rim of a wheel in a machine that can engage with similar teeth on other wheels and thus cause these wheels to turn and make the machine work.

coil (koil) *vb.* to curl or cause to curl round and round in circles: *the snake coiled its body around the tree.* —*n.* a length of rope, wire, etc., that has been coiled or made into a spiral shape.

coin (koin) *n.* a flat disk of metal, used as money, having a government stamp on it. —*vb.* 1. to make or produce (money). 2. to invent (a new word or phrase).

col·lapse (kə'laps) *vb.* **col·laps·ing, col·lapsed.** 1. to give way; fall to the ground: *the shed collapsed when a tree fell on it.* 2. (of balloons, etc.) to lose air suddenly; shrink down. 3. (of hopes, etc.) to fail: *his holiday plans collapsed at the last minute.* —*n.* the action or an instance of collapsing. **col'lap·si·ble** *adj.* able to be folded up, or be pushed inwards, in order to fit into a smaller space.

col·lar ('kolər) *n.* 1. the part of a shirt, jacket, etc., that encloses the neck. 2. a leather band round an animal's neck (esp. that of a dog). —*vb.* (informal) to seize; stop (someone) for a particular purpose: *the manager collared Bob to ask about work he should have done.* **'col·lar-·bone** *n.* either of two prominent bones at the base of the neck, joining the breastbone and the shoulder-blades.

col·lect (kə'lekt) *vb. 1. to bring together a group of things (stamps, coins, etc.). 2. to gather contributions: Valerie collected money for the old folks' party.* 3. to assemble or cause to assemble: *a large crowd collected to see the parade.* **col'lec·tion** *n.* 1. the act of collecting. 2. a group of things that have been collected together.

col·lege ('kolij) *n.* 1. an institution where one can continue one's education or obtain a professional training after leaving high school. 2. a body of scholars and students forming part of a university.

col·lide (kə'līd) *vb.* **col·lid·ing, col·lid·ed.** to run into; (often + *with*) crash: *the two cars collided with each other.* —**col·li·sion** (kə'lizhən) *n.*

co·lon ('kōlən) *n.* a punctuation mark (:) ranked between the semi-colon and the full stop and used to introduce an illustration or an example.

colo·nel ('kûrnəl) *n.* an army officer ranking above a lieutenant colonel and below a brigadier general and commanding a regiment.

col·o·ny ('kolənē) *n.,pl.* **col·o·nies.** 1. an area ruled by another country. 2. a group of foreigners in a country. 3. a group of similar animals that live together: *a colony of ants.* **'col·o·nist** *n.* a member of a colony. **co·lo·ni·al** (kə'lōniəl) *adj.* living in a colony: *prairie dogs are colonial animals.* —**co'lo·ni·al·ly** *adv.*

col·or ('kulər) *n.* 1. the appearance that light waves of a certain length or combinations of lengths present to the human eye. Light of a long wavelength is red; light of a short wavelength is blue. 2. the appearance of an object described in terms of the type of light it reflects: *the color of this sweater is red.* 3. **col·ors** (*pl.*) the flag of an army, regiment, etc. —*vb.* 1. to treat with color; paint. 2. to become red in the face, e.g. because of shame or anger. —'**col·ored** *adj.* —'**col·or·less** *adj.*

col·umn ('koləm) *n.* 1. a pillar, usu. with a decorated top. 2. a line of men, army vehicles, etc. 3. a list of figures for adding up. 4. a vertical section of print in a newspaper, book, etc. 5. anything rising straight up: *a column of smoke.*

column

comb (kōm) *n.* 1. a toothed device, for getting tangles out of the hair. 2. a similar device used for separating and cleaning fibers such as wool. 2. the red fleshy crest on the heads of domestic fowls. —*vb.* 1. to apply a comb to (one's hair, etc.). 2. to search very thoroughly: *they combed the countryside in their search for the escaped prisoners.*

com·bat *n.* ('kombat) a battle. —*vb.* ('kombat, kəm'bat) to do battle against; oppose: *the housewives tried to combat price rises.*

com·bine *vb.* (kəm'bīn) **com·bin·ing, com·bined.** to mix or join together. —*n.* ('kombīn) 1. a group of people brought together for a special purpose, esp. concerning business, politics, or finance. 2. a machine that combines the reaping and threshing of grain. **com·bi'na·tion** *n.* 1. the action or result of combining. 2. the group of people or things combined.

com·bus·tion (kəm'buschən) *n.* 1. the action of burning. 2. the chemical or physical process connected with burning. **com'bus·ti·ble** *adj.* able to be burnt.

com·e·dy ('komidē) *n.,pl.* **com·e·dies.** a play that is light and amusing and generally has a happy ending. **co·me·di·an** (kə'mēdēən) *n.* a comic actor. See also COMIC.

com·et ('komit) *n.* a CELESTIAL body that moves around the sun, consisting of a bright head and a very long tail.

com·fort ('kumfərt) *vb.* 1. freedom from pain, worry, hunger, poverty, etc.: *the old man sat in comfort in an armchair in front of the fire.* 2. help or kindness for someone in distress: *visits from friends brought Sam comfort when he was in hospital.* 3. something that provides help or relief: *a hot drink is a comfort on a cold day.* —*vb.* to provide comfort. '**com·fort·a·ble** *adj.* 1. providing comfort. 2. feeling at ease, free from pain, etc. —'**com·fort·a·bly** *adv.*

com·ic ('komik) *adj.* (also **com·i·cal**) funny; humorous. —*n.* 1. (also **comic strip**) a group of drawings, published in newspapers, etc., that tell a story. 2. an entertainer who tells jokes.

com·ma ('komə) *n.* a punctuation mark (,) used to show a slight break in a sentence.

com·mand (kə'mand) *vb.* 1. to give an order to (someone). 2. to lead. 3. to look out over: *the house on the cliff commanded a fine view.* —*n.* an order: *the general gave out his commands.*

com·mence (kə'mens) *vb.* **com·menc·ing, com·menced.** to begin; start. —**com'mence·ment** *n.*

com·mend (kə'mend) *vb.* 1. to give approval to; praise. 2. to entrust; give into the care of someone. **com'mend·a·ble** *adj.* praiseworthy.

com·ment ('koment) *n.* a statement or opinion about something; remark. —*vb.* (often + *about* or *on*) to make a comment or say as a comment. **com·men·tar·y** ('komənterē) *n.,pl.* **com·men·ta·ries.** 1. a spoken description of an event broadcast on radio or television. 2. the descriptive notes about the text of a book. '**com·men·ta·tor** *n.*

com·merce ('komûrs) *n.* trade or business, esp. on a large scale. **com'mer·cial** *adj.* 1. of or relating to trade or commerce. 2. able to be sold or make money. *n.* a radio or T.V. advertisement.

com·mis·sion (kə'mishən) *n.* 1. a military officer's post or a paper confirming this. 2. payment made to a salesman or saleswoman depending on the amount of goods that he or she sells. 3. a special job given to someone. 4. a group of people given power to carry out a special duty, esp. an investigation: *a government commission.* —*vb.* to pay (someone) to do a special job: *he was commissioned to write a symphony.*

com·mit (kə'mit) *vb.* **com·mit·ting, com·mit·ted.** 1. to do (something), esp. a crime or foolish action. 2. to entrust; give (something) up to someone's care or charge: *she decided to commit her jewels to the bank for safekeeping.* **com'mit·ment** *n.* a promise; pledge.

comet

com·mit·tee (kə'mitē) *n.* a group of people chosen by a larger group and given authority to carry out certain duties, such as the administration of a society, etc.

com·mon ('komən) *adj.* 1. usual; normal; most often seen, met with, etc.: *measles is a common illness in children.* 2. shared: *common knowledge.* 3. coarse or ill-mannered. —*n.* an open area of land for use by everyone.

com·mon·place ('komənplās) *adj.* ordinary; not very unusual: *the daisy is a commonplace flower.*

Common Market an economic and trading association of nine European countries (Italy, France, West Germany, Belgium, the Netherlands, Luxembourg, and (since 1973) Britain, Eire, and Denmark), established in 1958. It is also called the European Economic Community (EEC).

com·mon·wealth ('komənwelth) *n.* 1. the entire body of people in a country or state. 2. (usu. **Commonwealth**) a federation of colonies or former colonies, esp. those belonging to Britain. 3. the official name of certain U.S. states: Kentucky, Virginia, Massachusetts, Pennsylvania.

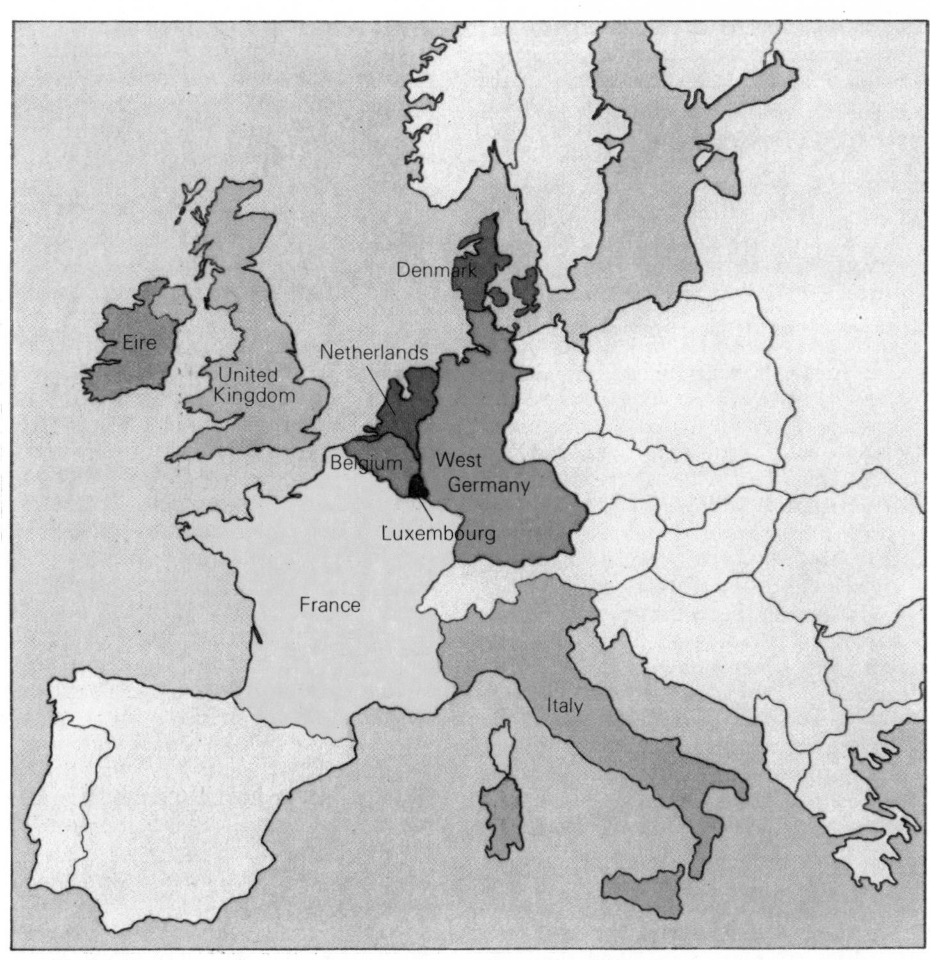

Common Market

com·mo·tion (kə'mōshən) *n.* a noisy, rushing, sometimes violent movement or disturbance.

com·mu·ni·cate (kə'myōōnəkāt) *vb.* **com·mu·ni·cat·ing, com·mu·ni·cat·ed.** 1. (+ *with*) to get in contact with. 2. (+ *to*) to pass (information, etc.) on to. 3. to pass (illness or disease) on to. **com·mu·ni'ca·tion** *n.* 1. the action of communicating. 2. something communicated, esp. a letter.

com·mu·ni·ty (kə'myōōnitē) *n.,pl.* **com·mu·ni·ties.** a group of people living together, esp. in a village, town, etc; any group of people with common interests.

com·mut·er (kə'myōōtər) *n.* a person living outside the large town or city where he works, and traveling in every day. **com'mute** *vb.* **com·mut·ing, com·mut·ed.** 1. to travel to work as a commuter. 2. to reduce the severity of (a punishment, sentence, etc.).

com·pact *adj.* (kəm'pakt) occupying little space; tightly packed; condensed. —*n.* ('kompakt) 1. an agreement, bargain, or treaty. 2. a flat, usu. circular box containing a woman's face powder and puff.

com·pan·ion (kəm'panyən) *n.* 1. a person with whom one keeps company: *a traveling companion.* 2. a person one likes to be with; friend. 3. someone hired to help or look after a sick or elderly person.

com·pa·ny ('kumpənē) *n.,pl.* **com·pa·nies.** 1. the state or condition of having visitors, or another person in one's presence. 2. a business; firm. 3. a small group of soldiers; sections of an army.

com·pare (kəm'peər) *vb.* **com·par·ing, com·pared.** 1. (+ *with* or *to*) to judge one thing as being like another: *her voice was compared to that of a nightingale.* 2. to look for the similarities and differences between one thing and another. **com·par·a·tive** (kəm'parətiv) *adj.* 1. of or concerning the action of comparing. 2. relative; approximate: *comparative safety.* *n.* a form of an adjective, e.g. *bigger* is the comparative of *big.* **com·par·i·son** (kəm'parisən) *n.* the act or an instance of comparing.

com·part·ment (kəm'pârtmənt) *n.* 1. a separate section of a container. 2. a part of a railway car.

com·pass ('kumpəs) *n.* 1. an instrument that indicates direction, consisting of a pivoted magnetized needle that always points north. 2. also **com·pass·es** (*pl.*) a geometrical instrument used for drawing circles and arcs. 3. range, scope: *the compass of his interests was great.*

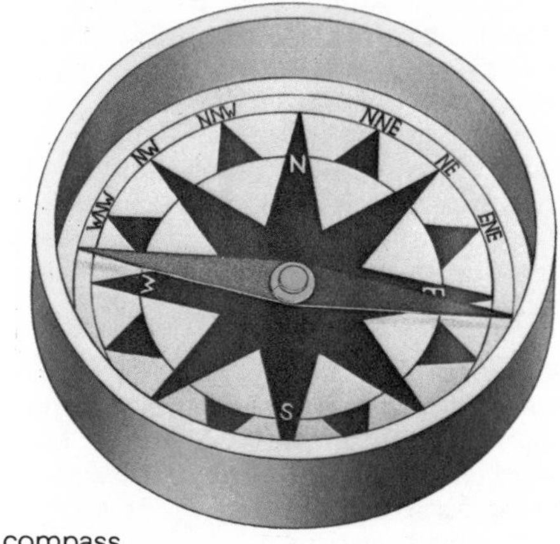

compass

com·pel (kəm'pel) *vb.* **com·pel·ling, com·pelled.** to make or force (someone) to do (something); bring pressure upon: *Brian compelled his sister to come with him.*

com·pete (kəm'pēt) *vb.* **com·pet·ing, com·pet·ed.** (+ *against, with,* etc.) 1. to take part in a game, sport, etc. 2. to rival: *the two boys competed for a place on the team.* **com·pe·ti·tion** (kompi'tishən) *n.* 1. the act of competing: *the competition for class prize was fierce.* 2. a game, etc., in which one competes. **com·pet·i·tor** (kəm'petitər) *n.* a person who competes.

com·plain (kəm'plān) *vb.* to express one's annoyance about something; grumble: *Mr Jones complained about the service in the store.* **com'plaint** *n.* 1. the action or an instance of complaining. 2. an illness: *Elizabeth suffers from a nervous complaint.*

com·ple·ment ('kompləmənt) *n.* 1. something necessary to make perfect or complete: *the new curtains made a nice complement to the the rest of the room.* 2. the full number of officers and men on a ship.

com·plete (kəm'plēt) *adj.* 1. full or finished; needing nothing more: *when the last chapter is finished the book will be complete.* 2. total: *complete silence.* —*vb.* **com·plet·ing, com·plet·ed.** to make complete. —**com'ple·tion** *n.*

com·plex (kəm'pleks, 'kompleks) *adj.* not simple; complicated. —*n.* ('kompleks) a large set of connected parts, esp. buildings, etc.: *a sports complex.* 2. a mental or psychological condition: *Jackie has an inferiority complex.* —**com'plex·i·ty** *n.,pl.* **com·plex·i·ties.**

com·plex·ion (kəm'plekshən) *n.* 1. the appearance of the face or skin: *a clear complexion.* 2. the appearance of a situation: *that puts a different complexion on matters.*

com·pli·cate ('kompləkāt) *vb.* **com·pli·cat·ing, com·pli·cat·ed.** to make (something) difficult or much less simple: *uncertainty over the weather complicated our plans for a picnic.* —**com·pli'ca·tion** *n.*

com·pli·ment *n.* ('kompləmənt) 1. an expression of admiration, respect, or praise. 2. **com·pli·ments** (*pl.*) a formal expression of greetings: *my compliments to your wife.* —*vb.* ('kompləment) 1. to express admiration; pay a compliment to: *he complimented her on her cooking.* 2. to congratulate. **com·pli'men·ta·ry** *adj.* 1. of or expressing a compliment; admiring. 2. free of charge: *complimentary tickets.*

com·pose (kəm'pōz) *vb.* **com·pos·ing, com·posed.** 1. to make up a whole out of several parts. 2. to write (music, poetry, a letter, etc.). 3. to calm (oneself): *she composed herself for her difficult task.* **com'poser** *n.* a writer of music. **com·po·si·tion** (kompə'zishən) *n.* something composed, esp. a musical or literary piece.

com·pound[1] *n.* ('kompound) 1. something formed by combining two or more ingredients. 2. (chemistry) a substance formed by the combination of two or more elements and having properties different from those of these elements: *water is a compound of two elements called hydrogen and oxygen.* 3. an enclosed area containing buildings: *a prison compound.* —*vb.* (kəm'pound) 1. to mix or combine. 2. to increase or be increased: *the farmer's misfortunes were compounded by the heavy rainfall.* —*adj.* ('kompound) composed of two or more parts, ingredients, etc.

com·pul·sion (kəm'pulshən) *n.* 1. the act of compelling or the state of being compelled. 2. a strong obsession, urge, etc. **com'pul·sive** *adj.* of or reflecting a strong urge: *a compulsive gambler.* **com'pul·so·ry** *adj.* required by law or some other authority.

com·pute (kəm'pyo͞ot) *vb.* **com·put·ing, com·put·ed.** to calculate; work out. **com'put·er** *n.* an electronic device able to carry out highly complex mathematical calculations, at great speed, and to store and give out information, according to instructions that are fed into it. —**com·pu·ta·tion** (kompyə'tāshən) *n.*

concertina

com·rade ('komrad) *n.* 1. a companion or friend. 2. **Comrade** a term of address used esp. in Communist countries to replace 'Mr', 'Sir', 'Mrs', 'Miss', etc. —'**com·rade·ship** *n.*

con·cave (kon'kāv) *adj.* (esp. of a LENS or mirror) tur ing inwards towards the center; resembling part of the inside of a sphere.

con·ceal (kən'sēl) *vb.* 1. to hide or keep out of sight: *her face was concealed under a mask.* 2. to keep secret: *he concealed the fact that he already knew the girl.* —**con'ceal·ment** *n.*

con·ceit (kən'sēt) *n.* excessive love and admiration of oneself; vanity. —**con'ceit·ed** *adj.*

con·cen·trate ('konsəntrāt) *vb.* **con·cen·trat·ing, con·cen·trat·ed.** 1. to direct thoughts or actions to one particular subject: *to concentrate on a problem.* 2. to increase the strength or intensity of: *the fruit juice was concentrated by boiling off the water.* 3. to come together; bring to a particular point: *most of the world's population is concentrated in cities.* —**con·cen'tra·tion** *n.*

con·cen·tric (kən'sentrik) *adj.* (of two or more circles or spheres) having a common central point, one circle or sphere lying within the other. See GEOMETRY.

con·cern (kən'sûrn) *n.* 1. something in which one has an interest, share, etc.; affairs; business. 2. anxiety; worry: *she showed great concern over the fate of the dog.* 3. a manufacturing or commercial firm; business: *he works for a shipping concern.* —*vb.* 1. to involve or be of interest or importance: *I am concerned with local politics.* 2. to worry or feel anxious: *I am concerned about her health.*

con·cert ('konsûrt) *n.* a musical entertainment given by an orchestra, soloist, etc., usu. before a large audience. **con·cert·ed** (kən'sûrtid) *adj.* done with all persons involved working together: *a concerted effort.*

con·cer·ti·na (konsər'tēnə) *n.* a small accordion.

con·clude (kən'klōōd) *vb.* **con·clud·ing, con·clud·ed.** 1. to finish; come or bring to an end. 2. to draw an impression or opinion: *may we conclude from your silence that you agree?* 3. to bring to a decision; settle: *they concluded a defense treaty.* **con'clu·sion** *n.* 1. the end or final part of something. 2. a result or outcome. 3. a deduction; inference: *she came to the conclusion that he was sick.* **con'clu·sive** *adj.* decisive or convincing: *conclusive evidence.*

con·crete ('konkrēt, kon'krēt) *adj.*1. firm or real: *he needed concrete facts to prove his case.* 2. made of concrete. —*n.* a hard material made by mixing sand, water, cement, pebbles, etc., together, used esp. in building.

con·cus·sion (kən'kushən) *n.* shock produced by a blow on the head, e.g. after a fall or collision, sometimes involving loss of consciousness. See CONSCIOUS.

con·demn (kən'dem) *vb.* 1. to sentence: *the judge condemned him to five years' imprisonment.* 2. to criticize strongly: *he condemned her action.* 3. to declare (a building) unfit for use. —**con·dem·na·tion** (kondem'nāshən) *n.*

con·dense (kən'dens) *vb.* **con·dens·ing, con·densed.** 1. to pack into a smaller space; make compact, small, etc. 2. (of a gas) to cool to liquid form. 3. to shorten (a story, article). **con·den·sa·tion** (konden'sāshən) *n.* 1. the action or process of condensing. 2. the condensed state or something in that state, e.g. water from water vapor: *there was condensation on the bathroom window.*

con·di·tion (kən'dishən) *n.* 1. state of being; situation: *the old house was in a poor condition.* 2. a necessary, agreed, or appropriate state; requirement or term: *conditions of surrender.* —*vb.* 1. to make terms. 2. to train (a person or animal) always to respond in the same way to certain treatment or actions: *the parrot was conditioned to speak when the door opened.* **con'di·tion·al** *adj.* depending on, containing, or imposing a condition or conditions: *the offer of a job was conditional on good references.* —**con'di·tion·al·ly** *adv.*

con·duct *vb.* (kən'dukt) 1. to guide or lead: *he conducted the blind man across the road.* 2. to manage or control (a meeting, business). 3. to direct (an orchestra, choir, etc.) by indicating time, etc., with one's hands or a stick called a baton. 4. to be able to transmit or pass on (heat, electricity, etc.): *a metal spoon conducts heat better than a wooden one.* —*n.* ('kondukt) behavior: *disobedience is bad conduct.* **con'duc·tor** *n.* 1. a person who directs an orchestra or choir. 2. a person in charge of a train who collects fares and tickets. 3. something that transmits heat, electricity, etc.

cone (kōn) *n.* 1. a solid pointed object with a circular base. See GEOMETRY. 2. a hollow cracker made in this shape to hold ice cream. 3. the scaly fruit of certain trees such as the pine. See CONIFER.

con·fess (kən'fes) *vb.* 1. to admit or acknowledge: *she confessed to having stolen the painting.* 2. to declare (one's sins) to a priest. —**con'fes·sion** *n.*

con·fide (kən'fīd) *vb.* **con·fid·ing, con·fid·ed.** to trust someone with a secret, etc.; entrust: *Ellen confided her problem to her mother.* **con·fi·dant** *or* **con·fi·dante** ('konfidânt) *n.* someone to whom secrets, feelings, etc., are confided. **con·fi·dence** ('konfidəns) *n.* 1. trust or belief in someone or something: *I have confidence in her ability.* 2. self-assurance: *he stepped onto the stage with great confidence.* **'con·fi·dent** *adj.* showing confidence; bold, assured, or positive. **con·fi·den·tial** (konfi'denshəl) *adj.* secret or characterized by secrecy: *a confidential message.*

con·fine *vb.* (kən'fīn) **con·fin·ing, con·fined.** 1. to imprison. 2. to set limits or bounds to (something): *Martin's broken leg confined his movements to slow walking.* —*n.* ('konfīn) a limit or boundary: *she stayed within the confines of the house.* **con'fine·ment** *n.* 1. imprisonment. 2. the period during which a woman gives birth to a child.

con·firm (kən'fûrm) *vb.* 1. to prove: *your wet umbrella confirms that you have been out.* 2. to make (something) certain: *a letter confirmed his appointment.* 3. to strengthen: *the news confirmed his doubts.* 4. to admit (a baptized person) as a full member of the church at a special service. —**con·fir'ma·tion** *n.*

con·fis·cate ('konfiskāt) *vb.* **con·fis·cat·ing, con·fis·cat·ed.** to seize, esp. legally or officially: *the teacher confiscated the child's chocolate.* —**con·fis'ca·tion** *n.*

cone

con·flict *n.* ('konflikt) 1. an argument, disagreement, or quarrel: *a conflict of opinion.* 2. a war or battle, esp. a prolonged struggle. —*vb.* (kən'flikt) 1. to clash or disagree. 2. to do battle; fight.

con·form (kən'fôrm) *vb.* 1. to act according to certain rules of behavior: *John would not conform to the rules of the club.* 2. to agree with or be similar to: *the shape of the house did not conform to the plans.* **con'form·i·ty** *n.* the act or an instance of conforming. **con'form·ist** *n.* a person who behaves like everyone else.

con·front (kən'frunt) *vb.* 1. to stand before (an enemy or opponent); face boldly. 2. to meet or face up to (a difficulty or problem).

con·fuse (kən'fyōōz) *vb.* **con·fus·ing, con·fused.** to bewilder, perplex, or muddle: *if you all talk at once you will confuse me.* —**con'fu·sion** *n.*

con·grat·u·late (kən'grachəlāt) *vb.* **con·grat·u·lat·ing, con·grat·u·lat·ed.** to compliment (someone) on success, good fortune, etc. —**con·grat·u'la·tion** *n.*

con·gre·gate ('konggrəgāt) *vb.* **con·gre·gat·ing, con·gre·gat·ed.** to assemble or gather together; collect: *the cattle congregated around the water tank.* **con·gre'ga·tion** *n.* 1. the action or an instance of congregating. 2. the whole group of worshipers in a church.

con·gress ('konggris) *n.* 1. a series of meetings for the exchange of views between representatives of different societies, professions, etc.: *a congress of dentists was held at the college.* 2. **Congress** the law-making assembly of the United States, consisting of the Senate and the House of Representatives. —**con·gres·sion·al** (kən'greshənəl) *adj.*

conifers

co·ni·fer ('konifə) *n.* a class of tree, including the pine and fir, that produces fruit in the form of CONES.

con·jur·er (k'unjərər, 'konjərər) *n.* a magician.

con·nect (kə'nekt) *vb.* 1. to join together or link up: *the mechanic connected the trailer to the car.* 2. to associate or be associated: *I always connect lavender with old ladies.* —**con'nec·tion** *n.*

con·quer ('kongkər) *vb.* 1. to win a victory over; subdue or gain by force: *they conquered new territory.* 2. to overcome (difficulty, etc.): *he conquered all his fears.* **con·quest** ('kongkwest) *n.* 1. the act or example of conquering. 2. the person, thing, or country conquered.

con·science ('konshəns) *n.* the ability to recognize a distinction between right and wrong: *my conscience will not let me deceive you.* **con·sci·en·tious** (konshē'enshəs) *adj.* guided by conscience; extremely careful, reliable, and scrupulous. —**con·sci'en·tious·ly** *adv.*

con·scious ('konshəs) *adj.* 1. fully aware of one's own sensations, etc. 2. mentally awake and alert. 2. deliberate and intentional: *his words were a conscious attempt to start a fight.* '**con·scious·ness** *n.* 1. the state of being fully awake and alert. 2. the mind. —'**con·scious·ly** *adv.*

con·sent (kən'sent) *vb.* to agree or approve; assent. —*n.* permission; approval: *the principal willingly gave his consent to the plan.*

con·se·quence ('konsəkwens) *n.* 1. an outcome, effect, or result: *the trick had an unfortunate consequence.* 2. importance, significance, or distinction: *a person of great consequence.* '**con·se·quent** *adj.* following; being the result of. —'**con·se·quent·ly** *adv.* **con·se·quen·tial** (konsə'kwenshəl) *adj.* 1. following as an outcome or result. 2. significant; important. —**con·se'quen·tial·ly** *adv.*

con·serv·a·tive (kən'sûrvətiv) *adj.* 1. tending or preferring to preserve existing institutions, conditions, etc.; resisting change. 2. cautious or moderate: *a conservative estimate.*

con·serve (kən'sûrv) *vb.* **con·serv·ing, con·served.** 1. to protect or keep safe (something highly valued); preserve. 2. to store up for later use: *conserve your energy for tomorrow's race.* **con·ser'va·tion·ist** *n., adj.* (of) a person who wishes to protect and preserve natural resources, the countryside, animals, etc. —**con·ser'va·tion** *n.*

con·sid·er (kən'sidər) *vb.* 1. to think about carefully; contemplate: *James considered the problem for a long time.* 2. to look upon; regard as: *I consider him a fool.* 3. to be kind and thoughtful; regard: *he never considered his mother.* **con'sid·er·a·ble** *adj.* 1. fairly large or great: *a considerable amount.* 2. important: *he was a considerable artist.* **con'sid·er·ate** *adj.* kind and thoughtful. **con·sid·er'a·tion** *n.* 1. kindness or thoughtfulness. 2. attention: *I will give the matter careful consideration.* 3. something taken or to be taken into account: *the cost of the plan was the most important consideration.* 4. a reward, payment, etc.: *for a small consideration he will take you there.*

con·sist (kən'sist) *vb.* 1. to be composed of: *the program consists of three short ballets.* 2. to be contained or based in. **con'sis·ten·cy** *n.,pl.* **con·sis·ten·cies.** 1. texture, density, firmness, etc.: *mix the ingredients to a thick consistency.* 2. constancy; lack of variation. **con'sis·tent** *adj.* 1. logically in agreement with: *his statement was not consistent with the facts of the case.* 2. unchanging; constant: *he showed a consistent dislike of her.* —**con'sis·tent·ly** *adv.*

con·so·nant ('konsənənt) *n.* 1. a speech sound made by blocking the passage of one's breath with the tongue or lips. 2. a letter of the alphabet representing such a sound, e.g. *b, d, l.* Compare VOWEL.

con·spic·u·ous (kən'spikyo͞oəs) *adj.* noticeable, striking, or eye-catching: *red is a conspicuous color.*

con·spire (kən'spīər) *vb.* **con·spir·ing, con·spired.** to plot or agree together, esp. in secret, to do something illegal, evil, etc.: *the customs man conspired with the smugglers to steal the diamonds.* —**con·spir·a·cy** (kən'spirəsē) *n.,pl.* **con·spir·a·cies.** —**con'spir·a·tor** *n.*

con·stant ('konstənt) *adj.* fixed or unchanging. —*n.* something fixed. —**'con·stan·cy** *n.* —**'con·stant·ly** *adv.*

con·stel·la·tion (konstə'lāshən) *n.* a pattern or grouping of stars, esp. one that has been given a name, e.g. Ursa Major, Orion.

con·struct (kən'strukt) *vb.* to build, create, make, or put together. **con'struc·tion** *n.* 1. the action or an instance of constructing. 2. anything constructed; structure, building, etc. 3. an explanation or interpretation: *there is only one construction that can be put on his conduct.* 4. (grammar) the form of words used in a sentence. 5. a special drawing made in geometry. **con'struc·tive** *adj.* 1. of, relating to, or tending to construct. 2. helpful; positive: *his comments on Jane's essay were very constructive.* —**con'struc·tive·ly** *adv.*

con·sult (kən'sult) *vb.* to ask or refer to for help, advice, an opinion, information, etc.: *Mark consulted the dictionary to check his spelling; Mr Brown consulted a lawyer when he was arrested.* **con'sult·ant** *n.* a specialist who gives professional advice, help, etc. —**con·sul·ta·tion** (konsəl'tāshən) *n.*

con·sume (kən'so͞om) *vb.* **con·sum·ing, con·sumed.** 1. to use up. 2. to drink or eat up: *he consumed two whole cakes.* 3. to destroy or be destroyed: *the building was consumed by fire.* **con'sum·er** *n.* a person who buys and uses goods and services. **con·sump·tion** (kən'sumpshən) *n.* the act of consuming: *his consumption of chocolate was so great that he was sick.*

con·tact ('kontakt) *n.* 1. the act or state of touching, meeting, etc. 2. a useful acquaintance; connection: *he has contacts in politics.* 3. the state of being in communication: *don't forget to get in contact with us.* **contact lenses** thin curved disks of plastic or glass worn on the eyeballs to aid defective vision. —*vb.* 1. to touch or to bring into contact: *his hand contacted the cold steel.* 2. to communicate with: *Peter contacted the doctor when he was ill.*

con·ta·gious (kən'tājəs) *adj.* 1. (of a disease) passed on by touch or close contact. 2. able to be spread to other people: *fear is contagious.*

con·tain (kən'tān) *vb.* 1. to hold or have inside: *the bottle contains a pint of milk.* 2. to include: *our team contains two fast forwards.* 3. to keep in check; restrain: *he was unable to contain his feelings.* **con'tain·er** *n.* a box, can, etc., for holding something.

con·tent[1] ('kontent) *n.* 1. usu. **con·tents** (*pl.*) all that is held in a container, area, etc.: *the contents of my room are private.* 2. usu. **contents**(*pl.*) the chief topics, chapters, items, or subject of a book, etc.

con·tent[2] (kən'tent) *adj.* (also **con·tent·ed**) satisfied; pleased: *he is content to stay at home.* —*vb.* to satisfy or please: *one large meal a day contents Stephen.* —**con'tent·ment** *n.*

con·test *n.* ('kontest) a struggle for victory, superiority, a prize, etc.: *a hard contest between the tennis players.* —*vb.* (kən'test) 1. to fight or struggle against; dispute: *I'll contest that decision.* 2. to fight or struggle for: *he contested the leadership.* —**con'test·ant** *n.*

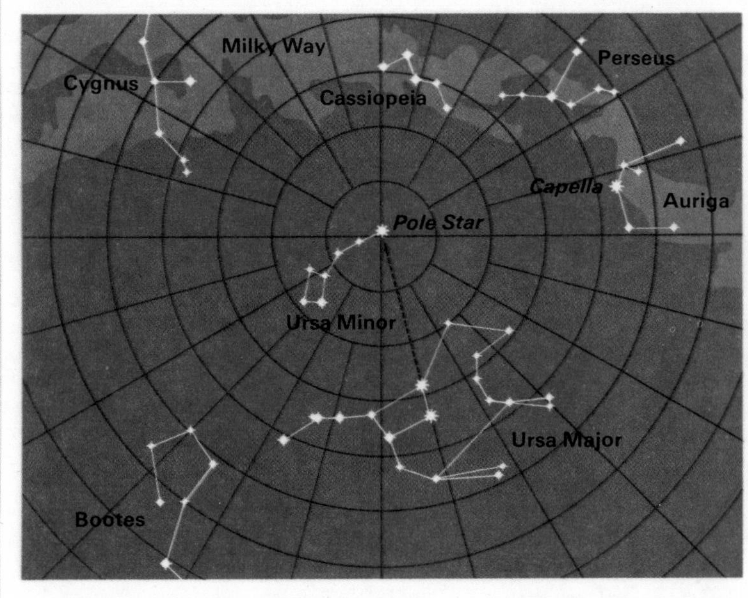

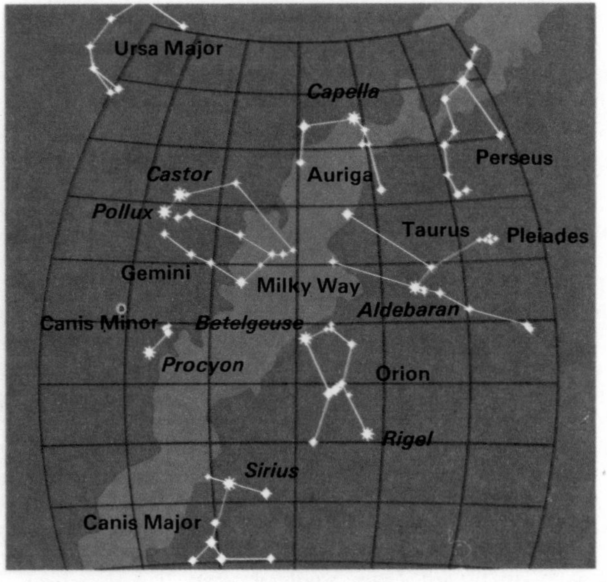

constellation

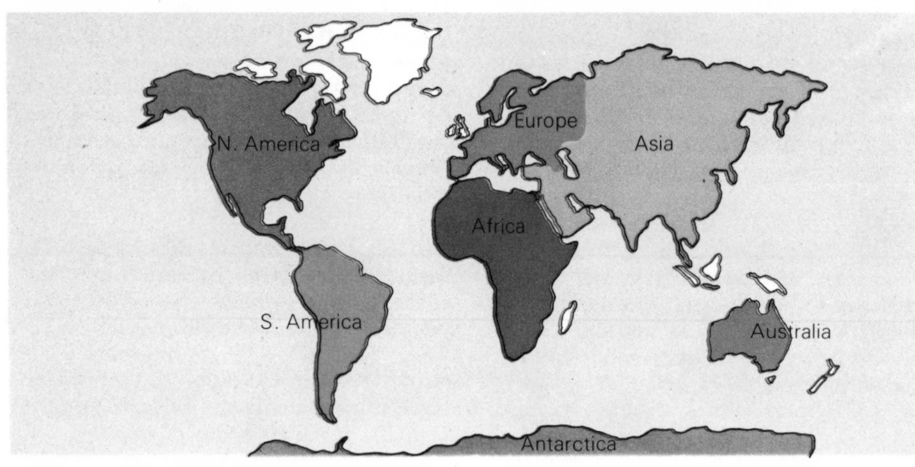

continent

con·ti·nent ('kontinənt) *n.* one of the seven great divisions of land on the earth's surface (Asia, Africa, Europe, Australia, Antarctica, North America, and South America). **the Continent** the mainland of Europe. —**con·ti·nen·tal** (konti'nentəl) *adj.*

con·tin·ue (kən'tinyo͞o) *vb.* **con·tin·u·ing, con·tin·ued.** 1. to last; endure: *the drought continued for four years.* 2. to carry on or take up again; resume: *the show will continue after an interval.* 3. to remain or stay: *John will continue as our team captain.* **con'tin·u·al** *adj* repetitive; following one after the other: *the continual beating of the waves on the shore.* **con'tin·u·ous** *adj.* connected or uninterrupted: *a continuous stream of traffic.* —**con'tin·u·al·ly** *adv.* —**con'tin·u·ous·ly** *adv.*

con·tract *n.* ('kontrakt) an agreement between two or more people or groups, esp. a written legal agreement. —*vb.* (kən'trakt) 1. to draw or be drawn together; make or become shorter, smaller, etc.; shrink: *the snail contracted into its shell.* 2. to acquire; start (e.g. an illness): *he contracted measles.*

con·tra·dict (kontrə'dikt) *vb.* 1. to be inconsistent with or state the opposite of; deny: *her bad behavior contradicts the sweetness of her face.* 2. to deny or speak against (the statements, comments, etc., of another or oneself): *you should not contradict your father.* **con·tra'dic·tion** *n.* the act or an instance of contradicting. —**con·tra'dic·to·ry** *adj.*

con·trast *n.* ('kontrast) 1. difference; dissimilarity. 2. a person or thing that is very different from another: *her good manners are a contrast to those of her brother.* 3. the use of dissimilar colors, etc., e.g. in painting. —*vb.* (kən'trast) to show differences; compare (several people or things) in order to demonstrate or discover the differences between them.

con·trib·ute (kən'tribyo͞ot) *vb.* **con·trib·ut·ing, con·trib·ut·ed.** (usu. + *to*) 1. to give (money, help, etc.) to a good cause: *we all contributed one dollar to the appeal fund.* 2. to write for a book, magazine, etc. 3. to have a share in; play a part in: *human error contributed to the disaster.* —**con·tri·bu·tion** (kontri'byo͞oshən) *n.* —**con'trib·u·tor** *n.*

con·trol (kən'trōl) *vb.* **con·trol·ling, con·trolled.** 1. to have power over; command. 2. to restrict, restrain, or check. —*n.* 1. power; command. 2. restriction; restraint: *his temper is out of control.* 3. an instrument for controlling a machine, etc. —**con'trol·ler** *n.*

con·ven·ient (kən'vēnyənt) *adj.* 1. well-situated; close by: *a convenient location.* 2. in accordance with one's needs; suitable: *a convenient arrangement.* **con'ven·ience** *n.* 1. the state of being convenient. 2. something that is convenient, esp. an aid or facility.

con·vent ('konvənt) *n.* 1. a community of nuns. 2. the buildings in which this community lives. 3. a girls' school run by nuns.

con·ven·tion (kən'venshən) *n.* 1. something or a way of doing something that is generally accepted; custom; usage. 2. an agreement. 3. a conference or meeting: *a political convention.* —**con'ven·tion·al** *adj.*

con·verge (kən'vûrj) *vb.* **con·verg·ing, con·verged.** to come together; meet at a certain place: *parallel lines never converge.* —**con'ver·gence** *n.*

con·verse (kən'vûrs) *vb.* **con·vers·ing, con·versed.** to talk together informally. **con·ver·sa·tion** (konvər'sāshən) *n.* an informal discussion. —**con·ver'sa·tion·al** *adj.*

con·vert *vb.* (kən'vûrt) 1. to change or transform: *they converted the old barn into a house.* 2. to change or cause to change in religious belief, etc.: *the people were converted to Christianity.* —*n.* ('konvûrt) a person whose principles, opinions, religious beliefs, etc., have been changed: *he is a recent convert to Christianity.* —**con'ver·sion** *n.* **con'vert·i·ble** *adj., n.* (of) something that can be altered or changed, e.g. an automobile with a folding top.

con·vex (kon'veks) *adj.* (esp. of a lens or mirror) curving or bulging outwards.

con·vict *vb.* (kən'vikt) to prove or declare guilty of an offense. —*n.* ('konvikt) a person convicted of a crime and serving a prison sentence. **con'vic·tion** *n.* 1. the act of proving or declaring a person guilty of a crime. 2. a firm belief.

con·vince (kən'vins) *vb.* **con·vinc·ing, con·vinced.** to make (someone) believe something; persuade: *she convinced him that he was wrong.* **con'vinc·ing** *adj.* believable; able to convince. —**con'vinc·ing·ly** *adv.*

cool (ko͞ol) *adj.* 1. fairly cold; not warm. 2. feeling or producing coolness: *a cool dress.* 3. unfriendly: *a cool welcome.* 4. calm: *keep cool in an emergency.* 5. (slang) excellent; fine. —*vb.* 1. (sometimes + *off* or *down*) to make or become cool. 2. (+ *off* or *down*) to become calmer.

co·op·er·ate (kō'opərāt) *vb.* **co·op·er·at·ing, co·op·er·at·ed.** to act as a single group; work together. **co'op·er·a·tive** *adj.* intending to or willing to cooperate. *n.* a business association in which profits are shared amongst its members. —**co·op·er'a·tion** *n.*

cope (kōp) *vb.* **cop·ing, coped.** (+ *with*) to handle successfully; deal with: *an astronaut has to cope with weightlessness.*

cop·per ('kopər) *n.* a reddish-brown metallic element used for wiring, plumbing, etc. Chemical symbol: Cu. —*adj.* made of copper.

cop·y ('kopē) *vb.* **cop·y·ing, cop·ied.** to produce an exact likeness or second example of; reproduce: *copy this poem.* —*n.,pl.* **cop·ies.** 1. an imitation or reproduction. 2. one of an edition of a book, magazine, etc. 3. manuscript or other material for printing.

cor·al ('kôrəl, 'korəl) *n.* the hard material forming sea reefs and formed from the skeletons of very small sea creatures.

coral

cord (kôrd) *n.* 1. a thick string consisting of several twisted or woven strands. 2. something resembling a cord: *the spinal cord.*

cor·du·roy ('kôrdəroi) *n.* 1. a strong fabric having ribs and grooves on its surface. 2. **cor·du·roys** (*pl.*) pants made of corduroy. —*adj.* made of corduroy.

core (kôr) *n.* 1. the central part of something: *the core of the earth.* 2. the basic or most important part of anything; heart: *the core of the problem.* 3. the middle of an apple or similar fruit, containing the seeds. —*vb.* **cor·ing, cored.** to remove the core from (apples, etc.).

cork (kôrk) *n.* 1. the light outer bark of a type of oak tree. 2. a stopper for bottles made of this bark. —*vb.* (sometimes + *up*) to stop up with a cork.

corn[1] (kôrn) *n.* a cereal plant widely cultivated for its grain, or kernels, that grow on large ears; maize. 2. the grain obtained from this plant. **'corn·y** *adj.* **corn·i·er, corn·i·est.** (informal) old-fashioned or unoriginal: *a corny joke.*

corn[2] (kôrn) *n.* a small painful area of hardened skin, esp. on the foot, caused by pressure or rubbing.

cor·ner ('kôrnər) *n.* 1. the place where two lines or surfaces meet. 2. the meeting place of two streets or where one street turns at a sharp angle. —*vb.* 1. to prevent from escaping: *the cat cornered the rat in the barn before pouncing on it.* 2. to go round a corner: *the car corners badly.*

cor·o·ner ('kôrənər, 'korənər) *n.* an official who organizes INQUESTs into unexplained or sudden deaths.

cor·po·ral ('kôrpərəl) *n.* a rank in the Army or Marine Corps directly below that of sergeant.

corpse (kôrps) *n.* a dead body.

cor·pus·cle ('kôrpusəl) *n.* one of the microscopic cells found in blood. The white corpuscles help the body to fight infection, while the smaller red corpuscles carry oxygen.

cor·rect (kə'rekt) *adj.* 1. having no mistakes; accurate: *a correct answer.* 2. observing the usual rules or conventions: *correct behavior.* —*vb.* to make correct: *the teacher corrected the child's mistakes.* —**cor'rec·tion** *n.*

cor·ri·dor ('kôridər, 'koridər) *n.* 1. an enclosed passageway in a building with rooms on one or both sides. 2. a narrow strip of land or air space, forming an access route for a country through neighboring countries, often unfriendly ones.

cor·rode (kə'rōd) *vb.* **cor·rod·ing, cor·rod·ed.** to wear or be worn away; eat or be eaten into: *acid corrodes metal.* —**cor'ro·sion** *n.*

cor·rupt (kə'rupt) *vb.* 1. to have an evil or destructive influence on: *some think that violence on television corrupts young people.* 2. to make rotten or foul. 3. to bribe (an official). —*adj.* dishonest or untrustworthy. —**cor'rup·tion** *n.*

cos·met·ic (koz'metik) *n.,* often **cos·met·ics** (*pl.*). a substance, such as lipstick, hair spray, etc., used to improve the skin or hair or make them appear more beautiful. —*adj.* relating to or acting like a cosmetic: *she had cosmetic surgery to improve the shape of her nose.*

cos·tume ('kostōōm, 'kostyōōm) *n.* 1. a set of clothes worn by an actor or a person in fancy dress. 2. any clothing or a set of clothes: *Elizabethan costume.*

cot·tage ('kotij) *n.* a small, simple house.

cot·ton ('kotən) *n.* 1. the soft white furry substance obtained from the pods (bolls) of the cotton plant. 2. thread or cloth made from cotton.

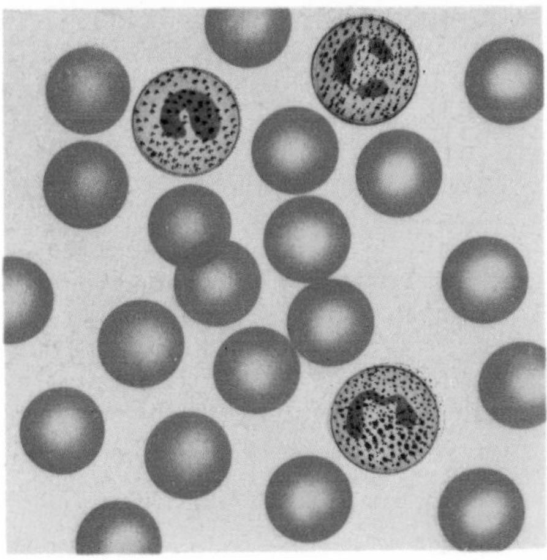
corpuscle

couch (kouch) *n.* an upholstered bench-like seat with a back, for two or more people; sofa.

cough (kôf, kof) *vb.* to force air from the lungs in a sudden noisy burst. —*n.* the action or an instance of coughing, esp. repeatedly.

coun·cil ('kounsəl) *n.* 1. a group of people who meet to discuss, organize, and make decisions on important matters. 2. a group appointed by an administrator to act in an advisory capacity. —**'coun·cil·lor** *n.*

coun·sel ('kounsəl) *n.* 1. guidance or advice. 2. a lawyer. —*vb.* to advise or guide.

count (kount) *vb.* (sometimes + *up*) 1. to recite the cardinal numbers in the correct order: *count from one to fifty.* 2. (sometimes + *up* or *out*) to work out; add up (the number of objects, items, etc., in a set): *count the cards in your hand.* 3. to come into consideration; be important: *good schooling counts when you apply for a job.* —*n.* the action or instance of counting: *a count was made of the people at the meeting.* **'count·down** *n.* a count of the hours, minutes, and seconds before an event, esp. a spacecraft launch, made backwards and ending at zero.

count·er¹ ('kountər) *n.* a table in a shop, bank, or similar place, at which goods are bought, money is exchanged, etc.

count·er² ('kountər) *vb.* to act against and thus destroy or reduce the effect of: *they countered his escape attempt by blocking all the roads.* **coun·ter'clock·wise** *adv.* circling in the direction opposite to that in which the hands of a clock turn. Compare CLOCKWISE.

coun·try ('kuntrē) *n., pl.* **coun·tries.** 1. a nation. 2. the area away from a city or town where houses and buildings are far apart.

coun·ty ('kountē) *n.,pl.* **coun·ties.** one of the areas into which some U.S. states are divided for administrative purposes. —*adj.* of or connected with a county.

cou·ple ('kupəl) *n.* 1. two; a pair. 2. a man and woman who are married, engaged, etc., or partners in some activity, e.g. dancing. —*vb.* **cou·pling, cou·pled.** to join together two things.

cour·age ('kûrij, 'kurij) *n.* bravery.

course (kôrs) *n.* 1. a route or direction: *the earth follows a course around the sun.* 2. passage of time: *much building was done during the course of the year.* 3. a piece of ground used for sport: *a golf course.* 4. a part of a meal: *soup is the first course.* 5. a subject of study: *a course in languages.* 6. a series: *a course of dental treatment.* —*vb.* **cours·ing, coursed.** (of liquids) to move or circulate quickly: *blood courses through one's body.*

crab

court (kôrt) *n.* 1. an enclosed ground marked out for certain ball games: *a tennis court.* 2. a group of buildings round an open space (**court·yard**). 3. the official home of a king or queen and his or her attendants (**cour·ti·ers**). 4. a place where legal cases are heard and judged. —*vb.* 1. (of a man) to pursue the favor of (a woman) in the hope of marrying her; woo. 2. to try to win (a person's favor or attention). 3. to risk: *the girl was courting disaster on the broken swing.*

cour·te·ous ('kûrtēəs) *adj.* polite, well-mannered, and considerate. '**cour·te·sy** *n.* politeness.

cov·er ('kuvər) *vb.* 1. (often + *up*) to put something over another in order to protect or hide it: *they covered the furniture with sheets before painting the walls.* 2. to lie or be spread on: *snow covered the ground.* 3. to conceal: *he covered his embarrassment by coughing.* 4. to extend or stretch over: *the farm covers 40 acres.* 5. to include or deal adequately with: *I hope I have covered everything.* 6. to aim a weapon at: *he covered the escaped tiger with a rifle.* —*n.* 1. something that covers. 2. a book or magazine binding. 3. shelter; concealment. 4. an activity or organization that conceals some other, often illegal, activity: *his business journeys were a cover for smuggling.*

cow·ard ('kouərd) *n.* a person who lacks courage and is easily frightened. '**cow·ard·ice** *n.* the behavior of a coward. —'**cow·ard·ly** *adj.*

crab (krab) *n.* a seashore animal having eight legs and two powerful front claws and a hard shell.

crack (krak) *n.* 1. a breakage line in an object caused by a sharp blow, exposure to heat, etc. 2. a small hole. 3. a sudden sharp noise. 4. (informal) a sharp blow. 5. (informal) a humorous or sarcastic remark. —*vb.* 1. to cause or get a crack. 2. to make or cause to make a sudden noise. 3. (informal) to strike (someone) a sharp blow. 4. (informal) to make a humorous or sarcastic remark. 5. (often + *up*) (informal) to suffer strain. 6. to break open (a safe).

craft (kraft) *n.* 1. a skill or ability. 2. a job requiring such skill, e.g. carpentry. 3. cunning or cleverness. 4. (*pl.* **craft**) a boat, ship, airplane, or spaceship. '**crafts·man** *n.,pl.* **crafts·men.** a skilled workman. '**craft·y** *adj.* **craft·i·er, craft·i·est.** clever; cunning.

cram (kram) *vb.* **cram·ming, crammed.** 1. to fill completely: *his pockets were crammed with apples.* 2. to study very hard at the last opportunity: *Dave crammed for the geography test.*

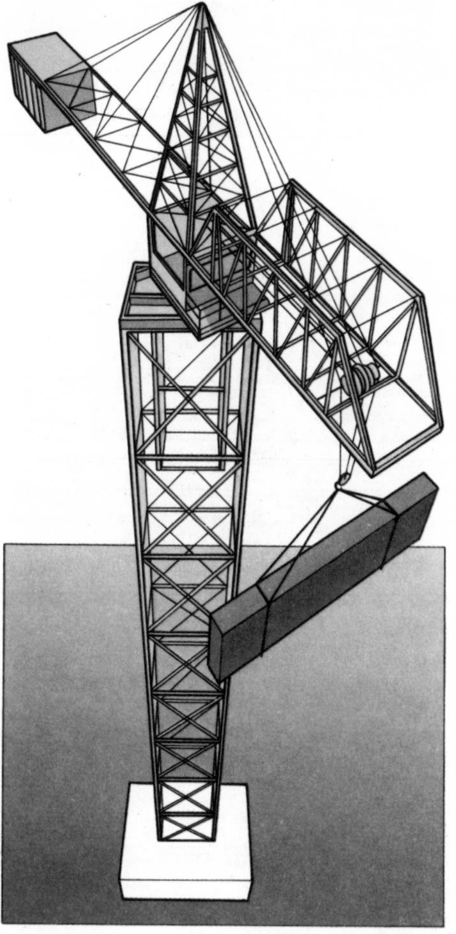
crane

crane (krān) *n.* 1. a type of large wading bird related to the heron. 2. a machine with a long beam for raising heavy weights. —*vb.* **cran·ing, craned.** to stretch (one's neck) in trying to see something.

crash (krash) *n.* 1. a harsh loud sound; clash. 2. a collision or accident involving one or more vehicles. —*vb.* to have or cause to have a crash.

cra·ter ('krātər) *n.* 1. the hole in the top of a volcano through which smoke and lava emerge during an eruption. 2. a hole in the ground caused by an explosion. 3. a saucer-shaped depression on the moon, often very large and often surrounded by very high ground.

crawl (krôl) *vb.* 1. to move along on one's hands and knees or on one's stomach. 2. to move very slowly: *the* *traffic crawled along.* —*n.* 1. the act of crawling. 2. a way of swimming in which a person moves by alternate movements of his arms over his head and kicking his legs.

craze (krāz) *n.* an activity, etc., followed enthusiastically by many people for a short time; fashion. —*vb.* **craz·ing, crazed.** to madden. **'craz·y** *adj.* **craz·i·er, craz·i·est.** 1. insane. 2. (informal) (usu. + *about*) very interested in: *crazy about pop music.*

cream (krēm) *n.* 1. the thick fatty substance that rises to the top in milk. 2. any substance made from, containing, or resembling cream: *face cream.* 3. the very best of something: *the cream of the class.* 4. a color between white and yellow. —*adj.* 1. made from or resembling cream. 2. having the color cream. —*vb.* to make (food) smooth like cream: *she creamed the potatoes.*

crease (krēs) *n.* a line produced in paper or cloth by folding it. —*vb.* **creas·ing, creased.** to have or cause to have creases: *Judy creases her clothes by packing them untidily.*

cre·ate (krē'āt) *vb.* **cre·at·ing, cre·at·ed.** to bring into existence; make: *the earth was created millions of years ago.* **cre'a·tion** *n.* 1. the act of creating or something created. 2. (often **Creation**) the origin of the whole world or universe. **crea·ture** ('krēchər) *n.* any living animal.

cred·i·ble ('kredəbəl) *adj.* able to be believed: *his story is not credible.* —**cred·i'bil·i·ty** *n.* —**'cred·i·bly** *adv.*

cred·it ('kredit) *n.* 1. just praise or acknowledgment: *give him credit for his achievement.* 2. confidence or trust placed in a buyer who receives goods before paying for them. 3. money or payments received. —*vb.* 1. to believe. 2. (+ *with*) to accept someone as having some quality, being the author of something, etc.: *she credited him with much intelligence.* **'cred·it·a·ble** *adj.* worthy. —**'cred·it·a·bly** *adv.*

creek (krēk) *n.* 1. a small river or stream. 2. a small inlet or bay.

creep (krēp) *vb.* **creep·ing, crept.** 1. to move along gradually, silently, and secretly: *Patrick crept out of the house to avoid doing his chores.* 2. (of plants) to spread along the ground or up a wall. **'creep·er** *n.* a type of plant that grows along the ground or up a wall.

crept (krept) *vb.* the past tense and past participle of CREEP.

cres·cent ('kresənt) *n.* the thin curved shape that the moon appears to have, as viewed from earth, when less than half its surface is lit by the sun. —*adj.* of, resembling, or describing this shape.

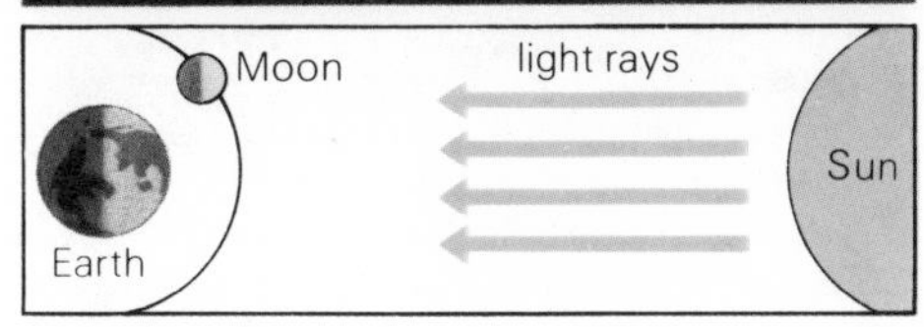

crescent

crest (krest) *n.* 1. the top of something, such as a wave or hill. 2. a group of feathers sticking upwards on a bird's head. 3. a special mark or design used by a family, business firm, etc., e.g. on letters.

crev·ice ('krevis) *n.* a deep narrow crack.

crew (kroo͞) *n.* all the people, except the captain, employed to take care of the management of a ship or aircraft.

crick·et ('krikit) *n.* an insect similar to the grasshopper that makes a distinctive sound by rubbing its wings together.

crime (krīm) *n.* 1. an act that is against the law: *armed robbery is a serious crime.* 2. an evil act; sin: *war is a crime against humanity.* **crim·i·nal** ('kriminəl) *n.* a person who commits a crime: *the escaped criminal was found hiding in a hut in the forest.* *adj.* of crime: *he had a criminal record.*

crim·son ('krimzən) *n.* a bright red color. —*adj.* having this color. —*vb.* to make or become red.

cringe (krinj) *vb.* **cring·ing, cringed.** 1. to shrink away in fear: *the dog cringed under the whip.* 2. to fawn or act in a slavish way: *the villain cringed before the hero in the hope that he would be set free.*

crip·ple ('kripəl) *n.* a lame person; someone who is disabled. —*vb.* **crip·pling, crip·pled.** 1. to make lame, or disable. 2. to hold back progress or reduce the efficiency of (something): *production at the new factory was crippled by strikes.*

cri·sis ('krīsis) *n.,pl.* **cri·ses** ('krisez). 1. an emergency. 2. a time of political, economic, or social difficulty: *when the chairman resigned there was a crisis in the company.* 3. a turning point in the course of a serious illness.

crisp (krisp) *adj.* 1. hard and crunchy: *crisp crackers.* 2. fresh or bracing; pleasantly cold: *a crisp morning.* 3. abrupt; brisk: *a crisp reply.* —*vb.* to make or become crisp. —**'crisp·ly** *adv.* —**'crisp·ness** *n.*

cri·te·ri·on (kri'tērēən) *n.,pl.* **cri·te·ri·a** (krī'tērēə). a standard against which examples may be measured.

crit·ic ('kritik) *n.* 1. a person who judges something or someone, esp. in a disapproving way: *the new housing plans had many critics.* 2. a person who judges literature, music, art, etc., esp. for a living: *a theater critic.* **'crit·i·cal** *adj.* 1. of a critic or criticism: *critical opinion.* 2. faultfinding: *why are you so critical of everything I do?* 3. at a crisis: *the injured man is in a critical condition.* **'crit·i·cize** *vb.* **crit·i·ciz·ing, crit·i·cized.** 1. to give an opinion. 2. to find fault; blame. **'crit·i·cism** *n.* 1. the action or an instance of criticizing. 2. the work of a professional critic: *he wrote a criticism of the new play.* —**'crit·i·cal·ly** *adv.*

crock·er·y ('krokərē) *n.* cups, saucers, plates, and dishes; china.

croc·o·dile ('krokədīl) *n.* a large REPTILE similar to the ALLIGATOR but with a longer narrower snout. It is found in Africa, Asia, Australia, and Central America.

crook (kro͝ok) *n.* 1. anything that is curved or bent: *she cradled the baby in the crook of her arm.* 2. a long stick with a curved hook at the top, formerly used by shepherds. 3. (slang) a criminal, esp. one who cheats or swindles. —*vb.* to curve or bend. **'crook·ed** *adj.* 1. not straight; curved or bent. 2. dishonest; criminal: *a crooked deal.* —**'crook·ed·ly** *adv.* in a lop-sided or crooked manner: *the picture hung crookedly on the wall.* —**'crook·ed·ness** *n.*

crop (krop) *n.* 1. the produce from a cultivated field, such as vegetables, fruit, etc. 2. the gullet of a bird, where food is stored and broken up to make it easier to digest. 3. (also **riding crop**) a short stick with a loop of leather on the end used as a whip. 4. a very short hair style. —*vb.* **crop·ping, cropped.** 1. to harvest or reap crops. 2. to cut (hair) very short. 3. (of animals) to feed on (plants): *the horse cropped the grass by the roadside.*

crow

cross[1] (krôs, kros) *adj.* feeling or expressing bad temper.

cross[2] (krôs, kros) *n.* 1. any two intersecting lines (×, +). 2. a wooden stake driven into the ground, with another nailed across it near the top, on which condemned men were once executed. 3. the symbol of Christianity. 4. a crucifix. 5. a cross-shaped monument. 6. a cross-shaped decoration in metal presented as an honor for some service or act of bravery. 7. an animal or plant of mixed breed: *a mule is a cross between a donkey and a horse.* —*vb.* 1. to go from one side to the other: *we crossed the road.* 2. (+ *out* or *off*) to draw a line across or through: *she crossed her name off the list.* 3. to breed from two different animals or plants in order to obtain a new type. 4. to anger or thwart: *it is not a good idea to cross your employer.* —*adj.* angry; annoyed. **cross section** 1. a view of something or a diagram representing such a view obtained by cutting part of it away, esp. to show how it is constructed. 2. a small number of items taken to represent the larger group of which they are members: *a cross section of the population.*

cross-eyed ('krôsīd, 'krosīd) *adj.* with one or both eyes looking inward toward the nose.

cross·roads ('krosrōdz) *pl.n.* a place where two or more roads cross.

cross·word ('krôswûrd, 'kroswûrd) *n.* (also **crossword puzzle**) a puzzle made up of numbered squares in which words are to be filled in according to clues given in a numbered table.

crouch (krouch) *vb.* to squat or bend down. —*n.* a squatting position.

crow[1] (krō) *n.* a bird with black plumage, dark bill, and hoarse call.

crow[2] (krō) *vb.* **crow·ing, crowed** *or* (for def. 1) **crew.** 1. (esp. of a rooster) to utter a shrill cry. 2. to boast triumphantly: *he crowed about winning the race.* —*n.* the cry of a rooster.

crowd (kroud) *n.* a large number of people in one place. —*vb.* 1. (of people) to gather together in a mass. 2. to press uncomfortably close to (someone): *don't crowd me!* 3. to pack into a confined space: *50 people crowded into the tiny room.*

crown (kroun) *n.* 1. a headgear, usu. a circle of gold or silver decorated with precious stones, worn by a king or queen as a symbol of rank, esp. at ceremonial occasions. 2. any headgear resembling this: *a crown of laurels.* 3. the top part of the head or the head itself. 4. the top of a hat. 5. the top of a hill, mountain, etc. —*vb.* 1. to place a crown upon (someone's head). 2. to make (someone) king or queen. 3. (informal) to hit someone over the head.

crude (krōōd) *adj.* 1. rough; unfinished: *a crude drawing.* 2. coarse or vulgar: *a crude joke.* 3. raw; untreated: *crude oil.* —'**crude·ly** *adv.* —'**crud·i·ty** *n.*

cru·el ('krōōəl) *adj.* taking pleasure in causing pain or suffering; unkind. —'**cru·el·ly** *adv.* —'**cru·el·ty** *n.*

crumb (krum) *n.* 1. a very small piece of bread, cake, etc. 2. any very small amount: *a crumb of comfort.*

crum·ble ('krumbəl) *vb.* **crum·bling, crum·bled.** to break up into small pieces; disintegrate or decay: *the bricks in the old house had begun to crumble.* —'**crum·bly** *adj.*

crush (krush) *vb.* 1. to squeeze hard, esp. causing injury. 2. to crease (a fabric). 3. to squash into a small space. 4. to defeat: *we crushed the enemy in the battle.* —*n.* 1. a dense crowd. 2. (Slang) (usu. + *on*) an infatuation (with): *the girl had a crush on her handsome teacher.*

crust (krust) *n.* 1. the hard crisp outer part of bread and other food. 2. any similar covering: *a crust of ice formed on the puddle.*

crutch (kruch) *n.* 1. a specially shaped wooden or metal stick designed to help a cripple or injured person to walk. 2. a support or aid: *she was a crutch to her sick sister.*

crys·tal ('kristəl) *n.* 1. a mineral that looks like clear glass. 2. the definite flat-sided regular shape natural to many solid substances: *sugar crystals.* 3. fine quality glassware. —*adj.* clear and bright, like crystal: *crystal water flowed from the spring.*

cube (kyōōb) *n.* 1. a solid block with six equal square sides. 2. (mathematics) the product of a number multiplied by itself twice: *the cube of 4 is 64* (4 × 4 × 4). '**cub·ic** *adj.* 1. with the shape of a cube. 2. of the measurements of volume.

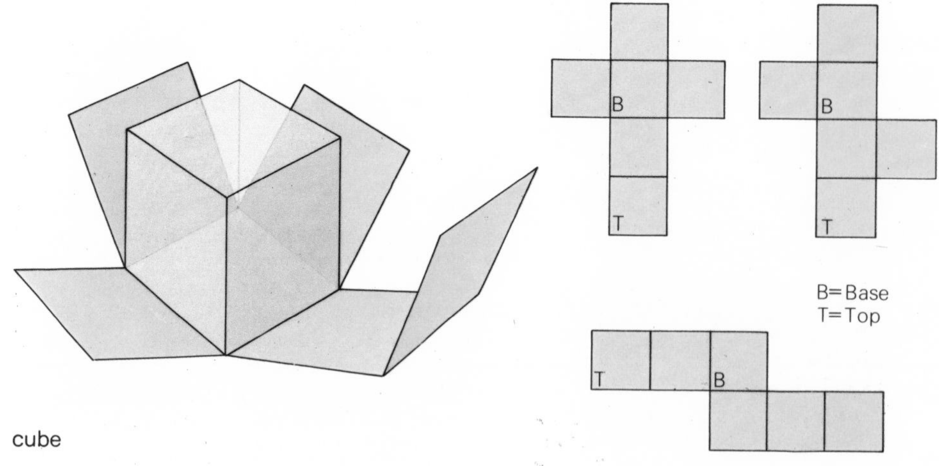

cube

cu·bi·cle ('kyo͞obikəl) *n.* a small area of a larger room, curtained off or divided from the rest: *the dressing room has eight cubicles.*

cuck·oo ('ko͞oko͞o, 'ko͝oko͞o) *n.* a long-tailed European bird that has a call that sounds like its name. The female cuckoo usu. lays her eggs in other birds' nests.

cu·cum·ber ('kyo͞okumbər) *n.* 1. a long fleshy green-skinned fruit used in salads or for pickles. 2. the creeping plant on which these fruits grow.

cuff (kuf) *n.* a band of material sewn at the end of a sleeve to make it fit around the wrist.

cul·prit ('kulprit) *n.* a person guilty of some crime or wrong-doing.

cul·ti·vate ('kultəvāt) *vb.* **cul·ti·vat·ing, cul·ti·vat·ed.** 1. to prepare and use (land) to grow crops. 2. to train and develop (the mind). 3. to encourage: *I cultivated her friendship.* **—cul·ti'va·tion** *n.*

cul·ture ('kulchər) *n.* 1. all the customs, beliefs, and arts of a particular people: *Chinese culture.* 2. high development of learning; possession of good taste and refined habits: *a man of great culture.* 3. the growing or developing of something, either by natural or artificial means: *the culture of pearls.* **'cul·tured** *adj.* 1. possessing culture; civilized. 2. artificially grown or produced. **—'cul·tur·al** *adj.* **—'cul·tur·al·ly** *adv.*

cun·ning ('kuniñg) *adj.* clever; sly.

cup·board ('kubərd) *n.* a closet, either built into the wall or made as a separate piece of furniture, for storing food, clothes, etc.

cu·ra·tor (kyo͞o'rātər) *n.* an official in charge of a museum or art gallery or of a special section of it.

cure (kyo͝or) *vb.* **cur·ing, cured.** 1. to heal; make (a sick person) better. 2. to preserve (meat, fish, skins) by drying, smoking, or salting. *—n.* something that restores health.

cu·ri·ous ('kyo͝orēəs) *adj.* 1. eager to find out; inquisitive: *the curious child was always asking questions.* 2. strange; unusual. **cu·ri·os·i·ty** (kyo͝orē'ositē) *n.,pl.* **cu·ri·os·i·ties.** 1. eagerness to find out. 2. a rare or strange object: *he brought several curiosities back from his travels.*

curl (kûrl) *vb.* 1. to form (hair) into ringlets or coils. 2. (often + *up*) to twist (something) into a spiral; coil. *—n.* a spiral coil, esp. of hair. **—'curl·y** *adj.* **curl·i·er, curl·i·est. —'curl·i·ness** *n.*

cur·rant ('kûrənt, 'kurənt) *n.* 1. a small dried seedless grape, like a raisin. 2. a small round berry that is the fruit of currant bushes.

cur·rent ('kûrənt, 'kurənt) *n.* 1. a flowing stream of water, air, etc., within a larger mass. 2. a flow of electricity. 3. a general trend: *the current of opinion. —adj.* 1. generally used or accepted. 2. of the present time: *current affairs.*

cur·ry ('kûrē, 'kurē) *n.,pl.* **cur·ries.** a spicy Indian dish, containing meat or vegetables, prepared in a sauce seasoned with **curry powder** (a mixture of spices). *—vb.* **cur·ry·ing, cur·ried.** to make a curry of.

curse (kûrs) *vb.* **curs·ing, cursed.** 1. to express a wish to bring harm upon (someone). 2. to use bad language; swear. *—n.* 1. a word or phrase used for cursing.

cus·tard ('kustərd) *n.* a pale yellow mixture of sweetened eggs and milk that is boiled or baked, and served either as a pudding or as a sauce on sweet dishes.

cus·tom ('kustəm) *n.* 1. a social habit, practice, or pattern of behavior that members of a group are expected to observe; tradition: *it is the custom to give presents at Christmas.* 2. an individual habit: *it was her custom to go abroad every year.* 3. patronage of a business or shop by persons (**cus·tom·ers**) who regularly trade there. 4. **cus·toms** (*pl.*) taxes or duty due on goods imported into a country, and the official body responsible for collecting them. **'cus·tom·ar·y** *adj.* usual; habitual.

cut·ler·y ('kutlərē) *n.* implements such as knives, forks, and spoons.

cy·cle ('sīkəl) *n.* a sequence of events, small units of time, etc., that is periodically repeated: *the cycle of day and night.* **cy·clic** ('sīklik, 'siklik) *adj.* repeated in cycles.

cy·clone ('sīklōn) *n.* a violent tropical storm; tornado.

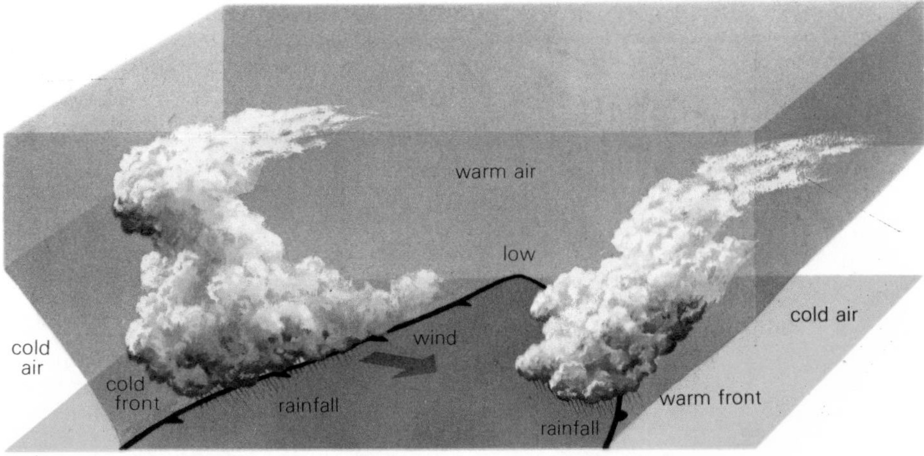

cyclone

cur·tain ('kûrtən) *n.* a hanging piece of cloth or other material used to shut out the light coming through a window, divide part of a room from the rest, etc.

curve (kûrv) *n.* a line, stretch of road, etc., that is not straight and keeps bending in a particular direction. *—vb.* **curv·ing, curved.** to have or cause to have a curved shape.

cush·ion ('ko͝oshən) *n.* a pad made of cloth, leather, plastic, etc., stuffed with soft material, such as feathers, and used for sitting on or against.

cyg·net ('signit) *n.* a young swan.

cyl·in·der ('silindər) *n.* 1. a solid or hollow tubular body, like a tin can, with round flat ends and straight sides. 2. a cylinder-shaped part of an engine. 3. the rotating part of a revolver, containing the bullets. **—cy'lin·dri·cal** *adj.*

cym·bal ('simbəl) *n.* a round metal plate that produces a ringing sound when struck, and used in music.

cy·press ('sīprəs) *n.* a type of CONIFER.

D

dab·ble ('dabəl) *vb.* **dab·bling, dab·bled.** 1. to splash (esp. one's fingers or toes) lightly in water. 2. (often + *in*) to engage in an activity, hobby, or interest with only casual concern. —'**dab·bler** *n.*

daffodil

daf·fo·dil ('dafədil) *n.* a garden plant grown from a bulb, having a yellow flower with a trumpet-shaped center.

dag·ger ('dagər) *n.* a short knifelike stabbing weapon with a sharp pointed blade.

dai·ly ('dālē) *adj.* occurring or appearing every day. —*n.,pl.* **dai·lies.** a newspaper published every weekday.

dain·ty ('dāntē) *adj.* **dain·ti·er, dain·ti·est.** 1. small, delicate, and neat in appearance. 2. of delicate taste; delicious. —'**dain·ti·ly** *adv.* —'**dain·ti·ness** *n.*

dair·y ('deərē) *n.,pl.* **dair·ies.** 1. a room or building on a farm where milk is kept and butter and cheese are made. 2. a store that sells milk and its products (butter, cheese, etc.). 3. a farm or section of a farm producing milk, butter, eggs, cheese, etc.

dai·sy ('dāzē) *n.,pl.* **dai·sies.** 1. a field flower with a yellow center and radiating white petals. 2. one of many similar kinds of garden flower, usu. with white, red, pink, or yellow petals.

dam (dam) *n.* 1. a barrier built across a stream, river, lake, etc., to obstruct or control the flow of water, e.g. to irrigate the land or to produce electricity. 2. a reservoir of water created by a dam. —*vb.* **dam·ming, dammed.** 1. to build a dam across. 2. to stop (a flow of water, tears, blood, etc.); keep in check or control.

dam·age ('damij) *n.* 1. harm or injury causing loss of value, usefulness, or efficiency. 2. **dam·ag·es** (*pl.*) money awarded by a court as compensation for loss or injury. —*vb.* **dam·ag·ing, dam·aged.** to injure, harm, or spoil.

damn (dam) *vb.* 1. to condemn to hell; curse. 2. to criticize severely. 3. to ruin the hopes or chances of: *lack of money and enthusiasm damned the new project.* —*interj.* an expression of impatience or annoyance. —**dam·na·ble** ('damnəbəl) *adj.* —**dam'na·tion** *n.*

damp (damp) *adj.* slightly wet; moist. —*n.* 1. (also **damp·ness**) humidity or moisture. 2. undesirable moisture on walls or other surfaces. —*vb.* (also **damp·en**) 1. to make slightly wet; moisten. 2. to check or restrain (spirits, action, etc.); discourage. 3. (often + *out*) to stifle or extinguish (fire). '**damp·er** *n.* 1. anything that discourages or depresses. 2. a felt pad in a piano that stops the vibration of the strings. 3. a movable piece of metal in a chimney for controlling the draft of a fire.

dan·druff ('dandrəf) *n.* small white scales found on the scalp and in the hair.

dan·ger ('dānjər) *n.* 1. risk of being harmed, injured, or killed; peril: *the explorers faced great danger in the jungle.* 2. somebody or something that causes danger. —'**dan·ger·ous** *adj.* —'**dan·ger·ous·ly** *adv.*

dan·gle ('dan͡ggəl) *vb.* **dan·gling, dan·gled.** to hang loosely or swing back and forth.

dare (deər) *vb.* **dar·ing, dared.** 1. to have enough courage to do something: *he didn't dare to move.* 2. to challenge (someone) to show his courage: *I dare you to jump.* —*n.* a challenge to someone to show his courage.

dam

dark (dârk) *adj.* 1. having little or no light; dim; gloomy: *the forest depths were dark even during the day.* 2. being of a deep color or shade that has some black in it. 3. (of hair or the complexion) brown or black. —*n.* (also **darkness**) 1. absence of light; blackness. 2. night time: *I'm not afraid of the dark.* '**dark·en** *vb.* to make or become dark or darker. '**dark·ly** *adv.* mysteriously or sinisterly: *he said darkly that there would be many changes when he took control of the business.*

darn (dârn) *vb.* to mend a hole (in socks, knitwear, etc.) by covering it with interwoven rows of wool or thread. —*n.* the area repaired in this way.

dart (dârt) *n.* 1. a small metal or wooden arrow, esp. one thrown by hand at a circular target (**dartboard**) in the game of **darts.** 2. a quick dash. 3. a short tapered seam used to shape a bodice, etc., in dressmaking. —*vb.* to move forward for a short distance suddenly and very fast: *she darted across the road just before the traffic moved.*

date[1] (dāt) *n.* 1. the time or period, expressed as day, month, year, on which any event takes place: *what is the date of your birthday?* 2. an appointment to meet on a specific day. —*vb.* **dat·ing, dat·ed.** 1. to mark (a letter, etc.) with the date. 2. to make an appointment with a member of the opposite sex, esp. habitually. 3. to estimate how old something is: *the archaeologist dated the vase to an early period.* 4. to show signs of age: *many fashions date quickly.* '**dat·ed** *adj.* old-fashioned.

date[2] (dāt) *n.* the sweet sticky fruit of the date palm tree.

daugh·ter ('dôtər) *n.* a female child or person in relation to her parents.

daw·dle ('dôdəl) *vb.* **daw·dling, daw·dled.** to move slowly, wasting time: *they dawdled on the way home and were late for supper.*

dawn (dôn) *n.* 1. sunrise. 2. the beginning of anything: *the beginning of this century saw the dawn of the movie age.* —*vb.* 1. to begin to grow light or appear. 2. (+ *on*) to become gradually clear to: *as he spoke, it dawned on me that his accent was French.*

day (dā) *n.* 1. the period of 24 hours in which the earth makes one turn around its axis. 2. the light part of this period.

daze (dāz) *vb.* **daz·ing, dazed.** to stun and confuse: *the uproar of the big city dazed the old man.* —*n.* the state of being bewildered.

daz·zle ('dazəl) *vb.* **daz·zling, daz·zled.** 1. to blind temporarily with bright light. 2. to stun with great beauty, brilliance, etc.: *the singer gave a dazzling performance.*

dart

dead (ded) *adj.* 1. without life; having died. 2. dull; boring. 3. no longer in use: *a dead language.* 4. accurate: *a dead shot.* —*n.* those who have died. —*adv.* (informal) completely or absolutely: *dead tired.* '**dead·ly** *adj.* **dead·li·er, dead·li·est.** likely to cause death: *arsenic is a deadly poison.*

dead·line ('dedlīn) *n.* the time by which a job must be finished.

dead·lock ('dedlok) *n.* the point in a situation where no progress, e.g. towards settling a dispute, can be made: *negotiations ended in a deadlock.*

deaf (def) *adj.* 1. unable to hear at all. 2. refusing to listen: *he was deaf to her pleading.* '**deaf·en** *vb.* to make partly or temporarily unable to hear: *he was deafened by the noise of the drill.* —'**deaf·ness** *n.*

deal (dēl) *vb.* **deal·ing, dealt** (delt). 1. to hand out, divide, or deliver: *she dealt the playing cards.* 2. (+ *with*) to do business with: *my family has dealt with your firm for years.* 3. (+ *with*) to manage or handle: *if he is troublesome I will deal with him!* —*n.* 1. quantity; amount: *I had a good deal of trouble finding the house.* 2. bargain; arrangement.

dear (dēr) *adj.* 1. beloved; highly thought of. 2. expensive; costly. —'**dear·ly** *adv.* —'**dear·ness** *n.*

death (deth) *n.* the end of life; condition of being dead. —'**death·ly** *adj.*

de·bate (di'bāt) *n.* a formal discussion or argument between several consecutive speakers in front of an audience: *our class had a debate about crime and punishment.* —*vb.* **de·bat·ing, de·bat·ed.** to discuss formally or consider.

deb·ris (də'brē, 'dābrē) *n.* scattered rubbish, wreckage, or fragments.

debt (det) *n.* something that is owed to another: *I owe you a debt of gratitude for your kindness.* **in debt** owing money. —'**debt·or** *n.*

dec·ade ('dekād) *n.* a period of ten years: *the years between 1960 and 1970 is the decade referred to as the sixties.*

de·cant·er (di'kantər) *n.* a fancy glass bottle into which wines, spirits, etc., are poured for serving.

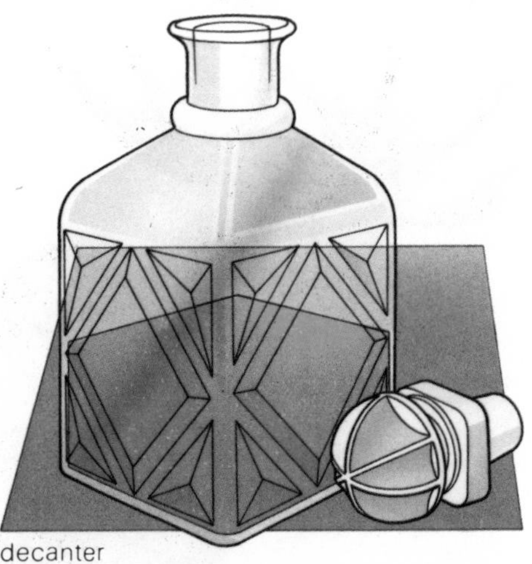

decanter

de·cay (di'kā) *vb.* to rot or waste away: *sugar can cause teeth to decay.* —*n.* state of rottenness or gradual decline.

de·ceive (di'sēv) *vb.* **de·ceiv·ing, de·ceived.** to mislead, cheat, or lie to: *though he was a cunning liar, he could not deceive his mother.* **de·ceit** (di'sēt) *n.* cheating, cunning falseness; act of deceiving. —**de'ceit·ful** *adj.* —**de'ceit·ful·ly** *adv.*

de·cent ('dēsənt) *adj.* 1. modest; respectable. 2. sufficient: *a decent portion.* 3. kind: *it was decent of you to give us supper.* —'**de·cen·cy** *n.* —'**de·cent·ly** *adv.*

de·cep·tion (di'sepshən) *n.* a deliberately misleading act or the practice of deceiving. **de'cep·tive** *adj.* likely to mislead; giving a false impression: *his appearance was deceptive —he looked young but was really quite old.*

de·cide (di'sīd) *vb.* **de·cid·ing, de·cid·ed.** to make up one's mind; choose or settle: *eventually she decided to buy the green dress.*

de·cid·u·ous (di'sijōōəs) *adj.* (of a tree, shrub, etc.) shedding its leaves every year, usu. in the fall or early winter: *the oak is a deciduous tree.* Compare EVERGREEN.

dec·i·mal ('desəməl) *adj.* of or based on units of 10 or tenth parts. —*n.* a number or part of a whole number expressed in tens or tenth parts, e.g. (three and a half expressed as) 3·5 is a decimal. Whole numbers and parts of numbers are separated by the **decimal point,** e.g. 6·4 is the decimal equivalent of six and four-tenths. **dec·i·mal·i'za·tion** *n.* the conversion from another system to a decimal system of units of money, weight, etc.

de·ci·pher (di'sīfər) *vb.* to work out the true meaning of (a piece of writing that is written in code, another alphabet, or just badly written): ***it is almost impossible to decipher John's untidy writing.***

de·ci·sion (di'sizhən) *n.* 1. the act of deciding. 2. judgment or course of action decided upon: ***a wise decision.*** 3. firmness and strength of character: ***he acted with decision on all occasions.*** **de·ci·sive** (di'sīsiv) *adj.* final, firm, and positive.

deck (dek) *n.* 1. the platform or floor of a ship, bus, etc. 2. a pack (of cards). —*vb.* to adorn or decorate: ***she was decked with jewels.***

de·clare (di'kleər) *vb.* **de·clar·ing, de·clared.** 1. to announce publicly or formally: ***I declare Jones the winner.*** 2. to state firmly. 3. to admit one has (taxable goods) when going through customs on entering a country. **dec·la·ra·tion** (deklə'rāshən) *n.* 1. the act of declaring. 2. a formal or legal statement or announcement: ***Britain made a declaration of war in 1939.***

de·cline (di'klīn) **de·clin·ing, de·clined.** 1. to become gradually less or worse: ***her health declined as she became old.*** 2. to refuse, esp. politely: ***he declined another cookie.*** 3. to slope downward. —*n.* 1. a gradual lessening, worsening, or downward turn: ***a decline in moral standards.*** 2. a downward slope.

dec·o·rate ('dekərāt) *vb.* **dec·o·rat·ing, dec·o·rat·ed.** 1. to make more beautiful by adding ornaments, etc.; adorn: ***on Christmas Eve we decorated the tree with colored lights.*** 2. to furnish, paint, or wallpaper (a room, house, office, etc.). 3. to award (someone) an honor or medal in recognition of courage, service, etc. **—dec·o'ra·tion** *n.* **—'dec·o·ra·tive** *adj.*

de·coy *n.* (di'koi, 'dēkoi) 1. a person or thing used to lure persons away from what they are seeking, to distract attention, etc.: ***the general sent a small force to attack from the west as a decoy.*** 2. a model of an animal, duck, etc., used to attract animals to where the hunters are. —*vb.* (di'koi) to deceive or trap in this way.

de·crease *vb.* (di'krēs) **de·creas·ing, de·creased.** to grow less; diminish. —*n.* ('dēkrēs, di'krēs) 1. the process of growing less. 2. the amount by which a thing is lessened: ***there has been a decrease in the demand for oil since the prices rose.***

ded·i·cate ('dedəkāt) *vb.* **ded·i·cat·ing, ded·i·cat·ed.** 1. to consecrate for a holy purpose: ***the church is dedicated to St. Joseph.*** 2. to devote wholly and exclusively: ***this department is dedicated to scientific research.*** 3. to inscribe (a book, piece of music, etc.) to someone as a mark of respect. **'ded·i·cat·ed** *adj.* devoted and hard-working: ***a dedicated nurse.*** **—ded·i'ca·tion** *n.*

de·duct (di'dukt) *vb.* to subtract or take away. **—de'duction** *n.*

deed (dēd) *n.* 1. an act or action: ***Peter's good deed for the day was to clean the windows.*** 2. a legal document to prove ownership.

deep (dēp) *adj.* 1. going very far down: ***a deep well.*** 2. wide: ***a deep shelf.*** 3. low in pitch: ***a deep voice.*** 4. dark in color: *deep blue.* 5. strong; intense: *deep sadness.* 6. far-reaching: *a deep thinker.* —*adv.* very far: *they pushed deep into the forest.* —'**deep·ly** *adv.* —'**deep·ness** *n.* See also DEPTH.

deer (dēr) *n.,pl.* **deer.** a four-legged hoofed animal, the male of which has antlers that are shed every year.

de·feat (di'fēt) *vb.* 1. to beat in a battle, game, etc.; overcome; conquer. 2. to frustrate, thwart, or prevent success in: *to give way now would defeat your purpose.* —*n.* the loss of a battle, game, etc. **de'feat·ist** *n.* a person who accepts defeat too easily.

de·fect *n.* ('dēfekt, di'fekt) a flaw; fault. —*vb.* (di'fekt) run away from one's country or duty: *the Russian scientist defected to America.* —**de'fec·tive** *adj.*

de·fend (di'fend) *vb.* 1. to protect against attack; keep safe. 2. to speak to prove someone's innocence in a law court. **de'fend·ant** *n.* a person called to a court of law to answer charges.

de·fense (di'fens) *n.* 1. protection against attack. 2. something used for this: *a shield is a defense.* 3. a legal case for proving the innocence of a defendant. 4. (sports) players who try to prevent opponents from scoring. **de'fen·si·ble** *adj.* able to be defended; justified. **de'fen·sive** *adj.* intended to defend or ward off attack. —**de'fen·sive·ly** *adv.*

de·fi·ance (di'fīəns) *n.* the act of defying; bold, often foolhardy opposition or disobedience. —**de'fi·ant** *adj.* —**de'fi·ant·ly** *adv.*

def·i·nite ('defənit) *adj.* 1. precise; clear: *a definite outline of a footprint.* 2. without a doubt; firm: *let's make a definite plan to meet on Thursday.* —'**def·i·nite·ly** *adv.*

def·i·ni·tion (defə'nishən) *n.* 1. an explanation of the meaning of a word or phrase. 2. degree of clearness: *the image looked hazy and lacked definition.* **de·fin·i·tive** (di'finitiv) *adj.* final; needing no further work or explanation: *the definitive edition of Shakespeare.*

de·flate (di'flāt) *vb.* **de·flat·ing, de·flat·ed.** to let out air or gas from (a tire, balloon, etc.).

de·form (di'fôrm) *vb.* to spoil the natural shape or look of; disfigure: *his right hand was deformed in an accident.* **de'form·i·ty** *n.,pl.* **de·form·i·ties.** a misshapen part (usu. of the body).

de·fy (di'fī) *vb.* **de·fy·ing, de·fied.** 1. to refuse to obey. 2. to challenge; dare: *I defy you to prove me wrong!* 3. to resist; prevent: *the beauty of the mountains defies description.*

de·gree (di'grē) *n.* 1. a unit for measuring heat; one of the divisions on a scale of temperature: *32 degrees Fahrenheit (freezing point) is equivalent to 0 degrees Celsius.* 2. the unit for measuring angles; there are 360 degrees in one complete turn. 3. amount or extent. 4. an award given to a person who attains a certain standard of knowledge at a university, etc.

de·ject·ed (di'jektid) *adj.* depressed, cast down; gloomy. —**de'jec·tion** *n.*

de·lay (di'lā) *vb.* to take a long time; be slow or make (something) late. —*n.* 1. the act of making late. 2. amount of time lost: *a delay of three hours.*

del·e·gate *vb.* ('deləgāt) **del·e·gat·ing, del·e·gat·ed.** to entrust (another person) with (a task, message, etc.): *Jane was delegated to give out the books.* —*n.* ('deləgāt, 'deləgit) a representative sent to a meeting on behalf of others. **del·e'ga·tion** *n.* a group of delegates.

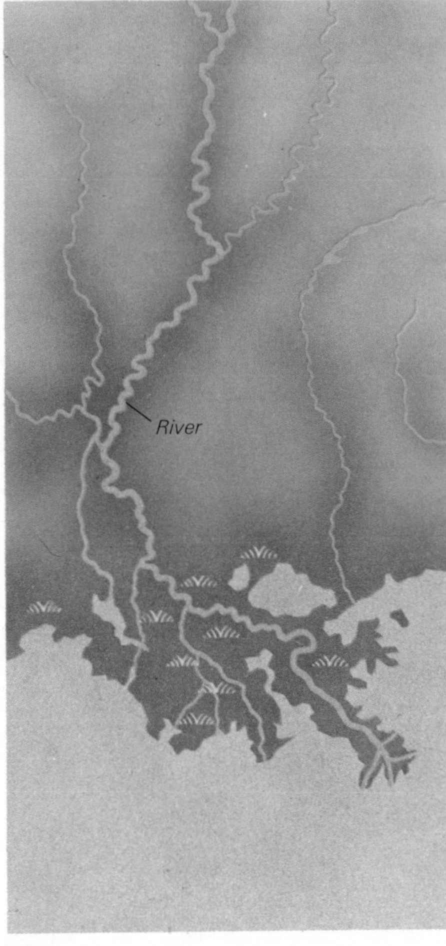

delta

de·lib·er·ate *adj.* (di'libərit) 1. not accidental; intentional. 2. careful or cautious; unhurried: *he walked with a deliberate pace.* —*vb.* (di'libərāt) **de·lib·er·at·ing, de·lib·er·at·ed.** to consider carefully possible courses of action. —**de'lib·er·ate·ly** *adv.* —**de·lib·er'a·tion** *n.*

del·i·cate ('deləkit) *adj.* 1. pretty and fragile: *a delicate china cup.* 2. weak; liable to sickness. 3. requiring careful handling: *a delicate situation.* —'**del·i·cate·ly** *adv.*

de·li·cious (di'lishəs) *adj.* 1. extremely good to eat. 2. very pleasant to the senses: *a delicious smell.* —**de'li·cious·ly** *adv.*

de·light (di'līt) *n.* 1. great pleasure or enjoyment. 2. something causing pleasure or enjoyment. —*vb.* to give or get great pleasure. —**de'light·ful** *adj.* —**de'light·ful·ly** *adv.*

de·lin·quent (di'lingkwənt) *n.* (also **juvenile delinquent**) a young person who has broken the law. —**de'lin·quen·cy** *n.*

de·liv·er (di'livər) *vb.* 1. to take (letters, goods, etc.) to the correct address. 2. to save; rescue from danger. 3. to say (a speech, sermon, sentence on a criminal, etc.) 4. to bring (a baby) into the world. 5. to aim or launch (a blow, etc.). —**de'liv·er·y** *n., pl.* **de·liv·er·ies.**

del·ta ('deltə) *n.* the triangular area where a river deposits silt and divides into branches as it reaches the sea.

de·luge ('delyo͞oj) *n.* 1. a flood or heavy storm. 2. an overwhelming amount: *she received a deluge of letters.* —*vb.* **de·lug·ing, de·luged.** to cover with or as if with a flood.

de·mand (di'mand) *vb.* to ask for strongly. —*n.* 1. a firm or urgent request. 2. requirement; need: *demand for holidays abroad has increased.*

de·mol·ish (di'molish) *vb.* 1. to destroy completely; tear down. 2. to disprove forcibly (someone's argument, theory, etc.). —**dem·o·li·tion** (demə'lishən) *n.*

dem·on·strate ('demənstrāt) *vb.* **dem·on·strat·ing, dem·on·strat·ed.** 1. to show how to do something, how a machine works, how to prove a geometric theorem, etc. 2. to take part in a demonstration: *the students demonstrated against the war.* **dem·on'stra·tion** *n.* 1. the act of demonstrating. 2. a meeting or rally held to protest against or support something. **de·mon·stra·tive** (di'monstrətiv) *adj.* showing one's feelings; warm and affectionate. **'dem·on·stra·tor** *n.* 1. one who demonstrates. 2. a product used by a retailer to exhibit its features to prospective customers.

de·ni·al (di'nīəl) *n.* 1. a refusal. 2. the action or an instance of denying: *he made a strong denial of the allegation that he had taken part in the robbery.*

de·note (di'nōt) *vb.* **de·not·ing, de·not·ed.** 1. to be a sign of: *red hair often denotes a fiery temperament.* 2. to be a symbol of: *'r' denotes the radius of a circle.* —**de·no'ta·tion** *n.*

dense (dens) *adj.* 1. solid; closely packed. 2. heavy in proportion to volume: *oil is less dense than water so it floats on its surface.* 3. (informal) slow-witted; dull. —**'dense·ly** *adv.* —**'den·si·ty** *n.,pl.* **den·si·ties.**

den·tal ('dentəl) *adj.* relating to the teeth.

den·tist ('dentist) *n.* a person who specializes in the care of the teeth. —**'den·tist·ry** *n.*

de·ny (di'nī) *vb.* **de·ny·ing, de·nied.** 1. to say that something is not true or non-existent: *she denied all knowledge of the plot.* 2. to deprive of; refuse: *they deny admittance to children.* See also DENIAL.

de·part (di'pârt) *vb.* 1. to go away (from); leave. 2. (+ *from*) to change (from the usual thing that is done); veer (from the truth). **de'part·ment** *n.* a section or subdivision of a large store, country, school, college, etc. —**de'par·ture** *n.*

de·pend (di'pend) *vb.* 1. (+ *on*) to rely on: *he depended on his wife's advice.* 2. to be decided or affected by: *the harvest will depend on the weather.* **de'pend·a·ble** *adj.* reliable; trustworthy. **de'pend·ant** (also **dependent**) *n.* a person who relies on another for support, e.g. a person's children. **de'pend·ence** *or* **de'pend·en·cy** *n.* 1. a state of relying. 2. a colonial territory: *India was once a dependency of Great Britain.* **de'pend·ent** *adj.* (+ *on*) relying on.

de·port·ment (di'pôrtmənt) *n.* the manner in which a person moves, stands, or behaves; carriage or bearing: *a fashion model must have graceful deportment.*

de·pos·it (di'pozit) *n.* 1. a layer of a substance left by nature; accumulation: *a deposit of mud.* 2. money put in a bank. 3. a first part payment on merchandise. —*vb.* to put or place: *she deposited her books on the table.* **de'pos·i·tor** *n.* a person who puts a deposit of money in a bank.

de·pot ('dēpō, 'depō) *n.* 1. a bus or railroad station. 2. a warehouse, esp. a military one.

de·press (di'pres) *vb.* 1. to make miserable or unhappy. 2. to press (a switch, etc.) down. **de'pres·sion** *n.* 1. a feeling of sadness and unhappiness. 2. a slackening off in trade, accompanied by high unemployment; slump: *there was a depression in the nineteen-thirties.* 3. low pressure in the atmosphere, usu. producing rain and high winds. 4. a hollow, e.g. in the ground.

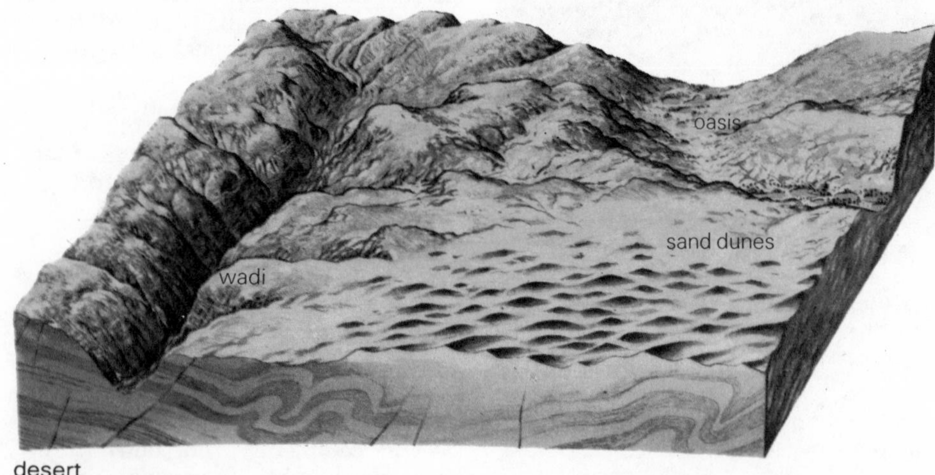

desert

de·prive (di'prīv) *vb.* **de·priv·ing, de·prived.** (+ *of*) to take away: *prison deprives people of their liberty.* **de'prived** *adj.* lacking normal comforts, rights, etc. —**dep·ri·va·tion** (deprə'vāshən) *n.*

depth (depth) *n.* 1. the state of being deep; deepness. 2. the extent or measure of how deep something is: *the depth of the pool is 3 feet.* 3. often **depths** (*pl.*) the most severe or intense stage: *the depths of winter.*

dep·u·ty ('depyətē) *n.,pl.* **dep·u·ties.** 1. a person appointed to stand in for or assist someone else: *a deputy sheriff.* 2. one of a group of people chosen to represent the views of others. **dep·u'ta·tion** *n.* a group chosen by a larger group to speak for or represent it. **'dep·u·tize** *vb.* **dep·u·tiz·ing, dep·u·tized.** to do something for or in the name of someone else.

der·e·lict ('derəlikt) *adj.* deserted, abandoned, or neglected and allowed to fall into ruin: *a derelict house.*

de·scend (di'send) *vb.* 1. to move or slope downward: *the road descends into the valley.* 2. (+ *from*) to have as an ancestor: *we are descended from 17th-century Dutch settlers.* 3. (+ *upon* or *on*) to attack or swoop down on. 4. (+ *to*) to lower oneself or stoop to: *don't descend to bullying.* **de'scend·ant** *n.* a person descended from others. **de'scent** *n.* 1. a passage or movement downward. 2. ancestry.

de·scribe (di'skrīb) *vb.* **de·scrib·ing, de·scribed.** 1. to state what someone or something is or was like. 2. to form the shape of (a geometrical figure). —**de·scrip·tion** (di'skripshən) *n.* —**de'scrip·tive** *adj.*

des·ert[1] ('dezərt) *n.* a large barren often sandy or rocky region with little vegetation or water.

de·sert[2] (di'zûrt) *vb.* 1. to abandon or forsake; go away from. 2. (of a soldier, etc.) to leave one's post; run away. —**de'sert·er** *n.* —**de'ser·tion** *n.*

de·serve (di'zûrv) *vb.* **de·serv·ing, de·served.** to have a right or be entitled to; merit: *he deserved promotion.* **de·serv·ed·ly** (di'zûrvidlē) *adv.* rightly; justifiably: *she was deservedly commended for her bravery.*

de·sign (di'zīn) *n.* 1. a plan or a preliminary sketch for a building, machine, dress, etc.: *the architect showed us the design for the new house.* 2. a pattern; ornamentation: *the material had a flowery design.* —*vb.* to make a preliminary sketch; plan. **de'sign·ing** *adj.* artful or cunning. —**de'sign·er** *n.*

de·sire (di'zīər) *n.* a strong longing, wish, or craving; passion: *he suddenly felt a desire for a cookie.* —*vb.* **de·sir·ing, de·sired.** to wish or long for. —**de'sir·a·ble** *adj.*

desk

desk (desk) *n.* a table-like piece of furniture often with drawers, used esp. in offices and schools.

de·spair (di'speər) *n.* a state or feeling of total hopelessness. —*vb.* to abandon hope.

des·patch (di'spach) *n., vb.* See DISPATCH.

des·per·ate ('despərit) *adj.* 1. acting or feeling reckless because of despair. 2. causing despair: *it was a desperate situation.* —**'des·per·ate·ly** *adv.* —**des·per·a·tion** (despə'rāshən) *n.*

de·spise (di'spīz) *vb.* **de·spis·ing, de·spised.** feel contempt or scorn for: *he despises cowards.* **de·spic·a·ble** ('despikəbəl, di'spikəbəl) *adj.* something to be despised.

de·spond·ent (di'spondənt) *adj.* downcast; in low spirits; near to despair: *he felt very despondent about the failure of his plans.*

des·sert (di'zûrt) *n.* a sweet course served at the end of the meal.

des·ti·na·tion (destə'nāshən) *n.* a place to which someone or something is going.

des·ti·ny ('destənē) *n.,pl.* **des·ti·nies.** an already determined or inescapable course of events; fate: *it was his destiny to die young.*

de·stroy (di'stroi) *vb.* to ruin or spoil completely: *rain destroyed the crop.* **de'stroy·er** *n.* a high-speed naval warship used to defend larger ships. —**de·struc·ti·ble** (di'struktəbəl) *adj.* —**de'struc·tion** *n.* —**de'struc·tive** *adj.* —**de'struc·tive·ly** *adv.*

de·tach (di'tach) *vb.* to separate (a part) from a larger whole; unfasten; remove: *we detached the trailer from the car.* **de'tached** *adj.* 1. separated. 2. without bias or special interest. **de'tach·ment** *n.* 1. aloofness; lack of involvement. 2. a section of an army separated for a special mission.

de·tail *n.* (di'tāl, 'dētāl) 1. a very small precise part of something. 2. a group of soldiers selected to do a particular job. —*vb.* (di'tāl) 1. to describe or list (every part). 2. to select and order (to do a particular job): *I was detailed to paint the walls.*

de·tect (di'tekt) *vb.* to discover by careful examination. **de'tec·tive** *n.* a person who hunts for evidence, usu. to solve crimes and catch the criminal. —**de'tec·tion** *n.* —**de'tec·tor** *n.*

de·ter (di'tûr) *vb.* **de·ter·ring, de·terred.** to prevent or discourage (someone) from doing something because of its unpleasant results; put off: *she was deterred from going for a walk by the heavy snowfall.*

de·ter·rent (di'tûrənt, di'terənt) *n.* something that deters.

de·ter·gent (di'tûrjənt) *n.* a cleaning or washing substance, esp. one used in place of soap.

de·te·ri·o·rate (di'tērēərāt) *vb.* **de·te·ri·o·rat·ing, de·te·ri·o·rat·ed.** to make or become worse: *the old cottage deteriorated because no one lived in it.* —**de·te·ri·o'ra·tion** *n.*

de·ter·mine (di'tûrmin) *vb.* **de·ter·min·ing, de·ter·mined.** 1. to decide; settle on: *we determined to go.* 2. to affect conclusively: *our refusal was determined by her rudeness.* 3. to establish or settle the facts about (something): *the explorers determined the course of the river.* **de'ter·mined** *adj.* trying hard to get what one wants; resolute. —**de·ter·mi'na·tion** *n.*

de·test (di'test) *vb.* to hate greatly; loathe.

de·tour ('dētŏŏr, di'tŏŏr) *n.* a route other than the usual or direct route: *we had to make a detour to avoid the floods.*

dev·as·tate ('devəstāt) *vb.* **dev·as·tat·ing, dev·as·tat·ed.** to destroy completely; make waste; ruin: *the floods devastated the countryside.* **'dev·as·tat·ing** *adj.* extremely effective: *they made a devastating attack and defeated the enemy.* —**dev·as'ta·tion** *n.*

de·vel·op (di'veləp) *vb.* 1. to grow or cause to grow and change to become larger, improved, etc.: *the foal developed into a horse.* 2. to treat (photographic film) with chemicals so that the picture appears. —**de'vel·op·er** *n.* —**de'vel·op·ment** *n.*

de·vice (di'vīs) *n.* 1. an object made for a specific working purpose or function; mechanical instrument: *he invented a device for lifting cattle onto ships.* 2. a cunning trick or plan: *giving free gifts with every purchase is just a device to get customers to buy more.*

dev·il ('devəl) *n.* 1. an evil spirit. 2. a mischievous or evil person. 3. a pitiable or unfortunate person. **the Devil** the chief wicked spirit who tries to possess men by evil; Satan. —*vb.* to prepare (eggs, etc.) using hot spices.

de·vote (di'vōt) *vb.* **de·vot·ing, de·vot·ed.** (+ *to*) 1. to give up (one's time, etc.) completely to. 2. to dedicate to: *a church devoted to St. John.* **de'vot·ed** *adj.* very fond or loving: *a devoted wife.* —**de'vo·tion** *n.*

dew (dōō, dyōō) *n.* drops of moisture that form out of the atmosphere as the air cools esp. at night and are found on the surfaces of leaves, etc.

di·ag·no·sis (dīəg'nōsis) *n.,pl.* **di·ag·no·ses** (dīəg'nōsēz). the careful examination and determination (sometimes after tests) of what is wrong with a person or thing. **di·ag·nose** ('dīəgnōs) *vb.* **di·ag·nos·ing, di·ag·nosed.** 1. to find out (what illness or injury a person has). 2. to find out the facts; analyze.

di·ag·o·nal (dī'agənəl) *adj.* slanting from or as if from one upper corner of a rectangle to the opposite lower one. —*n.* such a line. See GEOMETRY.

di·a·gram ('dīəgram) *n.* a line drawing used to show how something works, is built, etc.

dial

di·al ('dīəl) *n.* 1. the face of a clock or watch. 2. any face with numbers or markings on it often used for measuring electricity, pressure, etc., usu. by means of a movable indicator hand. —*vb.* to select (numbers on a dial), esp. to make a telephone call.

di·a·lect (dīəlekt) *n.* a way of speaking the language of a country that is typ·ical in pronunciation, words, and sometimes grammar, for a particular group of speakers.

di·a·logue ('dīəlôg, 'dīəlog) *n.* a conversation between two or more people.

di·am·e·ter (dī'amitər) *n.* 1. a line through the center of a circle from one side to the other. 2. the width of something round. See GEOMETRY.

dia·mond ('dīmənd, 'dīəmənd) *n.* 1. a very hard clear precious stone that is a form of CARBON. 2. a four-sided figure like a squashed square. 3. (usu. **diamonds**) a suit of playing cards marked with such figures.

di·a·ry ('dīərē) *n.,pl.* **di·a·ries.** 1. a personal account of daily events and thoughts. 2. a book marked out in days and with the date.

dice (dīs) *pl.n., sing.* **die** (dī). small cube-like shapes with from one to six dots marked on each side, thrown in games of chance. —*vb.* **dic·ing, diced.** to cut (food) into small cubes.

dic·tate *vb.* ('diktāt, dik'tāt) **dic·tat·ing, dic·tat·ed.** 1. to order; command. 2. to say (something) aloud so that another person can write it down. —*n.* ('diktāt) an order: *he obeys the dictates of his conscience.* '**dic·ta·tor** *n.* a ruler who has complete power. —**dic'ta·tion** *n.*

dic·tion·ar·y ('dikshənerē) *n.,pl.* **dic·tion·ar·ies.** a book in which words are listed in alphabetical order and either explained or defined or given an equivalent in another language.

die (dī) *vb.* **dy·ing, died.** 1. to stop living; perish. 2. to fade away; subside: *her anger died.*

die·sel ('dēzəl) *n.* 1. an engine that uses **diesel oil,** which is compressed until it is so hot it burns and drives the engine. 2. a vehicle e.g. a train, using a diesel engine.

di·et ('dīət) *n.* 1. the food that a person eats: *vegetables are essential for a healthy diet.* 2. a special selection of food eaten to lose weight, etc. —*vb.* to eat only certain food in order to lose weight.

dif·fer ('difər) *vb.* 1. to be unlike. 2. to disagree. '**dif·fer·ence** *n.* 1. the state of being unlike: *the only difference between the dresses was their color.* 2. amount between two different numbers: *the difference between 3 and 5 is 2.* 3. disagreement; argument: *they settled their differences and shook hands.* '**dif·fer·ent** *adj.* 1. unlike or separate. —'**dif·fer·ent·ly** *adv.*

dif·fi·cult ('difəkult) *adj.* 1. not easy; requiring effort to do, understand, etc.; hard. 2. awkward to get on with; uncooperative. —'**dif·fi·cul·ty** *n.,pl.* **dif·fi·cul·ties.**

di·gest (di'jest, dī'jest) *vb.* 1. to convert (food) into substances that the body can absorb and use. 2. to understand; take in: *he digested the news after a few minutes.* **di'gest·i·ble** *adj.* able to be digested. —**di'ges·tion** *n.*

dig·it ('dijit) *n.* 1. a finger or toe. 2. a whole number below ten.

dice

dig·ni·ty ('dignitē) *n.,pl.* **dig·ni·ties.** 1. calm composed seriousness; noble or important bearing. 2. a title or honor. '**dig·ni·fied** *adj.* calm; stately. '**dig·ni·fy** *vb.* **dig·ni·fy·ing, dig·ni·fied.** to bestow dignity on: *the king dignified the gathering by his presence.*

dike (dīk) *n.* a bank of earth, etc., built along the edges of a sea or river, esp. to control flooding.

di·lap·i·dat·ed (di'lapidātid) *adj.* run down through neglect or age: *a dilapidated house.* —**di·lap·i'da·tion** *n.*

di·lute (di'lo͞ot, dī'loot) *vb.* **di·lut·ing, di·lut·ed.** 1. to make weaker or thinner by adding water, etc.: *he diluted his drink.* 2. to reduce the strength, intensity, etc., of: *the serious message of the play was diluted by the humorous scenes.* —**di'lu·tion** *n.*

dim (dim) *adj.* **dim·mer, dim·mest.** 1. lacking in brightness; gloomy. 2. indistinct: *a dim outline.* 3. (also **dim-witted**) slow-witted. —*vb.* **dim·ming, dimmed.** to become or make dim. —'**dim·ly** *adv.* —'**dim·ness** *n.*

di·men·sion (di'menshən) *n.* 1. (usu. **di·men·sions**) size or measurement. 2. the characteristic of length, area, or volume. 3. extent; scope.

di·min·ish (di'minish) *vb.* to make or become smaller; reduce in size, scope, etc.: *the firm's profits diminished as business got worse.*

din·ghy ('dinggē) *n.,pl.* **din·ghies.** any small rowing or sailing boat.

din·gy ('dinjē) *adj.* **din·gi·er, din·gi·est.** dull or dark with dust, dirt, etc.; faded; shabby: *a dingy room.* —'**din·gi·ness** *n.*

di·no·saur ('dīnəsôr) *n.* one of the giant reptiles that lived from about 200 million to 65 million years ago.

di·o·cese ('dīəsēs, 'dīəsis) *n.* the district under the authority of a bishop.

di·plo·ma (di'plōmə) *n.* a certificate to show that someone has reached a required degree of knowledge or skill in a subject.

di·rect (di'rekt, dī'rekt) *adj.* 1. not stopping or turning off; straight: *a direct route.* 2. honest; frank: *a direct remark.* —*vb.* 1. to show the way to:

can you direct me to the station? 2. to manage; control. 3. to cause to head for or aim at. 4. to turn (one's attention). **di'rec·tion** *n.* 1. angle of movement toward a place; way. 2. instruction; order: *give me directions on how to do the job.* 3. control or management. **di'rec·to·ry** *n.,pl.* **di·rec·to·ries.** a list of names and addresses: *telephone directory.* **—di'rect·ly** *adv.* **—di'rect·ness** *n.* **—di'rec·tor** *n.*

dis·a·bil·i·ty (disə'bilitē) *n.,pl.* **dis·a·bil·i·ties.** lack of a physical or mental ability; handicap; incapacity: *being short is a disability if you want to become a policeman.* **dis·a·ble** (dis'ābəl) *vb.* **dis·a·bling, dis·a·bled.** to make (someone or something) unable to function. **dis'a·bled** *adj.* crippled.

dis·ad·van·tage (disəd'vantij) *n.* any unfavorable condition, situation, etc.; drawback.

dis·a·gree (disə'grē) *vb.* **dis·a·gree·ing, dis·a·greed.** 1. to differ in opinion; fail to agree. 2. to quarrel. 3. (+ *with*) to cause sickness in: *seafood disagrees with me.* **dis·a'gree·able** *adj.* unpleasant or bad-tempered.

dis·ap·pear (disə'pēr) *vb.* 1. to vanish; cease to be visible. 2. to cease to exist; become extinct: *dinosaurs disappeared millions of years ago.* **—dis·ap'pear·ance** *n.*

dis·ap·point (disə'point) *vb.* to fail to fulfill expectations, etc.; let down: *he was disappointed when his team lost the game.* **—dis·ap'point·ment** *n.*

dis·ap·prove (disə'proov) *vb.* **dis·ap·prov·ing, dis·ap·proved.** (+ *of*) to consider wrong; condemn.

dinosaur

dis·arm (dis'ârm) *vb.* 1. to remove weapons from; render harmless or defenseless. 2. to rid of suspicion, etc., by charm: *she disarmed him with a friendly smile.* **—dis'arm·a·ment** *n.* **—dis'arm·ing** *adj.*

dis·as·ter (di'zastər) *n.* a very unfortunate event. **—dis'as·trous** *adj.* **—dis'as·trous·ly** *adv.*

disc (disk) *n.* 1. (informal) a phonograph record. 2. an alternative spelling of DISK.

dis·card (dis'kârd) *vb.* to throw away; reject as unwanted.

dis·ci·ple (di'sīpəl) *n.* a follower, esp. of a religious leader, who tries to spread his teaching.

dis·ci·pline ('disəplin) *n.* 1. training to obey or behave well, esp. through strictness and punishment. 2. orderly behavior. 3. a subject of study: *the discipline of history.* —*vb.* **dis·ci·plin·ing, dis·ci·plined.** 1. to train. 2. to punish.

dis·close (dis'klōz) *vb.* **dis·clos·ing, dis·closed.** to reveal (a secret, etc.). **—dis'clo·sure** *n.*

dis·count *n.* ('diskount) a reduction in a price, given e.g. to those who buy in bulk or to attract customers. —*vb.* ('diskount, dis'kount) to reject as being untrue, worthless, or invalid; disbelieve.

dis·cour·age (dis'kûrij, dis'kurij) *vb.* **dis·cour·ag·ing, dis·cour·aged.** 1. to take away courage or confidence from. 2. to prevent or try to prevent (someone) from carrying out his intentions. Compare ENCOURAGE. **—dis'cour·age·ment** *n.*

dis·cov·er (dis'kuvər) *vb.* to reveal, find, or find out (something that was hidden or previously unknown). **—dis'cov·er·er** *n.* **—dis'cov·er·y** *n.,pl.* **dis·cov·er·ies.**

dis·crim·i·nate (dis'kriminā̆t) *vb.* **dis·crim·i·nat·ing, dis·crim·i·nat·ed.** 1. to see a difference between one thing and another; distinguish: *to discriminate right from wrong.* 2. (+ *against*) to make an unfair distinction; act in a biased way. **—dis·crim·i'na·tion** *n.*

dis·cus ('diskəs) *n.,pl.* **dis·cus·es.** a stone, wood, or metal disk used in throwing competitions.

dis·cuss (dis'kus) *vb.* to exchange ideas on a particular subject; talk over. **—dis'cus·sion** *n.*

dis·ease (di'zēz) *n.* an illness or disorder of health. **—dis'eased** *adj.*

dis·grace (dis'grās) *vb.* **dis·grac·ing, dis·graced.** to bring shame and dishonor to. —*n.* 1. a state of shame or dishonor. 2. anything that is shameful. **—dis'grace·ful** *adj.* **—dis'grace·ful·ly** *adv.*

dis·guise (dis'gīz) *vb.* **dis·guis·ing, dis·guised.** to change the appearance, sound, or flavor of (something) in order to conceal its true identity: *the bank robber disguised himself as an old lady to avoid recognition.* —*n.* anything that serves to disguise.

dis·gust (dis'gust) *n.* an intense dislike or loathing, e.g. strong enough to produce feelings of sickness; revulsion. —*vb.* to offend strongly; sicken. **—dis'gust·ing** *adj.*

dish (dish) *n.* 1. a shallow bowl or plate of china, glass, etc., used for serving food. 2. a particular kind of food.

dis·in·fect (disin'fekt) *vb.* to cleanse in order to get rid of germs. **dis·in'fect·ant** *n., adj.* (any chemical agent) that destroys germs.

dis·in·te·grate (dis'intəgrāt) *vb.* **dis·in·te·grat·ing, dis·in·te·grat·ed.** to fall apart; break or collapse into small pieces. **—dis·in·te'gra·tion** *n.*

disk (disk) *n.* an object that is flat and circular, like a coin.

dis·like (dis'līk) *vb.* **dis·lik·ing, dis·liked.** to find (something) unpleasant. —*n.* an idea that something is unpleasant: *a dislike of tea.*

dis·mal ('dizməl) *adj.* gloomy, dreary, or unhappy. —'**dis·mal·ly** *adv.*

dis·may (dis'mā) *vb.* to cause worry or alarm; discourage or sadden. —*n.* loss of hope or courage; alarm; worry: *the news filled him with dismay.*

dis·miss (dis'mis) *vb.* 1. to send away; give (soldiers, a class, etc.) permission to leave. 2. to end the employment of. 3. to put something out of one's mind. —**dis'miss·al** *n.*

dis·patch (dis'pach) *vb.* 1. to send (someone or something) off quickly to a place: she dispatched the parcel by airmail. 2. to settle quickly: *to dispatch a business matter.* 3. to kill; execute. —*n.* message; report.

dis·pense (dis'pens) *vb.* **dis·pens·ing, dis·pensed.** 1. to distribute or deal out; administer (justice, etc.). 2. to prepare (medicines). 3. (+ *with*) to cease using; do without. **dis'pen·sa·ble** *adj.* not absolutely necessary. **dis'pen·sa·ry** *n.,pl.* **dis·pen·sa·ries.** a place where medicines are prepared. **dis·pen'sa·tion** *n.* 1. the act of dispensing. 2. permission to do something that is normally forbidden, esp. according to Church law: *the pope granted them dispensation to marry.*

dis·play (dis'plā) *vb.* put on show; exhibit; reveal: *the pianist displayed his talent with a brilliant performance.* —*n.* an exhibition, demonstration, etc.: *a fireworks display.*

dis·pose (dis'pōz) *vb.* **dis·pos·ing, dis·posed.** (+ *of*) to get rid of. **dis'posed** *adj.* willing or likely; inclined: *he is not usually disposed to be friendly.* **dis·po·si·tion** (dispə'zishən) *n.* one's natural qualities of character: *a nervous disposition.*

dis·pute (dis'pyo͞ot) *vb.* **dis·put·ing, dis·put·ed.** 1. to argue or debate strongly. 2. to question the truth or validity of; contest: *do you dispute my reasons?* —*n.* a disagreement or quarrel.

dis·qual·i·fy (dis'kwoləfī) *vb.* **dis·qual·i·fy·ing, dis·qual·i·fied.** to take away the rights or privileges of, usu. because a law or rule has been broken. —**dis·qual·i·fi'ca·tion** *n.*

dis·re·gard (disri'gârd) *vb.* to ignore or pay no attention to. —*n.* indifference; lack of care or attention: *he showed an utter disregard for the feelings of his family.*

dis·solve (di'zolv) *vb.* **dis·solv·ing, dis·solved.** 1. to be or cause to be absorbed into a liquid: *sugar dissolves in hot coffee.* 2. to melt; change into a liquid: *the snow dissolved when it grew warmer.* 3. to end: *to dissolve a partnership.*

dis·suade (di'swād) *vb.* **dis·suad·ing, dis·suad·ed.** (+ *from*) to persuade (someone) not to do something. —**dis'sua·sion** *n.*

dis·tant ('distənt) *adj.* 1. far away in space or time. 2. related, but not in a close way: *a distant relative.* 3. reserved; unfriendly; aloof. '**dis·tance** *n.* 1. amount of space between two places, or time between two events: *the distance between the towns was ten miles.* 2. unfriendliness. —'**dis·tant·ly** *adv.*

dis·tinct (dis'tingkt) *adj.* 1. separate; having differences that mark out and set something apart. 2. clear; easily heard, seen, or understood: *she spoke in a very distinct fashion.* 3. definite: *a distinct possibility.* **dis'tinc·tion** *n.* 1. difference, esp. between things that are similar: *what is the distinction between a raven and a crow?* 2. excellence; superiority: *she was a woman of distinction.* —**dis'tinc·tive** *adj.* —**dis'tinc·tive·ly** *adv.* —**di'stinct·ly** *adv.* —**di'stinct·ness** *n.*

dis·tin·guish (dis'tinggwish) *vb.* 1. to recognize a difference; make a distinction. 2. to see or hear clearly; make out; recognize: *can you distinguish your friend in this crowd?* **distinguish oneself** to bring credit or honor to oneself; excel. **dis'tin·guished** *adj.* well known and honored.

dis·tract (dis'trakt) *vb.* 1. to attract the attention, concentration, etc., of (someone) from what he is doing: *noise distracts me from my work.* 2. to disturb or upset greatly: *they were distracted by grief.* —**dis'trac·tion** *n.*

dis·tress (dis'tres) *n.* suffering, esp. mental; grief; pain. —*vb.* to cause to suffer distress: *we were distressed by the news of his illness.*

dis·trib·ute (dis'tribyo͞ot) *vb.* **dis·trib·u·ting, dis·trib·u·ted.** 1. to give out or share amongst many; divide up: *the teacher distributed the books to the class.* 2. to spread or scatter over an area: *the leaflets were distributed from the air.* —**dis·tri'bu·tion** *n.* —**dis'trib·u·tive** *adj.* —**dis'trib·u·tor** *n.*

dis·trict ('distrikt) *n.* a division of land, e.g. into a county, borough, state, etc., for administrative, electoral, or other purposes.

dis·turb (dis'tûrb) *vb.* 1. to interrupt (a person, the silence, etc.). 2. to disarrange. 3. to cause worry or trouble to. —**dis'turb·ance** *n.*

ditch (dich) *n.* a long hollow channel dug in the earth, used for drainage, etc.; trench. —*vb.* (informal) to throw away; discard: *all the original plans were ditched when they made new ones.*

dit·to ('ditō) *n.* the same as already stated. Used in lists to avoid repeating the same information and indicated by **ditto marks** (").

di·van (di'van) *n.* a bed without sides, headboard, or footboard, that can be used as a seat during the day.

dive (dīv) *vb.* **div·ing, dived** *or* (informal) **dove, dived.** 1. to throw oneself into water, esp. headfirst, or with one's arms outstretched and hands together. 2. to move downward suddenly and quickly: *he dived into his seat.* 3. to reach for, into, etc., suddenly: *he dived into his pocket for money.* —*n.* the act of diving.

di·vert (di'vûrt, dī'vûrt) *vb.* 1. to turn aside, e.g. from a course or plan. 2. to entertain; amuse. —**di'ver·sion** *n.*

di·vide (di'vīd) *vb.* **di·vid·ing, di·vid·ed.** 1. to separate or become separated into parts. 2. to give out; share. 3. to calculate how many times one number is contained in another: *12 divided by 4 equals 3.* 4. to cause disagreement between: *jealousy divided the brothers.* **di·vi·sion** (di'vizhən) *n.* 1. the act of dividing. 2. a part or section, e.g. of an army. 3. the point at which something divides. 4. disagreement. **di·vis·i·ble** (di'vizibəl) *adj.* able to be divided.

di·vine (di'vīn) *adj.* 1. of or like a god. 2. (informal) wonderful; lovely.

di·vorce (di'vôrs) *n.* 1. the legal ending of a marriage. 2. any complete separation. —*vb.* **di·vorc·ing, di·vorced.** 1. to end one's marriage. 2. to separate: *his stories were completely divorced from reality.* **di·vor·će** (divôr'sā) *n.* a divorced

dogs

man. **di·vor·ćee** (divôr'sē) *n.* a divorced woman.

di·vulge (di'vulj, dī'vulj) *vb.* **di·vulg·ing, di·vulged.** to reveal or make public something previously unknown or secret; disclose.

diz·zy ('dizē) *adj.* **diz·zi·er, diz·zi·est.** 1. feeling an unbalanced or spinning sensation; giddy. 2. liable to cause giddiness: *a dizzy height.* —'**diz·zi·ly** *adv.* —'**diz·zi·ness** *n.*

do·cile ('dosəl) *adj.* easily managed or taught; tame. —**do·cil·i·ty** (do'silitē) *n.*

dock[1] (dok) *n.* a place where ships and boats are tied up for loading, repair, etc. —*vb.* 1. to enter or cause to enter a dock. 2. (of spacecraft) to link in space. '**dock·er** *n.* person who loads ships, etc.

dock[2] (dok) *n.* a small enclosed space in a courtroom where the accused is placed during his trial.

dock[3] (dok) *vb.* 1. to cut (a tail, etc.) short. 2. to deduct a part from (wages).

doc·tor ('doktər) *n.* 1. a person professionally qualified to practice medicine; physician. 2. a person who has been awarded one of the highest degrees conferred by a university. —*vb.* 1. to give medical treatment to. 2. (informal) to alter; falsify: *he doctored the entry date on the passport.*

doc·trine ('doktrin) *n.* a particular principle or system of belief, esp. a religious or established one.

doc·u·ment *n.* ('dokyəmənt) a written paper, esp. an official one providing evidence. —*vb.* ('dokyəment) to support or prove by documentary evidence: *the results of the scientific experiment were very carefully documented.* **doc·u'men·ta·ry** *adj.* relating to documents. *n.,pl.* **doc·u·men·ta·ries.** a film presenting a factual account of something: *a documentary about the wildlife of the Everglades.*

dodge (doj) *vb.* **dodg·ing, dodged.** 1. to move aside quickly to avoid (a blow, etc.). 2. to avoid by cleverness or trickery: *his answers dodged the question.* —*n.* the act of dodging.

dog (dôg, dog) *n.* any one of the family of warm-blooded flesh-eating animals, many kinds of which are kept as pets. —*vb.* **dog·ging, dogged.** to follow closely.

dog·wood ('dôgwood) *n.* 1. a small tree that is grown for ornament. It has dark red branches and its leaves turn bright red in the fall. 2. the wood of this tree.

dole (dōl) *n.* a regular distribution of money, food, clothing, etc., to the poor, esp. by a charitable organization. —*vb.* **dol·ing, doled.** (+ *out*) (informal) to parcel out.

doll (dol) *n.* a child's toy that looks like a human being.

dol·lar ('dolər) *n.* a unit of money in the U.S., Canada, Australia, and elsewhere.

dol·phin ('dolfin, 'dôlfin) *n.* a MAMMAL found in oceans and some rivers, that resembles a large fish with a beaklike mouth and numerous teeth. It is related to WHALES and is highly intelligent.

dome

dome (dōm) *n.* a roof like a hollow half sphere.

do·mes·tic (də'mestik) *adj.* 1. concerned with the home or household affairs. 2. living with man; tame: *the cat is a domestic animal.* 3. of the affairs of one's own country: *domestic policies.* —*n.* a household servant. —**do·mes·tic·i·ty** (dōmes'tisitē) *n.*

dom·i·nate ('domināt) *vb.* **dom·i·nat·ing, dom·i·nat·ed.** 1. to be the strongest force in; control. 2. to be the most important or noticeable feature or person in: *the Eiffel Tower dominates the Paris skyline.* —'**dom·i·nant** *adj.* —**dom·i'na·tion** *n.*

dom·i·no ('domənō) *n.,pl.* **dom·i·noes.** a small flat oblong piece of wood or plastic marked with spots, used in playing the game **dominoes.**

do·nate ('dōnāt, dō'nāt) *vb.* **do·nat·ing, do·nat·ed.** to give, esp. to charity: *they donated 20 dollars to the children's fund.* '**do·nor** *n.* a person who gives for a charitable or humane cause: *blood donor.* —**do'na·tion** *n.*

don·key ('doñgkē, d'uñgkē) *n.* a long-eared sure-footed animal of the horse family used chiefly as a beast of burden.

doo·dle ('do͞odəl) *vb.* **doo·dling, doo·dled.** to scribble or draw, usu. while thinking about something else. —*n.* an idle scribble or drawing. —'**doo·dler** *n.*

doom (do͞om) *n.* unpleasant fate or destiny; a harsh unavoidable end: *the prisoners went silently to their doom.* —*vb.* to condemn (to death, ruin, failure, or misfortune): *his plan was doomed from the start.*

dope (dōp) *n.* 1. (slang) narcotics or stimulants, esp. those given illegally to racehorses or sold illegally. 2. (informal) detailed or advance information. 3. (informal) a stupid person. 4. a thick varnish used for waterproofing aircraft, etc. —*vb.* **dop·ing, doped.** to drug. '**dop·ey** *or* '**dop·y** *adj.* **dop·i·er, dop·i·est.** (informal) 1. half asleep; half-conscious. 2. stupid; dim-witted.

dor·mi·to·ry ('dôrmitôrē) *n.,pl.* **dor·mi·to·ries.** 1. a building or part of one set aside for sleeping quarters for a number of people. 2. a building containing living and sleeping quarters for students.

dor·mouse ('dôrmous) *n.,pl.* **dor·mice** ('dôrmīs). a small furry squirrel-like animal with a bushy tail, found mainly in Europe. It is usu. nocturnal and hibernates in winter.

dose (dōs) *n.* an amount of medicine to be taken at one time. —*vb.* to administer medicine: *he dosed himself with aspirin when he had a pain.*

dormouse

dou·ble ('dubəl) *adj.* 1. twice as much. 2. paired; matching: *double doors.* 3. for two people: *a double bed.* —*adv.* 1 twice: *double the price.* 2. in two: *fold the blanket double.* —*n.* 1. an amount that is twice as much. 2. a person or thing that looks exactly like another. 3. **doubles** (*pl.*) (in tennis, etc.) a match with two players on each side. —*vb.* **dou·bling, dou·bled.** 1. to make or become double. 2. to fold or bend into two. —'**dou·bly** *adv.*

doubt (dout) *vb.* 1. to tend not to believe; be uncertain: *I doubt if he will come since the weather is so bad.* 2. to distrust; suspect: *I doubt his motives.* —*n.* often **doubts** (*pl.*) uncertainty, fear, distrust, or suspicion. —'**doubt·er** *n.* —'**doubt·ful** *adj.* —'**doubt·ful·ly** *adv.*

dough (dō) *n.* 1. a thick mixture of flour with water, milk, eggs, etc., that is baked to make bread, pastry, etc. 2. (slang) money.

doughnut ('dōnut) *n.* a type of cake, usu. ring-shaped, made of sweet dough and fried in fat.

douse (dous) *vb.* **dous·ing, doused.** to throw water over or thrust into water: *he doused the campfire with water.*

dove (duv) *n.* a bird of the pigeon family that is often used as a symbol of peace.

down·cast ('dounkast) *adj.* 1. discouraged; disappointed. 2. looking down: *downcast eyes.*

down·fall ('dounfôl) *n.* 1. sudden failure or ruin, esp. of a ruler. 2. something causing failure: *carelessness was her downfall.* 3. a heavy shower of rain or snow.

down·pour ('dounpôr) *n.* a very heavy rainfall.

down·right ('dounrīt) *adj.* 1. absolute; complete: *the party was a downright disaster* 2. honest; frank. —*adv.* thoroughly; completely: *downright foolish.*

doze (dōz) *vb.* **doz·ing, dozed.** 1. to sleep lightly, waking often. 2. (often + *off*) to fall asleep, esp. unintentionally. —*n.* a short light sleep. '**doz·y** *adj.* **doz·i·er, doz·i·est.** 1. sleepy; drowsy. 2. (informal) dull-witted. —'**doz·i·ly** *adv.* —'**doz·i·ness** *n.*

doz·en ('duzən) *n.* a set of twelve: *a dozen eggs.*

drab (drab) *adj.* **drab·ber, drab·best.** dull-colored or dreary; dull; shabby: *the room had a drab appearance.* —*n.* a dull yellow-brown or olive-brown color. —'**drab·ly** *adv.* —'**drab·ness** *n.*

draft (draft) *n.* 1. a rough sketch or plan; outline: *the first draft of a play.* 2. a group of men called upon for military service, etc. 3. a current of air inside a room, chimney, etc. 4. the taking of a liquid from a large container, e.g. a barrel: *beer on draft.* 5. a drink or gulp: *a draft of beer.* **draft animal** an ox. horse, etc., for pulling heavy loads. —*vb.* 1. to prepare preliminary (plans, etc.): *he drafted plans for the new sales campaign.* 2. to choose for or assign to a special purpose, esp. military service.— **draft·y** *adj.* **draft·i·er, draft·i·est.**

dragon

drafts·man ('draftsmən) *n., pl.* **drafts·men.** a person who prepares architectural plans, engineering drawings, etc.

drag·on ('dragən) *n.* a mythical fire-breathing winged reptile with a scaly skin.

drag·on·fly ('dragənflī) *n.,pl.* **drag·on·flies** a large colorful winged insect with a long thin body, that breeds in water.

drain (drān) *n.* 1. a channel or pipe for carrying away waste matter, such as sewage. 2. anything that uses up money, energy, etc.: *the new house was a drain on their finances.* —*vb.* 1. (sometimes + *off*) to channel or draw off (excess liquid). 2. to empty into a larger stretch of water: *the Nile drains into the Mediterranean Sea.* 3. to exhaust; use up: *his energy was drained at the end of the day.* —'**drain·age** *n.*

drain·pipe ('drānpīp) *n.* a pipe carrying water from a roof.

drake (drāk) *n.* a male duck, often more brightly colored than the female.

dram (dram) *n.* one-sixteenth part of an ounce.

dra·ma ('drâmə, 'dramə) *n.* 1. a play for stage, radio, or television. 2. plays in general; the theater. 3. an emotional or exciting scene; stir. **dra·mat·ic** (drə'matik) *adj.* 1. of or relating to drama. 2. exciting or vivid: *a dramatic landscape.* **dra·mat·ics** *pl.n.* 1. the staging of plays. 2. a fit of affected over-emotional behavior. '**dram·a·tize** *vb.* **dram·a·tiz·ing, dram·a·tized.** 1. to describe in an exaggerated or dramatic way: *the explorer dramatized the journey's dangers.* 2. to turn (a novel, poem, etc.) into a play: *the book* Oliver Twist *was dramatized for the movies.* —**dram·a·ti'za·tion** *n.*

drape (drāp) *vb.* **drap·ing, draped.** 1. to hang or arrange cloth so that it falls in loose folds. 2. to place one's arms or legs around something loosely or casually. —*n.,pl.* **drapes** hanging cloth; curtains.

dras·tic ('drastik) *adj.* highly effective or severe: *drastic action must be taken to save whales from extinction.* —'**dras·ti·cal·ly** *adv.*

draw (drô) *vb.* **draw·ing, drew, drawn.** 1. to pull in a specified direction: *the man drew me to one side.* 2. to move: *she drew near.* 3. to get or obtain: *he drew the money out of the bank.* 4. to pull (a weapon) from a sheath or holster: *he drew his gun.* 5. to pick or choose (a winning tickets, a playing card, etc.). 6. to attract: *he drew my attention to the time.* 7. to take in: *he drew a deep breath.* 8. to make a picture or design. 9. to neither win nor lose a contest or competition. 10. (+ *out*) to make or become longer in time. 11. (+ *out*) to persuade (a person) to talk or express his feelings. 12. (+ *up*) to set out or draft (a document, plans, etc.). 13. (+ *up*) to come to a halt: *the car drew up outside our house.* —*n.* 1. an attraction: *the new art exhibition was a big draw.* 2. the selection of the winning tickets in a lottery. 3. the selection of players for a team or the order in which they are to play. 4. a game or competition ending in a tie.

draw·back ('drôbak) *n.* a disadvantage or hindrance; inconvenience: *losing our best player was rather a drawback.*

draw·bridge ('drôbrij) *n.* 1. a bridge, across the moat of a castle, that can be drawn up to prevent access. 2. a bridge on a river or canal that can be pulled up to allow ships to pass.

draw·er ('drôər) *n.* 1. a boxlike compartment that slides in and out of a piece of furniture. 2. **drawers** (*pl.*) underpants.

drawl (drôl) *vb.* to speak very slowly, exaggerating the vowel sounds. —*n.* drawling or slow speech.

drawn (drôn) *vb.* the past participle of DRAW. —*adj.* tired or tense, as with worry, pain, etc.

dread (dred) *n.* great fear, alarm, or anxiety: *great dread came over him when he realised that he had made a big mistake.* —*vb.* to feel anxious and apprehensive; fear: *she dreaded going into the examination room.* '**dread·ful** *adj.* unpleasant; very bad; frightening. '**dread·ful·ly** *adv.* 1. extremely: *dreadfully tired.* 2. terribly or horribly.

dream (drēm) *n.* 1. a sequence of visual or verbal events that pass through the mind during sleep. 2. the state of being lost in thought and seeming not to notice one's surroundings. 3. an ambition or desire: *I have a dream that one day all wars will end.* —*vb.* **dream·ing, dreamed** *or* **dreamt** (dremt). to see in, or have, a dream. —'**dream·er** *n.* —'**dream·i·ly** *adv.* —'**dream·i·ness** *n.* —**dream·y** *adj.* **dream·i·er, dream·i·est.**

drear·y ('drērē) *adj.* **drear·i·er, drear·i·est.** 1. dull; gloomy: *a dreary view of factories.* 2. boring; tedious: *a dreary man.* —'**drear·i·ly** *adv.* —'**drear·i·ness** *n.*

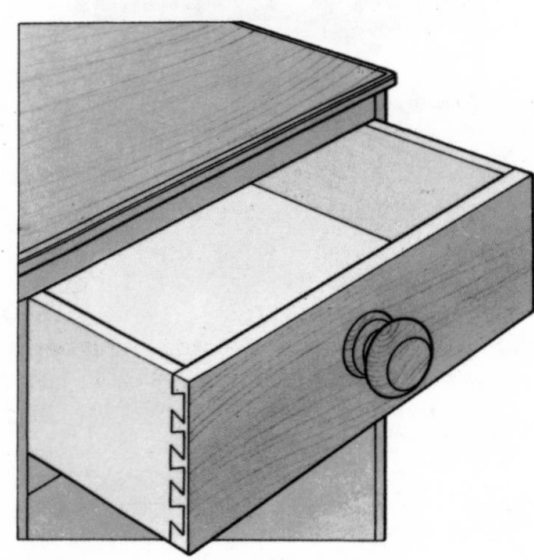
drawer

dredge (drej) *vb.* **dredg·ing, dredged.** to remove silt, mud, or other substances from the bottom of the sea, a river, etc. —*n.* a device for doing this. '**dredg·er** *n.* a ship used for dredging.

dregs (dregz) *pl.n.* 1. particles left at the bottom of a container of wine, coffee, etc. 2. the worthless parts, e.g. of life.

drench (drench) *vb.* to wet thoroughly; soak through; saturate: *the heavy rain drenched us before we could find shelter.*

dress (dres) *vb.* 1. to put on clothes or to clothe. 2. to decorate (a shop window, etc.). 3. to clean and bandage (a wound). —*n.* 1. a woman's or girl's one-piece garment with a top and skirt. 2. clothing; costume: *informal dress.* '**dress·ing** *n.* 1. a seasoned sauce made to put on foods, esp. salad. 2. a bandage, ointment, etc., used for cleaning and covering wounds.

dress·er[1] ('dresər) *n.* a person employed to help dress and look after the costumes of an actor or actress.

dress·er[2] ('dresər) *n.* 1. a chest of drawers. 2. a kitchen sideboard.

dresser

drib·ble ('dribəl) *vb.* **drib·bling, drib·bled.** 1. to allow SALIVA or liquid to escape from the mouth; slobber. 2. to trickle. 3. to send a ball forward while running. —*n.* 1. the fluid dribbled from the mouth. 2. the act of dribbling a ball.

dried (drīd) *vb.* the past tense and past participle of DRY.

drift (drift) *vb.* 1. to be carried along by wind or water. 2. to move into something without resistance: *they drifted into poverty.* 3. to wander aimlessly. 4. to leave a set course. —*n.* 1. a slow surface movement of the sea or sand, caused by wind or currents: *the North Atlantic Drift.* 2. a movement off course by a ship or aircraft due to wind or currents. 3. a slow general movement; trend. 4. (also **snowdrift**) a deep layer of snow. 5. (informal) general meaning: *do you get the drift of what I'm saying?* —'**drift·er** *n.*

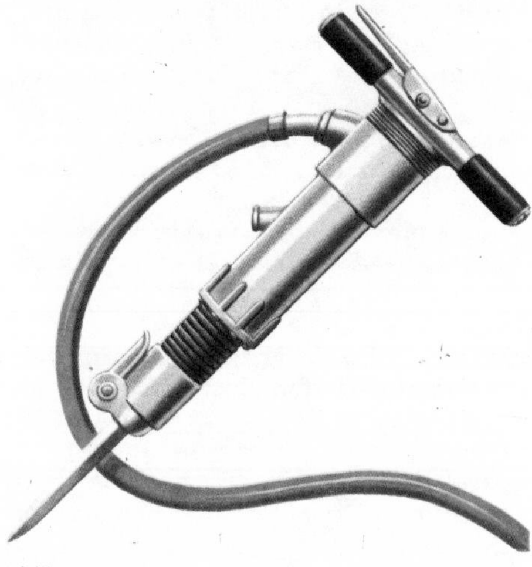

drill

drill[1] (dril) *n.* 1. a tool or machine used for boring holes in wood, teeth, etc. 2. a repetitive military training exercise involving marching and the handling of weapons. 3. disciplined instruction: *fire drill.* —*vb.* 1. to bore (a hole). 2. to train, instruct, or exercise by practice.

drill[2] (dril) *n.* a shallow trench or furrow in which seeds are planted.

drip (drip) *vb.* **drip·ping, dripped.** to fall or let fall in drops: *the rain dripped down the window.* —*n.* 1. a series of drops or the sound made as they fall. 2. (slang) a silly or weak person.

drive (drīv) *vb.* **driv·ing, drove, driv·en** ('drivən). 1. to push, press, or urge on or forward: *the waves drove the boat against the harbor wall.* 2. to control, transport, or travel in a car, bus, etc. 3. to force; compel: *he was driven to sell the house by lack of money.* 4. to send; render: *the noisy aircraft drove him mad.* 5. (+ *home*) to knock into position: *the nail was driven home by the hammer.* 6. (+ *home*) to emphasize strongly: *he drove home his points with some powerful examples.* —*n.* 1. energy and ambition. 2. a campaign: *the government drive to improve housing conditions.* 3. a journey made in a car, etc. 4. (also **driveway**) a private road leading up to a house or other building. 5. the apparatus for changing power into movement in a machine: *this car has front-wheel drive.* —'**driv·er** *n.*

driz·zle ('drizəl) *n.* very light rain. —*vb.* **driz·zling, driz·zled.** to rain lightly and steadily.

drone[1] (drōn) *n.* 1. a stingless male bee that produces no honey. 2. an idle person.

drone[2] (drōn) *vb.* **dron·ing, droned.** 1. to make a dull low continuous humming or buzzing noise. 2. to speak in a dull monotonous voice. 3. to continue in a boring way: *work droned on.* —*n.* a droning sound.

droop (dro͝op) *vb.* to sag; hang limply, bend over, or flag: *the flowers drooped because they had no water.* —*n.* a drooping movement or position.

drop (drop) *n.* 1. a small round or tear-shaped blob or spot of liquid. 2. a small amount of liquid: *just a drop, please.* 3. anything resembling a drop: *a cough drop.* 4. a sudden fall or decrease: *a drop in prices.* 5. a sudden fall between a high and lower level: *a steep drop.* —*vb.* **drop·ping, dropped.** 1. to fall or let fall: *he dropped the ball.* 2. (sometimes + *off*) to decrease: *demand for ice cream dropped in the winter.* 3. to give up, stop, omit, or abandon: *he was dropped from the team.*

drought (drout) *n.* a prolonged period in which little or no rain falls, causing water shortages.

drove (drōv) *vb.* the past tense of DRIVE.

drown (droun) *vb.* 1. to die or kill by suffocating in water or other liquid. 2. to drench or flood. 3. to muffle or prevent (something) being heard: *the noise of the party was so great that his words were drowned.*

drowse (drouz) *vb.* **drows·ing, drowsed.** to be half asleep or sleepy; doze; catnap. —'**drows·i·ly** *adv.* —'**drows·i·ness** *n.* —**drows·y** *adj.* **drows·i·er, drows·i·est.**

drug (drug) *n.* 1. any chemical substance used to treat a disease or disorder. 2. any chemical substance, whose overuse or misuse causes harmful dependence. —*vb.* **drug·ging, drugged.** to administer drugs to, usu. with the intention of putting to sleep or harming.

drum (drum) *n.* 1. a musical instrument consisting of a skin stretched over a hollow body and struck with sticks (**drumsticks**). 2. a large cylindrical container, esp. for oil. —*vb.* **drum·ming, drummed.** to beat rhythmically on a surface.

drum

drunk·ard ('drunkərd) *n.* a person who habitually drinks to much alcohol.

dry (drī) *adj.* **dri·er, dri·est.** 1. not wet or damp. 2. having little or no rainfall. 3. (of wines) not sweet. 4. unemotional but shrewd: *a dry sense of humor.* —*vb.* **dry·ing, dried.** to make or become dry. —'**dri·ly** *adv.*

du·al ('do͞oəl, 'dyo͞oəl) *adj.* double.

duch·ess ('duchis) *n.* 1. the wife or widow of a DUKE. 2. a woman equal in rank to a DUKE.

duck[1] (duk) *n.* a flat-billed webfooted water bird.

duck[2] (duk) *vb.* to bend down or lower the head quickly, esp. to avoid something.

duct (dukt) *n.* 1. a tube carrying fluid somewhere, esp. in the body. 2. a pipe enclosing electric wires.

due (do͞o, dyo͞o) *adj.* 1. owing; to be paid: *the rent is due.* 2. deserved, fair, or proper: *due respect.* 3. expected: *when is the bus due?*—*n.* 1. that which is owed or deserved. 2. **dues** (*pl.*) a fee; subscription. —*adv.* directly; straight: *the nearest town is due north.* —'**du·ly** *adv.*

du·el ('do͞oəl, 'dyo͞oəl) *n.* 1. (formerly) a sword or pistol fight between two men to settle a quarrel or decide a point of honor, usu. organized according to strict rules. 2. a contest or argument between two people or groups. —*vb.* to fight a duel. —'**du·el·er** *or* '**du·el·ist** *n.*

du·et (do͞o'et, dyo͞o'et) *n.* a work for two singers or instrumentalists.

duke (do͞ok, dyo͞ok) *n.* a nobleman next down in rank to a prince. —'**duke·dom** *n.*

dull (dul) *adj.* 1. not bright; cloudy. 2. boring; uninteresting. 3. blunt; not sharp: *a dull ache.* 4. stupid; slow: *a dull student.* 5. indistinct; deadened: *a dull thud.* —*vb.* to make or become dull. —'**dull·ness** *n.* —'**dul·ly** *adv.*

dumb (dum) *adj.* 1. unable or unwilling to speak. 2. (informal) stupid. —'**dumb·ly** *adv.* —'**dumb·ness** *n.*

dum·my ('dumē) *n.,pl.* **dum·mies.** a model, copy, or substitute, e.g. a figure used to display clothes. —*adj.* substitute; imitation.

dump (dump) *n.* 1. a pile of rubbish, etc. 2. a storage area where stocks are left for later use. —*vb.* to throw away or throw down.

duck

dune (do͞on, dyo͞on) *n.* a hill of light sand, formed by the wind, usu. on a beach or in a desert.

dun·geon ('dunjən) *n.* an underground prison, esp. below a castle.

du·pli·cate *vb.* ('do͞opləkāt, 'dyo͞opləkāt) **du·pli·cat·ing, du·pli·cat·ed.** 1. to make a copy of. 2. to imitate very closely. —*n.* ('do͞oplikit, 'dyo͞opləkit) something exactly like another. —*adj.* exactly like something else. '**du·pli·ca·tor** *n.* a machine that makes copies, usu. of letters, documents, pages etc. —**du·pli'ca·tion** *n.*

dusk (dusk) *n.* twilight; the darkening of the day just before night. '**dusk·y** *adj.* **dusk·i·er, dusk·i·est.** darkish.

dust (dust) *n.* fine dry particles of earth, dirt, etc. —*vb.* 1. to wipe or sweep dust from (furniture). 2. to sprinkle lightly, e.g. with flour. —'**dust·y** *adj.* **dust·i·er, dust·i·est.**

du·ty ('do͞otē, 'dyo͞otē) *n.,pl.* **du·ties.** 1. something a person knows he must do because it is right, because it is part of his job, etc. 2. tax on goods sold, brought into a country, etc. '**du·ti·ful** *adj.* aware of one's duty.

dwarf (dwôrf) *n.,pl.* **dwarfs** *or* **dwarves.** an abnormally short person, animal or plant —*vb.* to make look small; overshadow: *the skyscraper dwarfed the surrounding buildings.*

dwell (dwel) *vb.* **dwell·ing, dwelt.** to reside; live (at). **dwell on** to consider or speak about at length; linger over; emphasize: *in his speeches he always dwells on the importance of a steady food supply.* '**dwell·ing** *n.* a residence; place where someone lives.

dwin·dle ('dwindəl) *vb.* **dwin·dling, dwin·dled.** to grow gradually less; waste away; decline in importance or greatness.

dye (dī) *n.* a substance used to color cloth, hair, etc. —*vb.* **dye·ing, dyed.** to change the color of, using a dye. —'**dy·er** *n.*

dy·na·mite ('dīnəmīt) *n.* a highly explosive material, usu. used packed in sticks, esp. in mines.

dy·na·mo ('dīnəmō) *n.,pl.* **dy·na·mos.** a rotating machine that converts mechanical power into electrical power.

E

ea·ger ('ēgər) *adj.* keen; enthusiastic: *he was looking forward to the ball game and was eager to leave the house.* —**ea·ger·ly** *adv.* —**ea·ger·ness** *n.*

ea·gle ('ēgəl) *n.* a large bird of prey, usu. brown or black in color, with long broad wings and tail, feathered legs, strong sharp hooked beak, and talons.

earth (ûrth) *n.* 1. (also **Earth**) the planet on which we live; the third planet from the sun. 2. soil. —'**earth·y** *adj.* **earth·i·er, ear·th·i·est.** '**earth·en·ware** *n.* pottery made of baked clay. *adj.* made of such pottery. '**earth·quake** *n.* a violent shaking cracking, or folding of the earth's crust. '**earth·ly** *adj.* connected with or appearing in the world; not heavenly.

eaves·drop ('ēvzdrop) *vb.* **eaves·drop·ping, eaves·dropped.** to listen secretly to or intentionally overhear a private conversation. —'**eaves·drop·per** *n.*

ebb (eb) *n.* 1. the movement of a tide away from a beach or shore. 2. a decline; the process of becoming less: *after running a mile his strength began to ebb.*

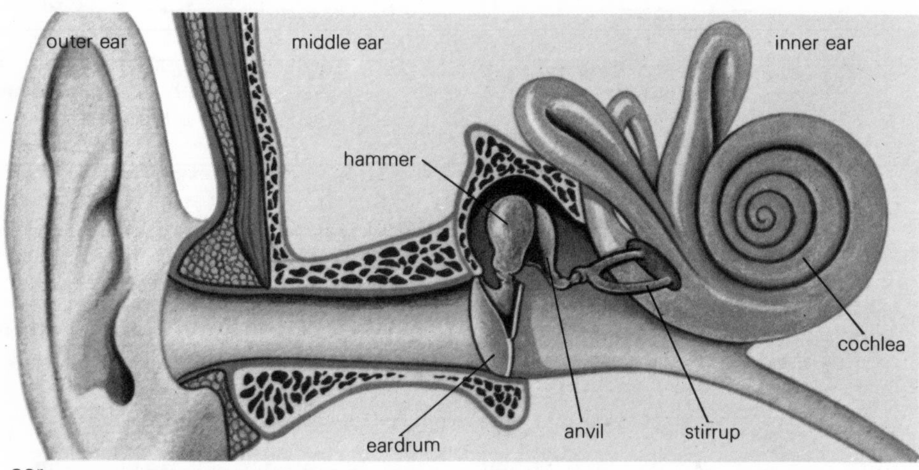

ear

ear (ēr) *n.* either of the two bodily parts, one each side of the head, through which sounds are perceived; one of the organs of hearing.

ear·ly ('ûrlē) *adj.* **ear·li·er, ear·li·est.** 1. near the beginning of something: *the early books on the subject were not very good.* 2. before an agreed or suitable time: *he had to wait for his friends because he arrived too early.* —*adv.* 1. at or near the beginning. 2. too soon.

earn (ûrn) *vb.* to deserve or gain something in return for work or as a direct result of some action, etc. '**earn·ings** *pl.n.* wages; regular payment for work.

ear·nest ('ûrnist) *adj.* 1. deeply serious or sincere: *his earnest wish was to help her in any way he could.* 2. needing serious thought and concern: *an earnest situation.* —'**ear·nest·ly** *adv.* —'**ear·nest·ness** *n.*

ease (ēz) *n.* freedom from worry, difficulty, or effort; comfort. —*vb.* **eas·ing, eased.** 1. to make easier or provide relief, e.g. from pain, etc. 2. to relax; make comfortable. 3. to move gently: *he eased the plant into the pot.*

ea·sel ('ēzəl) *n.* a frame, usu. of wood, upon which a painter's canvas can be mounted.

east (ēst) *n.* 1. the direction in which one turns to see the sunrise. 2. the part of a country lying in this direction. 3. **the East** the eastern part of the U.S. Also the countries of the east; the Orient. —*adj.* lying in or toward the east: *the east side.* —*adv.* toward the east: *moving east.* '**east·ern** *adj.* of or in the east, esp. in the U.S. or the Orient.

eas·y ('ēzē) *adj.* **eas·i·er, eas·i·est.** 1. not difficult; simple. 2. free from worry; comfortable. —'**eas·i·ly** *adv.* —'**eas·i·ness** *n.*

easel

eb·o·ny ('ebənē) *n.* a very hard, valuable, usu. black wood from a tree found mainly in India. —*adj.* 1. made from ebony. 2. (also **ebon**) of the color or toughness of ebony.

ec·cen·tric (ik'sentrik) *n.* a person who behaves in an unusual, strange, or fanciful way. —*adj.* irregular; strange. —**ec'cen·tri·cal·ly** *adv.* —**ec·cen·tric·i·ty** (eksen'trisitē) *n.,pl.* **ec·cen·tric·i·ties.**

ech·o ('ekō) *n.,pl.* **ech·oes.** 1. the repetition of a sound produced by the reflection of sound waves from a wall, cliff, etc. 2. any repetition or imitation. 3. a reminder: *an echo of the past.* —*vb.* **ech·o·ing, ech·oed.** to produce or return as an echo.

e·clipse (i'klips) *vb.* **e·clips·ing, e·clipsed.** 1. to hide the light from (the sun or moon). 2. to become more powerful, better known, etc., than someone else. —*n.* a time when the moon moves between the earth and the sun and blocks off its light (**eclipse of the sun**), or when the earth moves between the sun and the moon (**eclipse of the moon**).

e·con·o·my (i'konəmē) *n.,pl.* **e·con·o·mies.** 1. the way in which a country manages its money and industries. 2. the state of a country's money, etc.: *an increase in exports will help the economy.* 3. a method of saving money. **ec·o·nom·ic** (ekə'nomik) *adj.* 1. relating to a country's economy. 2. saving money. **ec·o'nom·ics** *sing.n.* the science concerning business and money and the best way to manage them. **ec·o'nom·i·cal** *adj.* 1. using little, esp. using little money: *they had an economical vacation by staying at home.* 2. brief: *an economical piece of writing.* **e·con·o·mize** (i'konəmīz) *vb.* **e·con·o·miz·ing, e·con·o·mized.** to keep low the amount of money one spends.

edge (ej) *n.* 1. the outer part of something, lying away from the center. 2. the sharp side of a knife, razor blade, sword, etc. —*vb.* **edg·ing, edged.** (+ *away, away from, toward,* etc.) to move sideways very slowly. **'edge·ways** *or* **'edge·wise** *adv.* with the edge first; sideways.

ed·it ('edit) *vb.* 1. to prepare (someone else's writing) for publication. 2. to organize the contents of and run (a magazine or newspaper). **'ed·i·tor** *n.* a person who edits. **ed·i'to·ri·al** *adj.* concerned with editors or editing. *n.* a newspaper article reflecting the views of the editor or owner of the paper.

ed·u·cate ('ejŏŏkāt) *vb.* **ed·u·cat·ing, ed·u·cat·ed.** to instruct, train, or teach (a person). —**ed·u'ca·tion** *n.* —**ed·u'ca·tion·al** *adj.*

eel

eel (ēl) *n.* a long snakelike fish.

ef·fect (i'fekt) *n.* 1. the result of some action or event. 2. **ef·fects** (*pl.*) one's belongings. **ef'fec·tive** *adj.* having an effect, esp. a good one. **ef'fec·tu·al** *adj.* able to bring about the desired effect.

ef·fi·cient (i'fishənt) *adj.* working or functioning well without wasting effort or time. —**ef'fi·cien·cy** *n.*

ef·fort ('efərt) *n.* 1. use of one's strength or energy, e.g. in working, facing a problem, etc. 2. an attempt: *he made no effort to escape.*

egg[1] (eg) *n.* 1. an object produced by female birds, insects, snakes, lizards, etc. inside which their young develop. 2. a hen's egg, or part of it, used as food.

egg[2] (eg) *vb.* (+ *on*) to urge or encourage someone: *they egged on the youngest boy to ring the doorbell.*

e·ject (i'jekt) *vb.* to throw or cast out: *lava and flames were ejected from the volcano.* —**e'jec·tion** *n.*

e·lab·o·rate *adj.* (i'labərit) done in very great detail; complicated: *an elaborate design.* —*vb.* (i'labərāt) **e·lab·o·rat·ing, e·lab·o·rat·ed.** to make complicated by adding many small details.

e·las·tic (i'lastik) *n.* a stretchable substance made from rubber or other material. —*adj.* 1. containing or using elastic. 2. able to be stretched or extended: *the time allowed for this job is very elastic.*

el·bow ('elbō) *n.* the joint in the middle of the arm. —*vb.* to hit or push with the elbow.

e·lect (i'lekt) *vb.* 1. to choose, esp. by voting (a person) to act as a representative. 2. to decide: *Jane elected to study art at college.* **e'lec·tion** *n.* the act or process of electing or being elected. —**e'lec·tive** *adj.* —**e'lec·tor** *n.*

e·lec·tric·i·ty (ilek'trisitē) *n.* energy produced by the presence and motion of charged particles such as electrons or protons. **e'lec·tric** *adj.* 1. operated by or resulting in electricity: *an electric light.* 2. thrilling; emotionally strong: *there was an electric atmosphere as the ball game was about to start.* **e'lec·tri·cal** *adj.* 1. relating to electricity: *an electrical fault.* 2. requiring electricity to operate: *an electrical appliance.*

el·e·ment ('eləmənt) *n.* 1. something forming part of a larger thing: *there was an element of truth in his argument.* 2. a chemical substance, such as oxygen or iron, that cannot be split into other substances. 3. a heating device in a kettle, fire, etc. **el·e·men·ta·ry** (elə'mentərē) *adj.* simple; basic.

elephant

el·e·phant ('eləfənt) *n.* an animal of Africa and India with a long trunk and tusks. Elephants are the largest land animals.

e·lim·i·nate (i'limənāt) *vb.* **e·lim·i·nat·ing, e·lim·i·nat·ed.** to reject; remove, esp. from a competition: *he was eliminated from the second round because of his low score in the first.* —**e·lim·i'na·tion** *n.*

elm (elm) *n.* 1. a tall tree often grown for shade or decoration. 2. the wood of this tree, used for furniture. —*adj.* made from or concerning elm.

e·lope (i'lōp) *vb.* **e·lop·ing, e·loped**

(of a young man or woman) to run away in order to marry secretly. —**e'lope·ment** *n.*

em·bark (em'bârk) *vb.* 1. to board a ship at the start of a voyage. 2. (+ *on* or *upon*) to begin; start: *he embarked on a new career in music.* —**em·bar'ka·tion** *n.*

em·bar·rass (em'barəs) *vb.* **em·bar·rass·ing, em·bar·rassed.** to cause (someone) to feel ashamed, nervous, uncomfortable, worried, etc. —**em'bar·rass·ment** *n.*

em·bas·sy ('embəsē) *n.,pl.* **em·bas·sies.** a place where the ambassador and other diplomats representing a foreign country live and work.

em·brace (em'brās) *vb.* **em·brac·ing, em·braced.** 1. to take in one's arms, usu. as a sign of affection. 2. to accept willingly: *he embraced Christianity.* 3. to include: *the book embraces many interesting ideas.* —*n.* the act of embracing; a hug.

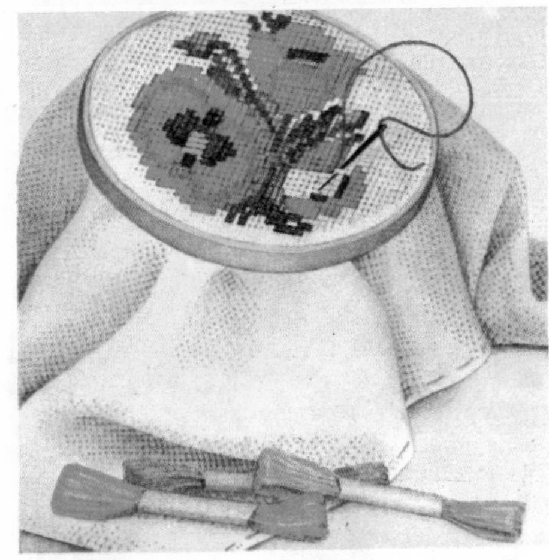

embroidery

em·broi·der (em'broidər) *vb.* 1. to decorate with ornamental designs in needlework. 2. to exaggerate or add invented detail to (a story, account, etc.). —**em'broi·der·y** *n.*

em·bry·o ('embrēō) *n.,pl.* **em·bry·os.** 1. a child or animal at the earliest stages of development inside the mother or egg. 2. the youngest stage of a plant within a seed. 3. the beginning or earliest stage of an idea, project, plan, etc. —**em·bry·on·ic** (embrē'onik) *adj.*

em·er·ald ('emərəld, 'emrəld) *n.* a rare green precious stone used in jewelry. —*adj.* 1. made of emerald: *an emerald brooch.* 2. having the color of emerald: *an emerald dress.*

e·merge (i'mûrj) *vb.* **e·merg·ing, e·merged.** 1. to appear; come out: *the moon emerged from behind the clouds.* 2. to develop: *new problems emerge every day.* —**e'mer·gence** *n.*

e·mer·gen·cy (i'mûrjənsē) *n.,pl.* **e·mer·gen·cies.** an unexpected or sudden event, situation, etc., requiring immediate action.

em·i·grate ('eməgrāt) *vb.* **em·i·grat·ing, em·i·grat·ed.** to leave one country or region to settle in another: *they emigrated from America to Australia.* **em·i·grant** ('eməgrənt) *adj., n.* (of) a person who emigrates. —**em·i'gra·tion** *n.*

em·i·nent ('emənənt) *adj.* high in rank or reputation; distinguished. —**'em·i·nence** *n.* —**'em·i·nent·ly** *adv.*

e·mit (i'mit) *vb.* **e·mit·ting, e·mit·ted.** 1. to send or be sent out: *she emitted a scream.* 2. to give out (radiation or other energy). —**e'mis·sion** *n.*

e·mo·tion (i'mōshən) *n.* a strong feeling, such as love, fear, hate, joy, etc.: *her voice trembled with emotion.* **e'mo·tion·al** *adj.* full of emotion. —**e'mo·tion·al·ly** *adv.*

em·per·or ('empərər) *n.* the supreme ruler of an empire. **em·press** ('empris) *n.* 1. a female emperor. 2. an emperor's wife.

em·pha·sis ('emfəsis) *n.,pl.* **em·pha·ses** ('emfəsēz). 1. importance or prominence given to anything by calling attention to it in some way. 2. the act of calling attention to something: *he laid emphasis on the word by repeating it.* 3. vigor; intensity of expression, action, etc. **em·pha·size** ('emfəsīz) *vb.* **em·pha·siz·ing, em·pha·sized.** to give emphasis to. **em·phat·ic** (em'fatik) *adj.* 1. using emphasis. 2. striking; clear. —**em'phat·i·cal·ly** *adv.*

em·pire ('empīər) *n.* a number of countries or states ruled over by a single person or government.

em·ploy (em'ploi) *vb.* 1. to use the services of or provide work for a person or persons: *that builder employs sixty men.* 2. to make use of: *Paul employed a boot to hammer in the nail.* **em·ploy'ee** *or* **em·ploy'e** *n.* a person working for another person or a company in exchange for wages. **em'ploy·ment** *n.* 1. work. 2. the act of using or the state of being applied: *the employment of new teaching methods.* —**em'ploy·er** *n.*

emp·ty ('emptē) *adj.* **emp·ti·er, emp·ti·est.** 1. unoccupied or containing nothing: *an empty box.* 2. worthless: *empty promises.* —*vb.* **emp·ty·ing, emp·tied.** to make or become empty: *empty the bucket.* —**'emp·ti·ness** *n.*

emu

e·mu ('ēmyōō) *n.* a large non-flying bird of Australia similar to the ostrich.

en·a·ble (en'ābəl) *vb.* **en·a·bling, en·a·bled.** to give (someone) the power, ability, or chance to do something.

e·nam·el (i'naməl) *n.* 1. a glossy material used as a protective or decorative coating on metal or pottery. 2. a paint or other coating resembling this. 3. the hard outer covering on teeth. —*adj.* of, resembling, or coated with enamel. —*vb.* to coat with enamel.

en·chant (en'chant) *vb.* 1. to cast a spell over (someone or something); bewitch. 2. to delight or charm: *the actors enchanted the audience with their performance.* —**en'chant·ing** *adj.* —**en'chant·ment** *n.*

en·close (en'klōz) *vb.* **en·clos·ing, en·closed.** 1. to shut in; surround: *the garden was enclosed by a high wall.* 2. to send in the same envelope or package as that containing the main letter, etc.: *I enclosed a check with the letter.* **en·clos·ure** (en'klōzhər) *n.* 1. the act of enclosing or the state of being enclosed. 2. an area of land surrounded by a fence or wall.

en·core ('onkôr) *n.* (in a concert, etc.) a repeat of a piece as demanded by the audience.

en·count·er (en'kountər) *vb.* 1. to meet unexpectedly. 2. to come across or struggle against (difficulties, opposition, etc.): *he encountered a number of obstacles on his journey.* —*n.* 1. a casual or unexpected meeting. 2. a hostile meeting; combat or battle.

en·cour·age (en'kûrij, en'kurij) *vb.* **en·cour·ag·ing, en·cour·aged.** to urge on by giving support, approval, etc.; inspire with hope or confidence: *Lucy's family encouraged her to continue with her piano lessons.* —**en'cour·age·ment** *n.*

en·cy·clo·pe·di·a (ensīklə'pēdēə) *n.* a book or set of volumes giving information on all branches of knowledge or all aspects of one subject. —**en·cy·clo'pe·dic** *adj.*

en·deav·or (en'devər) *vb.* to make an effort or attempt; try: *I will endeavor to be there on time.* —*n.* a strenuous effort or the use of it: *after great endeavor they reached the hilltop.*

en·dure (en'do͝or, en'dyo͝or) *vb.* **en·dur·ing, en·dured.** 1. to suffer or bear: *he was able to endure the cold.* 2. to last or continue: *their love endured for a lifetime.* —**en'dur·ance** *n.*

en·e·my ('enəmē) *n.,pl.* **en·e·mies.** 1. a person who hates an opponent and wishes to harm him. 2. a hostile nation or its armed forces; an opponent in war. 3. anything that threatens to harm or destroy: *fear is the great enemy.* —*adj.* of or belonging to a hostile force: *an enemy agent.*

en·er·gy ('enərjē) *n.,pl.* **en·er·gies.** 1. force; strength; vigor: *he had the energy to walk for miles without tiring.* 2. (physics) the capacity to do work. 3. power supplied by coal, gas, electricity, etc. **en·er·get·ic** (enər'jetik) *adj.* having plenty of energy. **en·er'get·i·cal·ly** *adv.* with great energy.

en·gage (en'gāj) *vb.* **en·gag·ing, en·gaged.** 1. to agree to pay for the services of (a person, etc.); employ. 2. to attract or occupy (one's interest or attention): *we were engaged in the conversation for hours.* 3. to fit; lock; match: *the two wheels of the machine engaged.* 4. to begin a battle with (an enemy). **en'gaged** *adj.* 1. (of a man and woman) intending to marry. 2. busy or occupied. **en'gage·ment** *n.* 1. the act of engaging. 2. a promise to marry. 3. a battle.

engines

en·gine ('enjin) *n.* a machine that drives or pulls something.

en·gi·neer (enjə'nēr) *n.* 1. a person employed on any of several practical scientific activities, e.g. building machines, roads, bridges, etc. 2. an engine driver. —*vb.* to make up (a clever plan): *the thief engineered a way of robbing the bank without being caught.* **en·gi'neer·ing** *n.* any of the applied sciences involving the techniques of the engineer.

en·grave (en'grāv) *vb.* **en·grav·ing, en·graved.** to cut (words, a design, etc.) into (stone or metal). **en'grav·ing** *n.* 1. the art of doing this. 2. a picture or design produced by engraving a piece of metal and printing it on paper.

e·nig·ma (i'nigmə) *n.* a person or thing that cannot be easily understood; something puzzling. **en·ig·mat·ic** (enig'matik) *adj.* mysterious; puzzling. —**en·ig'mat·i·cal·ly** *adv.*

en·large (en'lârj) *vb.* **en·larg·ing, en·larged.** 1. to make bigger. 2. (+ *on* or *upon*) to give further details about: *in the second lesson he enlarged upon the points he had made before.* —**en'large·ment** *n.*

en·light·en (en'lītən) *vb.* to help (someone) to increase his knowledge or understanding. **en'light·ened** *adj.* intelligent; knowledgable or civilized. **en'light·en·ment** *n.* the act of enlightening or being enlightened.

en·list (en'list) *vb.* 1. to enter or be entered into the army, navy, or air force. 2. to obtain (help): *he enlisted his father's aid in doing his homework.* —**en'list·ment** *n.*

e·nor·mous (i'nôrməs) *adj.* very big; huge. **e'nor·mi·ty** *n.,pl.* **e·nor·mi·ties.** very great evil or crime. —**e'nor·mous·ly** *adv.*

en·quire (en'kwīər) *vb.* **en·quir·ing, en·quired.** to seek information from someone; ask. **en'quir·y** *n.,pl.* **en·quir·ies.** a request for information. See also INQUIRE.

en·rage (en'rāj) *vb.* **en·rag·ing, en·raged.** to cause to be very angry: *her stupidity enraged him.*

en·sure (en'shoor) *vb.* **en·sur·ing, en·sured.** to make certain: *he ensured his success by practicing hard.*

en·ter·prise ('entərprīz) *n.* 1. having the initiative or ability to do something unusual: *she showed great enterprise in organizing a charity concert.* 2. a commercial business undertaking: *he began a fishing enterprise on the remote island.* **'en·ter·pris·ing** *adj.* bold; imaginative.

en·ter·tain (entər'tān) *vb.* 1. to provide amusement or distraction for (an audience). 2. to be prepared to think about: *I wouldn't entertain such an idea.* **en·ter'tain·er** *n.* a performer, esp. on the stage or television. **—en·ter'tain·ment** *n.*

en·thu·si·asm (en'thoozēazəm) *n.* very great interest, eagerness, or keenness. **en'thuse** *vb.* **en·thus·ing, en·thused.** to feel or express enthusiasm: *Peter enthused about his school project.* **en'thu·si·ast** *n.* someone full of enthusiasm. **—en·thu·si'as·tic** *adj.* **—en·thu·si'as·ti·cal·ly** *adv.*

en·tice (en'tīs) *vb.* **en·tic·ing, en·ticed.** (+ *into*) to encourage (someone) to do something, esp. something bad.

en·tire (en'tīər) *adj.* whole; complete; total: *he ate an entire batch of cookies.* **—en'tire·ly** *adv.* **—en'tire·ty** *n.*

en·vel·op (en'veləp) *vb.* to cover or surround totally: *smoke enveloped the scene.*

en·ve·lope ('envəlōp, 'ânvəlōp) *n.* a rectangular packet made of paper that can be sealed and used for mailing letters.

envelope

en·vi·ron·ment (en'vīrənmənt) *n.* the surroundings, situation, or circumstances in which a person or thing exists. **—en·vi·ron'men·tal** *adj.*

en·vy ('envē) *n.* the feeling of jealousy toward a person because of not being able to have what he possesses or experiences. *—vb.* **en·vy·ing, en·vied.** to feel envy: *Alan envied John his new book.*

ep·i·dem·ic (epi'demik) *n.* a disease that affects many people at the same time.

ep·i·sode ('episōd) *n.* 1. one of several sections of a story published in a periodical or broadcast over radio or television. 2. an event: *a happy episode in someone's life.*

ep·i·taph ('epitaf) *n.* a memorial inscription carved on a gravestone or tomb.

ep·och ('epək) *n.* a period in history, geology, etc., esp. one during which something important happens.

e·qual ('ēkwəl) *adj.* the same; (esp. of figures) coming to the same amount. *—vb.* 1. to come to an equal amount. 2. to make (something) equal to something else: *Tom equaled Steve's score by gaining another point.* **e·qual·i·ty** (i'kwolitē) *n.* the state of being equal, esp. of having the same rights as other people. **'e·qual·ize** *vb.* **e·qual·iz·ing, e·qual·ized.** to be or cause to be equal; balance. **—'e·qual·iz·er** *n.*

e·quate (i'kwāt) *vb.* **e·quat·ing, e·quat·ed.** 1. to consider or think of as equal. 2. to balance equally. **e'qua·tion** *n.* a mathematical expression in algebra in which one side is equal to the other and there is at least one unknown quantity, as in $x + 1$ 3.

e·qua·tor (i'kwātər) *n.* an imaginary line around the earth exactly halfway between the North and South Poles.

e·qui·nox ('ēkwənoks, 'ekwənoks) *n.* the two times during the year (in spring and autumn) when day and night are of equal length, occurring when the sun crosses the plane of the earth's equator.

e·quip (i'kwip) *vb.* **e·quip·ping, e·quipped.** to provide or supply with the apparatus, etc., necessary for some activity: *they equipped the team with rackets for the game.* **e'quip·ment** *n.* things with which someone or something can be equipped.

e·quiv·a·lent (i'kwivələnt) *adj.* matching something in effect, worth, or meaning: *10° Celsius is equivalent to 50° Fahrenheit.* **—e'quiv·a·lence** *n.*

e·ra ('ērə, 'erə) *n.* a period of time, esp. an age of history: *the Christian era.*

e·rase (i'rās) *vb.* **e·ras·ing, e·rased.** 1. to rub out (a mark, esp. a pencil mark). 2. to remove: *the memory of an unhappy time was erased as years passed.* **—e'ra·sure** *n.*

e·rect (i'rekt) *adj.* upright; vertical or straight. *—vb.* to build; put up: *the house was erected in a week.* **—e'rec·tion** *n.* **—e'rect·ly** *adv.*

ermine

er·mine ('ûrmin) *n.* 1. a weasel that has a white coat in winter. 2. the white fur grown by an ermine during the winter. *—adj.* trimmed with or made of ermine.

e·rode (i'rōd) *vb.* **e·rod·ing, e·rod·ed.** to wear away slowly over a long period: *water eroded the soft rock.* **—e'ro·sion** *n.*

err (ûr, er) *vb.* 1. to make a mistake. 2. (formerly) to commit a crime or sin.

er·rand ('erənd) *n.* a journey made in order to carry a message, fetch something, etc., for someone else: *Julie's mother sent her on an errand to the shop.*

er·ror ('erər) *n.* a mistake.

e·rupt (i'rupt) *vb.* to burst out unexpectedly: *lava erupted from the volcano.* **—e'rup·tion** *n.*

escalator

es·ca·la·tor ('eskəlātər) *n.* a staircase moving on a power-driven belt.

es·cape (is'kāp) *vb.* **es·cap·ing, es·caped.** 1. to get free from prison, danger, etc. 2. to avoid; elude: *Jim escaped his teacher's attention.* **es'cap·ism** *n.* the avoidance of all the problems of life and reality. **—es'cap·ist** *n., adj.*

es·cort *vb.* (e'skôrt) to go along with a person to a place as a protector, guard, or companion: *Sarah was escorted to the dance by her father.* **—*n.*** ('eskôrt) a person or group that escorts someone.

es·pi·o·nage ('espēənâzh) *n.* spying.

es·sence ('esəns) *n.* 1. the most important part or quality of a thing. 2. the concentrated form of a plant, drug, etc.: *vanilla essence.* **es·sen·tial** (i'senshəl) *adj.* 1. completely necessary and important. 2. concerning or produced by an essence. *n.* an essential part or element of something. **—es'sen·tial·ly** *adv.*

es·tab·lish (e'stablish) *vb.* 1. to organize, create, or set up: *to establish new laws.* 2. to prove: *can you establish that this is your car?* **es'tab·lish·ment** *n.* the action of establishing or something that is established, e.g. an organization or business.

es·tate (i'stāt) *n.* 1. everything a person owns; possessions: *she left her whole estate to her sister when she died.* 2. a large piece of land, usu. with a luxurious home, owned by a person.

es·ti·mate *vb.* ('estəmāt) **es·ti·mat·ing, es·ti·mat·ed.** to guess; judge: *he estimated that there were 30 people crowded into one room.* ('estəmit) 1. a guess or judgment. 2. a statement of the probable cost of some work, etc. **es·ti'ma·tion** *n.* a judgment or opinion.

es·tu·ar·y ('eschōōerē) *n.,pl.* **es·tu·ar·ies.** the mouth of a river, extending into the sea.

e·ter·nal (i'tûrnəl) *adj.* lasting forever; never ending: *he swore eternal loyalty.* **—e'ter·nal·ly** *adv.* **—e'ter·ni·ty** *n.,pl.* **e·ter·ni·ties.**

e·vade (i'vād) *vb.* **e·vad·ing, e·vad·ed.** to escape from or avoid: *he evaded my question by changing the subject.* **—e'va·sion** *n.* **—e'va·sive** *adj.*

e·van·ge·list (i'vanjəlist) *n.* 1. a person who spreads Christian religion in a vigorous way, esp. through public meetings. 2. **Evangelist** any of the four gospel writers, Matthew, Mark, Luke, and John. **—e'van·ge·lism** *n.*

e·vap·o·rate (i'vapərāt) *vb.* **e·vap·o·rat·ing, e·vap·o·rat·ed.** to change from a liquid to a vapor. **—e·vap·o'ra·tion** *n.*

e·ven ('ēvən) *adj.* 1. level; smooth: *an even surface.* 2. equal; matching: *the two boxers were even after the first round.* 3. (of a number) able to be divided by 2, without leaving a remainder: *2, 4, 6, and 8 are even numbers.*

e·vent (i'vent) *n.* something taking place at a certain time; an action or occurrence.

e·ven·tu·al (i'venchōōəl) *adj.* forming a result; final: *the eventual outcome of the game was a tie.* **e·ven·tu'al·i·ty** *n.* something that might occur; possible result: *Roger was prepared for every eventuality on his journey.* **e'ven·tu·al·ly** *adv.* at last; finally.

ev·er·green ('evərgrēn) *n.* a tree that does not shed its leaves in winter: *the fir tree is an evergreen.* **—*adj.*** of or concerning such a tree. Compare DECIDUOUS.

e·vict (i'vikt) *vb.* to remove (someone) from a place by legal methods or force. **—e'vic·tion** *n.*

ev·i·dence ('evidəns) *n.* a set of facts that support or disprove a case, esp. a legal case. **'ev·i·dent** *adj.* clear; obvious. **—'ev·i·dent·ly** *adv.*

e·vil ('ēvəl) *adj.* morally very bad; wicked. **—*n.*** anything that is evil.

e·vo·lu·tion ('evə'lōōshən) *n.* a process of evolving; development: *the evolution of farming methods since the turn of the century.*

e·volve (i'volv) *vb.* **e·volv·ing, e·volved.** to change gradually into a different form over a long period; develop: *most people think that men evolved from apes.*

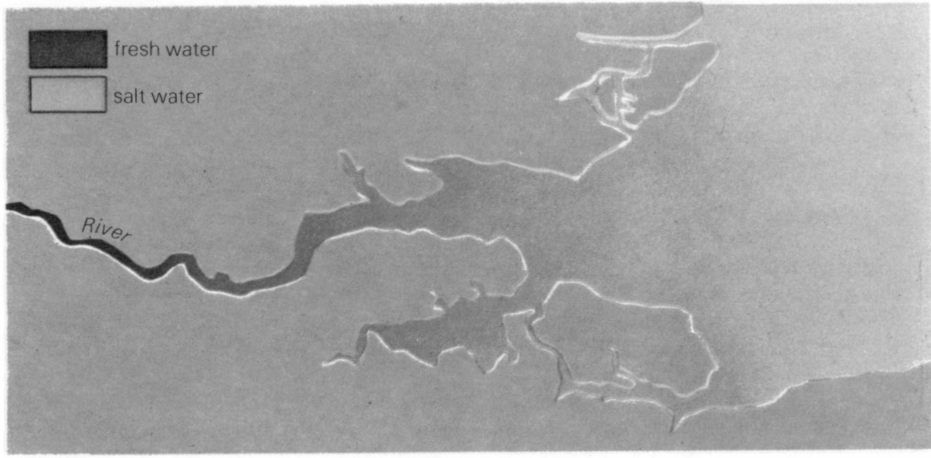

estuary

ewe

ewe (yo͞o) *n.* a female sheep.

ex·act[1] (ig'zakt) *adj.* accurate, correct, or precise. **ex'act·ly** *adv.* correctly; accurately. *interj.* quite right (used to indicate agreement).

ex·act[2] (ig'zakt) *vb.* to demand; get by power or authority: *the government exacted more money by raising taxes.*

ex·ag·ger·ate (ig'zajərāt) *vb.* **ex·ag·ger·at·ing, ex·ag·ger·at·ed.** to make something appear bigger, better, etc., than it really is: *John exaggerated when he said that he had caught a hundred fish.* **—ex·ag·ger'a·tion** *n.* **—ex'ag·ger·at·ed·ly** *adv.*

ex·am·ine (ig'zamin) *vb.* **ex·am·in·ing, ex·am·ined.** 1. to look at closely or thoroughly; inspect or investigate: *she examined the fruit carefully before she bought it.* 2. to put questions to (a student, pupil, etc.) in order to test his knowledge. **ex'am·in·er** *n.* someone who examines. **ex·am·i'nee** *n.* a person being examined, esp. a student or pupil. **—ex·am·i'na·tion** *n.*

ex·am·ple (ig'zampəl) *n.* 1. a person or thing that represents a class or group of similar people or things: *lions and tigers are examples of wild animals.* 2. an action or form of behavior worth copying or someone who provides this: *James was a good example to the class because he worked hard.*

ex·as·per·ate (ig'zaspərāt) *vb.* **ex·as·per·at·ing, ex·as·per·at·ed.** to annoy very much: *I was exasperated by Brian's irritating little habits.* **—ex·as·per'a·tion** *n.*

ex·ca·vate ('ekskəvāt) *vb.* **ex·ca·vat·ing, ex·ca·vat·ed.** 1. to hollow out; make a hole. 2. to dig up, esp. as part of an archaeological investigation.

ex·cel (ek'sel) *vb.* **ex·cel·ling, ex·celled.** to be very good, e.g. in an activity; do better than other people: *she excels at swimming.* **ex·cel·lent** ('eksələnt) *adj.* very good or fine. **'ex·cel·lence** *or* **'ex·cel·len·cy** *n.* 1. the quality of being excellent. 2. a term of address used to certain high-ranking officials, e.g. a foreign ambassador.

ex·cept (ek'sept) *prep.* (often + *for*) leaving out; not including or considering: *everyone came to the party except John.* —*vb.* to leave out; exclude. **ex'cep·tion** *n.* something outside or beyond what is allowed, usual, etc. **ex'cep·tion·al** *adj.* not ordinary or usual. **—ex'cep·tion·al·ly** *adv.*

ex·cess *n.* (ek'ses) 1. the state of exceeding or going beyond what is suitable or right: *he eats to excess.* 2. an amount or quantity that exceeds what is necessary, suitable, usual, etc.: *an excess of energy.* —*adj.* ('ekses, ek'ses) beyond what is needed, suitable, or usual: *excess weight.* **ex'ces·sive** *adj.* greater in amount, quantity, etc., than is usual.

ex·change (eks'chānj) *vb.* **ex·chang·ing, ex·changed.** to give one thing in return for another: *Benjamin exchanged his old car for a new one.* —*n.* 1. the act or an instance of exchanging. 2. a place where things are bought and sold: *people buy and sell financial shares at a stock exchange.*

ex·cite (ek'sīt) *vb.* **ex·cit·ing, ex·cit·ed.** to awaken (strong feelings or emotions, esp. of interest, anger, etc.) in (someone): *the news excited her.* **—ex'cite·ment** *n.*

ex·claim (eks'klām) *vb.* to shout in surprise, anger, etc. **ex·clam·a·tion** (eksklə'māshən) *n.* a shout.

ex·clude (iks'klo͞od) *vb.* **ex·clud·ing, ex·clud·ed.** to leave out; not consider or take account of: *he was excluded from the journey because of his age.* **ex'clu·sion** *n.* the act of excluding or state of being excluded. **ex'clu·sive** *adj.* 1. excluding something. 2. including only a few people or things; selective: *this club is exclusive.*

ex·cur·sion (ek'skûrzhən) *n.* a trip or journey, esp. a special trip organized for pleasure: *we went on an excursion to the country.*

ex·cuse *vb.* (ik'skyo͞oz) **ex·cus·ing, ex·cused.** 1. to forgive: *the teacher excused him for being late.* 2. to allow (someone) to be absent: *he excused her from school.* —*n.* (ik'skyo͞os) a reason given to explain something that might be thought wrong or bad: *David's excuse was that he was ill.*

ex·e·cute ('eksəkyo͞ot) *vb.* **ex·e·cut·ing, ex·e·cut·ed.** 1. to kill (someone) according to a law: *they executed him for murder.* 2. to perform (a task or duty): *he executed his task with great efficiency.* **—ex·e'cu·tion** *n.*

ex·ec·u·tive (ig'zekyətiv) *n.* 1. a person who organizes or administers a company or business firm. 2. a group responsible for organizing the work of a government, large association, union, or society.

ex·empt (ig'zempt) *adj.* (+ *from*) legally excluded from some law, rule, duty, etc.: *he is exempt from income tax.* —*vb.* to exclude (someone) in this way: *they exempted him from paying the usual fee.*

ex·er·cise ('eksərsīz) *vb.* **ex·er·cis·ing, ex·er·cised.** 1. to train or move the various parts of the body in order to build up one's strength, improve one's health and appearance, etc., e.g. by playing sport. 2. to use (one's power or authority): *he exercised his power as chairman to bring the meeting to order.* —*n.* 1. the act of exercising. 2. a piece of work done at school.

ex·ert (ig'zûrt) *vb.* to put into vigorous action (power, pressure, influence, etc.): *he exerted all his strength to move the rock.* **—ex'er·tion** *n.*

exhaust

ex·haust (ig'zôst) *vb.* 1. to use up (energy, food, etc.) completely: *after* *the long journey we exhausted our supply of food.* 2. to wear out: *Mark was exhausted by the long run.* —*n.* gases or steam given off by an engine, or the pipe through which the gases are expelled. **ex'haus·tive** *adj.* thorough. —**ex'haus·tion** *n.*

ex·hib·it (ig'zibit) *vb.* 1. to put on show; present for inspection: *to exhibit paintings in public.* 2. to make plain; display: *he exhibited delight at the suggestion.* —*n.* an object placed on show. **ex·hi'bi·tion** *n.* 1. a public presentation or show (of works of art, etc.). 2. a demonstration or public display.

ex·hil·a·rate (ig'zilərāt) *vb.* **ex·hil·a·rat·ing, ex·hil·a·rat·ed.** to excite in a lively happy way; stimulate: *she was exhilarated by the news that she was going home at last.* —**ex·hil·a'ra·tion** *n.*

ex·ile ('egzīl, 'eksīl) *n.* 1. prolonged enforced separation from one's native land or home: *she was sent into exile.* 2. a person living in exile. —*vb.* **ex·il·ing, ex·iled.** to send into exile; banish from one's native land.

ex·ist (ig'zist) *vb.* 1. to be real: *he does not believe that Martians exist.* 2. to continue to be or live over a period of time: *we existed on very little food.* 3. to occur or be found: *great poverty still exists in some parts of the world.* —**ex'ist·ence** *n.* —**ex'ist·ent** *adj.*

ex·it ('egzit, 'eksit) *n.* 1. a way out of a building or enclosure. 2. a departure, esp. the departure from the stage of an actor in a play etc.: *he made a quick exit at the left of the stage.* —*vb.* to leave or depart; go out.

ex·pand (ik'spand) *vb.* 1. to enlarge in size, volume, extent, etc.: *the school was expanded by building new classrooms.* Compare CONTRACT (*vb. def. 1*). 2. to develop; express in detail: *she expanded her notes into an essay.* —**ex'pan·sion** *n.* —**ex'pan·sive** *adj.*

ex·panse (ik'spans) *n.* a wide open space or area of water, sky, land, etc.

ex·pect (ik'spekt) *vb.* 1. to look forward to or consider likely: *I expect him to be here soon.* 2. to require or look for: *I expect complete obedience.* 3. to suppose: *I expect you are tired.* **ex·pec·ta·tion** (ekspek'tāshən) *n.* 1. the act of expecting. 2. something one expects or hopes for; a hope. —**ex'pec·tan·cy** *n.* —**ex'pect·ant** *adj.* —**ex'pect·ant·ly** *adv.*

ex·pe·di·tion (ekspi'dishən) *n.* 1. an organized journey made, usu. to a distant place, for a specific purpose. 2. the people, vehicles, ships, etc., engaged in such a journey. —**ex·pe'di·tion·ar·y** *adj.*

ex·pel (ik'spel) *vb.* **ex·pel·ling, ex·pelled.** 1. to drive out or away with force: *we shall expel the invaders from our country.* 2. to dismiss (from a club, community, school, etc.): *they expelled the student from college.* See also EXPULSION.

ex·pend (ik'spend) *vb.* to use up (money, energy, etc.), esp. without benefit to oneself: *he expended all his energy lifting heavy weights.* **ex'pen·di·ture** *n.* 1. the act of expending. 2. the amount of money that is spent or used up.

ex·pense (ik'spens) *n.* 1. cost or charge. 2. the occasion or cause for spending money: *a vacation abroad can be a great expense.* 3. **expenses** (*pl.*) money spent, esp. during the course of a job: *she was paid expenses for traveling to meetings.* **ex'pen·sive** *adj.* highly priced or costly. —**ex'pen·sive·ly** *adv.*

ex·pe·ri·ence (ik'spērēəns) *n.* 1. a particular event or series of events that happen to or have a personal effect on someone: *driving fast can be a frightening experience.* 2. the process of gaining knowledge and skill in life or in some activity, occupation, etc.: *he has business experience.* —*vb.* **ex·pe·ri·enc·ing, ex·pe·ri·enced.** to meet with; undergo; feel: *she experienced great joy.* **ex'pe·ri·enced** *adj.* well used to something; expert.

ex·per·i·ment *n.* (ik'sperəmənt) a test or series of tests carried out in order to discover something unknown or to test a principle or theory. —*vb.* (ik'sperəment) to make an experiment. —**ex·per·i'men·tal** *adj.*

ex·pert ('ekspûrt) *n.* a person having special skill or knowledge in some particular subject. —*adj.* 1. possessing special skill or knowledge, taught by practice: *an expert marksman.* 2. coming from or produced by an expert: *expert advice.*

ex·plain (ik'splān) *vb.* 1. to make clear or understandable: *the teacher explained the problem.* 2. to account for; give meaning to: *how do you explain your behavior?* **ex·pla·na·tion** (eksplə'nāshən) *n.* the act or an instance of explaining.

ex·plode (ik'splōd) *vb.* **ex·plod·ing, ex·plod·ed.** 1. to blow up or cause to blow up: *the bomb exploded after hitting the ground.* 2. to show sudden strong emotions: *she exploded with anger.* See also EXPLOSION.

ex·ploit *n.* ('eksploit) a daring or bold action, achievement, etc. —*vb.* (ik'sploit) 1. to employ or use, esp. for profit. 2. to take advantage of in a selfish way. —**ex·ploi'ta·tion** *n.*

ex·plore (ik'splôr) *vb.* **ex·plor·ing, ex·plored.** 1. to travel through (a region, country, etc.) for the purposes of discovery. 2. to examine thoroughly; look closely at. —**ex·plo'ra·tion** (eksplə'rāshən) *n.* —**ex'plor·a·to·ry** (eks'plôrətōrē) *adj.* —**ex'plor·er** *n.*

explosion

ex·plo·sion (ik'splōzhən) *n.* a sudden, violent, and often destructive bursting or breaking out. **ex'plo·sive** *adj.* capable of exploding or being exploded. *n.* an explosive substance.

ex·port *vb.* (ik'spôrt, 'ekspôrt) to take or send (manufactured goods, etc.) out of a country for sale abroad. —*n.* ('ekspôrt) 1. the act or process of exporting. 2. an item that is exported. **ex·por'ta·tion** *n.* —**ex·port·er** (ek'spôrtər, 'ekspôrtər) *n.* a person who exports goods.

ex·pose (ik'spōz) *vb.* **ex·pos·ing, ex·posed.** 1. to lay open (to danger, harm, etc.): *the army exposed itself to attack from the rear.* 2. to display or uncover: *he exposed his back to the sun.* 3. to make known; reveal or disclose: *the newspaper exposed the man as a criminal.* 4. to subject (a photographic film or plate) to the action of light. **ex'po·sure** *n.* 1. the action or an instance of exposing or being exposed. 2. the effects on the body of being without shelter or protection from severe weather.

ex·press (ik'spres) *vb.* 1. to put into words: *to express one's ideas.* 2. to reveal or communicate: *he expressed his anger by striking the table.* —*adj.* 1. clearly or definitely expressed: *express instructions.* 2. special; particular: *for an express purpose.* 3. traveling fast and directly: *express delivery.* —*n.* 1. a fast train or coach. 2. a system of sending letters, parcels, etc., quickly.

ex·pres·sion (eks'preshən) *n.* 1. an act or instance of expressing: *the expression of an opinion.* 2. a display of emotion or feeling: *the expression on someone's face.* 3. a particular phrase or form of words: *a slang expression.* **ex'pres·sive** *adj.* serving to express or having the force of expression: *an expressive gesture.*

ex·pul·sion (ik'spulshən) *n.* an instance of being expelled. See EXPEL.

ex·quis·ite ('ekskwizit, ik'skwizit) charming, excellent, perfect, or refined: *exquisite workmanship.* 2. showing delicate understanding or fine judgment: *an exquisite ear for music.* 3. (of pain or pleasure) sharp; strong. —**ex'quis·ite·ly** *adv.* —**ex'quis·ite·ness** *n.*

ex·tend (ik'stend) *vb.* 1. to increase in length, either in time or space: *we extended the pathway by 2 meters.* 2. to stretch out: *her land extends to the foot of the hills.* 3, to hold out (a hand, arm, etc.) or offer: *to extend one's thanks.*

ex·ten·sion (ik'stenshən) *n.* 1. the act of extending. 2. the additional part of something produced by extending. 3. an extra telephone in a house or building.

ex·tens·ive (ik'stensiv) *adj.* 1. covering a great area: *extensive grounds.* 2. thorough; comprehensive: *extensive knowledge.* —**ex'ten·sive·ly** *adv.*

ex·tent (ik'stent) *n.* 1. extended length or area; expanse. 2. amount; scope; range.

ex·te·ri·or (ik'stērēər) *n.* the outside of something, e.g. a building, person, etc.: *the exterior of a house.* —*adj.* occurring on or relating to the outside of something: *the exterior walls were white.*

ex·ter·mi·nate (ik'stûrmənāt) *vb.* **ex·ter·mi·nat·ing, ex·ter·mi·nat·ed.** to kill or destroy totally; put an end to: *all the rats in the barn have been exterminated with poison.* —**ex·ter·mi'na·tion** *n.* —**ex'ter·mi·na·tor** *n.*

ex·ter·nal (ik'stûrnəl) *adj.* coming from, occurring on, or connected with the outside of a person or thing. —**ex'ter·nal·ly** *adv.*

ex·tinct (ik'stingkt) *adj.* (of an animal, plant, etc.) no longer in existence; having died out entirely: *the dodo was a bird that became extinct in the 17th century.* —**ex'tinc·tion** *n.*

ex·tin·guish (ik'stinggwish) *vb.* to put out (a fire or something similar to fire): *they extinguished the flames.* —**ex'tin·guish·a·ble** *adj.*

ex·tol *or* **ex·toll** (eks'tōl) *vb.* **ex·tol·ling, ex·tolled.** to praise highly.

ex·tra ('ekstrə) *adj.* additional; more, esp. more than expected: *an extra helping of potatoes.* —*n.* 1. an additional thing or part. 2. a late or additional edition of a newspaper, esp. one published to give news of a major event.

ex·tract *n.* ('ekstrakt) 1. a part removed or chosen from a whole, e.g. an excerpt from a movie, story, play, etc. 2. a substance obtained from food, etc.: *malt extract.* —*vb.* (ik'strakt) 1. to draw (a part from a whole); select: *Martin extracted facts from the book to write his essay.* 2. to remove (a tooth). —**ex'trac·tion** *n.*

ex·traor·di·nar·y (ik'strôrdənerē) *adj.* very unusual; strange; amazing. **ex'traor·di·nar·i·ly** *adv.* 1. unusually; strangely. 2. very: *that's extraordinarily kind of you.*

ex·trav·a·gant (ik'stravəgənt) *adj.* 1. spending too much money; wasteful. 2. beyond what is sensible: *Bill has some extravagant ideas.* **ex'trav·a·gance** *n.* excessive spending; unrestrained excess.

ex·treme (ik'strēm) *adj.* 1. at the furthest outer limits of something: *Alaska is in the extreme north of America.* 2. on or over the limit of what is acceptable, reasonable, etc.: *extreme political measures.* 3. of the highest degree: *extreme heat.* —*n.* a limit. **ex'trem·ism** *n.* the holding of extreme, often violent or revolutionary political views. **ex'trem·ist** *adj., n.* (of) someone who holds extreme political views. **ex·trem·i·ty** (ik'stremitē) *n.,pl.* **ex·trem·i·ties.** 1. the very end of something.2. danger, poverty, or a similar extreme situation. 3. **extremities** (*pl.*) the toes or fingers.

ex·u·ber·ant (ig'zōōbərənt) *adj.* full of energy and cheerfulness. —**ex'u·ber·ance** *n.*

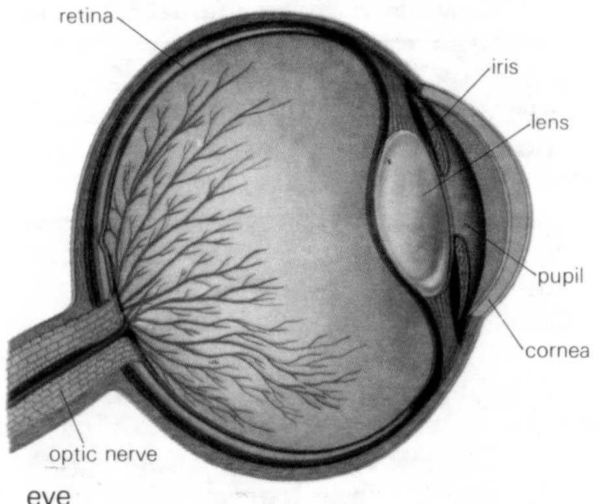

eye

eye (ī) *n.* 1. the part of the body that perceives light; the organ of sight. 2. something like an eye, e.g. the hole in the end of a needle through which the thread passes, or a bud on a potato. **keep an eye on** to keep a watch over. —*vb.* **ey·ing** *or* **eye·ing, eyed.** to look at closely or examine carefully, esp. with caution or envy: *Mr Brown eyed the man outside the bank suspiciously.*

eye·ball ('ībôl) *n.* the ball-like part of the eye, positioned in the eye socket and surrounded by the eyelids.

eye·brow ('ībrou) *n.* the hairy ridge above the eye.

eye·lash ('īlash) *n.* one of or all the hairs that grow around the edge of the eyelid.

eye·lid ('īlid) *n.* a protective piece of skin that is lowered in closing the eye and when blinking.

eye·wit·ness (ī'witnis) *n.* a person who is present at and observes an event, esp. an accident or crime.

F

fa·ble ('fābəl) *n.* a story, esp. one that teaches a lesson about life. **fab·u·lous** ('fabyələs) *adj.* 1. (informal) wonderful; excellent. 2. spoken of in fables: *the unicorn is a fabulous creature.*

fab·ric ('fabrik) *n.* 1. cloth or similar material. 2. the material that something is made out of: *the main fabric of the building was wood.*

fa·cade (fə'sâd) *n.* 1. the front view or face of a building. 2. an outward appearance, esp. a false or misleading one: *beneath his cold facade he was very friendly.*

face (fās) *n.* 1. the front part of the head, including the eyes, nose, and mouth. 2. a look or expression of the face: *Bill put on a happy face even though he was sad.* 3. the front or prominent part or surface of something: *the face of a clock.* 4. the outward appearance of something: *the face of the town is changing.* 5. (informal) boldness: *he had the face to challenge my decision.* —*vb.* **fac·ing, faced.** 1. to turn or be turned toward; look at: *face me when I'm talking to you.* 2. to meet directly; accept: *to face facts.* 3. to provide with a covering surface: *to face brick with a layer of plaster.* **face up to** to confront realistically; meet. '**fa·cial** *adj.* of or relating to the face. *n.* (informal) a massage or other treatment for making the face more beautiful, healthy, etc. —'**fa·cial·ly** *adv.*

fac·il·i·ty (fə'silitē) *n.,pl.* **fa·cil·i·ties.** 1. the ability for doing something easily; aptitude. 2. service, equipment, etc., that is useful: *the town has poor shopping facilities.*

fact (fakt) *n.* anything that is known to be true: *it is a fact that the U.S. became independent in the year 1776.* —'**fac·tu·al** *adj.*

fac·tion ('fakshən) *n.* a group of people having a common aim, esp. a small group within a political party, etc., that disagrees with the aims of that party.

fac·tor ('faktər) *n.* 1. a fact or element, esp. one of several connected with or contributing toward a subject or matter: *we must consider all the factors in this plan.* 2. one of several numbers or quantities which when multiplied together produce a given number: *5 and 3 are factors of 15 because* $5 \times 3 = 15$.

fac·to·ry ('faktərē) *n.,pl.* **fac·to·ries.** a building or group of buildings in which things are manufactured.

facade

fac·ul·ty ('fakəltē) *n.,pl.* **fac·ul·ties.** 1. any inborn ability of a living creature, such as hearing, sight, smell, etc. 2. any special mental or physical ability or power: *she has a faculty for mathematics.* 3. the teaching staff of a school, college, or university, or the staff in one particular department: *the history faculty.*

fad (fad) *n.* a fashion or craze; something of interest for a short time.

fade (fād) *vb.* **fad·ing, fad·ed.** 1. to become or make less bright; lose color: *that dress will fade if you wash it in hot water.* 2. to wither or lose strength: *the flowers have faded.* 3. to disappear gradually: *the music faded away.*

Fah·ren·heit ('farənhīt) *adj.* of a temperature scale on which the freezing point of water is set at 32° and the boiling point at 212°. Compare CELSIUS.

fail (fāl) *vb.* 1. to be unsuccessful in an attempt. 2. to stop working properly: *the radio has failed.* 3. to disappoint or be disappointing: *you have failed me.* '**fail·ure** *n.* 1. the action or an instance of failing. 2. a person or thing that fails.

faint (fānt) *adj.* 1. lacking in brightness or loudness; dim; unclear. 2. feeble or weak; lacking strength. —*vb.* to lose consciousness temporarily. —'**faint·ly** *adv.*

fair[1] (feər) *adj.* 1. free from bias; just: *the umpire made a fair decision.* 2. having light-colored skin, hair, etc. 3. attractive; pleasant-looking. 4. of moderate ability or achievement: *she is a fair swimmer.* 5. according to the rules; properly done: *a fair tackle.* 6. (of weather) fine and clear. '**fair·ly** *adv.* 1. justly: *Mother divided the candy fairly between the children.* 2. without cheating; legitimately: *he won fairly.* 3. moderately: *it was a fairly good game but it was not as exciting as usual.*

fair[2] (feər) *n.* 1. a temporary show with amusements, exhibits, contests, etc. 2. a show, market, or exhibition: *an antique fair.*

fair·y ('feərē) *n.,pl.* **fair·ies.** an imaginary tiny person with magical powers. —*adj.* of or concerning fairies. **fairy tale** 1. a story involving magic and fairies. 2. an invented or imaginary story or account.

faith (fāth) *n.* 1. a belief in something that cannot be proved true: *faith in magic.* 2. confidence or trust: *I have faith in your judgment.* 3. a religion or other belief: *the Christian faith.* **in good faith** honestly and sincerely. **'faith·ful** *adj.* 1. steady, honest, and loyal. 2. sticking closely to the truth; accurate: *he gave a faithful account of the accident.* —**'faith·ful·ly** *adv.*

fake (fāk) *vb.* **fak·ing, faked.** 1. to forge (something) and pass it off as true, real, etc.: *he faked the painting and sold it as a Picasso.* 2. to pretend: *he faked illness to avoid working.* —*n.* a forgery or deliberate deception. —*adj.* false or fraudulent.

fal·con ('falkən, 'fōlkən) *n.* a bird of prey belonging to the hawk family, with a powerful curved beak and hooked claws.

fall·out ('fôlout) *n.* radioactive dust falling onto the surface of the Earth after a nuclear explosion.

false (fôls) *adj.* 1. not true: *he gave a false account of the event.* 2. treacherous or untrustworthy: *a false friend gave away his secret.* 3. not real; artificial: *a false nose.* **'false·hood** *n.* an untruth; lie. **fal·si·fy** ('fôlsəfī) *vb.* **fal·si·fy·ing, fal·si·fied.** to alter (something) in order to deceive: *he falsified evidence so that he would win the case.* —**'false·ly** *adv.* —**'fal·si·ty** *n.*

fal·ter ('fôltər) *vb.* to lose confidence and hesitate for a moment: *the boy faltered as he read out loud.*

fame (fām) *n.* the quality of being widely known by many people; reputation. See also FAMOUS.

fam·il·iar (fə'milyər) *adj.* 1. commonly known; recognizable; not strange: *a familiar face.* 2. relaxed; friendly; informal: *Julie was on familiar terms with her friends' parents.* 3. (+ *with*) having good knowledge of something; well acquainted: *I'm familiar with his books.* —*n.* a close friend. **fa'mil·iar·ize** *vb.* **fa·mil·iar·iz·ing, fa·mil·iar·ized.** (+ *with*) 1. to make acquainted with something. 2. to make (something) well known. —**fa·mil·i·ar·i·ty** (fəmilē'aritē) *n.*

fam·i·ly ('faməlē) *n.,pl.* **fam·i·lies.** 1. a group of people who have a common ancestor or who are related by marriage. 2. any group of related things: *a plant family.*

fam·ine ('famin) *n.* 1. a widespread severe shortage of food, esp. one causing many people to starve to death. 2. an extreme shortage of anything: *a potato famine.*

fa·mous ('fāməs) *adj.* well known; having FAME.

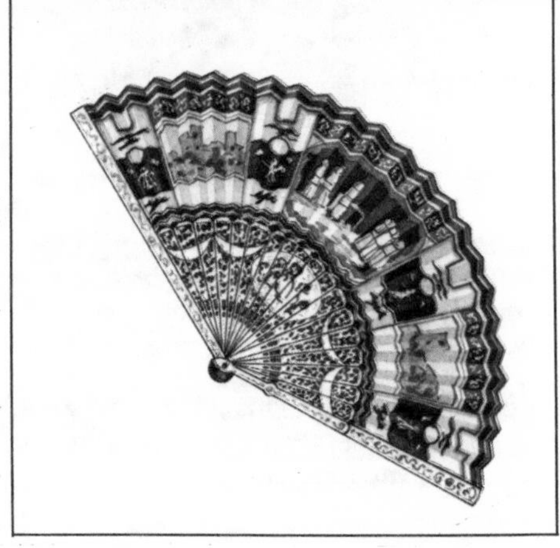

fan

fan[1] (fan) *n.* 1. a flat object of paper, feathers, etc., waved to produce a cooling draft. 2. a mechanical or electrical device with moving blades, used to produce a draft of air. 3. anything resembling a fan in its shape or action, e.g. a peacock's tail. —*vb.* **fan·ning, fanned.** 1. to move with or as if with a fan. 2. to encourage: *people's worries about rising prices were fanned by politicians.* **fan out** to spread out in the shape of a fan.

fan[2] (fan) *n.* a devoted and enthusiastic admirer. **fan club** an organized group of admirers.

fa·nat·ic (fə'natik) *n.* a person who is extremely enthusiastic or dedicated to a cause, pastime, etc. —*adj.* (also **fa·nat·ic·al**) concerning or typical of a fanatic: *he was so fanatical about music that he neglected his other studies.* —**fa'nat·i·cism** *n.*

fan·cy ('fansē) *n.,pl.* **fan·cies.** 1. an idea or impression; one's imagination: *he had a fancy that he was going to win the game.* 2. a desire or interest: *a pretty dress took her fancy.* —*vb.* **fan·cy·ing, fan·cied.** 1. to have an idea or impression; imagine: *I fancy I know that man.* 2. to like; want: *I fancy an apple now and then.* —*adj.* **fan·ci·er, fan·ci·est.** pretty; not plain or ordinary: *Jean wore a very fancy blouse.* —*interj.* an exclamation of surprise. **'fan·ci·ful** *adj.* produced in the imagination; not real: *she told us a fanciful story.*

fang (fang) *n.* any of the long sharp teeth of an animal, such as a wolf or snake.

fan·tas·tic (fan'tastik) *adj.* 1. of or happening in fantasy; unreal: *his story was so fantastic that no one believed it.* 2. (informal) wonderful; excellent. —**fan'tas·ti·cal·ly** *adv.*

fan·ta·sy ('fantəsē) *n.,pl.* **fan·ta·sies.** 1. a very strange or unreal experience, dream, or idea. Also (less common) **phan·ta·sy. 'fan·ta·size** *vb.* **fan·ta·siz·ing, fan·ta·sized.** to make up a dream or fantasy.

fare (feər) *n.* 1. money paid for a journey by bus, taxi, train, etc. 2. a bus or taxi passenger. 3. (old-fashioned) food or drink. —*vb.* **far·ing, fared.** to progress; get on: *I fared badly in the examinations.* **fare'well** *interj., n.* goodbye.

far-fetched (fâr'fecht) *adj.* very difficult to believe and therefore probably untrue: *John gave a rather far-fetched excuse for being late.*

far·ther ('fâdhər) *adv.* at a greater distance; to a greater degree: *the farther you go, the longer it will take you to get back.* —*adj.* more distant: *the farther house on the street is ours.*

fas·ci·nate ('fasənāt) *vb.* **fas·ci·nat·ing, fas·ci·nat·ed.** to attract all or most of the attention or interest of (a person): *he was fascinated by her beautiful eyes.* —**fas·ci'na·tion** *n.*

fash·ion ('fashən) *n.* 1. a style or activity that attracts general interest or enthusiasm for a short period; trend. 2. a way of doing something; manner: *Mark drove in a careless fashion.* —*vb.* to make or produce: *the carpenter fashioned the chair out of wood.*

fast[1] (fast) *adj.* 1. moving or able to move very quickly: *a fast car.* 2. allowing speedy movement: *a fast road.* 3. (of a clock) ahead of the right time. 4. loyal: *a fast friend.* 5. fixed; not easily removed: *fast colors do not run when washed.* 6. firmly stuck: *glue will hold the pieces fast.* —*adv.* 1. at high speed: *don't drive too fast.* 2. firmly; soundly: *fast asleep.*

fast[2] (fast) *n.* a period during which no food is eaten. —*vb.* to take part in a fast; do without food.

fast·en ('fasən) *vb.* to fix or be fixed firmly; hold or be held in place: *they* *fastened a square of carpet to the floor.* **'fast·en·er** *or* **fast·en·ing** *n.* a device used to fasten clothes.

fa·tal ('fātəl) *adj.* causing death; mortal: *a fatal wound.* **fa'tal·i·ty** *n.,pl.* **fa·tal·i·ties.** a person who dies in an accident, battle, etc. —**'fa·tal·ly** *adv.*

fate (fāt) *n.* a power supposed to control people's lives and futures; fortune; destiny. **'fat·ed** *adj.* brought about by fate; not able to be avoided: *it was fated that we should meet.* **'fate·ful** *adj.* decided by fate and usu. having unpleasant results.

fath·om ('fadhəm) *n.* a unit of length, used to measure the depth of the sea, equal to six feet (approximately 1·8 m). —*vb.* to discover the meaning of; get to understand thoroughly: *Barbara tried to fathom the meaning of the puzzle.*

fa·tigue (fə'tēg) *n.* 1. tiredness. 2. (military) a non military chore, e.g. cleaning floors, washing windows, etc. —*vb.* **fa·tigu·ing, fa·tigued.** to make tired.

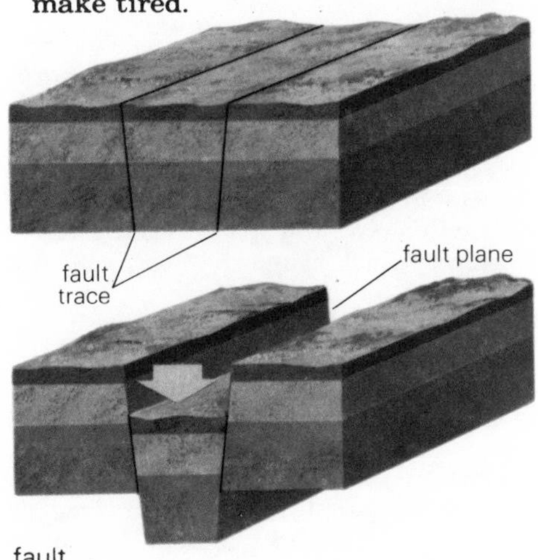

fault

fault (fôlt) *n.* 1. a mistake; error. 2. something that prevents something from being perfect or working properly: *there is a fault in the car's engine.* 3. (geology) a crack in the earth's crust. **at fault** in error; wrong. **find fault with** to criticize; find mistakes. —*vb.* to discover mistakes in: *we could not fault her singing.* —**'fault·y** *adj.* **fault·i·er, fault·i·est.**

fa·vor ('fāvər) *n.* 1. a kind action done to or for someone: *Ed did me a favor by lending me a book.* 2. consideration or special treatment: *she tried to win favor by giving presents.* 3. a badge or ribbon showing the wearer's loyalty to a party, team, etc. —*vb.* to support; show favor to. **'fa·vor·a·ble** *adj.* 1. giving approval: *a favorable report.* 2. good; fine: *favorable weather.* **'fa·vor·ite** *n., adj.* (something) that is liked best of all. —**'fa·vor·a·bly** *adv.*

fawn[1] (fôn) *n.* a young deer. —*adj., n.* (having) a light brown color.

fawn[2] (fôn) *vb.* (usu. + *on*) 1. to act in a slavish way in order to win someone's favor. 2. (of dogs) to show affection for (a human), esp. by wagging the tail, licking, etc.

fear (fēr) *n.* 1. the feeling or state of being afraid. 2. a worry or cause for worry. 3. deep respect or awe, esp. towards God. **for fear of** in order to avoid: *he wouldn't go out for fear of catching a cold.* —*vb.* to show fear of or for.

feast (fēst) *n.* 1. a rich or ceremonial meal, entertainment, etc.; banquet. 2. a special day on which a religious or other event is remembered. —*vb.* 1. to attend a feast or banquet. 2. to dine well or richly: *they feasted on venison.*

feat (fēt) *n.* a great deed or action.

feath·er ('fedhər) *n.* one of the light structures that form the outer covering of birds.

fea·ture ('fēchər) *n.* 1. a distinguishing mark or characteristic; important element: *the features of the man were his honesty and hard-working nature.* 2. often **fea·tures** (*pl.*) part of the face: *he had rugged features.* 3. a special article in a newspaper or magazine. —*vb.* **fea·tur·ing, fea·tured.** 1. to have or show as a feature. 2. to draw attention to (something); make prominent.

fed·er·a·tion (fedə'rāshən) *n.* 1. a group of connected states, societies, etc., organized together. 2. the formation of such a group.

fee (fē) *n.* a payment made to someone for a job or service.

fee·ble ('fēbəl) *adj.* weak; without force: *Steve made a feeble attempt to win the game.* —**'fee·bly** *adv.* —**'fee·ble·ness** *n.*

feed (fēd) *vb.* **feed·ing, fed.** 1. to provide (a person or animal) with food. 2. (+ *on*) to eat: *horses feed on hay.* 3. to supply material to be used: *he fed paper into the machine.* —*n.* food for chickens and other farm animals.

feel (fēl) *vb.* **feel·ing, felt.** 1. to touch, esp. with the hands, or experience: *she felt the sun on her back.* 2. to think; be of the opinion that: *I felt that he was wrong.* —*n.* 1. the impression of something to the touch: *the soft feel of silk.* 2. familiarity: *I don't yet have the feel of this job.* **'feel·er** *n.* a long jointed organ sticking out of an insect's head; antenna. **'feel·ing** *n.* 1. the ability to feel. 2. an emotion or opinion based on emotion.

feet (fēt) *n.* the plural of FOOT.

fe·line ('fēlīn) *adj.* of or like a cat. —*n.* a cat or a member of the cat family.

fel·low ('felō) *n.* 1. (informal) a man: *Paul is a nice fellow.* 2. a companion; friend: *Mark and his fellows went to the ball game.* 3. a senior member or research worker of a college or learned society. —*adj.* being a companion: *one's fellow workers.* **'fel·low·ship** *n.* 1. friendship; companionship. 2. a group or society.

felt[1] (felt) *n.* a material made from wool fibers matted together. —*adj.* made of felt.

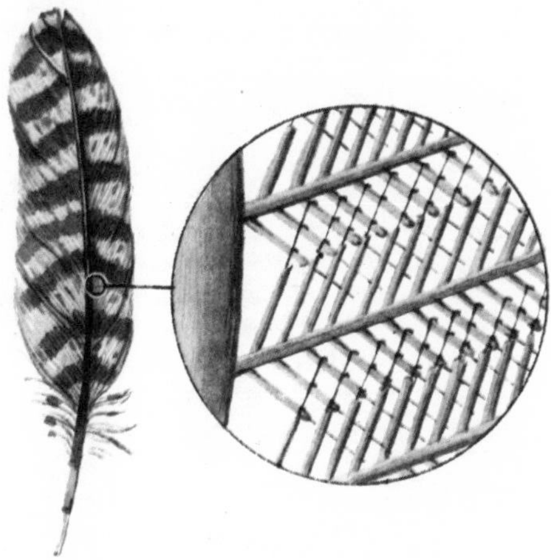
feather

felt[2] (felt) *vb.* the past tense and past participle of FEEL.

fe·male ('fēmāl) *adj.* of or concerning a woman or the sex that corresponds to that of women in animals. —*n.* a female animal.

fem·i·nine ('femənin) *adj.* 1. of, relating to, or suitable for a woman or girl: *feminine clothes.* 2. (grammar) denoting a gender (class of nouns) that concerns women or includes nouns of a specially defined type, e.g. *fiancée* is a feminine noun. —*n.* the feminine gender. **fem·i'nin·i·ty** *n.* the quality of being feminine.

fence[1] (fens) *n.* 1. a wooden or metal framework used for enclosing or dividing an area of land. 2. (informal) a person who buys and sells stolen property. —*vb.* **fenc·ing, fenced** (often + *off*) to separate or surround with a fence.

fence[2] (fens) *vb.* **fenc·ing, fenced.** to fight with swords as a sport.

fern (fûrn) *n.* a green nonflowering plant with large feathery leaves.

fe·ro·cious (fə'rōshəs) *adj.* fierce; aggressive and untamed: *the ferocious lion pounced on its prey.* —**fe'ro·cious·ly** *adv.* —**fe·roc·i·ty** (fə'rositē) *n.*

fer·ret ('ferit) *n.* a small aggressive animal of the weasel family often used to drive rats and rabbits from their holes. —*vb.* 1.to use a ferret in hunting. 2. (often + *out*) (informal) to search out or discover (information, facts, etc.): *George ferreted through the library to find a book.*

fer·ry ('ferē) *n.,pl.* **fer·ries.** a boat, plane, etc., that transports passengers or goods back and forth over a relatively short distance between two places. —*vb.* **fer·ry·ing, fer·ried.** to carry by ferry.

fer·tile ('fûrtəl) *adj.* 1. able to produce plants, fruit etc., easily: *fertile land.* 2. able to have children or young. 3. producing many ideas: *a fertile imagination.* **'fer·ti·lize** *vb.* **fer·ti·liz·ing, fer·ti·lized.** to make fertile. **'fer·ti·liz·er** *n.* a chemical or other substance used to make land fertile. —**fer·ti·li'za·tion** *n.*

fes·ter ('festər) *vb.* 1. (of a sore or wound) to produce pus. 2. to rot or decay. 3. to grow worse, as feelings of bitterness or resentment: *envy of Mike and his wealth festered in Tony's mind.*

fes·ti·val ('festəvəl) *n.* an occasion for public celebration or enjoyment. 2. a series of events or performances: *a music festival.*

fetch (fech) *vb.* 1. to go after and carry back: *David fetched the book from the library.* 2. to be sold for: *the painting fetched 10 000 dollars.*

fete (fāt, fet) *n.* a festival or outdoor entertainment, often one organized to raise money. —*vb.* **fet·ing, feted.** to welcome (an important or popular person) with public celebrations.

feud (fyo͞od) *n.* a bitter and long-standing quarrel between two people or groups. —*vb.* to conduct a feud.

feu·dal ('fyo͞odəl) *adj.* concerning a way of life in the Middle Ages in which people lived and worked on land in return for services given to the overlord who owned the land. —**'feu·dal·ism** *n.*

fe·ver ('fēvər) *n.* 1. an abnormally high body temperature. 2. any of several diseases normally associated with a very high temperature. 3. a state of great excitement or agitation: *Mary was in a fever of excitement on the day before her party.* **'fe·ver·ish** *adj.* 1. infected with or having a fever. 2. greatly excited or restless. —**'fe·ver·ish·ly** *adv.* —**'fe·ver·ish·ness** *n.*

fi·an·cé (fēân'sā) *n.* a man engaged to be married. **fi·an·cée** (feân'sā) *n.* a woman engaged to be married.

fi·as·co (fē'askō) *n.,pl.* **fi·as·cos.** a disastrous or complete failure: *because of the rain the outdoor show was a fiasco.*

fig

fi·ber ('fībər) *n.* 1. a fine thread or a threadlike part or structure. 2. any substance composed of threads. **moral fiber** strength of character; courage.

fi·ber·glass ('fībərglas) *n.* material made of glass that is spun into fibers. It is used in making cloth, and, when bonded by a resin, lightweight car bodies, boat hulls, etc.

fic·tion ('fikshən) *n.* literature produced by the writer's imagination: *novels and short stories are works of fiction.* **fic·ti·tious** (fik'tishəs) *adj.* false; made up.

fid·dle ('fidəl) *n.* (informal) a violin or similar musical instrument. —*vb.* **fid·dling, fid·dled.** (informal) 1. to play a fiddle. 2. (often + *with*) to touch or play with, esp. nervously: *Jean fiddled with her pen before the exam began.* —**'fid·dler** *n.*

fidg·et ('fijit) *vb.* to move about or play with or touch things in a nervous or restless way: *the class fidgeted during a boring lesson.* —*n.* a person who fidgets.

field (fēld) *n.* 1. an enclosed piece of land where crops are grown, animals grazed, etc. 2. an area or district from which a raw industrial material is obtained: *a coal field.* 3. a piece of land used for a special purpose: *a sports field.* 4. a branch of learning, experience, or knowledge: *the field of jazz.* —*vb.* (baseball) to take up a position in the field in order to stop or catch the ball hit by the batter. **'field·er** *n.* a person who fields. **field glasses** binoculars.

fiend (fēnd) *n.* 1. an evil spirit; devil or demon. 2. an evil person. —**'fiend·ish** *adj.* —**'fiend·ish·ly** *adv.*

fierce (fērs) *adj.* 1. aggressive and savage: *a fierce lion.* 2. angry, forceful, or dangerous: *a fierce attack.* —**'fierce·ly** *adv.* —**'fierce·ness** *n.*

fier·y (fīərē) *adj.* **fier·i·er, fier·i·est.** 1. of or resembling fire. 2. easily made angry; quick-tempered.

fig (fig) *n.* a soft pear-shaped fruit produced by a small tree (**fig tree**) growing in warm countries, and eaten fresh or in dried form.

fight (fīt) *n.* 1. a combat between two or more people using their fists or weapons. 2. any battle or hard struggle: *the townspeople fought against the development plan.* —*vb.* **fight·ing, fought.** (often + *with* or *against*) 1. to take part in a fight. 2. to struggle hard.

fig·ur·a·tive ('figyərətiv) *adj.* (of words) not used in a literal sense, e.g. the adjective *cool* used of a person's temperament; metaphorical.

fig·ure ('figyər) *n.* 1. a symbol used to represent anything other than a letter, esp. a number. 2. any geometrical drawing, or a diagram or illustration, as in a book or magazine. 3. a form or shape; the outline of something, esp. a human body: *Kate has a slender figure.* 4. a person, esp.

an important one: *Lincoln was an important figure in American history.* 5. the price of something: *I bought my bookcase at a low figure.* —*vb.* **fig·ur·ing, fig·ured.** 1. to use numbers to find the answer to a problem; calculate. 2. to be portrayed; feature: *his mother figures in most of his paintings.*

fig·ure·head ('figyərhed) *n.* 1. an ornamental figure, such as a statue, placed on the prow of a ship. 2. a person who seems to be in charge of something but has no real responsibility or authority.

fil·a·ment ('filəmənt) *n.* 1. a thin thread. 2. the metal wire that glows brightly in an electric light bulb.

file[1] (fīl) *n.* 1. a folder containing papers arranged in correct order. 2. a cabinet or drawer containing such papers or folders in a particular arrangement. 3. a line of people or things arranged one behind the other (in **single file**). —*vb.* **fil·ing, filed.** 1. to place or arrange in a file. 2. to send in; hand in a report: *he filed a complaint about the service.* 3. to march or walk in a file.

file[2] (fīl) *n.* a tool having an abrasive surface for smoothing or cutting metal, etc. —*vb.* **fil·ing, filed.** to cut or smooth with a file.

fi·let *or* **fil·let** (fi'lā, 'filit) *n.* a lean piece of fish or meat with the bones removed. —*vb.* to remove the bones from (a piece of fish or meat).

film (film) *n.* 1. a thin coating of anything: *a film of oil on water.* 2. a thin sheet of any material. 3. a roll of material coated with a light-sensitive chemical and used in photography. 4. a moving picture on a cinema screen. —*vb.* 1. to cover with a film. 2. to make a motion picture of.

fil·ter ('filtər) *n.* 1. a device for removing solid material from a liquid by allowing only the liquid to pass through. 2. a device used on a camera that allows only a certain color light to reach the film. —*vb.* 1. to pass through a filter. 2. (often + *out*) to remove with a filter. 3. (+ *through* or *down*) to move or come gradually: *news of the accident slowly filtered through to the town.*

filth (filth) *n.* 1. unpleasant dirt. 2. something disagreeable or disgusting. —**'filth·y** *adj.* **filth·i·er, filth·i·est.**

fin (fin) *n.* any of the parts projecting from the body of a fish, dolphin, whale, etc., or similar artificial devices on ships or aircraft, which are used to control movement.

fi·nal ('fīnəl) *adj.* 1. coming at or marking the end of something; last. 2. conclusive; not to be questioned or changed: *the referee's decision is final.* —*n.* the last game in a competition played to decide the overall winner. **'fi·nal·ize** *vb.* **fi·nal·iz·ing, fi·nal·ized.** to make the final arrangements for something; complete: *the plan was finalized and work began.* —**fi·nal·i·ty** (fī'nalitē) *n.* —**'fi·nal·ly** *adv.*

fi·nance ('fīnans, fi'nans) *n.* 1. the handling of money in business or other public matters. 2. often **fi·nanc·es** (*pl.*) the money required or used for something. —*vb.* **fi·nanc·ing, fi·nanced.** to provide money for (a plan, scheme, business, etc.): *Carol's uncle financed her music lessons.* **fi·nan·cial** (fi'nanshəl) *adj.* concerning money. **fin·an·cier** (finən'sēr, fīnan'sēr) *n.* a person concerned with money or its management.

fine[1] (fīn) *adj.* 1. excellent; very good: *he painted a fine picture.* 2. delicate or thin; easily broken or damaged: *the web was made of fine thread.* 3. made up of small particles: *a fine powder.* —*adv.* very well: *Tim gets on fine with his new team.* **'fin·er·y** *n.* decorative rich-looking clothes, jewels, etc.

fine[2] (fīn) *n.* a sum of money that a court of law or other authority compels a person to pay as a punishment for an offense. —*vb.* **fin·ing, fined.** to punish (someone) by making him pay a sum of money.

fin·ger ('finggər) *n.* 1. any of the flexible jointed parts of the hand joined to the palm opposite the thumb. 2. anything resembling a finger in shape or function: *Baja California is a finger of land projecting into the Pacific.* —*vb.* 1. to touch or handle (something) with fingers: *she fingered her hair when she was nervous.* **'fin·ger·print** *n.* the impression left on an object by the pattern of ridges on the tips of the fingers and thumb. —*vb.* to take the fingerprints of.

fin·ish ('finish) *vb.* **fin·ish·ing, fin·ished.** 1. (sometimes + *off* or *up*) to bring or come to an end: *we finished the job and had nothing to do.* 2. (+ *with*) to have no further need of: *I've finished with the bathroom.* —*n.* 1. a polished surface: *a smooth finish.* 2. an end or point at which something ends.

fiord *or* **fjord** (fyôrd) *n.* a long channel of the sea stretching far inland, esp. in Norway.

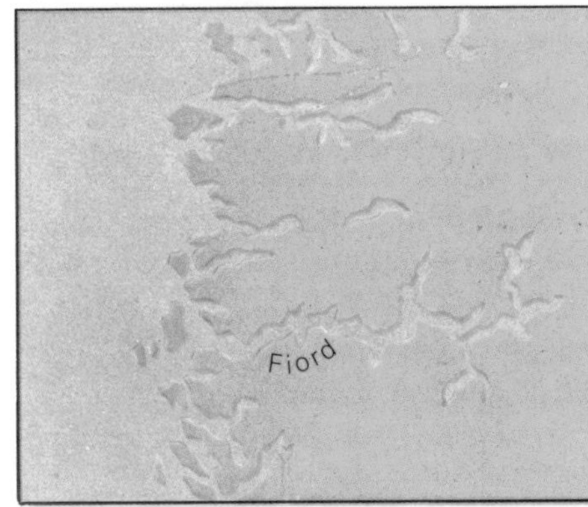

fiord

fir (fûr) *n.* 1. a cone-bearing evergreen tree. 2. the wood of this tree.

fire (fīər) *n.* 1. heat, light, flames, and smoke produced by burning. 2. fuel that is set burning for warmth. 3. shooting with guns: *they heard the fire of cannon in the distance.* 4. enthusiasm or passion. —*vb.* **fir·ing, fired.** 1. to shoot (a gun). 2. to set burning. 3. to fill with enthusiasm, passion, etc.: *the leader's speech fired them with enthusiasm.* 4. (slang) to dismiss (someone) from a job: *he was fired for constantly being late.*

fire·work ('fīərwûrk) *n.* a cardboard container filled with gunpowder and other chemicals, that makes a loud bang or displays brightly colored lights when burnt.

firm[1] (fûrm) *adj.* 1. strong; hard: *the teacher was firm in punishing the class.* 2. fixed, not easily moved. **stand firm** to stand still and not yield or retreat.

firm[2] (fûrm) *n.* a business or company.

first (fûrst) *adj., adv.* before everyone or everything else: *Christopher was first in the class.* —*n.* a person or thing that is first: *this car was the first of its kind.* **first aid** emergency treatment or care given to an injured person.

fish (fish) *n.,pl.* **fish·es** *or* **fish.** any of numerous types of animal living in seas or rivers, swimming by means of fins, and breathing through gills. —*vb.* to catch fish. **'fish·er·man** *n.,pl.* **fish·er·men.** a man who catches fish, esp. for a living.

fist (fist) *n.* the hand with the fingers closed tightly upon the palm.

fit[1] (fit) *adj.* **fit·ter, fit·test.** 1. suitable; appropriate: *the dinner is not fit to eat.* 2. strong and healthy. —*vb.* **fit·ting, fit·ted.** 1. to be suitable for: *he does not fit the job at all.* 2. to be the right size for: *this coat fits me perfectly.* 3. to put into place or position: *he fitted a new window in the bedroom.* **'fit·ter** *n.* 1. a mechanic who fits machine parts or equipment together. 2. a person who fits clothes on people at a shop.

fit[2] (fit) *n.* 1. a sudden attack of illness, often connected with uncontrollable movements of the body. 2. a sudden attack of anything: *a fit of coughing.* **'fit·ful** *adj.* with many interruptions: *she had a very fitful night's sleep.* —**'fit·ful·ly** *adv.*

fix (fiks) *vb.* 1. to place firmly in position; stick or fasten: *Willy fixed the shelves to the wall.* 2. (sometimes + *up*) to arrange; settle: *to fix the date for a meeting.* 3. to mend; repair: *he fixed the broken chair.* 4. to make (a color on cloth) stable; prevent from fading. 5. (slang) to arrange, dishonestly, as by bribery: *the race was fixed so that the favorite horse won.* —*n.* (informal) a difficult situation: *James was in a fix when his car broke down.* **fixed** *adj.* 1. sure; certain. 2. immovable: *the picture was in a fixed position and could not be moved.* **'fix·ture** *n.* 1. an item of equipment fixed or fitted, e.g. to a wall. 2. a traditional event, esp. one recurring regularly on the same date.

flab·by ('flabē) *adj.* **flab·bi·er, flab·bi·est.** 1. soft or limp to the touch; not firm: *he has flabby muscles from lack of exercise.* —**'flab·bi·ly** *adv.* —**'flab·bi·ness** *n.*

flags

flag[1] (flag) *n.* a piece of cloth bearing a design and used as a symbol, signal, decoration, etc. —*vb.* **flag·ging, flagged.** 1. to decorate, signal, warn, communicate, etc., with or as if with a flag. 2. (usu. + *down*) to wave to (a passing car, train, etc.) in order to make it stop.

flag[2] (flag) *vb.* **flag·ging, flagged.** to hang loosely; lose vigor; weaken: *his spirits flagged toward the end of the game.*

flair (fleər) *n.* natural talent or ability: *she had a flair for cooking.*

flake (flāk) *n.* a small thin piece of something, often a piece broken off; chip: *a flake of stone.* —*vb.* **flak·ing, flaked.** 1. (often + *off*) to peel off in tiny flakes: *the sun caused the paint to flake from the door.* 2. to form into flakes. —**'flak·y** *adj.* **flak·i·er, flak·i·est.**

flam·boy·ant (flam'boiənt) *adj.* outrageously bold or brilliant; showy; striking: *he was noticeable because of his extremely flamboyant clothes and manner.* **flam'boy·ance** *n.* the quality or state of being flamboyant. —**flam'boy·ant·ly** *adv.*

flame (flām) *n.* 1. a flickering light or glow produced when something burns. 2. anything like a flame in brilliance or intensity: *the sunset was a flame of color.* **in flames** ablaze. —*vb.* **flam·ing, flamed.** 1. to burn or glow with flames; blaze. 2. to burn or glow with strong emotion: *his eyes flamed with sudden anger.* **flam·ma·ble** ('flaməbəl) *adj.* easily set alight.

fla·min·go (flə'miṅggō) *n.,pl.* **fla·min·gos** *or* **fla·min·goes.** a long-legged wading bird with a long neck and usu. pale pink feathers.

flank (flaṅgk) *n.* 1. the fleshy sides of the body between the hips and the ribs. 2. the side of anything. 3. the right- or left-hand side of an army or group of soldiers. —*vb.* 1. to place or be located at the side of. 2. to attack or menace (an army, etc.) at its flank. 3. to protect or guard on the flanks.

flan·nel ('flanəl) *n.* a warm loosely-woven cloth of wool or wool blended with some other material. —*vb.* 1. to rub with flannel. 2. to cover or clothe with flannel.

flap (flap) *vb.* **flap·ping, flapped.** 1. to flutter or cause to flutter, esp. making a noise; wave: *the sail flapped in the breeze.* 2. to wave or move up and down: *the bird flapped its wings.* 3. (informal) to panic. —*n.* 1. any broad flat part that hangs loosely attached by one side only: *the flap of an envelope.* 2. the movement or noise made by something flapping: *we heard the flap of the bird's wings.* 3. (informal) a state of distress, emergency, or panic: *Margaret was in a flap about her homework.*

flare (fleər) *vb.* **flar·ing, flared.** 1. to burn very brightly; blaze. 2. to burst into activity, anger, etc: *he flared up when he was disobeyed.* 3. to spread outwards or widen: *her skirt flared at the hem.* —*n.* 1. a flickering flame or a sudden bright burst of light: *the rocket made a bright flare in the sky.* 2. such a light or a device producing it used as a distress signal, warning, etc. 3. a sudden violent outburst: *a flare of anger.* 4. a curve outward: *the flare of a trumpet.*

flash (flash) *n.* 1. a sudden bright flare of light lasting for only a moment: *a flash of lightning.* 2. a brief item of news. 3. a moment; instant: *he did it in a flash.* —*vb.* 1. to give out a flash: *the neon lights flashed all night.* 2. to pass before or into one's sight or mind very suddenly or quickly: *the racing car flashed past.* 3. (often + *around*) (informal) to display; show: *he flashed his money around.* —*adj.* (informal) showy or gaudy. **'flash·y** *adj.* **flash·i·er, flash·i·est.** 1. gaudy; showy. 2. sparkling or twinkling. —**'flash·i·ly** *adv.* —'flash·i·ness *n.*

flash·bulb ('flashbulb) *n.* a small glass bulb used in photography to light up the subject by a bright flash of light.

flash·light ('flashlīt) *n.* 1. a small portable electric light powered by batteries. 2. a light with a flashbulb used in photography.

flask (flask) *n.* a container made of metal, glass, etc. for liquids.

flat[1] (flat) *adj.* **flat·ter, flat·test.** 1. even; level; smooth. 2. spread out or levelled: *Angela lay flat on the grass sunbathing.* 3. absolute; complete: *a flat refusal.* 4. (of a tire) deflated by damage or wear. 5. (of effervescent drinks) having lost its sparkle. 6. (of a note) lowered from its ordinary pitch by an interval of a semitone. 7. out of tune by being too low in pitch. —*adv.* 1. in or into a horizontal position: *he fell down flat.* 2. (informal) completely; absolutely: *I'm flat broke.* 3. exactly: *she finished in ten minutes flat.* **flat out** at maximum speed or effort. —*n.* 1. a flat object, surface, part, etc.: *the flat of his hand.* 2. low-lying land, esp. a marsh. 3. a deflated tire. 4. (music) a note that is flat. **'flat·ten** *vb.* to make or become flat.

flask

flat[2] (flat) *n.* an apartment, usu. on one floor only.

flat·ter ('flatər) *vb.* 1. to praise or compliment, esp. insincerely. 2. to suit or show to advantage: *pink flatters you.* 3. to persuade (oneself) of something: *he flattered himself that he would get the job.* —**'flat·ter·y** *n.*

fla·vor ('flāvər) *n.* 1. the special taste of something. 2. a special characteristic: *the song had a nautical flavor.* —*vb.* to give a flavor to.

flea (flē) *n.* a small wingless bloodsucking animal living on the bodies of animals and sometimes humans.

fleck (flek) *n.* a spot or mark; speck: *a fleck of paint.* —*vb.* to mark with a fleck or flecks; speckle.

fled (fled) *vb.* the past tense and past participle of FLEE.

flee (flē) *vb.* **flee·ing, fled.** to run away from (danger, a threat, etc.); take flight from: *the animals fled the burning forest.*

fleece (flēs) *n.* the coat of wool covering a sheep or similar animal. —*vb.* **fleec·ing, fleeced.** 1. to shear the wool from (a sheep). 2. (informal) to rob by cheating; swindle.

fleet[1] (flēt) *adj.* rapid or swift.

fleet[2] (flēt) *n.* 1. the entire navy of a country or all the ships under a single command. 2. a number of ships, cars, etc., under a single ownership: *a fleet of taxis.*

fleet·ing ('flēting) *adj.* passing very quickly: *I had only a fleeting glimpse of the man.* —**fleet·ing·ly** *adv.*

flesh (flesh) *n.* 1. the soft tissues that cover the bones of an animal, consisting mainly of muscle and fat. 2. the meat of animals used as food. 3. the soft inner part of fruit and vegetables. —**'flesh·y** *adj.* **flesh·i·er, flesh·i·est.**

flew (flo͞o) *vb.* the past tense of FLY[1].

flex (fleks) *vb.* to bend: *he flexed his arm before lifting the weight.* **'flex·i·ble** *adj.* 1. able to be bent without breaking. 2. willing to adapt: *he was flexible enough to try any job.* 3. able to be modified or changed; able to be used for a number of applications. —**flex·i'bil·i·ty** *n.* —**'flex·i·bly** *adv.*

flick (flik) *vb.* to strike lightly and quickly, as in moving or removing something: *to flick a speck of dust from clothing.* —*n.* a light sudden movement.

flick·er[1] ('flikər) *vb.* 1. to burn with or give out an irregular wavering light: *the candle flickered in the drafty corridor.* 2. to make or cause brief fluttering movements. —*n.* 1. an unsteady flame or light. 2. a brief display of movement or emotion: *a flicker of hope.*

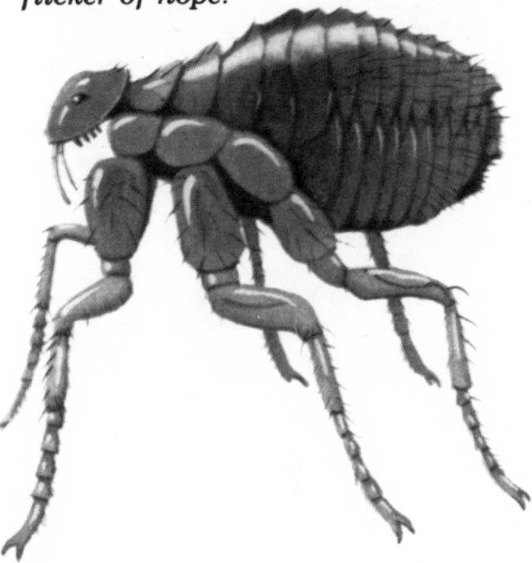
flea

flick·er[2] ('flikər) *n.* a North American woodpecker with yellow wing and tail markings.

flight (flīt) *n.* 1. the motion, power, or act of flying. 2. a journey by airplane or spacecraft: *we had a pleasant flight from New York.* 3. the act of fleeing; running away; escaping: *the flight of the defeated army.* 4. a series of steps or stairs between two landings. 5. the feathers on an arrow or dart that make it fly straight.

flim·sy ('flimzē) *adj.* **flim·si·er, flim·si·est.** 1. (of materials) thin; delicate; lacking strength: *she wore a flimsy dress and was cold.* 2. weak and insubstantial: *Robert gave a flimsy excuse for his lateness.* —**'flim·si·ly** *adv.* —**'flim·si·ness** *n.*

flinch (flinch) *vb.* to draw back in pain or fear: *Tim flinched as the ball flew past his ear.* —*n.* the act of flinching.

fling (fling) *vb.* **fling·ing, flung.** 1. to throw or hurl (something) violently: *he flung the money on the floor.* 2. to absorb oneself in some activity enthusiastically and wholeheartedly: *she flung herself into her work.* —*n.* 1. an energetic or violent movement. 2. (also **Highland fling**) a vigorous Scottish dance.

flint (flint) *n.* 1. a type of hard dark gray stone. 2. a hard material in a cigarette lighter that produces a hot spark when struck by steel.

flip·per ('flipər) *n.* 1. a broad flat limb of some animals such as seals, penguins, etc., adapted for swimming. 2. one of a pair of broad flat pieces of of rubber worn on the feet by swimmers, divers, etc.

flit (flit) *vb.* **flit·ting, flit·ted.** to move rapidly from one object or place to another; dart: *bees flit from flower to flower.* —*n.* a light rapid movement.

float (flōt) *vb.* 1. to move along on or be supported by a liquid or gas: *the petals floated away on the breeze.* 2. to cause to float: *the children floated the raft down stream.* —*n.* 1. a floating piece of cork, plastic, etc., used by fishermen to indicate a bite. 2. a platform for swimmers that floats on the water; raft. 3. a decorated vehicle used in a procession.

flock (flok) *n.* a collection of animals of one type, as sheep, goats, or birds. —*vb.* to move in a crowd: *the people flocked into the street to see the President.*

floodlight

flog (flog) *vb.* **flog·ging, flogged.** to punish (someone) by beating; cane or whip: *the cruel man flogged the old horse to make her move faster.*

flood (flud) *n.* 1. an overflow of water covering a large area of normally dry land after severe rain, etc. 2. a large amount of anything: *a flood of letters.* —*vb.* to cause (dry land) to be covered with water: *the bursting of the dam flooded the farmland around it.*

flood·light ('fludlīt) *n.* a powerful light used at night to light up buildings, sports events, etc. —*vb.* **flood·light·ing, flood·lit.** to light with a floodlight.

floor (flôr) *n.* the part of a building or room upon which people walk. —*vb.* to knock (someone) down: *she floored him with a blow on the jaw.*

flop (flop) *vb.* **flop·ping, flopped.** 1. to fall untidily or without control: *he flopped into his seat.* 2. to fail: *the show flopped after one performance.* —*n.* 1. the action or an instance of of flopping. 2. a failure, esp. in the theater.

floun·der[1] ('floundər) *vb.* to struggle awkwardly or helplessly; be in, or move with, difficulty: *Ann floundered in the water when it was too deep.*

floun·der[2] ('floundər) *n.* a common flatfish, used for food.

flour ('flouər) *n.* powdered wheat or similar cereal used for making bread, pastry, etc.

flour·ish ('flûrish, 'flurish) —*vb.* 1. to grow or live; thrive: *the plants flourished in the warm room.* 2. to make large gestures with; wave: *he flourished his handkerchief.* —*n.* 1. a large gesture; wave. 2. a curve or bold stroke, e.g. in handwriting or painting.

flow (flō) *vb.* 1. (of liquid) to move along; run down under the influence of gravity. 2. to move like a liquid: *time flows along.* —*n.* the movement of a liquid.

flow·er ('flouər) *n.* a part in some plants that contains the reproductive organs and often has colored petals; a bloom or blossom. —*vb.* to produce flowers.

flown (flōn) *vb.* the past participle of FLY[1].

flu (flo͞o) *n.* See INFLUENZA.

flu·ent ('flo͞oənt) *adj.* 1. able or competent in a foreign language: *she is fluent in French.* 2. flowing writing or speech; not hesitant or clumsy: *the senator was a fluent speaker.* —'**flu·en·cy** *n.* —'**flu·ent·ly** *adv.*

fluff (fluf) *n.* small bits of fiber, etc., that stick to cloth, esp. wool, collect in pockets, etc. —*vb.* (informal) to fail at; make a mess of: *the actor fluffed his lines.*

flu·id ('flo͞oid) *n.* a substance with no definite shape that is capable of flowing; a liquid or gas. —*adj.* 1. of or like a fluid; not solid. 2. (of arrangements or plans) not settled; easily changed: *my timetable is fluid enough for me to see you.* 3. easily flowing; fluent. —**flu'id·i·ty** *n.*

flung (flung) *vb.* the past tense and past participle of FLING.

flush (flush) *vb.* 1. to go red in the face as a result of some emotion; blush: *he flushed with pride.* 2. to drive away or make clean with a powerful flow of water. 3. (often + *out*) to force (a hunted animal) out of hiding: *they flushed the fox from its den.* —*n.* 1. a blush; redness of complexion. 2. a rushing flow, e.g. of water. —*adj.* 1. rich; wealthy; having money in plenty. 2. level or even: *tell the workmen to make sure that the door is flush with the wall.*

flute (flo͞ot) *n.* 1. a tubular musical wind instrument usu. equipped with keys, and with the mouth-hole in the side. 2. any sort of whistle.

flute

flowers

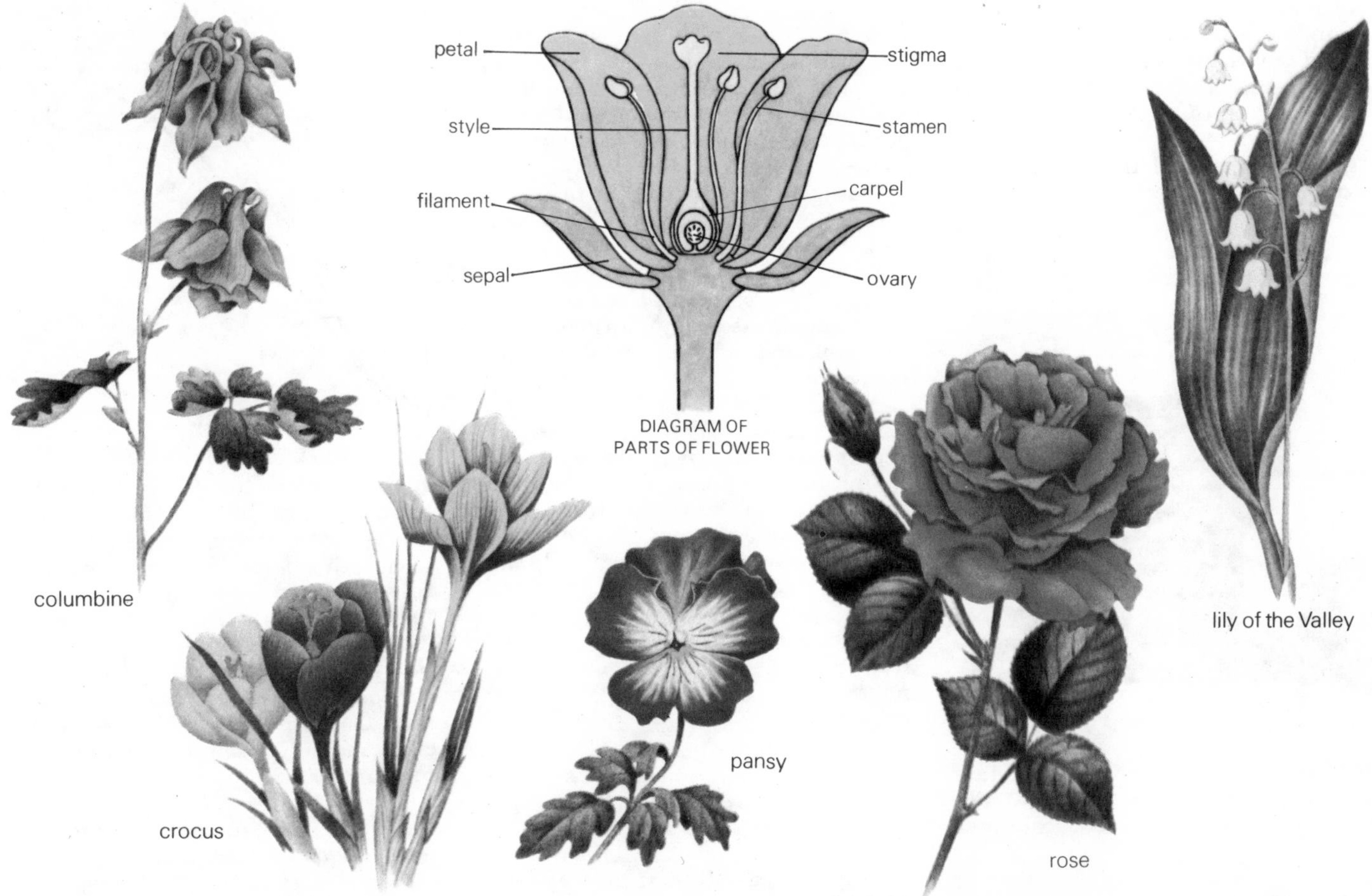

petal
style
filament
sepal
stigma
stamen
carpel
ovary
DIAGRAM OF PARTS OF FLOWER

columbine
crocus
pansy
rose
lily of the Valley

flut·ter ('flutər) *vb.* to move or flap quickly and lightly: *she fluttered her eyelashes shyly.* —*n.* 1. any light quick movement. 2. excitement or confusion: *a flutter of activity.* 3. (informal) a small bet on a horserace.

fly[1] (flī) *vb.* **fly·ing, flew, flown.** 1. to move through the air without touching the ground. 2. to control (an airplane) in flight. 3. to move quickly; rush. '**fli·er** *or* '**fly·er** *n.* an aircraft pilot.

fly[2] (flī) *n.,pl.* **flies.** 1. a common winged insect; housefly. 2. a lure of feathers and wire used as a bait in fishing.

foal (fōl) *n.* a newly born horse, mule, etc. —*vb.* to give birth to a foal.

foam (fōm) *n.* a large quantity of tiny bubbles produced on the surface of a liquid; froth. —*vb.* to produce foam: *the river foamed at the rapids.*

fo·cus ('fōkəs) *n.,pl.* **fo·cus·es** *or* **fo·ci.** 1. the point at which rays of light meet after passing through a lens or being reflected from a specially shaped mirror. 2. the central point or figure in something. —*vb.* 1. to bring to a focus. 2. to concentrate on. '**fo·cal** *adj.*

fog (fog) *n.* 1. a thick mist or cloud at low level occurring when a layer of hot moist air meets a layer of cold. 2. any mist or something that seems like a fog. —'**fog·gy** *adj.*

foil[1] (foil) *n.* 1. thin flexible material made of rolled and hammered metal. 2. a person or thing serving by contrast to make another person or thing appear good, clever, etc.: *the man in the audience was a perfect foil for the comedian.*

foil[2] (foil) *vb.* to prevent (someone) from achieving his aim; thwart: *bad weather foiled his attempt to climb the mountain.*

foil[3] (foil) *n.* a thin light flexible sword with a button on its point.

fold[1] (fōld) *vb.* to bend (paper, cloth, etc.) with one side overlapping the other. —*n.* a crease produced by folding.

fold[2] (fōld) *n.* a fenced enclosure for holding sheep.

fo·li·age ('fōlēij) *n.* the leaves of trees and other plants.

folk (fōk) *n.,pl.* **folk** *or* **folks.** 1. people in general, often those belonging to one tribe or area. 2. **folks** (*pl.*) (informal) one's parents or relatives. —*adj.* of or concerning the common people: *folk music.*

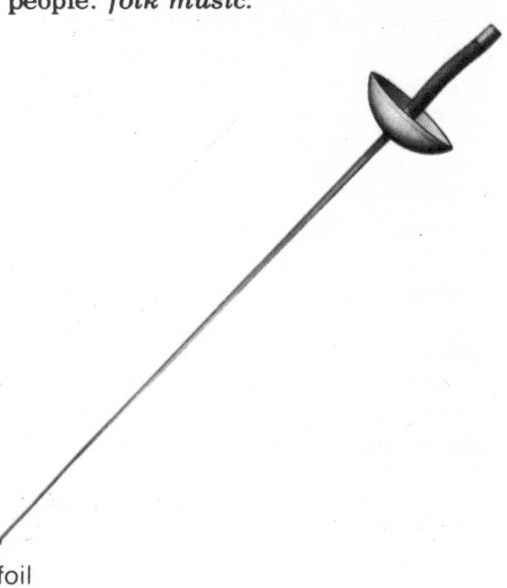
foil

fol·low ('folō) *vb.* 1. to go or come after (a person or thing) in space or time. 2. to understand; comprehend: *Dick followed the teacher's lecture.* 3. to act in agreement with: *to follow advice.* 4. to be interested in. —**'fol·low·er** *n.*

font (font) *n.* a basin in a church filled with water for baptisms.

font

fool (fo͞ol) *n.* a person who acts stupidly or absurdly; idiot. —**'fool·ish** *adj.* —**'fool·ish·ly** *adv.* —**'fool·ish·ness** *n.*

fool·proof ('fo͞olpro͞of) *adj.* totally reliable; unable to go wrong.

foot (fo͝ot) *n.,pl.* **feet.** 1. the part of the body at the bottom of the leg upon which a person or animal walks. 2. the base or lowest point of anything: *the foot of the mountain.* 3. a unit of length equal to 12 inches (30·5 cm) or one third of a yard.

foot·ball ('fo͝otbôl) *n.* 1. a game played on a field 160 feet wide and 360 feet long between two teams of eleven players each who try to kick or carry the ball into the goal area of their opponents. 3. the inflated, pigskin-covered ball used in this game, made as a long pointed oval.

foot·light ('fo͝otlīt) *n.* one of the row of lights at a front of the stage.

for·bid (fər'bid) *vb.* **for·bid·ding, for·bade** *or* **for·bad, for·bid·den.** to order (someone) not to do something; prevent (an action) by an explicit order: *she forbade her son to stay out late at night.* **for'bid·ding** *adj.* producing fear or worry.

force (fôrs) *n.* 1. strength or power: *the police used force to open the door.* 2. an organized group of people: *the police force.* 3. (physics) the influence on an object that causes it to move, change its motion, or stop. —*vb.* **forc·ing, forced.** 1. to use strength on. 2. to compel (someone) to do something: *his father forced him to do his homework before going out.* 3. to produce unnaturally rapid growth in (a plant). —**'force·ful** *adj.* —**'force·ful·ly** *adv.* —**'force·ful·ness** *n.*

for·ceps ('fôrseps) *n.,pl.* **for·ceps.** an instrument used by surgeons for grasping and holding, esp. during an operation.

fore·cast ('fôrkast) *n.* a statement or report about what is likely to happen in the future; prediction: *a weather forecast.* —*vb.* **fore·cast·ing, fore·cast.** to made a forecast; predict: *the man forecast that the game would end in a tie.*

fore·ground ('fôrground) *n.* the front part of a scene; the part that is nearest the observer. Compare BACKGROUND.

fore·head ('fôrid, 'forid) *n.* the front of the head; the part of the face between the eyebrows and the hair.

for·eign ('fôrin, 'forin) *adj.* coming from abroad; not native to the country in which it is found. **'for·eign·er** *n.* a foreign person.

fore·man ('fôrmən) *n.,pl.* **fore·men.** 1. a person in charge of a group of workers at a factory, building site, etc. 2. the man who speaks on behalf of a jury in a legal case.

fore·see (fôr'sē) *vb.* **fore·see·ing, fore·saw, fore·seen.** to see beforehand that something will happen; prophesy or predict. **'fore·sight** *n.* the ability to foresee future events.

for·est ('fôrist, 'forist) *n.* a large collection of trees; woodland or jungle. **'for·est·er** *n.* an official responsible for the management and protection of woodland. **'for·est·ry** *n.* forest management and protection.

for·feit ('fôrfit) *n.* something given up as a penalty: *Ben lost the game and had to give his bag of candy as a forfeit.* —*vb.* to loose something as a punishment, esp. according to rules or a law: *he forfeited his turn in the game because he cheated.* —*adj.* lost or taken away as a punishment: *the traitor's lands will be forfeit.*

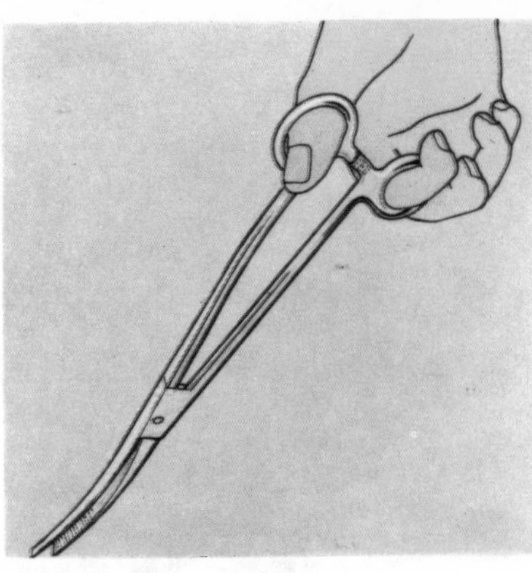
forceps

forge[1] (fôrj) *n.* 1. a furnace used for heating metal objects ready to be beaten into shape. 2. a workshop where this is done. —*vb.* **forg·ing, forged.** 1. to make on a forge: *he forged the horses shoes.* 2. to make or imitate (something) with the intention of deceiving someone: *he forged rare paintings and sold them as originals.* **'for·ger·y** *n.,pl.* **for·ger·ies.** the crime of making something to deceive someone.

forge[2] (fôrj) *vb.* **forg·ing, forged.** to move ahead in a determined way: *the explorer forged his way through the jungle.*

for·get (fər'get) *vb.* **for·get·ting, for·got, for·got·ten.** (often + *about*) to put out of one's memory, usu. unintentionally; fail to remember: *she soon forgot about the accident.* —**for·get·ful** *adj.*

for·give (fər'giv) *vb.* **for·giv·ing, for·gave, for·giv·en.** to pardon (someone who has done wrong): *Alice forgave her sister's lateness.* —**for'give·ness** *n.*

fork (fôrk) *n.* 1. an instrument with two or more pointed parts (tines) used in eating, serving, holding, etc., solid food. 2. a larger similar-shaped instrument used for turning over soil in a garden. 3. a point at which a road or path divides into two. —*vb.* to divide into two: *the road forked and we didn't know which way to choose.*

form (fôrm) *n.* 1. shape or a shape; outline: *the form of the tree stood on the skyline.* 2. a type or kind: *a duck is a form of bird.* 3. a way of doing things; accepted custom: *it is not good form to be rude.* 4. an official paper with spaces to be filled in by a person: *an application form.* 5. the performance or ability of a racehorse, athlete, or other type of competitor: *the horse's past form is excellent.* —*vb.* to produce or be produced: *the model was formed from clay.* **for'ma·tion** *n.* 1. the process or an instance of forming. 2. a shape or arrangement: *the aircraft flew in close formation.* **'form·a·tive** *adj.* of or during the time when something, esp. a person's character, is being formed.

form·al ('fôrməl) *adj.* done in the correct, approved, or official manner. **for'mal·i·ty** *n.,pl.* **for·mal·i·ties.** 1. the state of being formal. 2. a formal or official process, custom, or method.

for·mer ('fôrmər) *adj.* 1. concerning or belonging to an earlier time; previous. 2. the first of two things or people previously mentioned. Compare LATTER. —**'for·mer·ly** *adv.*

for·sake (fər'sāk) *vb.* **for·sak·ing, for·sook, for·sak·en.** to leave, give up, or abandon: *he forsook his family and left home.*

fort (fôrt) *n.* a building defended against enemy attacks; fortress.

forth·right ('fôrthrīt) *adj.* bold and frank in speech.

for·ti·fy ('fôrtəfī) *vb.* **for·ti·fy·ing, for·ti·fied.** 1. to build a protective wall, ditch, etc., around (a place) so it can be defended: *they fortified the top of the hill.* 2. to build up (someone's strength, spirits, or reputation): *the hot meal in camp fortified the climbers.* **for·ti·fi'ca·tion** *n.* 1. the act of fortifying a place. 2. usu. **for·ti·fi·ca·tions** (*pl.*) walls, ditches, etc., built for defense.

for·tress ('fôrtris) *n.* a strongly defended building; fort.

for·tune ('fôrchən) *n.* 1. luck or chance affecting the events of a person's life: *it was good fortune that he left before the storm.* 2. a large amount of money: *he made a fortune as a writer.* **'for·tu·nate** *adj.* lucky; having or causing good fortune. —**'for·tu·nate·ly** *adv.*

for·ward ('fôrwərd) *adj.* 1. moving toward, facing, or situated at the front. 2. bold, esp. too bold: *Edward is very forward with his elders.* **'for·ward** *or* **'for·wards** *adv.* in the direction of the front; ahead: *the car moved forward.*

fos·sil ('fosəl) *n.* the remains or trace of an ancient animal or plant, as a skeleton, footprint, etc. **'fos·sil·ize** *vb.* **fos·sil·iz·ing, fos·sil·ized.** to make into a fossil.

fos·ter ('fôstər, 'fostər) *vb.* 1. to help to grow or develop: *Julie's mother fostered her interest in dancing.* 2. to care in one's own home for (a child from another family). —*adj.* concerning, related by, or used for the process of fostering: *foster parents.*

fought (fôt) *vb.* the past tense and past participle of FIGHT.

foul (foul) *adj.* 1. filthy; dirty; polluted: *the effluent from the factories made the water foul.* 2. morally intolerable; disgusting: *a foul crime.* —*n.* (sport) a move, stroke, etc., that breaks the rules. —**'foul·ly** *adv.* —**'foul·ness** *n.*

found[1] (found) *vb.* the past tense of FIND.

fort

found[2] (found) *vb.* 1. to establish; bring into being. 2. to base: *the story was founded on fact.* **foun'da·tion** *n.* 1. the act of founding. 2. usu. **foun·da·tions** (*pl.*) the base of a building.

fowl (foul) *n.,pl.* **fowl** *or* **fowls.** any bird, esp. a domestic one, e.g. a chicken, turkey, or goose.

fox

fox (foks) *n.* 1. a bushy-tailed, doglike, reddish-brown animal hunted for sport. 2. a cunning person. —*vb.* to deceive; baffle: *the problem foxed him for a long time.*

foy·er ('foiər, 'foiā) *n.* 1. the lobby of a large public building, esp. a theater or hotel. 2. the entrance hall of a house or apartment.

frac·tion ('frakshən) *n.* 1. any quantity that is not a whole number, e.g. a half or a quarter. 2. a small part of a whole.

frac·ture ('frakchər) *n.* a break, esp. a break in a bone. —*vb.* **frac·tur·ing, frac·tured.** to break (a bone).

frag·ile ('frajəl) *adj.* easily broken or damaged; delicate: *that glass is fragile.* —**fra·gil·i·ty** (frə'jilitē) *n.*

frag·ment ('fragmənt) *n.* a small piece broken off or separated from the whole object: *after the explosion there were fragments of glass all over the road.* —'**frag·ment·ar·y** *adj.*

fra·grant ('frāgrənt) *adj.* having or producing a pleasant smell; scented. —'**fra·grance** *n.* —'**fra·grant·ly** *adv.*

frail (frāl) *adj.* 1. easily broken, damaged, or destroyed; delicate; fragile. 2. weak; easily tired: *the frail old man could not walk far.* —'**frail·ty** *n.*

frame (frām) *n.* 1. a structure of wood, metal, etc., usu. rectangular in shape, used to enclose and provide a firm border for a picture, window, etc. 2. the skeleton or supporting structure of a human or animal body or a building. —*vb.* **fram·ing, framed.** 1. to provide with a frame. 2. to shape or form (words, ideas, etc.): *the student framed his arguments very clearly.* 3. to arrange events and evidence to make someone appear guilty of a crime.

frame·work ('frāmwûrk) *n.* 1. a supporting structure for a building, machine, etc. 2. the basic or main ideas, actions, etc., of something: *the framework of his story was factual.*

frank (frangk) *adj.* direct, honest, and straightforward; open: *a frank statement.* —'**frank·ly** *adv.* —'**frank·ness** *n.*

frank·furt·er ('frangkfərtər) *n.* a reddish sausage made from ground beef, often with cereals as fillers, preservatives, etc.; hot dog.

fran·tic ('frantik) *adj.* in a great state of agitation; distracted with worry, etc. —'**fran·ti·cal·ly** *adv.*

fraud (frôd) *n.* 1. a crime involving trickery or deception in order to obtain money, etc. 2. a person or thing that is not genuine; impostor.

fray (frā) *vb.* to unravel or become unraveled, esp. by rubbing or wearing away material: *the sleeves of his jacket are frayed.*

freak (frēk) *n.* 1. an abnormal, usu. deformed living creature; monster. 2. an irregular or unusual event, mood, or object. 3. an unconventional or unusual person. —*adj.* unusual; irregular.

freck·le ('frekəl) *n.* one of a number of brownish marks on the skin of fair people, usu. produced through exposure to the sun. —*vb.* **freck·ling, freck·led.** to make or become covered with freckles.

free (frē) *adj.* **fre·er, fre·est.** 1. not under external control: *nobody is free to do what he likes.* 2. costing no money: *the air we breathe is free.* 3. generous; liberal: *he is free with his money.* 4. not occupied in business; without duties: *I'm free until three o'clock.* —*vb.* **free·ing, freed.** to set free: *he was freed after three years in prison.* —'**free·dom** *n.*

freeze (frēz) *vb.* **freez·ing, froze, fro·zen.** 1. to become or make very cold. 2. to make (a fluid) solid by lowering its temperature. 3. (of a fluid) to become solid in this way. 4. (+ *over*) (of water) to become covered with ice. 5. to stand very still. 6. to fix (prices or wages) at a certain level. —*n.* the action or an instance of freezing, esp. of fixing prices or wages: *a pay freeze.* '**freez·er** *n.* a special refrigerator for storing food at temperatures of 5°F or less.

freight (frāt) *n.* 1. the transport of goods by road, rail, air, or sea. 2. the goods being thus transported. —*vb.* to load (a ship) with freight. '**freight·er** *n.* a ship carrying freight.

fren·zy ('frenzē) *n.,pl.* **fren·zies.** a condition of an uncontrollable or mad excitement, passion, fear, joy, etc.: *the crowd went into a frenzy when the home team won.* —'**fren·zied** *adj.* —'**fren·zied·ly** *adv.*

fre·quent *adj.* ('frēkwənt) occurring regularly or often. —*vb.* (fri'kwent) to go to (a place) often. '**fre·quen·cy** *n.,pl.* **fre·quen·cies.** 1. the condition or fact of being frequent. 2. (physics) the rate or regularity of the movement of a radio signal, alternating electric current, etc. —'**fre·quent·ly** *adv.*

fresh (fresh) *adj.* 1. new or having the qualities of newness: *a fresh coat of paint brightened the walls.* 2. not stale or preserved in a tin or packet: *fresh fruit.* 3. (informal) impudent. 4. (of water) not salty. 5. bright; clean. 6. (of a breeze) strong. '**fresh·en** *vb.* to make or become fresh. —'**fresh·ly** *adv.* —'**fresh·ness** *n.*

fret[1] (fret) *vb.* **fret·ting, fret·ted.** to make or become anxious or irritable.

fret[2] (fret) *n.* 1. (also '**fret·work**) an angular design on wood, etc. 2. any of the raised pieces of metal, wood, etc., crossing the neck of a guitar, etc., against which the strings are pressed to produce different tones. —*vb.* **fret·ting, fret·ted.** to provide with frets or fretwork.

fric·tion ('frikshən) *n.* 1. the force that tends to prevent sliding and causes heat or wear when objects are rubbed together. 2. angry disagreement or quarreling.

friend (frend) *n.* a person whom one knows and likes. —'**friend·li·ness** *n.* —'**friend·ly** *adj.* —'**friend·ship** *n.*

frieze

frieze (frēz) *n.* a long narrow decorated band or border near the top of a wall in a room or building.

frig·ate ('frigit) *n.* a small fast warship, often used to escort and protect other ships.

fright (frīt) *n.* fear, esp. sudden fear: *she had a fright when the dog jumped at her.* '**fright·en** *vb.* to make afraid; cause fear in. '**fright·en·ing** *adj.* producing fear. '**fright·ful** *adj.* terrible; awful; disagreeable or unpleasant. —'**fright·en·ing·ly** *adv.*

frill (fril) *n.* 1. a decorative edging made from a strip of material fixed along one side and left loose and wavy on the other. 2. an ornamental or useless addition. '**fril·ly** *adj.* **fril·li·er, fril·li·est.** (also **frilled**) having frills.

fringe (frinj) *n.* 1. a decorative edge made of loose hanging threads, often gathered into bunches. 2. the outer parts of something: *the fringes of the city had easy access to the countryside.* —*vb.* **fringe·ing, fringed.** to provide with a fringe: *reeds fringed the edges of the lake.*

frog (frog, frôg) *n.* a small animal able to live both in water and on land and noted for its ability to jump quite long distances. See also TADPOLE. '**frog·man** *n.,pl.* **frog·men.** a diver equipped with a wet suit, air tanks, etc., who works underwater.

front (frunt) *n.* 1. the leading part, surface, or side of anything; the part that seems to look forward. 2. the part of a building containing the main door and having a façade. 3. the part of a battle area closest to the enemy. 4. (informal) a legal organization concealing the activities of a criminal one. 5. a group political parties acting as one. —*vb.* (of a building) to face onto (something): *the best hotel fronts the park.* '**front·age** *n.* the length of the front of a building along a street. **in front (of)** before; at the head (of). **put on a bold (*or* good) front** to act or appear brave or successful when one is not. '**fron·tal** *adj.* of or at the front. —**fron·tal·ly** *adv.*

fron·tier (frun'tēr) *n.* 1. the boundary between one country or state and another. 2. often **fron·tiers** (*pl.*) any limiting boundary: *the frontiers of science.*

frost (frôst, frost) *n.* 1. a weather condition occurring when the temperature falls below the freezing point of water. 2. a thin covering of icy particles formed from condensed water vapor. '**frost·bite** *n.* injury to parts of the body caused by exposure to extreme cold. —'**frost·bit·ten** *adj.* —'**frost·y** *adj.* **frost·i·er, frost·i·est.**

froth (frôth, froth) *n.* foam. —*vb.* (sometimes + *up*) to produce froth: *the water frothed where the river flowed over the rocks.* —'**froth·y** *adj.* **froth·i·er, froth·i·est.**

frown (froun) *n.* a sad, worried, or angry expression of the face, usu. with wrinkling of the forehead. —*vb.* to make a frown.

froze (frōz) *vb.* the past tense of FREEZE.

frozen ('frōzən) *vb.* the past participle of FREEZE.

fruit (froot) *n.* 1. the parts of a plant containing the seeds. In some plants e.g. apples, bananas, etc., these parts can be eaten. 2. something gained as the result of hard work, long careful handling, development, etc.: *the fruits of one's labor.* —*vb.* (of plants) to bring forth fruit. '**fruit·ful** *adj.* 1. producing much fruit. 2. producing great reward. '**fruit·less** *adj.* 1. producing no fruit. 2. achieving nothing; futile. **fru'i·tion** *n.* a condition of successful conclusion: *it was a long time before his idea came to fruition.* '**fruit·y** *adj.* **fruit·i·er, fruit·i·est.** tasting of fruit.

frus·trate ('frustrāt) *vb.* **frus·trat·ing, frus·trat·ed.** 1. to deprive of or keep from completion or success; make futile: *all our plans were frustrated by the bad weather.* 2. to cause (someone) to be angry because of failure, a handicap, etc.: *his inability to spell frustrated him.* —**frus'tra·tion** *n.*

fry[1] (frī) *vb.* **fry·ing, fried.** to cook in hot fat or oil.

fry[2] (frī) *pl.n.* tiny fish newly hatched out of their eggs. **small fry** (informal) 1. unimportant people. 2. children.

fuchsia

fuch·sia ('fyooshə) *n.* a garden plant producing fine drooping flowers.

fu·el ('fyooəl) *n.* 1. any material that can be converted into energy for operating a machine, providing heat, etc., usu. by the process of burning: *coal and oil are important fuels.* —*vb.* **fu·el·ing, fu·eled.** to provide with fuel.

fu·gi·tive ('fyoojitiv) *n.* a person who is running away, esp. someone trying to escape legal punishment or someone in search of freedom, such as a refugee.

ful·crum ('foolkrəm, 'fulkrəm) *n.,pl.* **ful·crums** *or* **ful·cra** ('foolkrə). the point of rest or support on which a LEVER turns; balancing point, as in a see-saw.

ful·fill (fo͝ol'fil) *vb.* 1. to bring to completeness or actual existence: *to fulfill a promise.* 2. to perform (one's duty) correctly and completely: *he fulfilled all the requirements of the job.* —**ful'fill·ment** *n.*

full (fo͝ol) *adj.* 1. having no room for any more; completely filled: *a full cup of coffee.* 2. containing a large amount or number: *the water is full of fish.* 3. rich; plentiful: *a full crop.* 4. well-rounded in form: *a full face.* 5. of the greatest size, amount, etc.: *at full speed.* —**'ful·ly** *adv.* —**'full·ness** *n.*

fum·ble ('fumbəl) *vb.* **fum·bling, fum·bled.** to make clumsy or awkward movements with the hands; handle clumsily: *he fumbled for his keys.*

fume (fyo͞om) *n.* usu. **fumes** (*pl.*) gas, smoke, or vapor, esp. when unpleasant or dangerous: *the fireman was almost overcome by fumes.* —*vb.* **fum·ing, fumed.** 1. to produce fumes. 2. to be very angry: *Ben's father was fuming because he came home late.*

func·tion ('fun͞gkshən) *n.* 1. the purpose or usual duty of a person or thing. 2. any formal event, e.g. a charity ball. —*vb.* 1. to serve as: *the kitchen also functions as a dining room.* 2. to operate; work: *this machine is not functioning.*

fund (fund) *n.* 1. often **funds** (*pl.*) money needed for something: *the committee is trying to raise funds.* 2. a large amount of: *he has a fund of knowledge.* —*vb.* to provide money for: *they persuaded the millionaire to fund the new hospital.*

fu·ner·al ('fyo͞onərəl) *n.* the religious ceremony concerning the burial or cremation of a dead person. **fu·ne·re·al** (fyo͞o'nērēəl) *adj.* gloomy; mournful: *the rooms in the old house were decorated in funereal colors.*

fun·fair ('funfeər) *n.* a fair full of various amusements and shows.

fun·gus ('fun͞ggəs) *n.,pl.* **'fun·gi** ('funjī) *or* **fun·gus·es.** a plant that lives on other plants or on rotting plant material: *mushrooms and toadstools are fungi.*

funnel

fun·nel ('funəl) *n.* 1. an open-ended, typically cone-shaped object through which liquid can be poured into a container with a narrow opening. 2. a large chimney-like object, e.g. on a steamship, through which smoke and steam escape. —*vb.* **fun·nel·ing, fun·neled.** to pass through a funnel.

fun·ny ('funē) *adj.* **fun·ni·er, fun·ni·est.** 1. amusing; humorous. 2. strange; odd: *Diane had a funny look on her face.* **funny bone** a part of the elbow which, when struck, produces a sharp tingling pain. —**'fun·ni·ly** *adv.*

fur (fûr) *n.* 1. the hair of certain animals, e.g. cats. 2. the skin of an animal, e.g. an ermine or mink, with the fur on it, used for clothes. 3. a garment made of or lined with fur. 4. a substance produced inside a kettle, etc., when hard water is boiled in it regularly. 5. a coating sometimes formed on the tongue during an illness. **'fur·ry** *adj.* **fur·ri·er, fur·ri·est.** 1. of or like fur. 2. covered with fur. **furred** *adj.* covered with fur.

fu·ri·ous ('fyo͝orēəs) *adj.* See FURY.

fur·nace ('fûrnis) *n.* an enclosed structure where a very hot fire can be made to provide heat for a building, melt metals, etc.

fur·nish ('fûrnish) *vb.* to provide a room, house, apartment, office, etc., with tables, chairs, beds, curtains, etc. **'fur·ni·ture** ('furnichər) *n.* movable objects, e.g. beds and chairs, used for furnishing.

fur·row ('fûrō 'furō) *n.* 1. a shallow trench cut along a field by a plow, into which seeds are sown. 2. a fold in the skin of a person's forehead, e.g. when frowning. —*vb.* to make a furrow or furrows in.

fur·ther ('fûrdhər) *adj.* 1. situated at or traveling to a greater distance: *Don walked further than he usually did.* 2. additional: *further work is required.* —*adv.* 1. at or to a greater distance: *I can't walk any further.* 2. to a greater degree; additionally. —*vb.* to advance; push forward: *his father helped to further his career.* **'fur·ther·ance** *n.* development.

fu·ry ('fyo͝orē) *n.,pl.* **fu·ries.** 1. madness, rage, or violence. 2. an instance of this. —**'fu·ri·ous** *adj: David was furious when he missed the bus.* —**'fu·ri·ous·ly** *adv.*

fuse (fyo͞oz) *n.* 1. a device in an electrical circuit that is designed to burn out and break the circuit if the current becomes too great. 2. also **fuze** a flammable length of cord, etc., ignited at one end to set off an explosive connected to the other. —*vb.* **fus·ing, fused.** 1. to melt. 2. to weld or be welded together under extreme heat. **'fus·ion** *n.* a joining together.

fu·se·lage ('fyo͞osəlâzh) *n.* the outer body or structure of an aircraft, excluding the wings and the tail.

fuss (fus) *n.* unnecessary or excessive worry, excitement, attention, etc. —*vb.* 1. (often + *over*) to make a fuss: *she fussed over her hair.* 2. to disturb or excite (someone); cause (someone) to make a fuss. —**'fuss·y** *adj.* **fuss·i·er, fuss·i·est.**

fu·tile ('fyo͞otəl) *adj.* having no useful result; useless; achieving nothing. —**fu·til·i·ty** (fyo͞o'tilitē) *n.*

fu·ture ('fyo͞ochər) *n.* 1. the time or set of events that will follow the present. 2. a successful life or career that is yet to come: *you have a great future.* 3. (grammar) the tense used for verbs describing actions that will happen after the present. —*adj.* 1. describing time or events that will follow the present. 2. concerning the future tense in grammar.

G

ga·ble ('gābəl) *n.* the triangular upper section of the side wall of a building formed by the two parts of a sloping roof.

gadg·et ('gajit) *n.* any sort of tool, machine, or device: *a gadget for opening bottles.* **'gadg·et·ry** *n.* a large number of gadgets.

gag (gag) *n.* a piece of cloth stuffed into someone's mouth to prevent him from making any sounds. —*vb.* **gag·ging, gagged.** to keep (someone) quiet with a gag.

gai·e·ty ('gāitē) *n.* cheerfulness; lightheartedness.

gain (gān) *vb.* 1. to win or acquire (what one wants or hopes for). 2. (often + *on*) come closer to or overtake: *looking back he saw that his opponent was gaining on him.* 3. (of a clock) to show a time later than the real time. 4. to increase in: *to gain weight.* —*n.* profit; advantage: *he made a gain of ten dollars in the deal.*

gait (gāt) *n.* a way of walking: *he had an awkward gait.* **'gait·ers** *pl.n.* ankle or leg coverings of cloth or leather, fastened by buttons.

gal·ax·y ('galəksē) *n.,pl.* **gal·ax·ies.** any of the huge collections of billions of stars scattered throughout space. **the Galaxy** the collection of stars to which the sun belongs; Milky Way. —**ga·lac·tic** (gə'laktik) *adj.*

gale (gāl) *n.* a very strong wind.

gal·lant *adj.* 1. ('galənt) brave. 2. (gə'lant, gə'lânt) (usu. of men in relation to women) polite or keen to show admiration or affection; chivalrous.

gal·ler·y ('galərē) *n.,pl.* **gal·ler·ies.** 1. a narrow passage or corridor, sometimes open on one side. 2. a narrow platform projecting from a wall and running around the inside or outside of a building. 3. an extended balcony in a theater, etc., usu. containing the cheapest seats. 4. a room or building used for displaying works of art.

galley

gal·ley ('galē) *n.* 1. a large single-decked ship used in ancient times, propelled by means of a number of oars rowed by slaves or prisoners. 2. a kitchen on a vessel or aircraft.

gal·lon ('galən) *n.* a measure of liquid equal to four quarts.

gal·lop ('galəp) *vb.* 1. (of a horse) to move at high speed. 2. to ride at high speed: *the rider galloped across the field.* —*n.* the action or an instance of galloping: *he went for a gallop on his pony.*

gal·lows ('galōz) *n.* a wooden scaffold for executing people by hanging.

ga·lore (gə'lôr) *adv.* abundantly; in plenty: *there wer flowers galore growing in his garden.*

ga·losh·es (gə'loshiz) *pl.n.* rubber or plastic shoes worn over other shoes to keep them dry or clean.

ga·lumph (gə'lumf) *vb.* to move about heavily and full of self-importance: *Patrick galumphed around boasting about his new car.*

gal·va·nize ('galvənīz) *vb.* **gal·van·iz·ing, gal·van·ized.** 1. to shock with electricity. 2. to startle into sudden action. 3. to coat (metal) with zinc to protect it.

gam·ble ('gambəl) *vb.* **gam·bling, gam·bled.** to take a risk, esp. on a game, horse race, etc., in order to gain money or some other advantage: *he gambles at the casino.* —*n.* the action or an instance of gambling. —**'gam·bler** *n.*

gam·bol ('gambəl) *vb.* to skip about; frolic: *lambs gamboled in the fields.*

game (gām) *n.* 1. a competition, as in a sport, played according to rules. 2. a self-contained part of a tennis or bridge match: *the tennis champion lost the first set six games to three.* 3. birds or animals hunted for sport and usu. used as food. 4. **games** (*pl.*) a series of competitions: *the Olympic Games.* —*adj.* eager or bold. —*vb.* **gam·ing, gamed.** to gamble.

game·keep·er ('gāmkēpər) *n.* a person employed to take care of a preserve where game is hunted for sport.

game re·serve *n.* an area set aside for the protection of wild animals.

gam·ete ('gamēt, gə'mēt) *n.* any of the two forms of mature reproductive cells, sperms or eggs, that are able to form a new animal or plant when they fuse together.

gam·ma rays ('gamə) rays similar to X–RAYs.

gan·der ('gandər) *n.* a male goose.

gang (gaṅg) *n.* 1. a group of criminals. 2. a group of workmen: *a road gang.* 3. (informal) a group of friends: *I saw the gang last night.* **'gang·ster** *n.* a criminal, esp. a member of a gang.

gang·way ('gaṅgwā) *n.* 1. a passage between two rows of seats; aisle. 2. a movable bridge from a ship to a pier allowing passengers to go aboard or ashore.

gaol (jāl) *n., vb.* See JAIL.

gape (gāp) *vb.* **gap·ing, gaped.** to open the mouth wide in surprise: *the children gaped at the strangely dressed man.* —*n.* an act of gaping.

ga·rage (gə'râzh) *n.* 1. a building or covered area where a car may be kept when not in use. 2. a place where repair work is done on cars.

gar·den ('gârdən) *n.* 1. an area, usu. next to or surrounding a house, where flowers, fruit, or vegetables are grown. 2. usu. **gardens** (*pl.*) a public park or open area in a city. **'gar·den·er** *n.* a person who takes care of a garden. **'gar·den·ing** *n.* the action or an instance of taking care of a garden.

gar·gle ('gârgəl) *vb.* **gar·gling, gar·gled.** to wash the inside of the mouth or throat by filling the mouth with liquid, leaning the head back, and exhaling to cause one's breath to bubble through the liquid. —*n.* 1. the action or an instance of gargling. 2. a liquid used for gargling.

gargoyle

gar·goyle ('gârgoil) *n.* a metal or stone figure of a very ugly man or animal whose mouth often forms the end of a spout for carrying rainwater off the roof of a building.

gar·lic ('gârlik) *n.* a plant with an onionlike root having a strong taste and smell and used in cooking.

gar·ment ('gârmənt) *n.* an item of clothing.

gar·ri·son ('garisən) *n.* a group of soldiers staying in a town, fort, etc., to protect it or keep control of it against enemy forces. —*vb.* to provide with a garrison.

gar·ter ('gârtər) *n.* a strip or band of elastic material worn around the leg or arm to hold up a sock, stocking, or shirt sleeve.

gas (gas) *n.* 1. the state of a substance, such as air, in which the atoms or molecules are sufficiently far apart to move freely so that they occupy all the space available to them. 2. the inflammable substance supplied to homes for cooking, heating, etc. 3. See GASOLINE. —*vb.* **gas·sing, gassed.** to kill or injure (a person or animal) with harmful gas. —**gas·e·ous** *adj.*

gash (gash) *n.* a deep cut, esp. a wound in someone's flesh. —*vb.* to make or cause a gash in something: *Robert gashed his thumb with the potato peeler.*

gas·o·line (gasə'lēn, 'gasəlēn) *n.* a highly flammable product made by refining oil, used as a fuel in engines.

gasp (gasp) *n.* a sudden sucking in of the breath, as in surprise, pain, etc.: *she gave a gasp when she saw the bath overflowing.* —*vb.* 1. to produce a gasp. 2. to breathe quickly, esp. when fighting for air. 3. to say with a gasp.

gate (gāt) *n.* 1. a type of door into a field, garden, etc., usu. in the form of a metal or wooden frame. 2. the people who pay to enter a sports ground. 3. the total of the money paid by such people: *the ball game drew a gate of 8,000 dollars.*

gate·crash ('gātkrash) *vb.* (slang) to attend an event without paying an admission or without having been invited. —**'gate·crash·er** *n.*

gath·er ('gadhər) *vb.* 1. to come or bring together; assemble: *a crowd gathered.* 2. to pick up and collect together. 3. to be led to understand: *I gather you're from abroad.* **'gath·er·ing** *n.* a crowd; assembly.

gaud·y ('gôdē) *adj.* **gaud·i·er, gaud·i·est.** bright and showy: *he wore a rather gaudy shirt.*

gauge (gāj) *n.* 1. a device for measuring something: *a pressure gauge.* 2. a measure of something, esp. of the distance between railway lines. —*vb.* **gaug·ing, gauged.** 1. to measure with or as if with a gauge. 2. to estimate; guess: *I gauged her to be 16.*

gaunt (gônt) *adj.* thin; having the appearance of being ill or hungry. —**'gaunt·ly** *adv.*

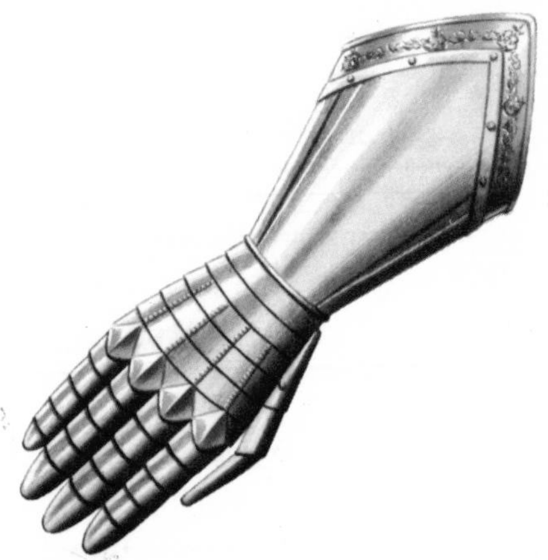

gauntlet

gaunt·let[1] ('gôntlit) *n.* a strong glove protecting the hand and wrist, esp. as worn by a knight in armor.

gaunt·let[2] ('gôntlit) *n.* used in the phrase **run the gauntlet.** 1. an old type of punishment in which two lines of people strike out at the offender who is made to run between them. 2. (often + *of* t) to make oneself open to blame or criticism (from someone or something): *to run the gauntlet of public opinion.*

gauze (gôz) *n.* a very thin finely woven transparent cloth often used to dress wounds. —**'gauz·y** *adj.* **gauz·i·er, gauz·i·est.**

gay (gā) *adj.* cheerful; happy; lively. **'gai·ly** *adv.* in a gay manner: *she skipped gaily along the street.* See also GAIETY.

gaze (gāz) *vb.* **gaz·ing, gazed.** to stare or look at; fix one's eyes upon something or look in a certain direction. —*n.* a long look or stare.

ga·zelle (gə'zel) *n.* a type of small ANTELOPE that is particularly graceful in its movements.

gear (gēr) *n.* 1. a device, often a toothed wheel that connects with a similar wheel, to change the speed or direction of rotation of a shaft in a machine. 2. tools, etc., for a job.

geese (gēs) *n.* the plural of GOOSE.

gel·a·tine *or* **gel·a·tin** ('jelətin) *n.* a substance used in cooking that forms a jelly upon cooling.

gel·ig·nite ('jelignīt) *n.* a type of explosive used esp. for blasting rock.

gem (jem) *n.* 1. a precious stone, such as a diamond; jewel. 2. something thought of or valued very highly.

gen·der ('jendər) *n.* (grammar) a class of nouns: *woman, mare, and cow are nouns of the feminine gender.*

gene (jēn) *n.* one of the tiny units carried in the CELLs of animals and plants by means of which their characteristics are passed from parents to offspring. **ge'net·ics** *sing.n.* the science concerned with the study of genes.

gen·er·al ('jenərəl) *adj.* 1. of, concerning, or applied to most or all persons and things; common. 2. showing no details; vague: *a general idea.* —*n.* a high-ranking military officer. **'gen·er·al·ize** *vb.* **gen·er·al·iz·ing, gen·er·al·ized.** 1. to make general. 2. to make a broad statement intended to include almost every case. **gen·er·al·i'za·tion** *n.* a vague general statement. **'gen·er·al·ly** *adv.* usually.

gen·er·ate ('jenərāt) *vb.* **gen·er·at·ing, gen·er·at·ed.** to produce, create, or cause: *the lights generated a great deal of heat.* **gen·er'a·tion** *n.* 1. all the people born at or about the same time: *the younger generation.* 2. the period between the beginning of one generation and the next, usu. about 30 years.

gen·er·ous ('jenərəs) *adj.* 1. giving freely: *he was very generous in giving the children presents.* 2. plentiful: *a generous helping of pie.* —**gen·er·os·i·ty** (jenə'rositē) *n.* —**'gen·er·ous·ly** *adv.*

gen·ius ('jēnyəs) *n.,pl.* **ge·nius·es.** brilliant intelligence, originality, or imagination.

gen·tle ('jentəl) *adj.* pleasantly soft or kind; not rough, harsh, etc.

gen·u·ine ('jenyo͞oin) *adj.* real; not forged: *a genuine painting.*

ge·og·ra·phy (jē'ogrəfē) *n.,pl.* **ge·og·ra·phies.** 1. the study of the earth's physical characteristics, industries, population, etc. 2. the distinctive features, landmarks, etc., of a district. —**ge·o·graph·ic** (jēə'grafik) *or* **ge·o'graph·i·cal** *adj.*

ge·ol·o·gy (jē'oləjē) *n.,pl.* **ge·ol·o·gies.** 1. the study of the rocks and layers of which the earth is made. 2. the local geological features of a district. —**ge·o·log·ic** (jēə'lojik) *or* **ge·o'log·i·cal** *adj.* —**ge'ol·o·gist** *n.*

ge·om·e·try (jē'omitrē) *n.* the branch of mathematics concerned with the properties of triangles, rectangles, circles, spheres, cubes, etc. —**ge·o·met·ric** (jēə'metrik) *or* **ge·o'met·ri·cal** *adj.*

geometry

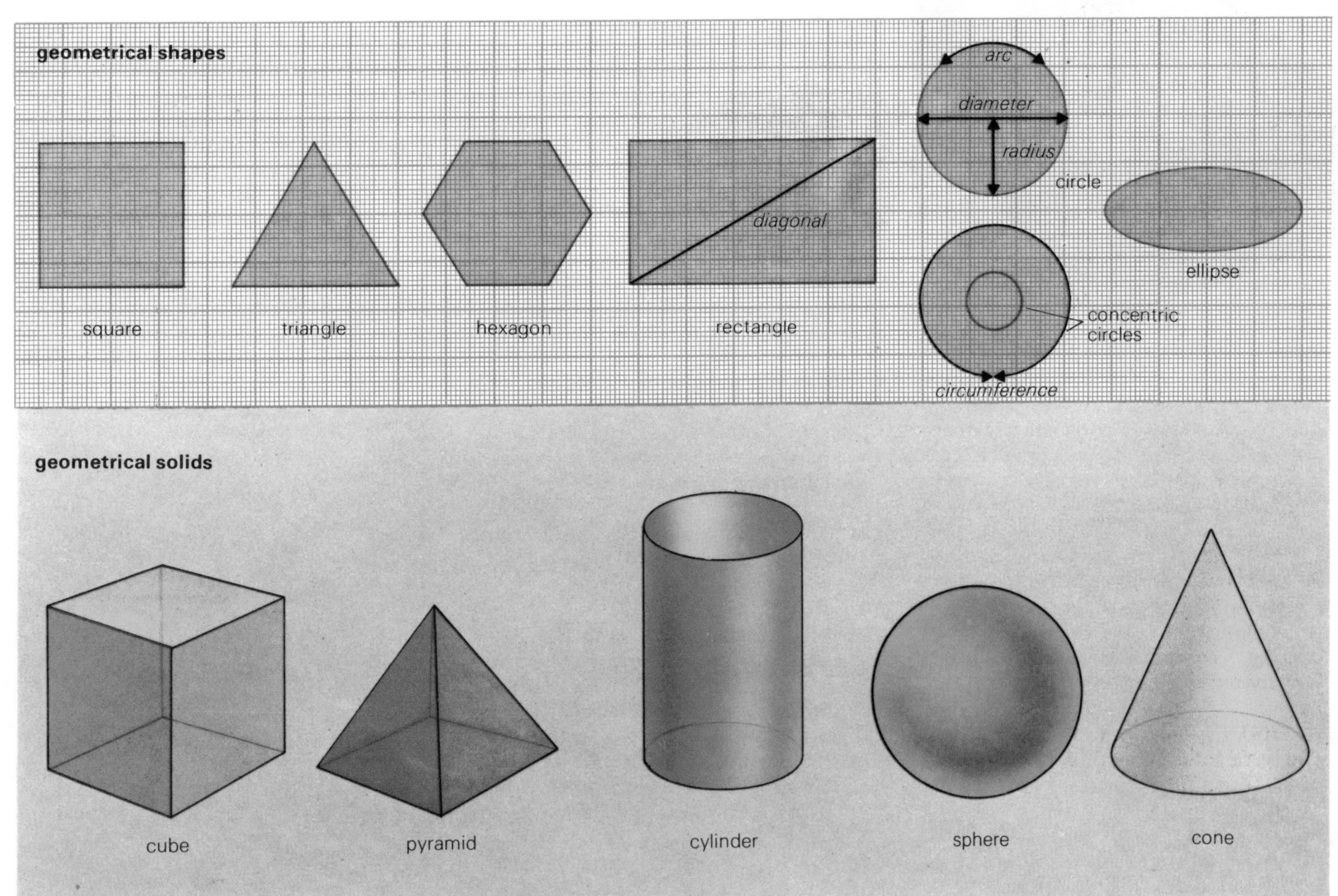

germ (jûrm) *n.* 1. a tiny organism (see BACTERIA and VIRUS) that often causes disease when present in or on the body. 2. a starting point from which something develops: *the germ of an idea.*

ger·mi·nate ('jûrmənāt) *vb.* **ger·mi·nat·ing, ger·mi·nat·ed.** 1. (of seeds) to begin to grow by producing roots and shoots. 2. to make (seeds) begin to grow. 3. to develop or cause to develop: *their plans germinated successfully.*

ges·ture ('jeschər) *n.* 1. a movement of the head, hands, etc., indicating or conveying an idea or emotion: *he shook his head in a gesture of refusal.* 2. any movement or action indicating intention, attitude, etc.: *a gesture of good will.* —*vb.* **ges·tur·ing, ges·tured.** to make a gesture.

gey·ser ('gīzər) *n.* 1. a natural spring in a volcanic area that shoots out hot water and steam. 2. a device for heating water.

geyser

ghost (gōst) *n.* 1. the soul or spirit of a dead person that is believed to be capable of haunting living people. 2. a shadow or pale likeness of something: *a ghost of an idea.*

gi·ant ('jīənt) *n.* 1. an imaginary human being of great height, size, strength, etc. 2. a person or thing of exceptional talents: *Bach is a giant among composers.* —*adj.* huge; enormous: *a giant ice cream cone.*

gib·bon ('gibən) *n.* a slender tailless ape with long arms that lives in trees in southern Asia and the East Indies.

gid·dy ('gidē) *adj.* **gid·di·er, gid·di·est.** 1. having or causing a dizzy or lightheaded feeling. 2. impulsive or frivolous: *a giddy adventure.* —'**gid·di·ness** *n.*

glacier

gift (gift) *n.* 1. a present. 2. a talent: *she has a gift for painting.*

gi·gan·tic (jī'gantik) *adj.* huge; enormous. —**gi'gan·ti·cal·ly** *adv.*

gig·gle ('gigəl) *vb.* **gig·gling, gig·gled.** to laugh in a silly manner. —*n.* a silly laugh. —'**gig·gler** *n.* —'**gig·gly** *adj.*

gild (gild) *vb.* to cover or coat with gold dust, gold leaf, gold paint, etc.

gill[1] (gil) *n.* the organ of breathing of fish and certain other animals that live in the water.

gill[2] (jil) *n.* a liquid measure equal to 1/4 pint.

gilt (gilt) *n.* gold leaf or gold paint. —*adj.* 1. having the color of gold. 2. (also **gilded**) covered in gold.

gim·mick ('gimik) *n.* a method, esp. an unusual or tricky one, used to attract attention, gain publicity, etc.: *free glasses are the store's latest gimmick to attract customers.*

gin (jin) *n.* an alcoholic drink made from grain and often flavored with the oil of juniper berries.

gin·ger ('jinjər) *n.* a tropical plant whose spicy underground stems are used in cooking. —*adj.* 1. containing ginger: *ginger cookies.* 2. of the color of ginger; reddish brown. '**gin·ger·ly** *adv.* cautiously or warily: *she gingerly put one foot into the pool to find out if the water was cold.*

Gip·sy ('jipsē) *n.,pl.* **Gip·sies.** See GYPSY.

gi·raffe (jə'raf) *n.* an African animal, having a very long neck and legs and a coat with regular dark brown markings.

gird·er ('gûrdər) *n.* any beam of steel, wood, etc., used as a support in a building, bridge, etc.

gir·dle ('gûrdəl) *n.* 1. a band, belt, etc., worn around the waist. 2. an undergarment designed to support or hold in the abdomen.

gla·cier ('glāshər) *n.* a large mass of ice produced by a build-up of snow that moves slowly down a mountain or toward the sea. —'**gla·cial** *adj.*

glad (glad) *adj.* **glad·der, glad·dest.** 1. happy; pleased; delighted. 2. causing joy or pleasure, etc.: *glad tidings.* —'**glad·ly** *adv.*

glad·i·a·tor ('gladēatər) *n.* an armed slave or captive who fought other gladiators, wild animals, etc., to entertain an audience in ancient Rome.

glam·our ('glamər) *n.* charm, beauty, attractiveness, etc., esp. of a rather

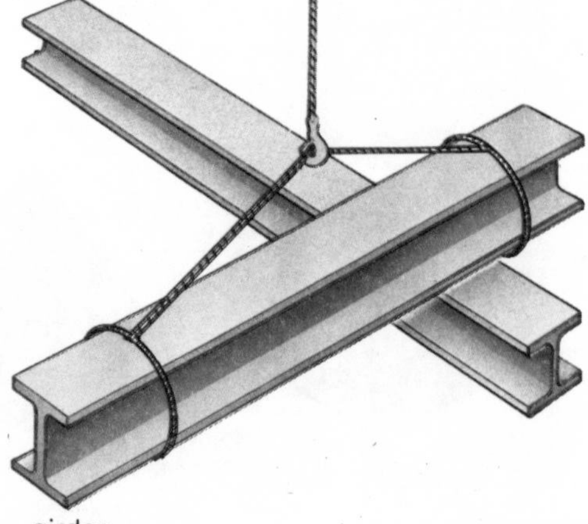

girder

superficial kind. **'glam·or·ize** *vb.* **glam·or·iz·ing, glam·or·ized.** to make more attractive, interesting, etc.: *newspapers often glamorize stories.* —**'glam·or·ous** *adj.* —**'glam·or·ous·ly** *adv.*

glance (glans) *vb.* **glanc·ing, glanced.** 1. to look briefly or quickly at, toward, through, etc. 2. (+ *off*) to strike against something and fly off at a narrow angle: *the tennis ball glanced off the top of the net.* —*n.* 1. a brief look: *Gary's aunt gave his dirty shoes a disapproving glance.* 2. a deflection.

gland (gland) *n.* any of various bodily organs, which pass natural substances directly into the blood or pass substances out of the body through special tubelike passages called ducts such as the pancreas, sweat glands, salivary glands. —**'glan·du·lar** *adj.*

glare (gleər) *n.* 1. a bright dazzling light. 2. a fierce or angry stare. —*vb.* **glar·ing, glared.** 1. to shine with a dazzling light. 2. to stare angrily.

glass (glas) *n.* 1. a hard usu. transparent breakable substance. 2. something made of glass, e.g. a drinking container. 3. (also **looking glass**) a mirror. 4. (also **spy·glass**) a small telescope. 5. the amount contained in a glass drinking vessel: *the bottle holds six glasses.* 6. **glass·es** (*pl.*) a pair of corrective lenses worn over the eyes to aid vision; spectacles. —*adj.* made of or fitted with glass.

glaze (glāz) *n.* a smooth glassy surface or coating, such as the finish given to pottery or porcelain. —*vb.* **glaz·ing, glazed.** 1. to give a smooth shiny surface to. 2. to fit or cover with glass.

gla·zier ('glāzhər) *n.* a person who fits panes of glass, e.g. for windows.

gleam (glēm) *n.* 1. a flash or beam of light. 2. a faint glow. 3. a slight or faint appearance; glimmer: *a gleam of hope.* —*vb.* to glow or catch the light, giving off a gleam or gleams.

glide (glīd) *vb.* **glid·ing, glid·ed.** to move gently and smoothly. —*n.* an effortless movement. **'glid·er** *n.* an aircraft without an engine, kept in flight by updrafts of air. **'glid·ing** *n.* the sport of flying a glider.

glim·mer ('glimər) *vb.* an unsteady flickering light. —*n.* 1. a dim flickering light. 2. a faint appearance; flicker: *a glimmer of hope.*

glimpse (glimps) *n.* 1. a brief and temporary view or sight of something: *I caught a glimpse of the train.* 2. a vague idea; hint. —*vb.* **glimps·ing, glimpsed.** 1. to obtain a brief view of. 2. to gain a vague idea of.

glis·ten ('glisən) *n.* to reflect the light, as when wet or polished.

glit·ter ('glitər) *vb.* to sparkle with a changing or flashing light. —*n.* a splendid or sparkling appearance, light, etc. **'glit·ter·ing** *adj.* 1. shining or sparkling. 2. splendid; fine: *a glittering success.*

gloat (glōt) *vb.* to take delight in or rejoice over (something) in a greedy or spiteful way. —*n.* the act or an example of gloating.

globe (glōb) *n.* 1. an object shaped like a ball; SPHERE. 2. an object of this shape used to represent the earth and having the continents and seas shown on its surface.

gloom (gloom) *n.* 1. deep shadow or dimness. 2. despair or depression. —**'gloom·y** *adj.* **gloom·i·er, gloom·i·est.** —**'gloom·i·ly** *adv.* —**'gloom·i·ness** *n.*

glo·ry ('glôrē) *n.,pl.* **glo·ries.** 1. honor; distinction; admiration: *he gained glory for his heroism in battle.* 2. brightness; splendor; brilliance: *the jewels were displayed in all their glory.* —*vb.* **glo·ry·ing, glo·ried.** (+ *in*) to rejoice in; express one's happiness; take pride in: *he gloried in his success.* **'glo·ri·fy** *vb.* **glo·ri·fy·ing, glo·ri·fied.** to praise or worship. **'glo·ri·ous** *adj.* splendid; wonderful. —**glo·ri·fi'ca·tion** *n.*

glow (glō) *vb.* 1. to emit a steady light. 2. to burn without flames. 3. to feel warmth: *he glowed after his run around the block.* 4. to feel a warmth of emotion; satisfaction: *she glowed with pride.* —*n.* 1. the light given out by a bright or burning object or substance. 2. a feeling of warmth. **'glow·ing** *adj.* 1. giving off a glow. 2. full of praise; fine; splendid: *glowing reports of someone's success.*

glu·cose ('glookōs) *n.* a type of sugar used by the tissues of the body to produce energy.

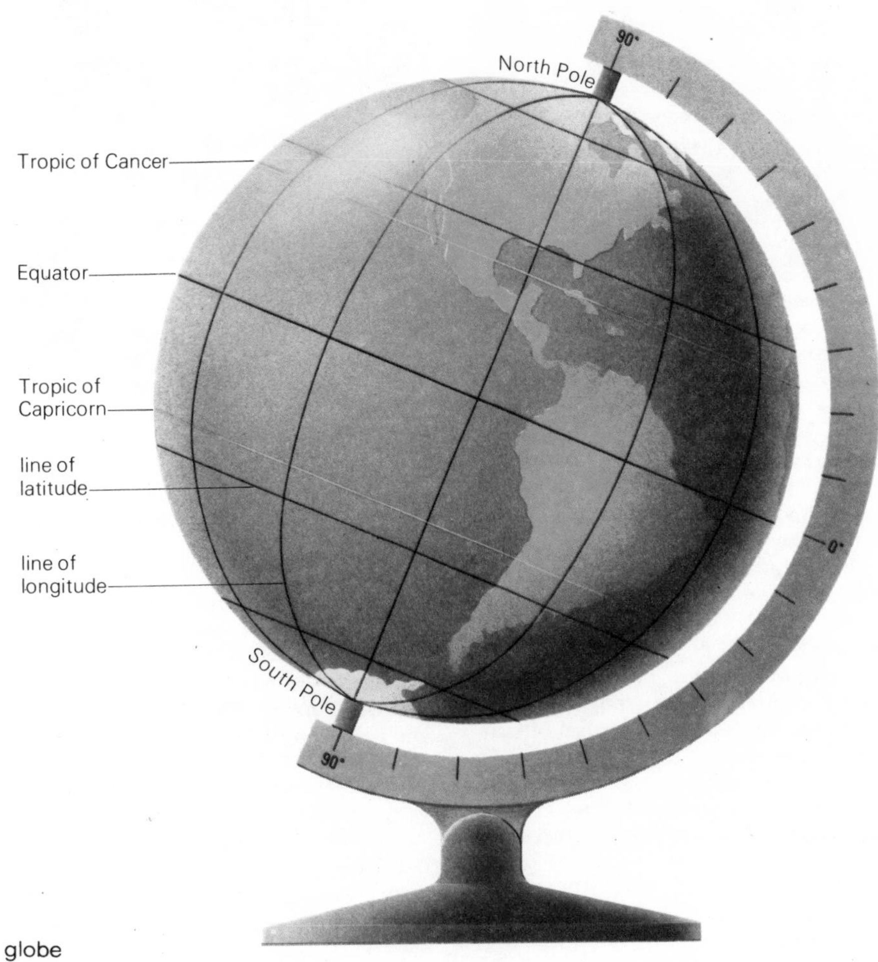

globe

glue (glōō) *n.* a substance for sticking things together. —*vb.* **glu·ing, glued.** 1. to stick or fasten with glue. 2. to be, stay, or put very close to something, as if stuck with glue: *he is glued to the television.*

gnarled (nârld) *adj.* rugged and wrinkled in appearance: *a gnarled tree.*

gnash (nash) *vb.* to force or grind (one's teeth) together in anger or pain.

gnat (nat) *n.* a tiny flylike insect related to the mosquito.

gnaw (nô) *vb.* 1. to bite or nibble persistently; wear away: *rats had gnawed through the floor.* 2. to trouble or worry: *the problem gnawed at his conscience.*

gnome (nōm) *n.* a type of FAIRY usu. described as a tiny old man.

gnu (nōō) *n.,pl.* **gnus.** a large ANTELOPE having curved horns and a long tail, that lives on the plains of south and east Africa.

goad (gōd) *vb.* to cause (someone) to become angry, esp. angry enough to commit some bad action; provoke: *the boy goaded Joe with his taunts.*—*n.* 1. a pointed stick for driving cattle. 2. any means of provocation.

goal (gōl) *n.* 1. an area marked by posts, lines, nets, etc., toward which players in some games, e.g. football and hockey, kick or direct a ball. 2. the action of directing a ball into or over a goal or the score made by doing this. 3. an end or aim; ambition: *his goal was to become the company president.* **'goal·ten·der** *n.* a player in soccer, hockey, etc., whose job is to defend the goal. Also **'goal·keep·er;** (informal) **goal·ie.**

goat (gōt) *n.* a sure-footed hairy animal having horns and a beard, closely related to the sheep, and often kept as a domestic animal.

god (god) *n.* 1. a being regarded as having power over nature and the affairs of men. 2. an image or other object worshiped as a symbol of supreme power; an idol. 3. **God** (in Christianity and some other religions) the one supreme being, creator and ruler of the universe. **'god·dess** *n.* a female god.

gold (gōld) *n.* 1. a heavy, yellowish metal that is very highly valued and used in jewelry, industry, and commerce, and formerly used for coins. Chemical symbol: Au. 2. a yellowish color. —*adj.* 1. made of or concerned with gold. 2. (also **gold·en**) of the color of gold.

gold·fish ('gōldfish) *n.* a small yellow or orange fish of the carp family, often kept in aquariums and pools.

golf (golf, gôlf) *n.* an outdoor game in which the player uses a number of clubs with wooden or metal heads to hit a small ball, using as few strokes as possible, into a series of holes set into the ground along a **golf course** with obstacles between them.

gong (gông, gong) *n.* a metal disk that produces a hollow vibrating note when struck.

goose (gōōs) *n.,pl.* **geese.** 1. a long-necked web-footed water bird, usu. larger than a duck and often domesticated. 2. the female bird as distinguished from the male (GANDER). 3. a silly or foolish person.

gooseberry

goose·ber·ry ('gōōsberē) *n.,pl.* **goose·ber·ries.** a small, rather acid-tasting fruit that grows on a prickly bush.

gorge (gôrj) *n.* a narrow steep-sided valley, often having a river or stream running through it. —*vb.* **gorg·ing, gorged.** (+ *on*) to swallow or eat greedily: *he gorged himself on apple pie and cream.*

gor·geous ('gôrjəs) *adj.* splendid or very beautiful. —**'gor·geous·ly** *adv.*

go·ril·la (gə'rilə) *n.* the largest of the apes, found in the forests of equatorial Africa. When upright, it stands six feet tall.

gos·pel ('gospəl) *n.* 1. the teaching of Christ. 2. the story of Christ's life and teaching, as told in the New Testament books of Matthew, Mark, Luke, and John. 3. one of these books.

gos·sip ('gosip) *n.* 1. idle talk, esp. about the private affairs of other people; rumor. 2. casual conversation. 3. a person who spreads rumors. —*vb.* to talk idly, esp. about the personal affairs of others. —**'gos·sip·er** *n.*

gov·ern ('guvərn) *vb.* 1. to rule with authority: *to govern a country.* 2. to influence; guide; control: *the reasons governing his actions were clear.* **'gov·ern·ment** *n.* 1. political administration and rule. 2. the system by which a community, country, etc., is governed. 3. the body of persons responsible for a country's government. **'gov·er·nor** *n.* the elected head of a state of the United States.

grace (grās) *n.* 1. ease or elegance in manner, movement, or form. 2. (in Christian religion) the love and favor freely granted by God to men. 3. an allowance of time to carry out some task: *he gave the boy three days' grace to finish his work.* 4. a term of address used to or in reference to a duke, duchess, or archbishop. —*vb.* **grac·ing, graced.** to favor or honor: *the princess graced the party with her presence.* **'grace·ful** *adj.* elegant or beautiful in manner, movement, or form. **gra·cious** ('grāshəs) *adj.* 1. kind; courteous. 2. characterized by good taste or elegance: *gracious living.* —**'grace·ful·ly** *adv.* —**'gra·cious·ly** *adv.*

grade (grād) *n.* 1. quality, value, or rank: *the store sells only high grade produce.* 2. a class at an elementary school. —*vb.* **grad·ing, grad·ed.** 1. to organize into a series of grades; place in order of quality, value, etc.; sort or classify. 2. to judge or mark (an essay, examination, etc.).

gra·di·ent ('grādēənt) *n.* a slope or a degree of slope: *the steep gradient forced the train to go slowly.*

grad·u·al ('grajōōəl) *adj.* happening or moving by slow degrees or very gently. —**'grad·u·al·ly** *adv.*

grain (grān) *n.* 1. the seed of one of the cereal plants (oats, wheat, barley, etc.). 2. any small hard particle: *a grain of sand.* 3. a tiny amount: *a grain of sense.* 4. a very small unit of weight equal to one seven-thousandth of a pound. 5. the arrangement of fibers in wood, as indicated by surface markings.

graph

gram (gram) *n.* the metric unit of mass or weight, approximately equal to one twenty-eighth of an ounce.

gram·mar ('gramər) *n.* 1. the description and classification of sounds and words in a language and the ways in which they are arranged and modified to form sentences. 2. a book about the grammar of a certain language: *a French grammar.* 3. speech or writing that agrees with accepted standards or rules: *bad grammar.* —**gram·mat·i·cal** (grə'matikəl) *adj.* —**gram'mat·i·cal·ly** *adv.*

grand (grand) *adj.* 1. very great in size or appearance: *the palace was very grand.* 2. very high in rank or dignity; of great importance: *a grand ruler.* 3. noble or admirable: *a grand old man.* 4. complete or final: *he added up the figures to find the grand total.* 5. (informal) very good: *we had a grand time.* '**grand·stand** *n.* the principal seating area in a stadium. —*n.* 1. a grand PIANO. 2. (slang) a thousand dollars. —'**grand·ly** *adv.* —'**grand·ness** *or* **grand·eur** ('granjər) *n.*

grant (grant) *vb.* 1. to give, esp. formally: *the king granted a new charter.* 2. to agree to: *he granted her request.* —*n.* something given formally such as a right, a piece of land, or a sum of money: *Christopher was given a grant to continue his studies.*

grape (grāp) *n.* a green or purple berry that grows in clusters on vines and is eaten or used to make wine.

grape·fruit ('grāpfro͞ot) *n.,pl.* **grape·fruit** *or* **grape·fruits.** a large round yellow-skinned edible CITRUS fruit with a juicy acid-tasting flesh.

graph (graf) *n.* a diagram showing by means of curves, lines, etc., how one quantity or factor changes with respect to another. '**graph·ic** *adj.* 1. of, concerning, or shown on a graph, diagram, or drawing. 2. vivid; clear: *she gave a graphic description of the event.* —'**graph·i·cal·ly** *adv.*

grasp (grasp) *vb.* 1. (often + *at*) to grip firmly with the hands or fingers: *he grasped the glass tightly.* 2. to get hold of mentally; understand: *do you grasp my meaning?* —*n.* 1. a hold or grip: *he held me in his grasp.* 2. the ability to understand: *this book is beyond my grasp.* '**grasp·ing** *adj.* greedy.

grass·hop·per ('grashopər) *n.* a plant-eating insect having strong hind legs with which it leaps considerable distances and which are rubbed against the wings to produce a ticking sound.

grate[1] (grāt) *vb.* **grat·ing, grat·ed.** 1. to rub together with a harsh scraping noise: *the knife grated against the plate.* 2. to reduce to small pieces by rubbing against a rough cutting surface: *she grated a carrot.* 3. (+ *on*) to have an irritating effect: *his constant chatter grates on my nerves.*

grate[2] (grāt) *n.* 1. a metal framework, esp. of iron, for holding burning fuel in a fireplace, furnace, etc. 2. (also **grat·ing**) a framework of bars used as a guard, cover, etc. 3. a fireplace.

grate·ful ('grātfəl) *adj.* 1. thankful to someone for benefits received, kindness, a gift, etc. —'**grate·ful·ly** *adv.* —**grat·i·tude** ('gratito͞od, 'gratityo͞od) '**grate·ful·ness** *n.*

grave[1] (grāv) *n.* 1. a pit or hole in the earth in which a dead body is buried. 2. any place of burial; tomb. '**grave·stone** *n.* a slab of stone placed over a grave and carved with the name and birth and death dates of the person buried there. '**grave·yard** *n.* a cemetery; burial ground.

grave[2] (grāv) *adj.* 1. serious or solemn in manner or expression. 2. important; involving serious matters: *grave news.* —'**grave·ly** *adv.*

grav·el ('gravəl) *n.* small stones and pebbles; a mixture of these with sand, used for making paths and roads. —*vb.* **grav·el·ing, grav·eled.** to cover with gravel. —'**grav·el·ly** *adj.*

grav·i·ty ('gravitē) *n.* 1. (also **grav·i·ta·tion**) the force that holds or pulls objects down toward the earth. 2. seriousness; importance: *Ted did not realise the gravity of the situation until it was too late.* —**grav·i'ta·tion·al** *adj.*

graze[1] (grāz) *vb.* **graz·ing, grazed.** 1. (of cattle, sheep, etc.) to feed on growing grass or pasture. 2. to cause cattle, sheep, etc., to feed on pasture or grassland: *the cattleman grazed his stock on a new pasture.*

graze[2] (grāz) *vb.* **graz·ing, grazed.** to scrape the surface from: *I fell and grazed my knee.* —*n.* a slight scratch on the skin.

grease (grēs) *n.* 1. soft animal fat. 2. any fatty or oily substance usu. used to reduce friction between the moving parts of a machine, etc. —*vb.* **greas·ing, greased.** to cover with grease. —'**greas·y** *adj.* **greas·i·er, greas·i·est.**

greed (grēd) *n.* excessive desire, esp. for food, money, or power. '**greed·y** *adj.* **greed·i·er, greed·i·est.** (often + *for* or *of*) excessively eager for: *he was always greedy for praise.* —'**greed·i·ly** *adv.*

greenhouse

green·house ('grēnhous) *n.* a building, mainly made of glass, for the cultivation of plants.

greet (grēt) *vb.* 1. to address (someone) with a special remark or form of words when meeting: *we greeted our guests cheerfully.* 2. to meet with or receive: *her speech was greeted with applause.* '**greet·ing** *n.* the words or actions of someone who greets.

gre·nade (grə'nād) *n.* 1. a small explosive shell thrown by hand or shot from a rifle. 2. a glass container that shatters and releases chemicals, such as tear gas, when thrown.

grew (gro͞o) *vb.* the past tense of GROW.

grey·hound ('grāhound) *n.* a tall slender short-haired dog, noted for its great speed and keen sight.

grid (grid) *n.* 1. a framework of crossed bars; grating. 2. a set of numbered squares on a map to indicate the accurate position of a place.

grief (grēf) *n.* 1. deep sorrow or distress over affliction or loss: *the loss of his wallet caused him a great deal of grief.* 2. a cause of such distress.

grieve (grēv) *vb.* **griev·ing, grieved.** (often + *over*) to feel or cause to feel deep sorrow or grief: *he grieved over the death of his friend.* **'griev·ance** *n.* 1. a real or imagined wrong; complaint. 2. a state of resentment. **'griev·ous** *adj.* extremely serious: *grievous injuries.*

grill (gril) *n.* 1. a kitchen device in which meat, fish, or vegetables are cooked by placing them on a metal grid directly under or over a source of heat. 2. a dish of meat, fish, or vegetables cooked in this way. —*vb.* to cook using a grill; broil.

grille

grille (gril) *n.* a gridlike screen or barrier usu. made of metal and often of decorative design.

grim (grim) *adj.* **grim·mer, grim·mest.** stern; fierce; bitter or harsh: *he worked with grim determination.* —**'grim·ly** *adv.* — **'grim·ness** *n.*

grime (grīm) *n.* dirt, dust, etc., ground into or covering the surface of something. —**'grim·y** *adj.* **grim·i·er, grim·i·est.** —**'grim·i·ness** *n.*

grin (grin) *vb.* **grin·ning, grinned.** to show the teeth in a broad smile. —*n.* the action or an instance of grinning.

grind (grīnd) *vb.* **grind·ing, ground.** 1. to crush into powder or tiny particles: *to grind coffee.* 2. to sharpen, shape, or smooth by means of friction: *to grind a knife.* 3. to rub (one's teeth) together, making a harsh scraping sound. 4. to work or study very hard. 5. (+ *down*) to wear down or oppress: *her constant nagging ground down his resistance to the plan.*

grip (grip) *vb.* **grip·ping, gripped.** 1. to take a firm hold of; grasp: *the little boy gripped his mother's hand when they crossed the street.* 2. to capture the interest or attention of someone: *the story gripped me right to the end.* —*n.* 1. a firm hold; grasp. 2. an understanding: *he has a good grip on the subject.*

gris·tle ('grisəl) *n.* a tough whitish elastic substance found in meat.

grit (grit) *n.* 1. small particles of stone or sand. 2. (informal) courage. —*vb.* **grit·ting, grit·ted.** to clench the teeth together in anticipation of pain or in anger. —**'grit·ty** *adj.* **grit·ti·er, grit·ti·est.** —**'grit·ti·ness** *n.*

groan (grōn) *n.* a low sound of distress, pain, disappointment, etc. —*vb.* 1. to make the sound of a groan: *Stan groaned when he heard the bad news.* 2. (of things) to be overloaded or weighed down: *the table groaned with food.*

gro·cer ('grōsər) *n.* a retail dealer who sells packaged foods and household goods, fresh fruits and vegetables, etc. **'gro·cer·y** *n.,pl.* **gro·cer·ies.** 1. a grocer's shop or business. 2. **groceries** (*pl.*) goods bought from a grocer's shop.

groom (gro͞om) *n.* 1. a person who takes care of the horses at a stable. 2. a bridegroom. See BRIDE. —*vb.* 1. to brush and clean the hair of a horse, dog, cat, etc. 2. to make oneself tidy or smart: *Olivia groomed herself before going dancing.*

groove (gro͞ov) *n.* a narrow channel or furrow on the surface of an object.

grope (grōp) *vb.* **grop·ing, groped.** 1. to move or search by feeling rather than looking: *Carol groped around in the dark.* 2. to make progress in a slow or hesitant manner: *to grope toward an understanding of a problem.* —**'grop·ing·ly** *adv.*

gross (grōs) *adj.* 1. whole; entire; without anything being taken away: *a gross wage.* Compare NET[2]. 2. very large or fat, often unpleasantly so. 3. rude; vulgar: *gross language.* —*n.* 1. the total amount of something. 2. a batch of 144 (12 dozen) items. —*vb.* to have as one's total earnings, before taxation. —**'gross·ly** *adv.*

gro·tesque (grō'tesk) *adj.* 1. fantastically ugly. 2. (in art) decorated with fantastic or monstrous human and animal forms intertwined with foliage.

ground[1] (ground) *n.* 1. the land surface of the earth. 2. the surface of cloth, a flag, etc., esp. with respect to its color: *her dress had blue flowers on a white ground.* 3. often **grounds** (*pl.*) a cause; basic reason: *he left his job on the grounds that he was underpaid.* 4. **grounds** (*pl.*) the land surrounding a large house, etc. —*vb.* 1. to keep (an aircraft pilot) from flying, esp. for medical reasons. 2.(+ *on*) to use (something) as a reason or basis for (some action): *his decision to leave was grounded in fear.*

ground[2] (ground) *vb.* the past tense of GRIND. —*n.* usu. **grounds** (*pl.*) something ground up or the remains of something ground up: *coffee grounds.*

group (gro͞op) *n.* a number of people or things considered together; assembly or collection. —*vb.* to form into a group.

grouse

grouse[1] (grous) *n.,pl.* **grouse.** a type of GAME bird, which includes the prairie chicken and ruffed grouse, that has feathered legs and brown, gray, or black plumage.

grouse² (grous) *vb.* **grous·ing, groused.** (informal) to grumble; complain. —*n.* (informal) an instance of grousing; complaint.

grov·el ('gruvəl, 'grovəl) *vb.* 1. to crawl on the ground with the head down in humility or fear: *the slaves groveled before the emperor.* 2. to fawn; flatter in the hope of gaining something.

grow (grō) *vb.* **grow·ing, grew, grown.** 1. to get bigger; develop. 2. to gradually become: *to grow tired.* 3. to raise plants: *he grows flowers in his garden.* **grow up** to become an adult; mature. **'grown-up** *n.* an adult. **growth** (grōth) *n.* 1. the process or amount of development or growing: *the growth of his savings pleased him.* 2. something that has grown, often something that develops in or on the body because of disease.

growl (groul) *vb.* 1. (of a dog) to make a deep angry throaty noise. 2. to express angrily or aggressively: *he growled an order.* —*n.* the sound of a growl.

grub (grub) *n.* 1. the wormlike LARVA of certain insects. 2. (informal) food. —*vb.* **grub·bing, grubbed.** to search for something by or as if by digging; dig up or uproot. **'grub·by** *adj.* **grub·bi·er, grub·bi·est.** *adj.* dirty.

grudge (gruj) *vb.* **grudg·ing, grudged.** to be jealous or resentful of: *I don't grudge him his wealth.* —*n.* an instance or cause of resentment.

grue·some ('groosəm) *adj.* horrifying; terrible to see: *a gruesome accident.* —**'grue·some·ly** *adv.* —**'grue·some·ness** *n.*

grum·ble ('grumbəl) *vb.* **grum·bling, grum·bled.** 1. to complain. 2. to murmur in low indistinct sounds. —*n.* 1. the action or an example of grumbling; complaint or murmur. 2. a rumble: *the volcano gave a grumble before erupting.* —**'grum·bler** *n.*

grunt (grunt) *n.* 1. a low short murmured sound: *he gave a grunt of agreement.* 2. the sound made by a pig. —*vb.* to make the sound of or express with a grunt.

guar·an·tee (garən'tē) *n.* 1. a promise, esp. a formal or official one, that something will be done, will work properly, etc.: *the radio was sold with a guarantee.* 2. a promise to accept responsibility for the actions, genuineness, or honesty of a person or thing. —*vb.* **guar·an·tee·ing, guar·an·teed.** to provide a guarantee for (a person or thing).

guinea pig

guard (gârd) *vb.* 1. to watch over; defend; protect. 2. to keep as a prisoner; prevent from escaping. —*n.* 1. a person who guards. 2. the action or an instance of guarding: *the police set a guard around the building.* 3. a man who looks after a train. 4. a defense or protection. **guard dog** a large dog especially trained to guard property. **'guard·i·an** *n.* a person who takes responsibility for an orphan.

guer·ril·la *or* **gue·ril·la** (gə'rilə) *n.* a fighter who is not part of a regular army but carries on war as a member of a small secret band.

guess (ges) *n.* an opinion, judgment, or estimate that one cannot be certain about. —*vb.* to make a guess about something.

guest (gest) *n.* a visitor or a person invited to someone's home or staying at a hotel, etc.

guide (gīd) *vb.* **guid·ing, guid·ed.** 1. to point out the way to; lead, as an expedition or tour. 2. to advise: *the principal tried to guide Don in his choice of career.* —*n.* 1. a person acting as a guide. 2. something such as a book, providing information or advice. **guide dog** a dog especially trained to lead a blind person. **'guid·ance** *n.* advice.

guild (gild) *n.* 1. an association of people with similar jobs or interests set up to help and protect its members. 2. one of many such organizations formed in England during the Middle Ages.

guil·lo·tine ('gilətēn) *n.* 1. a mechanical device, used mainly in France, for executing people by dropping a heavy blade onto the neck to cut off the head. 2. a device for cutting or trimming paper. —*vb.* **guil·lo·tin·ing, guil·lo·tined.** to execute by guillotine.

guilt (gilt) *n.* 1. the condition of being responsible for a crime or wrong. 2. the feeling connected with this. **'guilt·y** *adj.* **guilt·i·er, guilt·i·est.** responsible for a crime or wrong. —**'guilt·i·ly** *adv.* —**'guilt·i·ness** *n.*

guin·ea pig ('ginē) 1. a small ratlike animal without a tail often kept as a pet or used in scientific experiments. 2. any person or animal used in a scientific or other test.

gui·tar (gi'târ) *n.* a stringed musical instrument having a wooden body curving inward at the center and a narrow wooden neck crossed by small ridges called frets.

gulf (gulf) *n.* 1. a deep hole; ravine. 2. a stretch of sea partly surrounded by

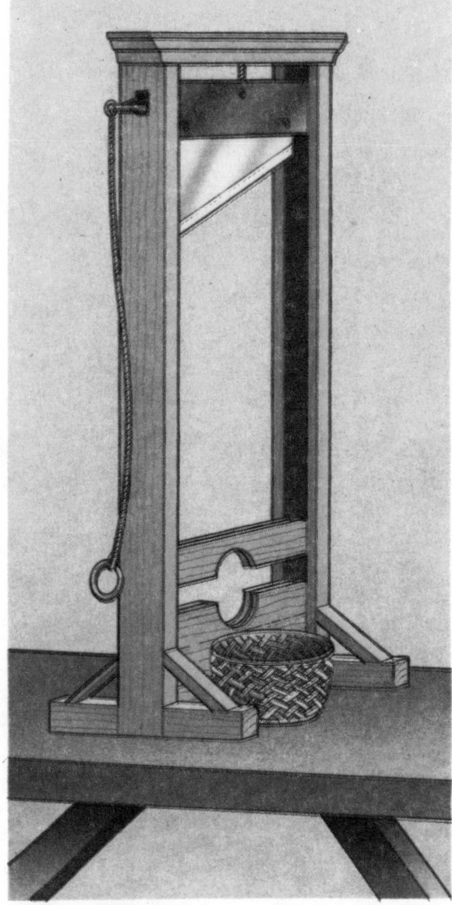

guillotine

land. 3. any wide gap or space: ***their different backgrounds formed a gulf between them.***

gull (gul) *n.* (also **sea·gull**) a type of seabird having webbed feet, a white front, a grayish back, and long grayish wings.

gul·let ('gulit) *n.* the passage along which food moves from the mouth to the stomach; throat.

gul·li·ble ('guləbəl) *adj.* easily deceived or tricked: ***the gullible customer was persuaded to buy a faulty machine.*** —**gul·li'bil·i·ty** *adj.*

gulp (gulp) *vb.* 1. to swallow quickly: ***he gulped his food.*** 2. to swallow as a sign of nervousness, fright, or surprise: ***he gulped when he saw how big his opponent was.*** —*n.* an instance of gulping.

gum[1] (gum) *n.* the soft flesh surrounding the base of a tooth.

gum[2] (gum) *n.* 1. a thick substance obtained from certain trees and used as glue. 2. a confection made from such a substance: ***chewing gum.*** 3. (also **gum tree**) a tree producing gum. —*vb.* **gum·ming, gummed.** 1. to stick with gum: ***he gummed the stamp onto the envelope.*** 2. (+ *up*) to make a mess of (something): ***your plan to finish the job in half the time really gummed up the works.***

gur·gle ('gûrgəl) *n.* a bubbling noise, as of boiling liquid. — *vb.* **gur·gling, gur·gled.** to make a bubbling sound: ***the water gurgled as it came out of the pipe.***

gush (gush) *vb.* 1.(often + *out, forth,* etc.) (of liquid) to rush out of somewhere in a flood. 2. to release (liquid) in a rushing flood: ***the crack in the pipe gushed oil onto the ground.*** 3. to talk enthusiastically. —*n.* 1. the action or an instance of gushing. 2. a flood of liquid. 3. a flow of enthusiastic talk.

gust (gust) *n.* 1. a sudden strong burst of wind, rain, smoke, sound, etc. 2. a burst of passion or emotion. —*vb.* (of the wind) to blow in gusts.

gut (gut) *n.* 1. the channel along which food travels through the body; intestine. 2. material prepared from the intestines of an animal, e.g. a sheep, and used for strings for violins, tennis-rackets, etc. 3. **guts** (*pl.*) (slang) courage. —*vb.* **gut·ting, gut·ted.** 1. to remove the insides from (a fish). 2. to burn completely the inside of (a building): ***fire gutted the apartment.***

gut·ter ('gutər) *n.* 1. a drainage channel at the side of a street for carrying away surface water. 2. a similar channel running around a roof.

gym·na·si·um (jim'nāzēəm) *n.* a special room or building fitted out with equipment for physical exercise. **gym·nast** ('jimnast) *n.* someone who performs physical exercises as a sport. **gym'nas·tic** *adj.* of or connected with physical exercises. **gym'nas·tics** *sing.n.* the sport involving such exercises.

Gyp·sy *or* **Gip·sy** ('jipsē) *n.,pl.* **Gyp·sies** *or* **Gip·sies.** a member of a group of nomadic people who came to Europe from India about 600 years ago. —*adj.* of or like a Gypsy. written **gip·sy** or **gyp·sy.**

gymnastics

H

hab·it ('habit) *n.* 1. a regularly repeated action, esp. one that is done without thinking about it: ***he has the habit of scratching his head when thinking.*** 2. a special form of clothing worn by certain people for a particular reason: ***a monk's habit.*** **'hab·i·tat** *n.* the natural surroundings of plants or animals: ***tigers have a jungle habitat.***

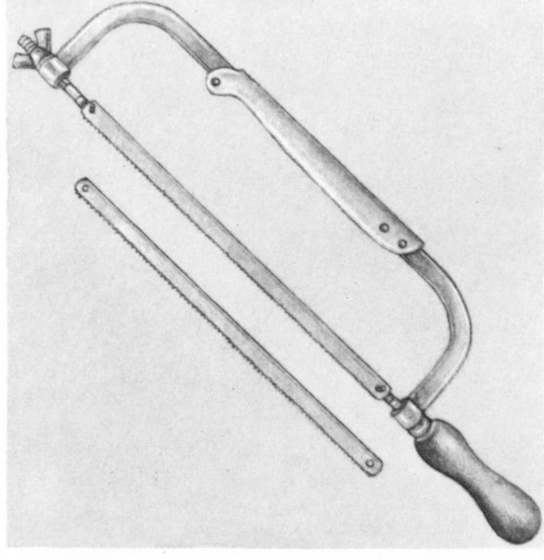

hacksaw

hack·saw ('haksô) *n.* a saw with a narrow replaceable blade used for cutting metals.

had·dock ('hadək) *n.* a deep-sea fish like a COD but smaller. It is found esp. in the eastern Atlantic around Britain, and is often eaten smoked.

hail[1] (hāl) *vb.* 1. to greet or call to (someone). 2. to come from a particular place: ***he hails from Texas.*** —*n.* a shouted greeting.

hail[2] (hāl) *n.* 1. balls of ice made from raindrops frozen together in a thundercloud and falling as a shower. 2. a shower of small missiles: ***a hail of bullets.*** —*vb.* 1. to fall as hailstones. 2. to cause (blows, words, etc.) to fall violently upon someone: ***he was hailed with abuse when he broke a glass.***

hair (heər) *n.* 1. one of the fine threadlike growths from the skin of mammals and certain other animals. 2. the mass of these growing on a human head. —**'hair·y** *adj.* **hair·i·er, hair·i·est.** —**'hair·i·ness** *n.*

hair-rais·ing ('heərrāziñg) *adj.* very frightening.

half (haf) *n.,pl.* **halves.** one of two equal parts into which a thing is divided. —*adj.* half of something: ***the ship slowed down to half speed.***

half-hearted *adj.* not very enthusiastic: ***they gave the team half-hearted support.***

hal·i·but ('halibət) *n.* the largest of the flatfishes, living on the bottom of the North Atlantic and Pacific Oceans. It is often used for food.

hall (hôl) *n.* 1. a building used for public gatherings, concerts, etc. 2. a large public room in a building. 3. a big house or other dwelling. 4. the entrance passage of a private house or apartment.

hall·mark ('hôlmârk) *n.* 1. a mark used by government offices for stamping silver or gold to indicate its quality. 2. a distinguishing characteristic: ***the hallmark of a gentleman is politeness.***

ha·lo ('hālō) *n.,pl.* **ha·los** *or* **ha·loes.** 1. a circle of light around the head of Christ and the saints, esp. in religious pictures. 2. a circle of light around a heavenly body, such as the moon.

halt (hôlt) *vb.* to stop or cause to stop, esp. on a journey: ***Frank halted at the end of the street.*** —*n.* a temporary stop on a journey.

halter (hôltər) *n.* a rope or strap that fits around the head or neck of a horse or other tame animal and is used to lead it.

halve (hav) *vb.* **halv·ing, halved.** to divide (something) into two equal parts.

ham (ham) *n.* 1. meat from the thigh of a pig. 2. (informal) an actor who overacts. —*vb.* to overact.

ham·burg·er ('hambûrgər) *n.* a flat round cake of minced beef, often grilled or fried and served in a split bread roll.

ham·let ('hamlit) *n.* a small group of houses in the country, smaller than a village.

ham·mer ('hamər) *n.* 1. a TOOL, usu. with a wooden handle and metal head, used for hitting nails and flattening or breaking wood, metal, etc. 2. one of the three small bones in the middle ear that transmit sounds to the inner ear. See EAR. —*vb.* to hit, join, or shape (nails, metal, etc.).

ham·mock ('hamək) *n.* a bed made of strong cloth or netting hung between two supports and swinging freely between them.

ham·per[1] ('hampər) *vb.* to hinder by getting in the way of (someone or something); to restrict.

ham·per[2] ('hampər) *n.* a large basket with a lid: ***a picnic hamper.***

ham·ster ('hamstər) *n.* a small furry animal rather like a rat with a short tail and pouched cheeks that is often kept as a pet.

ham·string ('hamstriñg) *n.* a cord (tendon) connecting the muscle with the leg bone at the back of the knee.

halo

hand (hand) *n.* 1. the part of the human body below the wrist. 2. a worker: *a factory hand.* 3. a pointer on a clock, watch, etc. 4. a style of writing: *her work was easy to read as she had a very clear hand.* —*vb.* (often + *over*) to give. **hand down** to pass on, esp. to an heir.

hand·cuff ('handkuf) *n.* one of a pair of locking metal bracelets joined by a short chain, used by police to restrict a prisoner's movements. —*vb.* to put (someone) in handcuffs.

hand·i·cap ('handēkap) *n.* a problem or circumstance tending to hold a person back, esp. a physical disability: *John's deafness is a handicap to him.* —*vb.* **hand·i·cap·ping, hand·i·capped.** 1. to hold back or restrict. 2. to create an infirmity or disability in (a person).

hand·ker·chief ('hangkərchif) *n.* a piece of cloth or tissue-like paper used for cleaning the nose, wiping away perspiration, etc.

han·dle ('handəl) *vb.* **han·dling, han·dled.** 1. to control or touch with the hands: *she handled the glass carefully.* 2. to deal with (a person, subject, business, etc.): *he handled his staff with tact.* —*n.* that part of a tool, object, etc., intended to be grasped or held by the hand, e.g. a doorhandle.

hand·some ('hansəm) *adj.* 1. pleasing to look at, esp. used of a good looking man. 2. ample in quantity; generous: *a handsome donation.* —'**hand·some·ly** *adv.*

hand·y ('handē) *adj.* **hand·i·er, hand·i·est.** 1. useful: *a handy tool.* 2. clever at using one's hands. 3. readily available: *keep the first-aid kit handy.*

hare

hang (hang) *vb.* **hang·ing, hung** *or* (for def. 2) **hanged.** 1. to hold or be held from above only, esp. so as to swing loosely. 2. to kill (a person) by suspending him by a rope around his neck. **hang about** to remain waiting: *we hung about in the garage while the car was being repaired.* **hang back** to be unwilling to act; hesitate. **hang onto** to hold onto; to refuse to let go of. **hang up** to end a telephone conversation by replacing the receiver.

hap·pen ('hapən) *vb.* 1. to take place; occur: *what happened yesterday?* 2. to take place by chance: *I happened to see Carol last night.* 3. to become of: *what happened to you when you left?* **happen on** *or* **upon** to come across by accident: *he happened on a clearing in the wood.* '**hap·pen·ing** *n.* an event.

hap·py ('hapē) *adj.* **hap·pi·er, hap·pi·est.** 1. expressing or feeling joy. 2. lucky: *that was a happy win.* —'**hap·pi·ly** *adv.* —'**hap·pi·ness** *n.*

har·bor ('hârbər) *n.* 1. a place of shelter for ships on a sea coast. 2. any place of refuge. —*vb.* 1. to give protection to (someone): *the criminal was harbored by friends.* 2. to keep (an idea, a feeling, etc.) in one's mind: *he harbored dreams of riches.*

hard (hârd) *adj.* 1. solid; firm. 2. difficult to understand or deal with: *a hard problem.* 3. strict; severe: *a hard man.* 4. violent: *a hard blow.* 5. energetic: *a hard worker.* —*adv.* 1. strenuously: *he tried hard to win the race.* 2. forcefully; violently: *he hit the ball hard.* 3. intently; earnestly: *he looked hard at the notice.* '**hard·en** *vb.* 1. to make or become hard or harder. 2. to make or become insensitive or indifferent: *Matthew hardened himself to the fact that he might fail his test.* —'**hard·ness** *n.*

hard·ly ('hârdlē) *adv.* scarcely: *he hardly moved an inch.*

hard·ship ('hârdship) *n.* something that is difficult to bear, esp. poverty, pain, hunger, etc.

hard·ware ('hârdweər) *n.* man-made metal goods.

har·dy ('hârdē) *adj.* **har·di·er, har·di·est.** able to survive hardship; tough. —'**har·di·ly** *adv.* '**har·di·ness** *n.* great physical endurance.

hare (heər) *n.* a wild animal similar to a rabbit but larger, with long ears and powerful hind legs.

harm (hârm) *n.* 1. injury; damage. 2. moral evil; wrong. —*vb.* to injure physically or mentally. —'**harm·ful** *adj.* '**harm·less** *adj.* —'**harm·ful·ly** *adv.* —'**harm·less·ly** *adv.*

har·mon·i·ca (hâr'monikə) *n.* a musical wind instrument consisting of reeds set in a box and sounded by blowing or sucking air over them. It is also called a mouth organ.

har·mo·ny ('hârmənē) *n.,pl.* **har·mo·nies.** 1. musical notes that are sounded together to make chords. 2. agreement; accordance. '**har·mo·nize** *vb.* **har·mo·niz·ing, har·mo·nized.** to be in harmony. —**har·mo·ni·ous** (hâr'mōnēəs) *adj.* —**har'mo·ni·ous·ly** *adv.*

har·ness ('hârnis) *n.* the leather straps and metal parts used to attach a work animal to a plow, carriage, etc. —*vb.* to put a harness on (an animal).

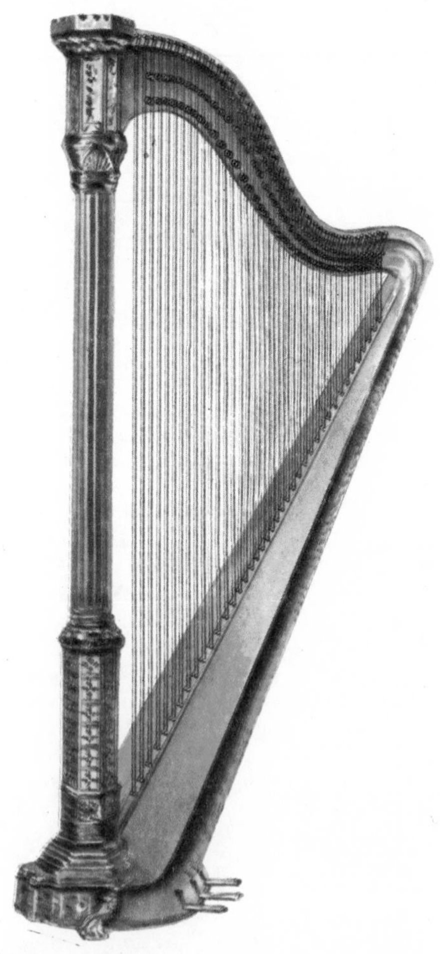

harp

harp (hârp) *n.* a large musical instrument with strings that are plucked by the player's fingers. **harp on** to talk about, too much; repeat.

har·poon (hâr'po͞on) *n.* a spearlike weapon with a rope attached to one end. It is shot from a gun or thrown by hand and used for spearing and capturing whales and fish. *—vb.* to use a harpoon to kill (whales, fish, etc.).

harsh (hârsh) *adj.* 1. unpleasant to any of the senses: *harsh sounds.* 2. cruel: *he is a harsh man.* —**'harsh·ly** *adv.* —**'harsh·ness** *n.*

har·vest ('hârvist) *n.* 1. the gathering in of ripe crops. 2. the crops so gathered. 3. the time of year when crops are gathered. 4. the results of actions, esp. the rewards of hard work: *the harvest of all his efforts was a pay raise.* *—vb.* 1. to gather in crops. 2. to obtain the results of one's deeds, esp. as reward or punishment.

haste (hāst) *n.* speed of movement or action: *Cathy finished the job with haste so that she could leave early.* **has·ten** ('hāsən) *vb.* to move or cause to move speedily: *she hastened home when it began to rain.* —**'hast·y** *adj.* **hast·i·er, hast·i·est.** —**'hast·i·ly** *adv.* —**'hast·i·ness** *n.*

hatch[1] (hach) *vb.* 1.(of young birds, snakes, etc.) to break out of their eggs. 2. to cause (chicks, snakes, etc.) to be born from eggs: *the farmer hatches chicks in an incubator.* 3. to think up a plan: *they hatched a plot.* **'hatch·er·y** *n.,pl.* **hatch·er·ies.** a place where young (chicks, fish, etc.) are reared from eggs.

hatch[2] (hach) *n.* 1. a trapdoor in a floor, deck, or roof.

hatch·et ('hachit) *n.* a small ax with a short handle, usu. held in one hand.

hate (hāt) *vb.* **hat·ing, hat·ed.** to have an extreme dislike or loathing for (someone or something): *he hates war.* *—n.* 1. the emotion or feeling of extreme dislike; loathing. 2. the object of the hate or dislike: *oranges are one of my pet hates.* **'hate·ful** *adj.* 1. full of hate. 2. causing or deserving hate: *making your little sister cry was a hateful thing to do.* —**'hate·ful·ly** *adv.* —**'hate·ful·ness** *n.* **'ha·tred** *n.* the feeling of hate: *there was a look of hatred on his face.*

haugh·ty ('hôtē) *adj.* **haugh·ti·er, haugh·ti·est.** being overproud of oneself and scornful of others; showing great arrogance, and disdain for others: *the haughty princess looked down on her servants.* —**'haugh·ti·ly** *adv.* —**'haugh·ti·ness** *n.*

haul (hôl) *vb.* to pull in or up; drag or carry something along: *we hauled the boat out of the water.* *—n.* 1. a strong pull; tug. 2. something obtained or taken: *the thieves got a good haul.* 3. a distance, esp. one that is long or difficult: *it was a long haul up the hill.* **'haul·age** *n.* 1. the transport of goods. 2. the charge made for transporting goods. **'haul·er** *n.* a person or company that transports goods.

haunch (hônch) *n.* the fleshy rear part of humans and animals between the waist and the thighs; hip.

haunt (hônt) *vb.* 1. (of ghosts) to cause trouble or disturbance by lingering in a place after death. 2. to visit (a place) often: *he haunted the football club.* 3. to fill the mind repeatedly: *the song haunted her.* *—n.* a place often visited by a particular person. **'haunt·ed** *adj.* visited by ghosts and spirits: *a haunted house.*

hatchet

ha·ven ('hāvən) *n.* 1. a place where ships may stay protected from rough weather, etc. 2. any place of safety and peace.

hav·er·sack ('havərsak) *n.* a bag made to be carried on a person's back and used by hikers, soldiers, etc.

hav·oc ('havək) *n.* destruction and disruption of normal activities, usu. caused by a huge force: *the floods caused havoc in the small town.*

hawk[1] (hôk) *n.* a bird of prey with broad wings, strong curved beak, and powerful clawed feet.

hawk[2] (hôk) *vb.* to offer (goods) for sale in the street.

haw·thorn ('hôthôrn) *n.* a thorny tree or shrub of the rose family with pink or white flowers and small red berries.

hay (hā) *n.* cut and dried grass used for feeding cattle, etc.

hay fe·ver ('hā fēvər) *n.* an unpleasant allergic reaction suffered by some people if they breathe in pollen, dust, etc. Hay fever causes sneezing and a runny nose.

haz·ard ('hazərd) *n.* 1. something causing danger of injury or damage: *high winds are a hazard to small boats.* 2. something that is a risk or left to chance. 3. a dice game. *—vb.* 1. to expose to danger or damage. 2. to take a chance with; risk: *I'll hazard a guess.* —**'haz·ard·ous** *adj.* —**'haz·ard·ous·ly** *adv.*

haze (hāz) *n.* a thin mist caused by smoke, water vapor, or dust in the air: *a heat haze.*

ha·zel ('hāzəl) *n.* a tree or bush that produces small edible nuts (**hazelnuts**). *—n., adj.* (having) a light reddish brown color.

head (hed) *n.* 1. the part of the body above the neck. 2. anything like a head in shape, function, or position. 3. the most important person: *Mr. Parker is the head of a large business.* *—vb.* 1. to be a leader of: *she headed an inquiry into the problem.* 2. (often + *for*) to move in a particular direction: *let's head for home.*

head·line ('hedlīn) *n.* the title of a newspaper story.

head·quar·ters ('hedkwôrtərz) *n.* the place from which an organization or operation is controlled.

head·strong ('hedstrông, 'hedstrông) *adj.* not easily guided or controlled; obstinate.

heal (hēl) *vb.* to make or become well, esp. after an injury.

health (helth) *n.* a state of physical or mental well-being, esp. being free from illness. **'health·y** *adj.* **health·i·er, health·i·est.** having or encouraging good health: *jogging around the park is a healthy pastime.*

hear (hēr) *vb.* **hear·ing, heard** (hûrd). to become aware of sounds through the ears. **'hear·ing** *n.* 1. the ability to hear: *his hearing is perfect.* 2. a trial in a court of law: *the case was given two hearings.*

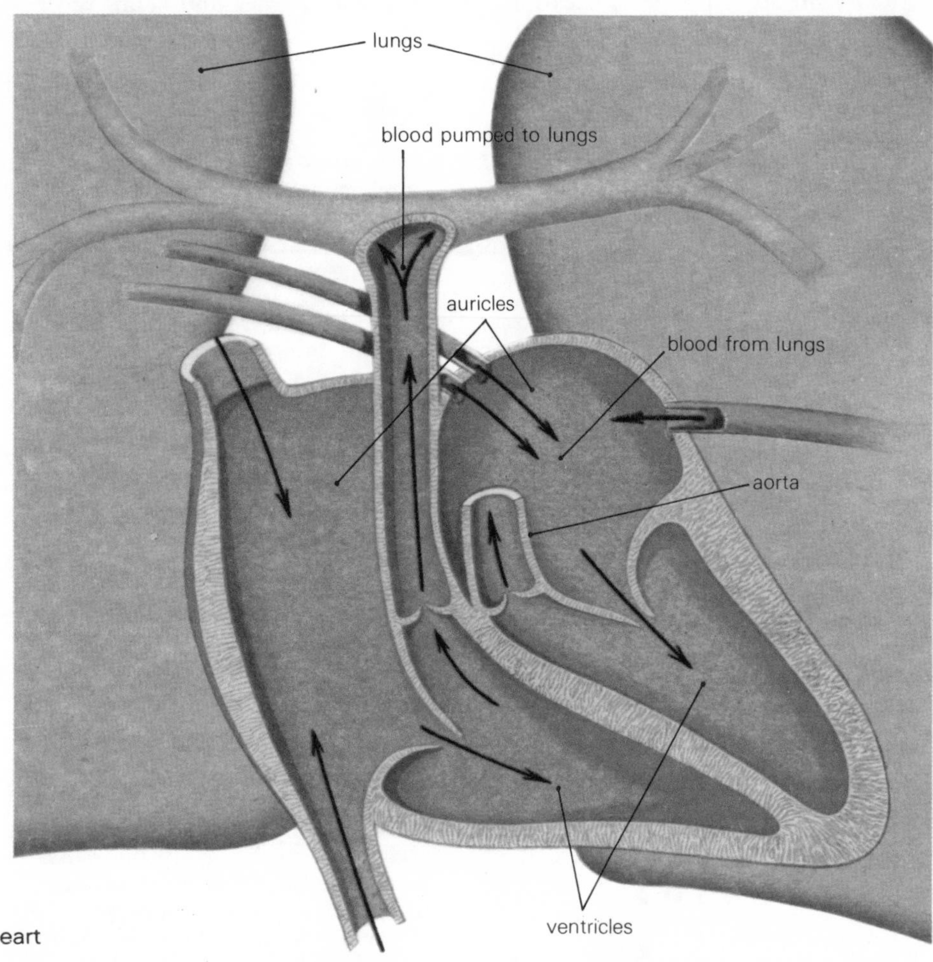

heart

heart (hârt) *n.* 1. the organ of the body that pumps blood. 2. the center of the emotions: *his heart was broken when the dog died.* 3. the center of any activity, organization, etc. **'heart·less** *adj.* unkind. **'heart·y** *adj.* **heart·i·er, heart·i·est.** 1. strong. 2. (of meals) big. —**'heart·i·ly** *adv.*

heath·er ('hedhər) *n.* a hardy evergreen shrub that has clusters of pink, purple, or white flowers.

heather

heav·en ('hevən) *n.* 1. (in religious belief) the place where God and his angels live and to which the souls of dead people go. 2. usu. **heav·ens** (*pl.*) the sky. 3. any delightful place or event. —**'heav·en·ly** *adj.*

heav·y ('hevē) *adj.* **heav·i·er, heav·i·est.** 1. difficult to lift; weighty: *a heavy sack.* 2. more than average: *a heavy rainfall.* **'heav·i·ly** *adv.* not lightly; clumsily: *the old lady fell quite heavily and hurt her leg.* —**'heav·i·ness** *n.*

hedge (hej) *n.* a barrier formed by bushes or trees planted close together. —*vb.* **hedg·ing, hedged.** 1. to form a fence with bushes or trees. 2. to avoid being committed: *he hedged on the issue.*

heed (hēd) *vb.* to pay careful attention to (someone or something): *Bob did not heed my advice and went out without a coat.* **'heed·ful** *adj.* careful. —**'heed·ful·ly** *adv.* **'heed·less** *adj.* unthinking; careless. —**'heed·less·ly** *adv.*

heel (hēl) *n.* 1. the rounded back part of a human foot. 2. the part of a sock or stocking covering it. 3. the part of a shoe underneath it.

height (hīt) *n.* 1. the distance between the top and bottom of anything: *the man was 6 feet in height.* 2. often **heights** (*pl.*) a high place. 3. a high point, esp. of success: *he died at the height of his fame.* **'height·en** *vb.* 1. to make or become higher. 2. to make (something or someone) more intense or dramatic: *the sun heightened the beauty of the lake.*

heir (eər) *n.* someone who receives a person's property, etc., after that person's death. **'heir·ess** *n.* a female heir.

heir·loom ('eərlo͞om) *n.* an object, esp. a valuable one, that has been owned by a family for many years and handed down from one generation to the next.

hel·i·cop·ter ('heləkoptər) *n.* an aircraft powered by long blades that rotate on top of it.

hell (hel) *n.* (in religious belief) a place of punishment for wicked souls after death. **'hell·ish** *adj.* horrible; wicked: *the hellish weather prevented them from going out.* —**'hell·ish·ly** *adv.* —**'hell·ish·ness** *n.*

helm (helm) *n.* the steering wheel or TILLER of a ship.

hel·met ('helmit) *n.* a hard hat (usu. metal) that prevents injuries to the head.

help (help) *vb.* 1. to aid or assist. 2. to avoid: *I couldn't help laughing.* —*n.* 1. an act of helping or assisting: *Susan gave help to the old man crossing the street.* 2. someone who gives assistance: *the help visits twice a week.* **'help·ing** *n.* an act of giving help. —**'help·ful** *adj.* —**'help·ful·ly** *adv.* —**'help·less** *adj.* —**'help·less·ly** *adv.*

hem (hem) *n.* the edge of a garment that has been made by turning over and stitching down the raw edge of the material. —*vb.* **hem·ming, hemmed.** to make a hem.

hem·i·sphere ('hemisfēr) *n.* half a sphere, esp. half the earth: *Australia is in the Southern Hemisphere.*

her·ald ('herəld) *n.* a messenger or carrier of news. —*vb.* to proclaim or announce: *the announcer heralded the arrival of the Senator at the car-*

heron

nival. **'her·ald·ry** *n.* the study of family histories, esp. in reference to the granting of family badges (coats of arms). —**he·ral·dic** (he'raldik) *adj.*

herb (ûrb) *n.* 1. a plant used to flavor food, e.g. parsley, sage, etc., and in making medicine and perfumes. 2. any plant that dies after flowering and does not have a woody stem.

herd (hûrd) *n.* a group of animals usu. of the same species that keeps together: *a herd of elephants.* —*vb.* 1. to come or cause to come together into a large group. 2. to drive (animals). **'herds·man** *n.,pl.* **herds·men.** a man in charge of a herd.

her·i·tage ('heritij) *n.* something that can be handed down from one generation to the next.

her·mit ('hûrmit) *n.* a person who lives alone, esp. a holy man. **'her·mit·age** *n.* a hermit's dwelling.

he·ro ('hērō) *n.,pl.* **he·roes.** 1. a man admired and respected for his great bravery. 2. the main male character in a play or book. **her·o·ine** ('herōin) *n.* a female hero. **he·ro·ic** (hi'rōik) *adj.* very brave. —**he'ro·i·cal·ly** *adv.* —**her·o·ism** ('herōizəm) *n.*

her·on ('herən) *n.* a large waterside bird that has a long slender bill for catching fish, a long neck, and long legs for wading.

her·ring ('heriñg) *n.,pl.* **her·rings** *or* **her·ring.** a small bony sea fish.

hes·i·tate ('hezitāt) *vb.* **hes·i·tat·ing, hes·i·tat·ed.** 1. to hang back or pause. 2. to show uncertainty: *he hesitated when telling us his tale.* —**'hes·i·tant** *adj.* —**'hes·i·tant·ly** *adv.* —**hes·i'ta·tion** *n.*

hex·a·gon ('heksəgon) *n.* a six-sided shape, usu. with sides of equal length. —**hex·ag·o·nal** (hek'sagənəl) *adj.*

hi·ber·nate ('hībərnāt) *vb.* **hi·ber·nat·ing, hi·ber·nat·ed.** (of some animals such as the ground squirrels) to spend the winter in very deep sleep. —**hi·ber'na·tion** *n.*

hic·cup ('hikup) *n.* often **hic·cups** (*pl.*) a jerky uncontrollable catching of breath, with a cough-like noise. —*vb.* to have an attack of hiccups. Also spelled **hic·cough.**

hide[1] (hīd) *vb.* **hid·ing, hid·den** *or* **hid.** 1. to keep secret; 2. to put or keep out of sight: *the trees hid the houses from view.*

hide[2] (hīd) *n.* 1. the skin of an animal, usu. a large one. 2. an animal skin treated for use in making clothing, shoes, bags, etc.; leather. **'hid·ing** *n.* a beating.

hid·e·ous ('hidēəs) *adj.* horrible or frightful: *the hideous crime shocked the whole town.* —**'hid·e·ous·ly** *adv.* —**'hid·e·ous·ness** *n.*

hi·er·ar·chy ('hīərâkē) *n., pl.* **hi·er·ar·chies.** people, institutions, etc., arranged in order of rank or authority: *he was near the top of the firm's hierarchy.*

hi·er·o·glyph·ic (hīərə'glifik) *n.* (also **hi·er·o·glyph**) a symbol or picture representing a word or sound, esp. in the writing (**hieroglyphics**) of the ancient Egyptians. —*adj.* of, or written in hieroglyphics.

high (hī) *adj.* 1. long from top to bottom; tall: *a high tower.* 2. much above ground or sea level: *he was high in the air.* 3. extending a specified distance upwards: *the tree is five feet high.* 4. relatively large or great in degree, intensity, importance, or amount: *high prices.* 5. (of sound, a note, etc.) at the upper end of the musical scale. 6. joyful; happy: *high spirits.* —*adv.* at or to a high place, level, degree, etc.: *he reached high to get the can from the shelf.* —*n.* something that is high: *prices reached a new high.* **'high·ly** *adv.* 1. very much. 2. with great respect, admiration, etc.: *we think highly of our teacher.* 3. at a high price. See also HEIGHT.

high·way ('hīwā) *n.* a main route, esp. a road between towns. **'high·way·man** *n.,pl.* **high·way·men.** (formerly) a robber, esp. one on horseback, who steals from travelers on public roads.

hi·jack ('hījak) *vb.* to seize control of or steal (a vehicle) in transit.

hike (hīk) *vb.* **hik·ing, hiked.** to go on a long walk through the countryside, esp. for pleasure. —*n.* a long walk.

hill (hil) *n.* 1. a raised area of land smaller than a mountain. 2. a small mound or pile: *an ant hill.*

hilt (hilt) *n.* the handle of a weapon or tool, esp. of a sword or dagger.

hin·der ('hindər) *vb.* to cause delay or difficulty. —**'hin·drance** *n.*

hinge (hinj) *n.* 1. a movable joint by which two things, e.g. a door and its frame, are connected, allowing one or both to turn or move. 2. a similar natural joint, e.g. in the knee. 3. something upon which other events, actions, etc., depend. —*vb.* **hing·ing, hinged.** 1. to turn on, supply with, or attach a hinge. 2. to depend or cause to depend.

hieroglyphic

hint (hint) *n.* 1. an indirect suggestion: *he dropped the hint that he wanted a new pen.* 2. a very slight amount: *a hint of garlic.* —*vb.* to make a hint or give a hint of.

hip (hip) *n.* the part of the body that sticks out below the waist at the sides and the back.

hip·po·pot·a·mus (hipə'potəməs) *n.,pl.* **hip·po·pot·a·mus·es** *or* **hip·po·pot·a·mi** (hipə'potəmī). often shortened to **hip·po.** a large plant-eating African animal with a tough hairless skin and short legs. It spends much time in the water.

hippopotamus

hire (hīər) *vb.* **hir·ing, hired.** 1. to engage the services or use of (someone or something) for payment: *he hired a boat.* 2. to grant the use or services of (someone or something) for payment: *the man hired boats to the campers.* —*n.* 1. the act of hiring. 2. the price paid or asked for hiring. **for hire** available or ready to be hired: *is this taxicab for hire?*

hiss (his) *vb.* to make a noise like the letter 's', as a snake does. —*n.* a hissing sound.

his·to·ry ('histərē) *n.,pl.* **his·to·ries.** 1. the branch of knowledge dealing with the past: *she was very interested in history.* 2. an account of past events relating to a particular nation, person, etc.: *a history of France.* **his·to·ri·an** (hi'stôrēən) *n.* a person who studies history as a profession. **his·tor·ic** (hi'stôrik, hi'storik) *adj.* having important connections with the past: *the signing of the treaty of Versailles was an historic occasion.* **his'tor·i·cal** *adj.* concerning history. —**his'tor·i·cal·ly** *adv.*

hit (hit) *vb.* **hit·ting, hit.** 1. to strike or knock against: *he hit his head on the low ceiling.* 2. to achieve (a desired target): *he hit the jackpot.* 3. to affect badly: *the manager's illness hit the business hard.* —*n.* 1. a blow or stroke, esp. one that reaches its target: *she scored three hits.* 2. (informal) popular success: *the song was a hit.*

hitch (hich) *vb.* 1. to move or pull something with a jerk: *he hitched his pants up.* 2. to tie up or fasten: *she hitched the horse to the rail.* —*n.* 1. a knot that can be quickly tied and untied. 2. a setback: *several hitches caused his late arrival.*

hitch·hike ('hichhīk) *vb.* **hitch·hik·ing, hitch·hiked.** to travel by taking free rides solicited from the drivers of passing vehicles.

hive (hīv) *n.* 1. a special box in which bees live and store their honey. 2. a busy scene: *a hive of activity.*

hoard (hôrd) *vb.* to collect and store, esp. in a secret place. —*n.* a hidden store (of food, money, etc.).

hoarse (hôrs) *adj.* (of a voice) husky; not clear. —**'hoarse·ly** *adv.* —**'hoarse·ness** *n.*

hoar·y ('hôrē) *adj.* whitened with age.

hoax (hōks) *n.* a trick or practical joke. —*vb.* to play a practical joke.

hob·ble ('hobəl) *vb.* **hob·bling, hob·bled.** 1. to limp. 2. to tie the legs of (a horse, etc.) together to prevent it running.

hob·by ('hobē) *n.,pl.* **hob·bies.** a favorite leisure-time activity.

hob·by·horse ('hobēhôrs) *n.* a toy made of a wooden horse's head stuck on a pole.

hock·ey ('hokē) *n.* a game played on a field by two teams of 11 players each. Sticks with curved ends are used to hit a small hard ball into the opposing team's goal. **ice hockey** a similar game played on ice by two teams of six players with a rubber disk (puck).

hoe (hō) *n.* a farming IMPLEMENT, consisting of a blade attached to a long handle and used for breaking up large lumps of soil. —*vb.* **hoe·ing, hoed.** to use a hoe.

hog (hôg, hog) *n.* 1. a pig. 2. (informal) a greedy person. —*vb.* **hog·ging, hogged.** to eat, consume, use, or take greedily.

hoist (hoist) *vb.* to pull up esp. by means of ropes and pulleys: *the sailors hoisted the sails.* —*n.* a device for lifting heavy goods.

hold (hōld) *vb.* **hold·ing, held.** 1. to grasp and keep a grip on something: *he held a pipe between his teeth.* 2. to keep in place or give support to: *this pillar holds the whole building up.* 3. to have or keep in one's possession or control: *they held the fort against many attacks.* 4. to contain or be able to contain: *this box holds all my marbles.* 5. to have (an opinion): *I hold that the earth is flat.* 6. (+ *back*) to deter or stop (someone) from doing something: *Andrew was held back in his career by his refusal to take advice.* 7. (+ *up*) to stop a person, vehicle, etc., with the intention of stealing: *the robbers held up a bank.* 8. (+ *up*) to delay or stop: *they were held up at the airport by fog.* —*n.* 1. a grasp; action of holding: *Mary had a firm hold on her mother's hand.* 2. an influence over someone: *she has a hold over him.* 3. storage space for goods below the deck of a ship, aircraft, etc.

hobbyhorse

honeycomb

hole (hōl) *n.* a space, gap, or hollow. —*vb.* **hol·ing, holed.** 1. to make a hole in (something): *he holed his sweater on the fence.* 2. (golf) to hit the ball into the hole.

hol·i·day ('holidā) *n.* one or more days recognized as a time when schools, banks, etc., and most businesses are closed: *the Fourth of July is a national holiday.*

hol·low ('holō) *n.* a space or groove in a solid object. —*adj.* 1. empty or with the center scooped out: *a hollow tree trunk.* 2. sunken: *his eyes were hollow.* —*vb.* to make a hollow; scoop out.

hol·ly ('holē) *n.,pl.* **hol·lies.** a small tree with dark green, prickly leaves and red berries, used for decoration at Christmas.

ho·ly ('hōlē) *adj.* **ho·li·er, ho·li·est.** 1. having special religious importance. 2. deeply religious: *St. Peter was a holy man.* **'hol·i·ness** *n.* the quality of being holy.

home (hōm) *n.* 1. the place where one lives. 2. the place where one was born and bred. 3. any place where people or animals are looked after: *a home for the aged.* —*adj.* 1. connected with one's home: *what is your home address?* 2. not foreign: *we found a home market for our goods.* —*adv.* 1. to or toward one's home: *he came home late.* 2. strongly touching one's feelings: *the photograph of his friends brought home his loneliness.* —*vb.* **hom·ing, homed.** to move naturally toward one's home. **'home·sick** *adj.* wishing one were at home. —**'home·less** *adj.*

hon·est ('onist) *adj.* trustworthy; not likely to cheat or tell lies. —**'hon·est·ly** *adv.* —**'hon·es·ty** *n.*

hon·ey ('hunē) *n.* sweet, yellow, sticky, edible syrup made by bees from the NECTAR inside flowers.

hon·ey·comb ('hunēkōm) *n.* the mass of six-sided cells made of wax in which bees store honey.

hon·ey·moon ('hunēmo͞on) *n.* a vacation that a bride and groom traditionally take directly after their wedding. —*vb.* to spend a honeymoon.

hon·ey·suck·le ('hunēsukəl) *n.* a climbing plant with sweet-smelling yellow, pink, and red flowers.

hon·or ('onər) *n.* 1. a strict standard of morals and behavior: *the new senator was considered a man of honor.* 2. title, privilege, award, etc., given as a mark of respect. —*vb.* to express respect for (someone). **'hon·or·a·ble** *adj.* having the quality of honor. —**'hon·or·a·bly** *adv.*

hon·or·ar·y ('onərerē) *adj.* 1. awarded as an honor: *he was given an honorary degree from the university when he became famous.* 2. holding a position or title without having the usual duties attached to it: *Mr White remained an honorary member of the board even after his retirement.*

hood (ho͝od) *n.* 1. a piece of clothing that covers the head and neck and is usu. attached to a coat, jacket, or cape. 2. the raisable lid over the engine of a car.

hoof (ho͝of, ho͞of) *n.,pl.* **hoofs** *or* **hooves.** the hard natural covering on the feet of certain animals, e.g. cows, horses, etc.

hook (ho͝ok) *n.* 1. a curved piece of wood, metal, etc., for hanging or fastening something: *a coat hook.* 2. a bent wire, usu. with a barb, for catching fish. 3. (in boxing) a short, swinging blow with the arm bent. —*vb.* 1. to curve into a hook; bend. 2. to catch (a fish). 3. to fasten or attach.

hoo·li·gan ('ho͞oləgən) *n.* a member of a gang of ruffians, esp. one who damages property.

hoot (ho͞ot) *n.* the cry of an owl, or a similar deep, hollow noise. —*vb.* 1. to make a noise like an owl's hoot. 2. to sound a car horn.

hop¹ (hop) *vb.* **hop·ping, hopped.** 1. to jump on one foot. 2. (of an animal) to jump using the hind legs held together. —*n.* a short jump.

hop

hop² (hop) *n.* a climbing plant that produces green cone-shaped flowers used in brewing beer.

hope (hōp) *vb.* **hop·ing, hoped.** to wish for or desire. —*n.* 1. a wish or desire. 2. something that one trusts will happen: *he has a hope of winning.* 3. a person or thing that raises expectations: *the passing ship was the castaway's only hope.* —**'hope·ful** *adj.* —**'hope·ful·ly** *adv.* —**'hope·ful·ness** *n.* —**'hope·less** *adj.* —**'hope·less·ly** *adv.* —**'hope·less·ness** *n.*

horde (hôrd) *n.* a very large crowd.

ho·ri·zon (hə'rīzən) *n.* the line in the distance at which the sky and the ground or sea seem to meet. **hor·i·zon·tal** (hôri'zontəl, hori'zontəl) *adj.* 1. parallel to the horizon. 2. parallel to the two eyes.

horn (hôrn) *n.* 1. a bony, pointed growth on the head of a cow, goat, etc. 2. the substance of which horns consist, often used to make other objects. 3. a type of brass musical instrument. **'horn·y** *adj.* **horn·i·er, horn·i·est.** hard like horn.

hor·ror ('hôrər, 'horər) *n.* 1. a feeling of terror or disgust: *I was filled with horror.* 2. something that causes fear, disgust, etc.: *the horrors of war.* **'hor·ri·ble** *adj.* 1. shocking; causing fear: *a horrible crime.* 2. very unpleasant: *a horrible smell.* **'hor·rid** *adj.* 1. disgusting; repulsive. 2. mean; nasty. **'hor·ri·fy** *vb.* **hor·ri·fy·ing, hor·ri·fied.** to disgust; cause shock or fear.

horse (hôrs) *n.* 1. a large hoofed four-legged animal, used for riding, carrying goods, pulling carts, etc. 2. a large wooden box with a padded top used in gymnastics.

hose[1] (hōz) *n.* stockings; socks.

hose[2] (hōz) *n.* a long flexible tube through which water is passed for watering gardens, putting out fires, etc. —*vb.* **hos·ing, hosed.** (often + *down*) to spray with water from a hose.

hos·pit·a·ble ('hospitəbəl, ho'spitəbəl) *adj.* offering a friendly welcome to visitors and treating them well.

hos·pi·tal ('hospitəl) *n.* a place in which people who are ill can be cared for by doctors, nurses, etc.

hos·pi·tal·i·ty (hospi'talitē) *n.* friendly and generous treatment of guests, esp. in one's home.

host[1] (hōst) *n.* 1. a man who receives guests. 2. a plant or animal on which another plant or animal, a PARASITE, depends for its existence. '**host·ess** *n.* 1. a woman who receives guests. 2. a woman who seats customers in a restaurant.

host[2] (hōst) *n.* a large number of people or things gathered in one place.

hos·tage ('hostij) *n.* a person who is kept as a prisoner until the captor receives money or some other thing he wants.

hos·tel ('hostəl) *n.* a building where people with very little money can stay overnight: *a youth hostel.*

hos·tile ('hostəl) *adj.* 1. of or concerning an enemy: *the spy crossed into hostile territory.* 2. unfriendly: *he was hostile to new ideas.* **hos·til·i·ty** (ho'stilitē) *n.,pl.* **hos·til·i·ties.** 1. unfriendliness. 2. (*pl.*) acts of war.

hot (hot) *adj.* **hot·ter, hot·test.** 1. having a high temperature; giving off, having, or feeling heat. 2. (of food) having a strong burning taste. 3. (informal) dangerous or uncomfortable: *the stolen goods were too hot to handle.* 4. very recent; having just come from: *the news was hot off the press.* '**hot·ly** *adv.* angrily.

ho·tel (hō'tel) *n.* a place where travelers can rent rooms, have meals, etc.

hound (hound) *n.* a dog trained for hunting, esp. a foxhound. —*vb.* to chase or worry persistently: *the outcast was hounded from town to town.*

hovercraft

hour (ouər) *n.* 1. one of the 24 equal parts of a day; 60 minutes. 2. **hours** (*pl.*) a period of time, esp. regular working time: *her hours are from 9:00 till 5:00.* 3. any particular time: *the hero of the hour.* —'**hour·ly** *adj., adv.*

house *n.* (hous), *pl.* **hous·es** ('houziz). 1. a building for people to live in. 2. the audience in a theater: *the group played to a full house every night.* 3. the legislating assembly of a country, e.g. the House of Representatives. 4. a family of importance including the ancestors and descendants: *the house of Tudor.* —*vb.* (houz) **hous·ing, housed.** 1. to provide with a house or shelter. 2. to act as a house for: *the old kettle housed the wren very well.*

house·wife ('houswīf) *n.,pl.* **house·wives.** a married woman who looks after her house and family.

hov·er ('huvər, 'hovər) *vb.* 1. to stay suspended in the air above one place: *the hawk hovered before swooping on its prey.* 2. to linger around close by: *Paul hovered by the kitchen door hoping to be given a cookie.*

Hov·er·craft ('huvərkraft) *n.* a trade name for a vehicle that moves at high speed on a cushion of air just above the surface of the ground or water.

howl (houl) *vb.* to make a long, wailing sound like that of a wolf. —*n.* a prolonged wailing cry.

hub (hub) *n.* 1. the solid central part of a wheel where it is joined to the AXLE. 2. the main point of activity, interest, etc.

hud·dle ('hudəl) *vb.* **hud·dling, hud·dled.** to gather together into a group, esp. for warmth or out of fear: *chicks huddle together in the nest to keep warm.* —*n.* a closely packed group.

huge (hyōōj) *adj.* enormous; very large.

hull (hul) *n.* the body of a hip or boat. the deck level.

hum (hum) *vb.* **hum·ming, hummed.** 1. to make a singing noise with the mouth closed. 2. to make a buzzing noise. —*n.* any humming noise.

hu·man ('hyo͞omən) *adj.* belonging to or concerning men and women: *apes have some human characteristics.* —*n.* a human being; a person. **hu·man·i·ty** (hyo͞o'manitē) *n.* 1. mankind; the human race: *his kindness arose from his love for humanity.* 2. kindness; the quality of being HUMANE. 3. human nature; the condition of being human.

hu·mane (hyo͞o'mān) *adj.* 1. kind; sympathetic. 2. minimizing the amount of pain to be suffered: *a quick death is more humane than a slow one.* —**hu'mane·ly** *adv.*

hum·ble ('humbəl) *adj.* 1. having a low opinion of oneself. 2. having a low or poor position. —*vb.* **hum·bling, hum·bled.** to make humble; humiliate. —'**hum·bly** *adv.*

hu·mid ('hyo͞omid) *adj.* (esp. of the weather) damp. —**hu'mid·i·ty** *n.*

hu·mor ('hyo͞omər) *n.* 1. the quality in an action, writing, etc., that causes amusement. 2. a mood or temper: *he is in good humor.* —*vb.* to please (someone) by adapting to his mood or opinions: *he tried to humor his father by agreeing with him.* —'**hu·mor·ous** *adj.* —'**hu·mor·ous·ly** *adv.*

hump (hump) *n.* 1. a large rounded lump as on a camel's back. 2. a small rise in the ground.

hunch (hunch) *vb.* to curve or bend in: *he hunched his shoulders against the cold wind.* —*n.* (informal) a feeling or guess without a logical basis: *I had a hunch that you would visit us today.*

hun·dred·weight ('hundridwāt) *n.* (often written **cwt.**) 100 pounds in weight.

hung (hung) *vb.* a past tense of HANG.

hun·ger ('hunggər) *n.* 1. the uncomfortable or painful feeling caused by lack of food. 2. the strong desire for (something). —*vb.* 1. to feel hungry. 2. to wish strongly for something: *Robert hungered for friends of his own age.* '**hun·gry** *adj.* **hun·gri·er, hun·gri·est.** 1. feeling hunger. 2. having a strong need or wish. —'**hun·gri·ly** *adv.*

hunt (hunt) *vb.* 1. to search for carefully. 2. to chase and kill (wild animals) for food, sport, etc. 3. to drive off: *the rogue was hunted out of town.* —*n.* 1. a chase. 2. a search: *Janet carried out a quick hunt for her lost sock.*

hur·dle ('hûrdəl) *n.* 1. a light fence that can be easily moved. 2. any obstacle that has to be surmounted before further progress can be made: *the final exam was the last hurdle before she started her career.* —*vb.* **hur·dling, hur·dled.** (sports) to run in a race in which hurdles are placed across the course (**hurdle race**).

hurl (hûrl) *vb.* to throw or cause to be thrown violently or with great force: *the giant wave hurled the boats onto the shore.*

hur·ri·cane ('hûrəkān, 'hurəkān) *n.* an enormously strong wind, esp. one developing over the North Atlantic Ocean. Compare TYPHOON.

hur·ry ('hûrē, 'hurē) *vb.* **hur·ry·ing, hur·ried.** 1. to act or move with speed. 2. to act or urge to act hastily or without due thought: *he hurried them into a decision.* —*n.* the need to hurry through eagerness, lack of time, etc.: *they are in a hurry to finish the job.* —'**hur·ried·ly** *adv.*

hurt (hûrt) *vb.* **hurt·ing, hurt.** 1. to injure; cause mental or physical pain or distress. 2. to feel sore or painful.

hus·band ('huzbənd) *n.* a man who has a wife.

husk (husk) *n.* the dry protective covering of a seed. —*vb.* to remove husks from (seeds).

husk·y[1] **husk**-('huskē) *adj.* **husk·i·er, ·i·est.** 1. (of a voice) deep and rough, esp. because of a dry throat. 2. (of a man) big and strong. —'**husk·i·ness** *n.*

husk·y[2] ('huskē) *n.,pl.* **husk·ies.** a strong thick-coated dog used by Eskimos to draw sledges.

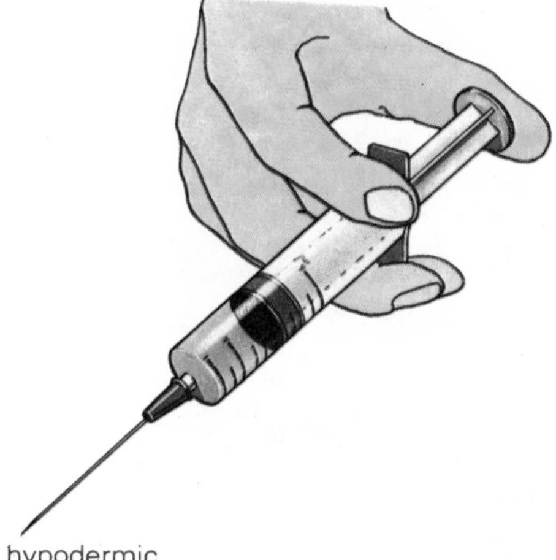
hypodermic

hus·tle ('husəl) *vb.* **hus·tling, hus·tled.** to push along roughly.

hutch (huch) *n.* a box with wire netting on one side, used to house small animals such as rabbits.

hy·a·cinth ('hīəsinth) *n.* a plant that grows from a bulb and produces thick clusters of small sweet-smelling flowers.

hy·dro·gen ('hīdrəjən) *n.* a gas that has no taste, smell, or color and combines with OXYGEN to form water. Chemical symbol: H.

hyena

hy·e·na (hī'ēnə) *n.* a flesh-eating dog-like animal with very powerful jaws and large shoulders.

hy·giene ('hījēn) *n.* conditions encouraging good health. —**hy·gi·en·ic** (hījē'enik, hī'jēnik) *adj.* —**hy·gi'en·i·cal·ly** *adv.*

hymn (him) *n.* a song of praise, esp. to God.

hy·phen ('hīfən) *n.* the sign (-), used in compound words, e.g. multi-colored, or indicating that a word has been split up at the end of a line.

hyp·no·tize ('hipnətīz) *vb.* **hyp·no·tiz·ing, hyp·no·tized.** to cause (someone) to fall into a state like a deep sleep in which his actions are controlled by the person who has hypnotized him. **hyp·not·ic** (hip'notik) *adj.* causing a sleep-like state. '**hyp·no·tist** *n.* a person who hypnotizes another. —**hyp'not·i·cal·ly** *adv.*

hy·po·der·mic (hīpə'dûrmik) *n.* an instrument with a hollow needle and a plunger for giving injections under the skin.

I

ice (īs) *n.* frozen water. —*vb.* **ic·ing, iced.** 1. to keep or make (something) cold by adding ice: *she iced the drinks.* 2. to cover (a cake) with a sweet-flavored coating (**icing**). 3. (often + *up* or *over*) to become coated with ice: *it was so cold this winter that the lake iced over.* '**ic·y** *adj.* **ic·i·er, ic·i·est.** 1. covered with ice. 2. as cold as ice: *icy weather.* —'**ic·i·ly** *adv.* —'**ic·i·ness** *n.*

ice·berg ('īsbûrg) *n.* a huge mass of ice, broken off a GLACIER or ice sheet. It floats in the sea and is a danger to ships.

iceberg

i·ci·cle ('īsikəl) *n.* a thin stick of ice formed by water that has frozen while dripping.

i·de·a (ī'dēə) *n.* a thought; a plan or picture formed in the mind.

i·de·al (ī'dēəl) *adj.* perfect; completely suitable: *you are ideal for the job.* —*n.* an idea, situation, person, etc, regarded as perfect or the best possible. **i'de·al·ism** *n.* the pursuit of noble or excellent aims or standards. **i'de·al·ist** *n.* a person who pursues or values such aims. —**i·de·al'is·tic** *adj.* —**i'de·al·ly** *adv.*

i·den·ti·cal (ī'dentikəl) *adj.* 1. the same in all respects: *she and her husband had identical cars.* 2. exactly the same as. —**i'den·ti·cal·ly** *adv.*

i·den·ti·fy (ī'dentəfī) *vb.* **i·den·ti·fy·ing, i·den·ti·fied.** 1. to recognize and give a name to (a specific person or thing): *he could identify the lost puppy.* 2. (+ *with*) to sympathize with or join: *she identifies with the prisoners.* 3. to mark: *the badge identifies a member of our club.* —**i·den·ti·fi'ca·tion** *n.*

i·den·ti·ty (ī'dentitē) *n.,pl.* **i·den·ti·ties.** 1. exactly who somebody is or what something is: *the identity of the masked man is not known.* 2. complete sameness: *they have an identity of interest in the matter.*

id·i·om ('idēəm) *n.* 1. a phrase that is used to mean something different from the strict and literal meaning of its individual words. For example, *to let the cat out of the bag* means to tell a secret. 2. a particular style of language. —**id·i·o'mat·ic** *adj.* —**id·i·o'mat·i·cal·ly** *adv.*

id·i·ot ('idēət) *n.* 1. a person who is lacking in mental abilities, usu. from birth. 2. someone who behaves in a foolish manner. —'**id·i·o·cy** *n.* —**id·i·ot·i·cal·ly** (idē'otiklē) *adv.*

i·dle ('īdəl) *adj.* **i·dler, i·dlest.** 1. not productive; unemployed: *during the strike the machines lay idle.* 2. lazy. 3. worthless: *idle chatter.* —*vb.* **i·dling, i·dled.** 1. to spend time being idle: *she idled away the afternoon.* 2. (of an engine) to be running without driving the machinery. —'**i·dle·ness** *n.* —'**i·dly** *adv.*

i·dol ('īdəl) *n.* 1. an image of a god used in worship. 2. a person (esp. an entertainer) who is greatly admired: *a movie idol.* **i·dol·a·try** (ī'dolətrē) *n.* the practice of worshiping images. '**i·dol·ize** *vb.* **i·dol·iz·ing, i·dol·ized.** to worship or admire greatly.

i·dyll ('īdəl) *n.* a short description, esp. in poetry, of a country scene. **i'dyl·lic** *adj.* simple and pleasant.

ig·loo ('iglo͞o) *n.,pl.* **ig·loos.** a dome-shaped Eskimo house made out of blocks of hard-packed snow or ice.

ig·nite (ig'nīt) *vb.* **ig·nit·ing, ig·nit·ed.** 1. to burst into flames: *the gas from the crashed car ignited.* 2. to cause (something) to explode or begin to burn, usu. by using a spark. **ig·ni·tion** (ig'nishən) *n.* 1. an instance of igniting. 2. the electrical system in a car engine, rocket, etc. that ignites the fuel.

ig·nor·ant ('ignərənt) *adj.* 1. generally ill-informed; not knowledgeable. 2. not aware of a particular fact or facts: *we are ignorant of the cause of the disaster.* —'**ig·nor·ant·ly** *adv.*

ig·nore (ig'nôr) *vb.* **ig·nor·ing, ig·nored.** to pay no attention to (someone or something): *she ignored her mother's advice.*

ill (il) *adj.* physically or mentally unwell. '**ill·ness** *n.* sickness; disease.

il·le·gal (i'lēgəl) *adj.* not allowed by law: *it is illegal to park here.* **il·le'gal·i·ty** *n.,pl.* **il·le·gal·i·ties.** something illegal. —**il'le·gal·ly** *adv.*

il·leg·i·ble (i'lejəbəl) *adj.* unable to be read: *illegible handwriting.*

il·lu·mi·nate (i'lo͞omənāt) *vb.* **il·lu·mi·nat·ing, il·lu·mi·nat·ed.** 1. to light (something) up: *the lamp illuminates the room.* 2. to explain something clearly: *he illuminated the meaning of the play.* **il·lu·mi'na·tion**

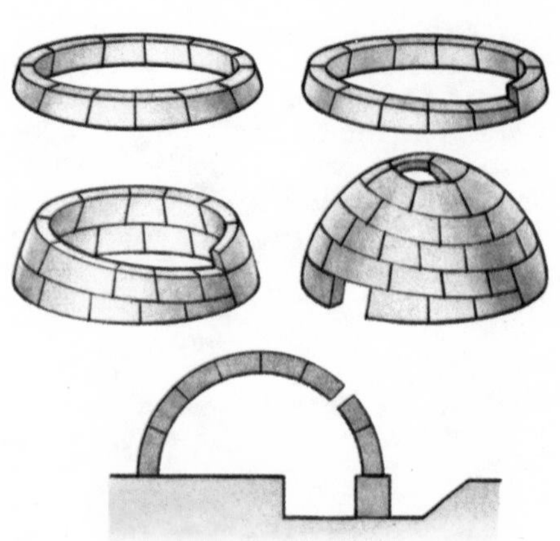

igloo

n. 1. light. 2. **illuminations** (*pl.*) an ornamental display of lights: *the amusement park illuminations.*

il·lu·sion (i'lo͞ozhən) *n.* a false idea, esp. one based on something one has perceived through the senses: *the water in the desert was an illusion.* Although line b looks longer than line a, that is an optical illusion.

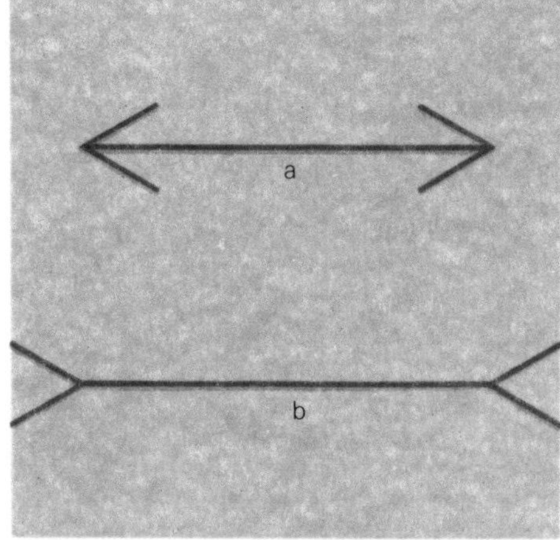

illusion

il·lus·trate ('iləstrāt) *vb.* **il·lus·trat·ing, il·lus·trat·ed.** 1. to provide (a book) with pictures. 2. to explain with the help of pictures or examples. **'il·lus·tra·tor** *n.* a person who draws pictures for a book, magazine, etc. —**il·lus'tra·tion** *n.*

im·age ('imij) *n.* 1. a mental picture: *the poem gave a gloomy image of city life.* 2. a statue or painting of a god or saint for worship. 3. something seen through or reflected by a lens or a mirror. 4. the aspect of personality presented to other people.

im·ag·ine (i'majin) *vb.* **im·ag·in·ing, im·ag·ined.** 1. to make or have a mental picture of: *I can imagine how sad you feel.* 2. to suppose: *I imagine it will be all right.* 3. to invent. **im'ag·i·na·ble** *adj.* able to be imagined. **im'ag·i·nar·y** *adj.* having no existence outside the mind. **im·ag·i'na·tion** *n.* 1. the mind's power to invent and picture, esp. in artistic and poetic matters. 2. fanciful invention. **im'ag·i·na·tive** *adj.* 1. having or resulting from a strong mental creative ability. 2. given to daydreaming. —**im'ag·i·na·tive·ly** *adv.* —**im'ag·i·na·tive·ness** *n.*

im·i·tate ('imitāt) *vb.* **im·i·tat·ing, im·i·tat·ed.** 1. to try to behave or appear like someone or something else; MIMIC. 2. to make a close copy of (something). —**im·i'ta·tion** *n.*

im·mac·u·late (i'makyəlit) *adj.* spotless; clean and tidy. —**im'mac·u·late·ly** *adv.* —**im'mac·u·late·ness** *n.*

im·ma·ture (imə'to͝or, imə'tyo͝or, imə'cho͝or) *adj.* youthful; not fully developed: *his behavior is very immature for his age.* —**im·ma'tur·i·ty** *n.*

im·me·di·ate (i'mēdēit) *adj.* 1. happening without delay: *an immediate answer.* 2. concerning the present time: *our immediate plans are vague.* 3. next or nearest: *my immediate neighbor.* 4. direct: *the immediate cause of the trouble.* —**im'me·di·a·cy** *n.* —**im'me·di·ate·ly** *adv.*

im·mense (i'mens) *adj.* very large; not easily measurable: *the Sahara is an immense desert.* —**im'mense·ly** *adv.* —**im'men·si·ty** *n.*

im·merse (i'mûrs) *vb.* **im·mers·ing, im·mersed.** 1. to dip under the surface of a liquid so as to cover completely: *she immersed her hands in water.* 2. to involve deeply: *I immersed myself in a book.* —**im'mer·sion** *n.*

im·mi·grate ('imigrāt) *vb.* **im·mi·grat·ing, im·mi·grat·ed.** to come into a country where one was not born in order to settle permanently. —**'im·mi·grant** *n.* —**im·mi'gra·tion** *n.*

im·mo·bile (i'mōbəl) *adj.* not moving or not capable of movement. **im'mo·bi·lize** *vb.* **im·mo·bi·liz·ing, im·mo·bi·lized.** to make incapable of moving or of being moved. —**im·mo'bil·i·ty** *n.* —**im·mo·bi·li'za·tion** *n.*

im·mor·al (i'môrəl, i'morəl) *adj.* contrary to the proper standards of personal and social behavior; wicked. —**im·mo'ral·i·ty** *n.*

im·mor·tal (i'môrtəl) *adj.* 1. not having to suffer death. 2. remembered or admired for all time: *the immortal plays of Shakespeare.* —*n.* 1. a being that will always exist. 2. a person of enduring fame. —**im·mor'tal·i·ty** *n.* —**im'mor·tal·ly** *adv.*

im·mune (i'myo͞on) *adj.* 1. protected from a disease (often by vaccination or inoculation; see INOCULATE and VACCINATE). 2. not affected by people's remarks, etc., or any other outside influence: *he was immune to all criticism.* **im·mu·nize** ('imyənīz) *vb.* **im·mu·niz·ing, im·mu·nized.** to protect from disease: *to immunize against measles.* —**im'mu·ni·ty** *n.,pl.* **im·mu·ni·ties.**

imp (imp) *n.* 1. a little devil or wicked spirit. 2. (informal) a mischievous child. —**'imp·ish** *adj.*

im·pact ('impakt) *n.* 1. the blow of a body in motion striking another; collision: *the car hit the wall with a tremendous impact.* 2. an influence: *the impact of new ideas changed their lives.*

im·par·tial (im'pârshəl) *adj.* not showing favor to one side; just: *to judge fairly you need to be impartial.* —**im·par·ti·al·i·ty** (impârshē'alitē) *n.* —**im'par·tial·ly** *adv.*

im·pa·tient (im'pāshənt) *adj.* 1. showing lack of patience; unable to wait, listen, etc., calmly. 2. (+ *of*) intolerant: *impatient of new ideas.* 3. (+ *for*) restlessly eager: *impatient for adventure.* —**im'pa·tience** *n.* —**im'pa·tient·ly** *adv.*

im·pede (im'pēd) *vb.* **im·ped·ing, im·ped·ed.** to obstruct or hinder: *the explorers' progress was impeded by thick jungle.* **im·ped·i·ment** (im'pedəmənt) *n.* 1. an obstacle or hindrance. 2. a physical defect, esp. a disorder preventing ease in speaking: *a speech impediment made him shy.*

im·per·a·tive (im'perətiv) *adj.* 1. urgently necessary: *it is imperative that the message reach them today.* 2. indicating or expressing a command; commanding: *the general addressed his troops in imperative tones.* —**im'per·a·tive·ly** *adv.*

im·per·fect (im'pûrfikt) *adj.* having faults or defects: *imperfect eyesight.* **imperfect tense** (in grammar) the tense denoting action going on but not completed, e.g. *he was walking.* —**im'per·fect·ly** *adv.*

im·pe·ri·al (im'pērēəl) *adj.* of, like, or relating to an empire, emperor, or empress: *the imperial throne.* **im'pe·ri·al·ism** *n.* the policy of extending the rule of an empire or nation over other countries. **im'pe·ri·al·ist** *n.* a person who believes in imperialism.

im·per·son·al (im'pûrsənəl) *adj.* 1. not connected with any individual person: *as an outsider, I can give an impersonal opinion.* 2. having little or no concern for individual feelings: *an impersonal governmental department.* —**im'per·son·al·ly** *adv.*

im·per·son·ate (im'pûrsənāt) *vb.* **im·per·son·at·ing, im·per·son·at·ed.** to pretend to be (some other person) by assuming his character, appearance, or manner: *he escaped from prison by impersonating one of the guards.* —**im·per·son'a·tion** *n.*

im·per·ti·nent (im'pûrtənənt) *adj.* rude; impudent: *he made some impertinent remarks to the chairman and as a result he lost his job.* —**im'per·ti·nence** *n.* —**im'per·ti·nent·ly** *adv.*

im·pet·u·ous (im'pecho͞oəs) *adj.* acting rashly; over-eager; impulsive: *he regretted his impetuous remarks when he saw that he had upset his friends.* —**im·pet·u'os·i·ty** *n.* —**im'pet·u·ous·ly** *adv.*

im·ply (im'plī) *vb.* **im·ply·ing, im·plied.** 1. to suggest without directly stating; hint: *he implied that I was lying.* 2. to involve necessarily: *a competition implies competitors.* —**im·pli'ca·tion** *n.*

im·port *vb.* (im'pôrt) to bring (something) into a country from somewhere else. —*n.* ('impôrt) 1. often **im·ports** (*pl.*) goods imported. 2. the meaning of something: *I understood the import of her words.*

im·por·tant (im'pôrtənt) *adj.* 1. of great significance, effect, etc.: *she wrote an important book on the subject.* 2. of considerable authority: *the mayor is an important official in the city.* —**im'por·tance** *n.* —**im'por·tant·ly** *adv.*

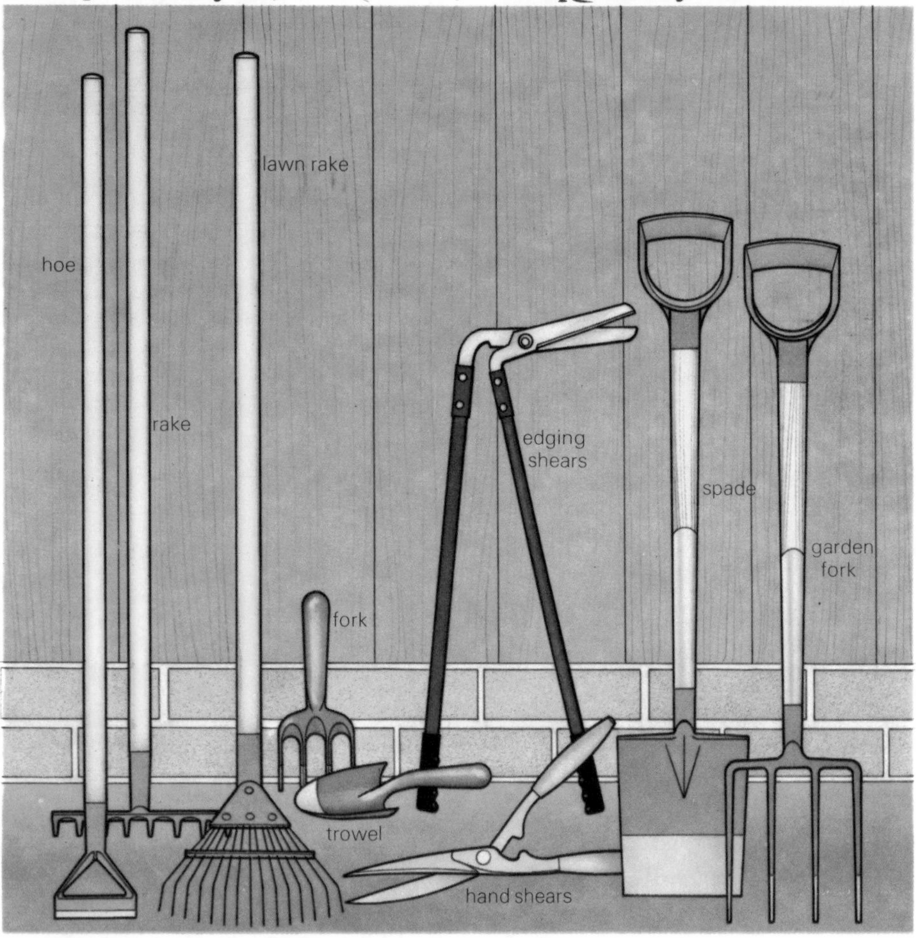

implements

im·ple·ment *n.* ('impləmənt) a tool, utensil, or instrument. —*vb.* ('impləment) to fulfill or perform: *his plans were soon implemented.* —**im·ple·men'ta·tion** *n.*

im·plore (im'plôr) *vb.* **im·plor·ing, im·plored.** to ask earnestly; entreat: *I implored you to have mercy.*

im·pose (im'pōz) *vb.* **im·pos·ing, im·posed.** 1. to put upon by authority or force: *I shall impose a severe punishment.* 2. (+ *upon* or *on*) to take unfair advantage of (patience, kindness, etc.): *he imposed upon our friendship.* **im'pos·ing** *adj.* making a strong impression on the mind. —**im·po·si·tion** (impə'zishən) *n.*

im·pos·si·ble (im'posəbəl) *adj.* 1. not possible; not capable of existing, being done, or being true: *it is impossible to live without food and water for long.* 2. hopelessly unsuitable or objectionable: *Mary-Jane is an impossible child.* —**im·pos·si'bil·i·ty** *n.* —**im'pos·si·bly** *adv.*

im·pos·tor (im'postər) *n.* someone who deceives by pretending to be someone else.

im·press (im'pres) *vb.* **im·press·ing, im·pressed.** 1. to produce a deep effect (esp. on the mind or feelings): *his knowledge will impress you.* 2. to mark by pressure: *I impress the design of the ring in the soft wax.* **im'pres·sion** *n.* 1. the effect left in the mind by a person, experience, etc.: *my impression of him was unfavorable.* 2. a vague, uncertain memory. 3. a mark produced by pressure: *an impression of a foot in the sand.* **im'pres·sion·a·ble** *adj.* easily influenced. **im'pres·sive** *adj.* capable of producing a deep effect. —**im'pres·sive·ly** *adv.* —**im'pres·sive·ness** *n.*

im·print *n.* ('imprint) a mark made by pressure: *the imprint of a hoof in the mud.* —*vb.* (im'print) 1. to make a mark on (something) by pressure; stamp. 2. to fix (in the mind).

im·promp·tu (im'prompto͞o, im'prompty͞oo) *adj.* done without preparation; improvised: *he gave an impromptu speech*

im·prove (im'pro͞ov) *vb.* **im·prov·ing, im·proved.** to make or become better in quality. —**im'prove·ment** *n.*

im·pro·vise ('imprəvīz) *vb.* **im·pro·vis·ing, im·pro·vised.** 1. to speak or perform without previous preparation: *she improvised a tune on the violin.* 2. to make (a substitute for something) from materials available: *they improvised a sail for their boat from a piece of old canvas.* —**im·pro·vi'sa·tion** *n.*

im·pu·dent ('impyədənt) *adj.* disrespectful; rude. —'**im·pu·dence** *n.* —'**im·pu·dent·ly** *adv.*

im·pulse ('impuls) *n.* 1. a force acting on the mind or a body, causing a particular result: *the impulse of the current in the river pushed the boat onward.* 2. a sudden inclination to do something. 3. a single movement of electrical current in one direction. —**im'pul·sive** *adj.*

in·au·gu·rate (i'nôgyərāt, i'nôgərāt) *vb.* **in·au·gu·rat·ing, in·au·gu·rat·ed.** 1. to begin or open in a formal manner: *the mayor inaugurated the conference.* 2. to install (a person) in office with formal ceremony: *we shall inaugurate the new president tomorrow.* —**in'au·gu·ral** *adj.* —**in·au·gu'ra·tion** *n.*

in·cense[1] ('insens) *n.* a substance that is burned to produce sweet-smelling fumes, esp. during religious ceremonies.

in·cense[2] (in'sens) *vb.* **in·cens·ing, in·censed.** to inflame with anger; enrage.

in·cen·tive (in'sentiv) *n.* something that provides a strong reason for action; motive: *money and power were the incentives that kept him working.*

in·ces·sant (in'sesənt) *adj.* going on without interruption; continual: *I could not study because of their incessant chattering.* —**in'ces·sant·ly** *adv.*

inch (inch) *n.* a measure of length equal to one twelfth of a foot.

in·ci·dent ('insidənt) *n.* 1. an occurrence, esp. something of minor importance that happens in connection with something else: *various incidents caused delays on the journey.* 2. an event involving hostility: *an international incident that could lead to war.* **in·ci'den·tal** *adj.* happening in connection with something else but of less importance: *she came to see my father and meeting me was incidental.* —**in·ci'den·tal·ly** *adv.*

in·cite (in'sīt) *vb.* **in·cit·ing, in·cit·ed.** to urge (someone) on to do something; to stir up: *the leader incited the mob to violence.* —**in'cite·ment** *n.*

in·cline *vb.* (in'klīn) **in·clin·ing, in·clined.** 1. to have a preference for; be disposed: *I incline to the belief that he is lying.* 2. to lean or slant: *the road inclines upward.* —*n.* ('inklīn) a slope: *the horses struggled up the steep incline.* —**in·cli'na·tion** *n.*

in·clude (in'klōōd) *vb.* **in·clud·ing, in·clud·ed.** to take in as part of something: *he was included in the team.* —**in'clu·sion** *n.* —**in'clu·sive** *adj.*

in·come ('inkum) *n.* the financial gain that comes from work, business, investment, etc.: *during the strike Tom's family depended on his wife's income.*

in·cor·po·rate (in'kôrpərāt) *vb.* **in·cor·po·rat·ing, in·cor·po·rat·ed.** 1. to combine; include: *the book incorporates some new ideas.* 2. to form a corporation: *to incorporate a business.* —**in·cor·po'ra·tion** *n.*

in·crease *vb.* (in'krēs) **in·creas·ing, in·creased.** to make or become greater in size: *the tree's height increased with age.* —*n.* ('inkrēs) 1. growth. 2. the amount by which something grows. —**in'creas·ing·ly** *adv.*

in·cred·i·ble (in'kredəbəl) *adj.* 1. impossible to believe. 2. (informal) very surprising. —**in'cred·i·bly** *adv.*

in·crim·i·nate (in'krimənāt) *vb.* **in·crim·i·nat·ing, in·crim·i·nat·ed.** to say or suggest that (someone) is guilty of wrongdoing: *the evidence incriminates the entire class.*

in·cu·bate ('inkyəbāt) *vb.* **in·cu·bat·ing, in·cu·bat·ed.** to keep at the right temperature for aiding development, esp. in hatching eggs. **'in·cu·ba·tor** *n.* an apparatus in which a steady temperature is maintained for hatching eggs, for rearing prematurely born babies, etc. —**in·cu'ba·tion** *n.*

in·def·i·nite (in'defənit) *adj.* not fixed or certain; vague: *she will be away for an indefinite length of time.* —**in'def·i·nite·ly** *adv.*

in·del·i·ble (in'deləbəl) *adj.* unable to be removed or rubbed out: *indelible stains.* —**in'del·i·bly** *adv.*

in·de·pend·ent (indi'pendənt) *adj.* 1. not relying on or influenced by others. 2. not subject to another's authority. —*n.* (politics) a person who acts and votes without being a member of any party. —**in·de'pend·ence** *n.* —**in·de'pend·ent·ly** *adv.*

in·dex ('indeks) *n.,pl.* **in·dex·es** (or, esp. for def. 4., **in·di·ces** ('indisēz)). 1. an alphabetical list of things in a book, showing the numbers of the pages on which they are mentioned. 2. anything that gives a sign or indication. 3. a pointer or hand on a dial, scale, etc. 4. (mathematics) a symbol denoting a power, e.g. $3^3 (3 \times 3 \times 3)$. **index finger** the finger nearest the thumb on either hand. —*vb.* to compile an index for (a book).

in·di·cate ('indəkāt) *vb.* **in·dic·at·ing, in·di·cat·ed.** 1. to point out: *he indicated the road we should follow.* 2. to show or be a sign of: *their smiles indicated friendliness.* —**'in·di·ca·tor** *n.* —**in·di'ca·tion** *n.*

in·dif·fer·ent (in'difərənt) *adj.* 1. not caring; unconcerned: *they were indifferent to my problems.* 2. undistinguished in quality: *he gave an indifferent performance of the song.* —**in'dif·fer·ence** *n.* —**in'dif·fer·ent·ly** *adv.*

in·di·ges·tion (indi'jeschən) *n.* 1. difficulty in digesting food. 2. any minor stomach disorder. 3. pain caused by this.

in·dig·nant (in'dignənt) *adj.* affected by mingled anger and scorn, usu. caused by something unjust, wicked, etc.: *I was indignant at his unfair accusations.* —**in'dig·nant·ly** *adv.* —**in·dig'na·tion** *n.*

in·di·go ('indigō) *n.* a dark blue dye obtained from the leaves of various plants. —*adj.* deep violet-blue in color.

in·di·vid·ual (indi'vijōōəl) *adj.* 1. relating to or provided for one only: *each person had his individual place at the dinner table.* 2. unique or unusual: *she has some highly individual ideas.* —*n.* any single person, animal, plant, etc. —**in·di·vid·u·al·i·ty** *n.*

in·duce (in'dōōs, in'dyōōs) *vb.* **in·duc·ing, in·duced.** 1. to persuade or influence (someone to do something): *they induced him to betray his friends.* 2. to cause: *the noise induced a headache.* —**in'duce·ment** *n.*

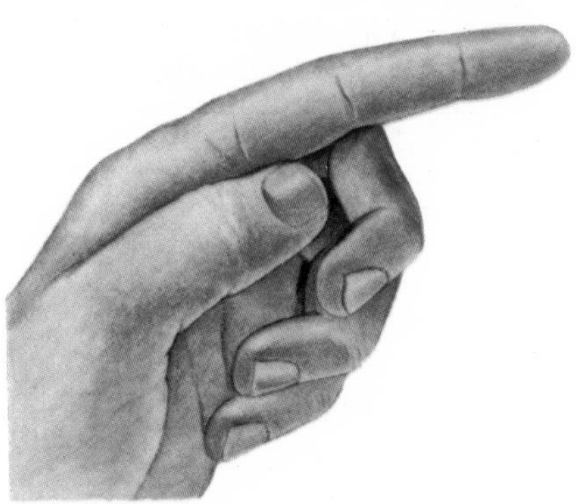

index finger

in·dulge (in'dulj) *vb.* **in·dulg·ing, in·dulged.** 1. to yield to the wish or desires (of oneself or another person): *Mike's mother indulges him too much.* 2. (+ *in*) to enjoy freely: *I indulged in an enormous meal.* —**in'dul·gence** *n.* —**in'dul·gent** *adj.* —**in'dul·gent·ly** *adv.*

in·dus·try ('indəstrē) *n.,pl.* **in·dus·tries.** 1. manufacture or trade in general: *industry suffered during the Depression.* 2. any particular branch of manufacture, trade, or business: *the steel industry.* 3. steady application to work: *they worked with great industry.* —**in·dus·tri·al** (in'dustrēəl) *adj.*

in·ert (i'nûrt) *adj.* 1. without life or energy. 2. (chemistry) not likely to combine or react with another chemical. **in·er·tia** (i'nûrshə) *n.* the state of being without energy. —**in'ert·ly** *adv.*

in·ev·i·table (in'evitəbəl) *adj.* certain to happen or unavoidable; not capable of being stopped: *it was inevitable that his driving would cause an accident.* —**in·ev·i·ta'bil·i·ty** *n.*

in·fa·mous ('infəməs) *adj.* of very bad reputation; famed for being evil: *an infamous murderer.* —'**in·fa·mous·ly** *adv.* —'**in·fa·my** *n.*

in·fant ('infənt) *n.* a baby or young child. —*adj.* very young. —'**in·fan·cy** *n.*

in·fan·try ('infəntrē) *n.* soldiers who normally fight on foot (not in tanks, aircraft, or ships).

in·fect (in'fekt) *vb.* 1. to pass a disease on to (someone else). 2. to influence (someone) in a particular way: *her happiness infected us all.* —**in'fec·tion** *n.* —**in'fec·tious** *adj.* —**in'fec·tious·ly** *adv.*

in·fe·ri·or (in'fērēər) *adj.* 1. of lower quality. 2. lower in rank: *patrolmen are inferior to police sergeants.* —*n.* someone of lower rank. —**in·fe·ri'or·i·ty** *n.*

in·fil·trate ('infiltrāt) *vb.* **in·fil·trat·ing, in·fil·trat·ed.** 1. to pass or cause to pass into by filtering. 2. to place agents secretly in a rival organization or among one's enemies. —**in·fil'tra·tion** *n.* —'**in·fil·tra·tor** *n.*

in·fi·nite ('infənit) *adj.* without any limit or boundary.

in·fin·i·tive (in'finitiv) *n.* the form of a verb not made particular as to subject or object, e.g. *to walk, to run.*

in·flame (in'flām) *vb.* **in·flam·ing, in·flamed.** 1. to make (part of the body) hot, swollen, and painful. 2. to arouse (temper, passion, or desire).

in'flam·ma·ble *adj.* likely to burn easily. —**in·flam'ma·tion** *n.*

in·flate (in'flāt) *vb.* **in·flat·ing, in·flat·ed.** to fill (a balloon, tire, etc.) with gas or air. **in'fla·tion** *n.* 1. the act of inflating. 2. an increase in the usual price of goods and services, causing the cost of living to rise. —**in'fla·tion·ar·y** *adj.*

in·flict (in'flikt) *vb.* to cause (something unpleasant) to happen to another person: *the boys inflicted a beating on the bully.* —**in'flic·tion** *n.*

in·flu·ence ('inflo͞oəns) *vb.* **in·flu·enc·ing, in·flu·enced.** to affect; to change or modify. —*n.* 1. ability to affect people, objects, events, etc.: 2. a force affecting the mind or feelings. —**in·flu'en·tial** *adj.*

in·flu·en·za (inflo͞o'enzə) *n.* (often abbreviated to **flu**) a common and infectious disease, causing a high temperature, sore throat, etc.

in·form (in'fôrm) *vb.* to pass facts on to (another person). **in'form·ant** *n.* a person who informs. **in'form·er** *n.* a person who passes on damaging facts to harm someone else: *the police used an informer to discover when the robbery would take place.* **in·for'ma·tion** *n.* the facts that are passed on. —**in'form·a·tive** *adj.*

infantry

in·for·mal (in'fôrməl) *adj.* without ceremony; casual. —**in'for·mal·ly** *adv.*

in·fra·red (infrə'red) *adj.* of light waves that are too long to be seen by the human eye; found below red in the visible color SPECTRUM.

in·fur·i·ate (in'fyo͝orēāt) *vb.* **in·fur·i·at·ing, in·fur·i·at·ed.** to arouse anger in (someone): *John's constant whining infuriates me.* —**in·fur·i'a·tion** *n.*

in·gen·ious (in'jēnyəs) *adj.* 1. clever at inventing things, solving problems, etc. 2. cleverly made, designed, or solved: *ingenious plans.* —**in'gen·ious·ly** *adv.* —**in·ge·nu·i·ty** (injə'no͞oitē, injə'nyo͞oitē) *n.*

in·gre·di·ent (in'grēdēənt) *n.* a substance that forms part of a mixture: *flour is an ingredient of bread.*

in·hab·it (in'habit) *vb.* to live in. —**in'hab·it·ant** *n.*

in·her·it (in'herit) *vb.* 1. to receive (money or goods) from someone who has died: *she inherited her mother's jewels.* 2. to have looks, skills, or habits in common with an ancestor: *he inherited his father's red hair.* —**in'her·it·ance** *n.*

in·i·tial (i'nishəl) *n.* the first letter of a word, esp. of a name: *Howard Alec Jones has the initials H.A.J.* —*adj.* to do with the first stages of. —*vb.* to sign (a document) using only one's initials. —**in'i·tial·ly** *adv.*

in·i·ti·ate *vb.* (i'nishēāt) **in·i·ti·at·ing in·i·ti·at·ed.** 1. to begin; take the first steps in (a project or plan). 2. to instruct (someone) in the basic ideas of (a subject of study, secret society, etc.). —*n.* (i'nisheit) a beginner who has taken the first steps. —**in·i·ti'a·tion** *n.*

in·i·ti·a·tive (i'nishēətiv) *n.* 1. the very first step in a new policy or action: *Alan took the initiative.* 2. the ability to begin things or make changes.

in·ject (in'jekt) *vb.* 1. to force a liquid (under someone's skin, into a blood vessel, etc.) through a hollow needle. 2. to force (something) into (something else): *in some engines fuel is injected at high pressure.*

in·jure ('injər) *vb.* **in·jur·ing, in·jured.** 1. to damage (the body). 2. to do an injustice or cause other damage to (someone). —**in·ju·ri·ous** (in'jo͝orēəs) *adj.* —**in'ju·ri·ous·ly** *adv.* —**'in·ju·ry** *n.,pl.* **in·ju·ries.**

ink (ingk) *n.* a black or colored liquid used for writing, drawing, or printing. —*vb.* to smear or cover with ink. —**'ink·y** *adj.* **ink·i·er, ink·i·est.**

in·mate ('inmāt) *n.* one who lives in an INSTITUTION, esp. a mental hospital or prison.

in·nate (i'nāt) *adj.* inborn; natural.

in·ner ('inər) *adj.* 1. inside; further in. 2. private; personal: *inner thoughts.*

in·no·cent ('inəsənt) *adj.* 1. free from guilt or fault. 2. inexperienced; without cunning. —*n.* 1. a blameless person. 2. a simple person who does not suspect another's motives. —**'in·no·cence** *n.* —**'in·no·cent·ly** *adv.*

in·no·vate ('inəvāt) *vb.* **in·no·vat·ing, in·no·vat·ed.** to make changes by introducing a new idea or method. —**in·no'va·tion** *n.*

in·oc·u·late (i'nokyəlāt) *vb.* **in·oc·u·lat·ing, in·oc·u·lat·ed.** to inject a living, but weakened, disease-carrying VIRUS into a body, whose own defenses learn how to kill the weak virus and can quickly react and protect the body against a strong virus for some time afterwards. —**in·oc·u'la·tion** *n.*

in·quest ('inkwest) *n.* a legal inquiry by a CORONER into the causes of a person's death.

in·quire (in'kwīər) *vb.* **in·quir·ing, in·quired.** to ask questions about; look into or investigate. See also ENQUIRE. **in'quir·y** *n.,pl.* **in·quir·ies.** an investigation, esp. a public one. **in·quis·i·tive** (in'kwizitiv) *adj.* always asking questions, esp. about other people's business; showing curiosity. —**in'quis·i·tive·ly** *adv.* —**in'quis·i·tive·ness** *n.*

in·scribe (in'skrīb) *vb.* **in·scrib·ing, in·scribed.** to write, mark, carve, or engrave words upon. —**in·scrip·tion** (in'skripshən) *n.*

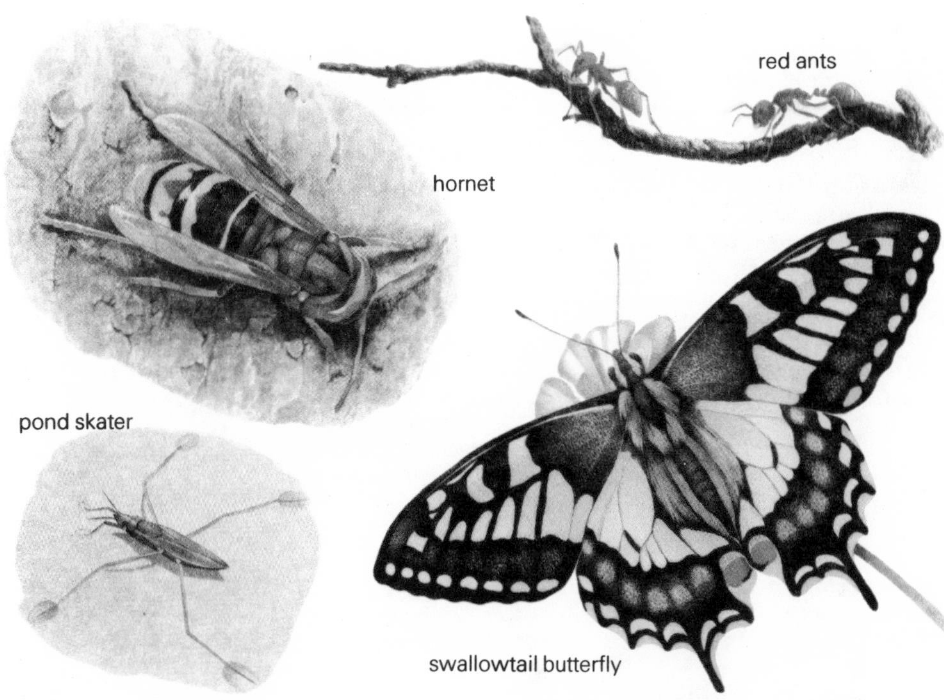

in·sect ('insekt) *n.* any creature that has no backbone, a body in three parts (head, thorax, abdomen), and three pairs of jointed legs. **in'sec·ti·cide** *n.* a chemical made to kill insects.

in·sert (in'sûrt) *vb.* 1. to put inside: *he inserted the coin into the drinks machine.* 2. to place something extra in or among: *the teacher inserted three words into my sentence.* —**in'ser·tion** *n.*

in·sight ('insīt) *n.* an understanding that goes deeper than normal: *my day at the farm gave me an insight into a farmer's life.*

in·sist (in'sist) *vb.* to demand urgently and firmly: *when my new iron broke, I insisted upon having my money back.* —**in'sist·ence** *n.* —**in'sist·ent** *adj.* —**in'sist·ent·ly** *adv.*

in·so·lent ('insələnt) *adj.* rude; disrespectful; insulting. —**'in·so·lence** *n.* —**'in·so·lent·ly** *adv.*

in·som·ni·a (in'somnēə) *n.* inability to sleep. **in'som·ni·ac** *n.* a person who frequently cannot sleep.

in·spect (in'spekt) *vb.* to examine carefully, esp. looking for faults. **in'spec·tor** *n.* 1. an official responsible for examining and checking. 2. a rank in some police forces, next below a superintendent. —**in'spec·tion** *n.*

in·spire (in'spīər) *vb.* **in·spir·ing in·spired.** to stir up noble or creative thoughts, feelings, or actions in someone: *her love inspired her to write beautiful poetry.* —**in·spi·ra·tion** (inspə'rāshən) *n.*

in·stall (in'stôl) *vb.* 1. to place or fix into position for use: *the plumber installed a new basin.* 2. to place (someone) ceremoniously in an official position. **in·stal·la·tion** (instə'lāshən) *n.* 1. the act of installing. 2. something that has been installed: *a radar installation.*

in·stall·ment (in'stôlmənt) *n.* 1. an amount of money paid at intervals, esp. to pay off part of a larger debt or loan. 2. a single episode in a series or serial.

in·stance ('instəns) *n.* an example or particular case: *the soldier's rescue of his wounded friend was an instance of great courage.* —*vb.* **in·stanc·ing, in·stanced.** to quote an example.

in·stant ('instənt) *n.* a brief or particular moment of time: *for an instant he almost smiled.* —*adj.* immediate: *he gave an instant reply.* —**'in·stant·ly** *adv.*

in·step ('instep) *n.* the arched top of the foot, between the ankle and toes.

in·stinct ('instingkt) *n.* an inborn ability to act in a certain way: *some animals can find their way home by instinct, even if they are taken miles away.* —**in'stinc·tive** *adj.* —**in'stinc·tive·ly** *adv.*

in·sti·tute ('institoot, 'instityoot) *vb.* **in·sti·tut·ing, in·sti·tut·ed.** to start (a process, system, etc.); establish. —*n.* an organization set up to study or promote a particular cause: *she works at the medical institute.*

in·sti·tu·tion (insti'tooshən), insti-'tyooshən) *n.* 1. an organization, or its buildings, devoted to a public or social cause. 2. a long-standing custom: *the institution of marriage.* —**in·sti'tu·tion·al** *adj.*

in·struct (in'strukt) *vb.* 1. to teach; inform. 2. to give orders. —**in'struc·tion** *n.* —**in'struc·tor** *n.*

in·stru·ment ('instrəmənt) *n.* 1. a tool or object used for doing work, esp. in science or medicine. 2. a device for making musical sounds. **in·stru'men·tal** *adj.* 1. serving as an instrument or means: *his help was instrumental in getting the project started.* 2. of musical instruments. —**in·stru'men·tal·ly** *adv.*

in·su·late ('insəlāt, 'insyəlāt) *vb.* **in·su·lat·ing, in·su·lat·ed.** to seal off; protect against heat, cold, electrical current, etc. **'in·su·la·tor** *n.* a device often made of glass, pottery, or plastic, which will hold a live electrical wire without passing its current to ground. —**in·su'la·tion** *n.*

in·sult *vb.* (in'sult) to make hurtful or rude remarks to or about (someone). —*n.* ('insult) a rude remark.

in·sur·ance (in'shoorəns) *n.* arrangement to ensure that in the event of loss (damage, fire, death, etc.) another person or company will pay a sum of money as compensation. **in'sure** *vb.* **in·sur·ing, in·sured.** 1. to make a contract whereby compensation will be paid if property or life is lost or damaged. 2. to make or be safe against.

in·tact (in'takt) *adj.* whole; undamaged: *suprisingly, the car was intact after the accident.*

in·te·grate ('intəgrāt) *vb.* **in·te·grat·ing, in·te·grat·ed.** 1. to make available to people of all races and social groups: *our sports club is integrated.* 2. to bring together in a whole; combine; unite. **in·te'gra·tion** *n.* the act of making (schools, social facilities, etc.) available to all races.

in·teg·ri·ty (in'tegritē) *n.* complete honesty; honor: *we need a man of integrity to be president.*

in·tel·lect ('intəlekt) *n.* cleverness. **in·tel'lec·tu·al** *adj.* concerned with using the mind: *chess is an intellectual game. n.* a clever, educated person who is good at using his or her brains. —**in·tel'lec·tu·al·ly** *adv.*

in·tel·li·gence (in'teləjəns) *n.* 1. the ability to think quickly, solve problems, etc. 2. high intellectual ability. 3. news, esp. secret information of military importance. **in'tel·li·gent** *adj.* 1. showing the ability to think well. 2. (of plans, ideas, etc.) well thought out. —**in'tel·li·gent·ly** *adv.*

in·tend (in'tend) *vb.* to mean; plan: *she intended to return early, but was delayed.*

in·tense (in'tens) *adj.* 1. extreme or very great: *intense heat.* 2. (of people) apt to feel or express emotions very strongly. **in'ten·si·fy** *vb.* **in·ten·si·fy·ing, in·ten·si·fied.** to make intense. **in'ten·sive** *adj.* thorough; concentrated. —**in'tense·ly** *adv.* —**in'ten·si·ty** *n.* —**in'ten·sive·ly** *adv.*

in·tent (in'tent) *adj.* (often + *on*) with mind firmly fixed on something: *he was intent on going.* —*n.* an aim or purpose.

in·ten·tion (in'tenshən) *n.* a purpose or desire. **in'ten·tion·al** *adj.* deliberate; done on purpose. —**in'ten·tion·al·ly** *adv.*

in·ter·cept (intər'sept) *vb.* to catch (someone or something) on the way to somewhere else. —**in·ter'cep·tion** *n.*

in·ter·est ('intərist, 'intrist) *n.* 1. the desire to be involved with or know about something: *his interest was aroused by this incident.* 2. something that one is involved with: *though confined to a wheelchair he had plenty of interests.* 3. a private advantage, esp. a monetary one: *they put their own interest before the public good.* 4. a sum of money charged periodically by a lender in return for use of a sum of money lent or invested. —*vb.* to involve or be concerned.

in·ter·fere (intər'fēr) *vb.* **in·ter·fer·ing, in·ter·fered.** 1. (of people) to meddle with. 2. to cause disturbance (esp. to sound or radio waves): *passing traffic can interfere with radio reception.* —**in·ter'fer·ence** *n.*

in·ter·im ('intərim) *n.* an interval. —*adj.* temporary: *the countries made an interim settlement while a peace treaty was drawn up.*

in·te·ri·or (in'tērēər) *adj.* inside; the further in of two. —*n.* 1. the inner part of something. 2. the home affairs or inland regions of a country.

in·ter·jec·tion (intər'jekshən) *n.* 1. a remark put in while someone else is speaking: *interjections from the audience interrupted his speech.* 2. (grammar) a natural exclamation, e.g. *hey! phew!* etc. classified as a part of speech. **in·ter'ject** *vb.* to interrupt suddenly with an exclamation or remark.

in·ter·lude ('intərlood) *n.* 1. a happening, often amusing in character, that is not part of the main course of events. 2. an interval between two acts of a play, opera, etc.

in·ter·me·di·ate (intər'mēdēit) *adj.* coming between two places, grades, or points in time; in between: *the express train does not stop at intermediate stations.*

in·ter·mis·sion (intər'mishən) *n.* a brief pause or rest, esp. between two parts of a play.

in·ter·nal (in'tûrnəl) *adj.* 1. situated inside something else: *the internal organs of the body.* 2. concerning the inner part or workings of something: *this is an internal matter and does not concern outsiders.* 3. to do with the domestic affairs of a country: *internal politics.* —**in'ter·nal·ly** *adv.*

in·ter·na·tion·al (intər'nashənəl) *adj.* 1. between nations: *the international telephone exchange.* 2. of many nations: *an international gathering.* —**in·ter'na·tion·al·ly** *adv.*

in·ter·pret (in'tûrprit) *vb.* 1. to translate the words of a speaker into a different language, sentence by sentence. 2. to explain, bring out, or understand the meaning of (a play, writings, dreams, etc.). **in'ter·pret·er** *n.* someone who translates for a speaker. —**in·ter·pre'ta·tion** *n.*

in·ter·rupt (intə'rupt) *vb.* 1. to break in while someone else is speaking. 2. to interfere with so as to stop (the flow of traffic, an electric current, etc.): *T.V. programs were interrupted by a newsflash.* —**in·ter'rup·tion** *n.*

in·ter·sect (intər'sekt) *vb.* (of roads, railways, etc., also of lines, surfaces, and solids) to cross or run into one another. **in·ter'sec·tion** *n.* the point at which two lines, roads, etc., cross.

in·ter·val ('intərvəl) *n.* 1. a pause between two events. 2. the distance between objects or places.

in·ter·vene (intər'vēn) *vb.* **in·ter·ven·ing, in·ter·vened.** to come between or interrupt: *he intervened in the dispute and eventually persuaded them to make peace.* —**in·ter·ven·tion** (intər'venshən) *n.*

in·ter·view ('intərvyōō) *n.* a prearranged formal meeting, e.g. one to decide on someone's suitability for a job, or one between a reporter and another person from whom he wishes to obtain information. —*vb.* to question (someone) at an interview.

in·tes·tine (in'testin) *n.* often **in·tes·tines** (*pl.*) the long twisty tubelike part of the body through which food is passed after it has been digested in the stomach and from which it is absorbed. —**in'tes·tin·al** *adj.*

in·ti·mate ('intəmit) *adj.* 1. very close and familiar: *intimate friends.* 2. private; personal: *an intimate diary.* —*n.* a close friend. —**'in·ti·ma·cy** *n.* —**'in·ti·mate·ly** *adv.*

in·tri·cate ('intrəkit) *adj.* delicate and complicated: *an intricate design.* —**'in·tri·ca·cy** *n.,pl.* **in·tri·ca·cies.** —**'in·tri·cate·ly** *adv.*

in·trigue *vb.* (in'trēg) **in·trigu·ing, in·trigued.** 1. to plot: *the army intrigued against the government.* 2. to arouse the interest of: *the rumor intrigues me.* —*n.* (in'trēg, 'intrēg) a secret plan.

in·tro·duce (intrə'dōōs, intrə'dyōōs) *vb.* **in·tro·duc·ing, in·tro·duced.** 1. to start; bring into use or consideration. 2. to present (a person) formally. —**in·tro·duc·tion** (intrə'dukshən) *n.* —**in·tro'duc·to·ry** *adj.*

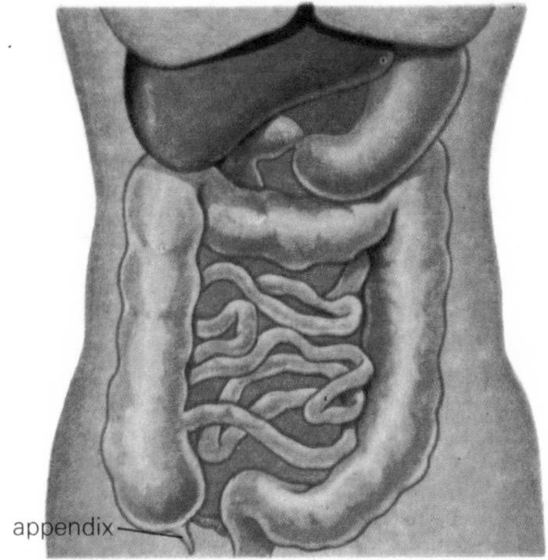

intestine

in·trude (in'trōōd) *vb.* **in·trud·ing, in·trud·ed.** to come into a place or another person's company uninvited, and usu. unwanted. —**in'tru·sion** *n.*

in·vade (in'vād) *vb.* **in·vad·ing, in·vad·ed.** 1. to enter and overrun (another country) with an army. 2. to intrude on (another person's privacy). —**in'va·sion** *n.*

in·va·lid[1] ('invəlid) *n.* a person in need of nursing because of illness or injury. —*vb.* to remove from active service because of sickness or injury. —*adj.* ill.

in·val·id[2] (in'valid) *adj.* not valid; with no legal value.

in·val·u·a·ble (in'valyōōəbəl) *adj.* too valuable to be measured: *she was an invaluable help when I was sick.*

in·vent (in'vent) *vb.* 1. to design (something new) or discover (a new way of doing something): *he invented a new airplane.* 2. to make up (a story, excuse, etc.). —**in'ven·tion** *n.* —**in'ven·tive** *adj.* —**in'ven·tor** *n.*

in·ver·te·brate (in'vûrtəbrit, in'vûrtəbrāt) *n.* an animal without a backbone. —*adj.* having no backbone. Compare VERTEBRATE.

in·vest (in'vest) *vb.* (+ *in*) to put money into the full or partial purchase of an interest in a company, product, work of art, etc., in the expectation of an increase in its value.

in·ves·ti·gate (in'vestigāt) *vb.* **in·ves·ti·gat·ing, in·ves·ti·gat·ed.** to inquire carefully into (a problem, a crime, etc.): *the police investigated the murder.* —**in·ves·ti'ga·tion** *n.* —**in'ves·ti·ga·tor** *n.*

in·vite (in'vīt) *vb.* **in·vit·ing, in·vit·ed.** to ask (someone) to come to a meal, party, etc. **in'vit·ing** *adj.* attractive or tempting: *those home-made cakes look very inviting.* —**in·vi'ta·tion** *n.*

in·voice ('invois) *n.* a bill; a list of goods sent and services rendered, with prices.

invertebrates

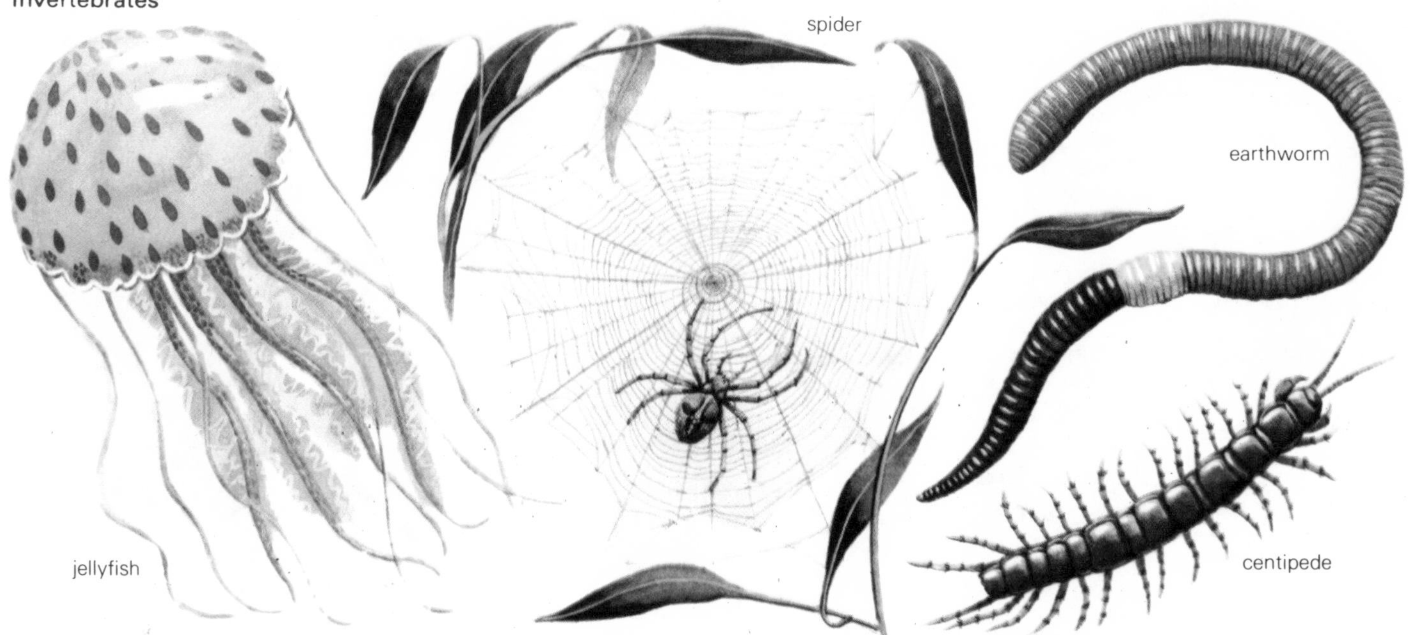

in·volve (in'volv) *vb.* **in·volv·ing, in·volved.** 1. to include; entangle in (a mystery, a plot, etc.). 2. to make necessary; entail: *this job involves hard work.* —**in'volve·ment** *n.*

i·o·dine ('iədīn) *n.* 1. a chemical element, found esp. in seaweed. Chemical symbol: I. 2. a brown strong-smelling medicine used as an ANTISEPTIC.

i·on ('īən) *n.* an electrically charged atom.

i·ris ('īris) *n.* 1. a plant that has long sword-shaped leaves and handsome flowers, usu. of purple, blue, yellow, or white. 2. the colored circular part of the eye surrounding the PUPIL[2].

iris

i·ron ('īərn) *n.* 1. the most common metallic chemical element. It is greyish white in color. Chemical symbol: Fe. 2. an object made from iron. 3. a household device with a flat heated lower surface used to smooth clothes after they have been washed. —*adj.* 1. made of iron. 2. hard and not easily broken: *he has an iron will.*

Iron Curtain the informal name for the barrier set up by Russia and her allied countries against the rest of the world, forming a barrier against free communications and trade.

i·ro·ny ('īrənē) *n.,pl.* **i·ro·nies.** 1. saying the opposite of what one means, for the sake of emphasizing one's meaning; e.g. on hearing of some personal disaster, to say 'What great news!' would be a use of irony. 2. the arrival of a hoped-for event too late or at a bad moment. —**i·ron·ic** (ī'ronik) *adj.* —**i'ron·i·cal·ly** *adv.*

ir·ra·tion·al (i'rashənəl) *adj.* not reasonable. —**ir'ra·tion·al·ly** *adv.*

ir·reg·u·lar (i'regyələr) *adj.* 1. not regular or according to the usual standards : *irregular handwriting.* 2. (grammar) of word patterns not formed according to the usual rules. —**ir·reg·u'lar·i·ty** *n.,pl.* **ir·reg·u·lar·i·ties.** —**ir'reg·u·lar·ly** *adv.*

ir·rel·e·vant (i'reləvənt) *adj.* pointless; of no importance to the matter in hand. —**ir'rel·e·vance** *or* **ir'rel·e·van·cy** *n.*

ir·re·sist·i·ble (iri'zistəbəl) *adj.* too strong to be resisted: *the cakes were an irresistible temptation to the hungry child.* —**ir·re'sist·i·bly** *adv.*

ir·re·spon·si·ble (iri'sponsəbəl) *adj.* 1. (of behavior) thoughtless; done without regard to the consequences: *it was irresponsible of Bill to spend all his pocket money in one day.* 2. (of people) not to be trusted; unreliable. —**ir·re·spon·si'bil·i·ty** *n.*

ir·ri·gate ('irəgāt) *vb.* **ir·ri·gat·ing, ir·ri·gat·ed.** to supply water to (fields and crops) by means of man-made channels, dams, canals, ditches, or pipes, or by sprinkling or spraying. —**ir·ri'ga·tion** *n.*

ir·ri·tate ('iritāt) *vb.* **ir·ri·tat·ing, ir·ri·tat·ed.** 1. to annoy. 2. to make (an itch or a sore place) worse by rubbing, etc. —**ir·ri·ta·ble** ('iritəbəl) *adj.* —**ir·ri'ta·tion** *n.*

is·land ('īlənd) *n.* any area of land entirely surrounded by water.

i·so·late ('īsəlāt) *vb.* **i·so·lat·ing, i·so·lat·ed.** to take or put (something) apart from other things; separate: *he isolated the cause of the trouble.* **'i·so·lat·ed** *adj.* 1. distant from other people: *they live in an isolated part of the country.* 2. single; unique: *an isolated case of measles.* —**i·so'la·tion** *n.*

is·sue ('ishōō) *vb.* **is·su·ing, is·sued.** 1. to come out from; emerge: *clear water issued from the little spring.* 2. to hand out; distribute. —*n.* 1. the act of giving or sending out: *the governor ordered an issue of food to the poor.* 2. something sent or given out: an issue of a magazine. 3. the problem or point (of a discussion, argument etc.): *they debated the issue of capital punishment.*

isth·mus ('isməs) *n.,pl.* **isth·mus·es.** a narrow piece of land with water on two sides that joins together two larger areas of land.

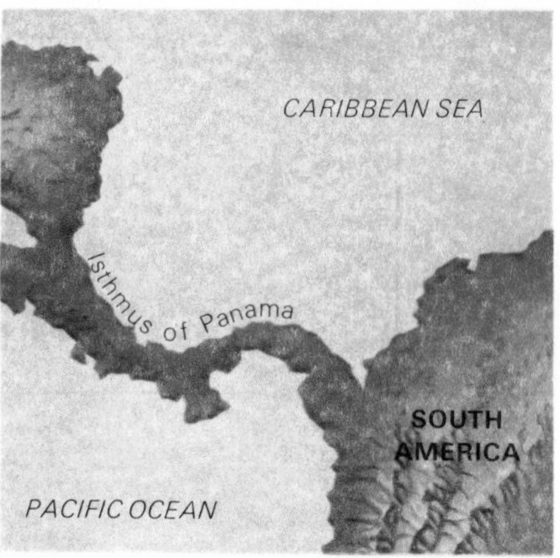

isthmus

i·tal·ic (i'talik) *adj.* of a style of printing type with sloping letters: *this sentence is printed in italic type.* **i·tal·ics** *pl.n.* italic print.

itch (ich) *n.* 1. a tickling feeling on the skin that makes one want to scratch. 2. a nagging desire: *I have had an itch to visit India for several years.* —*vb.* to have or feel an itch. —**'itch·i·ness** *n.* —**'itch·y** *adj.* **itch·i·er, itch·i·est.**

i·tem ('ītəm) *n.* 1. one article from a list, collection, etc.: *one item is missing.* 2. a short piece of information or news, esp. in a newspaper. **'i·tem·ize** *vb.* **i·tem·iz·ing, i·tem·ized.** to make a list of items.

i·vor·y ('īvərē) *n.* 1. the hard white bony substance of elephants' and walruses' tusks, used for making ornaments and piano keys. 2. a pale cream color.

i·vy ('īvē) *n.,pl.* **i·vies.** an evergreen plant with shiny, often star-shaped leaves that climbs up and covers walls, trees, etc.

ivy

J

jab (jab) *vb.* **jab·bing, jabbed.** to thrust (something pointed) sharply into or at something else: *he jabbed the knife into the wood.* —*n.* 1. a quick thrust; poke. 2. (informal) an injection: *have you had a flu jab?*

jack (jak) *n.* 1. a tool or machine for raising cars or other heavy objects short distances. 2. **jacks** (*pl.*) a game in which small pieces of metal, stones, pebbles, or similar (jacks) are thrown into the air, caught and moved on the ground according to certain rules, generally while the player bounces a small rubber ball. 3. a playing card with the picture of a young man (knave) on it. —*vb.* (often + *up*) 1. to raise with a jack. 2. (informal) to increase (prices, demands, etc.).

jack·al ('jakəl) *n.* a wild dog of Africa and Asia that hunts in packs at night, and often eats animals killed by larger beasts of prey.

jack·et ('jakit) *n.* 1. a short coat, usu. extending only down to the waist or seat. 2. an outer covering: *the book jacket was made of plastic.*

jade (jād) *n.* a hard, usu. pale green stone that is much prized for ornaments.

jad·ed ('jādid) *adj.* tired or worn out, as by overwork or overuse: *she had a jaded look after her long journey.*

jag·ged ('jagid) *adj.* (of a line or edge) having sharp, irregular points or notches: *the broken bottle had a jagged edge.*

jail (jāl) *n.* a prison. —*vb.* to put in jail; imprison.

jar[1] (jâr) *n.* a container made of glass, pottery, etc., usu. with a wide mouth.

jar[2] (jâr) *vb.* **jar·ring, jarred.** 1. to jerk or jolt: *he jarred my elbow.* 2. to cause an unpleasant grating noise or effect: *his voice jarred* (on) *my nerves.* 3. to conflict: *his ideas jarred with my plans.* —*n.* 1. a jolt or jerk. 2. an unpleasant grating noise.

jackal

jar·gon ('jârgən) *n.* 1. language that is full of scientific or technical words. 2. (informal) any speech or writing that is difficult to understand because it uses unnecessarily difficult words.

jaun·dice ('jôndis) *n.* a sickness that tints the skin, whites of the eyes, and body fluids yellow. —*vb.* **jaun·dic·ing, jaun·diced.** to prejudice.

jaunt (jônt) *n.* a short journey made for pleasure: *let's go for a jaunt in the country.* —*vb.* to go on a short pleasure trip.

jaun·ty ('jôntē) *adj.* **jaun·ti·er, jaun·ti·est.** lively or carefree.

jav·e·lin ('javəlin) *n.* a light spear for throwing, now used in athletic competitions.

jaw (jô) *n.* 1. either of the two bones that form the frame of the mouth and in which the teeth are set. 2. the lower part of the face. 3. **jaws** (*pl.*) anything resembling a pair of jaws in shape or function, such as the parts of a tool used for gripping.

jay (jā) *n.* any of a number of birds related to the crow and usu. having brightly colored feathers and a harsh noisy call.

jazz (jaz) *n.* a type of music that has strong rhythms with the beat on notes that normally would not be accented.

jeal·ous ('jeləs) *adj.* 1. envious of another person's advantages: *Tony is jealous of Susie's wealth.* 2. watchful and alert in guarding something: *he was a jealous guardian of his country's freedom.* —'**jeal·ous·ly** *adv.* —'**jeal·ous·y** *n.,pl.* **jeal·ous·ies.**

jeans (jēnz) *pl.n.* a pair of trousers, usu. made out of denim and worn for heavy work and as informal leisure wear.

jeep (jēp) *n.* a strong motor vehicle used by farmers, soldiers, etc., for driving over rough country.

jeep

jel·ly ('jelē) *n.,pl.* **jel·lies.** 1. a preserve usu. made from fruit juice and sugar, and eaten on bread. 2. anything resembling jelly. —*vb.* **jel·ly·ing, jel·lied.** to make into, put into, or become jelly.

jel·ly·fish ('jelēfish) *n.* any of various soft boneless sea animals that have a jelly-like body and (usu.) tentacles.

jeop·ard·y ('jepərdē) *n.* danger; risk. '**jeop·ard·ize** *vb.* **jeop·ard·iz·ing, jeop·ard·ized.** to risk (something); endanger: *Andy jeopardized our safety by driving fast.*

jerk (jûrk) *vb.* to pull, twist, or move abruptly or suddenly: *she jerked her hand away from the fire.* —*n.* a sudden movement such as a twitch or quick pull.

jest (jest) *vb.* 1. to make jokes. 2. to scoff: *the girls jested at their brother.* —*n.* 1. a joke. 2. something or someone to scoff at. '**jest·er** *n.* a person who jests, esp. one who was paid to amuse a noble household in former times.

jet[1] (jet) *n.* 1. a stream of gas, liquid, or small particles shot out from a narrow opening: *a jet of hot steam burst from the pipe.* 2. a nozzle or other device through which fluid, gas, etc., is shot: *the jets on the gas stove are blocked.* 3. an engine that provides a thrust forward by shooting out a stream of gas in the opposite direction. It is widely used for powering aircraft. 4. an airplane powered by such an engine. —*vb.* **jet·ting, jet·ted.** 1. to shoot out forcefully in a stream. 2. (informal) to travel in a jet plane.

jet[2] (jet) *n.* a hard black mineral like a stone, often cut and highly polished for jewelry.

jet·ty ('jetē) *n.,pl.* **jet·ties.** 1. a wooden or stone structure built out into a lake, river, sea, etc., from the shore, to protect a harbor or beach from the force of currents and waves. 2. a similar structure to which boats can be tied.

jew·el ('jo͞oəl) *n.* 1. a precious stone, e.g. a diamond, that has been cut and polished; gem. 2. an ornament made of gems. 3. a person or thing that is valued highly: *she's a real jewel.* '**jew·el·er** *n.* a person who makes, sells, or repairs jewelry. '**jew·el·ry** *n.* ornaments often made of metal set with real or fake gems.

jig·saw puzzle ('jigsô) a puzzle consisting of a picture mounted on cardboard or wood and cut up into small curved pieces. The pieces must be fitted together to make the complete picture.

jin·gle ('jinggəl) *n.* 1. a clinking sound. 2. a short song or rhyme, esp. one used in advertisements. —*vb.* **jin·gling, jin·gled.** to clink and tinkle.

job (job) *n.* 1. a trade or profession: *she had a good job as a teacher.* 2. a particular piece of work: *can you do a job for me?* 3. (informal) an effort: *they had a job deciding what to do.*

jock·ey ('jokē) *n.* a person who rides racehorses for a living. —*vb.* to trick or cheat.

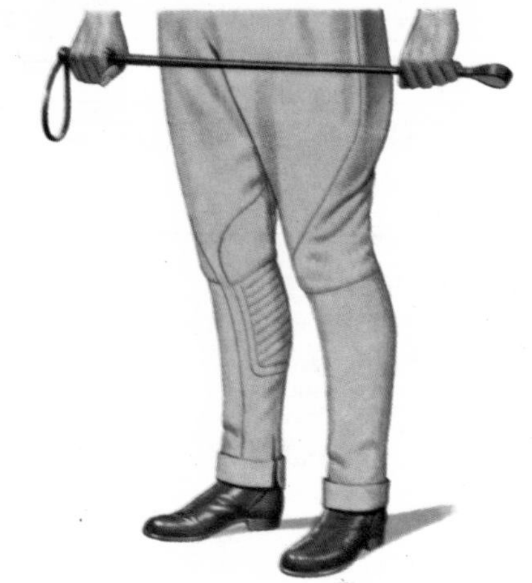

jodhpurs

jodh·purs ('jodpərz) *pl.n.* riding trousers that are wide around the thigh and hip and tight-fitting from knee to ankle.

jog (jog) *vb.* **jog·ging, jogged.** 1. to bump; jolt: *you jogged my elbow.* 2. to run at a slow steady pace.

join (join) *vb.* 1. to unite or connect: *the Panama Canal joins the Atlantic to the Pacific Ocean:* 2. to come together or merge: *the river joins the sea at the coast.* 3. to become a member of: *she joined a club.* —*n.* a place where two things meet or are joined. '**join·er** *n.* a skilled carpenter. **joint** *n.* 1. a structure that connects two bones in the body: *the knee joint connects the shin and thigh bones.* 2. the point at which two or more things are joined, or the method of joining them: *father mended the joint between the chair leg and seat. adj.* shared; done by two or more people: *Fred and Charles were joint owners of the business.*

joke (jōk) *n.* 1. a short funny story. 2. (often **practical joke**) an amusing trick played on another person to make him look foolish. 3. something said or done in fun. —*vb.* **jok·ing, joked.** 1. to make jokes. 2. to say (something) in fun. '**jok·er** *n.* 1. a person who loves playing or telling jokes. 2. a playing card, usu. with a jester's head on it.

jol·ly ('jolē) *adj.* **jol·li·er, jol·li·est.** full of cheerfulness and high spirits. —'**jol·li·ty** *n.,pl.* **jol·li·ties.**

jolt (jōlt) *vb.* to jerk or bump: *the train jolted and stopped.* —*n.* a sudden bump or jerk.

jos·tle ('josəl) *vb.* **jos·tling, jos·tled.** to push roughly; shove: *we were jostled by the crowd.*

jour·nal ('jûrnəl) *n.* 1. a magazine or newspaper, usu. on a special subject. 2. a full daily diary. '**jour·nal·ism** *n.* the job of writing for, editing, and publishing newspapers, magazines, etc. —'**jour·nal·ist** *n.*

jour·ney ('jûrnē) *n.* a long trip. —*vb.* to travel.

joust (joust) *vb.* to fight in armor on horseback with lances, as knights did in the Middle Ages. —*n.* a jousting contest.

jo·vi·al ('jōvēəl) *adj.* hearty and jolly. —**jo·vi'al·i·ty** *n.* —'**jo·vi·al·ly** *adv.*

joy (joi) *n.* 1. great happiness or pleasure. 2. a cause of happiness or pleasure: *your singing is a joy to hear.* —'**joy·ful** *adj.* —'**joy·ful·ly** *adv.*

ju·bi·lee ('jo͞obəlē, jo͞obə'lē) *n.* a celebration to mark a special anniversary. **silver (golden, diamond) jubilee** a twenty-fifth (fiftieth, sixtieth) anniversary.

judge (juj) *n.* 1. the official in charge of court cases, who decides on and announces punishments. 2. any person appointed to give a decision or ruling in a contest or dispute. 3. a person qualified to form an opinion: *she is a good judge of character.* —*vb.* **judg·ing, judged.** 1. to act as a judge. 2. to form an opinion about: *I judge his age to be about fifty.* '**judg·ment** *n.* (sometimes spelled **judge·ment**) 1. a law court's final decision, sentence, or ruling. 2. the ability to look at things in a critical and discerning way. 3. opinion: *in my judgment he is not to be trusted.*

judo

ju·do ('jo͞odō) *n.* a Japanese form of fighting without weapons, similar to wrestling, and engaged in as a sport.

jug (jug) *n.* a container with a handle and lip or spout, used for holding and pouring liquids.

jug·ger·naut ('jugərnôt) *n.* an overpowering, unstoppable force or object that destroys everything in its way.

jug·gle ('jugəl) *vb.* **jug·gling, jug·gled.** to do tricks that involve throwing, catching, and balancing a number of balls, bottles, rings, etc.

juice (jo͞os) *n.* liquid found in fruit, vegetables, and meat, that runs out when the substance is cooked, crushed, etc. —'**juic·y** *adj.* **juic·i·er, juic·i·est.**

juke-box ('jo͞okboks) *n.* a coin-operated machine for playing popular records.

jum·ble ('jumbəl) *n.* a mess or a muddle; confusion. —*vb.* **jum·bling, jum·bled.** to mix up.

junc·tion ('juñgkshən) *n.* 1. a place where two or more roads, railroad lines, etc., meet or cross. 2. any place where objects are joined or meet.

jun·gle ('juñggəl) *n.* 1. a dense, wild, tropical forest. 2. an area of life that is fiercely competitive and ruthless: *the world of business is a jungle.*

jun·ior ('jo͞onyər) *adj.* 1. younger (added to the name of a son whose father has the same name). 2. lower in rank or less experienced: *a junior partner.* —*n.* a lower-ranking, younger, or less experienced person.

junk¹ (juñgk) *n.* rubbish; something worthless or useless: *that car is complete junk.*

junk² (juñgk) *n.* a Chinese boat with large sails.

ju·ry ('jo͞orē) *n.,pl.* **ju·ries.** twelve people chosen from all areas of life who listen to evidence in a law court and decide whether the person being tried is guilty or not guilty. '**jur·or** *n.* a member of a jury.

junk

just (just) *adj.* 1. fair and right: *the judge made a just decision.* 2. suitable; deserved: *a just reward.* —*adv.* 1. exactly: *the bell rang just as the door opened.* 2. barely; hardly: *I just had time to comb my hair.* 3. a moment ago: *he's just gone.* 4. a short time or distance: *it's just round the corner.* 5. merely; only: *I just thought you might know.* '**just·ly** *adv.* fairly; with justice.

jus·tice ('justis) *n.* 1. sense of fairness. 2. fair treatment: *the expelled student demanded justice.* 3. the carrying out of the law: *not all thieves are brought to justice.* 4. a judge.

jus·ti·fy ('justəfī) *vb.* **jus·ti·fy·ing, jus·ti·fied.** to have or give good reason for: *can you justify your outrageous behavior?* —'**jus·ti·fi·a·ble** *adj.* —**jus·ti·fi'ca·tion** *n.*

jut (jut) *vb.* **jut·ting, jut·ted.** (often + *out*) to stick out or project: *Florida juts out into the ocean.*

jute (jo͞ot) *n.* a strong fiber from an Asian plant used to make rope or coarse material for potato sacks, etc.

ju·ve·nile ('jo͞ovənəl) *n.* a young person or animal. —*adj.* relating to or intended for children.

K

ka·lei·do·scope (kə'līdəskōp) *n.* an instrument with small pieces of colored glass or plastic at one end. When viewed through a hole at one end, mirrors inside reflect snowflakelike patterns.

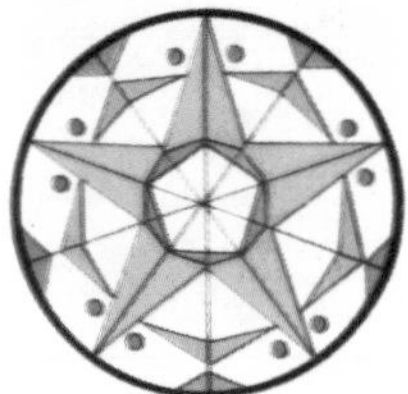

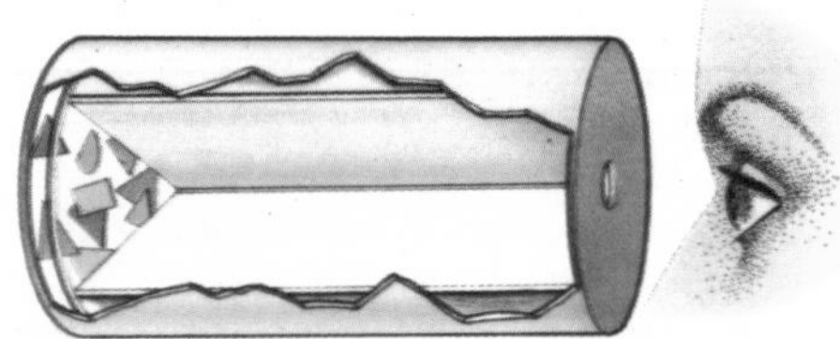

kaleidoscope

kan·ga·roo (kaṅggə'rōō) *n.* an Australian MARSUPIAL that carries its young in a pouch and bounds along on powerful hind legs.

ka·ra·te (kə'râtē) *n.* a Japanese form of fighting without weapons. Fighters use sharp blows, esp. from the side of the hand and forearm.

keel (kēl) *n.* the central bottom part of a boat running along its wide length. —*vb.* (+ *over*) 1. to capsize: *the boat keeled over in the high wind.* 2. (informal) to fall down: *the blow made him keel over.*

keen (kēn) *adj.* 1. (often + *on*) very interested (in); enthusiastic: *Elaine is keen on dancing.* 2. acute or active: *a keen sense of responsibility.* 3. sharply edged; cutting: *a keen wind.* —'**keen·ly** *adv.* —'**keen·ness** *n.*

ken·nel ('kenəl) *n.* 1. a small hut for a dog. 2. often **ken·nels** (*pl.*) a place where dogs are bred or boarded.

ker·nel ('kûrnəl) *n.* 1. the part of a nut inside its hard shell. 2. a grain (of wheat, corn, etc.).

ker·o·sene ('kerəsēn) *n.* (also **ker·o·sine**) a strong smelling oil obtained from petroleum and used as fuel in lamps and stoves.

ket·tle ('ketəl) *n.* a metal pot with a spout and handle, used for boiling water.

key (kē) *n.* 1. a device used to open and close locks. 2. something similar in shape or function. 3. something that explains or solves: *the detective discovered the key to the mystery.* 4. a means of attaining something: *hard work is the key to success.* 5. a part of a machine or musical instrument that is pressed down to operate the machine: *typewriter keys; piano keys.* 6. a musical scale: *the symphony was written in the key of B flat.* —*adj.* very important; vital: *he is a key figure in the movie.*

key·board ('kēbôrd) *n.* the part of a machine or musical instrument on which keys are situated: *a piano keyboard.*

khak·i ('kakē, 'kâkē) *n.* 1. a dull brown or olive green color. 2. a thick cotton cloth in this color, used esp. for soldiers' uniforms to provide camouflage.

kib·butz (ki'bŏŏts) *n.,pl.* **kib·but·zim** (kibŏŏt'sēm). a farming settlement in Israel where land is owned jointly by those who live on the kibbutz and the work and profits are shared among everyone.

kid·nap ('kidnap) *vb.* **kid·nap·ping, kid·napped.** to steal a person, often for ransom: *the crook kidnapped the millionaire.* —'**kid·nap·per** *n.*

kid·ney ('kidnē) *n.* one of the two organs in the body that filter waste matter from the bloodstream and turn it into URINE.

kiln (kil) *n.* a furnace or large oven used in various manufacturing processes, e.g. for baking or drying bricks, pottery, corn, etc., or for burning lime.

kil·o·gram ('kiləgram) *n.* a unit for measuring weight in the metric system. It is equal to 1000 grams (about 2 pounds 3 ounces).

ki·lom·e·ter ('kiləmētər, ki'lomitər) *n.* a unit for measuring length in the metric system. It is equal to 1000 meters (about 0·67 mile).

kil·o·watt ('kiləwât) *n.* a unit for measuring electrical power. A kilowatt is equal to 1000 watts. See WATT.

kilt (kilt) *n.* a short pleated skirt, usu. TARTAN, originally worn by Highland Scotsmen.

kind[1] (kīnd) *adj.* gentle; considerate: *the children loved the kind old man.* —'**kind·ness** *n.*

kind[2] (kīnd) *n.* a sort, variety, or type: *there are several kinds of musical instruments.*

king (kiṅg) *n.* 1. the male SOVEREIGN or ruler of a nation. 2. a playing card with a picture of a king. 3. a chess piece to be defended against checkmate. '**king·dom** *n.* a state ruled by a king or queen.

kingfisher

king·fish·er ('kiṅgfishər) *n.* a bird with a long pointed beak and brilliantly colored feathers. It dives into the water to catch fish for food.

kip·per ('kipər) *n.* a fish, esp. a HERRING, split open, smoked, salted, and used for food.

kitch·en ('kichən) *n.* a place where food is prepared and cooked.

kite (kīt) *n.* 1. a toy made of paper or cloth stretched over a light frame and flown in the air at the end of a long string. 2. a bird of the hawk family that hunts other birds.

kit·ten ('kitən) *n.* a young cat.

knack (nak) *n.* the special ability to do something; skill: ***she has the knack of making people happy.***

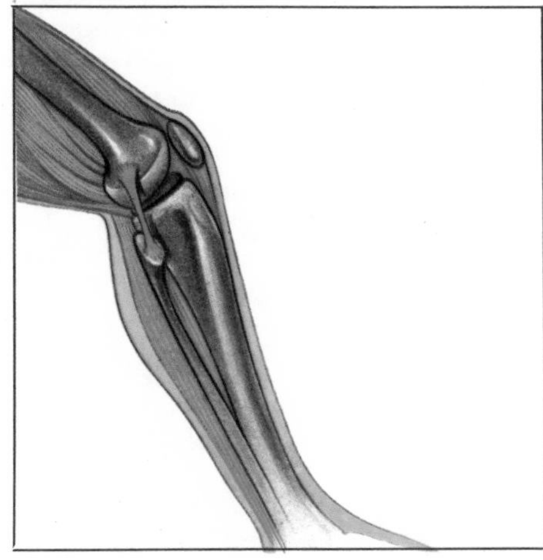

knee

knee (nē) *n.* the joint that is found in the human leg between the thigh and shin bones. **'knee·cap** *n.* the flat round bone in front of the knee that protects the knee.

kneel (nēl) *vb.* **kneel·ing, knelt.** to bend the legs and rest on the knees: ***the children knelt down to say their prayers.***

knew (noo, nyoo) *vb.* the past tense of KNOW.

knife (nīf) *n.,pl.* **knives.** a cutting instrument made of a sharp blade set either in a handle or a machine. —*vb.* **knif·ing, knifed.** to cut or stab with a knife: ***the thief knifed the policeman in the back.***

knight (nīt) *n.* 1. a soldier of high rank who fought on horseback in the Middle Ages. 2. a man with the title 'Sir.' 3. a chess piece in the shape of a horse's head. —*vb.* to make (someone) a knight. —**'knight·hood** *n.*

knit (nit) *vb.* **knit·ting, knit·ted** *or* **knit.** 1. to form fabric by closely interlocking loops of wool using two or more long straight needles or a machine. 2. to make or become well joined: ***her broken leg knitted well in three months.*** **'knit·ting** *n.* a piece of work being knitted.

knob (nob) *n.* 1. a rounded handle: ***the knob fell off the door.*** 2. a small lump, e.g. of sugar or coal.

knock (nok) *vb.* 1. to hit with a hard sharp blow: ***he knocked the nail into the wood with a hammer.*** 2. (of an engine) to rattle as a result of faulty mechanism. 3. (slang) to run down; belittle. —*n.* a short sharp blow (on a door or other surface). **'knock·er** *n.* 1. a person who knocks. 2. a shaped piece of metal attached to a door so that people can strike it to attract attention.

knock·out ('nokout) *n.* 1. the blow that knocks a boxer down and makes him unable to get up again before the referee has counted to ten. 2. (informal) anything that is remarkably successful or beautiful.

knot (not) *n.* 1. a fastening made of tightly tied loops of thread, string, etc. 2. any similar lump or tangle: ***her hair was so full of knots it took an hour to comb.*** 3. a measure of speed at sea, equivalent to one nautical mile (about 1·85 kilometers or 6076 feet) per hour. 4. a compact group of persons or things. 5. a hard lump in a sawn piece of timber. —*vb.* **knot·ting, knot·ted.** to tie in knots.

know (nō) *vb.* **know·ing, knew, known.** 1. to be acquainted with; to be familiar with. 2. to be certain about: ***I know you have made a mistake.*** **knowl·edge** ('nolij) *n.* information; a body of facts gained from experience. **'knowl·edge·able** *adj.* well informed.

knuck·le ('nukəl) *n.* any of the bony joints in a finger or between the finger and hand.

ko·a·la (kō'âlə) *n.* a small bearlike animal that lives in Australia. It eats eucalyptus leaves and carries its young in a pouch.

koala

L

la·bel ('lābəl) *n.* a small piece of paper, card, materialse etc., attached to an object to give information about the object: *the label in the shirt gave instructions on how to wash it.* —*vb.* to attach to a label to (something): *Ellen labeled all her clothes with her name.*

la·bor ('labər) *n.* 1. hard work, esp. physical work done for money. 2. people who do hard work for a living: *there was not enough labor on the building site.* 3. the pains and effort undergone in giving birth. —*vb.* 1. to work hard mentally or physically: *they had labored in the fields all summer.* 2. to have difficulty in doing, moving, etc.: *the old car labored up the hill in first gear.* —**la·bor·i·ous** (lə'bôrēəs) *adj.*

lab·o·ra·to·ry ('labrətôrē) *n.,pl.* **lab·o·ra·to·ries.** a building or room equipped for carrying out scientific experiments, research, and tests.

lab·y·rinth ('labərinth) *n.* 1. a complicated arrangement of passages, streets, etc. 2. the inside part of the ear.

lace (lās) *n.* 1. a delicate patterned netlike material, used for decorating dresses, underwear, etc. 2. a piece of string that is threaded through holes to hold two pieces of material, leather, etc., together as in shoes. —*vb.* **lac·ing, laced.** 1. to tie up by means of laces. 2. to thread a lace through holes. —'**lac·y** *adj.* **lac·i·er, lac·i·est.**

lack (lak) *n.* shortage or absence of something much needed or wanted: *there was a lack of sunshine during the vacation.* —*vb.* to be without (something): *Martin lacked good manners.*

lad·der ('ladər) *n.* a device of metal or wooden bars, fixed one above the other between two parallel poles. It is used for climbing up trees, buildings, etc.

la·dy ('lādē) *n.,pl.* **la·dies.** 1. (polite) any woman. 2. a woman of high social rank. 3. a woman with good manners.

ladybug

la·dy·bug ('lādēbug) *n.* a small flying beetle, usu. red or yellow, with black spots.

lag[1] (lag) *vb.* **lag·ging, lagged.** to drop behind: *he was lagging at the end of the long walk.* —*n.* a delay; time lapse: *after the overture there was a lag before the play began.*

lag[2] (lag) *vb.* **lag·ging, lagged.** to wrap thick material around (hot water pipes, boilers, etc.) to prevent loss of heat. '**lag·ging** *n.* any material used for this purpose.

la·goon (lə'gōōn) *n.* a shallow stretch of water enclosed by coral reefs or sandbanks.

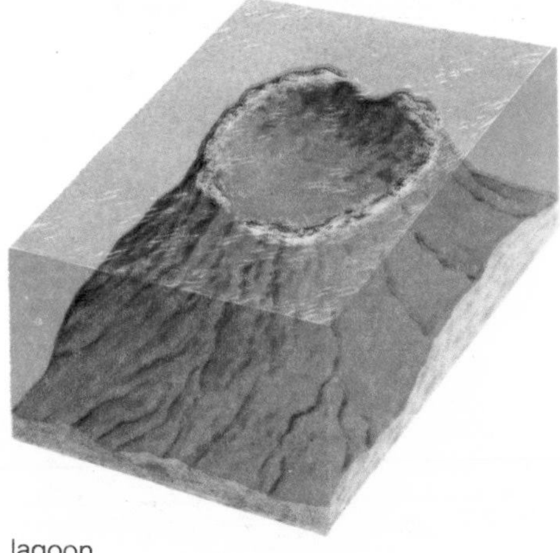

lagoon

laid (lād) *vb.* the past tense of LAY[1].

lain (lān) *vb.* the past participle of LIE[2].

lake (lāk) *n.* a large inland stretch of water.

lamb (lam) *n.* 1. a young sheep. 2. the meat from a young sheep. 3. (informal) a very gentle and defenseless person. —*vb.* to give birth to lambs.

lame (lām) *adj.* **lam·er, lam·est.** unable to walk properly due to injury to the legs or feet. 2. feeble: *a lame excuse.* —*vb.* **lam·ing, lamed.** to make (someone) lame. —'**lame·ly** *adv.* —'**lame·ness** *n.*

lamp (lamp) *n.* a device that produces light by means of electricity, oil, gas, etc.

lance (lans) *n.* a long spearlike weapon with a sharp metal point used in the past by mounted soldiers.

land (land) *n.* 1. the dry, solid part of the earth's crust. 2. a country: *the land of Norway.* 3. the people of a country: *the whole land rejoiced.* 4. that part of a country devoted mainly to farming: *he returned from Chicago to the land.* —*vb.* 1. to arrive on land from water or the air: *the airplane landed.* 2. (fishing) to catch (a fish): *Ken landed a large trout.* 3. (informal) to get or win: *he landed a big contract.* 4. to get into a situation or place: *his temper landed him in trouble.*

land·lord ('landlôrd) *n.* a man who owns property and lets other people (tenants) occupy it in return for money (rent). **land·lady** *n.,pl.* **land·la·dies.** a female landlord.

land·mark ('landmârk) *n.* 1. something fixed and clearly visible that serves as a guide to travelers. 2. a marker at the boundary of a piece of land. 3. something that marks a major change or turning point: *the invention of the automobile was a landmark in history.*

land·scape ('landskāp) *n.* 1. a stretch of countryside seen from a particular position. 2. a picture of such a view. —*vb.* **land·scap·ing, land·scaped.** to improve the appearance of (land) by planting trees, lawns, etc.

land·slide ('landslīd) *n.* 1. the fall of a mass of rocks and earth down a steep slope. 2. an overwhelming majority of votes in an election: *the President's victory at the last election was a landslide.*

lane (lān) *n.* 1. a narrow country road. 2. a route that airplanes and ships use regularly. 3. part of a road marked out for traffic moving in a particular direction.

lan·guage ('langgwij) *n.* 1. spoken or written human speech. 2. any particular form of this used for communication between people: *the German language.* 3. a way of expressing feelings or thoughts with or without words: *sign language; animal language.*

lantern

lan·tern ('lantərn) *n.* a case, usu. of glass and metal, intended to protect a light inside it.

lap¹ (lap) *n.* the area between the front part of the waist and the knees of a seated person.

lap² (lap) *vb.* **lap·ping, lapped.** to take (liquid) into the mouth by scooping it up with the tongue: *the cat lapped the milk.*

lap³ (lap) *n.* one circuit of a running or race track. —*vb.* **lap·ping, lapped.** 1. to place or be placed so as to lie partly over something else: *birds' feathers lap over each other.* 2. (sports) to overtake competitors still completing a previous lap in a race.

lapse (laps) *n.* 1. a slight and easily made mistake: *Tom's failure to reply to her letter was a lapse of memory.* 2. a slip away from normal standards or behavior: *a lapse into a life of crime.* 3. that which has passed: *a time lapse.* —*vb.* **laps·ing, lapsed.** 1. to fail to keep to accepted standards: *he lapsed into idleness during the vacation.* 2. to become void: *my driver's license has lapsed.*

lard (lârd) *n.* soft white pig fat often used in cooking. —*vb.* to grease (food) with fat before cooking to improve its flavor.

large (lârj) *adj.* **larg·er, larg·est.** big or bigger than usual: *a large meal.* **at large** 1. free: *the escaped lion was at large.* 2. everyone or everything: *the crowd at large.* **'large·ly** *adv.* mainly: *his success was largely due to hard work.* —**'large·ness** *n.*

lark¹ (lârk) *n.* one of several kinds of small dull-colored bird, noted for its beautiful song.

lark² (lârk) *n.* a bit of fun; romp. —*vb.* (usu. + *about* or *around*) to frolic: *he told us to stop larking around and finish the job.*

lar·va ('lârvə) *n.,pl.* **lar·vae** ('lârvē). the young of many types of insect at the stage of hatching from the egg. Larvae often look very different from the adult forms.

lash (lash) *vb.* 1. to strike violently and repeatedly: *the hailstones lashed against the window.* 2. to urge (someone) into actions, etc.: *his angry words lashed them on to finish the job.* 3. to attack in writing, speech, etc. 4. to tie: *we lashed the sail to the mast.* —*n.* 1. a whip made from a thong attached to a handle. 2. a blow from a lash or whip. 3. an EYELASH.

las·so ('lasō, la'sōō) *n.,pl.* **las·sos.** a long rope with a loop at one end, used by cowboys to catch horses, cattle, etc. —*vb.* **las·so·ing, las·soed.** to catch (an animal) with a lasso.

last¹ (last) *adj.* 1. coming at the end: *he was last in the lunch line.* 2. most recent: *his last song.* 3. remaining: *her last dime.* 4. least satisfactory: *the tropics are the last place to go in midsummer.* —*adv.* 1. after everyone or everything else: *he spoke last.* 2. most recently: *she was last seen in Paris.* **last·ly** *adv.* finally; in conclusion.

last² (lâst) *vb.* 1. to remain: *the bowl of apples lasted for three days.* 2. to survive in good repair: *her shoes lasted three years.* —*n.* that which is left; remainder: *they drank the last of the wine.* **last·ing** *adj.* continuing; remaining: *she achieved lasting fame.*

latch (lach) *n.* a fastener for doors, windows, or gates made from a bar that drops into a notch. —*vb.* to fasten with a latch.

late (lāt) *adj.* **lat·er, lat·est.** 1. arriving or happening after the expected time: *the late guests could not find seats at the table.* 2. coming near the end. 3. recently dead: *the late Mr Smith.* —*adv.* 1. after the expected time. 2. toward the end of a period. **'late·ly** *adv.* not long ago. —**'late·ness** *n.*

lat·ent ('lātənt) *adj.* present but not used or able to be seen; hidden or concealed: *Tim has considerable latent ability.*

lathe (lādh) *n.* a machine that holds a piece of metal, wood, etc., to be shaped by spinning it while a stationary cutting tool is held against it in order to shape it.

lathe

lath·er ('la<u>th</u>ər) *n.* 1. bubbly foam made by soap and water. 2. the foam caused by heavy sweat: *the racehorse was covered in lather after the race.* —*vb.* 1. to make lather. 2. to cover with lather: *Robin lathered himself all over with soap.*

lat·i·tude ('latito͞od, 'latityo͞od) *n.* the distance north or south of the equator. Latitude is measured in degrees and each degree is equal to about 69 miles: *the latitude of Peking is 40 degrees north.*

lat·ter ('latər) *adj.* 1. the second of two. 2. toward the end: *the latter part of the morning.* '**lat·ter·ly** *adv.* of late; recently.

laugh (laf) *vb.* to express merriment, joy, scorn, etc., by smiling and making other movements and sounds. —*n.* 1. the act or sound of laughing. 2. (slang) something which causes amusement or scorn; a joke: *if we played a trick on my teacher it might be a laugh.* '**laugh·a·ble** *adj.* likely to make people laugh; ridiculous: *his dancing was laughable.* '**laugh·ter** *n.* continuous laughing.

launch[1] (lôn<u>ch</u>) *vb.* 1. to send off (a ship, rocket, etc.) esp. for the first time. 2. to start (a course of action, a career, etc.): *Peter launched out into business on his own.*

launch[2] (lôn<u>ch</u>) *n.* an open motorboat used mainly in harbors and on rivers and lakes.

Laun·dro·mat ('lôndrəmat) *n.* (trademark) a storelike business with several coin-operated washing machines and (usu.) dryers.

laun·dry ('lôndrē) *n.,pl.* **laun·dries.** 1. a place where clothes and linens are washed and (usu.) ironed. 2. the items that are laundered. '**laun·der** *vb.* to wash (clothes).

lau·rel ('lôrəl, 'lorəl) *n.* a small evergreen tree with smooth shiny leaves that have long been the symbol of victory and honor.

la·va ('lâvə) *n.* 1. melted rock flowing from an erupting volcano. 2. rock formed when this cools.

lav·a·to·ry ('lavətôrē) *n.,pl.* **lav·a·to·ries.** 1. a room fitted with a sink and (usu) one or more toilets; washroom. 2. a basin for washing, esp. a fixed one with running water.

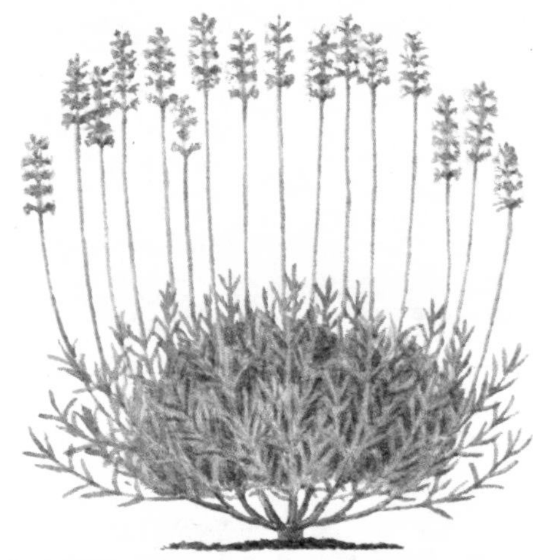

lavender

lav·en·der ('lavəndər) *n.* 1 a plant with pale purple strong-smelling flowers used to make perfume, lavender water, etc. 2. pale purple color.

lav·ish ('lavi<u>sh</u>) *adj.* generous; extravagent: *the mansion had lavish furnishings.* —*vb.* to give generously; waste: *the doting aunt lavished presents on her nephews.*

law (lô) *n.* 1. a rule or set of rules laying down what may and may not be done by people: *laws of a country.* 2. the basic facts and principles: *laws of science.* 3. the legal profession. 4. (informal) the police. '**law·ful** *adj.* obeying or allowed by law. —'**law·ful·ly** *adv.*

lawn (lôn) *n.* a stretch of ground with very closely cut grass growing on it.

law·yer ('lôyər) *n.* a member of the legal profession whose job is to advise people about the law and to represent people in court.

lay[1] (lā) *vb.* **lay·ing, laid.** 1. to put down, fasten, or place in a certain position: *he laid the knives in the drawer where they are kept.* 2. (of birds) to produce eggs.

lay[2] (lā) *adj.* 1. of someone who is not in holy orders. 2. nonprofessional: *in lay opinion, doctors often do not explain things clearly enough to their patients.* '**la·i·ty** *n.* everyone who is not a clergyman.

lay[3] (lā) *vb.* the past tense of LIE[2].

lay·er ('lāər) *n.* 1. a single coating or thickness: *the wall needed an extra layer of paint.* 2. a hen that lays eggs. —*vb.* to form layers: *he layered the crackers on a plate.*

la·zy ('lāzē) *adj.* **la·zi·er, la·zi·est.** idle; not liking activity. **laze** *vb.* **laz·ing, lazed.** to be idle: *they lazed in the sun during the vacation.* —'**la·zi·ly** *adv.* —'**la·zi·ness** *n.*

lead[1] (lēd) *vb.* **lead·ing, led.** 1. to guide esp. by walking ahead of (someone or something). 2. to live or experience: *she led a happy life.* 3. to be a way to: *jealousy leads to hate.* 4. to be the first, best, etc.: *she led the class.* —*n.* 1. the most important position: *a famous actor took the lead.* 2. the ability to act first and make others follow: *we followed his lead.* 3. a clue or hint: *the fingerprints on the safe gave the police a lead.* '**lead·er** *n.* someone who leads or guides. —'**lead·er·ship** *n.*

lead[2] (led) *n.* 1. a very heavy soft gray metal that melts and bends easily. Chemical symbol: Pb. 2. the black substance (graphite) in a pencil.

leaf (lēf) *n.,pl.* **leaves.** 1. the flat green part of plants that grows from the stem. 2. a sheet of paper. —*vb.* (+ *through*) to turn over (pages of a book, magazine) rapidly.

league (lēg) *n.* 1. an agreement, esp. between nations. 2. an association with members who have common interests.

leak (lēk) *vb.* 1. to pass slowly through a hole, crack, etc.: *the ice cream leaked out of the packet.* 2. to become known by accident: *the news leaked out.* —*n.* 1. a crack, hole, etc., through which fluids or gases leak: *the leak in the bucket made it impossible to carry water.* 2. the revealing of news that should have been kept secret. '**leak·age** *n.* the act of leaking. —'**leak·i·ness** *n.*

lean[1] (lēn) *vb.* 1. to slope or slant: *the old house leans to the left.* 2. to rely on for support: *she leaned heavily on the stick.* 3. to prefer: *his talents lean toward the arts.*

lean[2] (lēn) *adj.* 1. thin; having no fat: *lean meat.* 2. poor: *a lean income.* —'**lean·ness** *n.*

leap (lēp) *vb.* **leap·ing, leaped** *or* **leapt** (lept). to jump high into the air and cover a long distance; to spring up. —*n.* a jump.

leap·frog ('lēpfrog, 'lēpfrôg) *n.* a game in which players take turns in jumping over players who are bending over.

leapt (lept) *vb.* a past tense and past participle of LEAP.

leap year a year that has 366 days. Leap years occur every four years when February has 29 days.

learn (lûrn) *vb.* **learn·ing, learned** *or* **learnt** (lûrnt). 1. to acquire knowledge, skills, etc.: *she learned to speak Italian.* 2. to find out: *he learned the truth.* 3. to commit (something) to memory: *she learned the poem.* **'learn·ing** *n.* 1. the process of gaining knowledge, skills, etc. 2. knowledge acquired by studying.

lease (lēs) *n.* an agreement by which one person lets another occupy his house, land, etc., for a certain time in return for money. —*vb.* **leas·ing, leased.** to rent (property) on a lease.

least (lēst) *adj.* smallest. —*adv.* to the smallest degree: *he was least loved of all.* —*n.* the smallest amount.

leath·er ('ledhər) *n.* animal skin treated so as to be tough but soft enough to make into shoes, bags, coats, etc. —**'leath·er·y** *adj.*

leave[1] (lēv) *vb.* **leav·ing, left.** 1. to depart; to go away from (a place or situation). 2. to allow to remain behind: *she left the box on the table.* 3. to give in a will: *he left the house to his wife.*

leave[2] (lēv) *n.* 1. permission to do or not to do something: *Don was given leave to stay out late.* 2. permission to be absent, usu. for a holiday: *the soldiers were on leave.*

lec·tern ('lektərn) *n.* a sloping surface or stand on which a reader, preacher, or lecturer places a book, notes, a speech, etc.

lectern

lec·ture ('lekchər) *n.* 1. an educational speech to a class or audience: *a lecture on Africa.* 2. a warning. —*vb.* **lec·tur·ing, lec·tured.** 1. to give a lecture. 2. to rebuke: *the principal lectured the naughty girl.*

led (led) *vb.* the past tense and past participle of LEAD[1].

ledge (lej) *n.* 1. a narrow shelf that sticks out from a wall. 2. a rocky shelf projecting from the side of a cliff or steep slope.

ledg·er ('lejər) *n.* a book containing a record of all sums of money coming in or going out of a business.

leek (lēk) *n.* a winter vegetable similar to an onion in taste and having an edible bulb and broad green leaves.

left[1] (left) *vb.* the past tense and past participle of LEAVE[1].

left[2] (left) *adj.* on the west side of your body as you face north. —*n.* the left side or direction.

le·gal ('lēgəl) *adj.* 1. concerning the law: *legal papers.* 2. allowed by law. **'le·gal·ize** *vb.* **le·gal·iz·ing, le·gal·ized.** to make (something) legal. —**le·gal·i'za·tion** *n.*

leg·end ('lejənd) *n.* a story handed down, usu. by word of mouth, for many years, sometimes based on truth but sometimes just an imaginary tale. —**'leg·end·ar·y** *adj.*

leg·i·ble ('lejəbəl) *adj.* clear enough to be read: *neat writing is usually legible.* —**'leg·i·bly** *adv.*

le·gion ('lējən) *n.* 1. a division of the army in ancient Rome, consisting of about 5000 soldiers on foot and horseback. 2. a huge number. **'le·gion·ar·y** *n.,pl.* **le·gion·ar·ies.** a Roman soldier.

lei·sure ('lēzhər, 'lezhər) *n.* a time for relaxing and enjoying oneself; spare time. **'lei·sure·ly** *adv.* without haste: *they walked along the river bank in a leisurely way.*

lem·on ('lemən) *n.* 1. a yellow CITRUS fruit with sour juice. 2. the tree on which lemons grow. —*adj.* 1. made or tasting of lemons. 2. pale yellow.

lend (lend) *vb.* **lend·ing, lent.** 1. to allow someone the use of (something) for a time. 2. to give: *the music lent gaiety to the evening.*

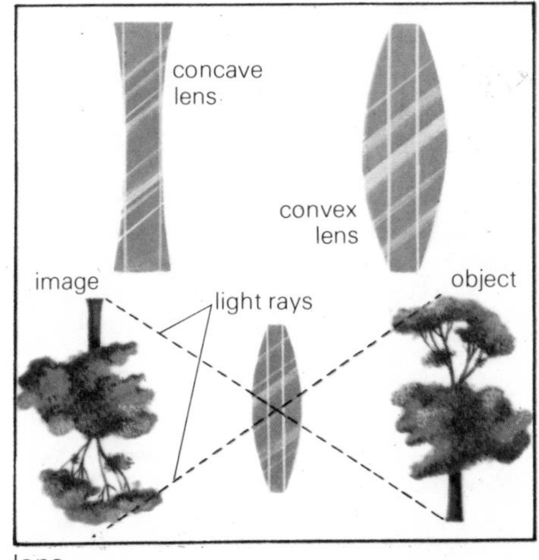

lens

length (length) *n.* 1. the distance from one end of a thing to another: *the length of a river.* 2. the extent in time from the beginning to the end: *the length of a day.* 3. a measured piece of something: *a length of material.* **'length·en** *vb.* to make or become long or longer. —**'length·i·ness** *n.* See also LONG[1].

lens (lenz) *n.* 1. a piece of clear glass or plastic with surfaces curved to focus light rays. Lenses are used in magnifying glasses, telescopes, eyeglasses, and microscopes. 2. the part of the eye that focuses the light rays entering it.

lent (lent) *vb.* the past tense and past participle of LEND.

Lent (lent) *n.* the 40 days before Easter when Christians (traditionally) FAST[2].

leop·ard ('lepərd) *n.* a large wild animal belonging to the cat family and having a golden-brown coat with black spots. It lives in Africa and Asia.

lemon

lep·ro·sy ('leprəsē) *n.* a crippling disease that is now mainly confined to tropical countries. '**lep·er** *n.* a person suffering from leprosy. —'**lep·rous** *adj.*

less (les) *adj.* not as much: *she eats less food than her brother.* —*adv.* to a smaller extent: *he tried smoking less.* —*n.* a smaller amount: *he earned less this year.* '**less·en** *vb.* to make or become smaller. '**less·er** *adj.* 1. smaller of two. 2. less in extent, amount, etc.

les·son ('lesən) *n.* 1. something taught at school or college: *a science lesson.* 2. anything taught by experience: *the accident taught Peter a lesson.*

let (let) *vb.* **let·ting, let.** 1. to permit; allow. 2. to turn over the use of (property) in return for payment: *she let her house to some students.* 3. (+ *down*) to disappoint.

le·thal ('lēthəl) *adj.* deadly; able to kill: *a lethal weapon.* —'**le·thal·ly** *adv.*

let·ter ('letər) *n.* 1. a symbol representing a speech sound: *there are 26 letters in the English alphabet.* 2. a written message sent from one person to another: *did you mail that letter?*

let·tuce ('letis) *n.* a plant that has large bright green leaves commonly eaten in salads.

lev·el ('levəl) *adj.* 1. having a flat surface; even: *it is easy to cycle on a level road.* 2. at the same distance or height: *the shelf was level with his eyes.* —*n.* height: *the flood reached the level of the window sills.* —*vb.* to flatten.

lev·er ('levər, 'lēvər) *n.* 1. a bar or other tool used to raise things or force things open. 2. a bar or rod by which a machine is operated. —*vb.* to use a lever to do or move (something): *Ted levered the lid from the crate with an iron bar.* '**lev·er·age** *n.* force obtained by using a lever.

lev·y ('levē) *vb.* **lev·y·ing, lev·ied.** to collect (troops, taxes, etc.) by force or authority. —*n.,pl.* **lev·ies.** troops or money collected by levying.

li·ar ('līər) *n.* someone who does not tell the truth.

lib·er·al ('libərəl) *adj.* 1. generous: *a liberal helping of cake.* 2. broad-minded; tolerant: *a man of liberal views.* —*n.* a person who believes in religious or political progress or in moderate reform. '**lib·er·al·ize** *vb.* **lib·er·al·iz·ing, lib·er·al·ized.** to make liberal or more liberal. **lib·er·al·i'za·tion** *n.* the act of making more liberal. —'**lib·er·al·ism** *n.*

lifeboat

lib·er·ate ('libərāt) *vb.* **lib·er·at·ing, lib·er·at·ed.** to set free; release: *the police liberated the hostages.* —**lib·er'a·tion** *n.* —'**lib·er·a·tor** *n.*

lib·er·ty ('libərtē) *n.,pl.* **lib·er·ties.** 1. freedom to act without foreign or government control: *liberty is much prized in democratic countries.* 2. freedom to act as one chooses: *she was given liberty to come and go as she pleased.* 3. a rude or disrespectful act: *he took a liberty with the manager by demanding a day off.*

li·brar·y ('lībrerē) *n.,pl.* **li·brar·ies.** 1. a collection of books, journals, etc., owned by a person or institution. 2. a room or building where books are kept and people can go to read or borrow them. **li·brar·i·an** (lī'brerēən) *n.* a person in charge of a library.

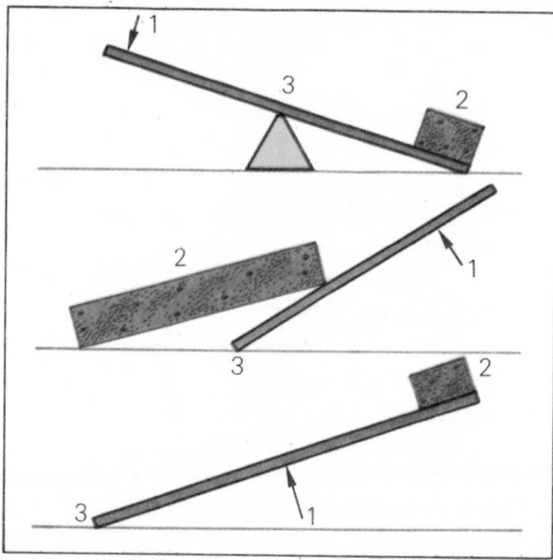

lever: 1 effort; 2 load; 3 fulcrum.

lice (līs) *n.* the plural of LOUSE.

li·cense ('līsəns) *n.* 1. a paper, cardboard disk, etc., proving that a tax has been paid or permission (for something) has been given: *dog license.* 2. a symbol, usu. in the form of a metal tag or plate, showing that a license certificate has been issued. 3. excessive or unreasonable freedom of action: *his parents gave him too much license as a child.* —*vb.* **li·cens·ing, li·censed.** 1. to grant a license (def. 1). 2. to give (someone) permission to do something.

li·chen ('līkən) *n.* a plant that is composed of a FUNGUS and an ALGA growing together and is found on trees, rocks, etc. A lichen can be leafy, branched, or, commonly, looks like a flat rough green, gray brown, or yellow patch.

lick (lik) *vb.* 1. to move one's tongue across (something): *Joanna licked her ice cream cone.* 2. (informal) to defeat: *the champion licked his opponent.* —*n.* 1. act of licking with the tongue. 2. a block of salt or other mineral for cattle to lick.

lid (lid) *n.* 1. a cover used to close open vessels. 2. the movable skin that covers the eyes to close them.

lie[1] (lī) *vb.* **ly·ing, lied.** to say something that one knows is not true. —*n.* an untrue statement: *when asked where he had gone, he told a lie.*

lie[2] (lī) *vb.* **ly·ing, lay, lain.** 1. to be in a horizontal position; stretch out flat. 2. to be in a certain position: *America lies across the Atlantic Ocean from Britain.*

lieu·ten·ant (lōō'tenənt) *n.* a junior officer in the army, navy, or marines.

life (līf) *n.,pl.* **lives.** 1. the quality that enables animals and plants to grow and reproduce. 2. the period between birth and death or between start and finish. 3. a way of living: *a monk's life is a hard one.* 4. activity; bustle: *there is plenty of life in this town.* 5. a biography: *she is writing a life of Abraham Lincoln.*

life·boat ('līfbōt) *n.* 1. a small boat equipped with provisions and carried aboard ships for use in case of shipwreck.

life·guard ('līfgârd) *n.* a very good swimmer employed at beaches and swimming pools to rescue swimmers in danger of drowning.

lilac

lift (lift) *vb.* 1. to raise from a lower to a higher level. 2. to cancel; call off: *speed restrictions were lifted temporarily.* —*n.* a ride in somebody else's vehicle: *John gave Mary a lift to the station.*

lig·a·ment ('ligəmənt) *n.* white connecting tissue that joins bones to each other and holds organs in place.

light[1] (līt) *n.* 1. a form of energy that makes things visible. 2. rays of visible energy from a fire, lamp, the sun, etc.: *the light from the spotlight was bright.* 3. something that produces light rays, e.g. a candle, lamp, etc. —*vb.* **light·ing, light·ed** *or* **lit.** 1. to set alight; cause to burn: *she lit the bonfire.* 2. to burn or start to burn: *the bonfire lit after three attempts to start it.* 3. (+ *up*) to show interest or pleasure: *his face lit up when his mother gave him a new watch.* —*adj.* 1. bright and clear; not dark. 2. pale in color. **'light·en** *vb.* to make or become light or lighter. **'light·er** *n.* a portable device that produces a flame for lighting cigarettes, cigars, etc.

light[2] (līt) *adj.* 1. not heavy; easy to lift or handle. 2. (of food) easy to digest. 3. mild; not severe: *the light fall of snow did not block the roads.* **'light·en** *vb.* to make or become less heavy. **'light·ly** *adv.* 1. not heavily; not pressing hard: *the ladder rested lightly against the wall.* 2. nimbly; in an agile way: *he hopped lightly across the stepping-stones.* 3. not seriously; without complaining: *she treated the accident lightly.*

light·heart·ed ('līt'hârtid) *adj.* happy; carefree. —**'light'heart·ed·ly** *adv.* —**'light'heart·ed·ness** *n.*

light·house ('līthous) *n.* a tall, towerlike building, built near or just off the coast, with a powerful lamp at the top to guide ships.

light·ning (lītniŋ) *n.* a sudden brilliant flash of light in the sky caused by electricity in the clouds.

like[1] (līk) *adj.* similar to or the same as: *this cloth feels like silk.* **'like·ness** *n.* a resemblance; similarity: *I can see a likeness to her mother in her face.*

like[2] (līk) *vb.* **lik·ing, liked.** to enjoy; be fond of: *I like ice cream on a hot summer's day.* **likes** *pl.n.* things one enjoys: *swimming is one of my likes.* **'lik·ing** *n.* fondness: *Wendy has a liking for apples.* —**'lik·a·ble** *or* **'like·a·ble** *adj.*

like·ly ('līklē) *adj.* **like·li·er, like·li·est.** 1. expected: *it is likely that I shall return home in time for dinner.* 2. possibly or apparently suitable: *the man who was interviewed for the job is a likely young fellow.* —**'like·li·hood** *or* **'like·li·ness** *n.*

li·lac ('līlək, 'līlak) *n.* a small tree that has clusters of sweet-smelling purple or white flowers.

lil·y ('lilē) *n.,pl.* **lil·ies.** 1. a plant, grown from a bulb, that has long narrow leaves and ornamental flowers. 2. any plant like a lily: *water lily.*

limb (lim) *n.* 1. a part of the body that is attached to the trunk, e.g. a leg. 2. a large branch of a tree.

lime[1] (līm) *n.* a white powdery substance made by burning limestone (a chalky rock) and used as a fertilizer or in cement.

lime[2] (līm) *n.* a small oval pale green CITRUS fruit with acid-tasting juice.

lime·light ('līmlīt) *n.* the center of attention: *the President's whole family was placed in the limelight after he had won the election.*

lim·er·ick ('limərik) *n.* a funny poem five lines long. Lines 1, 2, and 5 have one rhyme, and lines 3 and 4 another.

At beauty I am not a star.
The others outshine me by far.
My face I don't mind it,
Because I'm behind it,
It's those out in front that I jar.

lim·it ('limit) *n.* 1. a place, point, or boundary that cannot or may not be passed: *the limit of man's endurance.* 2. also **lim·its** (*pl.*) boundary: *the city limits.* —*vb.* to put a limit or limits to; restrict: *we must limit the amount we eat in order to stay healthy.*

lim·ou·sine ('liməzēn, limə'zēn) *n.* 1. a large luxurious automobile. 2. a small bus for transporting people: *an airport limousine.*

limp[1] (limp) *vb.* to move unsteadily or unevenly usu. because of an injured foot or leg. —*n.* a halting or unsteady step; lameness.

limp[2] (limp) *adj.* not firm or crisp; flabby: *the lettuce was not fresh and had become limp.*

lim·pet ('limpit) *n.* a small MOLLUSK that lives in a flat conical shell and is able to cling very tightly to the surface of rocks.

limpet

line[1] (līn) *n.* 1. a thin mark which may be straight or curved: *he drew a line across the page.* 2. a geometric figure having length but not breadth. 3. a boundary or border: *county line.* 4. a wrinkle or fold: *Alan has lines of worry on his brow.* 5. a row of people or things: *a line of soldiers.* 6. a single row of words on a page, in a poem, etc. 7. a succession of ancestors; family: *his is an aristocratic line.* 8. any course, route, or direction: *a line of action.* 9. a career, hobby, or activity: *Stephen is in the catering line.* 10. a type of product: *the shop carries only one line of clothing.* 11. **lines** (*pl.*) the speeches delivered by an actor in a play: *try to remember your lines.* 12. **lines** (*pl.*) the outlines of any object, esp. when judging whether it is pleasing: *that new model car has nice lines.* 13. a length of cord, wire, etc., used or designed for a specific purpose: *a fishing line.* 14. a transportation system for the public, traveling regular routes: *a rail line, a bus line.* 15. a wire or wires connecting points in a telephone or telegraph system. 16. (football) the row of players arranged in front of the backfield. —*vb.* **lin·ing, lined.** 1. to mark with a line. 2. to form a row or rows.

line[2] (līn) *vb.* **lin·ing, lined.** to cover the inside of (a coat, box, room, etc.) with some material. **'lin·ing** *n.* material used to cover the inside of something, esp. a coat.

lin·e·ar ('linēar) *adj.* 1. composed of, concerning, or depending mainly on lines: *linear art.* 2. straight; not curved: *linear motion.*

line·man ('līnman) *n.* 1. (also **'lines·man**) a person who repairs and installs telephone, telegraph, or power lines. 2. a football player in the forward line.

lin·en ('linən) *n.* 1. cloth woven from flax fibers. 2. household items made or formerly made from linen cloth, e.g. sheets, tablecloths.

lin·er ('līnər) *n.* an airplane or ship, esp. a large passenger ship, controlled by a shipping line and usually sailing regularly on the same voyage.

liner

lin·ger ('liñggər) *vb.* 1. to delay or move slowly: *he lingered on his way to school.* 2. to remain.

link (liñgk) *n.* 1. one of the rings in a chain. 2. anything that connects or holds things together: *Mr Wilson had a number of links with the town.* —*vb.* to join, esp. with a link.

li·no·le·um (li'nōliəm) *n.* a tough, hard-wearing material used to cover floors.

li·on ('līən) *n.* a large wild animal of Africa and South Asia belonging to the cat family and having a golden-brown coat. The fully grown male has a shaggy mane of hair framing his face. **'li·on·ess** *n.* a female lion.

lip (lip) *n.* 1. the outline of pink flesh around the mouth. 2. the edge or rim of something: *the lip of a jug.* 3. (informal) impudent and disrespectful talk: *I won't stand for any lip from my children.*

liq·uid ('likwid) *n.* a substance that is neither a solid nor a gas and is able to flow freely, e.g. oil, water. —*adj.* in the form of a liquid. **'liq·uid·ize** *vb.* **liq·uid·iz·ing, liq·uid·ized.** to make into a liquid.

liq·uor ('likər) *n.* 1. an alcoholic drink, e.g. brandy. 2. a liquid.

lisp (lisp) *n.* a speech habit that causes people to make a *th* sound when they try to make an *s* sound: *a lithp.* —*vb.* to speak with a lisp.

list (list) *n.* a series of names, things, etc., set down one after the other: *a shopping list.* —*vb.* 1. to write down a list. 2. to state in a systematic way: *he listed his objections.*

lis·ten ('lisən) *vb.* to make a conscious effort to hear.

list·less ('listlis) *adj.* lacking energy or interest; indifferent: *the heat made everyone listless.* —**'list·less·ly** *adv.* —**'list·less·ness** *n.*

lit (lit) *vb.* a past tense and past participle of LIGHT[1].

li·ter ('lētər) *n.* a unit for measuring fluids in the metric system. One liter equals about 1·056 liquid quarts.

lit·er·al ('litərəl) *adj.* 1. exactly following the words of a text: *I made a literal translation of the book into Italian.* 2. unimaginative; lacking artistic expression; ignoring symbolism: *a literal interpretation of the Bible.* —**'lit·er·al·ly** *adv.*

lit·er·a·ture ('litərəchər) *n.* 1. creative written works of permanent value or interest. 2. written works on a particular subject: *chemical literature.* 3. leaflets or other printed matter given out to people for advertising purposes. **lit·er·ar·y** ('litərerē) *adj.* of or connected with literature.

lit·mus ('litməs) *n.* a vegetable dye that is blue in an ALKALI solution and turns red in an ACID solution. **litmus paper** a paper soaked in litmus and used to test whether substances are acids or alkalis.

lit·ter ('litər) *n.* 1. rubbish dropped in public places. 2. straw or other material used as bedding for animals. 3. a number of kittens, puppies, etc., produced at one birth. 4. a stretcher on which injured people are carried. —*vb.* to make untidy by carelessly throwing rubbish around: *Ralph's bedroom floor was littered with old comics and toys.*

lit·tle ('litəl) *adj.* **lit·tler, lit·tlest** *or* **less, least.** 1. small in size. 2. short. —*adv.* **less, least.** to a small extent; hardly at all. —*n.* 1. a small amount. 2. a short distance or time.

live[1] (liv) *vb.* **liv·ing, lived.** 1. to have life; remain alive: *he lived through the war.* 2. to occupy: *she lived in an apartment.* 3. (+ *on* or *by*) to support oneself; depend on something for survival: *he lived on his savings.* 4. to spend one's life in a certain way: *he lived a carefree life.* **liv·ing** *n.* one's means of keeping alive.

live[2] (līv) *adj.* 1. alive: *a live fish.* 2. charged with electricity: *a live rail.* 3. (of a television or radio program) broadcast while being performed; not pre-recorded.

live·ly ('līvlē) *adj.* **live·li·er, live·li·est.** 1. cheerful, active, and full of life: *a lively party is fun to go to.* 2. stimulating; stirring: *a lively discussion.* —'**live·li·ness** *n.*

liv·er ('livər) *n.* 1. the large reddish-brown organ in the body that carries out a number of functions and is the largest GLAND in the body. 2. animal's liver used for food.

live·stock ('līvstok) *n.* animals such as cows, sheep, and pigs that are raised on a farm for profit.

liz·ard ('lizəd) *n.* 1. a REPTILE with four legs and a long body and tail. 2. the leather made from this reptile's skin that is sometimes used to make bags, belts, etc.

load (lōd) *n.* 1. something that is carried; a burden, esp. if heavy or big: *a load of sand.* 2. a weight on the mind; a worry. —*vb.* 1. (often + *on* or *up*) to put a load or burden into a vehicle or onto someone's back: *they loaded the cases into the trunk of the car.* 2. to put ammunition into (a gun). 3. to put film into (a camera).

loaf[1] (lōf) *n.,pl.* **loaves.** 1. a large portion of bread dough baked in one piece. 2. a quantity of food shaped like a bread loaf: *a meat loaf.*

loaf[2] (lōf) *vb.* (informal) to be idle: *he loafed in the garden all summer.* '**loaf·er** *n.* 1. an idle or lazy person. 2. a soft shoe, like a slipper, for casual wear.

loan (lōn) *n.* 1. something lent or borrowed, esp. money to be paid back after a certain length of time with INTEREST (def.4). 2. the act of lending something. —*vb.* to make a loan.

loathe (lōdh) *vb.* **loath·ing, loathed.** to hate very strongly.

loaves (lōvz) *n.* the plural of LOAF[1].

lob·by ('lobē) *n.,pl.* **lob·bies.** 1. an entrance hall. 2. a group of people who try to put pressure on government members to vote in a particular way. —*vb.* **lob·by·ing, lob·bied.** to try to get one's way by forming a lobby (def. 2): *the townspeople lobbied the mayor for a better bus service.*

lob·ster ('lobstər) *n.* an edible sea creature, with a dark colored shell that turns bright red when it is cooked. It has five pairs of legs, with very large claws on the front pair.

lizard

lo·cal ('lōkəl) *adj.* belonging to one particular place: *the local shops.* **lo'cal·i·ty** *n.,pl.* **lo·cal·i·ties.** place; area.

lo·cate ('lōkāt, lō'kāt) *vb.* **lo·cat·ing, lo·cat·ed.** 1. to find or note the position of (something): *he located the mine field.* 2. to be positioned or placed: *the church was located on a hill.* **lo'ca·tion** *n.* 1. a place where something is positioned. 2. a place outside a studio where scenes from a film are made: *they shot the skiing scene on location in Switzerland.* 3. the act of locating something.

lock[1] (lok) *n.* 1. a device for securing a door, box, desk, etc., so it cannot be opened without a key. 2. a grip or hold in wrestling. 3. a system of watertight gates in a canal that enable the level of the water between them to be raised or lowered. —*vb.* 1. to fasten with a lock. 2. to become fixed or immovable: *the wheel locked and would not budge.*

lock[2] (lok) *n.* a piece of hair; a curl.

lock·er ('lokər) *n.* a box or small cupboard in a public place, gym, club, etc., in which people can leave and lock up their possessions.

lo·cust ('lōkəst) *n.* a plant-eating insect, similar to the grasshopper, that often occurs in great numbers and destroys large areas of crops.

lodge (loj) *n.* 1. a small country house or hut used as a base for sporting activities: *a hunting lodge.* 2. a small house at the gateway of a large estate. 3. a local branch of a secret society such as the Freemasons. 4. a beaver's nest. —*vb.* **lodg·ing, lodged.** 1. to stay in a house, esp. temporarily as a paying guest. 2. to become firmly fixed: *the arrow lodged in the tree.* 3. to put forward formally (a complaint, statement). '**lodg·er** *n.* someone who pays to live in part of another person's house. '**lodg·ing** sometimes **lodg·ings** (*pl.*) sleeping accommodation for rent.

loft (lôft) *n.* 1. an attic; room or space just under the roof of a house, church, stables, etc. 2. a pigeon house.

loft·y ('lôftē) *adj.* **loft·i·er, loft·i·est.** 1. very high: *a lofty tree.* 2. noble; dignified: *the hero had lofty ideals.* —'**loft·i·ness** *n.*

log (lôg, log) *n.* 1. a rough thick chunk of tree-trunk or branch. 2. (also **log·book**) the daily record of a journey, esp. a ship's voyage. —*vb.* **log·ging, logged.** 1. to cut down trees and trim the wood into logs. 2. to record (progress) in a ship's logbook.

loi·ter ('loitər) *vb.* to delay; linger idly: *Tom loiters on his way to school.*

lone·ly ('lōnlē) *adj.* **lone·li·er, lone·li·est.** 1. sad because alone: *I was lonely when my friends left town.* 2. alone: *a lonely tree.*

lobster

long[1] (lông) *adj.* **long·er** ('lônggər), **long·est** ('lônggist). 1. great in length or distance; not short. 2. being great in length of time: *the days are long in summer.* 3. being of a certain measurement in length: *the car is twelve feet long.* —*adv.* 1. for a long time. 2. for a certain time: *it rained all day long.* See also LENGTH.

long[2] (lông) *vb.* to want (something) very badly; desire: *he longed for water.* **'long·ing** *n.* the state of wanting something badly.

lon·gi·tude ('lonjitōōd, 'lonjityōōd) *n.* the angular distance east or west of an imaginary line on the earth's surface drawn between the North Pole and the South Pole and passing through Greenwich, England. Longitude is measured in degrees: *the longitude of Seville is six degrees east.*

long·wind·ed ('lông'windid) *adj.* (of a speech, letter) tediously long.

look (lŏŏk) *vb.* 1. to observe, study, or watch: *he looked at the flowers.* 2. to appear; seem: *she looked a mess.* 3. to face: *the palace looked northwards.* 4. (often + *for*) to search: *they looked for the lost puppy.* 5. to attend to; consider: *look at the problem from a different viewpoint.* —*n.* 1. the act of looking. 2. expression: *a naughty look.* 3. (often **looks** *pl.*) the appearance of something: *he has good looks.*

look·out ('lŏŏkout) *n.* 1. the act of keeping watch for someone or something. 2. a person who keeps watch. 3. the place from which the person on the watch looks out. 4. (slang) problem; worry: *finding the money is his lookout.*

loom[1] (lōōm) *n.* a machine on which yarn or thread is woven into cloth.

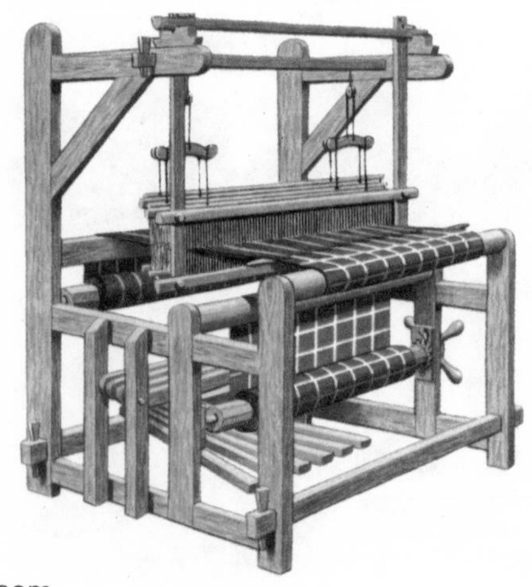

loom

loom[2] (lōōm) *vb.* (often + *up*) to seem huge and frightening: *the examinations loomed ahead.*

loop (lōōp) *n.* 1. a circle formed by bending one end of a piece of string, wire, etc., over the other. 2. something like a loop in shape: *her writing had many loops.* —*vb.* to make a loop.

loop·hole ('lōōphōl) *n.* a legal chance of escaping control: *he found a loophole in the tax laws.*

loose (lōōs) *adj.* **loos·er, loos·est.** 1. able to move freely; at liberty: *a loose dog.* 2. not firmly fixed in place: *a loose tooth.* 3. not packaged: *loose candy.* 4. inaccurate; not exact: *a loose account.* —*vb.* **loos·ing, loosed.** 1. to set (someone, something) free: *he loosed the guard dog onto the intruder.* 2. to shoot (an arrow). **'loos·en** *vb.* 1. to make or become loose or looser: *Jim loosened his tie in the hot room.* 2. (+ *up*) to make one's body supple by exercises: *he loosened up in preparation for the race.* —**'loose·ly** *adv.* —**'loose·ness** *n.*

loot (lōōt) *n.* 1. property taken by an army or rioters; plunder. 2. goods stolen by a thief.

lord (lôrd) *n.* 1. a male ruler, esp. in the Middle Ages. 2. (Britain) **Lord** the ceremonial or courtesy title of bishops and certain noblemen. 3. **the Lord** God.

lose (lōōz) *vb.* **los·ing, lost.** (lôst, lost). 1. to mislay (something); be unable to find: *he lost his suitcase.* 2. to fail to win: *they lost the game.* 3. to be without (someone or something) as the result of death, accident, etc.: *he lost his grandfather.* 4. to be or become totally absorbed in something: *he lost himself in the music.* 5. to waste (money, time): *six days' work was lost when the machine broke.* 6. (of a clock) to show a time earlier than the real time; be slow. **loss** *n.,pl.* **loss·es.** 1. the act of losing. 2. something lost: *they had a loss of 50 dollars.* 3. soldiers dead and wounded: *heavy losses in the battle.* **'los·er** *n.* 1. a person who fails to win. 2. (informal) someone who is constantly unsuccessful in life. **lost** *adj.* 1. misplaced; not able to be found: *a lost purse.* 2. unable to find the way; not knowing one's location: *we had gone so far into the woods that we realized we were lost.* 3. no longer practiced or known: *lost customs.* 4. ruined: *a lost hope.* 5. helpless; bewildered: *he is lost without his glasses.*

lot (lot) *n.* 1. a large amount: *a lot of noise.* 2. a thing or a group of things to be sold at an auction. 3. a small unit of land: *a parking lot.* 4. something that happens to one as the result of fate: *he had a happy lot in life.* 5. one of a set of marked papers, pebbles, etc., drawn at random to decide something: *they drew lots to decide who would begin the game.*

lot·ter·y ('lotərē) *n.,pl.* **lot·ter·ies.** a competition in which those taking part buy numbered tickets and one or more numbers are drawn out at random to win prizes.

loud (loud) *adj.* 1. having a great volume of sound; noisy: *a loud bang.* 2. flashy or vulgar: *loud colors.* —*adv.* (also **'loud·ly**) in a loud manner: *please try not to talk too loud.* —**'loud·ness** *n.*

lounge (lounj) *vb.* **loung·ing, lounged.** to relax or move lazily: *Howard lounged in a chair in front of the television.* —*n.* 1. a room with comfortable seats, esp. in a hotel, theater, etc., where people can relax: *he waited for Jim in the lounge.* 2. a couch.

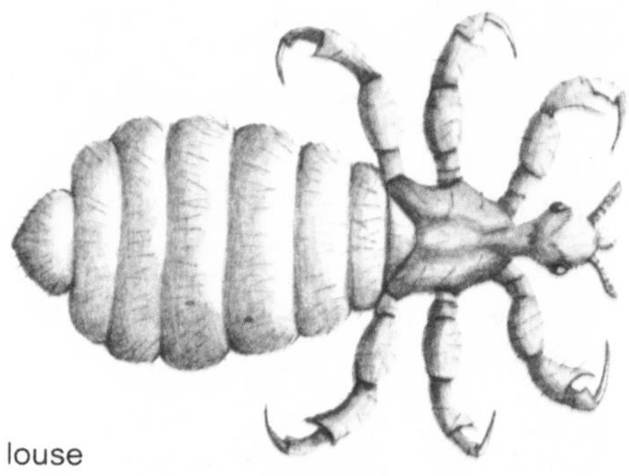

louse

louse (lous) *n.,pl.* **lice.** a small insect that lives on man and some animals, and sucks their blood. **lous·y** ('louzē) *adj.* **lous·i·er, lous·i·est.** 1. infested by lice. 2. (slang) very bad: *he did a lousy job.*

love (luv) *n.* 1. the emotion felt for people one is very fond of. 2. a strong liking: *she has a great love of reading.* 3. someone beloved: *he wrote a letter to his love.* 4. a zero score in tennis. —*vb.* **lov·ing, loved.** 1. to feel a strong affection for (someone or something). 2. to like very much. **'lov·a·ble** *adj.* causing a feeling of affection: *a lovable baby.*

love·ly ('luvlē) *adj.* **love·li·er, love·li·est.** 1. beautiful: *a lovely garden.* 2. delightful: *we had a lovely time.*

lunar module

low[1] (lō) *adj.* 1. not high; not far off the ground: *a low ceiling.* 2. less in quantity, value, etc., than is usual: *low prices.* 3. quiet and soft: *he spoke in a low whisper.* 4. miserable; suffering from ill-health: *he felt very low.* 5. not having enough: *low on food.* 6. vulgar; morally base: *stealing from the old lady was a very low act.* —*n.* 1. lowest point: *the market reached a new low.* 2. (cars) first gear. **'low·er** *vb.* to make or become low or lower: *he lowered the sacks onto the ground.*

low[2] (lō) *vb.* to make the deep throaty noise of cattle. —*n.* the sound of lowing.

loy·al ('loiəl) *adj.* faithful; true to one's country, friends, etc. —**'loy·al·ly** *adv.* —**'loy·al·ty** *n.,pl.* **loy·al·ties.**

luck (luk) *n.* 1. chance: *having a puncture twice in one day was bad luck.* 2. good fortune: *she was in luck.* —**'luck·i·ly** *adv.* —**'luck·y** *adj.* **luck·i·er, luck·i·est.**

lug·gage ('lugij) *n.* a traveler's suitcases, bags, etc., and their contents.

luke·warm ('lo͝ok'wôrm) *adj.* 1. barely warm; tepid: *lukewarm soup.* 2. not enthusiastic; reserved: *a lukewarm welcome.*

lull·a·by ('luləbī) *n.,pl.* **lull·a·bies.** a quiet, gentle song meant to put children to sleep.

lum·ber ('lumbər) *n.* timber cut and ready for use; boards and planks. —*vb.* 1. to cut timber to get it ready for use. 2. to move heavily and clumsily. **'lum·ber·jack** *n.* a person who cuts down trees and prepares logs for the sawmill.

lump (lump) *n.* 1. a shapeless solid mass: *there are lumps in the gravy.* 2. a swelling on the body. —*vb.* (often + *together*) to put, treat, or bring (different things) together: *I lumped together all the books even though some weren't mine.* —**'lump·y** *adj.* **lump·i·er, lump·i·est.**

lu·na·cy ('lo͞onəsē) *n.* 1. insanity. 2. great stupidity: *it was lunacy to swim in the flooded river.* **'lu·na·tic** *n.* 1. a crazy person. 2. a foolish person. —*adj.* 1. crazy. 2. very stupid..

lu·nar ('lo͞onər) *adj.* of or relating to the moon: *lunar exploration.* **lunar module** a small spacecraft, which is part of a larger one, that can be put into a separate orbit round the moon, land on its surface, and return to the parent spacecraft.

lung (lung͟) *n.* one of the two spongy inflatable organs in the chests of people and animals, used for breathing.

lurk (lûrk) *vb.* 1. to lie in wait; hide: *the thief lurked in the shadows.* 2. to move furtively or in a sneaky manner.

lux·u·ry ('lukshərē, 'lugzhərē) *n.,pl.* **lux·u·ries.** 1. an expensive and very comfortable way of life: *the rich man lived in luxury.* 2. an expensive and unnecessary comfort or pleasure: *a private yacht is a luxury few can afford.* **lux·u·ri·ate** (lug'zho͝orēāt, luk'sho͝orēāt) *vb.* **lux·u·ri·at·ing, lux·u·ri·at·ed.** to enjoy greatly. **lux·u·ri·ious** *adj.*

lynch (linch) *vb.* to put to death without trial: *an angry mob threatened to lynch the murderer.*

M

mac·a·ro·ni (makə'rōnē) *n.* a food made from flour paste shaped into small hollow tubes. It is boiled and often eaten with a cheese sauce.

ma·chine (mə'shēn) *n.* a device made up of a number of different parts and used to apply power to do a particular job: *a sewing machine.* **ma'chin·er·y** *n.* machines collectively.

mack·er·el ('makrəl) *n.,pl.* **mack·er·el** *or* **mack·er·els.** a small silvery ocean fish caught for food.

mad (mad) *adj.* **mad·der, mad·dest.** 1. out of one's mind; crazy. 2. feeling or expressing rage. 3. very interested in or fond of: *Mike is mad about butterflies.* —**'mad·ly** *adv.* —**'mad·ness** *n.*

magnet

mag·a·zine (magə'zēn, 'magəzēn) *n.* 1. a collection of stories and articles by different authors, bound in paper covers and published at regular intervals. 2. the part of a gun that holds the ammunition. 3. a storehouse for ammunition.

mag·got ('magət) *n.* the small white wormlike LARVA of a fly.

mag·ic ('majik) *n.* 1. the art of using or appearing to use mysterious hidden powers to control events. 2. the skill of performing tricks to entertain people. **black magic** evil magic, using wicked spirits or demons. **white magic** magic intended to do good. —*adj.* (also **mag·ic·al**) used in or caused by magic. **ma·gi·cian** (mə'jishən) *n.* a conjurer; one who is skilled in magic. —**'mag·i·cal·ly** *adv.*

mag·is·trate ('majistrāt) *n.* 1. a person who acts as a judge in minor court cases. 2. a government official who enforces the law.

mag·net ('magnit) *n.* a piece of metal, esp. iron, that has the power to attract other pieces of iron. **mag·net·ic** (mag'netik) *adj.* 1. having the power of a magnet. 2. attracting attention or admiration: *William has a magnetic personality.* —**mag'net·i·cal·ly** *adv.* —**'mag·net·ism** *n.*

mag·nif·i·cent (mag'nifisənt) *adj.* splendid; exceptionally great or beautiful: *a magnificent red and golden sunset.* —**mag'nif·i·cence** *n.* —**mag'nif·i·cent·ly** *adj.*

mag·ni·fy ('magnəfī) *vb.* **mag·ni·fy·ing, mag·ni·fied.** to make something seem bigger than it really is. **magnifying glass** a LENS used to make things look bigger.

mag·pie ('magpī) *n.* a long-tailed black and white bird of the crow family known for its noisy chattering song and habit of stealing small glittering objects.

ma·hog·a·ny (mə'hogənē) *n.* 1. reddish-brown hard wood used in making furniture, planks for boats, etc. 2. the tropical tree from which this wood comes. 3. a reddish brown color. —*adj.* made from or of the color of mahogany.

mail[1] (māl) *n.* 1. letters and parcels sent through the postal system: *is there any mail today?* 2. the system by which mail is sent, carried, and delivered. —*vb.* to send by mail. **'mail·box** 1. a box in which mail is delivered at a person's home. 2. a box from which mail is collected by the Post Office.

mail[2] (māl) *n.* body armor made of interlocking steel rings and plates worn for protection by medieval warriors.

main (mān) *adj.* the first or most important: *the main reason for his visit was curiosity.* —*n.* often **mains** the largest pipe or cable carrying water, gas, electricity, etc. —**'main·ly** *adv.*

main·land ('mānland, 'mānlənd) *n.* the area of land forming the major part of a country or continent rather than islands or peninsulas.

main·stream ('mānstrēm) *n.* the principal tradition or trend: *the mainstream of art.*

main·tain (mān'tān) *vb.* 1. to continue to have or do: *the car main-*

magpie

tained a steady speed. 2. to care for: *he maintained his garden carefully.* 3. to say with conviction: *he maintained he knew the way.* **main·te·nance** ('māntənəns) *n.* the act of caring for or maintaining: *the maintenance of the family is in father's hands.*

maj·es·ty ('majistē) *n.* 1. grandeur; dignity: *the majesty of a state funeral.* 2. **Majesty,** *pl.* **Maj·es·ties** a title used in talking to or about kings and queens. **ma·jes·tic** (mə'jestik) *adj.* very noble, dignified, and grand: *Georgina walked onto the platform in a majestic fashion.*

mammoth

ma·jor ('mājər) *adj.* 1. great in size, age, importance, value, etc.: *the Mississippi is one of the major rivers of the world.* 2. (of a musical scale) using a particular sequence of notes in which the intervals between the notes are always the same as those between the white keys of a piano beginning on the note C: *a major key.* Compare MINOR. —*n.* an army officer between captain and lieutenant-colonel. —*vb.* to specialize in a particular subject: *she majored in physics at university.* **ma·jor·i·ty** (mə'joritē) *n.,pl.* **ma·jor·i·ties.** 1. a larger part or number: *the majority of people enjoy sunshine.* 2. the age of full legal responsibility.

make-be·lieve ('mākbilēv) *n.* fantasy; indulgence in the belief that something obviously false is true: *his idea of himself as a great hero is just make-believe.* —*adj.* not real; imaginary. **make believe** to pretend.

make-up ('mākup) *n.* 1. cosmetics for the face. 2. the way in which something is put together or composed, esp. a person's character: *it is not in her make-up to be rude.*

male (māl) *adj.* 1. of or concerning the sex that can father young: *a male pig is called a boar.* 2. of or concerning men or boys: *the male teachers formed a team to play the students at football.* —*n.* a male person or animal.

mal·ice ('malis) *n.* spitefulness; ill will towards other people. **ma·li·cious** (mə'lishəs) *adj.* feeling or showing ill will. —**ma'li·cious·ly** *adv.*

mal·let ('malit) *n.* a heavy wooden hammer used as a tool.

malt (môlt) *n.* substance made by soaking grain, usu. barley, in water, allowing it to sprout, and then drying it. Malt is used in making beer and other drinks and in cooking.

mam·mal ('maməl) *n.* an animal that has warm blood, a bony SKELETON, and hair or fur on its body. A female mammal feeds its young on milk that it produces from GLANDs in its body. Human beings, sheep, and whales are all mammals.

mam·moth ('maməth) *n.* a very large hairy elephant-like mammal that lived many thousands of years ago. —*adj.* huge; very large: *clearing up after the party was a mammoth task.*

man·age ('manij) *vb.* **man·ag·ing, man·aged.** 1. to control or handle: *she managed the galloping horse skillfully.* 2. to succeed, often against difficulties: *despite his ill-health, he managed to become a lawyer.* **'man·age·ment** *n.* 1. act or method of managing. 2. the group of people concerned with running a business, factory, etc. **'man·a·ger** *n.* a supervisor of other employees in a company.

mane (mān) *n.* the long thick hair that grows on the backs of some animals' necks: *the lion had a fine mane.*

ma·neu·ver (mə'nōōvər) *n.* 1. a clever or crafty movement: *Graham maneuvered through the crowd until he reached the front row.* 2. often **ma·neu·vers** (*pl.*) movement of armed forces to gain advantage over an enemy. —*vb.* to make moves to try to gain an advantage.

man·gle ('manggəl) *vb.* **man·gling, man·gled.** to damage badly by force or clumsiness; destroy by twisting and crushing: *in the accident the truck mangled the small car.* —*n.* a machine for ironing flat laundry like sheets, tablecloths, etc.

ma·ni·a ('mānēə) *n.* 1. violent madness. 2. an unreasonably strong enthusiasm or craze: *he has a mania for old motorcycles.* **ma·ni·ac** ('mānēak) *n.* a person suffering from mania; a madman. —**man·ic** ('manik) *adj.*

ma·nip·u·late (mə'nipyəlāt) *vb.* **ma·nip·u·lat·ing, ma·nip·u·lat·ed.** 1. to control or operate with the hands: *she manipulated the puppet's strings.* 2. to manage skillfully, esp. by underhand means: *he manipulated the committee to achieve his desires.* —**ma·nip·u·la·tion** *n.*

man·ner ('manər) *n.* 1. a particular way of doing something: *Jeff was whistling in a cheerful manner.* 2. a way of behaving: *she has a sullen manner.* 3. **man·ners** (*pl.*) polite or correct ways of behaving: *he has good manners.* **'man·ner·ism** *n.* a noticeable and unusual characteristic.

mantelpiece

man·tel·piece ('mantəlpēs) *n.* the shelf jutting out from the wall or chimney front above a fireplace.

man·u·al ('manyōōəl) *adj.* done by hand: *gardening is mainly manual labor.* —*n.* a book that gives instructions how to do or use something: *I consulted my car manual.*

man·u·fac·ture (manyəfakchər) *vb.* **man·u·fac·tur·ing, man·u·fac·tured.** 1. to make (goods) on a large scale using machinery: *the factory manufactures electrical goods.* 2. to invent (an excuse). —*n.* the act of manufacturing.

ma·nure (mə'nōōr, mə'nyōōr) *n.* animal waste, e.g. from horses, cows, and sheep, used to enrich the soil. —*vb.* **ma·nur·ing, ma·nured.** to spread manure.

man·u·script ('manyəskript) *n.* 1. books, letters, etc., in handwritten form. 2. a book in its original form before it has been printed.

map (map) *n.* an outline drawing of the surface of the earth or part of it, showing towns, rivers, roads, and other features. —*vb.* **map·ping, mapped.** 1. to make a map of. 2. (+ *out*) to plan thoroughly: *father mapped out the vacation so that it would run smoothly.*

mar·a·thon ('marəthon) *n.* 1. a long-distance running race. 2. a long and exhausting struggle, task, etc.

mar·ble ('mârbəl) *n.* 1. a hard stone, often handsomely marked, that is cut and polished and used in buildings, statues, and furniture. 2. a small glass ball used in games.

march (mârch) *vb.* to walk at a regular pace as soldiers do. —*n.* 1. the steady walking pace of soldiers. 2. the act of marching. 3. a piece of music to accompany marching.

mare (meər) *n.* a female horse, pony, donkey, or zebra.

mar·ga·rine ('mârjərin) *n.* a mixture of vegetable oils and skimmed milk used in place of butter.

mar·gin ('mârjin) *n.* 1. the edge of something, esp. the area around the written or printed part of a page. 2. an amount allowed in addition to what is necessary: *leave a margin of an hour for your journey.* **'mar·gin·al** *adj.* 1. in or of the margin: *marginal notes.* 2. small: *the delay is of marginal importance.* —**'mar·gin·al·ly** *adv.*

ma·rine (mə'rēn) *adj.* 1. of or found in the sea: *marine animals.* 2. concerned with shipping or naval matters: *a marine insurance company.* —*n.* a member of a military unit serving on land and aboard ships, esp. a member of the U.S. Marine Corps.

mark (mârk) *n.* 1. a spot, scratch, etc., made accidentally. 2. a sign made as a reminder, to help identification, etc. 3. a letter or figure indicating the standard of a person's performance: *Patrick got the best mark in the class.* 4. a line or object showing position: *the horses passed the two-mile mark.* —*vb.* 1. to put a mark or marks on. 2. to indicate (position). 3. to give marks (def. 3) to.

mar·ket ('mârkit) *n.* 1. the open or covered area where people meet to buy and sell goods or animals. 2. the demand for something that is for sale: *there is a poor market for fresh fruit now.* —*vb.* to sell or put up for sale: *the company markets televisions.*

mar·ma·lade ('mârməlād) *n.* jam made from oranges or other citrus fruit.

ma·roon[1] (mə'ro͞on) *vb.* to abandon (someone) on a lonely island or leave in a similar difficult position: *the tide marooned them on the rock.*

ma·roon[2] (mə'ro͞on) *n., adj.* (having) a dark crimson color with a brownish tinge.

mar·row ('marō) *n.* the soft fatty substance inside hollow bones.

mar·ry ('marē) *vb.* **mar·ry·ing, mar·ried.** to join legally as husband and wife. **'mar·riage** *n.* 1. the state of living together as husband and wife. 2. a wedding.

marsh (mârsh) *n.* an area of low-lying waterlogged ground on which reeds and grasses grow.

mar·shal ('mârshəl) *n.* 1. an official with duties similar to those of a sheriff. 2. a police or fire department chief in a city. 3. a person who arranges important public ceremonies. —*vb.* to gather together and arrange in proper order: *he marshaled his thoughts before writing the essay.*

mar·su·pi·al (mârso͞opēəl) *n.* one of a class of animals (e.g. Virginia possum, kangaroo) found mainly in Australia and also in America, whose young are carried by their mothers in a pouch.

mar·tial ('mârshəl) *adj.* of warfare; military: *martial discipline.*

mar·tyr ('mârtər) *n.* a person who dies or suffers for a cause: *St Stephen was the first Christian martyr.* —*vb.* to torture or put (someone) to death for his beliefs.

mar·vel·ous ('mârvələs) *adj.* 1. astonishing: *the Grand Canyon is a marvelous sight.* 2. (informal) excellent; wonderful: *a marvelous idea.* —**'mar·vel·ous·ly** *adv.*

mar·zi·pan ('mârzəpan) *n.* paste with an almond and sugar base used in making sweets.

mas·car·a (ma'skarə) *n.* a dark substance used to color the eyelashes.

mas·cot ('maskot) *n.* something reputed to bring good luck.

mas·cu·line ('maskyəlin) *adj.* of or like the male sex: *beards are a masculine feature.* —**mas·cu'lin·i·ty** *n.*

mash (mash) *n.* 1. animal feed esp. a mixture of warm boiled bran. 2. any soft pulp. —*vb.* to make into a soft pulp.

mask (mask) *n.* 1. a covering worn to protect or hide the face. 2. anything that conceals or covers up. —*vb.* 1. to put on or wear a mask. 2. to hide: *the cracks in the wall were masked with a coat of paint.*

mass[1] (mas) *n.* 1. a quantity of matter without a specific shape: *a mass of snow slid off the roof.* 2. a large number: *a mass of people.* 3. the quantity of matter in a body: *a feather has a low mass.* —*vb.* to gather or be gathered into a mass.

mass[2] (mas) *n.* the principal religious ceremony of the Roman Catholic Church.

mas·sa·cre ('masəkər) *n.* the brutal killing of many people. —*vb.* **mas·sa·cring, mas·sa·cred.** to kill brutally.

mas·sage (mə'sazh) *n.* the rubbing of body muscles and joints in order to improve their function. —*vb.* **mas·sag·ing, mas·saged.** to give a massage to.

mas·sive ('masiv) *adj.* very big; on a very large scale: *the new campaign gathered massive public support.* —**'mas·sive·ly** *adv.*

mast (mast) *n.* 1. a vertical pole supporting the sails of a ship. 2. an upright metal pole or pylon used to transmit radio or television broadcasts.

mas·ter ('mastər) *n.* 1. a man who controls or has power. 2. a skilled craftsman or person with great knowledge of a particular thing: *a master butcher.* 3. **Master** the title used on letters as a form of address for a young boy. —*vb.* to achieve control of: *he mastered his anger.*

mas·ter·mind ('mastərmīnd) *n.* a person of superior intelligence. —*vb.* to plan and direct (a scheme, etc.):

marsupials

mas·ter·piece ('mastərpēs) *n.* a work of expert skill or craftsmanship.

match[1] (mach) *n.* 1. a person or thing exactly equal to another: *Jane is Carol's match at chess.* 2. a contest of skill between individuals or teams: *a hockey match.* 3. a marriage. —*vb.* 1. to be the equal of. 2. to correspond to something else: *the pieces of the puzzle don't match.* 3. to harmonize with in color, quality, etc.: *her gloves match her handbag.*

match[2] (mach) *n.* a small piece of wood or cardboard tipped with a substance that bursts into flame when rubbed on a treated surface.

mate (māt) *n.* 1. the male or female of a pair of animals. 2. fellow-worker or assistant. 3. an officer on a ship below the rank of captain. —*vb.* **mat·ing, mat·ed.** to join together as a pair for breeding.

ma·te·ri·al (mə'tērēəl) *n.* anything used to make something, esp. a fabric: *she used a light material for her dress.* —*adj.* 1. physical: *material well-being.* 2. important: *a material witness.* **ma'te·ri·al·ism** *n.* the stressing of physical values. **ma'te·ri·al·ize** *vb.* **ma·te·ri·al·iz·ing, ma·te·ri·al·ized.** to become a fact. —**ma'te·ri·al·ist** *n.* —**ma·te·ri·al'is·tic** *adj.*

ma·ter·ni·ty (mə'turnətē) *n.* the state of being a mother.

math·e·mat·ics (mathə'matiks) *n.* the study of numbers, quantities, sizes, and shapes. Algebra, arithmetic, geometry, and trigonometry are all branches of mathematics. **math·e·ma·ti·cian** (mathəmə'tishən) *n.* someone who studies mathematics.

mat·i·nee (matə'nā) *n.* an afternoon performance at a theater or movie house.

mat·ri·mo·ny ('matrəmōnē) *n.* the state of being married; marriage. —**mat·ri'mo·ni·al** *adj.*

ma·tron ('mātrən) *n.* 1. a woman in charge of female prisoners. 2. the chief nurse in a hospital.

mat·ter ('matər) *n.* 1. substance having weight and taking up space; substance of which all physical things are made. 2. a subject of interest, importance, discussion, etc. 3. trouble; difficulty: *what's the matter?* —*vb.* to be of interest or importance: *it mattered to him that his team should win the cup.*

mat·tress ('matris) *n.* a thick pad, usu. made to fit a bed frame, and made up of a fabric case containing either stuffing or springs.

ma·ture (mə'choor, mə'toor, mə'tyoor) *adj.* fully grown; adult. —*vb.* **ma·tur·ing, ma·tured.** 1. to develop completely. 2. to ripen. —**ma'ture·ly** *adv.* —**ma'tur·i·ty** *n.*

mauve (mōv) *n., adj.* (having) a delicate purple color.

max·i·mum ('maksəməm) *n.* the greatest or highest point or value: *the temperature reached its maximum at noon.* —*adj.* greatest possible: *the maximum number of schoolchildren should be vaccinated against polio.*

may·or ('māər) *n.* the head of the government of a town or city.

maze (māz) *n.* 1. a confusing layout of paths with high hedges on either side, forming a puzzle in which people can wander for amusement. 2. any puzzle with alternative routes, only one of which leads to the goal.

maze

mead·ow ('medō) *n.* a field of long grass used for hay or as grazing.

meal[1] (mēl) *n.* a type or quantity of food served and eaten at any one time: *fried chicken is my favorite meal.*

meal[2] (mēl) *n.* the edible part of wheat, corn, or any other grain ground into a coarse powder for use as food.

mean[1] (mēn) *vb.* **mean·ing, meant** (ment). 1. to want to say or do; intend: *she meant to leave at six o'clock.* 2. to signify or have (a certain sense): *mensa means table in Latin.* **'mean·ing** *n.* something that is meant or intended. —**'mean·ing·ful** *adj.* —**'mean·ing·ful·ly** *adv.*

mean[2] (mēn) *adj.* 1. unkind: *he played a mean trick on his brother.* 2. selfish; ungenerous: *he is too mean to buy his nephew a present.* 3. poor in quality or social position: *a mean dwelling.*

means (mēnz) *pl.n.* 1. the way in which a particular result is obtained: *she won by honest means.* 2. property or money: *only a man of means can afford to keep racehorses.*

meant (ment) *vb.* the past tense and past participle of MEAN[1].

mea·sles ('mēzəlz) *n.* a VIRUS disease that causes a high fever and a rash of bright red spots all over the body.

meas·ure ('mezhər) *vb.* **meas·ur·ing, meas·ured.** 1. to find or show the size, degree, weight, etc., of something: *I measured the table and found it was six feet long.* 2. to be a certain size: *the car measured fourteen feet in length.* 3. (+ *off* or *out*) to separate (a measured amount of something) from the rest: *I measured out four cups of flour for the cake.* —*n.* 1. the size, amount, weight, etc., of something. 2. a standard or unit of measuring: *a yard is a measure of length.* 3. a device used for measuring: *I found a pint measure in the kitchen drawer.* 4. often **meas·ures** (*pl.*) a proposed law or course of action: *the police take strong measures against speeding.* **'meas·ure·ment** *n.* 1. the act of measuring. 2. the size, weight, etc., shown by measuring. —**'meas·ur·a·ble** *adj.*

me·chan·ic (mə'kanik) *n.* a person who is skilled at repairing or operating machinery: *Charlie is an automobile mechanic.* **me'chan·i·cal** *adj.* of or like machinery: *his actions were mechanical.* **mech·a·nism** ('mekənizəm) *n.* 1. the working parts of a machine or other device. 2. any kind of mechanical device or system that operates like a machine.

med·al ('medəl) *n.* a flat piece of metal, usu. on a ribbon and bearing some form of design, given as a reward for an achievement. **me·dal·lion** (mi'dalyən) *n.* a large medal or something resembling this.

medal

med·dle ('medəl) *vb.* **med·dling, med·dled.** to interfere in other people's affairs. —**'med·dle·some** *adj.*

med·i·cine ('medisin) *n.* 1. a drug used to prevent or treat disease. 2. the science and skill of preventing or treating disease or injury: *he studied medicine for six years.* **'med·i·cal** *adj.* of the science of medicine: *Sarah sought medical advice.*

me·di·e·val (mēdē'ēvəl, medē'ēvəl) *adj.* of the Middle Ages (usu. reckoned to be between 1000 and 1500 A.D.).

me·di·um ('mēdēəm) *n.,pl.* **me·di·a** ('mēdēə). a means by which something is done or acts: *radio is an important medium of communication.* —*adj.* halfway between extremes of size, amount, etc.: *Chris is of medium weight.*

meg·a·phone ('megəfōn) *n.* a cone-shaped device used to direct one's voice in a certain direction and make it louder.

mel·an·chol·y ('melənkolē) *n.* sadness; lowness of spirits. —*adj.* 1. sad; gloomy. 2. causing sadness.

mel·o·dy ('melədē) *n.,pl.* **mel·o·dies.** the sequence of musical notes that make up a tune: *she played a gay melody on the flute.* **me·lo·di·ous** (mə'lōdēəs) *adj.* tuneful.

mel·on ('melən) *n.* one of several kinds of large fruits with a hard outer covering and juicy sweet-tasting flesh inside.

melt (melt) *vb.* 1. to become or cause to become liquid as a result of heating: *the butter melted in the hot kitchen.* 2. (often + *away*) to disappear; dwindle away: *the crowd melted away after the parade.* 3. to blend into (something): *a tiger's stripes help it to melt into its background.*

mem·ber ('membər) *n.* 1. an individual (person, animal, etc.) that is part of a group: *only members may use the club's swimming pool.* 2. (old-fashioned) a part of the body. **'mem·ber·ship** *n.* 1. the state of belonging to a society, club, etc. 2. the total number of members: *the society has a membership of 147.*

mem·brane ('membrān) *n.* a very thin soft layer of skin or similar tissue that covers or lines parts of the body.

me·mo·ri·al (mə'môrēəl) *n.* something that acts as a reminder of a person or event.

mem·o·ry ('memərē) *n.,pl.* **mem·o·ries.** 1. the power of storing information in the mind for future recall: *Penny has a good memory for figures.* 2. a person, thing, or event that is remembered. **'mem·o·rize** *vb.* **mem·o·riz·ing, mem·o·rized.** to learn (something) by heart. **'mem·o·ra·ble** *adj.* worthy of being remembered: *a memorable dance.* —**'mem·o·ra·bly** *adv.*

men·ace ('menəs) *n.* a danger; threat: *the savage dog was a menace.* —*vb.* **men·ac·ing, men·aced.** to threaten.

men·tal ('mentəl) *adj.* 1. of or in the mind: *mental arithmetic.* 2. suffering from an illness of the mind: *a mental patient.* —**'men·tal·ly** *adv.*

men·tion ('menshən) *vb.* to speak or write briefly about. —*n.* a reference (to a subject): *he made no mention of his vacation.*

men·u ('menyōō) *n.,pl.* **men·us.** a list of the food that can be obtained in a restaurant, cafe, etc.

melon

mer·chant ('mûrchənt) *n.* a person whose work is buying and selling things, esp. in large quantities: *Simon's father is a grain merchant.*

mer·cu·ry ('mûrkyərē) *n.* a heavy silver-colored metallic chemical element that is liquid at normal temperatures and is used in thermometers and barometers. Chemical symbol: Hg.

mer·cy ('mûrsē) *n.,pl.* **mer·cies.** 1. the treating of wrong-doers or enemies with more forgiveness or kindness than is deserved or expected: *the judge had a reputation for mercy.* 2. a blessing; relief: *it was a mercy that no one was killed in the crash.* **'mer·ci·ful** *adj.* showing mercy. **'mer·ci·less** *adv.* showing no mercy.

mere (mēr) *adj.* no more than; only: *the dog that Walter had told us was so savage turned out to be a mere puppy.* **'mere·ly** *adv.* only; simply.

merge (mûrj) *vb.* **merg·ing, merged.** to become or cause to become one: *the roads merged in the valley.* **'merg·er** *n.* the combining of two or more companies into one large one.

me·ringue (mə'rang) *n.* a mixture of sugar and egg whites baked until it is crisp and eaten as small cakes or used as a topping for desserts.

mer·it ('merit) *n.* 1. value; excellence: *his work has the merit of thoroughness.* 2. **mer·its** (*pl.*) the facts or particular circumstances of something: *we consider each case on its merits.* —*vb.* to deserve: *his work merited high rewards.*

mer·maid ('mûrmād) *n.* a legendary sea-creature that was believed to have the head and body of a woman and the tail of a fish. **'mer·man** *n.,pl.* **'mer·men.** a male mermaid.

mes·sage ('mesij) *n.* a request, piece of news, information, etc., passed in written form or by word of mouth from one person to another.

mes·sen·ger ('mesənjər) *n.* a person who carries messages or runs errands.

met·al ('metəl) *n.* a substance, such as iron, silver, lead, bronze, etc., that conducts heat and electricity. —**me·tal·lic** (mə'talik) *adj.*

me·te·or ('mētēər) *n.* matter that falls from space into the earth's atmosphere and burns up, causing the bright fiery streak in the sky that is known as a shooting star. **'me·te·or·ite** *n.* a meteor that has fallen to earth.

me·te·or·ol·o·gy (mētēə'roləjē) *n.* the study of the weather and the changes and conditions of the earth's atmosphere. —**me·te·or·o·log·i·cal** (mētēərə'lojikəl) *adj.*

me·ter[1] ('mētər) *n.* a device that measures and records the amount of electricity used, the money to be charged so that correct payment can be made.

me·ter[2] ('mētər) *n.* verse rhythm or a particular form of this. —**met·ri·cal** ('metrikəl) *adj.*

me·ter[3] ('mētər) *n.* a unit for measuring length in the metric system. A metre is equal to about 39 inches. **met·ric** ('metrik) of or measured in meters. **metric system** the decimal measuring system that has the meter as the basic unit of length. The KILOGRAM is the unit of weight and the LITER the unit of capacity.

meth·od ('methəd) *n.* 1. a way of doing something: *which method shall I use?* 2. system; orderliness in actions or speech: *the letters were filed without method.* **me·thod·i·cal** (mə'thodikəl) *adj.* orderly and thorough.

me·trop·o·lis (mə'tropəlis) *n.* a very large city, esp. the largest in a country, state, etc. —**met·ro·pol·i·tan** (metrə'politən) *adj.*

mice (mīs) *n.* the plural of MOUSE.

mi·crobe ('mīkrōb) *n.* a very small living creature that can be seen only through a MICROSCOPE.

mi·cro·phone ('mīkrəfōn) *n.* an instrument that changes sound waves into electrical currents so that they can be recorded, made louder, etc.

mi·cro·scope ('mīkrəskōp) *n.* an instrument with a LENS or lenses, used to make very small things appear larger. **mi·cro·scop·ic** (mīkrə'skopik) *adj.* too small to be seen, except under a microscope.

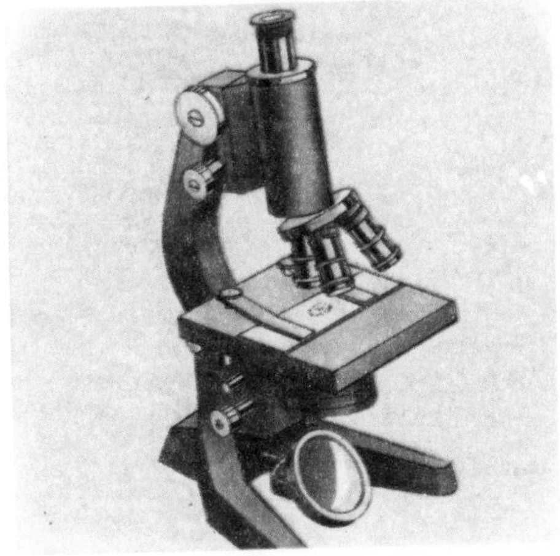

microscope

mid·dle ('midəl) *adj.* 1. halfway between two ends, sides, times, etc.: *ours is the middle house in the row.* 2. medium: *he bought a middle-sized car.* —*n.* a point halfway between two edges, ends, times, etc.

midg·et ('mijit) *n.* a very small person.

mid·wife ('midwīf) *n.,pl.* **mid·wives.** a person trained to assist at the birth of a baby.

might (mīt) *n.* strength; force: *he threw the ball with all his might.* **'might·y** *adj.* **might·i·er, might·i·est.** great in size, force, or amount.

mi·grate ('mīgrāt) *vb.* **mi·grat·ing, mi·grat·ed.** 1. to move from one place to another, often a long distance away. **mi·grant** ('mīgrənt) *n.* a person or animal that migrates. —**mi'gra·tion** *n.*

mild (mīld) *adj.* not severe or harsh: *in a mild winter we have little snow.* —**'mild·ly** *adv.* —**'mild·ness** *n.*

mile (mīl) *n.* a measure of distance equal to 1760 yards (5280 feet). **'mile·age** *n.* distance traveled measured in miles.

mile·stone ('mīlstōn) *n.* 1. a stone or other marker set up beside a road to show how many miles one has to travel to reach certain places. 2. an important happening: *the Emancipation Proclamation was a milestone in American history.*

mil·i·tant ('militənt) *adj.* actively supporting the use of force to achieve political or other ends. —*n.* an active supporter of force or violent tactics.

mil·i·tar·y ('militerē) *adj.* of or relating to the army, land warfare, etc.: *military uniform.*

milk (milk) *n.* 1. the white liquid produced by female MAMMALs to feed their young. 2. a similar liquid found in some plants: *coconut milk.* —*vb.* to take milk from (a cow, goat, or sheep).

mill (mil) *n.* 1. a building containing machinery for grinding grain: *a flour mill.* 2. a device for grinding: *a pepper mill.* 3. a factory producing certain materials: *a paper mill.* —*vb.* to put something through a mill.

mil·li·gram ('miləgram) *n.* a very small unit of weight in the metric system; one-thousandth part of a GRAM.

mil·li·me·ter ('miləmētər) *n.* a very short unit of length in the metric system; one-thousandth part of a METER[1].

mil·li·ner·y ('milənerē) *n.* 1. women's hats. 2. the business of making women's hats. —**mil·li·ner** *n.*

mil·lion ('milyən) *n., adj.* one thousand thousand (1,000,000). **mil·lion·aire** (milyə'neər) *n.* a person who owns money and property worth over a million dollars.

mime (mīm) *n.* 1. a play or method of acting without using words. The actors tell the story by means of facial expression and hand and body movements. 2. an actor who specializes in this form of acting.

mim·ic ('mimik) *vb.* **mim·ick·ing, mim·icked.** to imitate. —*n.* a person or thing that mimics.

minaret

min·a·ret (minə'ret) *n.* a tall tower attached to a MOSQUE from the top of which a crier calls Muslims to prayer five times a day.

mince (mins) *vb.* **minc·ing, minced.** to cut up into tiny pieces with a knife or a grinder.

mince·meat ('minsmēt) *n.* a sweet mixture of dried fruit, sugar, apples, and spices, used as a pie filling.

mind (mīnd) *n.* 1. a person's ability to think, understand, remember, learn, etc.: *he cannot keep his mind on his work.* 2. something that is thought; an intention, wish, or opinion: *I changed my mind about buying the dress.* —*vb.* 1. to dislike, be unhappy about, or object to something: *she minded being left behind when all her friends went to the movies.* 2. to pay attention to; be careful about: *your own business!* 3. to take care of: *Jill minds her baby sister while her mother is out.* **'mind·less** *adj.* lacking in thought or not needing intelligence.

mine (mīn) *n.* 1. a series of holes, pits, and passageways dug underground so that people can remove valuable substances from the earth. 2. a bomb placed underground or underwater. —*vb.* **min·ing, mined.** 1. to dig out from under the ground. 2. to place bombs in.

min·er·al ('minərəl) *n.* a natural substance, such as silver or salt, that is found in the ground, water, or rocks. —*adj.* belonging to or containing this class of substances: *mineral water.* **min·er·al·o·gy** (minə'roləjē) *n.* the study of minerals.

min·gle ('minggəl) *vb.* **min·gling, min·gled.** to mix together; blend: *the speakers mingled with the audience after the meeting.*

min·i·a·ture ('minēəchər, 'minəchər) *adj.* very small in size. —*n.* something made in a very small size, esp. a painted portrait of someone.

min·i·mum ('minəməm) *n.* the least possible amount: *she does the minimum of work.* —*adj.* lowest; smallest. **'min·i·mal** *adj.* very little.

mink (mingk) *n.,pl.* **mink** *or* **minks.** a small animal like a weasel with a soft thick fur that is highly valued for making coats.

mi·nor ('mīnər) *adj.* 1. small in size, age, importance, value, etc.: *it was a minor accident and no one was hurt.* —*n.* a person who has not yet reached the age of full legal responsibility. **mi·nor·i·ty** (mi'nôritē) *n.,pl.* **mi·nor·i·ties.** a smaller part or number: *a minority of people own motorcycles.*

mint[1] (mint) *n.* 1. one of several plants with strongly smelling leaves that are used for flavoring, e.g. peppermint, spearmint. 2. a mint-flavored piece of candy.

mint[2] (mint) *n.* 1. a place where coins are made. 2. (informal) a lot of money: *repairs to the house have cost me a mint.* —*vb.* to make coins.

minus ('mīnəs) *prep.* 1. less: *ten minus five equals five.* 2. without: *a table minus one leg.* —*adj.* denoting subtraction or a negative quantity: *minus seven degrees.*

min·ute[1] ('minit) *n.* 1. a sixtieth part of an hour. 2. a very short space of time: *wait a minute.* 3. (geometry) a sixtieth part of a DEGREE (def. 2). 4. **min·utes** (*pl.*) the detailed record of an official meeting.

mint

mi·nute² (mī'nōōt, mī'nyōōt) *adj.* 1. tiny. 2. very detailed: *they made a minute investigation of the evidence.*

mir·a·cle ('mirəkəl) *n.* 1. an event that cannot be explained by natural causes. 2. something amazing: *the miracle of space flight.* **mi·rac·u·lous** (mi'rakyələs) *adj.* 1. amazing; hardly believable: *she made a miraculous recovery after her long illness.* 2. able to work miracles. 3. caused by a miracle.

mir·ror ('mirər) *n.* a sheet of glass coated with silvery paint on the back so that it reflects the image of whatever is in front of it. —*vb.* to reflect an image as a mirror does.

mis·chief ('mischif) *n.* 1. playful malice or annoying behavior: *the puppy was full of mischief.* 2. trouble; damage: *the rats caused mischief in the barns by eating the corn.* —**mis·chie·vous** ('mischəvəs) *adj.* —'**mis·chie·vous·ly** *adv.*

mi·ser ('mīzər) *n.* a person who hoards money and refuses to spend it. —'**mi·ser·ly** *adj.*

mis·er·y ('mizərē) *n.,pl.* **mis·er·ies.** unhappiness or great distress. '**mis·er·a·ble** *adj.* 1. very sad. 2. valueless; bad: *that's a miserable piece of work.* 3. causing misery or distress. —'**mis·er·a·bly** *adv.*

mis·fit ('misfit) *n.* something or someone that does not fit properly into an intended role, situation, etc.

mis·for·tune (mis'fôrchən) *n.* 1. bad luck. 2. an unlucky event.

mis·lay (mis'lā) *vb.* **mis·lay·ing, mis·laid.** to put (something) away and then forget where it is.

mis·lead (mis'lēd) *vb.* **mis·lead·ing, mis·led.** 1. to cause (someone) to go wrong. 2. to give the wrong idea: *you misled me with your description.*

miss¹ (mis) *vb.* **miss·ing, missed.** 1. to fail to do, hear, see, etc.: *I missed the next words.* 2. to feel the loss of: *I shall miss you.* 3. to avoid; escape: *I just missed bumping into him.* —*n.* the failure to hit a target or achieve an aim.

miss² (mis) *n.* **Miss** the formal way of addressing an an unmarried woman or girl.

mis·sile ('misəl) *n.* anything that can be thrown or shot through the air: *bricks, bottles, and other missiles were thrown at the police during the riot.*

miss·ing ('mising) *adj.* lost; absent.

mis·sion ('mishən) *n.* 1. a group of people sent to carry out a particular task for which they are specially trained. 2. the task that they are sent to do: *Trevor was sent on a business mission abroad.* 3. a building used by missionaries. 4. a purpose in life: *Ellen felt that her mission was to teach.* '**mis·sion·ar·y** *n.,pl.* **mis·sion·ar·ies.** a person sent out to preach and convert unbelievers to Christianity. *adj.* of missions and their work.

mist (mist) *n.* 1. a cloud of tiny water droplets at or near ground level; thin fog. 2. anything that blurs or obscures. —*vb.* (often + *over*) to be or become misty. —'**mist·y** *adj.* **mist·i·er, mist·i·est.**

mis·take (mi'stāk) *n.* 1. a fault; unintentionally wrong thought or action. —*vb.* **mis·tak·ing, mis·took, mis·tak·en.** 1. to understand wrongly. 2. to make a mistake: *I mistook her for Sue.*

mis·un·der·stand ('misundər'stand) *vb.* **mis·un·der·stand·ing, mis·un·der·stood.** 1. to interpret (a person's behavior) wrongly. 2. to fail to understand (the true meaning of words, etc.): *I misunderstood the question and gave the wrong answer.*

mi·ter ('mītər) *n.* the tall official headdress worn by a bishop.

mix (miks) *vb.* 1. to combine two or more different things. 2. (+ *up*) to confuse. '**mix·ture** *n.* the result of mixing things together: *the cake mixture contained sugar, flour, and fruit.*

moan (mōn) *n.* a low sound expressing pain or sadness. —*vb.* 1. to make a soft, pained sound. 2. to complain.

moat (mōt) *n.* a deep ditch, usu. filled with water, surrounding a castle or town as a defense against attack.

mo·bile ('mōbəl) *adj.* able to move or be moved easily. —*n.* a work of art or decoration consisting of a series of objects hung up and balanced so as to move in air currents. —**mo'bil·i·ty** *n.*

mock (mok) *vb.* 1. to laugh at or speak of in a contemptuous way. 2. to imitate (a person, manner, etc.) so as to make seem ridiculous; mimic. —*adj.* false; imitation: *a mock examination.* '**mock·er·y** *n.,pl.* **mock·er·ies.** 1. mocking behavior. 2. an insulting imitation.

mod·el ('modəl) *n.* 1. a particular style or pattern. 2. an exact copy of something on a much smaller scale: *he collects models of ships.* 3. someone or something worthy of imitation: *his work is a model that others should follow.* 4. a person who poses for an artist or photographer or who demonstrates clothes. —*vb.* 1. to shape or construct: *he modeled the statue out of clay.* 2. to act as an artist's or fashion model. —*adj.* excellent: *model behavior.*

mod·er·ate *adj.* ('modərit) 1. not extreme in opinions, wishes, or needs: *a moderate eater.* 2. fairly good: *the play was a moderate success.* —*n.* 1. a person who holds moderate (def. 1) views. 2. a person who acts as a referee between two opposing persons of groups. —*vb.* ('modərāt) **mod·er·at·ing, mod·er·at·ed.** to make or become less extreme: *he had to moderate his ideas to fit in with the others.* —**mod·er'a·tion** *n.*

miter

mod·ern ('modərn) *adj.* to do with the present or recent times. '**mod·ern·ize** *vb.* **mod·ern·iz·ing, mod·ern·ized.** to make modern. **mod·ern·i'za·tion** *n.* the process of making modern or more modern.

mod·est ('modist) *adj.* 1. having a fairly humble opinion of oneself. 2. just adequate; not excessive: *he earned a modest wage.* —'**mod·est·ly** *adv.* —'**mod·est·y** *n.*

mod·i·fy ('modəfī) *vb.* **mod·i·fy·ing, mod·i·fied.** 1. to make slight changes to: *she modified the dress by removing the sleeves.* 2. to moderate; make less extreme: *he modified his demands.* —**mod·i·fi'ca·tion** *n.*

moist (moist) *adj.* damp; slightly wet. **mois·ten** ('moisən) *vb.* to make damp or damper. '**mois·ture** *n.* dampness; slight wetness. —'**moist·ly** *adv.* —'**moist·ness** *n.*

mole[1] (mōl) *n.* a small mammal with dark gray-brown fur and tiny eyes that digs underground tunnels using its strong broad feet as shovels. It feeds mainly on worms.

mole

mole[2] (mōl) *n.* a permanent brown spot on a person's skin.

mol·e·cule ('moləkyōōl) *n.* the smallest particle, consisting of one or more ATOMs, into which a substance can be broken down without undergoing a change in its chemical make-up. —**mo·lec·u·lar** (mə'lekyələr) *adj.*

mol·lusk ('moləsk) *n.* one of a group of soft-bodied animals, usu. living in water and usu. having a hard shell to protect their bodies. Oysters, clams, snails, slugs, and octopuses are all mollusks.

molt (mōlt) *n.* the seasonal shedding of old fur or feathers to make way for new growth. —*vb.* to pass through this process.

mo·ment ('mōmənt) *n.* 1. a very short time: *I won't be gone a moment.* 2. a specific point in time: *it is the right moment to start.*

mon·arch ('monərk) *n.* the supreme single ruler of a state; king; queen. '**mon·ar·chy** *n.* 1. a country ruled by a monarch. 2. the government or rule of a monarch.

mon·as·ter·y ('monəsterē) *n.,pl.* **mon·as·ter·ies.** the building in which monks live and work. —**mo·nas·tic** (mə'nastik) *adj.*

mon·ey ('munē) *n.* coins and banknotes; cash. **mon·e·tar·y** ('moniterē) *adj.* concerning money.

mon·grel ('monggrəl) *n.* a dog having parents of different breeds.

monk (mungk) *n.* a man who has joined a religious society and lives his life in obedience to its rules.

mon·key ('mungkē) *n.* one of a large group of intelligent animals closely related to man and having long limbs and grasping hands and feet. They often live in trees. —*vb.* (+ *around*) to interfere or play with.

mo·nop·o·ly (mə'nopəlē) *n.,pl.* **mo·nop·o·lies.** the complete control of trade in a product or service by one person or firm. **mo'nop·o·lize** *vb.* **mo·nop·o·liz·ing, mo·nop·o·lized.** to gain or hold exclusive control over: *he monopolized all the books that they needed.* —**mo·nop·o·li'za·tion** *n.*

mo·not·o·nous (mə'notənəs) *adj.* dull; lacking in interest or variety. —**mo'not·o·nous·ly** *adv.*

mon·soon (mon'sōōn) *n.* 1. a strong seasonal wind of the Indian Ocean and South Asia that blows from the southwest in summer and the northeast in winter. 2. the summer period of heavy rains in India and nearby regions.

mon·ster ('monstər) *n.* 1. any huge imaginary beast, usu. ugly and terrifying. 2. a grotesque or deformed animal or plant. 3. a cruel and inhuman person. —*adj.* extraordinarily large: *a monster fish.* '**mon·strous** *adj.* 1. abnormally or frighteningly large. 2. evil; horrible. 3. (informal) outrageous; scandalous: *your behavior last night was monstrous!* —'**mon·strous·ly** *adv.*

month (munth) *n.* one of the twelve divisions of the year. '**month·ly** *adj.* 1. happening once a month. 2. happening throughout a month: *the monthly output of the factory.* —*adv.* once a month.

mon·u·ment ('monyəmənt) *n.* a statue, building, ornamental slab, etc., erected to keep alive the memory of some person, event, or discovery. **mon·u'men·tal** *adj.* 1. connected with monuments: *a monumental sculpture.* 2. enduring and important: *landing on the moon was a monumental achievement.* 3. (informal) enormous: *he made a monumental blunder when he bought the old car.*

mood (mōōd) *n.* an emotional state of mind: *the crowd was in a happy mood.* '**mood·y** *adj.* **mood·i·er, mood·i·est.** likely to have fits of depression. —'**mood·i·ly** *adv.* —'**mood·i·ness** *n.*

moon (mōōn) *n.* 1. often **Moon** the heavenly body that orbits the earth once every 29·5 days and shines by reflecting light from the sun. 2. a similar body moving around another planet; SATELLITE: *Mars has two moons.*

moor[1] (mōōər) *n.* a wide expanse of wild land with heather, grass, and marshy areas, but few trees.

moor[2] (mōōər) *vb.* to tie up (a boat) to a fixed place by rope or chain. '**moor·ing** *n.* a place where boats can be safely tied up.

mop (mop) *n.* an absorbent wad of material on the end of a long pole, used for cleaning floors. —*vb.* **mop·ping, mopped.** to clean with a mop.

mor·al ('môrəl) *adj.* 1. concerning the choice between right and wrong and how to apply it in life: *whether to fight or not was a moral decision.* 2. of or following the rules for right conduct: *moral life.* —*n.* 1. the moral teaching given in a story or event. 2. **mor·als** (*pl.*) a person's moral character or conduct. **mo·ral·i·ty** (mə'ralitē) *n.* standards of morally right behavior. '**mor·al·ize** *vb.* **mor·al·iz·ing, mor·al·ized.** to talk on moral subjects, esp. in a tedious way.

more·o·ver (môr'ōvər) *adv.* besides; in addition; furthermore: *he is handsome; moreover, he's very intelligent.*

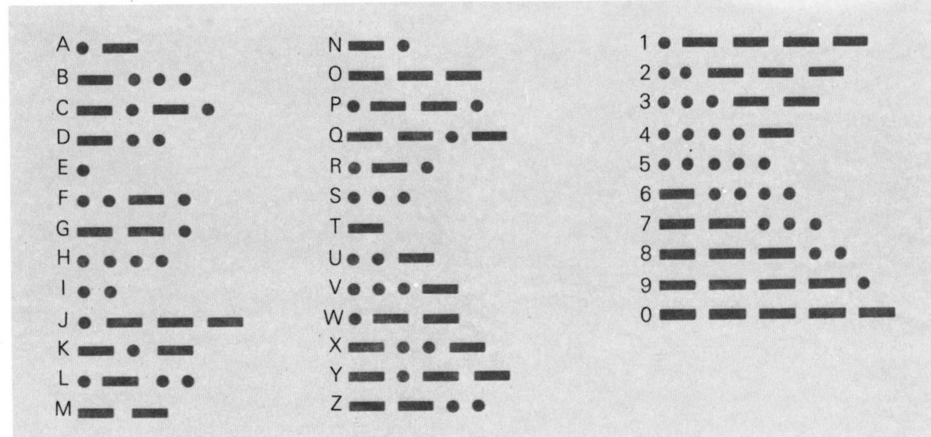

Morse code

Morse code (môrs) a code invented by Samuel Morse in 1837 and used for sending messages by wire, radio, or flashlight. Each letter of the alphabet is coded into combinations of long or short dots and dashes which may be represented by buzzes and flashes.

mor·tal ('môrtəl) *adj.* 1. not living forever. 2. causing death: *a mortal blow.* —*n.* a human being.

mort·gage ('môrgij) *n.* a loan of money given in exchange for property that is paid off over a fixed time. —*vb.* **mort·gag·ing, mort·gaged.** to give property as security for a money loan.

mo·sa·ic (mō'zāik) *n.* a decorative design made up of tiny colored pieces of stone, ceramic, or some other durable material cemented together. —*adj.* made of or decorated with mosaics: *the Romans made mosaic floors in their villas.*

mosque (mosk) *n.* a place of worship for MUSLIMS.

mos·qui·to (mə'skēto) *n.,pl.* **mos·qui·toes.** a small long-legged type of fly. The female sucks animals' blood and in some cases transmits the disease malaria.

moss (môs) *n.* a small soft green plant that grows in damp places, on stones, tree trunks, and similar surfaces, often in dense spongy clumps. —'**moss·y** *adj.* **moss·i·er, moss·i·est.**

moth (moth) *n.,pl.* **moths** (môdhz, môths) an insect like a butterfly with large colored wings and feathery ANTENNAe. Most moths are active at night.

mo·tion ('mōshən) *n.* 1. the act of changing position; movement: *he set the swing in motion by pushing it hard.* 2. a suggestion made formally at a meeting: *the committee was asked to vote on the motion.* —*vb.* to show or indicate by a movement: *the stewardess motioned us to go out to the aircraft.*

motion picture a series of pictures projected on to a screen so rapidly that the objects seen seem to move; MOVIE.

mo·tive ('mōtiv) *n.* a reason or emotion that causes or influences an action, decision, wish, etc. —*adj.* capable of setting something going: *gasoline provides the motive power in a car.* '**mo·ti·vate** *vb.* **mo·ti·vat·ing, mo·ti·vat·ed.** to give a motive (for doing something): *Roger was motivated by a desire to become rich.* **mo·ti'va·tion** *n.* force, reason, etc., encouraging one to act.

mo·tor ('mōtər) *n.* a machine that uses fuel or electricity to produce the power to make another machine or a vehicle work. —*adj.* having to do with or powered by a motor: *Carol bought a motor scooter.* —*vb.* to travel by motorcar. '**mo·tor·ist** *n.* a person who drives an automobile.

mot·to ('motō) *n.,pl.* **mot·tos** *or* **mot·toes.** a short phrase that sums up a belief, e.g. *do unto others as you would have them do unto you.*

mound (mound) *n.* a heap or small hill of rocks, earth, or other material.

mount (mount) *vb.* 1. to climb onto (a horse, motorcycle, etc.). 2. to go up (stairs); get onto (a platform). 3. to increase: *his debts mounted daily.* 4. to arrange or set up: *the art class mounted an exhibition of paintings.* 5. to fix onto a backing or support: *to mount a painting.* —*n.* 1. something ridden: *her mount was a small black pony.* 2. the cardboard surround or backing for a photograph, painting, etc. 3. a hill or mountain: *Mount Everest.*

moun·tain ('mountən) *n.* 1. a very large mass of land that rises steeply from the surrounding country, often reaching a very great height, e.g. the Rocky Mountains. 2. (informal) a large amount or heap: *there was a mountain of vegetables on the plate.* —'**moun·tain·ous** *adj.* —**moun·tain·eer** (mountən'ēr) *n.* a person who climbs mountains.

mourn (môrn) *vb.* to be sorrowful about a loss; grieve: *Beverley mourned for weeks after her little puppy died.* '**mourn·ful** *adj.* sad; gloomy. —'**mourn·ful·ly** *adv.*

mouse (mous) *n.,pl.* **mice.** a small furry animal with large ears, beady eyes, and a long almost hairless tail. They are usually brownishgray but white ones are bred as pets.

mouth *n.* (mouth), *pl.* **mouths** (moudhz). 1. the opening in a person's or animal's face through which food is taken in. 2. any opening similar to this in shape: *the mouth of a jar.* 3. the opening of a river into a larger body of water.

mov·ie ('mōōvē) *n.* 1. usu. **movies** a theater where motion pictures are screened: *they go to the movies every week.* 2. a motion picture: *which movie is showing this week?* 3. **movies** the industry concerned with the production of motion pictures.

mow (mō) *vb.* **mow·ing, mowed, mown.** to cut down (grass or grain). '**mow·er** *n.* a machine for cutting the grass on lawns.

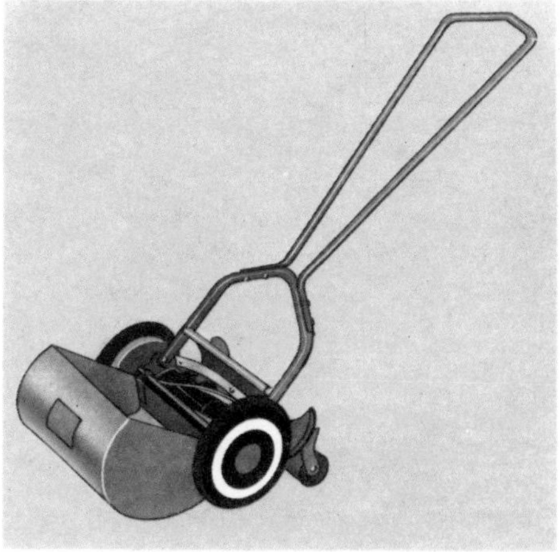
mower

muf·fle ('mufəl) *vb.* **muf·fling, muf·fled.** 1. to wrap up in order to keep warm. 2. to deaden sound (of engines, traffic, etc.). '**muf·fler** *n.* 1. a woollen scarf to wear round the neck. 2. a device for quietening engine noise.

mummy

mug (mug) *n.* 1. a large straight-sided cup with a handle. 2. (informal) someone who is easily deceived. 3. (slang) face or mouth. —*vb.* **mug·ging, mugged.** 1. to attack and rob (someone) in the street. 2. to make funny faces.

mule (myo͞ol) *n.* an animal that has a horse as its mother and a donkey as its father.

mul·ti·ply ('multəplī) *vb.* **mul·ti·ply·ing, mul·ti·plied.** 1. to add (a given number) to itself a certain number of times: *adding 5 to itself 3 times* 5 + 5 + 5=15. Another way of writing this is 5 × 3=15. **mul·ti·ple** ('multəpəl) *adj.* with or concerning many parts: *multiple injuries.* —*n.* a number produced by multiplying two or more smaller numbers together: *15 is a multiple of 5.* —**mul·ti·pli'ca·tion** *n.*

mum·my ('mumē) *n.,pl.* **mum·mies.** a dead body, prepared and wrapped for burial by a special method used esp. by the ancient Egyptians to preserve it from decay. '**mum·mi·fy** *vb.* **mum·mi·fy·ing, mum·mi·fied.** to preserve (something dead) by a special method.

mu·nic·i·pal (myo͞o'nisəpəl) *adj.* owned or employed by local government: *municipal workers care for the town parks.* **mu·nic·i'pal·i·ty** *n.,pl.* **mu·nic·i·pal·i·ties.** a town or area that is self-governing within a county, state, or federal government.

mur·der ('mûrdər) *n.* the intentional and unlawful killing of a person. —*vb.* to kill a person on purpose. '**mur·der·ous** *adj.* of or concerning murder. —'**mur·der·ous·ly** *adv.*

mur·mur ('mûrmər) *n.* 1. a quiet steady sound: *we heard the murmur of a brook in the distance.* 2. a subdued protest: *he made murmurs about the poor quality of the meal.* —*vb.* to make a murmuring sound.

mus·cle ('musəl) *n.* a fibrous tissue in the body that causes movement of bones, organs, etc., when contracted: *long bicycle rides developed his leg muscles.* **mus·cu·lar** ('muskyələr) *adj.* 1. having large muscles. 2. of or concerning muscles.

mu·se·um (myo͞o'zēəm) *n.* a building where things of historic or scientific interest are displayed.

mush·room ('mushro͞om) *n.* a FUNGUS with a stout central stem and an umbrella-shaped cap. Some mushrooms are edible. —*vb.* to grow rapidly: *sales mushroomed after the publicity campaign.*

mu·sic ('myo͞ozik) *n.* 1. the arrangement of sounds into expressive or pleasing combinations. 2. written symbols representing these sounds; notes or a score. '**mu·si·cal** *adj.* 1. referring to or using music. 2. showing a feeling, talent, or ability regarding music. **mu'si·cian** *n.* someone able to play or produce music well.

Mus·lim ('muzlim, 'mo͞ozlim) *adj., n.* (of) a person who follows the teachings of the prophet Muhammad, which are embodied in the religion known as Islam.

mus·sel ('musəl) *n.* an edible shellfish with a dark-blue or purplish shell.

mussel

mus·tache (mə'stash, 'mustash) *n.* the hair growing on a man's upper lip.

mus·tard ('mustərd) *n.* a hot-tasting relish made from the tiny bright yellow seeds of the mustard plant.

mute (myo͞ot) *adj.* 1. silent, e.g. the *b* in *comb* is a mute letter. 2. not able to speak. —*n.* 1. a person who is unable to speak. 2. a device to soften the sound of a musical instrument.

mu·ti·ny ('myo͞otənē) *n.,pl.* **mu·ti·nies.** a rebellion against authority. —*vb.* **mu·ti·ny·ing, mu·ti·nied.** to join in a rebellion: *the ship's crew mutinied because they were ill-treated.* **mu·ti'neer** *n.* a person who takes part in a mutiny. —'**mu·ti·nous** *adj.*

mut·ton ('mutən) *n.* the meat from a full-grown sheep.

muz·zle ('muzəl) *n.* 1. the nose and mouth of an animal. 2. a device to fit over an animal's muzzle to prevent it from biting. 3. the open end of a gun. —*vb.* **muz·zling, muz·zled.** to put a muzzle (def. 2) on (an animal).

mys·ter·y ('mistərē) *n.,pl.* **mys·ter·ies.** something strange or inexplicable. **mys·te·ri·ous** (mi'stērēəs) *adj.* difficult to understand; arousing curiosity. —**mys'te·ri·ous·ly** *adv.*

myth (mith) *n.* 1. a story relating to a people's beliefs about their distant past, their ancestors, etc., and not based on facts: *the myths of ancient Greece include many stories about Zeus.* 2. (informal) a story, belief, etc., that is totally untrue. **my'thol·o·gy** *n.* 1. the study of myths and legends. 2. the myths of a particular people collected together. —'**myth·i·cal** *adj.* —**myth·o'log·i·cal** *adj.*

N

nail (nāl) *n.* 1. a metal spike with a flattened head and pointed tip, used for fastening together pieces of wood and other materials. 2. (also **fin·ger·nail** *or* **toe·nail**) the hard protective covering on the upper tips of fingers and toes. —*vb.* to fasten with nails.

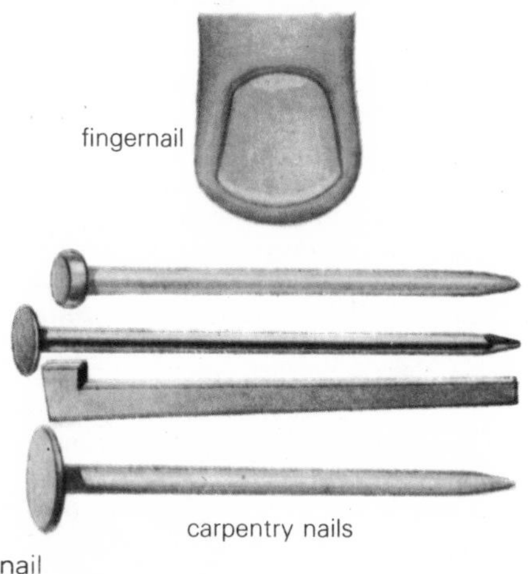

nail

na·ked ('nākid) *adj.* 1. without clothes or covering. 2. (of the eye) unaided by an instrument such as a telescope, microscope, binoculars, etc.: *I could see the comet with my naked eye.* —'**na·ked·ly** *adv.* —'**na·ked·ness** *n.*

name (nām) *n.* 1. the word or words given to people, places, or things, by which they are spoken of or addressed: *my dog's name is Spot.* 2. character or reputation: *his cheating gave him a bad name.* 3. (informal) a well-known person: *a big name in politics.* —*vb.* **nam·ing, named.** 1. to give a name to. 2. to put into words or state: *name a price for your old skates.* '**name·ly** *adv.* that is to say: *three of us went, namely Donna, Pete, and Ed.*

nap·kin ('napkin) *n.* a piece of cloth or paper that is used to protect clothing and for wiping fingers and lips at mealtimes.

nar·rate ('narāt) *vb.* **nar·rat·ing, nar·rat·ed.** to tell or relate (a series of events or story). **nar·ra·tive** ('narətiv) *n.* a story. *adj.* of a story; telling a story: *a narrative poem.* —**nar'ra·tion** *n.* —**nar'ra·tor** *n.*

nar·row ('narō) *adj.* 1. not wide: *a narrow path.* 2. with little to spare: *a narrow escape.* —'**nar·row·ly** *adv.* —'**nar·row·ness** *n.*

nas·ty ('nastē) *adj.* **nas·ti·er, nas·ti·est.** 1. unpleasant; disagreeable: *a nasty temper.* 2. severe or dangerous: *there was a nasty accident between two cars.* 3. mean and disagreeable. —'**nas·ti·ly** *adv.*

na·tion ('nāshən) *n.* a country and the people who live there and share the same government and culture.

na·tion·al ('nashənəl) *adj.* of or concerning a nation. —*n.* a person belonging to a particular country: *Henri is a Belgian national.* '**na·tion·al·ism** *n.* a powerful feeling of loyalty to one's country. '**na·tion·al·ist** *n.* someone who supports or fights for his country. **na·tion'al·i·ty** *n.,pl.* **na·tion·al·i·ties.** 1. the condition of belonging to a particular nation. 2. people who have the same language, history, and culture. '**na·tion·al·ize** *vb.* **na·tion·al·iz·ing, na·tion·al·ized.** to make (an industry, service, etc.) the property of the nation. —**na·tion·al·i'za·tion** *n.*

na·tive ('nātiv) *n.* 1. someone born in a particular place: *a native of Rome.* 2. a person, plant, or animal belonging naturally in a certain place: *Caribou are natives of North America.* —*adj.* 1. natural: *native wit.* 2. belonging to a person's birthplace: *one's native land.* 3. living or growing naturally in a certain place: *eagles are native to wild and mountainous regions.*

nat·u·ral ('nachərəl) *adj.* 1. not artificial; produced or caused by nature: *natural beauty.* 2. normal; expected: *Ed's failure was the natural result of his laziness.* 3. closely imitating nature: *his photograph of the baby looks very natural.* —*n.* a successful example of something achieved without special training: *she is a natural at ballet.*

na·ture ('nāchər) *n.* 1. the physical world esp. those things not made by man. 2. a person's character; the essential qualities of a thing: *it is in his nature to keep busy.* 3. type; kind: *she hates work of that nature.*

naugh·ty ('nôtē) *adj.* **naugh·ti·er, naugh·ti·est.** (of children) badly behaved; mischievous or disobedient. —'**naugh·ti·ly** *adv.* —'**naugh·ti·ness** *n.*

nau·ti·cal ('nôtikəl) *adj.* having to do with sailors, ships, or the sea.

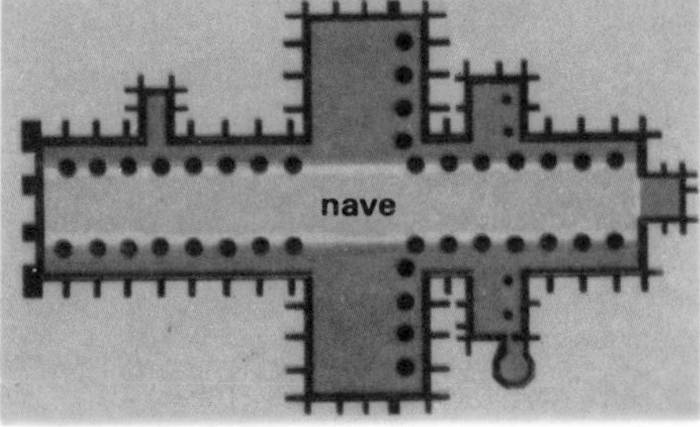

nave

nave (nāv) *n.* the main central part of a church, where the congregation sits, usu. separated from the side AISLEs by pillars.

na·vel ('nāvəl) *n.* the little hollow in the middle of the abdomen, where the cord joining a newborn baby to its mother was detached at birth.

nav·i·gate ('navəgāt) *vb.* **nav·i·gat·ing, nav·i·gat·ed.** 1. to steer a ship or aircraft by means of instruments and charts. 2. to sail. **'nav·i·ga·ble** *adj.* suitable for shipping: *a navigable river.* **nav·i'ga·tion** *n.* 1. the science of navigating. 2. the act of steering. —**'nav·i·ga·tor** *n.*

na·vy ('nāvē) *n.,pl.* **na·vies.** 1. the whole fleet of warships possessed by a state, together with their officers and crews. 2. (also **navy blue**) the very dark blue color used for naval uniforms.

near (nēr) *adj.* 1. close in space or time: *the near future.* 2. close in relationship or association: *a near relative.* —*adv.* close at hand: *the time is near for our departure.* —*prep.* close to; not far from. —*vb.* to approach: *the boat neared the beach.* **'near·by** *adj.* close at hand. *adv.* not far off. **'near·ly** *adv.* almost.

neat (nēt) *adj.* 1. orderly; carefully arranged. 2. skillful: *a neat dive.* 3. (informal) wonderful; attractive: *a neat car.* **'neat·en** *vb.* to make neat or neater.—**'neat·ly** *adv.* —**'neat·ness** *n.*

nec·es·sar·y ('nesiserē) *adj.* 1. essential: *water is necessary for living things.* 2. unavoidable; not governed by one's free will: *prison was the necessary result of his crimes.* **ne·ces·si·tate** (ni'sesitāt) *vb.* **ne·ces·si·tat·ing, ne·ces·si·tat·ed.** to make (something) necessary: *the car's breakdown necessitated a change in our plans.* **ne'ces·si·ty** *n.,pl.* **ne·ces·si·ties.** something that cannot be avoided or done without.

neck (nek) *n.* 1. the part of the body connecting the head to the trunk. 2. a narrow necklike part of anything.

neck·lace ('nekləs) *n.* an ornament of beads or jewels threaded or linked together and worn round the neck.

nec·tar ('nektər) *n.* a sweet substance produced by flowers to attract the insects and birds that pollinate them.

need (nēd) *vb.* 1. to be in want; lack: *the plant needed water.* 2. to be obliged to; to have to: *need we go now?* —*n.* 1. a want or necessity. 2. poverty: *need drove him to steal.* 3. a time of crisis or danger. **'need·y** *adj.* **need·i·er, need·i·est.** very poor. —**'need·ful** *adj.*

nee·dle ('nēdəl) *n.* 1. a slender sharp-pointed instrument with a hole at one end, used to draw thread through fabric. 2. any object of similar shape used for various purposes: *knitting needle.* 3. a stiff, thin leaf: *a pine needle.* —*vb.* **nee·dling, nee·dled.** (informal) to irritate; annoy.

neg·a·tive ('negətiv) *adj.* 1. expressing denial or refusal. 2. not enthusiastic or helpful; uncomplimentary: *he made some negative comments on her work.* 3. having a particular type of electrical charge that which is opposite to positive. 4. of numbers that are less than zero. —*n.* 1. a word or statement by which something is denied or refused. 2. a photographic plate on which areas of light and shade are reversed.

nests

ne·glect (ni'glekt) *vb.* 1. to fail to take care of: *Russell neglected his hamster.* 2. to fail to do: *he neglected to fetch the newspaper.* —*n.* lack of proper care or attention.

ne·go·ti·ate (ni'gōshēāt) *vb.* **ne·go·ti·at·ing, ne·go·ti·at·ed.** 1. to settle by discussions or bargaining: *the manager negotiated a wage agreement.* 2. to pass over or through with skill or care: *the driver negotiated the muddy, steep lane in low gear.* —**ne'go·ti·a·ble** *adj.* —**ne·go·ti·'a·tion** *n.* —**ne'go·ti·a·tor** *n.*

neigh·bor ('nābər) *n.* a person who lives in the next house or nearby. **'neigh·bor·hood** *n.* 1. a particular area of a town or city. 2. the people in the area where one lives. **'neigh·bor·ly** *adj.* friendly; helpful.

neph·ew ('nefyo͞o) *n.* the son of one's brother or sister.

nerve (nûrv) *n.* 1. a fiber that carries messages between the brain or spinal cord and other parts of the body. 2. bravery: *have you the nerve to ride the racehorse?* 3. (informal) impudence: *he had the nerve to try to borrow money again.* **'nerv·ous** *adj.* fearful: *I am nervous of swimming.* —**'nerv·ous·ly** *adv.*

nest (nest) *n.* 1. a structure built by birds and some other animals as shelter for themselves and their young. 2. a cluster or group occupying a nest: *a nest of ants.* 3. a set of objects neatly fitting inside one another: *a nest of tables.* —*vb.* to make, have, or settle in a nest.

net[1] (net) *n.* a fabric of loose open meshes, fastened at the points where the strands of thread, wire, cord, etc., cross. —*vb.* **net·ting, net·ted.** 1. to catch with a net. 2. to cover with a net.

net[2] (net) *adj.* 1. remaining after all necessary deductions have been made: *after tax his net income was not enough to live on.* 2. (of weights) not including packaging. —*vb.* **net·ting, net·ted.** to make as clear profit: *he netted a hundred dollars on the sale.*

net·tle ('netəl) *n.* a wild plant with hairs on the leaves and stalk that cause a stinging sensation to the human skin. —*vb.* **net·tling, net·tled.** to irritate.

net·work ('netwûrk) *n.* 1. a system of many crossing and connecting lines: *the highway network.* 2. a system of radio or television stations, stores, warehouses, offices, etc., under the same ownership. 3. a group of interacting people: *a spy network.*

neu·tral ('no͞otrəl, nyo͞otrəl) *adj.* 1. not taking sides in a dispute. 2. not distinctively marked or colored: *the wallpaper was a neutral shade.* 3. (chemistry) neither ACID nor ALKALI. —*n.* 1. a person or group that does not take sides in a dispute. 2. the position of gears in which an engine cannot send power to the wheels or other working parts. **neu'tral·i·ty** *n.* a state of not taking sides. **'neu·tral·ize** *vb.* **neu·tral·iz·ing, neu·tral·ized.** to make or become neutral.—**neu·tral·i'za·tion** *n.*

new (no͞o, nyo͞o) *adj.* 1. only recently existing, made, or done: *a new book.* 2. unknown or undiscovered before: *a new star.* 3. beginning again: *a new moon.* 4. unaccustomed; strange: *a new pupil at the school.* —**'new·ly** *adv.*

news (no͞oz, nyo͞oz) *n.* information not heard before; recent and interesting events.

news·deal·er ('no͞ozdēlər, 'nyo͞ozdēlər) *n.* a person whose business is selling newspapers.

news·pa·per ('no͞ozpāpər, 'nyo͞ozpāpər) *n.* printed sheets of paper published daily or weekly to give the latest news.

newt (no͞ot, nyo͞ot) *n.* a small AMPHIBIAN that looks like a lizard but has smooth skin and spends most of its time in water.

nice (nīs) *adj.* **nic·er, nic·est.** 1. pleasant; attractive: *a nice day.* 2. delicate; calling for care or accuracy: *he kept a nice balance between the disputing groups.* **nic·e·ty** ('nīsitē) *n.,pl.* **nic·e·ties.** exact or perfect detail. —**'nice·ly** *adv.*

nick·el ('nikəl) *n.* 1. a hard silvery metal much used in industry. Chemical symbol: Ni. 2. a coin in the U.S., worth five cents.

nick·name ('niknām) *n.* a name given to someone and used instead of his real name: *Paul's nickname was Freckles.* —*vb.* **nick·nam·ing, nick·named.** to give a nickname to.

nic·o·tine ('nikətēn) *n.* an oily poisonous substance that is found in tobacco plants.

niece (nēs) *n.* the daughter of one's brother or sister.

night (nīt) *n.* the period of darkness between sunset and sunrise. **'night·ly** *adj.* of or happening in the night. *adv.* every night.

nightingale

night·in·gale ('nītiṅggāl) *n.* a small European reddish-brown bird famous for its beautiful song that is heard mainly at night.

night·mare ('nītmeər) *n.* 1. a very unpleasant dream. 2. any horrible experience causing terror or frustration. —**'night·mar·ish** *adj.*

nim·ble ('nimbəl) *adj.* **nim·bler, nim·blest.** moving or working lightly and quickly; agile. —**'nim·ble·ness** *n.*—**'nimb·ly** *adv.*

nip·ple ('nipəl) *n.* 1. the small tip in the center of a breast or udder through which a mammal's young can suck milk from its mother. 2. any similar small projection, e.g. the rubber tip of a baby's feeding bottle.

ni·tro·gen ('nītrəjən) *n.* a colorless odorless gas that makes up about four fifths of the earth's atmosphere. Chemical symbol: N.

no·ble ('nōbəl) *adj.* **no·bler, no·blest.** 1. having or showing high ideals and a worthy character. 2. of high social rank. **no'bil·i·ty** *n.,pl.* **no·bil·i·ties.** the quality of being noble.

noc·tur·nal (nok'tûrnəl) *adj.* happening or active at night: *badgers are nocturnal animals.*

noise (noiz) *n.* 1. a loud unpleasant sound. 2. any sound. —**'nois·i·ly** *adv.* —**'nois·y** *adj.* **nois·i·er, nois·i·est.**

no·mad ('nōmad) *n.* a person who has no settled home but wanders from place to place.

nom·i·nal ('nomənəl) *adj.* 1. existing in name only, not in fact: *he was the nominal leader of the group.* 2. very slight: *nominal damage.* —'**nom·i·nal·ly** *adv.*

non·sense ('nonsens) *n.* something that lacks sense or reason. —**non'sen·si·cal** *adj.*

noon (nōōn) *n.* twelve o'clock in the daytime; midday.

noose (nōōs) *n.* a loop of rope with a knot that can slide along the rope to make the loop smaller or larger.

nor·mal ('nôrməl) *adj.* fitting in with accepted standards; typical: *she has normal eyesight.* —'**nor·mal·ly** *adv.*

north (nôrth) *n.* 1. the point on the compass that is on your right if you stand facing the sunset. 2. (often **North**) a region lying in this direction: *Canada is in the North of the American continent.* —*adj.* toward, from, or in the north. —*adv.* toward the north: *we turned north.* **north·ern** ('nôrdhərn) *adj.* of or in the north.

nose (nōz) *n.* 1. the part of a human's or animal's head used for smelling and breathing. 2. the front end of something: *the nose of an airplane.* —*vb.* **nos·ing, nosed.** 1. (+ *out*) to find out or discover: *the detective nosed out some new clues.* 2. to move very slowly and carefully: *the boat nosed into the harbor.* '**nos·y** *or* '**nos·ey** *adj.* **nos·i·er, nos·i·est.** (slang) inquisitive.

nos·tril ('nostrəl) *n.* one of two openings in the nose.

note (nōt) *n.* 1. a short written record made to explain something or help a person remember: *we took notes on the lecture.* 2. a short letter or message. 3. a single sound or the sign that stands for that sound in music: *the singer could not reach the high notes.* 4. importance: *he is an actor of note.* —*vb.* **not·ing, not·ed.** 1. to record in writing or in the mind. 2. to pay attention to. '**not·ed** *adj.* famous.

no·tice ('nōtis) *n.* 1. a written or printed poster giving information or warning. 2. attention: *the broken window escaped his father's notice.* —*vb.* **no·tic·ing, no·ticed.** to observe. '**no·tice·a·ble** *adj.* easily seen.

no·ti·fy ('nōtəfī) *vb.* **no·ti·fy·ing, no·ti·fied.** to give notice to; inform: *she notified the bank about her lost checks.* —**no·ti·fi'ca·tion** *n.*

no·tion ('nōshən) *n.* an idea or general impression: *he had a notion it would rain.*

no·to·ri·ous (nō'tôrēəs) *adj.* well-known and generally disapproved of; infamous: *Jesse James was a notorious outlaw in America.* —**no'to·ri·ous·ly** *adv.*

noun (noun) *n.* a word belonging to a class of words in a language that express the names of things, people, ideas, etc., e.g. *sheep, Peter, botany, inflation.*

nour·ish ('nûrish, 'nurish) *vb.* to feed (an animal, plant, person, etc.) to keep healthy. '**nour·ish·ment** *n.* food and other things necessary for life.

nov·el[1] ('novəl) *adj.* new; unusual: *she has some novel ideas for raising money for the homeless.* '**nov·el·ty** *n.,pl.* **nov·el·ties.** 1. a new experience, esp. an enjoyable one. 2. a small cheap toy, ornament, etc.

nov·el[2] ('novəl) *n.* a long story written about the lives of imaginary people. '**nov·el·ist** *n.* a person who writes novels.

nov·ice ('novis) *n.* a beginner or inexperienced person, esp. a new member of a religious order.

nu·cle·us ('nōōklēəs, 'nyōōklēəs) *n.,pl.* **nu·cle·i** ('nōōklēī, 'nyōōklēī). 1. the center of an atom, made up of protons and neutrons. 2. the center of a plant or animal cell. '**nu·cle·ar** *adj.* 1. of a nucleus. 2. of or coming from atomic energy.

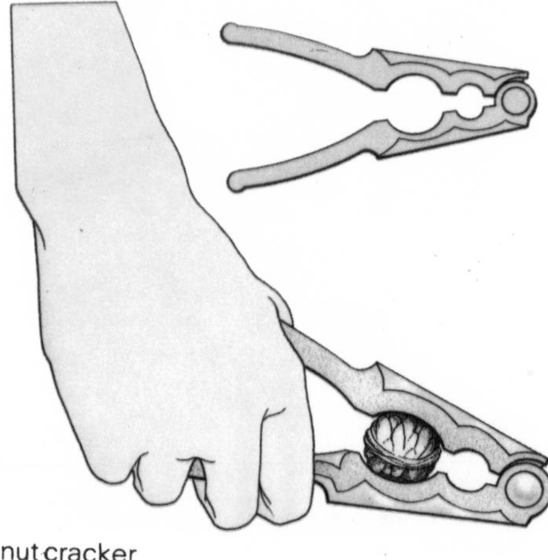

nutcracker

nude (nōōd, nyōōd) *adj.* naked; not wearing clothes. —*n.* a person who is wearing no clothes. —'**nud·i·ty** *n.*

nudge (nuj) *vb.* **nudg·ing, nudged.** to push onward slightly. —*n.* a slight push, usu. given with the elbow, esp. as a signal or to urge someone on.

nui·sance ('nōōsəns, 'nyōōsəns) *n.* something that causes trouble, annoyance, etc.

numb (num) *adj.* without feeling in the body or mind, often as a result of cold, or shock. —*vb.* to make numb.

num·ber ('numbər) *n.* 1. the total of a quantity of things or people. 2. a NUMERAL. 3. an issue of a magazine. 4. a song or melody: *the band rehearsed the number.* —*vb.* 1. to count. 2. to count out; assign numerals to: *number these pages from 1 to 125.* '**num·ber·less** *adj.* consisting of an enormous quantity.

nu·mer·al ('nōōmərəl, 'nyōōmərəl) *n.* a figure or sign standing for a number: *the numeral for six is 6.*

nu·mer·ous ('nōōmərəs, 'nyōōmərəs) *adj.* 1. many. 2. containing many: *a numerous herd of cattle.*

nun (nun) *n.* a woman who has joined a Christian religious order and has taken vows to live in poverty and not to marry.

nurse (nûrs) *n.* 1. a person trained to help doctors to care for sick people, e.g. in hospitals. 2. a woman whose job is to care for young children. —*vb.* **nursing, nursed.** to care for.

nurs·er·y ('nûrsərē) *n.,pl.* **nurs·er·ies.** 1. a room in which babies and children sleep and play. 2. a place where young plants are reared.

nut (nut) *n.* 1. a dry often edible fruit in a hard shell, e.g. walnut, pecan, cashew. 2. a small piece of metal with a threaded central hole made to screw on to BOLTs (defs. 1 and 2). 3. (slang) a person who behaves in a crazy way.

nut·crack·er ('nutkrakər) *n.* often **nut·crack·ers** (*pl.*) a device for breaking the shells of nuts.

nut·meg ('nutmeg) *n.* a hard spicy seed ground up to flavor food.

ny·lon ('nīlon) *n.* a tough manmade material used to make thread, textiles, parachutes, etc.

O

oak (ōk) *n.* 1. one of a large family of DECIDUOUS or EVERGREEN trees that grow in temperate climates and produce acorns. 2. the wood of this tree. *—adj.* made of this wood.

oar (ôr) *n.* 1. a long wooden pole with a flattened end, used to row a boat. 2. (also **oars·man**) a rower.

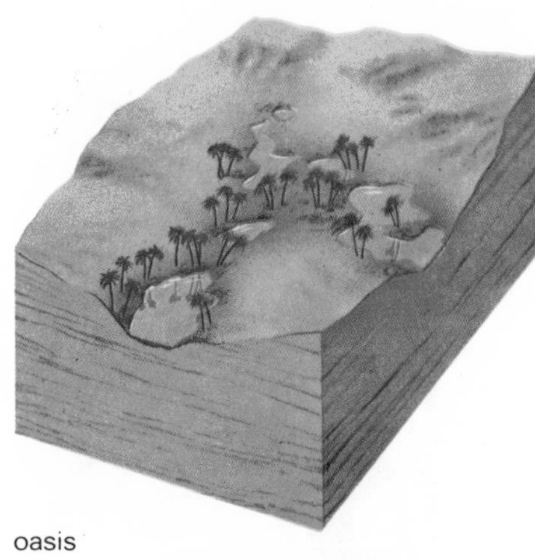

oasis

o·a·sis (ō'āsis) *n.,pl.* **o·a·ses** (ō'āsēz). 1. a fertile area with water in the middle of a desert. 2. a place of safety or comfort; haven.

oat (ōt) *n.* 1. a type of cereal plant yielding grain used for food. 2. **oats** (*pl.*) the grains used as food.

oath (ōth) *n., pl.* **oaths** (ōdhz, ōths). 1. a solemn formal promise, usu. involving calling God as a witness, to tell the truth, be loyal, etc. 2. a curse; swear word.

o·bey (ō'bā) *vb.* to act in accordance with an order, rule, etc: *John was punished for not obeying the teacher's orders.* **o·be·di·ent** (ō'bēdēənt) *adj.* yielding willingly to the orders of someone else. **—o'be·di·ence** *n.* **—o'be·di·ent·ly** *adv.*

object[1] ('objekt) *n.* 1. a real physical thing; something that can be seen or touched. 2. aim; goal: *his object was to get home.* 3. a person or thing toward which a feeling or action is directed: *she was the object of their pity.* 4. (grammar) a word or phrase that bears the action of a verb or follows a preposition, e.g. *ball* is the object in the sentence *Bill kicked the ball.*

ob·ject[2] (əb'jekt) *vb.* 1. (+ *to*) to disapprove of or disagree with: *I object to such rudeness.* 2. to express a reason for not favoring or agreeing: *John objected to Alan's plans.* **ob'jec·tion** *n.* the reason for not doing or favoring something; drawback.

ob·ject·ive (əb'jektiv) *adj.* impartial; not taking sides: *an objective opinion.* *—n.* a goal; target; purpose.

o·blige (ə'blīj) *vb.* **o·blig·ing, o·bliged.** 1. to do something in order to help or as a favor to. 2. to force; compel: *Roger was obliged to pay for the damage he did.* **ob·li·ga·tion** (oblə'gāshən) *n.* a duty to do something; debt; promise. **ob·lig·a·to·ry** (ə'bligətəri) *adj.* necessary; compulsory. **o'blig·ing** *adj.* willing to help.

ob·long ('oblông, 'oblong) *n.* a geometric figure like a square but having two opposite sides shorter than the other two sides; RECTANGLE. *—adj.* of this shape.

o·boe ('ōbō) *n.* a musical instrument of the woodwind family, having a double reed and a high-pitched tone. **—'o·bo·ist** *n.*

oboe

ob·scure (əb'skyoor) *adj.* 1. not clear; difficult to understand: *the explanation was made obscure by the use of long words.* 2. not well known; hidden: *nobody had heard of the obscure poet.* *—vb.* **ob·scur·ing, ob·scured.** 1. to darken or hide from view: *clouds obscured the moon.* 2. to make (someone's meaning, etc.) less clear or understandable; confuse. **—ob'scure·ly** *adv.* **—ob'scur·i·ty** *n.*

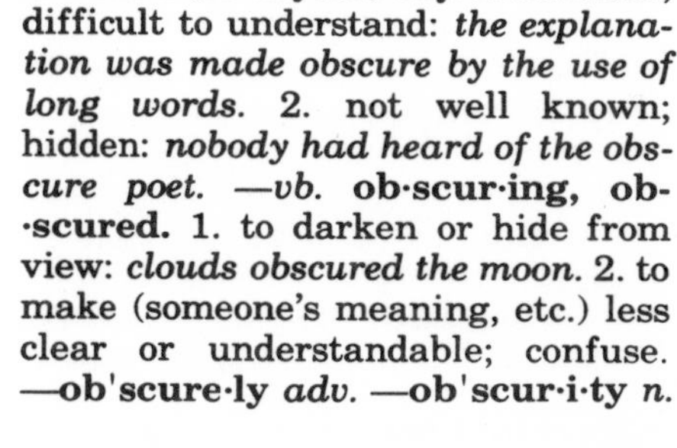

ob·serve (əb'zûrv) *vb.* **ob·serv·ing, ob·served.** 1. to regard; look at; watch carefully: *Pat observed the chipmunks for hours.* 2. to obey; follow; take notice of: *he observed the speed limit.* 3. to remark on; notice: *he observed that the weather was fine.* **ob'serv·ance** *n.* 1. the keeping (of a custom, etc.): *the observance of Thanksgiving Day is a tradition.* 2. a custom or usual celebration. **ob'serv·ant** *adj.* noticing small details; alert and watchful. **ob·ser'va·tion** *n.* 1. watch; study. 2. the state of being observed. 3. remark; comment. **ob'serv·a·to·ry** *n.,pl.* **ob·serv·a·to·ries.** a building, usu. containing a large telescope, from which the stars, etc., are observed.

ob·so·lete (obsə'lēt) *adj.* no longer used, done, or made; out-of-date: *the old car was an obsolete model.*

ob·sta·cle ('obstəkəl) *n.* something that stands in the way of someone's progress; hindrance.

ob·sti·nate ('obstinət) *adj.* unmoving in opinion, habits, etc.; stubborn: *the obstinate donkey refused to move.* **—'ob·sti·na·cy** *n.* **—'ob·sti·nate·ly** *adv.*

ob·struct (əb'strukt) *vb.* 1. to block; get in the way of: *the new building obstructed the view.* 2. to be a hindrance or obstacle to: *he obstructed our plans.* **—ob'struc·tion** *n.*

ob·tain (əb'tān) *vb.* to get; acquire.

ob·tuse (əb'toos, əb'tyoos) *n.* 1. stupid. 2. (of an ANGLE[1], def. 1) between 90° and 180°.

ob·vi·ous ('obvēəs) *adj.* clear; easily seen or understood. —'**ob·vi·ous·ly** *adv.* —'**ob·vi·ous·ness** *n.*

oc·ca·sion (ə'kāzhən) *n.* 1. the time when a particular event happens. 2. a special event: *they had a party to celebrate the occasion of her birthday.* 3. a cause or reason for something: *he had no occasion to be upset.* —*vb.* to cause. **oc'ca·sion·al** *adj.* 1. not frequent: *there was occasional rain.* 2. on or for a particular occasion. —**oc'ca·sion·al·ly** *adv.*

oc·cu·py ('okyəpī) *vb.* **oc·cu·py·ing, oc·cu·pied.** 1. to take up time or space; fill: *the visit occupied an hour.* 2. to live in: *he occupies the top story of the house.* 3. to seize and keep possession of: *the Germans occupied Paris in 1940.* **oc·cu'pa·tion** *n.* 1. job; business: *Jerry's occupation is teaching.* 2. the act of occupying: *the students' occupation of the building ended when the Principal agreed to their demands.* —**oc·cu'pa·tion·al** *adj.*

oc·cur (ə'kûr) *vb.* **oc·cur·ring, oc·curred.** 1. to come to pass; happen: *a strange thing occurred on the way to work.* 2. to come into someone's mind: *it occurs to me that I have heard his name before.* 3. to be found; exist: *tigers occur in India.* **oc'cur·rence** *n.* a happening.

o·cean ('ōshən) *n.* 1. the mass of salt water that covers about 70% of the earth's crust. 2. one of the five main areas of this (Indian, Pacific, Antarctic, Arctic, Atlantic). —**o·ce·an·ic** (ōshē'anik) *adj.*

octopus

oc·to·pus ('oktəpəs) *n.,pl.* **oc·to·pus·es.** a sea creature, ranging from 6 inches to 32 feet in length, with a soft rounded body and eight arms bearing rows of suckers.

odd (od) *adj.* 1. unusual; different; peculiar. 2. not important; extra: *the odd jobs were left until the weekend.* 3. (arithmetic) not capable of being exactly divided by two: *3, 5, and 9 are odd numbers.* 4. part of a set now incomplete; the only remaining one of a pair: *an odd glove.* '**odd·i·ty** *n.,pl.* **odd·i·ties.** a peculiar or unusual person or thing. —'**odd·ly** *adv.* —'**odd·ness** *n.*

odds (odz) *pl.n.* the chances of something happening: *the odds are against our team's winning.*

o·dor ('ōdər) *n.* a smell.

of·fense (ə'fens) *n.* 1. the breaking of a law, rule, etc.; crime. 2. the act of hurting, disgusting, or annoying someone. 3. something that causes disgust or annoyance: *the smoke from the factory was an offense to the neighborhood.* **of'fend** *vb.* 1. to make (someone) angry, upset, etc.: *Janet was offended by his unkind words.* 2. to cause disgust. 3. to break the law. **of'fen·sive** *adj.* 1. causing offense; displeasing. *the manners of the thugs were offensive.* 2. used for attacking: *offensive weapons. n.* an attitude or policy of attack. —**of'fen·sive·ly** *adv.*

of·fer ('ôfər, 'ofər) *vb.* to put forward or present (something) to be accepted or refused: *I offered ten dollars for the radio.* —*n.* 1. the act of offering. 2. something that is offered, such as money.

of·fice ('ôfis, 'ofis) *n.* 1. a room or suite of rooms where business is carried out. 2. a responsible position, esp. in government: *the office of mayor.* 3. **of·fic·es** (*pl.*) acts done to help someone: *his friend's kind offices got him the job.*

of·fic·er ('ôfisər, 'ofisər) *n.* 1. a person who holds a responsible position in government, a police force, etc. 2. a person in the army, navy, or air force with a certain rank and authority.

of·fi·cial (ə'fishəl) *n.* someone who is authorized to carry out particular duties. —*adj.* 1. holding a position of authority: *an official agent.* 2. authorized: *an official statement.* 3. formal; ceremonious: *an official banquet was held for the President.*

off·spring ('ôfspring, 'ofspring) *n.,pl.* **off·spring.** 1. child or children. 2. result or development: *the new book was the offspring of Ed's original idea.*

oil (oil) *n.* a thick greasy liquid that will not mix with water. There are many different kinds of oil. —*vb.* to put oil into or onto something. '**oil·y** *adj.* **oil·i·er, oil·i·est.** of, like, or soaked in oil.

oint·ment ('ointmənt) *n.* a soft greasy paste used as a medicine to heal or protect sore places on the skin.

old (ōld) *adj.* 1. not young; having existed, grown, developed, etc., for a long time. 2. of a certain age: *Sally is twelve years old.* 3. belonging to the past; former. **the old** old people.

ol·ive ('oliv) *n.* 1. a southern European evergreen tree. 2. the small oval fruit of this tree, used as a relish or made into oil. *n., adj.* (having) a dark yellowish-green color.

olive

om·e·let *or* **om·e·lette** ('omlit) *n.* a food made of eggs beaten together and fried in a flat pan.

o·men ('ōmən) *n.* an event or thing that is thought to indicate good or bad luck in the future: *it was an ill omen for our team when our mascot was stolen.*

om·i·nous ('omənəs) *adj.* giving an advance warning, esp. of something evil or threatening: *the ominous black clouds indicated a storm approaching.* —'**om·i·nous·ly** *adv.*

o·mit (ō'mit) *vb.* **o·mit·ting, o·mit·ted.** 1. to leave out: *he omitted chapter six.* 2. to fail to make or do: *he omitted to turn the lights off.* **o'mis·sion** *n.* 1. the act of omitting. 2. something left out.

on·ion ('unyən) *n.* the bulb of a vegetable with a strong taste and smell, often used in cooking.

ooze (o͞oz) *vb.* **ooz·ing, oozed.** to leak very slowly; seep: *mud oozed through his boots.* —*n.* liquid mud found on ocean and river beds.

opal

o·pal ('ōpəl) *n.* a beautiful semiprecious stone much valued as a gemstone because of its quality of displaying colors in shifting patterns.

o·paque (ō'pāk) *adj.* not allowing light to pass through. —**o·pac·i·ty** (ō'pasitē) *n.*

op·er·a ('opərə, 'oprə) *n.* a form of stage play in which all or most of the words are sung. —**op·er·'a·tic** *adj.*

op·er·ate ('opərāt) *vb.* **op·er·at·ing, op·er·at·ed.** 1. to act; carry out a function; control (a machine). 2. to perform surgery on a person. **op·er'a·tion** *n.* 1. the act of working. 2. a task; project: *the operation was completed very easily.* 3. an act of surgery. **op·er·a·tive** ('opərətiv) *adj.* 1. in working order: *the machine is operative.* 2. effective: *the new law is now operative.* *n.* 1. a worker: *a machine operative.* 2. (informal) a detective or secret agent. **'op·er·a·tor** *n.* a person who works a machine, etc.

o·pin·ion (ə'pinyən) *n.* a view or judgment held by someone about a subject: *in my opinion it will rain.*

o·pos·sum (ə'posəm) *n.* (also **pos·sum**) a small furry American animal that lives in trees and carries its young in a pouch.

op·por·tu·ni·ty (opər'to͞onitē, opər'tyo͞onitē) *n.,pl.* **op·por·tu·ni·ties.** a good, and often lucky, chance coming at a convenient time. **op·por'tun·ist** *n.* a person who makes clever use of opportunities when they occur. —**op·por'tun·ism** *n.*

op·pose (ə'pōz) *vb.* **op·pos·ing, op·posed.** to argue, vote, or fight against: *the neighbors opposed the plan to build a new factory.* **op·po·site** ('opəzit) *adj.* 1. on the other side of. 2. completely different; contrary: *the two children have opposite natures; one is good, the other bad.* *n.* someone or something that is contrary or opposing: *they are opposites; one is fair, the other dark.* *prep.* facing; in front of; across from: *the car stood opposite the house.*

op·press (ə'pres) *vb.* **op·press·ing, op·pressed.** 1. to keep down by force; to treat cruelly. 2. to overwhelm mentally or physically: *the heat oppressed us.* —**op'pres·sion** *n.* —**op'pres·sive** *adj.*

op·ti·cal ('optikəl) *adj.* of or concerning the sense of sight. **op'ti·cian** *n.* a person who makes or sells spectacles and, sometimes, other optical devices.

op·tion ('opshən) *n.* 1. the power or ability to make a choice: *I lost the bus fare and had no option but to walk.* 2. something chosen or available to be chosen: *Tom's option was to study science.* **'op·tion·al** *adj.* left to one's choice.

or·ange ('ôrinj, 'orinj) *n.* 1. a round sweet juicy CITRUS fruit with a tough skin. —*n., adj.* (having) a reddish-yellow color.

orange

or·bit ('ôrbit) *n.* the path along which a planet, satellite, or other body travels when revolving round another body in space. —*vb.* to move in an orbit: *the satellite orbited the earth.*

or·chard ('ôrchərd) *n.* a place where fruit trees are grown.

or·ches·tra ('ôrkistrə) *n.* 1. a group of musicians who play together, esp. for the performance of large-scale musical works such as symphonies. 2. the seats in a theater that are on the main floor.—**or·ches·tral** (ôr'kestrəl) *adj.*

or·chid ('ôrkid) *n.* one of many types of flower prized on account of their strange and beautiful shapes and brilliant colors.

or·deal (ôr'dēl) *n.* an experience that is exhausting, painful, or unpleasant: *the storm was an ordeal for the passengers.*

or·der ('ôrdər) *n.* 1. a rule or command. 2. a condition in which things are neat, in their proper places, etc.: *mother keeps the house in order by tidying every day.* 3. the way in which things are arranged: *alphabetical order.* 4. working condition: *my watch is out of order.* 5. peace and quiet: *the army restored order after the riot.* 6. an instruction to buy or sell goods or send money. 7. an organized group of people or things. —*vb.* 1. to command: *the general ordered the troops to advance.* 2. to request (food, goods, etc.) to be supplied: *they ordered four pounds of nails.* 3. to put in order; arrange. **'or·der·ly** *adj.* 1. neatly arranged or organized according to a system: *an orderly bookcase.* 2. well-behaved: *an orderly class.* *n.,pl.* **or·der·lies.** 1. a person who keeps things clean and tidy in a hospital. 2. a soldier who runs errands for an officer. —**'or·der·li·ness** *n.*

or·di·nar·y ('ôdənerē) *adj.* 1. common; normal. 2. below average quality; poor: *a very ordinary play.*

ore (ôr) *n.* a rock, soil, or mineral containing a metal or other useful substance: *iron ore.*

or·gan ('ôrgən) *n.* 1. a musical keyboard instrument in which the sound is made by air forced through a number of pipes. 2. a part of the body of an animal: *the liver is an essential organ.* **or·gan·ic** (ôr'ganik) *adj.* 1. of, obtained from, or concerned with living plants or animals. 2. (of chemicals) containing carbon. **'or·gan·ism** *n.* a living plant or animal.

or·gan·ize ('ôrgənīz) *vb.* **or·gan·iz·ing, or·gan·ized.** 1. to put together in an orderly way. 2. to arrange for something to happen: *Susan organized a picnic.* **or·gan·i'za·tion** *n.* an organized group of people or things.

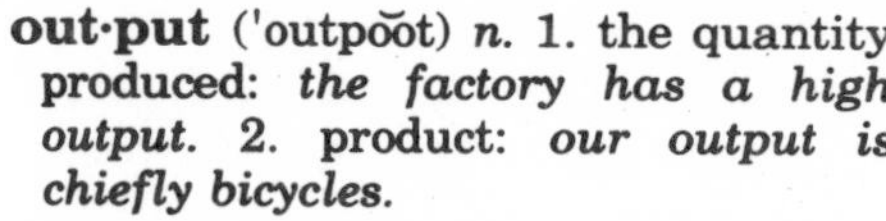

or·i·gin ('ôrijin, 'orijin) *n.* the source or cause of something. **o·rig·i·nal** (ə'rijənəl) *adj.* 1. first; earliest. 2. new or fresh. —*n.* something that is not a copy or translation of anything else: *the painting was an original by Michelangelo.* **o'rig·i·nate** *vb.* **o·rig·i·nat·ing, o·rig·i·nat·ed.** to begin; start.

or·phan ('ôrfən) *n.* a child whose parents have died. —*vb.* to deprive of parents. **or·phan·age** (ôrfənij) *n.* a home for orphans.

os·trich ('ôstrich, 'ostrich) *n.* a flightless long-legged bird that runs very quickly. It lives in Africa and Arabia and is the largest existing bird.

out·put ('outpoot) *n.* 1. the quantity produced: *the factory has a high output.* 2. product: *our output is chiefly bicycles.*

out·rage ('outrāj) *n.* 1. great fury: *Neil felt outrage at being insulted.* 2. a cruel or violent act. —*vb.* **out·rag·ing, out·raged.** to cause to feel great anger: *the plan for a new factory outraged the local people.* —**out'ra·geous** *adj.*

out·skirts ('outskûrts) *pl.n.* an area on the edge of a town or city.

otter

ot·ter ('otər) *n.* a web-footed fish-eating animal that lives near water and is an excellent swimmer.

ounce (ouns) *n.* (usu. shortened to oz.) a unit of weight equal to one sixteenth of a pound. **fluid ounce** a liquid measure equal to one sixteenth of a pint.

out·come ('outkum) *n.* a result: *the outcome of the game was a tie.*

out·law ('outlô) *n.* a criminal. —*vb.* 1. to make unlawful: *people have tried to outlaw alcohol.* 2. to make an outlaw of someone.

out·let ('outlet) *n.* 1. a point at which something can come out, e.g. a water outlet. 2. a means of getting rid of something: *football is a good outlet for his energy.*

out·line ('outlīn) *n.* 1. a line around the edge or limits of an object. 2. a drawing on which only the main lines or features are marked. 3. the main features of something; a summary: *give us an outline of the plot.* —*vb.* **out·lin·ing, out·lined.** 1. to draw the outer lines of. 2. to give the main features of.

out·stand·ing (out'standing) *adj.* 1. excellent; distinguished: *an outstanding athlete.* 2. not yet dealt with: *David has some outstanding debts.*

o·val ('ōvəl) *n., adj.* (having) a shape like an egg.

ov·en ('uvən) *n.* an enclosed cupboard-like space, usu. part of a stove, in which food is cooked.

o·ver·board ('ōvərbôrd) *adv.* over the side of a boat or ship into the water: *the sailor tripped and fell overboard.*

o·ver·come (ōvər'kum) *vb.* **o·ver·com·ing, o·ver·came, o·ver·come.** to be too strong for: *the heat overcame the firemen.*

o·ver·haul *vb.* (ōvər'hôl) to examine carefully and make changes or repairs: *the garage overhauled our car before we took it on vacation.* —*n.* ('ōvərhôl) a thorough examination.

o·ver·hear (ōvər'hēr) *vb.* **o·ver·hear·ing, o·ver·heard** (ōvər'hûrd). to hear something by chance without the knowledge of the speaker: *I overheard my parents saying they would me a fishing rod for Christmas.*

o·ver·look (ōvər'look) *vb.* 1. to have a view of: *my window overlooks the river.* 2. to ignore; excuse: *he overlooked his son's faults.* 3. to fail to see, think of, etc.: *in his hurry, the thief overlooked the radio.*

o·ver·pow·er (ōvər'pouər) *vb.* to be too strong for; overwhelm: *the policeman overpowered the bank robber.*

o·ver·see (ōvər'sē) *vb.* **o·ver·see·ing, o·ver·saw, o·ver·seen.** to supervise, organize, or manage (work or workers). **'o·ver·se·er** *n.* a person who is responsible for overseeing; foreman.

o·ver·take (ōvər'tāk) *vb.* **o·ver·tak·ing, o·ver·took, o·ver·tak·en.** 1. to catch up and pass: *the sports car overtook the bus.* 2. to happen to or come upon suddenly: *disaster overtook the aircraft.*

o·ver·time ('ōvərtīm) *n.* time spent in working outside normal working hours. — *adv.* after the usual hours.

o·ver·ture ('ōvərchər) *n.* 1. a piece of music played to introduce an opera, ballet, etc.

o·ver·whelm (ōvər'hwelm, ōvər'welm) *vb.* crush; destroy by too much force or weight.

owe (ō) *vb.* **ow·ing, owed.** 1. to have to give or pay: *he owes me an apology.* 2. to be grateful to: *I owe my aunt a great deal for her kindness.*

owl (oul) *n.* a bird with big staring eyes and strong beak and talons. It hunts small animals by night. **'owl·ish** *adj.* like an owl, esp. looking solemn or wise.

own (ōn) *adj.* relating to or belonging to oneself: *my own hat.* —*pron.* something that belongs to one: *this book is my own.* —*vb.* to have or possess: *do you own a bicycle?* **own up** to admit one's guilt: *Jane owned up to breaking the window.* **'own·er** *n.* a person who owns or possesses.

ox·y·gen ('oksijən) *n.* a colorless odorless gas that makes up about one fifth of the world's atmosphere. Oxygen is necessary for animals to breathe and for combustion. Chemical symbol: O.

oys·ter ('oistər) *n.* a shellfish valued as food and for the pearls that some of them produce.

P

pace (pās) *n.* 1. a single step: *she took a pace forward.* 2. a rate or tempo of movement: *he drove at a rapid pace.* 3. a particular gait of a horse whereby both legs on one side are lifted when those on the other side are lowered. —*vb.* **pac·ing, paced.** to move or walk with regular steps.

pack (pak) *n.* 1. a number of objects tied or wrapped together for carrying; bundle. 2. a group with something in common: *a pack of wolves.* 3. a set of playing cards. 4. a large number; great deal: *a pack of nonsense.* —*vb.* 1. to put together into a bundle. 2. to fill (a container): *he packed his suitcase.* 3. to crowd tightly together: *hundreds of people packed into the hall.*

pack·age ('pakij) *n.* one or more objects wrapped or tied together; parcel. —*vb.* **pack·ag·ing, pack·aged.** to make or put into a package, esp. for selling.

pack·et ('pakit) *n.* a small package or bundle.

pad[1] (pad) *n.* 1. a soft thick piece of any material used for protection or as stuffing: *I slept on a foam rubber pad on the floor.* 2. a number of sheets of paper fastened together along one edge. 3. the soft spongy underneath part of the feet of certain animals, e.g. dogs. 4. (also **launching pad**) the area from which a rocket is launched. 5. (slang) a room or apartment of one's own. —*vb.* **pad·ding, pad·ded.** 1. to stuff or protect with a pad. 2. to cover or fill with pads. 3. to add unnecessary material: *he padded his lecture with irrelevant quotations.*

pad[2] (pad) *vb.* **pad·ding, pad·ded.** to move so that one's feet make only a quiet dull sound.

pad·dle[1] ('padəl) *n.* 1. a short oar with a wide flat blade at one or both ends, used esp. for moving a canoe. 2. any implement with a wide flat blade: *a table tennis paddle.* 3. any of the wide boards on the outside of a waterwheel. —*vb.* **pad·dling, pad·dled.** to move (a boat) with paddles; row.

pad·dle[2] ('padəl) *vb.* **pad·dling, pad·dled.** 1. to wade about in shallow water. 2. to swim or splash about using rapid movements of the limbs.

pad·lock ('padlok) *n.* a lock with a curved movable bar that can be snapped shut and opened with a key. —*vb.* to fasten with a padlock.

page[1] (pāj) *n.* one side of a sheet of paper, with or without printing or writing on it.

padlock

page[2] (pāj) *n.* 1. a servant, often a boy, who runs errands for members of a legislative assembly, e.g. in Congress, or for guests in a hotel. 2. (in the Middle Ages) a boy training to become a knight. —*vb.* **pag·ing, paged.** to try to contact (someone) by calling out his name.

pag·eant ('pajənt) *n.* 1. a colorful and exciting parade. 2. a theatrical presentation about historical events or legends.

paid (pād) *vb.* the past tense and past participle of PAY.

pain (pān) *n.* suffering in the body or in the mind: *my broken arm caused me great pain.* 2. **pains** (*pl.*) effort: *John took pains over his work.* —*vb.* to cause to suffer. —'**pain·ful** *adj.* —'**pain·ful·ly** *adv.* —'**pain·ful·ness** *n.*

paint (pānt) *n.* a mixture of coloring matter and oil, water, or some other liquid that can be spread on a surface to color or protect it. —*vb.* 1. to apply paint to. 2. to make (a picture) by using paint.

pair (peər) *n.* 1. two people, objects, or animals that are alike, are used together, or are related in some way; set of two: *a pair of socks.* 2. something made up of two similar parts: *a pair of scissors.* —*vb.* to arrange or form into a pair or pairs.

pa·ja·mas (pə'jâməz) *pl.n.* a pair of loose-fitting trousers with a jacket worn in bed.

pal·ace ('paləs) *n.* a large impressive building, esp. one where a king, archbishop, or other important person lives. —**pa·la·tial** (pə'lāshəl) *adj.*

pale (pāl) *adj.* **pal·er, pal·est.** 1. having a whitish complexion, e.g. from illness. 2. lacking brightness of color: *pale blue.* —*vb.* to become pale.

palm[1] (pâm) *n.* the area on the front of the hand between the fingers and the wrist. —*vb.* 1. to hide in the hand: *the gambler palmed an extra card.* 2. (+ *off*) to get rid of (an undesirable object): *she palmed off her old radio on her brother.*

palm[2] (pâm) *n.* any of various tropical trees with tall unbranched stems topped by bunches of large leaves.

pam·phlet ('pamflit) *n.* a thin printed book with few pages and paper covers; booklet.

pan·da ('pandə) *n.* a large bearlike animal that lives in Tibet and Southern China and has a white coat with black legs, shoulders, and ears.

pane (pān) *n.* a sheet of glass set in a window or door.

pan·el ('panəl) *n.* 1. an area or part of something that is raised, sunk, or otherwise distinct from the rest: *her blue dress has panels of red on the* *skirt* 2. a body of people selected for a special task, e.g. a jury. 3. a surface or board with the controls of a machine: *an instrument panel.* —*vb.* to furnish with panels: *they paneled the hall with oak.*

pan·ic ('panik) *n.* a sudden unreasoning fear, often spreading rapidly through a group: *when the fire broke out, panic struck the audience.* —*vb.* **pan·ick·ing, pan·icked.** to affect or be affected by panic. —'**pan·ic-strick·en** *adj.*

pan·o·ra·ma (panə'ramə, panə'râmə) *n.* a view over a wide expanse of territory: *from the hill top we could see a beautiful panorama of unbroken forest.*

pant (pant) *vb.* to breathe in quick gasps: *he panted after the long run.* —*n.* a short quick breath.

pan·ther ('panthər) *n.* 1. a leopard, esp. one that has a black coat. 2. a jaguar, cougar, or other large wild cat.

pan·to·mime ('pantəmīm) *n.* a play without words, in which the actors use movements and expressions of the face instead of speech. —*vb.* **pan·to·mim·ing, pan·to·mimed.** to act in a pantomime or express with gestures only.

pan·try ('pantrē) *n.,pl.* **pan·tries.** a small room for storing food, tableware, or glass; larder.

pa·per ('pāpər) *n.* 1. a flexible material, usu. made in very thin sheets from wood pulp, rags, or other matter, and used for writing, printing, wrapping, etc. 2. a piece of paper that provides information, often officially; document: *a secret paper was stolen from the office.* 3. a newspaper. 4. an essay or article. —*vb.* to decorate (a room, wall) with wallpaper.

pap·ri·ka (pa'prēkə, 'paprəkə) *n.* a red spice that is not as strong as red pepper. It is made from the dried fruit of certain sweet peppers.

par·a·chute ('parəshōōt) *n.* an umbrella-like apparatus of silk or nylon with ropes attached to it, used to slow down something or someone falling through the air. —*vb.* **par·a·chut·ing, par·a·chut·ed.** to use a parachute to come or send down.

pa·rade (pə'rād) *n.* 1. a march or procession. 2. a military display. —*vb.* **pa·rad·ing, pa·rad·ed.** 1. to march or cause to march in a parade. 2. to display or show off: *he is always parading his cleverness.*

par·a·dise ('parədīs) *n.* 1. heaven. 2. a condition of extreme happiness.

par·af·fin ('parəfin) *n.* a white or colorless waxy substance obtained from petroleum and used to make candles, waxed paper, etc.

par·a·graph ('parəgraf) *n.* 1. a group of sentences in a piece of writing that deals with one topic. A paragraph begins on a new line and its first word is usu. set in from the margin. 2. a short article or note.

par·al·lel ('parəlel) *adj.* 1. going or pointing in the same direction and keeping the same distance apart: *the gymnast did stunts on the parallel bars.* 2. similar: *we had parallel experiences.* —*n.* 1. a parallel line, esp. a line of LATITUDE. 2. something that is similar: *there was a parallel in the careers of the two friends.* —*vb.* to develop or move in a similar direction: *the line of trees paralleled the road.* **par·al'lel·o·gram** *n.* (geometry) a four-sided figure the opposite sides of which are parallel.

par·a·lyze ('parəlīz) *vb.* **par·a·lyz·ing, par·a·lyzed.** to destroy the power to move or feel: *the accident paralyzed her right leg.* **pa·ral·y·sis** (pə'ralisis) *n.* loss of feeling or motion. —**par·a·lyt·ic** (parə'litik) *adj.*

parachute

par·a·site ('parəsīt) *n.* 1. a plant or animal that lives on or in a plant or animal of a different kind and takes its food from its host: *fleas are parasites on cats, dogs, and humans.* 2. a person who is supported by other people in return. —**par·a·sit·ic** (parə'sitik) *adj.*

par·a·sol ('parəsôl) *n.* a sunshade, usu. decorated with frills or lace.

par·a·troops ('parətrōōps) *n.* soldiers who are taken by aircraft to the site of a battle where they are dropped by parachute. —'**par·a·troop·er,** *n.*

par·cel ('pârsəl) *n.* 1. a single item or a number of objects packed together; package. 2. a part or section, esp. of land. —*vb.* (usu. + *out*) to divide into portions; distribute.

par·don ('pârdən) *n.* 1. forgiveness; an excusing: *I beg your pardon.* 2. a release from punishment. —*vb.* 1. to forgive or excuse. 2. to free from punishment: *the governor pardoned four prisoners.* —'**par·don·a·ble** *adj.*

par·ent ('peərənt) *n.* 1. a father or mother. 2. a plant or animal that produces offspring. —**pa·ren·tal** (pə'rentəl) *adj.*

par·ish ('parish) *n.* 1. a small area with its own church and minister. 2. the people who live there. 3. a district, corresponding to a county, in Louisiana.

park (pârk) *n.* an area of land set aside for public use and pleasure. —*vb.* to leave (a car, luggage, etc.) in a certain place for a time.

par·lia·ment ('pârləmənt) *n.* (in some countries) an assembly or assemblies of people have the power to make the laws of the land. —**par·lia'men·ta·ry** *adj.*

par·lor ('pârlər) *n.* 1. (old-fashioned) a room used for receiving guests. 2. a room or rooms used for a business: *a beauty parlor.*

pa·role (pə'rōl) *n.* the release of a prisoner on condition that he keeps certain promises about his behavior or obeys certain rules. —*vb.* **pa·rol·ing, pa·roled.** to free (someone) on parole.

parrot

par·rot ('parət) *n.* a tropical bird with a hooked bill and often brightly colored feathers. Some parrots can learn to copy human words.

pars·ley ('pârslē) *n.* a garden herb with crinkly leaves that are used to flavor food.

pars·nip ('pârsnip) *n.* 1. a plant, related to the carrot, that has a long whitish root. 2. the root of this plant, eaten as a vegetable when cooked.

part (pârt) *n.* 1. a division or section of a whole: *we saw only part of his face.* 2. one of the sides in an argument, arrangement, etc.: *on our part, we will sell the car at the agreed price.* 3. a share: *we did our part in the work.* 4. a replacement section: *parts for a car.* 5. a role in a play, opera, etc.: *the part of* Hamlet *was played by a famous actor.* 6. a line in the hair caused by combing it in opposite directions. —*vb.* 1. to separate or cause to separate; divide. 2. to go one's separate ways. 3. to make a dividing line in one's hair. **part with** to be separated from or let go: *Jane would not part with her dog.* —*adj.* incomplete; not all: *part payment.* —*adv.* to a certain extent, not completely. '**part·ing** *n.* a separation from another person. —'**part·ly** *adv.*

par·tial ('pârshəl) adj. 1. not complete: *a partial victory.* 2. biased; prejudiced: *a partial reporter.* 3. (+ *to*) fond (of): *partial to cream.* —**par·ti·al·i·ty** (pârshē'alitē) *n.* —'**par·tial·ly** *adj.*

par·ti·ci·ple ('pârtisipəl) *n.* the form of a verb that can be used as an adjective or noun or with a helping verb, such as *has* or *was,* to form certain tenses, e.g. *working* (present participle), *worked* (past participle).

par·ti·cle ('pârtikəl) *n.* a very small bit or item: *a particle of dust.*

par·tic·u·lar (pâr'tikyələr) *adj.* 1. relating to one and not to all; not general: *his particular problem is his handwriting.* 2. individual; separate: *I like this particular dress.* 3. to a high degree; special: *Ronald is his particular friend.* 4. very careful; precise: *Sheila is very particular about doing a good job.* 5. hard to please; fussy: *she is most particular about her tea.* —*n.* often **particulars** (*pl.*) details: *please give me the particulars of the job.* —**par'tic·u·lar·ly** *adv.*

part·ner ('pârtnər) *n.* 1. a person who shares in an activity; colleague: *a partner in crime.* 2. one of two or more people who together own a business, sharing its profits and losses. 3. a husband or wife. 4. the person with whom one dances. 5. (games) a player on the same side. '**part·ner·ship** *n.* 1. the condition of being a partner. 2. a business run by partners.

par·tridge ('pârtrij) *n.* any of various game birds that belong to the same family as the chicken.

par·ty ('pârtē) *n.,pl.* **par·ties.** 1. a gathering of people for the purpose of enjoying themselves. 2. a body of people who join together because they have common political goals: *which party will you vote for?* 3. a person or group taking part in some activity: *he was a party to the crime.* —*adj.* of or relating to a party.

pass (pas) *vb.* 1. to go by, over, beyond, through, etc.: *I passed him in the street.* 2. to go from one place or state to another: *she passed into unconsciousness.* 3. to send, move, or deliver: *pass the salt.* 4. to undergo or complete satisfactorily: *to pass an examination.* 5. (+ *for*) to be regarded as: *in his disguise he was able to pass for a woman.* 6. to spend (time, etc.). —*n.* 1. a narrow way by which one may travel: *a mountain pass.* 2. a ticket or permit for travel or entry: *a bus pass.* 3. (games) the movement of the ball from one player to another. 4. a success in an examination, etc.

pas·sage ('pasij) *n.* 1. a narrow corridor or hallway. 2. a progress (of time, events, etc.). 3. an extract from a book, a piece of music, etc. 4. the act of going from one place or state to another.

pas·sen·ger ('pasənjər) *n.* a traveler on a bus, train, airplane, etc.

pas·sion ('pashən) *n.* 1. a powerful emotion or agitation of the mind, e.g. rage, hate, etc. 2. a very strong enthusiasm or desire for anything: *he has a passion for poetry written by Wordsworth.* —'**pas·sion·ate** *adj.*

pas·sive ('pasiv) *adj.* 1. not reacting to something that might be expected to produce some response; inactive: *she remained passive when he shouted at her.* 2. indicating that the subject of a verb is affected by an action, *e.g. painted* in the sentence *the picture was painted by John* is in the passive voice. Compare ACTIVE. —'**pas·sive·ly** *adv.* —**pas'siv·i·ty** *n.*

pass·port ('paspôrt) *n.* an official document serving as a means of identification and permitting a person to travel to foreign countries and to re-enter his own country.

past (past) *adj.* gone by; in time already over. **past tense** the construction of a verb that refers to action, etc., in time gone by. —*n.* that which has happened in earlier times; history. —*adv.* so as to go by: *he hurried past.* —*prep.* beyond or farther than in amount, position, time, etc.: *it is past three o'clock.*

paste (pāst) *n.* 1. a mixture used for sticking things together. 2. any material in a similar soft thick form: *salmon paste.* —*vb.* **past·ing, past·ed.** to cover, fasten, or stick with paste.

pas·teur·ize ('paschərīz) *vb.* **pas·teur·iz·ing, pas·teur·ized.** to kill harmful germs in (milk or other food) by a process of heating.

pas·try ('pāstrē) *n.,pl.* **pas·tries.** 1. a floury paste or dough that is baked and used for pies, tarts, etc. 2. a food item made of this dough, baked and sweetened, usu. filled with jam, fruit, or cream.

pas·ture ('paschər) *n.* land covered with grass, used for the grazing of cattle, sheep, etc. —*vb.* **pas·tur·ing, pas·tured.** to feed animals by allowing them to graze on grassland.

pat (pat) *vb.* **pat·ting, pat·ted.** 1. to strike gently with something flat in order to smooth or flatten: *he carefully patted the sandcastle into shape.* 2. to tap or stroke gently with the hand as a sign of affection or approval. —*n.* 1. a gentle tap. 2. a small shaped lump e.g. of butter.

patch (pach) *n.* 1. a piece of material used to cover a hole or worn place. 2. a small area, e.g. of ground. —*vb.* 1. to mend with a patch. 2. (usu. + *up*) to repair in a makeshift way. —'**patch·i·ness** *n.* —'**patch·y** *adj.* **patch·i·er, patch·i·est.**

pat·ent ('patənt) *n.* 1. a government permit to an inventor giving him the sole right to manufacture and sell his invention. 2. something invented and protected by a patent. —*vb.* to obtain a patent for (something). —*adj.* 1. protected by a patent. 2. obvious: *his irritation was patent.* —'**pa·tent·ly** *adv.*

path (path) *n.,pl.* **paths** (padhz, paths). 1. a way or narrow road for passing on foot: *a path through the woods.* 2. the direction in which something moves: *the path of the storm.*

pa·thet·ic (pə'thetik) *adj.* 1. arousing pity. 2. (informal) very incompetent or unsuitable. —**pa'thet·i·cal·ly** *adv.*

pa·tient ('pāshənt) *adj.* 1. putting up with trouble, misfortune, etc., without complaint: *it will be a long wait so you will have to be patient.* 2. careful: *her patient work produced splendid results.* —*n.* a person undergoing medical treatment. '**pa·tience** *n.* 1. the quality of waiting or enduring without complaint. 2. diligence. —'**pa·tient·ly** *adv.*

pa·trol (pə'trōl) *vb.* **pa·trol·ling, pa·trolled.** to go around (an area, district, town, etc.) in order to watch and protect. —*n.* 1. a man, esp. a policeman, or group of men who patrol. 2. a small scouting party of soldiers.

pat·tern ('patərn) *n.* 1. a decorative design arranged in a regular manner. 2. a thing or person to be copied.

pause (pôz) *n.* a temporary ceasing of speech or action; rest. —*vb.* **paus·ing, paused.** to make a short stop.

pa·vil·ion (pə'vilyən) *n.* 1. an ornamental building used for exhibitions, concerts, etc. 2. one of a collection of connected buildings forming part of a complex, e.g. a hospital.

paw (pô) *n.* the foot of an animal with claws.

pawn[1] (pôn) *vb.* to deposit (something) as security for money borrowed. —*n.* the state of being pledged for money: *my watch is in pawn.*

pawn[2] (pôn) *n.* 1. one of the sixteen pieces of the lowest value in the game of chess. 2. a person who is used as a tool by another without consideration for his fate or rights.

pay (pā) *vb.* **pay·ing, paid.** 1. to give money in return for goods or services, as a reward, etc. 2. to yield profit or advantage: *it pays to be careful.* 3. to make (a call, visit, etc.). —*n.* salary; wages. —**pay·ment** *n.*

pea (pē) *n.* 1. a small, round, green seed that is eaten as a vegetable. 2. the climbing plant on which peas grow.

peace (pēs) *n.* 1. freedom from war or civil disturbance. 2. state of quiet, stillness, calm, or tranquillity. —'**peace·ful** *adj.* —'**peace·ful·ly** *adv.*

peach (pēch) *n.* a sweet, juicy, velvety-skinned fruit, yellow and red in color, with a rough stone inside.

pea·cock ('pēkok) *n.* the male peafowl. It is a large bird with splendid feathers and a tail that can be spread out like a fan.

peacock

peak (pēk) *n.* 1. a high point: *a mountain peak.* 2. the highest level: *the peak of his achievements.* 3. the projecting front of a cap.

pear (peər) *n.* a sweet juicy fruit that has a smooth yellow, green, or brownish skin and a shape that is wide at one end and tapers toward the stalk.

pearl (pûrl) *n.* a smooth rounded object, lustrous white or gray, formed within the shell of an oyster and valued as a gem. —'**pearl·y** *adj.* **pearl·i·er, pearl·i·est.**

peas·ant ('pezənt) *n.* a country person who owns or rents a small farm or works on one for wages.

peat (pēt) *n.* decayed vegetable matter that is found in marshy regions and is dug up and dried for use as fuel and to improve garden soil.

peb·ble ('pebəl) *n.* a small rounded stone, esp. one worn smooth by water.

peck (pek) *vb.* 1. to strike or pick up with the beak: *Jane's parrot pecked me.* 2. to eat small quantities without enjoyment: *Stan pecked at his meal.* 3. to give a hasty kiss. —*n.* 1. a stroke with the beak. 2. a hasty kiss.

pe·cu·liar (pi'kyoolyər) *adj.* 1. strange or unaccustomed. 2. special; distinctive: *a book of peculiar interest.* **pe·cu·li·ar·i·ty** (pikyoolē'aritē) *n., pl.* **pe·cu·li·ar·i·ties.** odd or distinctive features.

ped·al ('pedəl) *n.* 1. a lever pressed by the foot in order to drive a machine. 2. a foot-operated lever on a musical instrument, e.g. a piano. —*vb.* to operate a pedal.

ped·dle ('pedəl) *vb.* **ped·dling, ped·dled.** to take small goods from place to place, offering them for sale. **ped·dler** *n.* a person who travels around peddling goods.

pe·des·tri·an (pə'destrēən) *n.* a person who travels on foot. —*adj.* 1. of walkers and walking: *a pedestrian crossing.* 2. dull; commonplace: *the writer's pedestrian style bored me.*

ped·i·gree ('pedəgrē) *n.* a line of ancestors that can be traced: *the dog had a good pedigree.*

peel (pēl) *vb.* to remove skin or bark from (something): *he peeled an orange.* —*n.* the skin of fruit and vegetables.

peep (pēp) *vb.* 1. to look secretly, esp. through a narrow opening: *I peeped through the crack in the door.* 2. to be just showing: *the sun peeped through the mist.* —*n.* a quick look.

peer[1] (pēr) *n.* 1. a person of the same rank or standing; an equal: *his classmates were his peers.* 2. a nobleman.

peer[2] (pēr) *vb.* to look narrowly or closely: *he peered at the page.*

pel·i·can ('peləkən) *n.* a large water bird with a long beak under which is an enormous pouch for storing the fish that it catches.

pel·let ('pelit) *n.* 1. a small hard ball or pill: *he fed food pellets to the goldfish.* 2. a small lead shot used in a gun.

pen[1] (pen) *n.* a slender instrument for writing or drawing with ink. —*vb.* **pen·ning, penned.** to write.

pen[2] (pen) *n.* a small enclosure, esp. one for animals. —*vb.* **pen·ning, penned.** to confine within a small space.

pedal

pe·nal ('pēnəl) *adj.* concerned with punishment, esp. legal punishment. **'pe·nal·ize** *vb.* **pe·nal·iz·ing, pe·nal·ized.** to impose a penalty or punishment. **pen·al·ty** ('penəltē) *n.,pl.* **pen·al·ties.** 1. a punishment enforced because of the breaking of the law or a rule or agreement. 2. (in games) a free shot, kick, etc., awarded to one side if the other breaks the rules.

pen·cil ('pensəl) *n.* 1. an instrument for writing or drawing, usu. consisting of a core of graphite, crayon etc., enclosed in a thin tube of wood. 2. anything shaped like a pencil. —*vb.* to write, draw, or mark with a pencil.

pendulum

pen·du·lum ('penjələm) *n.* a weight hung from a fixed point by a string, rod, etc., so that it swings freely to and fro. Pendulums are sometimes used as part of a clock's mechanism.

pen·e·trate ('penitrāt) *vb.* **pen·e·trat·ing, pen·e·trat·ed.** to pierce or force a way into: *the enemy penetrated beyond our defenses.* —**pen·e·tra·ble** ('penitrəbəl) *adj.* —**pen·e'tra·tion** *n.*

pen·guin ('peñggwin) *n.* a flightless black and white sea bird found only in the southern hemisphere. They are good swimmers and feed on fish.

pen·i·cil·lin (peni'silin) *n.* a powerful drug that is made from a type of mold and is widely used by doctors to kill harmful bacteria.

pen·in·su·la (pə'ninsələ, pə'ninsyələ) *n.* a piece of land jutting out from a larger mass of land and almost completely surrounded by water: *most of Florida is a peninsula.* —**pen'in·su·lar** *adj.*

pen·sion ('penshən) *n.* a regular payment of money from a former employer or the government to a person who has stopped working because of old age or illness. —*vb.* (often + *off*) to cause to retire.

peo·ple ('pēpəl) *n.* 1. all the persons making up a community, nation, or race: *the American people.* 2. human beings in general. —*vb.* **peo·pling, peo·pled.** to stock with human beings.

pep·per ('pepər) *n.* 1. a seasoning for food obtained from the dried berries of certain plants, either used whole (**pep·per·corns**) or ground into powder. 2. the red or green fruit of the capsicum plant. —*vb.* 1. to sprinkle, or spray: *he peppered the wall with gunshot.* —**'pep·per·y** *adj.*

pep·per·mint ('pepərmint) *n.* 1. a plant cultivated for its strong-tasting oil. 2. candy flavored with this oil.

per·ceive (pər'sēv) *vb.* **per·ceiv·ing, per·ceived.** 1. to become aware of (something) through the senses. 2. to understand: *I perceived what he was trying to tell us.* **per·cep·tion** (pər'sepshən) *n.* understanding.

per cent (pər 'sent) (often represented by the symbol %) one hundredth part: *three per cent of $100 is $3.* **per'cent·age** *n.* a rate or amount per hundred.

perch (pûrch) *n.* 1. a bar or rod on which birds alight. 2. any high seat or position. —*vb.* to settle or rest in some high place.

per·cus·sion (pər'kushən) *n.* 1. the class of musical instruments that make a sound by striking or clashing together. 2. the effect of hitting together two hard objects.

per·en·ni·al (pə'renēəl) *adj.* 1. lasting for a long time. 2. (of plants) living for more than two years. —*n.* a perenniel plant. —**per'en·ni·al·ly** *adv.*

per·fect *adj.* ('pûrfikt) absolutely without fault; beyond improvement. **perfect tense** the construction of a verb expressing an act completed, e.g. *I have returned.* —*vb.* (pər'fekt) to make perfect. —**per'fec·tion** *n.* —**'per·fect·ly** *adv.*

per·form (pər'fôrm) *vb.* 1. to do. 2. to act in a play, sing, or play music, etc. **per'for·mance** *n.* 1. a theatrical or musical entertainment. 2. the act of doing or fulfilling.

per·fume *n.* ('pûrfyōōm, pər'fyōōm) 1. a pleasant smelling liquid. 2. a sweet smell: *the perfume of flowers.* —*vb.* (pər'fyōōm) **per·fum·ing, per·fumed.** to give a pleasant smell to.

pe·ri·od ('pērēəd) *n.* 1. a stage or portion of time. 2. a mark of punctuation (·) used at the end of a sentence, in abbreviations, and elsewhere. **pe·ri·od·i·cal** (pērē'odikəl) *n.* a magazine or other publication that appears at regular intervals. *adj.* (also **pe·ri·od·ic**) happening or appearing at intervals of time. —**pe·ri'od·i·cal·ly** *adv.*

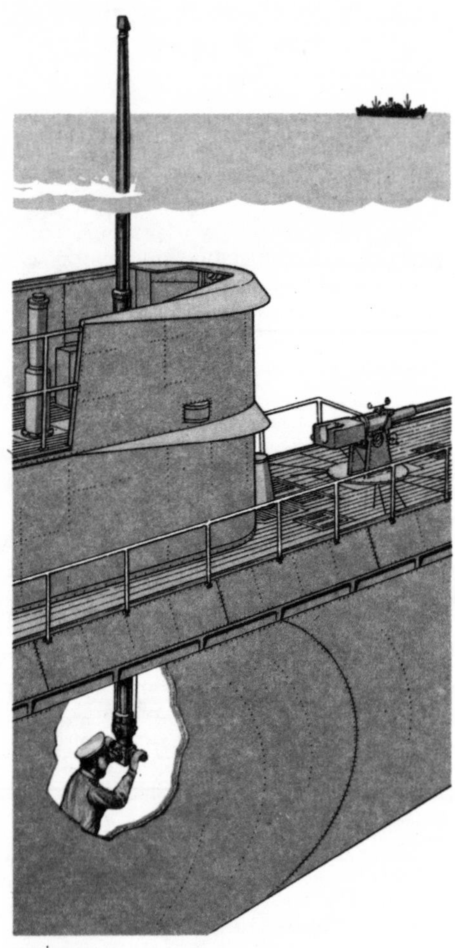
periscope

per·i·scope ('periskōp) *n.* a tube with an arrangement of mirrors or prisms for looking at objects above the direct line of vision, e.g. in a submarine.

per·ish ('perish) *vb.* 1. to die: *the crew perished when the ship sank.* 2. to decay; rot: *the rubber tubes had perished in the heat.* **'per·ish·a·ble** *adj.* liable to decay. *n.* usu. **per·ish·a·bles** (*pl.*) food that is liable to decay.

per·ma·nent ('pûrmənənt) *adj.* remaining or intended to remain for an indefinite period; everlasting. —**'per·ma·nence** *n.* —**'per·ma·nent·ly** *adv.*

per·mit *vb.* (pər'mit) **per·mit·ting, per·mit·ted.** to allow. —*n.* ('pûrmit) an official document allowing a person to do something: *you will need a permit to visit the bird sanctuary.* **per'mis·sion** *n.* consent granted to do something. **per'mis·sive** *adj.* 1. granting permission. 2. allowing great freedom of action and behavior. —**per'mis·sive·ly** *adv.*

per·pen·dic·u·lar (pûrpən'dikyələr) *adj.* 1. straight up and down: *perpendicular walls.* 2. set at right angles to a line or surface. —*n.* a line that forms a right angle with another line or surface. —**per·pen'dic·u·lar·ly** *adv.*

per·pet·u·al (pər'pechōōəl) *adj.* lasting forever without stopping or changing. —**per'pet·u·al·ly** *adv.*

per·se·vere (pûrsə'vēr) *vb.* **per·se·ver·ing, per·se·vered.** to continue steadily with an activity despite discouragement or difficulties. —**per·se'ver·ance** *n.*

per·sist (pər'sist) *vb.* 1. to continue with a course of action despite opposition or warning. 2. to last; survive: *belief in magic still persists.* —**per'sist·ence** *n.* —**per'sist·ent** *adj.* —**per'sist·ent·ly** *adv.*

per·son ('pûrsən) *n.* 1. a single human being. 2. the living body of a human being: *she had no money on her person.* **'per·son·al** *adj.* relating to, belonging to, or coming from a particular person; private: *do not interfere in my personal affairs.* **'per·son·al·ly** *adv.* 1. done by a particular person, not a substitute: *he saw to the matter personally.* 2. as far as oneself is concerned: *personally, I believe we should go ahead.* **per·son'al·i·ty** *n.,pl.* **per·son·al·i·ties.** 1. the impression made on others of all the aspects of a person's character: *she has a very pleasant personality.* 2. a well-known person: *a television personality.*

per·son·nel (pûrsə'nel) *n.* the body of people engaged in some particular work or activity, e.g. the workers in an office.

per·spec·tive (pər'spektiv) *n.* 1. the art of drawing to give the appearance of depth and distance. 2. a view or viewpoint: *take a look at the problem from a different perspective.*

per·spire (pər'spīər) *vb.* **per·spir·ing, per·spired.** to sweat. **per·spi·ra·tion** (pûrspə'rāshən) *n.* 1. sweat. 2. the act of sweating.

per·suade (pər'swād) *vb.* **per·suad·ing, per·suad·ed.** to convince or win over to a point of view, usu. by polite arguments. —**per'sua·sion** *n.* —**per'sua·sive** *adj.*

pes·si·mist ('pesəmist) *n.* a person who always looks on the gloomy side, convinced that the worst will always happen. —**'pes·si·mism** *n.* —**pes·si'mis·ti·cal·ly** *adv.*

pet (pet) *n.* 1. a tame animal kept as company. 2. a spoiled or favorite child. —*adj.* 1. tame: *a pet squirrel.* 2. favorite: *the scientist proved his pet theory.* —*vb.* **pet·ting, pet·ted.** to treat as a pet; cuddle and stroke.

pet·al ('petəl) *n.* one of the usu. colored leaflike parts of a flower.

pe·ti·tion (pə'tishən) *n.* a formal request addressed to a court, employer, or other authority, asking for a reform or favor. —*vb.* 1. to present a petition. 2. to ask.

pe·tro·le·um (pə'trōlēəm) *n.* a flammable black oily liquid obtained by drilling deep into the earth and used, when refined, as a fuel for heating, automobiles, etc.

pet·ti·coat ('petēkōt) *n.* a garment worn by women under an outer skirt, dress, etc.

pet·ty ('petē) *adj.* **pet·ti·er, pet·ti·est.** 1. minor; unimportant. 2. spiteful in a narrow-minded way: *he can be very petty over small matters.*

pew (pyōō) *n.* a long seat or bench in a church.

phan·tom ('fantəm) *n.* 1. a ghost. 2. anything that appears to exist but does not really.

phase (fāz) *n.* 1. a stage in development or growth: *my children went through a very rebellious phase.* 2. the shape and appearance of the moon at a given time. —*vb.* **phas·ing, phased.** 1. to separate (a plan, activity, etc.) into its different stages: *the government phased the introduction of the new plans.* 2. (+ *out*) to do away with or get rid of gradually.

pheas·ant ('fezənt) *n.* a large bird with a long tail that is hunted for sport and for food. The male birds have brightly colored feathers.

pho·to·graph ('fōtəgraf) *n.* often **pho·to** ('fōtō), *pl.* **pho·tos.** a picture made by recording the action of light on a specially prepared film or plate. —*vb.* to take a picture of (something) with a camera. **pho·tog·ra·phy** (fə'togrəfē) *n.* art of making pictures with a camera. —**pho·to'graph·ic** *adj.*

phrase (frāz) *n.* 1. a group of words forming part of a sentence, e.g. *in the boat* in the sentence *six men sat in the boat.* 2. (music) a group of notes.

phys·i·cal ('fizikəl) *adj.* 1. of the body: *he suffers from poor physical health.* 2. of or concerning material things, forces, etc.: *what are the physical characteristics of this metal?* 3. of nature: *the mountain was the chief physical feature of the area.* —'**phys·i·cal·ly** *adv.*

phy·si·cian (fi'zishən) *n.* a doctor.

phys·ics ('fiziks) *sing.n.* the science of energy and matter that deals with the nature of light, heat, motion, electricity, etc. '**phys·i·cist** *n.* a person who studies physics.

piano

pi·an·o (pē'anō) *n.,pl.* **pi·an·os.** a large musical instrument. The player produces sounds by pressing keys that cause small felt-covered hammers to strike metal strings. —**pi·an·ist** (pē'anist, 'pēənist) *n.*

pic·co·lo ('pikəlō) *n., pl.* **pic·co·los.** a small type of FLUTE producing notes of a higher pitch than an ordinary flute.

pick[1] (pik) *vb.* 1. to choose. 2. to poke or probe, esp. with the fingers or a sharp pointed tool: *she picked at the threads to untangle them.* 3. to gather, esp. by hand. 4. to open (a lock) without a key. 5. to start (a fight) on purpose.

pick[2] (pik) *n.* a large tool having a heavy curved metal head with pointed ends, used for breaking up stones, concrete, etc.

pick·et ('pikit) *n.* 1. a striker or group of strikers, parading or standing outside a place of work to persuade other workers to join a strike, to call attention to complaints, persuade the public not to do business with the company, etc. 2. a stake driven into the ground, esp. part of a fence. —*vb.* to act as a picket (def. 1).

pick·le ('pikəl) *vb.* **pick·ling, pick·led.** to preserve (food) in vinegar or salt water. —*n.* 1. often **pick·les** (*pl.*) vegetables, esp. cucumbers, pickled and used as a condiment. 2. (informal) a difficult situation.

pic·nic ('piknik) *n.* an outing that includes a meal eaten out of doors, usu. in the country, for fun. —*vb.* **pic·nick·ing, pic·nicked.** to take part in a picnic.

pic·ture ('pikchər) *n.* 1. a drawing, painting, or photograph representing a person or thing. 2. an image seen on a television or motion-picture screen. 3. a type or symbol: *Tom is the picture of happiness.* —*vb.* 1. to describe (something) in words. 2. to imagine. **pic·to·ri·al** (pik'tôrēəl) *adj.* of or like pictures. **pic·tur·esque** (pikchə'resk) *adj.* pretty or interesting enough to be the subject of a picture.

piece (pēs) *n.* 1. a part, portion, or fragment. 2. a literary, artistic, or musical composition. 3. an individual thing that is part of a set or large number: *a chess piece.* —*vb.* **piec·ing, pieced.** (often + *together*) to join up scattered fragments, clues, etc., to make a whole.

pier (pēr) *n.* 1. a structure extending into the water at the shore, used esp. as a landing place for boats. 2. a pillar supporting a bridge, jetty, etc.

pierce (pērs) *vb.* **pierc·ing, pierced.** to make a hole in or through. '**pierc·ing** *adj.* 1. perceptive: *he gave her a piercing stare.* 2. penetrating: *a piercing scream.*

pig·eon ('pijən) *n.* a common bird of the dove family. Tame pigeons are often used for racing.

pig·eon·hole ('pijənhōl) *n.* a small boxlike compartment of a desk, used for storing documents. —*vb.* **pig·eon·hol·ing, pig·eon·holed.** 1. to classify: *the boy was pigeonholed as a trouble-maker.* 2. to put off or postpone.

pig·my ('pigmē) *n.,pl.* **pig·mies.** See PYGMY.

pike (pīk) *n.* a large green freshwater fish with long jaws and very sharp teeth.

pile[1] (pīl) *n.* 1. a heap. 2. (informal) a very large amount, esp. of money. —*vb.* **pil·ing, piled.** (often + *on* or *up*) to heap up.

pile[2] (pīl) *n.* the thick fibers on the surface of velvet, carpeting, etc.

pil·grim ('pilgrim) *n.* 1. a person who travels to a holy place as an act of religious devotion. 2. **Pilgrim** one of the people who left England and settled in America in 1620. '**pil·grim·age** *n.* a pilgrim's journey.

pill (pil) *n.* a small tablet of medicine, usu. made to be swallowed whole.

pil·lar ('pilər) *n.* a tall column supporting a building or standing as a monument.

pil·low ('pilō) *n.* a soft cushion used to support the head of someone who is asleep or resting.

pi·lot ('pīlət) *n.* a person who guides a ship, airplane, or spacecraft. —*vb.* to act as a pilot.

pin·cers ('pinsərz) *n.* (*pl.* or *sing.*) 1. a tool for gripping and pulling or twisting: *she pulled the rusty nails from the plank with pincers.* 2. the claws of crabs, lobsters, etc.

pinch (pinch) *vb.* to nip or squeeze painfully, esp. between finger and thumb. —*n.* 1. a squeeze; sharp pressure. 2. the amount that can be held between finger and thumb: *a pinch of salt.* **pinched** *adj.* ill-looking.

pigeon

pine[1] (pīn) *n.* a widespread, hardy, evergreen tree with needle-shaped leaves, whose wood is used for telegraph poles, building, etc. —*adj.* made of pinewood.

pine[2] (pīn) *vb.* **pin·ing, pined.** 1. to suffer because of sorrow or illness. 2. to long for (something): *I pine for sunshine in winter.*

pineapple

pine·ap·ple ('pīnapəl) *n.* 1. the large sweet juicy fruit of a tropical plant, with a rough skin and yellow flesh. 2. the plant producing this fruit.

pin·na·cle ('pinəkəl) *n.* 1. a tall pointed structure on a building. 2. a natural rock formation with a similar shape. 3. the highest point: *the pinnacle of achievement.*

pint (pīnt) *n.* a liquid measure equal to one eighth of a gallon or 16 fluid ounces.

pi·o·neer (pīə'nēr) *n.* 1. a person who explores and settles in new territory. 2. a person who develops new fields of research methods, etc.

pipe (pīp) *n.* 1. a tube of metal, glass etc., used for carrying fluids or gas. 2. a wooden or clay tube with a little bowl at one end used for smoking tobacco. 3. a tubelike musical instrument played by blowing into the end. —*vb.* **pip·ing, piped.** 1. to play a pipe. 2. to send (oil, water, etc.) through a pipe. **'pip·ing** *n.* 1. the sound of pipe-playing, birdsong, etc. 2. a narrow cord or strip used as decoration on clothes, furniture, etc.

pipe·line ('pīplīn) *n.* a long continuous line of pipes transporting something a great distance, e.g. oil from a desert oilwell.

pi·rate ('pīrət) *n.* 1. a robber who plunders ships at sea. 2. a person who illegally takes over another's rights of trading, manufacturing, broadcasting, etc. —*vb.* **pi·rat·ing, pi·rat·ed.** to publish illegally a version of another's writings, records, etc. —**'pi·ra·cy** *n.*

pis·til ('pistəl) *n.* the seed-bearing part of a flower.

pis·tol ('pistəl) *n.* a small gun held in one hand for firing.

pis·ton ('pistən) *n.* a metal cylinder that fits closely inside a tube in which it moves backward and forward, producing motion in car engines, pumps, etc.

pit (pit) *n.* 1. a hole dug in the earth. 2. an open mine for chalk, gravel, etc. 3. a natural hollow in the body or skin, e.g. armpit. 4. an area sunk below that of the surroundings. —*vb.* **pit·ting, pit·ted.** 1. to make holes or dents (in something). 2. (+ *against*) to set or match against: *the wrestlers pitted their strength against each other.*

pitch[1] (pich) *vb.* 1. to toss; throw. 2. to set up (a tent, camp, etc.). 3. to plunge violently forward: *the boat capsized and they were pitched into the sea.* 4. to set the TONE of a sound: *can you pitch your voice a little higher?*—*n.* 1. a throw or way of throwing in some sports, e.g. baseball. 2. a degree or extent: *we were in a high pitch of excitement.* 3. the highness or lowness of a tone, esp. in music.

pitch[2] (pich) *n.* a sticky black substance made from tar and used to waterproof roofs, ships' decks, etc.

pit·fall ('pitfôl) *n.* a hidden trap or danger.

pith (pith) *n.* 1. a spongy material in the center of the stems of some plants. 2. a similar white tissue under the skins of some fruits, e.g. oranges. 3. the essential part: *the pith of her argument.* **'pith·y** *adj.* **pith·i·er, pith·i·est.** 1. of or like pith. 2. brief and to the point.

pit·y ('pitē) *n.,pl.* **pit·ies.** 1. a feeling of sympathy for those in trouble. 2. something to be regretted. —*vb.* **pit·y·ing, pit·ied.** to feel sympathy for (someone in distress). **'pit·i·ful** *adj.* 1. arousing pity. 2. arousing scorn: *pitiful cowardice.* —**'pit·i·ful·ly** *adv.*

place (plās) *n.* 1. a particular position; area of space. 2. one's home. 3. a position or rank: *an important place in history.* 4. duty; job: *its not my place to criticize.* —*vb.* **plac·ing, placed.** 1. to put or be in a particular spot or position. 2. to identify: *I can't place her, but I have seen her somewhere else.*

plac·id ('plasid) *adj.* calm; serene. —**'plac·id·ly** *adv.* —**'plac·id·ness** *n.*

plague (plāg) *n.* 1. a very serious infectious disease, causing widespread deaths, esp. in the Middle Ages. 2. a persistent nuisance: *a plague of mosquitoes.* —*vb.* **pla·guing, plagued.** to annoy repeatedly.

plain (plān) *adj.* 1. clear; easy to understand or see: *I made it plain that I was cross.* 2. undecorated; simple: *a plain gray dress.* 3. of no great beauty, luxury, or richness. —*n.* a flat stretch of land without hills or valleys. —**'plain·ly** *adv.* —**'plain·ness** *n.*

plait (plāt, plat) *n.* three strands of rope, straw, etc., woven into one thick strand; a braid. —*vb.* to weave or twist into a plait.

plan (plan) *n.* 1. a method of doing or achieving something that is worked out beforehand; scheme. 2. often **plans** (*pl.*) a large-scale diagram or detailed drawing of the layout or design of a house, etc. —*vb.* **planning, planned.** 1. to make a plan or plans. 2. to intend. 3. to design.

plane (plān) *n.* 1. a completely level surface. 2. a standard of achievement or a stage of development: *his work often reached a very high plane. 3. an* AIRPLANE. 4. a tool for smoothing wood by scraping off very thin layers. —*vb.* **plan·ing, planed.** to smooth with a plane.

plane

plan·et ('planit) *n.* a celestial object orbiting around a star and made visible only by reflecting starlight. **plan·et·oid** ('planitoid) *n.* (also **minor planet**) a small planet.

plank (plangk) *n.* a long narrow piece of sawn wood. —*vb.* to cover with planks.

plank·ton ('plaŋktən) *pl.n.* tiny plants and animals that float in the sea or fresh water.

plant (plant) *n.* 1. a living organism that manufactures food from air, water, and soil, using sunlight. Unlike most animals, a plant does not move about and has no nervous system. 2. a complete set of equipment including machinery, instruments, etc., esp. for a factory. 3. a factory. 4. a person or thing put in a place to deceive or trick: *Bob claimed that the stolen goods found in his garage were a plant, put there by someone who hated him.* —*vb.* 1. to set a plant, seed, bulb, etc., in the soil to grow. 2. to set down firmly; establish: *she planted herself near the entrance.* 3. to place a person or object to serve as a plant (def. 3): *detectives were planted in the crowd.* **plan'ta·tion** *n.* 1. an area planted with trees. 2. a large farm or estate on which single crops such as tea, sugar, or cotton are cultivated, often employing resident workers.

plas·ter ('plastər) *n.* 1. a combination of lime, sand, and water used to give walls a smooth surface. 2. bandages soaked in a white paste that sets hard to form a cast to keep broken limbs in a fixed position. 3. a pasty medicine applied to the body for curing: *a mustard plaster.* —*vb.* 1. to cover with plaster. 2. to cover over with: *his boots were plastered with mud.*

plas·tic ('plastik) *n.* a manmade substance that can be easily shaped when hot. —*adj.* 1. able to be shaped. 2. made of plastic.

plate (plāt) *n.* 1. a flat dish on which food is eaten or served. 2. a sheet or thin smooth piece (of metal, glass, etc.). 3. an illustration in a printed book. 4. a structure for supporting false teeth or correcting badly positioned teeth. 5. silver and gold covered objects, esp. cutlery and household articles. —*vb.* **plat·ing, plat·ed.** to coat with metal.

pla·teau (pla'tō) *n.,pl.* **pla·teaus** *or* **pla·teaux** (pla'tōz). a flat expanse of land raised above the surrounding country.

plat·form ('platfôrm) *n.* 1. a raised area of floor. 2. the part of a railroad station next to which trains stop.

plat·i·num ('platənəm, 'platnəm) *n.* a precious metal that looks like silver and is used for making watch parts and jewelry. Chemical symbol: Pt.

play (plā) *vb.* 1. to amuse oneself. 2. to take part in (a game or sport). 3. to compete against (someone) in a game or sport. 4. to produce sound from: *will you play your violin?* 5. to act as: *who is playing Cinderella?* 6. to have one's turn (at a game). —*n.* 1. a story written for the theater; drama. 2. the act or activity of playing. 3. scope for freedom of movement and development: *he gave free play to his fears.*

plea (plē) *n.* 1. an appeal or earnest entreaty. 2. an excuse: *she made the plea that she had too much work to do and could not come out.* 3. a statement in a court of law: *he changed his plea to "guilty".*

plead (plēd) *vb.* **plead·ing, plead·ed, plead** (pled), *or* **pled.** 1. to beg; implore. 2. to give as an excuse. 3. to enter a plea in a legal proceeding: *do you plead guilty or not guilty?*

pleas·ant ('plezənt) *adj.* 1. enjoyable. 2. agreeable; likable.

please (plēz) *vb.* **pleas·ing, pleased.** 1. to give pleasure to; make happy. 2. to choose or desire: *he does as he pleases.* —*adv.* kindly; if you please.

pleas·ure ('plezhər) *n.* 1. a feeling of deep enjoyment. 2. anything causing pleasure. —**'pleas·ur·a·ble** *adj.* —**'pleas·ur·a·bly** *adv.*

pleat (plēt) *n.* a flat fold made by doubling cloth and then fastening it, e.g. by stitching. —*vb.* to make pleats in.

plen·ty ('plentē) *n.* 1. a large quantity; good supply: *we have plenty of food for the winter.* 2. riches: *the good harvest gave the farmers a feeling of plenty.* —**'plen·ti·ful** *adj.*

pleat

pli·ers ('plīərz) *pl.n.* a TOOL for gripping, bending, and cutting.

plod (plod) *vb.* **plod·ding, plod·ded.** to walk with a slow heavy regular tread. **'plod·der** *n.* 1. a person who plods. 2. a person who works hard but slowly: *he is a plodder but his work is always good.*

plot[1] (plot) *n.* 1. a secret plan: *the Gunpowder Plot.* 2. the main story (of a book, film, etc.). —*vb.* **plot·ting, plot·ted.** 1. to make a plot. 2. to plan (something) secretly. 3. to record on a chart or graph: *he plotted the ship's progress.*

plot[2] (plot) *n.* a small area of land: *she made a vegetable garden on a plot behind the house.*

plow (plou) *also* **plough** *n.* 1. a farming implement used for making furrows in the earth before sowing seed. 2. a machine for clearing a way through snow. —*vb.* 1. to use a plow on (land). 2. to move heavily or with difficulty: *he plowed through the math problems.*

pluck (pluk) *vb.* 1. to pull sharply or pick. 2. to remove feathers from (birds). —*n.* (informal) bravery.

plug (plug) *n.* 1. something used to close a hole. 2. a pronged object used for connecting an electrical appliance to the power supply. —*vb.* **plug·ging, plugged.** 1. to stop up by means of a plug. 2. (informal) to recommend or advertise heavily: *they're plugging the new record on the radio stations.* 3. (+ *in*) to connect (an electrical appliance) to a power supply.

plum (plum) *n.* the fruit of the plum tree, which can be purple, red, orange, or yellow in color, with sweet edible flesh and a hard flat stone.

plumb·er ('plumər) *n.* a person whose job is to fit and repair the water and drainage pipes and the equipment associated with them.

plume (plo͞om) *n.* 1. a large fluffy feather, esp. when worn as a decoration. 2. a feather-like streak, e.g. of smoke.

plump (plump) *adj.* rounded; fat in a pleasing way. —*vb.* (+ *up*) to make nicely rounded: *she plumped up the cushions.*

plunge (plunj) *vb.* **plung·ing, plunged.** to move violently and suddenly in some direction: *Sarah plunged into the swimming pool to cool off after cutting the lawn.* —*n.* the act of plunging.

plu·ral ('plo͝orəl) *adj.* of or expressing more than one; not singular. —*n.* the plural grammatical form: *fungi is the plural of fungus.*

pneu·mo·nia (nə'mōnyə, no͞o'mōnyə, nyo͞o'mōnyə) *n.* a serious disease, caused by a bacterium, in which the lungs become inflamed, making breathing difficult.

poach[1] (pōch) *vb.* to steal game, e.g. rabbits, pheasants, salmon, etc., from land, a stretch of river, etc., owned by someone else.

poach[2] (pōch) *vb.* to cook in gently boiling liquid.

pock·et ('pokit) *n.* 1. a small pouch or bag, esp. one attached to a garment for holding small objects. 2. a small area that is different in some way from that surrounding it: *there are pockets of sand between the rocks.* —*vb.* to put in one's pocket: *don't pocket that pen—it's mine!*

pod (pod) *n.* the small case that contains the seeds of such plants as peas, beans, etc. —*vb.* **pod·ding, pod·ded.** 1. to develop pods. 2. to remove from the pod.

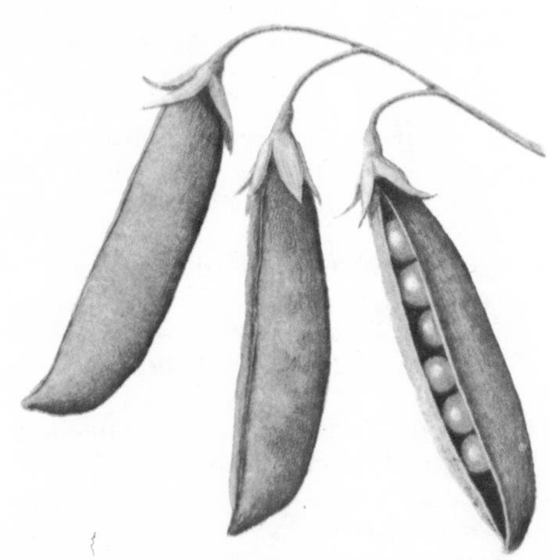
pod

po·em ('pōəm) *n.* an arrangement of words using rhythm, imaginative forms of expression, and sometimes rhyme, to convey an important idea or intensely felt experience often in a relatively short space. **'po·et** *n.* a writer of poetry. **po·et·ic** (pō'etik) *or* **po'et·i·cal** *adj.* relating to, like, or suitable for a poem. **'po·et·ry** *n.* 1. the art and practice of writing poems. 2. poems in general.

point (point) *n.* 1. a sharp end or tip: *the point of a needle.* 2. a dot, esp. in punctuation or expressing decimals. 3. a specific position on a scale, course, compass, etc.: *a good starting point.* 4. a time or moment: *we were interrupted at that point.* 5. an argument or opinion: *the speaker made several good points.* 6. a basic essential: *did you get the point of the joke?* 7. purpose or use: *there's no point in continuing.* 8. a narrow strip of land jutting into the sea, a lake, etc. 9. a unit used in counting, scoring, or rating. —*vb.* to aim or direct; indicate or show position or direction by stretching out a hand and forefinger. **'point·ed** *adj.* 1. having a point. 2. (of remarks) deliberately wounding; meaningful. **'point·less** *adj.* useless; futile.

poi·son ('poizən) *n.* a substance that injures or kills plants or animals. —*vb.* 1. to give poison to. 2. to kill with poison. —**'poi·son·ous** *adj.*

pok·er[1] ('pōkər) *n.* a metal rod used for moving lighted coals in a fire.

pok·er[2] ('pōkər) *n.* a card game in which the players make bets on the value of the cards in their hands.

po·lar ('pōlər) *adj.* of or relating to a pole, esp. the North or South Pole.

po·lar bear a very large shaggy coated white bear that lives in the regions of the North Pole.

pole[1] (pōl) *n.* a long straight rod of metal, wood, etc.

pole[2] (pōl) *n.* 1. either end of the axis about which the earth rotates, i.e. the North Pole and South Pole. 2. either terminal of a magnet. 3. either end of the terminals in a battery.

po·lice (pə'lēs) *pl.n.* an organization of men and women responsible for seeing that the law is obeyed and for preventing crime and violence. —*vb.* **po·lic·ing, po·liced.** to guard, regulate, or control.

pol·i·cy ('polisē) *n.,pl.* **pol·i·cies.** 1. a plan of action or declaration of principles and aims, esp. by an institution or government: *the government's policy was not to interfere.* 2. a written contract of insurance: *he has a policy with his insurance company that covers medical costs.*

pol·ish ('polish) *vb.* 1. to make shiny by rubbing. 2. to make elegant or stylish: *the president polished his speech.* —*n.* 1. shine; glossiness. 2. material used to produce a shine: *boot polish.* 3. elegance or refinement.

po·lite (pə'līt) *adj.* having or showing good manners; courteous and considerate: *Alan was always very polite when people visited his home.* —**po'lite·ly** *adv.*

pol·i·tics ('politiks) *sing.* or *pl.n.* 1. the work, management, or structure of a government or political party. 2. the tactics and schemes involved in the management of power: *business politics is often complicated.* 3. political opinions or beliefs: *what are your politics?* **po·lit·i·cal** (pə'litikəl) *adj.* 1. relating to the affairs of government. 2. relating to the organization or management of any kind of power. **pol·i·ti·cian** (poli'tishən) *n.* a person directly involved in the government of a country, esp. as a member of a political party. —**po'lit·i·cal·ly** *adv.*

pol·len ('polən) *n.* the fine, usu. yellow powder produced by flowering plants and carried by the wind, birds, insects, etc., to fertilize plants of the same species. **'pol·li·nate** *vb.* **pol·li·nat·ing, pol·li·nat·ed.** to fertilize with pollen. —**pol'li'na·tion** *n.*

pol·lute (pə'lo͞ot) *vb.* **pol·lut·ing, pol·lut·ed.** to make impure or dirty: *the factory polluted the river with chemicals.* —**pol'lu·tion** *n.*

pom·e·gran·ate ('poməgranit) *n.* a reddish fruit, the size of an orange, with a hard rind covering a mass of seeds in an edible semi-sweet jelly.

pomegranate

pomp (pomp) *n.* splendid ceremonious display: *the royal wedding was an*

ponies

Australian Waler

Appaloosa

Exmoor

Highland

occasion of very great pomp. **'pomp·ous** *adj.* self-important and full of one's own dignity.

pond (pond) *n.* a pool of still water smaller than a lake.

po·ny ('pōnē) *n.,pl.* **po·nies.** a horse of a small breed.

pool[1] (po͞ol) *n.* 1. a puddle. 2. a small pond. 3. a deep part of a river. 4. a large tank of water for swimming in, diving into, etc.

pool[2] (po͞ol) *n.* 1. an arrangement by which resources are combined and shared: *a typing pool.* 2. a form of billiards. 3. the total amount bet by a group of gamblers that is paid to the winner or winners at the outcome of an event; lottery. —*vb.* to combine resources.

poor (po͝oər) *adj.* 1. not rich; needy. 2. unfortunate; pitiful. 3. inferior; not good: *the meal was poor.* —**'poor·ly** *adv.*

pope (pōp) *n.* the head of the Roman Catholic Church.

pop·py ('popē) *n.,pl.* **pop·pies.** a plant that grows wild and in gardens and has red, yellow, or pink flowers.

pop·u·lar ('popyələr) *adj.* 1. liked and appreciated by many people: *a popular lecturer.* 2. of, for, or in connection with the majority of people: *the book appealed to popular taste.* —**pop·u'lar·i·ty** *n.* —**'pop·u·lar·ly** *adv.*

pop·u·la·tion (popyə'lāshən) *n.* 1. the number of people living in a town, country, etc. 2. people: *the population fled from the earthquake.*

porch (pôrch) *n.* 1. a roofed area or platform attached to a house. 2. a roofed and sometimes enclosed doorway or entrance built onto a house; lobby.

por·cu·pine ('pôrkyəpīn) *n.* a smallish, short-legged animal whose body is covered in spines that it can raise when attacked.

pore (pôr) *n.* a tiny opening in the skin or some other surface through which liquid can pass. —**'por·ous** *adj.*

pork (pôrk) *n.* meat from a pig.

por·poise ('pôrpəs) *n.* a fish-eating MAMMAL like a DOLPHIN.

port[1] (pôrt) *n.* 1. a harbor used for trading or passenger ships. 2. a town or city with a harbor.

port[2] (pôrt) *n.* the left-hand side of a ship or airplane for someone on board facing the bow or nose.

porcupine

port[3] (pôrt) *n.* a sweet strong red or white wine from Portugal.

por·ter (pôrtə) *n.* a person employed to carry goods or baggage.

por·tion ('pôrshən) *n.* a part of a whole. —*vb.* to divide into parts.

por·trait ('pôrtrit) *n.* a painting, photograph, or account that depicts or describes a person or group. **por·tray** (pôr'trā) *vb.* to make a portrait: *the hero is portrayed as a brave man.*

pose (pōz) *vb.* **pos·ing, posed.** 1. to take up a position consciously, esp. when having one's picture taken. 2. to appear to be something that one is not. 3. to state or present a problem or question: *the breakdown posed a great problem for us.* —*n.* 1. a way of sitting or standing. 2. a pretense: *a pose of self-confidence.*

po·si·tion (pə'zishən) *n.* 1. a place: *take up your positions for the parade.* 2. an arrangement, posture, or state of affairs. 3. someone's social status, occupation, rank, or role on a sports team. 4. a point of view; opinion. —*vb.* to put in a particular place.

pos·i·tive ('pozitiv) *adj.* 1. without doubt. 2. self-confident; optimistic. 3. (of a number) greater than zero. 4. (of a photographic print) having the areas of light and dark in their normal relation to one another. 5. having a relatively high electric potential. —*n.* 1. a photographic print showing objects either light or dark, as they appear in nature. 2. an electric charge with a relatively high electric potential. 3. a number greater than zero. —'**pos·i·tive·ly** *adv.*

postmark

pos·sess (pə'zes) *vb.* **pos·sess·ing, pos·sessed.** 1. to have (esp. a personal quality): *she possesses great talent.* 2. to own: *do you possess a watch?* 3. to influence strongly: *he was possessed by a great fear.* —**pos'ses·sion** *n.* **pos'ses·sive** *adj.* 1. jealously guarding one's property. 2. treating other people as if they were one's property. 3. (of a part of speech) expressing the relation of possession, e.g. *his, Jim's.* —**pos'ses·sive·ly** *adv.* —**pos'ses·sive·ness** *n.*

pos·si·ble ('posəbəl) *adj.* 1. capable of being; capable of happening. 2. reasonable; able to be considered: *he is a possible leader for the expedition.* —**pos·si'bil·i·ty** *n.,pl.* **pos·si·bil·i·ties.** —'**pos·si·bly** *adv.*

post[1] (pōst) *n.* a stake of wood or metal placed upright in the ground and used as a support or marker. —*vb.* to put up a public notice: *he posted the announcement on the bulletin board.*

post[2] (pōst) *n.* a job. —*vb.* to send (someone) to a different place in the course of his work, esp. in the armed services.

post[3] (pōst) *vb.* to send a letter or parcel through the mail. '**post·age** *n.* the amount charged for sending an item through the mail. '**post·al** *adj.* of the post office.

post·er ('pōstər) *n.* a large notice, advertisement, or decorative picture, put up in a public place for people to read, or on walls for decoration.

post·mark ('pōstmârk) *n.* a mark stamped at a post office on a letter or parcel, recording the place and time of mailing.

post·pone (pōst'pōn) *vb.* **post·pon·ing, post·poned.** to arrange (something) at a later time than that originally planned: *the tennis match was postponed because of rain.* —**post'pone·ment** *n.*

pos·ture ('poschər) *n.* the characteristic position of a person's body: *she sat in a dignified posture.* —*vb.* **pos·tur·ing, pos·tured.** to pose.

po·ta·to (pə'tātō) *n.,pl.* **po·ta·toes.** the swollen starchy underground stem (tuber) of the potato plant, cultivated as a vegetable and eaten boiled, roasted, fried, etc.

pot·hole ('pothōl) *n.* 1. a small pit in the surface of a road. 2. an underground cave.

pottery

pot·ter·y ('potərē) *n.,pl.* **pot·ter·ies.** 1. vases, pots, bowls, etc., collectively, shaped in moist clay and hardened by baking. 2. the practice or craft of making such vessels. 3. a workshop where such vessels are made. '**pot·ter** *n.* a person who makes pottery.

pouch (pouch) *n.* 1. a small bag; sack. 2. a baglike receptacle like the pocket in which a kangaroo carries its young.

poul·try ('pōltrē) *n.* chickens, turkeys, geese, ducks, and other domestic birds reared for their eggs and flesh.

pound (pound) *n.* 1. a unit for measuring weight, equivalent to 16 ounces. 2. a unit of British currency equivalent to one hundred pence.

pour (pôr) *vb.* 1. to flow or cause to flow in a stream or as if in a stream. 2. to rain steadily and hard.

pout (pout) *vb.* to thrust the lower lip forward in an expression of sympathy, dejection, or displeasure. —*n.* the expression itself.

pov·er·ty ('povərtē) *n.* 1. a lack of money. 2. any lack or deficiency.

pow·der ('poudər) *n.* a dry material of fine particles. —*vb.* 1. to apply fine particles to a surface. 2. to break up into fine particles. —'**pow·der·y** *adj.*

pow·er ('pouər) *n.* 1. ability to act; authority: *the judge had the power to imprison the criminal.* 2. working energy: *a car with little power.* 3. a person or state with strength and influence: *Russia is a world power.* 4. the amount of times a number is multiplied by itself: *3 to the power of 4 is 81* (i.e. $3 \times 3 \times 3 \times 3$). —'**pow·er·ful** *adj.* —'**pow·er·ful·ly** *adv.*

prac·tice ('praktis) *n.* 1. a habit or customary action. 2. the repeated performance of some action as a way of learning or perfecting a skill. 3. a professional person's business: *a doctor's practice.* 4. the act of doing something: *the idea did not work in practice.* —*vb.* **prac·tic·ing, prac·ticed.** 1. to perform some action habitually. 2. to perform some action repeatedly as a way of learning a skill. 3. to be engaged in a profession: *Mary practices law.* **prac·ti·ca·ble** ('praktəkəbəl) *adj.* capable of being done. **'prac·ti·cal** *adj.* 1. concerned with action rather than theory. 2. good at doing things or carrying out ideas. 3. useful; functional. **'prac·ti·cal·ly** *adv.* 1. almost; virtually. 2. in a practical manner.

praise (prāz) *vb.* **prais·ing, praised.** to show approval or admiration of. —*n.* an expression of approval or admiration. —**'praise·wor·thy** *adj.*

prawn (prôn) *n.* one of several kinds of small edible SHELLFISH.

pray (prā) *vb.* 1. to try to communicate through speech or thought with God or other holy beings. 2. to ask earnestly. **pray·er** (preər) *n.* the message of one who prays.

preach (prēch) *vb.* **preach·ing, preached.** 1. to deliver a sermon. 2. to give moral advice in a tedious or patronizing manner.

pre·cau·tion (pri'kôshən) *n.* something done in advance in order to prevent troublesome consequences: *when I go out I take the precaution of locking the door.* —**pre'cau·tion·ar·y** *adj.*

pre·cious ('preshəs) *adj.* of great value.

prec·i·pice ('presəpis) *n.* a high vertical, or nearly vertical, cliff.

pred·a·tor ('predətər) *n.* an animal that lives by hunting and eating other animals. —**'pred·a·to·ry** *adj.*

pre·dict (pri'dikt) *vb.* to tell in advance: *he tried to predict the outcome of the game.* —**pre'dict·a·ble** *adj.* —**pre'dict·a·bly** *adv.* —**pre'dic·tion** *n.*

pre·fer (pri'fûr) *vb.* **pre·fer·ring, pre·ferred.** to like better: *I prefer dogs to cats.* **pref·er·ence** ('prefərəns) *n.* 1. the act of preferring: *I have a preference for jazz.* 2. something chosen because it is liked better: *my preference is skiing.* **pref·er·en·tial** (prefə'renshəl) *adj.* treated with preference.

pre·fix ('prēfiks) *n.* a part of a word placed before a word, and usu. joined to it, to affect its meaning, e.g. *un-* in *unable.* —*vb.* **pre·fix·ing, pre·fixed.** to put before or at the beginning.

preg·nant ('pregnənt) *adj.* 1. (of a woman or female animal) having a child or young developing inside the body. 2. implying more than is expressed: *a glance pregnant with warning.*

pre·his·tor·ic (prēhi'stôrik, prēhi'storik) *adj.* concerning or belonging to a period before the existence of written historical documents. —**pre·his·to·ry** (prē'histərē) *n.*

prej·u·dice ('prejədis) *n.* 1. an opinion formed beforehand without proper consideration; bias. 2. unreasonably hostile feelings or attitudes: *racial prejudice.* 3. damage or harm. —*vb.* **prej·u·dic·ing, prej·u·diced.** 1. to bias the mind of: *they prejudiced her against him.* 2. to injure: *you will prejudice your chances of success.* **prej·u·di·cial** (prejə'dishəl) *adj.* harmful.

pre·mi·um ('prēmēəm) *n.* 1. a reward: *a premium for extra work.* 2. payment for insurance: *what is the annual premium on your car?* 3. great value: *the teacher put a premium on accuracy.*

pre·pare (pri'peər) *vb.* **pre·par·ing, pre·pared.** to make ready. **prep·a·ra·tion** (prepə'rāshən) *n.* 1. the act of preparing. 2. something made ready for a purpose, e.g. a medicine.

prep·o·si·tion (prepə'zishən) *n.* a word placed before a noun or pronoun to show its relationship to another word, e.g. *at* in *Pete stood at the door.*

precipice

pre·scribe (pri'skrīb) *vb.* **pre·scrib·ing, pre·scribed.** to advise or order the use of a particular medicine, treatment, etc. **pre·scrip·tion** (pri'skripshən) *n.* 1. instructions written by a doctor regarding the preparation and use of a medicine. 2. a rule to be followed: *a prescription for success.*

pres·ence ('prezəns) *n.* 1. the fact of being in a particular place at a particular time. 2. immediate vicinity. 3. striking personal appearance and manner: *the actor had great presence on the stage.*

pres·ent[1] ('prezənt) *adj.* 1. being in a particular place at a particular time: *he was present at the party.* 2. existing, dealt with, or occurring at this time: *our present headmaster is more popular than the last one.* **present tense** the construction of a verb that refers to action, etc., now going on, e.g. *he walks.* —*n.* this time; now. **'pres·ent·ly** *adv.* 1. soon. 2. at the present time.

pre·sent[2] *vb.* (pri'zent) 1. to give, often formally: *they presented him with a gold watch.* 2. to introduce (one person) to another: *may I present my son?* 3. to show: *they will present a new play.* 4. to send or put forward for consideration or examination: *I will present my proposals.* —*n.* ('prezənt) a gift. **pre'sent·a·ble** *adj.* fit to be seen. **pres·en·ta·tion** (prezən'tāshən) *n.* 1. a formal act of giving. 2. something that is presented.

pre·serve (pri'zûrv) *vb.* **pre·serv·ing, pre·served.** 1. to keep safe or in existence: *we must preserve our rights.* 2. to keep food from decay by treating it in a particular way. —*n.* 1. a place set apart for the protection of animals or birds. 2. usu. **pre·serves** (*pl.*) fruit that has been preserved in a particular way, e.g. jam or chutney. **pre'serv·a·tive** *n.* a substance for preserving foodstuffs from decay. *adj.* tending to preserve. —**pres·er·va·tion** (prezər'vāshən) *n.*

pre·side (pri'zīd) *vb.* **pre·sid·ing, pre·sid·ed.** to be at the head or in charge of. **pres·i·dent** ('prezidənt) *n.* 1. the head of a republic: *the President of the United States.* 2. the head of an organization, committee, etc. —**'pres·i·den·cy** *n.,pl.* **pres·i·den·cies.** —**pres·i'den·tial** *adj.*

press

press (pres) *vb.* 1. to push with force. 2. to squeeze or clasp. 3. to trouble. 4. to urge strongly: *he pressed me to come.* 5. to iron. —*n.* 1. an apparatus for pressing, shaping, etc. 2. a printing machine. 3. the profession of journalism, newspapers, and broadcasting collectively: *the story was reported in the press.* 4. stress: *the press of business worries.*

pres·sure ('preshər) *n.* 1. force caused by one thing pushing on or against something else: *the pressure of the crowd broke the police barriers.* 2. strong influence: *his friends put pressure on him to come to the party.* 3. strain and stress: *the pressure of work.* —*vb.* to put pressure on. **'pres·su·rize** *vb.* **pres·su·riz·ing, pres·su·rized.** 1. to regulate the air pressure in an aircraft or submarine. 2. to keep under pressure.

pre·sume (pri'zo͞om, pri'zyo͞om) *vb.* **pre·sum·ing, pre·sumed.** 1. to take as true without proof; suppose: *I presume that you are hungry.* 2. to take liberties; venture. —**pre·sump·tion** (pri'zumpshən)*n.*—**pre'sump·tu·ous** *adj.* —**pre'sump·tu·ous·ly** *adv.*

pre·tend (pri'tend) *vb.* 1. to speak or act falsely in order to deceive: *he pretended he could not hear* 2. to make believe: *they pretended they were cowboys and Indians.* **pre'tend·er** *n.* 1. one who pretends. 2. a claimant to a throne. —**pre·tense** (pri'tens, 'prētens) *n.*

pret·ty ('pritē) *adj.* **pret·ti·er, pret·ti·est.** pleasing to the eye or ear. —*adv.* quite: *it hit him pretty hard.* —**'pret·ti·ness** *n.*

pre·vail (pri'vāl) *vb.* 1. to be general or common: *cheerfulness prevailed among the people.* 2. to succeed: *our armies prevailed over the enemy.* 3. to persuade: *he prevailed upon me to stop.* —**prev·a·lent** ('prevələnt) *adj.*

pre·vent (pri'vent) *vb.* to keep from happening. —**pre'ven·tion** *n.*

prey (prā) *n.* 1. an animal that is killed and eaten by another. 2. a victim: *Steve fell prey to the big bully.* —*vb.* (+ *on* or *upon*) 1. to hunt, kill, and eat. 2. to distress or trouble: *his problems preyed on his mind.*

price (prīs) *n.* the amount of money established for something that is to be sold. —*vb.* **pric·ing, priced.** to fix or find out the price of something.

pride (prīd) *n.* 1. pleasure or self-esteem derived from achievements, possessions, etc.: *he took great pride in his garden.* 2. self-respect: *have you no pride?* 3. arrogant behavior; exaggerated opinions of one's qualities, abilities, etc. 4. the best or most highly regarded: *the painting was the pride of his collection.* 5. a group of lions. See also PROUD.

priest (prēst) *n.* a person whose duty it is to perform religious ceremonies.

pri·ma·ry ('prīmerē) *adj.* 1. chief or most important. 2. first or original; basic: *primary education.* —*n.,pl.* **pri·ma·ries** an election in which members of the same political party choose candidates for public office. **'pri·mar·i·ly** *adv.* in the first place.

prime (prīm) *adj.* 1. first in order of time, rank, value, etc. 2. of the highest quality: *prime beef.* —*n.* the best or most flourishing part of anything: *the prime of life.* —*vb.* **prim·ing, primed.** to make ready for a particular purpose: *the woodwork was primed with its first coat of paint.*

prim·er ('primər) *n.* an elementary textbook, esp. one for teaching reading.

prim·i·tive ('primitiv) *adj.* 1. belonging to the earliest times: *primitive man.* 2. simple or crude: *a primitive hut.* —**'prim·i·tive·ly** *adv.*

prim·rose ('primrōz) *n.* a plant with a pale yellow flower, common in woodlands and meadows.

prince (prins) *n.* 1. a male member of a royal family. 2. the ruler of a principality or other small state. **'prin·cess** *n.* 1. a female member of a royal family. 2. the wife of a prince.

prin·ci·pal ('prinsipəl) *adj.* chief; highest in rank or achievement: *the principal reason for the strike was the poor pay.* —*n.* 1. the most important person in an organization, esp. the head of a grammar, junior high, or high school. 2. anyone who plays a chief part in some activity. 3. invested or borrowed money on which interest is paid. —**'prin·ci·pal·ly** *adv.*

prin·ci·ple ('prinsipəl) *n.* 1. a fundamental truth or basic law: *his argument was based on sound principles.* 2. a settled rule of conduct: *I make it a principle never to borrow money.*

print (print) *vb.* 1. to produce a book, newspaper, etc., by pressing inked type, blocks, or plates onto paper or some other surface. 2. to write in separate letters like those made by type. 3. (photography) to produce a positive picture from a negative. —*n.* 1. printed lettering; printed matter, such as a newspaper. 2. a picture or design produced by printing. 3. a mark made by pressure. 4. a photographic picture made from a negative.

primrose

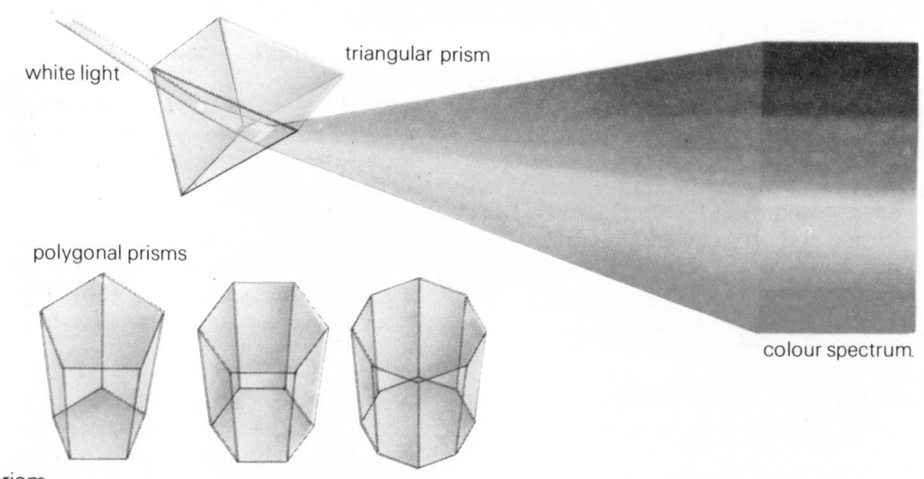

prism

prism ('prizəm) *n.* a solid transparent object that breaks up rays of white light into the colors of the rainbow. —**pris·mat·ic** (priz'matik) *adj.*

pris·on ('prizən) *n.* a secure building where criminals are locked up. '**pris·on·er** *n.* 1. a person sent to prison. 2. any person kept locked up by others.

pri·vate ('prīvit) *adj.* belonging to or concerning some particular person or persons: *my private room.* —*n.* a soldier of the lowest rank. —'**pri·va·cy** *n.* —'**pri·vate·ly** *adv.*

priv·i·lege ('privəlij) *n.* a special right or advantage granted to, or enjoyed by, one person or a few: *the privilege of a good education.* '**priv·i·leged** *adj.* enjoying special rights or advantages.

prize (prīz) *n.* 1. a reward for success in a sport, competition, etc. 2. anything that is highly valued or worth striving for. —*vb.* **priz·ing, prized.** to value something highly.

prob·a·ble ('probəbəl) *adj.* 1. likely to happen; expected: *the probable result.* 2. having more evidence for than against: *the probable cause of death was cancer.* —**prob·a'bil·i·ty** *n.* —'**prob·a·bly** *adv.*

probe (prōb) *vb.* **prob·ing, probed.** to investigate or search thoroughly. —*n.* 1. a thorough investigation. 2. a fine surgical instrument. 3. a space vehicle designed to send information back to earth.

prob·lem ('probləm) *n.* a matter or question that is difficult to solve.

proc·ess ('proses) *n.* 1. a series of actions carried out for a purpose: *the process of making steel.* 2. a sequence of changes: *the process of growing up.* —*vb.* to treat by some series of operations, as in manufacturing.

pro·ces·sion (prə'seshən) *n.* a company of people or vehicles moving forward in a formal or ceremonious manner. —**pro'ces·sion·al** *adj.*

pro·claim (prə'klām) *vb.* to announce formally in public. —**proc·la·ma·tion** (proklə'māshən) *n.*

pro·duce *vb.* (prə'dōōs, prə'dyōōs) **pro·duc·ing, pro·duced.** 1. to make, provide, or yield. 2. to bring out for inspection: *please produce your passport.* 3. to bring before the public (a play, film, etc.) —*n.* ('prodōōs, 'prodyōōs, 'prōdōōs, 'prōdyōōs) things produced on farms, such as eggs, fruit, etc. **prod·uct** ('prodəkt) *n.* 1. a thing produced; a result. 2. the result of mathematical multiplication. **pro'duc·tion** *n.* 1. the act or process of producing. 2. the presentation of a play or other entertainment to the public. **pro'duc·tive** *adj.* producing abundantly. —**pro·duc'tiv·i·ty** *n.*

pro·fes·sion (prə'feshən) *n.* 1. an occupation requiring a lengthy process of training, e.g. law or medicine. 2. the people engaged in such an occupation. 3. declaration: *a profession of love.* —**pro'fes·sion·al** *adj.*

pro·fes·sor (prə'fesər) *n.* a university teacher of the highest rank.

prof·it ('profit) *n.* 1. financial gain. 2. advantage; benefit. —*vb.* to benefit; gain advantage. —'**prof·it·a·ble** *adj.*

pro·gram ('prōgram) *n.* 1. a scheme or plan: *the government promised the country a program of reform.* 2. a production of a dramatic, quiz, interview, or other show, esp. on radio or television. 3. a booklet giving details about a ceremony, concert, or theatrical performance. 4. instructions given to a computer. —*vb.* **pro·gram·ming, pro·grammed.** to plan, or include in, a computer program.

prog·ress *n.* ('progres) 1. a forward movement in space or time. 2. improvement. —*vb.* (prə'gres) 1. to go forward. 2. to improve. **pro'gres·sion** *n.* a growth or development in successive stages. **pro'gres·sive** *adj.* 1. of a progression. 2. favoring new methods, etc. —**pro'gres·sive·ly** *adv.*

pro·ject *vb.* (prə'jekt) 1. to throw forward. 2. to stick out. 3. to cause light, shadows, images, etc., to fall on a surface: *she projected the movie.* 4. to predict what will happen. —*n.* ('projekt) a scheme for a new undertaking. **pro'jec·tile** *n.* something that is thrown or shot from a gun. **pro'jec·tion** *n.* 1. the act of projecting. 2. something that sticks out. **pro'jec·tor** *n.* a machine used for showing movies and picture slides.

projector

prom·ise ('promis) *vb.* **prom·is·ing, prom·ised.** 1. to give one's word; vow. 2. to look likely to be or have: *this book promises to be interesting.* —*n.* 1. a vow. 2. the indication of future excellence: *this young actor shows great promise.*

pro·mote (prə'mōt) *vb.* **pro·mot·ing, pro·mot·ed.** 1. to advance (someone) to a better job, higher rank, etc. 2. to give active support. 3. to advertise (a product). —**pro'mo·tion** *n.*

prompt (prompt) *adj.* quick and punctual in action: *he was always prompt in paying.* —*vb.* 1. to urge (someone) into action. 2. to supply (an actor) with lines that he has forgotten. —'**prompt·ly** *adv.* —'**prompt·ness** *n.*

pro·noun ('prōnoun) *n.* a word used in place of a noun, e.g. *he, she, it, who.*

pro·nounce (prə'nouns) *vb.* **pro·nounc·ing, pro·nounced.** 1. to utter (words, syllables, etc.) in a particular way. 2. to declare formally: *the judge pronounced sentence on the man.* **pro'nounce·ment** *n.* a formal declaration. **pro·nun·ci·a·tion** (prənunsē'āshən) *n.* the manner or act of pronouncing (def. 1.)

proof (proof) *n.* the evidence establishing the facts of an action, incident, etc. —*adj.* able to withstand: *the castle was proof against attack.*

propeller

pro·pel (prə'pel) *vb.* **pro·pel·ling, pro·pelled.** to drive or cause to move forward. **pro·pel·ler** *n.* a device made of two or more spinning blades, used to drive a ship or aircraft.

prop·er·ty ('propərtē) *n.,pl.* **prop·er·ties.** 1. the things belonging to a person. 2. a house or other building, usu. with its land. 3. a distinctive quality.

proph·e·cy ('profisē) *n.,pl.* **proph·e·cies.** a statement that foretells a future event.

proph·e·sy ('profisī) *vb.* **proph·e·sy·ing, proph·e·sied.** to say what will happen in the future. '**proph·et** *n.* one who prophesies.

pro·por·tion (prə'pôrshən) *n.* 1. the comparative relation of one thing to another: *the proportion of oil to vinegar in a salad dressing is three to one.* 2. correct balance: *try to get things in proportion.*

pro·pose (prə'pōz) *vb.* **pro·pos·ing, pro·posed.** 1. to put forward (a suggestion) for consideration. 2. to nominate (someone) for office: *he was proposed as president.* 3. to make an offer of marriage. **pro'pos·al** *n.* 1. a suggested plan or scheme. 2. an offer of marriage. **prop·o·si·tion** (propə'zishən) *n.* a scheme, plan, etc., put forward for approval.

pro·pri·e·tor (prə'prīitər) *n.* the owner of something, esp. a business.

pro·pul·sion (prə'pulshən) *n.* force causing a forward motion.

pros·e·cute ('prosəkyoot) *vb.* **pros·e·cut·ing, pros·e·cut·ed.** to take legal proceedings against (someone). —**pros·e'cu·tion** *n.*

pros·pect ('prospekt) *n.* 1. the outlook for the future: *the prospect of fame thrilled the young actor.* 2. usu. **pros·pects** (*pl.*) future expectations, esp. of success, promotion, etc.: *her prospects look good since she left the firm.* —*vb.* to explore, esp. for mining opportunities. **pro'spec·tive** *adj.* relating to the future: *a prospective candidate.* '**pros·pec·tor** *n.* a person who explores for gold, oil, etc.

pros·per ('prospər) *vb.* to do well, esp. financially; succeed. **pros·per·i·ty** (pros'peritē) *n.* financial success. '**pros·per·ous** *adj.* flourishing, esp. financially. —'**pros·per·ous·ly** *adv.*

pro·tect (prə'tekt) *vb.* to shield from harm. —**pro'tec·tion** *n.* —**pro'tec·tive** *adj.*

pro·tein ('prōtēn) *n.* one of a large number of chemical compounds that forms an essential part of the bodies of plants and animals.

pro·test *vb.* (prə'test) to express an objection or disapproval. —*n.* ('prōtest) an expression of disapproval.

proud (proud) *adj.* 1. having a sense of honor and pleasure because of one's achievements, possessions, etc. 2. having a high opinion of one's own importance. 3. having a sense of self-respect: *he was too proud to accept charity.* —'**proud·ly** *adv.*

prove (proov) *vb.* **prov·ing, proved.** 1. to show to be true. 2. to be found to be.

prov·erb ('provûrb) *n.* a short well-known saying illustrating a popular moral or belief, e.g. *too many cooks spoil the broth.* —**pro'ver·bi·al** *adj.*

pro·vide (prə'vīd) *vb.* **pro·vid·ing, pro·vid·ed.** to make ready; supply. **prov·i·dent** ('providənt) *adj.* careful; thrifty.

prov·ince ('provins) *n.* 1. a division of a country: *Saskatchewan is a province of Canada.* 2. an area of knowledge, experience, etc.: *mathematics is not my province.*

pro·vi·sion (prə'vizhən) *n.* 1. the act of providing. 2. a condition: *we made the provision that we were to be paid in cash.* 3. **pro·vi·sions** (*pl.*) a supply of food. **pro'vi·sion·al** *adj.* conditional; not definitely settled or permanent.

pro·voke (prə'vōk) *vb.* **pro·vok·ing, pro·voked.** 1. to irritate; annoy. 2. to cause (action or response): *his remarks provoked a lively discussion.* **pro·voc·a·tive** (prə'vokətiv) *adj.* likely to cause interest, anger, etc. **prov·o·ca·tion** (provə'kāshən) *n.* the act or an instance of making somebody angry, etc.

prow

prow (prou) *n.* the pointed front part of a ship.

prune[1] (proon) *n.* a dried plum.

prune[2] (proon) *vb.* **prun·ing, pruned.** to cut back (a tree or plant) to encourage better growth.

pry[1] (prī) *vb.* **pry·ing, pried.** to try to discover other people's secrets.

pry[2] (prī) *vb.* (usu. + *up, open, apart,* etc.) to force (up, open, apart, etc.) by leverage: *pry the lid off that can.*

psy·chol·o·gy (sī'koləjē) *n.* the study of the mind and the way it works. **psy'chol·o·gist** *n.* a person who studies the mind.

pub·lic ('publik) *adj.* of, concerning, open to, or owned by the whole community. —*n.* people in general: *open to the public.* **pub·lic·i·ty** (pu'blisitē) *n.* 1. state of being widely known; fame. 2. advertising matter. —'**pub·lic·ly** *adv.*

pub·li·ca·tion (publə'kāshən) *n.* 1. the act of publishing. 2. something that is published, e.g. a magazine.

pub·lish ('publish) *vb.* 1. to print and sell to the public: *his novel was published after his death.* 2. to make known to the public.

pul·ley ('poolē) *n.* a wheel with a grooved outer edge for a rope or chain that is used to help raise heavy loads.

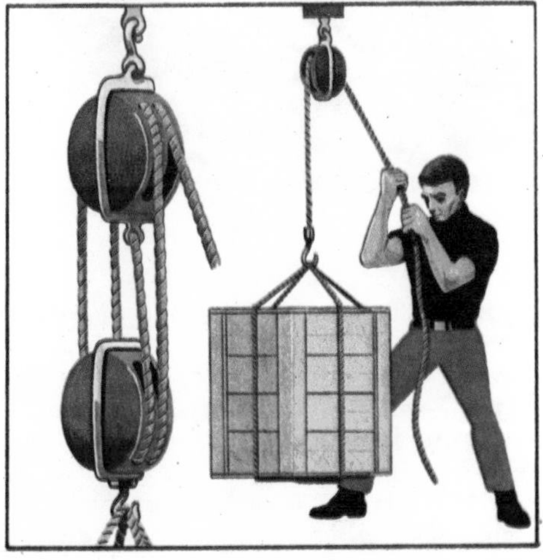

pulley

pulp (pulp) *n.* 1. a soft damp mass of material: *paper is made from wood pulp.* 2. the soft juicy part of a fruit. —*vb.* to make into pulp.

pul·pit ('poolpit, 'pulpit) *n.* a raised boxed-in stand where the clergyman stands during church services.

pulse (puls) *n.* the regular throbbing of the blood in the arteries as it is pumped around the body by the heart, e.g. as felt at a person's wrist.

pump (pump) *n.* a machine or device for forcing fluids or gases through a tube or pipe. —*vb.* 1. to use a pump. 2. (+ *up*) to force air into.

pump·kin ('pumpkin) *n.* 1. a large round yellow fruit eaten as a vegetable. 2. the vine on which the fruit grows.

pun (pun) *n.* the witty use of words that sound similar but have different meanings, e.g. they went and *told* the sexton, and the sexton *tolled* the bell.

pumpkin

punch[1] (punch) *vb.* to hit hard with the fist. —*n.* a sharp blow from a fist.

punch[2] (punch) *n.* 1. a tool for making holes through paper, leather, etc., or for impressing a design on a surface.

punch[3] (punch) *n.* a drink made from fruit juices, often mixed with alcoholic beverages and spices.

punc·tu·al ('pungkchooəl) *adj.* being on time. —**punc·tu'al·i·ty** *n.* —'**punc·tu·al·ly** *adv.*

punc·tu·ate ('pungkchooāt) *vb.* **punc·tu·at·ing, punc·tu·at·ed.** to break up a piece of writing into sentences and clauses by means of commas (,), periods (.), colons (:), etc., to make reading easier and the sense clearer. —**punc·tu'a·tion** *n.*

punc·ture ('pungkchər) *vb.* **punc·tur·ing, punc·tured.** to make a hole using a sharp object; pierce. —*n.* a hole made by a pointed object.

pun·ish ('punish) *vb.* to make (someone) suffer for wrongdoing. '**pun·ish·a·ble** *adj.* likely to be punished. —'**pun·ish·ment** *n.*

pu·pa ('pyoopə) *n.,pl.* **pu·pae** ('pyoopē). an insect at the stage in its life during which it rests, e.g. in a cocoon, and gradually changes to become an adult.

pu·pil[1] ('pyoopəl) *n.* a person who is learning from a teacher; student.

pu·pil[2] ('pyoopəl) *n.* a circular opening in the center of the eyeball that controls the amount of light entering the eye. See EYE.

pur·chase ('pûrchəs) *vb.* **pur·chas·ing, pur·chased.** to buy. —*n.* 1. the act of buying. 2. something bought. 3. a firm grip: *he got a good purchase on the rope.*

pure (pyoor) *adj.* 1. unmixed with anything else. 2. clean; spotless. 3. nothing but: *it was pure chance that I saw Bob there.* **pu·ri·fy** ('pyoorəfī) *vb.* **pu·ri·fy·ing, pu·ri·fied.** to make or become pure or purer. —**pu·ri·fi'ca·tion** *n.* —'**pur·i·ty** *n.*

pur·pose ('pûrpəs) *n.* 1. plan; intention. 2. use; function: *what is the purpose of the dial on this machine?*

pur·sue (pər'soo) *vb.* **pur·su·ing, pur·sued.** 1. to chase. 2. to carry on; continue to follow: *he pursued his career as a dentist.* **pur·suit** (pər'soot) *n.* the act of pursuing.

pus (pus) *n.* a thick fluid formed in a sore, infected wound, etc.

puz·zle ('puzəl) *n.* 1. a question or problem that is hard to understand. 2. a toy or problem that tests a person's skill, knowledge, etc. —*vb.* **puz·zling, puz·zled.** 1. to confuse or be hard to understand. 2. (+ *over*) to think hard about.

pyg·my *or* **pig·my** ('pigmē) *n.,pl.* **pyg·mies** *or* **pig·mies.** a member of one of the races of very small people (between 4 and 5 feet tall when fully grown) who live in Africa and certain islands off Asia.

pyramid

pyr·a·mid ('pirəmid) *n.* 1. an object with a square base and four triangular sides that meet in a point at the top. See GEOMETRY. 2. a structure shaped like this, esp. one of the tombs in ancient Egypt.

py·thon ('pīthon) *n.* a large snake that suffocates its prey.

quack (kwak) *n.* 1. the cry of a duck. 2. (informal) an unqualified doctor. —*vb.* to make a noise like a duck's quack.

quad·ran·gle ('kwodrang̃gəl) *n.* 1. a plane figure with four sides, esp. a square or rectangle. 2. an open space or courtyard surrounded by buildings.

quad·rant ('kwodrənt) *n.* 1. the fourth part of a circle or its circumference. 2. an instrument used by sailors to find the position of their ship at sea.

quad·ri·lat·er·al (kwodri'latərəl) *n.* a plane figure with four sides. —*adj.* four-sided.

quad·ru·ped ('kwodro͝oped) *n.* any four-footed animal.

quad·ru·plet (kwo'druplit, kwo-'dro͝oplit) *n.* (often shortened to **quad**) one of four babies born to one mother at the same time.

quail[1] (kwāl) *vb.* to feel or show fear; flinch or draw back in fright.

quail

quail[2] (kwāl) *n.* a small plump bird often hunted for food or sport.

quaint (kwānt) *adj.* pleasingly unusual, esp. in an old-fashioned way. —'**quaint·ly** *adv.* —'**quaint·ness** *n.*

quake (kwāk) *vb.* **quak·ing, quaked.** to tremble; shiver, esp. with fear, strong emotion, illness, etc.: ***the sight of the huge dog made him quake.*** —*n.* (informal) earthquake.

qual·i·fy ('kwoləfī) *vb.* **qual·i·fy·ing, qual·i·fied.** 1. to obtain the necessary training or standard to fit oneself for a job, career, competition, etc.: ***she qualified as a doctor.*** 2. to limit or impose restrictions or conditions (on something): ***the store qualified the offer of low prices by accepting cash only.*** **qual·i·fi'ca·tion** *n.* 1. something that makes someone or something fit to undertake a task. 2. a restriction.

qual·i·ty ('kwolitē) *n.,pl.* **qual·i·ties.** 1. a degree of excellence; high grade, standard, etc.: ***the workmanship is of very high quality.*** 2. a personal characteristic, esp. a moral or mental virtue: ***she has the qualities of gentleness and generosity.*** 3. the basic character of a thing. **qual·i·ta·tive** ('kwolitātiv) *adj.* relating to quality.

quan·ti·ty ('kwontitē) *n.,pl.* **quan·ti·ties.** 1. a known or measurable amount, number, weight, etc. 2. often **quantities** (*pl.*) large amounts; plenty: ***they supplied quantities of food at their party.***

quar·an·tine ('kwôrəntēn 'kworəntēn) *n.* a stretch of time during which people or animals that may be carrying infectious diseases are kept completely cut off from others to prevent the infection from spreading. —*vb.* **quar·an·tin·ing, quar·an·tined.** to isolate to prevent disease spreading.

quar·rel ('kwôrəl, 'kworəl) *n.* an angry or unfriendly argument; dispute. —*vb.* 1. to argue; fight. 2. (+ *with*) to find fault with. '**quar·rel·some** *adj.* fond of quarreling.

quar·ry[1] ('kwôrē, 'kworē) *n.,pl.* **quar·ries.** a person or animal that is being hunted or chased: ***the dog pounced on its quarry, which was a small rabbit.***

quarry

quar·ry[2] ('kwôrē, 'kworē) *n,pl.* **quar·ries.** a large open pit in the ground from which stone, sand, flint, etc., is dug. —*vb.* **quar·ry·ing, quar·ried.** to dig out from a quarry.

quart (kwôrt) *n.* a measurement of liquid equal to one quarter of a gallon or two pints.

quar·ter ('kwôrtər) *n.* 1. one of four equal parts: ***a quarter of an hour is equal to 15 minutes.*** 2. a U.S. coin equal to 25 cents, or one-quarter of a dollar. 3. a district of a city: ***Plaka is the old Turkish quarter of Athens.*** 4. source; direction from which something comes: ***children ran from every quarter to see the parade.*** 5. **quar·ters** (*pl.*) a place to stay; lodgings: ***the soldiers returned to their quarters.*** —*vb.* 1. to divide into four equal sections. 2. to find lodgings for (soldiers).

quar·ter·ly ('kwôrtərlē) *adj., adv.* once every three months. *n.,pl.* **quar·ter·lies.** a magazine published four times a year.

quar·tet (kwôr'tet) *n.* 1. a piece of music written to be performed by four musicians or singers. 2. a group of four musicians or singers who perform together.

quay (kē) *n.* a manmade landing place, usu. built of stone, alongside which ships can be tied; wharf.

queen (kwēn) *n.* 1. a SOVEREIGN or ruler of a nation. 2. the wife or widow of a king. 3. a woman or thing of particular beauty or importance: *the aircraft carrier was queen of the fleet.* 4. an egglaying bee, ant, wasp, or termite. 5. the most powerful piece in the game of chess. 6. a playing card with a picture of a queen on it. **'queen·ly** *adj.* majestic; regal: *she walked in a queenly manner.*

queer ('kwēr) *adj.* peculiar; unusual; differing from normal.

quench (kwench) *vb.* 1. to satisfy; put an end to: *I quenched my thirst.* 2. to put out; extinguish: *the firemen quenched the flames.*

que·ry ('kwērē) *n.,pl.* **que·ries.** a question, esp. one that expresses doubt about the truth of something. —*vb.* **que·ry·ing, que·ried.** to express doubt or uncertainty about: *she queried her bank statement.*

quest (kwest) *n.* a search or hunt, esp. of an adventurous sort: *the explorers went in quest of tigers.*

ques·tion ('kweschən) *n.* 1. a sentence that demands an answer; enquiry. 2. a matter to be talked about; something doubtful or uncertain: *the chairman raised the question of money.* —*vb.* 1. to ask questions of (someone). 2. to express doubt about: *she questioned his fitness for the job.* **'ques·tion·a·ble** *adj.* doubtful; likely to be challenged. **question mark** a punctuation mark (?) placed at the end of a written question.

quib·ble ('kwibəl) *vb.* **quib·bling, quib·bled.** to argue about petty details; find trivial faults in: *the teacher quibbled about some of the points in my essay, but admitted that it was mostly very good.* —*n.* a small objection or criticism. —**'quib·bler** *n.*

quick (kwik) *adj.* 1. happening or done in a short space of time: *quick results.* 2. understanding or working easily and swiftly: *a quick intelligence.* —*n.* sensitive flesh, esp. that in which fingernails and toenails are set. **'quick·en** *vb.* to make or become quick or quicker: *he quickened his step when it began to snow.* —**'quick·ly** *adv.* —**'quick·ness** *n.*

qui·et ('kwīit) *adj.* 1. making little or no noise: *quiet footsteps.* 2. having little or no movement; peaceful; inactive: *a quiet day.* 3. subdued; not too bright or loud: *a quiet color.* —*n.* state of calm or silence. **'qui·et·en** *vb.* to make or become quiet or quieter. —**'qui·et·ly** *adv.* —**'qui·et·ness** *n.*

quilt (kwilt) *n.* a warm bedcover made of two pieces of cloth stitched together with thick padding between them. —*vb.* 1. to make a quilt. 2. to make (something) in the same pattern as a quilt: *to quilt a jacket.*

quin·tet (kwin'tet) *n.* 1. a piece of music written to be performed by five musicians or singers. 2. a group of five musicians or singers who perform together.

quin·tu·plet (kwin'tuplit, kwin'tooplit) *n.* (often shortened to **quint**) one of five babies born to one mother at the same time.

quip (kwip) *n.* a short and sharp witty or clever remark. —*vb.* **quip·ping, quipped.** to make such a remark.

quit (kwit) *vb.* **quit·ting, quit** *or* **quit·ted.** 1. to leave: *Bill quit school to find work.* 2. to stop; cease doing something: *he would not quit working even when he was ill.*

quiv·er[1] ('kwivər) *vb.* to tremble; shake slightly with fear or excitement. —*n.* the act of quivering.

quiver

quiv·er[2] ('kwivər) *n.* a long narrow case for carrying arrows.

quiz (kwiz) *n.* a test or contest, esp. one consisting of a few short questions. —*vb.* **quiz·zing, quizzed.** to examine or test by asking questions.

quo·ta ('kwōtə) *n.* the limited portion that each person receives after whatever is to be shared out has been divided: *you have had your quota of cake.*

quote (kwōt) *vb.* **quot·ing, quot·ed.** 1. to repeat (something that someone else has said or written): *the President quoted Shakespeare in his speech.* 2. to inform about the cost of something: *to quote a price.* —*n.* (informal) quotation. **quo'ta·tion** *n.* 1. someone else's words or phrases repeated in a speech, article, etc. 2. an estimate of the current cost of anything. **quotation mark** a punctuation mark placed at the beginning (m‘ or “m) and end (m’ or ”m) of a written quotation.

quo·tient ('kwōshənt) *n.* the answer or number obtained when one number is divided by another: *when eighteen is divided by three, the quotient is nine.*

R

rab·bi ('rabī) *n.* the religious head of a Jewish community, who is also a teacher of Jewish law. —**rab·bin·i·cal** (rə'binikəl) *adj.*

rab·bit ('rabit) *n.* a small furry burrowing animal with long ears and a short tail.

ra·bies ('rābēz) *n.* a VIRUS disease affecting people and warm-blooded animals that is passed on by the bite of an animal already having the disease, and nearly always causes death. —**rab·id** ('rabid) *adj.*

race[1] (rās) *n.* a competition to find out who or which is the fastest at a sport or other activity. —*vb.* **rac·ing, raced.** 1. to compete or cause to compete in races: *he races pigeons.* 2. to move at speed: *Jane raced for the bus.*

race[2] (rās) *n.* a large group of people with a common origin and the same physical characteristics that distinguish them from people with different origins. '**ra·cial** *adj.* of or concerning a race of people.

rack·et[1] ('rakit) *n.* 1. a very loud and confusing noise; din. 2. (informal) a scheme, often of a criminal nature, for making money.

rack·et[2] *or* **rac·quet** ('rakit) *n.* a wooden or metal device with a long handle and a flat circular or oval head supporting a tight network of gut or nylon. Rackets are used to hit the ball in tennis, squash, etc.

racket

radar

ra·dar ('rādâr) *n.* electronic apparatus used to find and mark the positions of distant objects, e.g. aircraft, ships at sea, etc., by sending out radio waves and measuring the reflection of these waves from the objects.

ra·di·ant ('rādēənt) *adj.* 1. shining brightly; showing joy or excitement: *the bride's face was radiant.* 2. sending out or given out in rays: *radiant heat is given off by the sun.* —'**ra·di·ant·ly** *adv.*

ra·di·ate ('rādēāt) *vb.* **ra·di·at·ing, ra·di·at·ed.** 1. to give off or be given off in rays. 2. to move or spread out from the center like the spokes of a bicycle wheel: *streets radiate from the central square.* **ra·di'a·tion** *n.* the sending out of energy, light, etc., in rays. '**ra·di·a·tor** *n.* 1. an apparatus that heats a room. 2. a device for cooling a car's engine.

ra·di·o ('rādēō) *n.,pl.* **ra·di·os.** 1. a method of sending and receiving sounds through the air or space by means of waves that are similar to light waves but have a much longer wavelength. 2. an apparatus for receiving these sounds. —*vb.* **ra·di·o·ing, ra·di·oed.** to send a message by radio.

ra·di·o·ac·tive (rādēō'aktiv) *adj.* having atoms that break up and give out energy in the form of very short radio waves or of electrically charged particles that are able to penetrate solid bodies; emitting radiation. —**ra·di·o·ac'tiv·i·ty** *n.*

rad·ish ('radish) *n.* a small strongly flavored white salad vegetable with a red skin.

ra·di·us ('rādēəs) *n.,pl.* **ra·di·i** ('rādēī) *or* **ra·di·us·es.** 1. a straight line from the center to the outside of a circle or sphere. See GEOMETRY. 2. an area measured in terms of radius: *there are no trees within a radius of 50 yards.*

raft (raft) *n.* a flat floating structure usu. made from lengths of tree trunks fastened together.

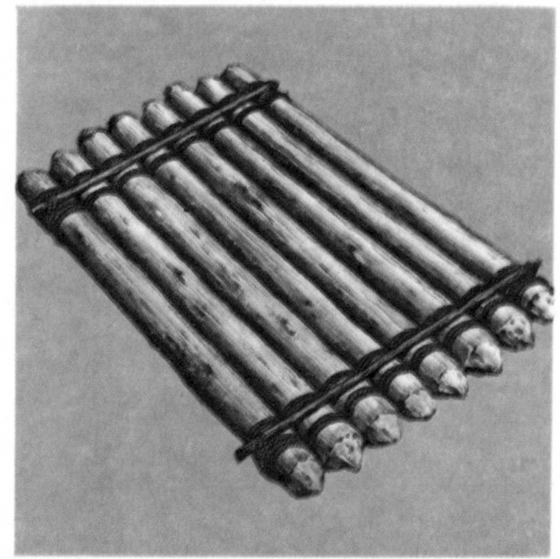

raft

raft·er ('raftər) *n.* a beam or timber that supports a roof.

rag (rag) *n.* 1. a torn piece of material. 2. **rags** (*pl.*) old shabby clothes.

rage (rāj) *n.* 1. violent anger; fury: *Alan flew into a rage.* 2. (informal) someone or something that is currently very fashionable: *straw hats are all the rage this year.* —*vb.* **rag·ing, raged.** to feel and express great anger.

rag·ged ('ragid) adj. 1. torn and tattered; shabby: *a ragged suit.* 2. rough; not well put together: *a ragged piece of music.*

raid (rād) *n.* 1. a sudden military attack. 2. a sudden invasion of people looking for something: *a police raid.* —*vb.* 1. to attack. 2. to search.

rail (rāl) *n.* 1. a strong metal or wooden bar. 2. one of a pair of parallel steel tracks along which trains run. —*vb.* 1. to fence with rails. 2. to send by train. **'rail·ing** *n.* a fence made from rails (def. 1).

rail·road ('rālrōd) *n.* 1. a track made from two parallel steel rails on which trains run. 2. the system of transportation that uses trains.

rain (rān) *n.* 1. water condensed from vapor in the clouds to form drops that fall to earth. 2. a shower of this water. —*vb.* to fall as rain. **'rain·y** *adj.* **rain·i·er, rain·i·est.** having much rain.

rain·bow ('rānbō) *n.* an arc of seven colors seen in the sky during or after a shower of rain on a sunny day.

raise (rāz) *vb.* **rais·ing, raised.** 1. to move or cause to move to a higher level; increase the amount of: *he raised their wages.* 2. to produce; grow: *he raised a good crop of potatoes.* 3. to stir up; cause: *the joke raised a laugh.* 4. to collect; gather together: *we raised money for charity.* 5. to suggest (something) for discussion or consideration: *Mike raised some questions.*

rai·sin ('rāzin) *n.* a dried grape often used in cakes and breads.

rake (rāk) *n.* a tool with many teeth and a long handle, used to level soil or gather leaves. See IMPLEMENT. —*vb.* **rak·ing, raked.** 1. to use a rake. 2. to search carefully. 3. to spray with gunfire. 4. to gather in large amounts.

ral·ly ('ralē) *vb.* **ral·ly·ing, ral·lied.** 1. to bring (soldiers) together and encourage them to further efforts. 2. to revive; recover health, spirits, etc. 3. to assemble for a common purpose. —*n.,pl.* **ral·lies.** 1. the act of gathering and preparing for further action. 2. a recovery or attempt at recovery made by a sick person. 3. a number of people who have assembled for a common purpose. 4. (esp. in tennis) an exchange of several strokes before a point is won. 5. (also **ralley**) a competition to test a car driver's skill over a difficult course.

ram (ram) *n.* 1. an adult male sheep. 2. a device for driving repeated and heavy blows: *the battering ram broke through the city gates.* —*vb.* **ram·ming, rammed.** 1. to hit (something) repeatedly with heavy blows. 2. to crash into (something) violently. 3. to cram; stuff: *he rammed the clothes into the suitcase.*

ram·ble ('rambəl) *vb.* **ram·bling, ram·bled.** 1. to walk for pleasure. 2. (often + *on*) to wander aimlessly in speech: *he rambled on about golf.* —*n.* a walk taken for pleasure.

ramp (ramp) *n.* a sloping roadway, passageway, etc., connecting different levels: *we walked up the ramp into the aircraft.*

ram·part ('rampârt) *n.* a bank of earth or thick wall which serves as part of a fort's defenses.

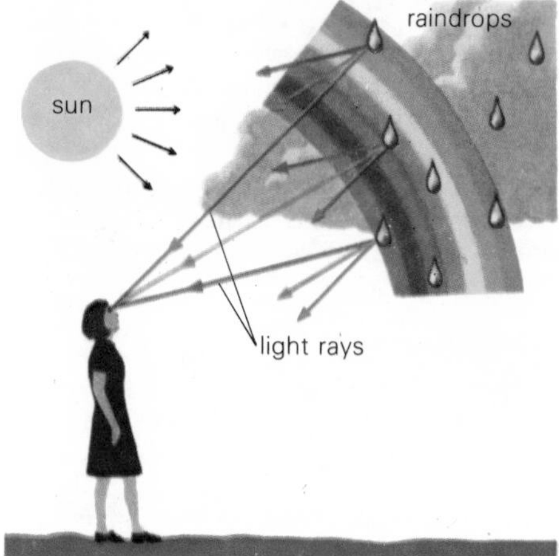

rainbow

ram·shack·le ('ramshakəl) *adj.* falling to pieces through age or neglect; badly built: *a ramshackle old bus.*

ranch (ranch) *n.* a big farm where horses, cattle, sheep, etc., are reared in large numbers. —*vb.* to work on, manage, or own a ranch.

ran·dom ('randəm) *adj.* haphazard; relying on chance: *as she did not know the answer, she made a random guess.* —**'ran·dom·ly** *adv.*

rang (rang) *vb.* the past tense of RING[2].

range (rānj) *n.* 1. the area or extent over which anything can reach, move, or operate: *the missile's range was 450 miles.* 2. the extent or scope of something: *the range of a subject.* 3. a large kitchen stove. 4. a row, line, or group: *a mountain range.* 5. a large open area of land on which livestock can roam. —*vb.* **rang·ing, ranged.** 1. to arrange in a line, row, etc. 2. to roam. 3. to extend between limits: *their ages ranged from six to nine.* **'rang·er** *n.* a person who guards a forest or park.

rank (rangk) *n.* 1. high social position; degree of standing or excellence. 2. a position of authority: *the rank of Captain.* 3. **ranks** (*pl.*) *or* **rank and file** all soldiers who are not officers. —*vb.* to have the position or status of; be considered as: *she ranked high in our estimation.*

ran·som ('ransəm) *n.* the price paid to obtain the release of a person or thing in captivity. —*vb.* to pay a ransom to obtain someone's release.

rap (rap) *vb.* **rap·ping, rapped.** 1. to tap or strike sharply and quickly; knock: *she rapped on the door.* 2. (+ *out*) to say something sharply: *he raps out orders.* —*n.* a sharp quick blow: *a rap on the door.*

rap·id ('rapid) *adj.* 1. moving with great speed; quick. 2. **rap·ids** (*pl.*) a part of a river where the current is very swift. —**ra·pid·i·ty** (rə'piditē) *n.* —**'rap·id·ly** *adv.*

rare[1] (reər) *adj.* unusual; not frequent in occurrence and therefore highly valued. **'rar·i·ty** *n.,pl.* **rar·i·ties.** 1. the state of being rare. 2. something that is rare.

rare[2] (reər) *adj.* cooked so that it is still red inside: *a rare steak.*

ras·cal ('raskəl) *n.* rogue; mischievous person.

rash[1] (rash) *adj.* hasty; lacking in caution: *Richard regretted his rash decision to leave his job.* —**'rash·ly** *adv.* —**'rash·ness** *n.*

rash[2] (rash) *n.* an outbreak of red spots or blotches on the skin.

raspberry

rasp·ber·ry ('razberē) *n.,pl.* **rasp·ber·ries.** 1. a small sweet soft juicy red fruit. 2. the prickly plant that bears this fruit.

rasp·ing ('rasping) *adj.* harsh: *the saw made a rasping sound.*

rat (rat) *n.* 1. an animal like a mouse but larger, often inhabiting buildings where grain and other foodstuffs are kept. See RODENT. 2. a person who deserts a cause or his friends in time of difficulty. —*vb.* **rat·ting, rat·ted.** 1. to hunt rats. 2. (+ *on*) (slang) to desert; betray.

rate (rāt) *n.* 1. a standard or proportion by which a quantity or value may be fixed: *the rate for the job is 3 dollars an hour.* 2. speed: *the mountaineers climbed at a rate of 1000 feet a day.* 3. quality or standard: *his work is first rate.* —*vb.* **rat·ing, rat·ed.** to estimate (value, rank, class, etc.) or to be placed in such a class or position. **'rat·ing** *n.* 1. the credit standing of a company or individual. 2. the degree of popularity of TV or radio programs.

rath·er ('rathər) *adv.* 1. preferably; more willingly: *I would rather ride than walk.* 2. somewhat: *rather small.* 3. more properly; instead: *I asked Kate rather than Tom.*

rat·i·fy ('ratəfī) *vb.* **rat·i·fy·ing, rat·i·fied.** to confirm or approve: *now that he has ratified the plan we can go ahead.* —**rat·i·fi'ca·tion** *n.*

ra·tion ('rashən, 'rāshən) *n.* 1. a fixed allowance or portion of something. 2. usu. **ra·tions** (*pl.*) a fixed quantity of food to last for a certain length of time. —*vb.* 1. to share out (food, etc.) in fixed portions, esp. when supplies are limited. 2. to limit or restrict.

ra·tion·al ('rashənəl) *adj.* reasonable and sensible; involving reason and sound judgment. **ra·tion'al·i·ty** *n.* reasonableness.

rat·tle ('ratəl) *vb.* **rat·tling, rat·tled.** 1. to make or cause to make a rapid series of short sharp sounds. 2. to move briskly and noisily: *the bus rattled along.* 3. (+ *on*) (informal) to speak at length: *he rattled on about his garden.* 4. (slang) to cause alarm to; fluster: *the crisis at the office rattled him.* —*n.* 1. a rapid series of sharp noises. 2. a baby's toy or other device that will make such noises when shaken.

rau·cous ('rôkəs) *adj.* harsh; hoarse: *the parrot gave a raucous cry.* —**'rau·cous·ly** *adv.*

rave (rāv) *vb.* **rav·ing, raved.** 1. to talk wildly and uncontrollably. 2. (+ *about*) (informal) to praise very enthusiastically: *Sally raved about her favorite pop singer.*

rav·en ('rāvən) *n.* a large glossy black bird of the crow family that has a harsh voice and feeds chiefly on flesh.

rav·en·ous ('ravənəs) *adj.* intensely hungry. —**'rav·en·ous·ly** *adv.*

ra·vine (rə'vēn) *n.* a deep narrow gorge or valley.

raw (rô) *adj.* 1. uncooked. 2. in the natural state; not manufactured: *raw material.* 3. having the skin rubbed off: *a raw spot on the heel.* 4. chilly and damp: *a raw February morning.* 5. untrained: *raw recruits.* 6. without a smooth finish: *a raw edge.*

ray[1] (rā) *n.* 1. a narrow beam of light, heat, etc. 2. one of a number of lines or parts spreading out from a central point.

ray[2] (rā) *n.* one of several kinds of deep-sea fish with a broad flattened body and fins.

ray·on ('rāon) *n.* an artificial fabric with a fine silky texture, made from a substance called cellulose that is obtained from plants.

raze (rāz) *vb.* **raz·ing, razed.** to destroy totally; demolish: *the old buildings were razed and a new park was built.*

ra·zor ('rāzər) *n.* an implement with a sharp blade or cutters used for shaving off hair.

reach (rēch) *vb.* 1. to get as far as; arrive at. 2. to achieve: *the singer reached the top in a year.* 3. to be long enough or go far enough to touch, pierce, etc.; extend: *the shelves reached from floor to ceiling.* 4. to stretch out one's hand or arm; touch, take, or hand over with outstretched arm: *he reached out to take the book from me.* 5. to try to attain: *he reached for the presidency.* —*n.* 1. the act of stretching out: *the outlaw made a reach for his gun.* 2. range of someone's abilities. 3. a stretch between defined limits: *the lower reaches of the Mississippi pass through New Orleans.*

re·act (rē'akt) *vb.* 1. to act in return; respond to a stimulus: *he did not react to the bully's threats.* 2. (chemistry) (+ *to* or *with*) to cause or be involved in change: *how does silver react to this acid?* **re'ac·tion** *n.* 1. an action in response to another action: *the audience's reaction to his speech was enthusiastic.* 2. (chemistry) chemical change. 3. resistance to revolution or progress. **re'ac·tion·ar·y** *n.,pl.* **re·ac·tion·ar·ies.** a person who opposes change, esp. in politics. *adj.* of or relating to resistance to change or progress. **re'ac·tor** *n.* an apparatus for producing controlled atomic energy.

read (rēd) *vb.* **read·ing, read** (red). 1. to interpret (written or printed words). 2. to utter aloud something written or printed. 3. to record or show information or measurement: *the speedometer read 80 m.p.h.* —*n.* 1. the act of reading. 2. (informal) something that is read. **'read·er** *n.* 1. a person who reads. 2. a textbook designed to teach children and learners of a foreign language to read. **'read·able** *adj.* 1. able to be read easily. 2. worth reading.

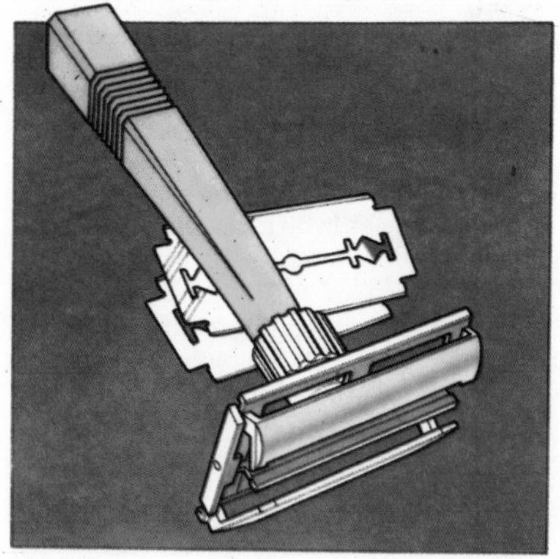

razor

read·y ('redē) *adj.* **read·i·er, read·i·est.** 1. prepared; fit to act or be used at once: *the dinner will be ready in five minutes.* 2. willing. 3. likely; inclined: *he was ready to desert at a moment's notice.* 4. quick: *a ready reply.* 5. near at hand: *he had no ready cash.* —*adv.* prepared beforehand. —'**read·i·ly** *adv.* —'**read·i·ness** *n.*

re·al (rēəl) *adj.* 1. actually existing; not imaginary. 2. not false; genuine: *are these spoons made of real silver?* '**re·al·ism** *n.* 1. ability or willingness to face facts or to concentrate on the practical. 2. (in art or literature) the attempt to convey life accurately, not hiding unpleasant aspects. '**re·al·ist** *n.* a person who concentrates on practical issues and claims to be without illusions. **re·al'is·tic** *adj.* 1. practical; clear-sighted. 2. life-like; true to the object or situation represented. **re'al·i·ty** *n.* actual fact. —'**re·al·ly** *adv.*

re·al·ize ('rēəlīz) *vb.* **re·al·iz·ing, re·al·ized.** 1. to understand clearly; become aware: *he realized it was raining.* 2. to make real; achieve: *she realized her ambition to be a singer.* —**re·al·i'za·tion** *n.*

realm (relm) *n.* 1. a kingdom. 2. an area of interest or knowledge: *the realm of science.*

reap (rēp) *vb.* 1. to cut (crops) with a sickle, scythe, or reaping machine; harvest. 2. to obtain (penalties or rewards) for past actions: *he reaped the rewards of his hard work.*

rear[1] (rēr) *n.* the part or position at the back. —*adj.* hind; at the back: *rear wheels.*

rear[2] (rēr) *vb.* 1. to bring up; raise (cattle, plants, children, etc.). 2. to rise on the hind legs: *the horse reared in fright.* 3. to rise or cause to rise steeply: *the cliff reared behind the house.*

rea·son ('rēzən) *n.* 1. a cause; motive. 2. excuse; logical argument. 3. the mind's power of thinking logically. —*vb.* 1. to think clearly and step by step. 2. to persuade or try to persuade by argument: *she tried to reason with him.* '**rea·son·a·ble** *adj.* 1. acting according to reason. 2. sensible; moderate. —'**rea·son·a·bly** *adv.*

re·as·sure ('rēəshoor) *vb.* **re·as·sur·ing, re·as·sured.** to restore confidence: *your promises reassure me.*

reb·el *n.* ('rebəl) 1. a person who resists social pressures or authority. 2. a person who tries to overthrow the legal government by force. —*vb.* (ri'bel) **re·bel·ling, re·belled.** 1. to resist authority. 2. to try to overthrow a government. 3. to feel or show extreme dislike or resentment. **re'bel·lion** *n.* an organized and open resistance to authority. —**re'bel·lious** *adj.* —**re'bel·lious·ly** *adv.* —**re'bel·lious·ness** *n.*

re·bound *vb.* (ri'bound) to bounce back after a collision. —*n.* ('rēbound) the act of rebounding.

re·buke (ri'byōōk) *vb.* **re·buk·ing, re·buked.** to scold; reprimand. —*n.* a reproof; a scolding.

re·call *vb.* (ri'kôl) 1. to call back. 2. to remember; bring back to mind. —*n.* ('rēkôl) 1. a message ordering return. 2. the power to remember: *her recall of the event was very good.*

re·cant (ri'kant) *vb.* to admit that one's former beliefs are wrong.

rear

re·ceipt (ri'sēt) *n.* 1. the act of receiving or being received. 2. a written acknowledgment that money or goods have been received. 3. **re·ceipts** (*pl.*) the money taken by a business. —*vb.* to make out a written receipt.

receiver

re·ceive (ri'sēv) *vb.* **re·ceiv·ing, re·ceived.** 1. to get; accept. 2. to take in as guest; greet. **re'ceiv·er** *n.* 1. a person or thing that receives. 2. the earpiece of a telephone. 3. an apparatus, e.g. a TV or radio set, for transforming electrical waves into pictures or sounds.

re·cent ('rēsənt) *adj.* begun or happening not long ago; modern: *recent events.* —'**re·cent·ly** *adv.*

re·cep·ta·cle (ri'septəkəl) *n.* a container or place to put things.

re·cep·tion (ri'sepshən) *n.* 1. the act or manner of receiving or being received: *a favorable reception.* 2. the way in which radio or TV signals are received: *radio reception was poor because of the thunderstorms.* 3. a formal party or receiving of guests: *a champagne reception.* **re'cep·tion·ist** *n.* a person employed to greet and guide visitors to a business office, hospital, etc. **re'cep·tive** *adj.* quick and eager to receive new ideas, impressions, etc. —**re'cep·tive·ly** *adv.* —**re'cep·tive·ness** *n.*

re·cess (ri'ses, 'rēses) *n.* 1. an alcove; part of a room or wall set back from the rest. 2. a temporary halt to work.

re·ci·pe ('resəpē) *n.* 1. a list of ingredients and instructions for making something to eat or drink. 2. a well-known way of achieving a particular result: *the recipe for success.*

re·cite (ri'sīt) *vb.* **re·cit·ing, re·cit·ed.** 1. to repeat aloud from memory. 2. to quote (a list) item by item. **re'cit·al** *n.* 1. a detailed account or story. 2. the performance of music by a soloist or a small group of musicians. **rec·i·ta·tion** (resi'tāshən) *n.* 1. the act of reciting, esp. from memory. 2. the repeating of a prepared lesson.

reck·less ('reklis) *adj.* not thinking of the consequences; careless. —**reck·less·ly** *adv.* —'**reck·less·ness** *n.*

reck·on ('rekən) *vb.* 1. to count or estimate: *we reckoned on 50 people attending the party.* 2. to consider; suppose: *I reckon we'll get there in time.*

re·cline (ri'klīn) *vb.* **re·clin·ing, re·clined.** to lie back or down so as to rest comfortably.

rec·og·nize ('rekəgnīz) *vb.* **rec·og·niz·ing, rec·og·nized.** 1. to be or become aware that one knows (someone or something). 2. to acknowledge or accept (a fact): *Dave recognized that he had to help his father.* —**rec·og·ni·tion** (rekəg'nishən) *n.*

re·coil (ri'koil) *vb.* 1. to jump or move back from; shrink: *Maria recoiled when she saw the snake.* 2. (of a gun) to kick back sharply when fired.

rec·om·mend (rekə'mend) *vb.* 1. to speak well of: *she recommended her dentist to her friend.* 2. to advise: *the doctor recommends a long rest.* **rec·om·men'da·tion** *n.* 1. the act of recommending. 2. a favorable statement about someone or something.

re·cord *n.* ('rekərd) 1. a permanent account in writing, on film, tape, etc., of facts or events. 2. a person's known previous behavior: *she has a record of lateness.* 3. an achievement, esp. in sport, that surpasses everything previously achieved: *Joanna broke the school's high jump record.* 4. a thin disk on which music or other sounds have been registered to be played back later. —*vb.* (ri'kôrd) 1. to put down in writing. 2. to show or indicate. 3. to make a musical record. **re'cord·er** *n.* 1. a person or machine that records. 2. a small musical wind instrument with finger holes to change the pitch.

re·cov·er (ri'kuvər) *vb.* 1. to get well again. 2. to return to normal. 3. to get back (something): *the police recovered the stolen car.* —**re'cov·er·y** *n.,pl.* **re·cov·erries.**

rec·re·a·tion (rekrē'āshən) *n.* a sport, hobby, or other activity that a person does in his free time.

re·cruit (ri'kro͞ot) *n.* a new member of an organization, esp. army, navy, or air force. —*vb.* to get (people) to join an organization. **re'cruit·ment** *n.* the process of obtaining recruits.

rec·tan·gle ('rektanggəl) *n.* a figure with four sides and four right angles. See GEOMETRY. —**rec·tan·gu·lar** (rek'tanggyələr) *adj.*

re·deem (ri'dēm) *vb.* 1. to buy or get back. 2. to exchange: *she redeemed her trading stamps for an alarm clock.* 3. to make up for: *the excellent food redeemed the slow service at the restaurant.* 4. to save; rescue. —**re·demp·tion** (ri'dempshən) *n.*

re·duce (ri'do͞os, ri'dyo͞os) *vb.* **re·duc·ing, re·duced.** (often + *to*) 1. to lessen or make smaller in amount, size, strength, or position. 2. to change the form of; to simplify: *he reduced his essay to a short list of facts.* —**re·duc·tion** (ri'dukshən) *n.*

re·dun·dant (ri'dundənt) *adj.* unnecessary; repetitious: *a redundant remark.* —**re'dun·dan·cy** *n.,pl.* **re·dun·dan·cies.**

reed (rēd) *n.* 1. one of many tall moisture-loving grasses with hollow stems and narrow leaves. 2. a thin piece of wood, metal, etc., in the mouth of certain wind instruments that vibrates to produce a sound.

reef (rēf) *n.* a ridge of rock, coral, etc., near the surface of the sea or other stretch of water.

reel

reel[1] (rēl) *n.* a cylinder or spool around which rope, fishing line, film, etc., is wound for storage. —*vb.* to wind or unwind using a reel.

reel[2] (rēl) *vb.* 1. to move unsteadily; stagger: *Philip reeled across the field when the ball hit him.* 2. to turn round and round. —*n.* 1. a lively dance such as the Virginia Reel. 2. the music for this dance.

re·fer (ri'fûr) *vb.* **re·fer·ring, re·ferred.** 1. to mention. 2. to indicate or concern. 3. to consult for information: *to refer to a dictionary.* 4. to send or pass on: *her doctor referred her to a specialist.* **ref·er·ee** (refə'rē) *n.* 1. a person who acts as a judge, esp. in certain sports; umpire. 2. a person who supports or recommends another by making a statement about his character, abilities, financial status, etc. —*vb.* to act as a referee. **ref·er·ence** ('refərəns) *n.* 1. an act or instance of referring. 2. the source of a piece of information. 3. a written recommendation of a person.

re·fine (ri'fīn) *vb.* **re·fin·ing, re·fined.** to make (oil, sugar, etc.) pure by removing other substances. **re'fined** *adj.* 1. made pure. 2. behaving in an elegant or polite way. **re'fine·ment** *n.* 1. elegant or delicate manners. 2. improvement. **re'fin·er·y** *n.,pl.* **re·fin·er·ies.** a factory that refines oil, sugar, etc.

re·flect (ri'flekt) *vb.* 1. to throw back (light, heat, etc.). 2. to give (an image of something: *the calm lake reflected the hills.* 3. to think deeply and carefully. 4. to represent; give an impression of: *the records he brought reflected his taste in music.* 5. to discredit, hurt the reputation of: *his behavior reflected on his parents.* **re'flec·tion** *n.* 1. an image that is reflected. 2. the act of reflecting. —**re'flec·tor** *n.*

re·flex ('rēfleks) *n.* an action that is carried out by the muscles without thinking about it: *the doctor tested his reflexes by tapping his knee.* —*adj.* of or by a reflex. **reflex angle** an ANGLE[1] (def. 1) greater than 180°.

re·form (ri'fôrm) *vb.* to make or become better; improve by making changes. —*n.* a change for the better.

re·fract (ri'frakt) *vb.* to cause (rays of sound, light, etc.) to bend aside: *the curved surface of the telescope lens refracts the light.* —**re'frac·tion** *n.*

re·fresh (ri'fresh) *vb.* to restore strength and energy, esp. by giving or consuming food or drink. **re'fresh·ment** *n.* often **re·fresh·ments** (*pl.*) food and drink.

re·frig·er·ate (ri'frijərāt) *vb.* **re·frig·er·at·ing, re·frig·er·at·ed.** to make or keep cold, esp. in order to preserve food. **re'frig·er·a·tor** *n.* an insulated box that preserves food by keeping it cold.

ref·uge ('refyo͞oj) *n.* a place of shelter or safety. **ref·u·gee** (refyo͞o'jē) *n.* a person who has been forced by war or other disaster to leave his home.

re·fund *vb.* (ri'fund) to pay back money: ***the cost of faulty goods will be refunded by the store.*** —*n.* ('rēfund) a repayment.

re·fuse[1] (ri'fyo͞oz) *vb.* **re·fus·ing, re·fused.** 1. to turn down or reject (something offered). 2. to be unwilling to do or give (something): *to refuse permission.*

ref·use[2] ('refyo͞os) *n.* garbage; waste matter.

re·gard (ri'gârd) *vb.* 1. to consider; give thought to. 2. to think well of; esteem. 3. to observe; stare at. —*n.* 1. admiration; respect. 2. concern: ***he has no regard for anyone else.*** 3. **re·gards** (*pl.*) best wishes. **re'gard·less** *adj.* having no concern for.

re·gat·ta (ri'gatə, ri'gâtə) *n.* a sailboat or rowboat race.

reg·i·ment *n.* ('rejəmənt) a large military unit, usu. made up of several battalions and commanded by a colonel. —*vb.* ('rejəment) to organize strictly.

re·gion ('rējən) *n.* an area or part of a country or the world, often without any exact boundaries: ***the Arctic region.*** —**'re·gion·al** *adj.*

reg·is·ter ('rejistər) *n.* 1. an official book or list containing a record, e.g. of marriages, voters, etc. 2. a machine or device used to record amounts, e.g. a cash register. 3. a part of the range of a human voice or musical instrument. 4. a device that controls the flow of air in a heating or air-conditioning system. —*vb.* 1. to make an entry, or put one's name, in a register. 3. to show or indicate: ***his face registered hatred.*** 4. to pay a fee for (mail) in order to have it officially recorded. **reg·is·trar** ('rejistrâr) *n.* an official responsible for making registrations and keeping records. **'reg·is·try** *n.,pl.* **reg·is·tries.** the place where registers are kept. —**reg·is'tra·tion** *n.*

re·gret (ri'gret) *vb.* **re·gret·ting, re·gret·ted.** to feel sorry or repentant about (something). —*n.* a feeling of sadness or disappointment. **re'gret·ful** *adj.* feeling regret. **re'gret·ta·ble** *adj.* causing regret; unfortunate. —**re'gret·ful·ly** *adv.* —**re'gret·ta·bly** *adv.*

reg·u·lar ('regyələr) *adj.* 1. evenly set out in time or space: ***he walked with a regular step.*** 2. usual; according to habit: ***a regular customer.*** —*n.* a professional soldier. **'reg·u·lar·ize** *vb.* **reg·u·lar·iz·ing, reg·u·lar·ized.** to make regular or more regular. —**reg·u'lar·i·ty** *n.* —**'reg·u·lar·ly** *adv.*

reg·u·late ('regyəlāt) *vb.* **reg·u·lat·ing, reg·u·lat·ed.** 1. to check by means of rules or controls: ***the factory regulates the quality of its products.*** 2. to adjust in order to make regular or accurate: ***the alarm clock needs regulating.*** **reg·u'la·tion** *n.* 1. the act of regulating. 2. a rule or law. —*adj.* as demanded by the rules; standard.

re·hearse (ri'hûrs) *vb.* **re·hears·ing, re·hearsed.** 1. to practice (a play, speech, etc.) before a public performance. 2. to recite or relate: ***he rehearsed the sad tale to his friends.*** —**re'hears·al** *n.*

reign (rān) *vb.* 1. to rule as sovereign or supreme power. 2. to be the main influence; prevail. —*n.* the period during which someone or something rules or prevails.

rein (rān) *n.* often **reins** (*pl.*) the long narrow strap joined to a horse's bit, used for guiding and controlling the animal. —*vb.* to control with a rein.

reindeer

rein·deer ('rāndēr) *n.,pl.* **rein·deer.** a large deer with branched antlers found in Arctic regions and sometimes kept in herds for its milk, meat, and hide.

re·in·force (rēin'fôrs) *vb.* **re·in·forc·ing, re·in·forced.** to give support or added strength to. **re·in'force·ment** *n.* 1. the act of reinforcing. 2. something that reinforces.

re·ject *vb.* (ri'jekt) to turn down; refuse to allow or accept (something offered or proposed): ***he rejected her advice.*** —*n.* ('rējekt) something that is rejected as damaged, unwanted, or worthless. —**re'jec·tion** *n.*

re·joice (ri'jois) *vb.* **re·joic·ing, re·joiced.** to express great joy.

re·late (ri'lāt) *vb.* **re·lat·ing, re·lat·ed.** 1. to tell the story of; describe: ***he related his vacation experiences.*** 2. to concern; to have, make, or find a connection with: ***the description relates to someone else.*** **re·lat·ed** *adj.* connected by blood ties or marriage.

re·la·tion (ri'lāshən) *n.* 1. a person connected with another by blood ties or marriage: ***aunts and uncles are relations.*** 2. a connection or point of similarity: ***this problem has no relation to the previous one.*** 3. the telling of a story: ***his relation of the tale was not accurate.*** 4. **re·la·tions** (*pl.*) the feelings that exist between people or groups of people dealing together. **re'la·tion·ship** *n.* 1. the way in which one person deals with and interacts with another: ***a stormy relationship.*** 2. the state of being related; a point of connection; link.

rel·a·tive ('relətiv) *n.* a person connected to another by blood ties or marriage; relation. —*adj.* 1. comparative: ***relative calm was restored.*** 2. strictly connected with: ***state only the details relative to the problem.*** 3. (grammar) noting or concerning a kind of connecting pronoun, e.g. ***who, which,*** used to begin a clause. **'rel·a·tive·ly** *adv.* comparatively; fairly.

re·lax (ri'laks) *vb.* 1. to make or become less tense in body and mind. 2. to make easier or less strict: ***discipline has slowly been relaxed in the office.*** **re·lax·a·tion** (rēlak'sāshən) *n.* 1. the act of relaxing. 2. a means of relaxing; pastime.

re·lay *n.* ('rēlā) 1. a fresh group of workers, team of animals, etc., that takes over from another: ***clearing the wreckage will be done in relays.*** 2. an electrical apparatus for increasing the strength and range of radio messages. **relay race** a race in which each member of competing teams covers only part of the course and is then replaced by another member. —*vb.* ('rēlā, ri'lā) 1. to pass on (information). 2. to receive and transmit (a radio message, broadcast, etc.) to a wider area.

re·lease (ri'lēs) *vb.* **re·leas·ing, re·leased.** 1. to let go; set free. 2. to make (information, a record, film, etc.) available to the public. —*n.* 1. the act of releasing. 2. freedom from something. 3. a discharge from prison. 4. a device for unfastening: *seat belts have quick releases.* 5. a current record, film, etc.

re·li·a·ble (ri'līəbəl) *adj.* dependable; trustworthy. —**re·li·a'bil·i·ty** *n.* —**re'li·a·bly** *adv.*

re·lieve (ri'lēv) *vb.* **re·liev·ing, re·lieved.** 1. to ease or remove (pain, anxiety, etc.). 2. to free (a besieged town, castle, etc.). 3. to take over (duties) from another person. 4. to provide a break from or a contrast to: *no sunshine relieved the foggy day.* **re'lief** *n.* 1. the act of relieving. 2. someone or something that relieves. 3. a method of carving designs, figures, etc., so that the pattern stands out from the background. 4. variation in the surface of the land esp. as shown on a relief map.

re·li·gion (ri'lijən) *n.* 1. a particular system of belief, worship, etc. 2. belief in and worship of a supernatural power. —**re'li·gious** *adj.* —**re'li·gious·ly** *adv.*

rel·ish ('relish) *n.* 1. spicy or strongly flavored food used to improve the taste of other food. 2. a liking for; enthusiasm. —*vb.* to enjoy: *he relished the thought of going to Europe.*

re·luc·tant (ri'luktənt) *adj.* unwilling; unenthusiastic. —**re'luc·tance** *n.* —**re'luc·tant·ly** *adv.*

re·ly (ri'lī) *vb.* **re·ly·ing, re·lied.** (+ *on* or *upon*) to depend on; be able to trust. —**re'li·ance** *n.*

re·main (ri'mān) *vb.* 1. to be left after the rest or a part has gone away or been changed. 2. to continue; go on being: *they remained at home all evening.* **re'main·der** *n.* the remaining portion. **re'mains** *pl.n.* 1. a thing or things left over. 2. ruins.

re·mark (ri'mârk) *vb.* 1. to say or state briefly or casually. 2. (+ *on*) to mention specially. —*n.* a short statement; comment. **re'mark·a·ble** *adj.* out of the ordinary; unusual or unexpected.

rem·e·dy ('remidē) *n.,pl.* **rem·e·dies.** something that heals or improves. —*vb.* **rem·e·dy·ing, rem·e·died.** to put right, heal, or improve.

re·mem·ber (ri'membər) *vb.* 1. to bring back to mind. 2. to keep in mind: *I will always remember this occasion.* —**re'mem·brance** *n.*

re·mind (ri'mīnd) *vb.* to cause to remember or think of: *remind me to buy some eggs.*

rem·nant ('remnənt) *n.* a small piece of something left over or amount left behind.

re·mote (ri'mōt) *adj.* 1. distant; isolated: *he lived in a remote hut in the mountains.* 2. very slight: *a remote chance of success.* —**re'mote·ly** *adv.* —**re'mote·ness** *n.*

re·move (ri'mōōv) *vb.* **re·mov·ing, re·moved.** to take or move away. **re'mov·al** *n.* the act or process of removing.

rent (rent) *n.* regular payment for the use of a house or other property belonging to another person. —*vb.* 1. to have the right to use (something) in return for payment: *we rented a villa for our holiday.* 2. to give the right to use (something) in return for payment: *the farmer rents his cottages to vacationers.*

re·pair (ri'peər) *vb.* to mend; put in working order again. —*n.* 1. the act of repairing. 2. the condition of something: *Sam kept his bicycle in good repair.*

re·peat (ri'pēt) *vb.* to say or do (something) again. —*n.* something that is repeated: *this broadcast is a repeat of last week's concert.* **rep·e·ti·tion** (repi'tishən) *n.* the act of repeating. —**re'peat·a·ble** *adj.*

re·pel (ri'pel) *vb.* **re·pel·ling, re·pelled.** 1. to drive away; force back. 2. to cause a feeling of disgust in: *the smell of the rotting fish repelled them.* 3. to keep out: *the raincoat repels rain.* **re'pel·lent** *adj.* able to repel; disgusting: *his habits are repellent.* *n.* something that repels, esp. a spray or ointment that drives away insects.

re·pent (ri'pent) *vb.* to feel sorrow, guilt, or shame about (something one has done). —**re'pent·ance** *n.* —**re'pent·ant** *adj.*

re·place (ri'plās) *vb.* 1. to provide a substitute for: *plastics have replaced leather for many uses.* 2. to return or restore (something) to its proper place.

re·ply (ri'plī) *vb.* **re·ply·ing, re·plied.** to say or do (something) in answer to something else; respond. —*n.,pl.* **re·plies.** an answer.

re·port (ri'pôrt) *n.* 1. a statement, description, or account often set out in a formal way: *the journalist wrote a report on the event.* 2. a bang: *the report of a gun.* —*vb.* 1. to make or give a report about: *she reported the faulty telephone.* 2. to present oneself: *Mike reported for work late.* **re'port·er** *n.* a person who reports news for a newspaper, radio, etc.

rep·re·sent (repri'zent) *vb.* 1. to stand for; be a symbol of. 2. to act on behalf of: *his lawyer represented him in court.* **rep·re·sen'ta·tion** *n.* the act of representing. **rep·re'sent·a·tive** *adj.* characteristic or typical: *a representative selection.* *n.* a person who acts or speaks for others.

re·proach (ri'prōch) *vb.* to blame; make (someone) feel ashamed or guilty: *his mother reproached him for not wiping his muddy shoes.* —*n.* 1. sorrowful disapproval or accusation. 2. disgrace. —**re'proach·ful** *adj.* —**re'proach·ful·ly** *adv.*

re·pro·duce (rēprə'dōōs, rēprə'dyōōs) *vb.* **re·pro·duc·ing, re·pro·duced.** 1. to produce an exact copy. 2. to produce young.

re·pro·duc·tion (rēprə'dukshən) *n.* 1. the process of reproducing. 2. a copy; something reproduced from an original, e.g. a painting.

rep·tile ('reptīl) *n.* one of a large group of cold-blooded animals that have scaly or horny skins and generally reproduce by laying eggs. —**rep·til·i·an** (rep'tilēən, rep'tilyən) *adj.*

re·pub·lic (ri'publik) *n.* 1. a form of government in which power is held by the people and their elected representatives. 2. a country or state with this form of government. **re'pub·li·can** *adj.* of or favoring a republic. *n.* a person who favors the republican system.

rep·u·ta·tion (repyə'tāshən) *n.* the general public opinion of a person, place, or thing.

re·pute (ri'pyōōt) *n.* public opinion; reputation. *vb.* **re·put·ing, re·put·ed.** to be said or generally thought to be: *he is reputed to be rich.* **rep·u·ta·ble** ('repyətəbəl) *adj.* well-known to be trustworthy, respectable, etc.

re·quest (ri'kwest) *n.* 1. the act of asking for something. 2. something that is asked for: *her request was granted.* —*vb.* to ask for politely.

re·quire (ri'kwīər) *vb.* **re·quir·ing, re·quired.** to need; demand: *knitting requires patience.* **re'quire·ment** *n.* something that is needed.

res·cue ('reskyōō) *vb.* **res·cu·ing, res·cued.** to save from danger, captivity, or death. —*n.* the act of setting free or saving.

re·search (ri'sûrch, 'rēsûrch) *n.* detailed investigation to discover fresh facts: *she was doing research into cures for cancer.* —*vb.* to carry out research.

re·sem·ble (ri'zembəl) *vb.* **re·sem·bling, re·sem·bled.** to be like or similar to, either in general appearance or in some detail. —**re'sem·blance** *n.*

re·sent (ri'zent) *vb.* to be angered or hurt by another's action: *I resent your interference.* —**re'sent·ful** *adj.*

re·serve (ri'zûrv) *vb.* **re·serv·ing, re·served.** 1. to keep aside for a special purpose. 2. to save up for future use. —*n.* 1. something reserved or stored for future use: *they had a reserve of canned food in the house.* 2. the habit of not expressing one's thoughts or feelings. 3. land set aside as a protected area for animals. 4. emergency forces, players, etc., only to be used if really necessary. **re'served** *adj.* 1. shy; quiet: *a reserved person.* 2. kept for a special purpose: *reserved seats.* **res·er·va·tion** (rezər'vāshən) *n.* 1. act of reserving. 2. something that is reserved, e.g. a booked seat on a train. 3. doubt or uncertainty: *I have reservations about his honesty.* 4. land set aside for a purpose.

res·er·voir ('rezərvwâr) *n.* an artificial lake or tank where water supplies are stored.

re·sign (ri'zīn) *vb.* 1. to give up (a job, position, etc.). 2. to submit patiently to something unpleasant. **res·ig·na·tion** (rezig'nāshən) *n.* 1. the act of giving up. 2. calm acceptance.

re·sist (ri'zist) *vb.* to stand up to or fight against. **re'sist·ance** *n.* 1. the act of resisting. 2. an opposing force: *water resistance reduces a boat's speed.* —**re'sist·ant** *adj.*

reso·lu·tion (rezə'lōōshən) *n.* 1. firm determination: *he made a resolution to give up smoking.* 2. a decision: *the council approved the resolution to buy extra land.* **'res·o·lute** *adj.* determined; showing will power.

re·solve (ri'zolv) *vb.* **re·solv·ing, re·solved.** 1. to make up one's mind; decide. 2. to solve or settle: *the difficult situation was resolved by his departure.* —*n.* a firmly fixed purpose.

re·sort (ri'zôrt) *n.* 1. a place popular with vacationers. 2. a person or thing that one goes to for advice, protection, etc. —*vb.* 1. to visit regularly. 2. to turn to: *he was so poor that he resorted to stealing.*

re·sound (ri'zound) *vb.* to make a loud or echoing sound: *the crash resounded through the neighborhood.*

reptiles

chameleon

tortoise

rattlesnake

re·source ('rēsôrs, ri'sôrs) *n.* 1. usu. **re·sourc·es** (*pl.*) supplies of minerals, power, etc., that form the basis of a country's wealth. 2. a person or thing from which one can seek support or help. 3. skill; powers of invention. —**re'source·ful** *adj.* —**re'source·ful·ly** *adv.*

re·spect (ri'spekt) *vb.* 1. to honor; admire. 2. to treat with attention or consideration: *he respected his grandfather's need for peace and quiet.* —*n.* 1. admiration. 2. politeness; consideration. **re·spect·a'bil·i·ty** *n.* the condition of having an assured and respected social position. **re'spect·a·ble** *adj.* 1. decent; well-behaved. 2. deserving admiration: *a respectable essay.* **re'spec·tive** *adj.* referring individually to particular people or things: *the runners went to their respective starting positions.*

re·spond (ri'spond) *vb.* 1. to reply or answer. 2. to react. **re'sponse** *n.* an answer or reaction. **re'spon·sive** *adj.* quick to react. —**re'spon·sive·ly** *adv.* —**re'spon·sive·ness** *n.*

re·spon·si·ble (ri'sponsəbəl) *adj.* 1. accountable; having the job of caring for something: *the guide was responsible for our safety.* 2. reliable. 3. being the cause of: *several years of drought were responsible for the famine.* —**re·spon·si'bil·i·ty** *n.* —**re'spon·si·bly** *adv.*

rest[1] (rest) *n.* 1. a pause for relaxation, sleep, or refreshment. 2. a prop or support, e.g. a head rest. 3. a silent interval in music. —*vb.* 1. to have or cause to have a rest. 2. to lean on or place something on: *rest the load on the step.* —**'rest·ful** *adj.* —**'rest·ful·ly** *adv.* —**'rest·ful·ness** *n.* —**'rest·less** *adj.*

rest[2] (rest) *n.* 1. remainder; that which is left: *take what you want, they can have the rest.* 2. all the others: *I go today, the rest go tomorrow.*

res·tau·rant ('restərânt) *n.* a place where meals are sold and eaten.

re·store (ri'stôr) *vb.* **re·stor·ing, re·stored.** 1. to give or bring back: *the lost child was restored to his parents.* 2. to repair or renew. **res·to·ra·tion** (restə'rāshən) *n.* 1. the act of giving or bringing back. 2. the work of restoring old buildings, paintings, etc., to their original condition.

re·strain (ri'strān) *vb.* to hold in or back; check.

re·strict (ri'strikt) *vb.* to limit; confine: *her diet restricts her eating habits.* —**re'stric·tion** *n.*

re·sult (ri'zult) *vb.* to have or follow as a consequence: *his carelessness resulted in an accident.* —*n.* outcome; consequence: *the results of the tests were good.* —**re'sult·ant** *adj.*

res·ur·rect (rezə'rekt) *vb.* 1. to bring back to use after disuse: *she resurrected her grandmother's shawl for the play.* 2. to bring back to life. **res·ur'rec·tion** *n.* 1. act of resurrecting. 2. the Christian doctrine that Christ rose from the dead.

re·tail ('rētāl) *n.* sale of goods in small quantities direct to the customer. —*adj.* selling goods by retail: *a retail dress shop.* —*vb.* 1. to sell or be sold to the consumer. 2. to repeat in detail: *she retailed the whole incident to everyone she met.*

re·tain (ri'tān) *vb.* 1. to keep hold of: *though poor, she retained her dignity.* 2. to reserve (someone's services) by paying a fee: *the racehorse trainer retains two jockeys.* **re'tain·er** *n.* a fee paid to secure services. **re·ten·tion** (ri'tenshən) *n.* the act or ability of retaining: *the retention of water by sand is low.* —**re'ten·tive** *adj.*

re·tal·i·ate (ri'taleāt) *vb.* **re·tal·i·at·ing, re·tal·i·at·ed.** to take vengeance; repay a wrong with a similar action. —**re·tal·i'a·tion** *n.*

ret·i·na ('retənə) *n.* the layer of cells inside the back of the eyeball that are sensitive to light and transmit images to the brain. See EYE.

re·tire (ri'tīər) *vb.* **re·tir·ing, re·tired.** 1. to give up full-time work usu. because of age. 2. to withdraw; go away: *the runner retired from the race with a strained leg muscle.* 3. to go to bed: *we usually retire before midnight.* **re'tire·ment** *n.* 1. the act of giving up work. 2. the state of being retired.

re·tort (ri'tôrt) *vb.* to answer back quickly, esp. in anger. —*n.* a quickly made angry or witty reply: *Joy made a sharp retort to my complaint.*

re·treat (ri'trēt) *vb.* to go back or withdraw, esp. under attack. —*n.* 1. the act of retreating. 2. a place of safety or peace.

re·trieve (ri'trēv) *vb.* **re·triev·ing, re·trieved.** 1. to fetch or recover. 2. to make good or repair: *he retrieved his losses by hard work.* **re'triev·er** *n.* a breed of dog often trained to fetch game that has been shot. —**re'triev·a·ble** *adj.*

re·turn (ri'tûrn) *vb.* 1. to go, come, give, send, take, or answer back. 2. to make an official statement or election: *the town returned four women to the council this year.* —*n.* 1. the act of returning. 2. an official statement, e.g. an income tax return. 3. **re·turns** (*pl.*) proceeds or profit. —**re'turn·a·ble** *adj.*

re·un·ion (rē'yo͞onyən) *n.* a meeting of family members, old friends, etc., after separation: *Carol goes to her college reunion every year.* **re·u·nite** (rēyo͞o'nīt) *vb.* **re·u·nit·ing, re·u·nit·ed.** to come or bring together again.

re·veal (ri'vēl) *vb.* 1. to cause or allow to be seen. 2. to make known: *the newspaper revealed the shocking facts.* **rev·e·la·tion** (revə'lāshən) *n.* 1. the act of revealing. 2. something that is revealed, esp. something surprising.

re·venge (ri'venj) *vb.* **re·veng·ing, re·venged.** to do harm in return for an injury suffered. —*n.* the act of revenging. —**re'venge·ful** *adj.*

re·verse (ri'vûrs) *vb.* **re·vers·ing, re·versed.** 1. to turn back to front, upside down, the other way round, etc. 2. to change to the opposite: *he reversed his decision.* 3. to move or be moved backward. —*n.* 1. the opposite: *he thought she was rich but the reverse is true.* 2. a setback or defeat: *the army suffered a reverse.* 3. the back or side opposite the head. 4. the gear of a vehicle that makes it go backward: *he shifted into reverse.* —*adj.* opposite; back. —**re'vers·i·ble** *adj.*

revolver

re·view (ri'vyōō) *vb.* 1. to look at again; reconsider: *Martin reviewed his essay and found several mistakes.* 2. to write a critical report of (a play, book, opera, etc.) for a newspaper or magazine. 3. to inspect (troops, ships, etc.). —*n.* 1. a critical report of a play, book, etc. 2. a general reconsideration or summing-up. 3. an inspection of troops, ships, etc.

re·vise (ri'vīz) *vb.* **re·vis·ing, re·vised.** to reconsider and change for the better: *we revised our plans.* —**re·vi·sion** (ri'vizhən) *n.*

re·vive (ri'vīv) *vb.* **re·viv·ing, re·vived.** 1. to bring or come back to life, health, popularity, etc. 2. to put on a new production of (an old play, opera, etc.) —**re'viv·al** *n.*

re·volt (ri'vōlt) *vb.* 1. to rebel or rise up against authority. 2. to disgust: *your table manners revolt me.* —*n.* a rebellion or uprising. **re'volt·ing** *adj.* disgusting; loathsome.

rev·o·lu·tion (revə'lōōshən) *n.* 1. a rebellion or violent upheaval that overthrows the government. 2. a complete movement or rotation around a central point. **rev·o'lu·tion·ar·y** *n.,pl.* **rev·o·lu·tion·ar·ies.** a person who promotes revolution. *adj.* causing great or violent changes.

re·volve (ri'volv) *vb.* **re·volv·ing, re·volved.** 1. to turn or rotate about a central point or axis. 2. to turn over in one's mind; ponder.

re·volv·er (ri'volvər) *n.* a small hand-held gun that has ammunition placed in a revolving cylinder, so that it does not need reloading after every shot.

re·ward (ri'wôrd) *n.* 1. something given in return for help or merit. 2. a sum of money offered in return for a lost person, thing, etc. —*vb.* to give a reward to.

rheu·ma·tism ('rōōmətizəm) *n.* a painful disease in which the the joints and muscles swell and stiffen. —**rheu·mat·ic** (rōō'matik) *adj.*

rhi·noc·er·os (rī'nosərəs) *n.,pl.* **rhi·noc·er·os·es.** a large heavily built African or Indian animal with a thick skin and one or two upright horns on its snout.

rhom·bus ('rombəs) *n.,pl.* **rhom·bus·es** *or* **rhom·bi** ('rombī). a figure with four sides of equal length and angles that are not right angles.

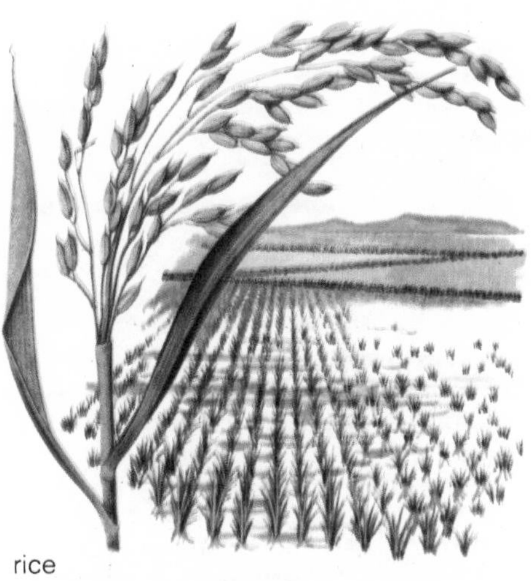

rice

rhu·barb ('rōōbârb) *n.* a plant whose reddish leaf stalks are cooked and eaten as a dessert or used for preserves.

rhyme (rīm) *n.* 1. the similarity of sounds in words, esp. at the ends of lines of verses, e.g. *take, make, bake.* 2. verse or verses containing rhymes. —*vb.* **rhym·ing, rhymed.** to make a rhyme or rhymes.

rhythm ('ridhəm) *n.* a regular sequence of sounds: *the rhythm of a waltz.* —'**rhyth·mic** *adj.*

rib (rib) *n.* 1. one of the slender curved bones extending from the backbone to the front of the chest. 2. something resembling a rib in shape: *the ribs of an umbrella.*

rib·bon ('ribən) *n.* a flat narrow band or strip of material, paper, etc.

rice (rīs) *n.* 1. a type of grain used as food. 2. the plant that grows in warm countries and produces this grain.

rich (rich) *adj.* 1. wealthy; owning a great deal of money, property, etc. 2. fertile; having plenty: *the desert is rich in oil.* 3. (of food) containing much butter, cream, or seasoning. 4. splendid: *rich furnishings.* '**rich·es** *pl.,n.* great wealth.

rid (rid) *vb.* **rid·ding, rid.** to make free from: *we rid the garden of weeds.*

rid·dle[1] ('ridəl) *n.* a puzzling question that is made deliberately difficult to understand, e.g. *what has four wheels and flies?* Answer: *a garbage truck.*

rid·dle[2] ('ridəl) *vb.* **rid·dling, rid·dled.** to pierce with many holes: *the timber was riddled with termite holes.*

ridge (rij) *n.* 1. the raised line made by the meeting of two sloping surfaces: *the ridge of a tent.* 2. any raised strip, as on cloth. 3. a long line of hills or high ground.

rid·i·cule ('ridəkyōōl) *vb.* **rid·i·cul·ing, rid·i·culed.** to make fun of; mock. —*n.* mockery; scorn. **ri·dic·u·lous** (ri'dikyələs) *adj.* laughable; absurd. —**ri'dic·u·lous·ly** *adv.*

ri·fle[1] ('rīfəl) *n.* a gun with spiral grooves inside its long barrel that spin the bullet and increase its speed.

ri·fle[2] ('rīfəl) *vb.* **ri·fling, ri·fled.** to search thoroughly in order to steal from: *the burglar rifled all the drawers in the house.*

rift (rift) *n.* 1. a split; crack: *the sun came through a rift in the clouds.* 2. a quarrel or lack of understanding.

rig (rig) *vb.* **rig·ging, rigged.** 1. to arrange (something) to benefit oneself: *the race was rigged so that Arthur would win.* 2. to provide with necessary equipment. 3. (+ *up*) to make hastily or in a makeshift way: *they rigged up a shelter when they were caught in the storm.* —*n.* 1. the tall drilling tower used in mining and oil extraction. 2. an outfit of clothing, equipment, etc., for a special purpose: *diving rig.* 3. (also **rig·ging**) the arrangement of ropes, cables, chains, etc., that braces the masts and works the sails of a sailboat.

right (rīt) *adj.* 1. fair; just. 2. correct; true. 3. proper; suitable: *it was only right to help.* 4. on the east side of your body as you face north. **right angle** an angle of 90°. —*n.* 1. that which is naturally just and fair. 2. a just, moral, or legal claim to possess something or act in a certain way. 3. the

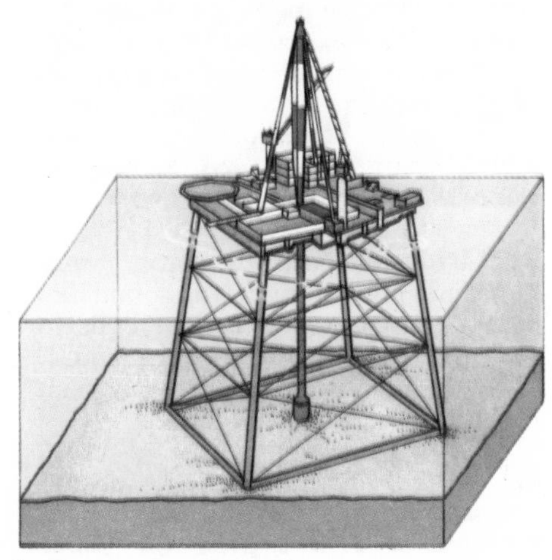

rig

right side or direction. —*vb.* 1. to recover an upright or normal position after being upset or overturned: ***after capsizing it was difficult to right the boat.*** 2. to set right; correct. —*adv.* 1. straight; directly; all the way: ***he went right up to him.*** 2. correctly; properly. **'right·ful** *adj.* legal; legitimate: ***the stolen goods were returned to their rightful owners.***

right·eous ('rīchəs) *adj.* of an honest and morally upright character; virtuous; just. —**'right·eous·ly** *adv.* —**'right·eous·ness** *n.*

rig·id ('rijid) *adj.* 1. firm and unbending: ***a rigid iron bar.*** 2. severe; inflexible in character: ***rigid rules.*** —**ri'gid·i·ty** *n.* —**'rig·id·ly** *adv.*

rim (rim) *n.* the curved and raised outer edge of something, e.g. a wheel or a glass.

rind (rīnd) *n.* the coarse protective outer skin of fruit, vegetables, bacon, and cheese.

rind

ring[1] (ring) *n.* 1. a circle; closed curved line or arrangement. 2. a circular metal band, esp. one worn on a finger as an ornament. 3. an enclosed piece of ground used for boxing, circus events, etc. —*vb.* to form the shape of a ring around: ***he ringed the items in the catalog that he wanted.***

ring[2] (ring) *vb.* **ring·ing, rang, rung.** 1. to make a clear vibrating sound like a bell. 2. to cause a bell or bells to sound. 3. to re-echo; be full of sound. 4. (+ ***up***) to enter (a sale) on a cash register. —*n.* a ringing sound.

rink (ringk) *n.* 1. an artificial sheet of ice used for skating and playing ice hockey. 2. a flat area for roller skating.

rinse (rins) *vb.* **rins·ing, rinsed.** to wash out (soap or impurities) from (something) with clean water. —*n.* 1. the act of rinsing. 2. a semi-permanent hair dye.

ri·ot ('rīət) *n.* violent and uncontrolled disorder caused by a crowd. —*vb.* to make or join in a riot. —**'ri·ot·ous** *adj.* —**'ri·ot·ous·ly** *adv.*

ripe (rīp) *adj.* 1. ready for eating or harvesting; mature. 2. prepared; ready: ***the children were ripe for mischief.*** **'rip·en** *vb.* to make or become ripe or riper. —**'ripe·ness** *n.*

rip·ple ('ripəl) *n.* a small smooth wave; small disturbance on the surface of water. —*vb.* **rip·pling, rip·pled.** to make or move in ripples.

rise (rīz) *vb.* **ris·ing, rose, ris·en** ('rizən). 1. to move or slope upwards: ***the hills rise gently.*** 2. to get up onto the feet from a seated or lying position. 3. to gain higher rank, office, or social position. 4. to increase; reach a higher level: ***the tide rose up the beach.*** 5. to rebel. —*n.* 1. an upward movement. 2. an upward slope.

risk (risk) *n.* the likelihood of danger. —*vb.* to do or use something knowing there is a chance of failure, danger, etc.; take a chance on. —**'risk·y** *adj.* **risk·i·er, risk·i·est.**

rite (rīt) *n.* a formal or customary act or ceremony, esp. as part of religious worship. **rit·u·al** ('richooəl) *n.* 1. the official order of words and actions at sacred ceremonies. 2. habitual or generally expected actions and words. —*adj.* ceremonial or customary.

ri·val ('rīvəl) *n.* a competitor; someone who strives against another person for the same object. —*vb.* to claim to be as good as; compete against: ***Ken and Chris rivaled each other for first position in the class.*** —**'ri·val·ry** *n.,pl.* **ri·val·ries.**

riv·er ('rivər) *n.* a large natural stream of fresh water that flows toward the sea, a lake, or another river.

road (rōd) *n.* 1. a smooth or paved strip used by people and vehicles to get from one place to another; track; highway. 2. a course towards some end or goal: ***determination was his road to success.***

roam (rōm) *vb.* to wander; walk about without a fixed goal.

roar (rôr) *n.* 1. a loud throaty sound made by a large animal. 2. any loud deep prolonged sound. —*vb.* to make a roaring sound.

roast (rōst) *vb.* to cook steadily in an oven or over a fire.

rob (rob) *vb.* **rob·bing, robbed.** to steal; take someone else's property by force, fraud, or threat. **'rob·ber·y** *n.,pl.* **rob·ber·ies.** an act of robbing.

robe (rōb) *n.* 1. a long loose flowing garment. 2. often **robes** (*pl.*) a garment of a particular color, cut, and material to show the wearer's rank or office: ***the judge's robes.*** —*vb.* **rob·ing, robed.** to dress in robes.

rob·in ('robin) *n.* 1. a type of thrush with a reddish-colored breast and black head and tail that lives in North America. 2. a small brown bird with a red breast living in Europe.

ro·bot ('rōbət) *n.* a machine that is able to do certain jobs that human beings can do.

ro·bust (rō'bust, 'rōbust) *adj.* strong; healthy.

rock[1] (rok) *n.* 1. a large mass of stone; boulder. 2. the dense hard mineral substance of varying kinds and characteristics that composes the earth's surface. —**'rock·y** *adj.* **rock·i·er, rock·i·est.**

rock[2] (rok) *vb.* 1. to move gently back and forth or from side to side. 2. to cause to sway violently.

rock·et ('rokit) *n.* a tube-shaped device that is driven forward by a powerful stream of hot gases that are released from one end when the fuel is burned.

river

rodents

rat

squirrel

rod (rod) *n.* 1. a thin straight flexible pole, e.g. a fishing rod. 2. a long metal bar that links moving parts of a machine.

ro·dent ('rōdənt) *n.* one of a large family of MAMMALS with large strong front teeth that are used for gnawing. Rats, squirrels, beavers, and hamsters are rodents.

ro·de·o ('rōdēō, rō'dāō) *n.,pl.* **ro·de·os.** an exhibition in which cowboys show off their skills in riding untamed horses, roping calves, etc.

roe (rō) *n.* the eggs of a fish.

rogue (rōg) *n.* 1. a dishonest person. 2. a mischievous person. '**ro·guish** *adj.* playful.

role (rōl) *n.* 1. the part of a character in a play: *John played the role of Othello.* 2. someone's function in a particular situation: *his role in the office was to make coffee.*

roll (rōl) *vb.* 1. to move by turning over and over. 2. to move on wheels or by means of a wheeled vehicle. 3. to curl or wind up into a ball or cylindrical shape. 4. to press out flat with a roller: *she rolled out the pastry.* 5. to trill the letter 'r' in speech. 6. to sweep along with a gentle rising and falling motion: *the boat rolled along in the heavy swell.* 7. to rumble or reverberate: *the drums rolled in the distance.* —*n.* 1. material rolled up into a cylindrical bale: *a blanket roll.* 2. a small bread loaf. 3. a rolling movement or sound. 4. an official list of names. '**roll·er** *n.* 1. a metal or wooden cylinder that rolls on its axis and has many uses in machines for crushing and smoothing (e.g. a steam roller), for moving loads, processing continuous sheets of paper, metal, etc. 2. a long swelling ocean wave.

ro·mance (rō'mans, 'rōmans) *n.* 1. a love affair. 2. the quality of mystery, adventure, or excitement: *the romance of the Wild West.* 3. a story or poem dealing with love and adventure. —**ro'man·tic** *adj.*

roof (ro͞of, ro͝of) *n.* 1. the protective outer covering on top of a building. 2. the topmost part of anything: *the roof of one's mouth.* —*vb.* to provide with a roof.

rook[1] (ro͝ok) *n.* a European bird of the crow family, with black plumage, a strong gray beak, and a hoarse call.

rook[2] (ro͝ok) *n.* a chess piece, also known as a castle.

room (ro͞om, ro͝om) *n.* 1. a space enclosed by walls inside a building. 2. sufficient space: *there is room for five people in my car.* 3. scope for doing something; opportunity: *his words left no room for argument.* 4. **rooms** (*pl.*) lodgings. '**room·y** *adj.* **room·i·er, room·i·est.** with plenty of space.

roost (ro͞ost) *vb.* (of birds) to perch and settle down for sleep or rest. —*n.* the place where birds settle for the night. '**roost·er** *n.* a male chicken.

root[1] (ro͞ot, ro͝ot) *n.* 1. the part of a plant that usu. grows underground, serving to anchor it in the soil and to absorb water and nutrients. 2. a part resembling a root in function or structure: *the root of a hair.* 3. the source; origin: *love of money is the root of all evil.* 4. a word from which other words are formed, e.g. *truth* in *truthful, truthfully,* and *truthfulness.* —*vb.* 1. to grow or put down roots. 2. to fix firmly or establish.

root[2] (ro͞ot, ro͝ot) *vb.* 1. to turn up the soil with the snout when looking for food: *the pigs rooted for acorns.* 2. to search around: *Clive rooted around in his desk for a pen.*

rope (rōp) *n.* 1. a length of thick cord made by twisting together strands of hemp, wire, etc. 2. a number of objects strung or twisted together like a rope: *a rope of beads.* —*vb.* **rop·ing, roped.** to catch or tie with rope.

rose[1] (rōz) *n.* a garden flower that grows on a thorny bush or climbing plant, and has fragrant blooms usu. in shades of red, pink, yellow, or white. '**ros·y** *adj.* **ros·i·er, ros·i·est.** 1. having a pinkish-red color. 2. promising; bright: *she has rosy prospects as an actress.*

rose[2] (rōz) *vb.* the past tense of RISE.

ro·sette (rō'zet) *n.* an imitation rose made of paper, ribbon, etc., used as a decoration or emblem.

rosette

ro·tate ('rōtāt) *vb.* **ro·tat·ing, ro·tat·ed.** 1. to move round a center or axis: *wheels rotate on an axle.* 2. to change regularly; take turns in a fixed order: *the farmer rotates beans and potatoes with barley in his large field.* —**ro'ta·tion** *n.*

rote (rōt) *n.* a mechanical routine.

rough (ruf) *adj.* 1. not smooth; uneven. 2. showing force or violence: *a rough game of hockey.* 3. unfinished; not perfectly made or finished off: *a rough sketch.* 4. unpleasant; hard: *a rough time.* —*vb.* 1. to make rough, or treat roughly. 2. (+ *out*) to plan or make in an incomplete way: *he roughed out a plan of the house.* —'**rough·ly** *adv.* —'**rough·ness** *n.*

rouse (rouz) *vb.* **rous·ing, roused.** 1. to cause to get up; awaken from sleep, rest, etc. 2. to stir up: *his rudeness roused the teacher's anger.*

route (ro͞ot, rout) *n.* the road or way one follows from one place to another. —*vb.* **rout·ing, rout·ed.** to send by or arrange a particular route.

rou·tine (ro͞o'tēn) *n.* 1. a regular pattern or schedule for doing things. 2. dull sameness in work or other actions: *Betty hated routine schoolwork.* —*adj.* regular; habitual: *a routine checkup with the doctor.*

row[1] (rō) *n.* a number of people or things set side by side in a line: *a row of chairs.*

row[2] (rō) *vb.* 1. to propel a boat with oars. 2. to transport in a rowboat: *she rowed her parents upstream.* —*n.* a journey in a rowboat.

row[3] (rou) *n.* 1. a quarrel; noisy argument. 2. an uproar; din: *he shouted above the row of the pneumatic drill.*

roy·al ('roiəl) *adj.* 1. of, concerning, or belonging to a king or queen. 2. like or suitable for a king or queen: *Sarah's grandparents gave her a royal welcome.* '**roy·al·ist** *n.* a loyal supporter of a monarch. '**roy·al·ty** *n.,pl.* **roy·al·ties.** 1. a royal person or persons. 2. the office or power of a king or queen. 3. usu. **royalties** (*pl.*) money paid to a writer or composer for each copy of his work that is sold.

rub·ber ('rubər) *n.* a strong, flexible, waterproof substance made from the sap of a tree that grows in hot countries, and used in manufacturing many products. '**rub·ber·y** *adj.* having the texture of rubber.

rubber

rub·bish ('rubish) *n.* 1. waste material; garbage. 2. anything that is inferior or worthless.

ru·by ('ro͞obē) *n.,pl.* **ru·bies.** 1. a rare precious stone with colors ranging from deep crimson to pale pink. 2. a dark red color. —*adj.* dark red.

rucksack

ruck·sack ('ruksak, 'ro͝oksak) *n.* a type of knapsack carried on straps over the shoulders and used by hikers, soldiers, etc.; a backpack.

rud·der ('rudər) *n.* 1. a flat broad movable piece of wood or metal attached to the stern of a boat and used for steering. 2. a similar structure on the tail of an airplane.

rud·dy (rudē) *adj.* **rud·di·er, rud·di·est.** having a rosy glow of health.

rude (ro͞od) *adj.* 1. bad-mannered; impolite. 2. roughly or crudely made: *the shepherd slept in a rude hut made out of stones.* —'**rude·ly** *adv.* —'**rude·ness** *n.*

ruf·fle ('rufəl) *vb.* **ruf·fling, ruf·fled.** 1. to disturb the smoothness of: *the wind ruffled his hair.* 2. to upset: *her laughter ruffled them.* —*n.* a strip of material gathered into a frill and used as decoration, e.g. on curtains or clothes.

rug (rug) *n.* 1. a carpet used to cover part of a floor. 2. an animal hide used for this purpose: *a bearskin rug.*

rug·ged ('rugid) *adj.* 1. rough and uneven in surface or outline: *rugged cliffs.* 2. tough; strong: *a rugged fighter.* 3. harsh; uncomfortable: *a rugged life in the Arctic.*

ru·in ('ro͞oin) *n.* 1. downfall; collapse: *eating too much has been the ruin of his health.* 2. often **ru·ins** (*pl.*) the remains of decayed or destroyed buildings. —*vb.* 1. to cause the downfall of. 2. to reduce to ruins; destroy. —'**ru·in·ous** *adj.*

rule (ro͞ol) *n.* 1. a principle or instruction, either formally set out or generally accepted, that controls action or behavior: *do you know the rules of chess?* 2. government; control: *the rule of a king.* 3. (also **rul·er**) a marked strip of wood, plastic, etc., used for measuring and drawing straight lines. —*vb.* **rul·ing, ruled.** 1. to govern; exercise control over. 2. to make a decision from a position of authority: *the judge ruled that the trial should continue.* 3. to draw lines with the aid of a ruler.

rum·ble ('rumbəl) *vb.* **rum·bling, rum·bled.** to make a dull rolling sound like distant thunder. —*n.* a dull rolling noise.

ru·mor ('ro͞omər) *n.* a report or story that is based on gossip and may be totally untrue. —*vb.* to spread (information) by rumor: *it is rumored that he is bankrupt.*

rump (rump) *n.* 1. the hind end or buttocks of an animal. 2. a cut of meat cut from this part.

rung[1] (rung) *n.* a short piece of wood or metal fitted between the uprights of a ladder to form one of a series of footholds.

rung[2] (rung) *vb.* the past participle of RING[2].

rush[1] (rush) *vb.* 1. to hurry; move very fast: *she rushed past me.* 2. to make a sudden violent move against: *the police rushed the armed criminal.* —*n.* 1. the act of rushing. 2. intense activity: *the Christmas rush in the stores.*

rush[2] (rush) *n.* a tall grasslike plant with straight hollow stems that grows near water.

rut (rut) *n.* 1. a track or groove worn into the ground by the passage of wheels. 2. a dull routine.

ruth·less ('ro͞othlis) *adj.* without pity; merciless. —'**ruth·less·ly** *adv.* —'**ruth·less·ness** *n.*

rye (rī) *n.* a grain that grows on a grasslike plant and is used to make bread and whiskey and to provide fodder for cattle.

S

Sab·bath ('sabəth) *n.* the day of the week on which God was said to have rested after creating heaven and earth; the day of religious observance for Christians and Jews and the day when people rest from their work. For Christians the Sabbath falls on each Sunday and for Jews it falls on each Saturday.

sa·ber ('sābər) *n.* 1. a heavy, slightly curved sword with one sharpened edge, used by cavalry soldiers. 2. a light sword used in fencing, having two sharpened edges and a blunt end.

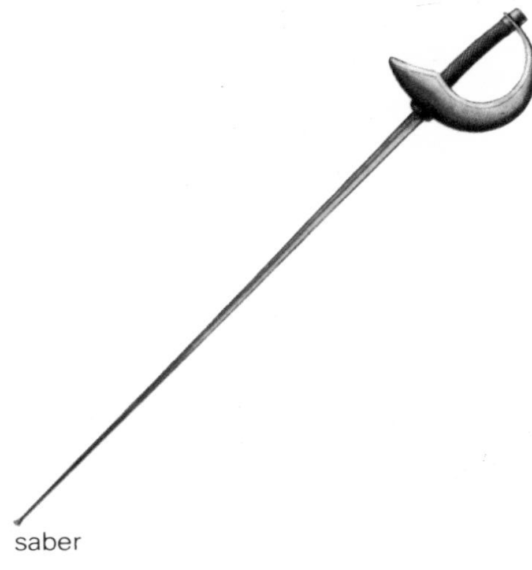
saber

sab·o·tage ('sabətâzh) *n.* the deliberate destruction or damage of machinery, etc., esp. as done by enemy agents in wartime. —**sab·o·tag·ing, sab·o·taged.** *vb.* to damage or destroy (something) by sabotage.

sac·cha·rin ('sakərin) *n.* a sweet chemical compound used instead of sugar, often by people trying to lose weight. **sac·cha·rine** *adj.* sickly sweet; like sugar: *she gave him a saccharine smile.*

sa·chet (sa'shā) a small, usu. decorated bag, for holding sweet-smelling dried flowers, perfumed powder, etc., that give a pleasant odor to closets, drawers, etc.

sack[1] (sak) *n.* 1. a large bag made from a rough cloth, used for shipping potatoes, coffee, etc. 2. the amount a sack holds. —*vb.* to put (something) in a sack. **hit the sack** (informal) go to bed.

sack[2] (sak) *vb.* to steal from and destroy or burn (a town captured in war).

sack·ing ('saking) *n.* a coarse cloth used for making sacks.

sac·ra·ment ('sakrəmənt) *n.* an act, ceremony, or object that is regarded as especially holy, esp. the bread and wine taken by Christians as symbols of Jesus's body and blood.

sa·cred ('sākrid) *adj.* 1. concerned with God or a god; holy. 2. deserving respect or reverence: *a sacred law.* 3. devoted to, in honor of, or used for a certain purpose, esp. a religious one: *this church is sacred to St. Andrew.* —**'sa·cred·ly** *adv.*

sac·ri·fice ('sakrəfīs) *n.* 1. the ritual killing of an animal or other victim in honor of a god. 2. an offering made to a god. 3. the act of giving up (something dear to one) as part of one's duty or in order to get something better: *she made a sacrifice by giving up her job to look after him.* 4. the thing given up. —*vb.* **sac·ri·fic·ing, sac·ri·ficed.** to make a sacrifice of (an animal or thing).

sac·ri·lege ('sakrəlij) *n.* an act that harms or is disrespectful of something sacred. **sac·ri·le·gious** *adj.*

sad·dle ('sadəl) *n.* 1. a rider's seat, usu. of leather, strapped to a horse's back. 2. a bicycle seat. 3. that part of an animal between the shoulders and the lower back from which a cut of meat may be taken: *saddle of lamb.* —*vb.* **sad·dling, sad·dled.** 1. to put a saddle on (a horse). 2. (+ *with*) to load with: *John is saddled with heavy responsibilities.*

sa·fa·ri (sə'fârē) *n.,pl.* **sa·fa·ris.** a journey or expedition carried out in order to hunt or study wild animals, esp. in Africa.

safe (sāf) *adj.* **saf·er, saf·est.** 1. not in danger; not hurt or damaged: *they were safe at home.* 2. not dangerous; unlikely to cause damage or injury: *that swing is not safe.* 3. reliable; sure; trustworthy. —*n.* a strong metal box or secure room in which money, jewels, etc., are locked away for safety. —**'safe·ly** *adj.* —**'safe·ty** *n.*

sag (sag) *vb.* **sag·ging, sagged.** 1. to bend downward because of pressure, weight, etc. 2. to weaken because of tiredness, lack of determination, etc.: *he was sagging after the ten-mile walk and refused to go on.* —*n.* the state of sagging or the extent to which something sags.

said (sed) *vb.* the past tense and past participle of SAY.

sail (sāl) *n.* 1. a large piece of canvas or similar material attached to the mast of a yacht, ship, etc., to catch the wind and thus move the boat. 2. a trip in a sailing boat. 3. anything that resembles a sail, e.g. the arm of a windmill. **set sail** to begin a voyage or trip. —*vb.* 1. to manage a sailing boat. 2. to begin a voyage or trip on a boat: *they sailed at dawn.* 3. to move like a sailing boat; glide smoothly: *she sailed around the dance floor in her long dress.* **'sail·or** *n.* a person who sails, esp. a seaman in the navy.

saint (sānt) *n.* 1. a person of almost divine goodness whose holiness is officially recognized by the Christian Church after death. 2. any very good and kind person. —**'saint·ly** *adj.* **saint·li·er, saint·li·est.**

sal·ad ('saləd) *n.* a dish usu. consisting of raw lettuce, cucumbers, tomatoes, etc., often served with a spicy dressing. —*adj.* relating to or prepared for salads.

sal·a·ry ('salərē) *n.,pl.* **sal·a·ries.** a payment of money made monthly or yearly in return for work. **'sal·a·ried** *adj.* earning a salary.

sale (sāl) *n.* 1. the act or process of selling. 2. an auction. 3. the selling of goods at reduced prices. 4. demand; market: *there is no sale for bathing suits in winter.*

sa·li·va (sə'līvə) *n.* liquid formed in the mouth; spit. It helps the chewing and swallowing of food.

sal·mon ('samən) *n.* a large edible fish having a delicate pink flesh and a brownish skin. It lives in the North Atlantic and travels up rivers to lay eggs. **salmon pink** *n., adj.* (having) the color of a salmon.

salmon

salt (sôlt) *n.* a naturally occurring substance, formed from the elements sodium and chlorine, that is found esp. in the sea and used for flavoring food. —*vb.* to flavor with salt.

sa·lute (sə'lo͞ot) *n.* 1. a sign of greeting or respect, esp. as given by a serviceman to another of higher rank: *the lieutenant greeted the general with a salute.* 2. the firing of a gun as a sign of respect for a president, king, etc. —*vb.* **sa·lut·ing, sa·lut·ed.** 1. to make a salute. 2. to give (someone) a salute.

sal·va·tion (sal'vāshən) *n.* 1. the act of saving or the person or thing that saves. 2. (Christianity) the rescue of someone's soul.

sam·ple ('sampəl) *n.* a piece or part of something representing the whole object, etc., from which it was taken: *this essay is a sample of his work.* —*vb.* **sam·pling, sam·pled.** to test a sample from (something): *please sample some of my cheesecake.*

sanc·tu·ar·y ('sangkcho͞oerē) *n., pl.* **sanc·tu·ar·ies.** 1. a place of safety or protection: *a wildlife sanctuary.* 2. the altar of a Christian church or the area in which it is placed.

sand (sand) *n.* 1. a natural substance consisting of small particles of worn rock. 2. (also **sands**) a beach, shore, or desert. —*vb.* 1. to spread sand upon or around: *the men sanded the icy roads.* 2. to rub or smooth (wood, metal, etc.) with sandpaper. —'**sand·i·ness** *n.* —'**sand·y** *adj.* **sand·i·er, sand·i·est.**

san·dal ('sandəl) *n.* a shoe made of a sole fastened to the foot by straps.

sand·pa·per ('sandpāpər) *n.* stiff paper that has sand particles stuck to it, used for smoothing wood, metal, etc. —*vb.* to sand.

sand·wich ('sandwich) *n.* a piece of food usu. consisting of two slices of bread with filling placed between them: *a peanut-butter sandwich.* —*vb.* to place (a person or thing) between two others.

sane (sān) *adj.* **san·er, san·est.** not suffering from mental illness; not mad. —'**sane·ly** *adv.* —**san·i·ty** ('sanitē) *n.*

san·i·tar·y ('saniterē) *adj.* 1. healthy: *sanitary conditions.* 2. connected with health, cleanness, and prevention of disease. —'**san·i·tar·i·ly** *adv.* —'**san·i·tar·i·ness** *n.*

sank (sangk) *vb.* the past tense of SINK.

sap (sap) *n.* the juice of a plant carrying the minerals and water necessary for it to live. —*vb.* **sap·ping, sapped.** to remove or exhaust (a person's strength or energy): *the long illness slowly sapped his strength until he was too weak to move.*

sap·phire ('safīər) *n.* a hard clear mineral used as a gem, usu. deep blue in color. —*adj.* having the color of a sapphire.

sar·dine (sâr'dēn) *n.* the young of a pilchard or similar small fish, often preserved in oil for food.

sash (sash) *n.* 1. a strip of cloth worn around the waist or over one shoulder as decoration, e.g. as part of a uniform. 2. a metal or wooden window frame that opens by sliding up or down.

sat·el·lite ('satəlīt) *n.* 1. a natural or artificial object that orbits around a larger object in space, esp. a planet: *the moon is a natural satellite of the earth.* 2. a person or country under the influence of a more powerful person or country.

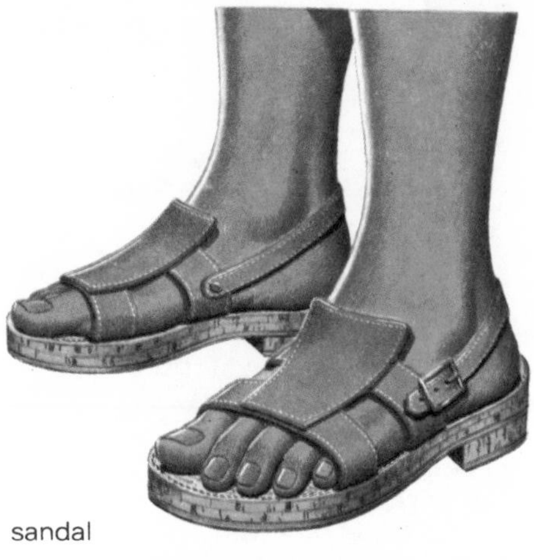

sandal

sat·in ('satən) *n.* a fabric made from silk, cotton, or manmade fibers, having a shiny, slippery surface. —*adj.* 1. made of satin. 2. glossy; smooth: *satin skin.*

sat·is·fy ('satisfī) *vb.* **sat·is·fy·ing, sat·is·fied.** 1. to supply (someone or something) with what is wanted, needed, or expected; make content. 2. fulfill (a desire, need, or demand): *that pie satisfied my hunger.* 3. to convince: *I satisfied myself that he was telling the truth.* 4. to meet the needs or requirements of. —**sat·is·fac·tion** (satis'fakshən) *n.* —**sat·is'fac·to·ry** *adj.*

sauce (sôs) *n.* a pleasantly flavored liquid or creamy mixture served with different foods to improve their tastes. '**sauc·y** *adj.* **sauc·i·er, sauc·i·est.** impertinent or impudent: *a saucy smile.* —'**sauc·i·ly** *adv.* —'**sauc·i·ness** *n.*

sauce·pan ('sôspan) *n.* a metal pot with a handle and usu. a cover, used for cooking food.

sau·cer ('sôsər) *n.* 1. a small shallow dish in which a cup stands. 2. anything shaped like a saucer: *some people believe that flying saucers come from outer space.*

sau·na ('sônə) *n.* (also **sauna bath**) (originally in Finland) a place where one takes a steam bath followed by a cold shower or swim.

sau·sage ('sôsij) *n.* a type of food consisting of chopped pork or other meat seasoned with herbs and spices and stuffed into a tubular skin.

sav·age ('savij) *adj.* 1. dangerous, untamed, or wild: *a savage beast.* 2. cruel, vicious, or brutal: *a savage crime.* —*n.* 1. anyone who is wild or cruel. 2. an uncivilized. person. —**'sav·age·ly** *adv.* —**'sav·age·ry** *n.*

save (sāv) *vb.* **sav·ing, saved.** 1. to preserve, rescue, or keep safe from harm, destruction, or loss. 2. (often + *up*) to keep or store up for future use: *Pete saved his allowance for a year so that he could buy a car.* 3. (Christianity) to rescue from sin. **'sav·ings** *pl.n.* money that has been saved.

sav·ior ('sāvyər) *n.* 1. a person who saves or rescues. 2. **'Savior** Jesus Christ, as the Son of God who, as Christians believe, saved men from sin.

sa·vor ('sāvər) *vb.* 1. to taste with satisfaction: *Tom savored the dessert.* 2. to take pleasure in: *Julie savored the memories of her vacation.*

sa·vor·y ('sāvərē) *adj.* 1. tasty in flavor, but not sweet: *cheese is a savory food.* 2. respectable: *the less savory part of town.*

saw[1] (sô) *n.* a cutting TOOL with a sharp-toothed blade used to cut wood, metal, etc. —*vb.* **saw·ing, sawed, sawn.** to cut wood, metal, etc., with a saw. **circular saw** an electrically operated cutting tool consisting of a sharp-toothed rotating disk. **'saw·dust** *n.* the wood particles produced when a piece of wood is sawn.

saw[2] (sô) *vb.* the past tense of SEE[1].

sax·o·phone ('saksəfōn) *n.* a wind instrument having a single reed set in its mouthpiece, used mainly in jazz and pop music.

saxophone

say (sā) *vb.* **say·ing, said.** 1. to speak, tell, state, or express by word of mouth: *he said he was going away until the end of the month.* 2. to decide or give an opinion: *I say you ought to go to school.* 3. to repeat or recite: *the children were taught to say their prayers before school.* 4. to guess or suppose; assume: *I'd say we can expect him to come on time.* —*n.* the right or chance to express a view or make a decision: *he was told to have his say.* **'say·ing** *n.* a well-known or often repeated phrase, e.g. *a stitch in time saves nine.*

scab (skab) *n.* 1. a crust that forms over a wound to protect the new skin being produced underneath. 2. (slang) a contemptible person, esp. one who continues to work after a strike has been called. **'scab·by** *adj.* **scab·bi·er, scab·bi·est.** 1. covered with a scab or scabs. 2. contemptible.

scaf·fold ('skafəld, 'skafōld) *n.* 1. (also **scaf·fold·ing**) a temporary structure of platforms and metal bars, used by workers for building work, etc. 2. a platform from which criminals were formerly executed, usu. by hanging.

scald (skôld) *vb.* 1. to burn with boiling liquid or steam. 2. to kill all the germs on (something) by putting it in boiling water. —*n.* a burn caused by scalding.

scale[1] (skāl) *n.* 1. a range of measurements as marked in a scientific instrument. 2. a group of musical notes in ascending or descending order. 3. any system consisting of gradual steps: *a scale of charges.* 4. also **scales** (*pl.*) a balance for weighing things. 5. the size of a drawing, map, etc., as compared with the thing it represents: *this map has a scale of one inch to every hundred miles.* 6. amount; size; extent: *his business was on a small scale.* —*vb.* **scal·ing, scaled.** to climb or climb over. **scale up** (*or* **down**) to increase (or decrease) some quantity or value: *the firm scaled up its prices by 10 per cent.*

scale[2] (skāl) *n.* any of the hard flat horny plates making up the skin covering on certain animals, e.g. fishes and lizards. —**'scal·y** *adj.* **scal·i·er, scal·i·est.**

scal·lop ('skoləp) *n.* a sea animal whose body is contained in two ridged shells hinged together and is eaten as a delicacy. See SHELL.

scalp (skalp) *n.* the skin on top of the head, usu. covered with hair. —*vb.* (esp. among certain Indian tribes) to tear or cut the scalp from the head of (a person) as a sign of victory.

scal·pel ('skalpəl) *n.* a small very sharp knife used in surgery.

scam·pi ('skampē) *n.* a dish consisting of very large shrimps split and broiled with a sauce of garlic butter.

scan (skan) *vb.* **scan·ning, scanned.** 1. to look over; survey: *he scanned the horizon.* 2. to look rapidly through something; read quickly: *he scanned the newspapers.* 3. (of verse) to conform to a consistent rhythm. **'scan·ner** *n.* a thing that scans, esp. a radar antenna surveying the area near it.

scan·dal ('skandəl) *n.* 1. gossip or talk about a person, esp. when damaging to his reputation. 2. a disgraceful act or event that causes angry talk or gossip among the public: *the disappearance of the money was a scandal.* **'scan·dal·ize** *vb.* **scan·dal·iz·ing, scan·dal·ized.** to cause shame, disgrace, or embarrassment to. —**'scan·dal·ous** *adj.* —**'scan·dal·ous·ly** *adv.*

scant (skant) *adj.* not enough: *Ben could not understand the math problem as he had paid scant attention to the lesson.* **'scanty** *adj.* **scant·i·er, scant·i·est.** of small size or amount: *the food seems scanty for a party of this size.*

scape·goat ('skāpgōt) *n.* a person who bears the blame for others' faults, mistakes, etc.

scar (skâr) *n.* 1. a mark left on the skin when a wound, cut, etc., has healed. 2. a permanent effect left by experience, suffering, etc.: *her mother's death left Jane with a scar.* —*vb.* **scar·ring, scarred.** to leave or mark with a scar.

scarce (skeərs) *adj.* **scarc·er, scarc·est.** not plentiful; rare: *strawberries are scarce in winter.* **'scarce·ly** *adv.* hardly; not much: *I scarcely saw him after that night.* —**'scar·ci·ty** *n.,pl.* **scar·ci·ties.**

scare (skeər) *vb.* **scar·ing, scared.** 1. to frighten (a person or animal). 2. (+ *off* or *away*) to drive (someone or something) away by frightening them. —*n.* the act of scaring or state of being scared.

scarecrow

scare·crow ('skeərkrō) *n.* 1. a model of a man dressed in old clothes and placed in the fields to frighten birds away from crops. 2. an untidy or very thin person.

scarf (skârf) *n.,pl* **scarves** (skârvz). a square or long narrow strip of cloth worn around the neck or on the head.

scar·let ('skârlit) *adj.* a very bright red or slightly orange-red color. **scarlet fever** a serious infectious illness characterized by a red rash, sore throat, etc.

scat·ter ('skatər) *vb.* 1. to throw around: *Betty scatters seeds for the birds.* 2. to send or be sent off in different directions; disperse. —*n.* the act of scattering.

scene (sēn) *n.* 1. the place where something happens; the background of an event: *a witness at the scene of the accident.* 2. a view or landscape: *a country scene.* 3. a section of an act in a play. 4. a display of anger, etc.: *Sam made a scene about having to stay at home.* '**scen·e·ry** *n.* 1. the look of a landscape: *the scenery is beautiful.* 2. the painted screens, etc., used on stage for a play in a theatre.

scent (sent) *n.* 1. a smell, usu. a pleasant one: *the scent of flowers.* 2. perfume. 3. the smell left by an animal as it moves, which dogs and other animals can detect and follow. 4. any trail of clues, etc. —*vb.* 1. to detect the scent of. 2. to detect as if by smell: *he scented danger.* 3. to cover, sprinkle, etc., with scent.

scep·ter ('septər) *n.* a rod or staff usu. made of precious metals and jewels and carried by a king or queen on important occasions as a symbol of power.

sched·ule ('skejōōl) *n.* a list of things to be done and the times at which they are to be done; timetable: *a full schedule.* —*vb.* **sched·ul·ing, sched·uled.** 1. to make out a schedule. 2. to arrange (something) according to a schedule.

scheme (skēm) *n.* 1. a plan or arrangement. 2. a design made according to a definite plan: *a color scheme.* —*vb.* **schem·ing, schemed.** 1. to make plans; work out a scheme. 2. to make secret or dishonest plans.

schol·ar ('skolər) *n.* 1. a well-educated or learned person. 2. a student, esp. one awarded a special grant of money because of merit, etc. '**schol·ar·ship** *n.* 1. the state of being a scholar. 2. a special grant of money given to certain students, usu. because of merit, etc. —'**schol·ar·ly** *adj.*

school[1] (skōōl) *n.* 1. a place of education. 2. a department in a college or university teaching a particular subject or subjects: *a school of medicine.* 3. a group of writers, artists, etc., all using the same methods. —*vb.* to educate; train.

school[2] (skōōl) *n.* a large group of fish, porpoises, etc., swimming along together; shoal.

schoon·er ('skōōnər) *n.* a type of sailing ship with two masts, the one nearer the bow being shorter than the other.

sci·ence ('sīəns) *n.* knowledge about the physical character of things and events occurring in nature or the universe. **sci·en·tif·ic** (sīən'tifik) *adj.* 1. relating to science. 2. skilled or expert. '**sci·en·tist** *n.* an expert in science. —**sci·en'tif·i·cal·ly** *adv.*

scin·til·late ('sintəlāt) *vb.* **scin·til·lat·ing, scin·til·lat·ed.** 1. to twinkle; sparkle. 2. to spark; emit sparks. **scin'til·la** *n.* trace; spark: *he was convicted without a scintilla of evidence.* '**scin·til·lat·ing** *adj.* sparkling; enchantingly lively: *she found him to be scintillating company.*

scis·sors ('sizərz) *pl.n.* a cutting instrument in which two blades with finger and thumb holes at their ends are pivoted about a central point so that their cutting edges work against each other.

scoop (skōōp) *n.* 1. an instrument similar to a shovel or ladle used to lift or move things. 2. (informal) a news story of great public interest obtained and published before other newspapers get it. —*vb.* 1. (often + *up*) to move or pick up with a scoop or something similar. 2. (+ *out*) to make (a hollow) with or as if with a scoop. 3. (informal) to get hold of a good news story before (rival newspapers).

scoot·er ('skōōtər) *n.* 1. a child's wheeled toy consisting of an oblong platform with a single wheel at each end and a vertical handle for steering. 2. (also **motor scooter**) a lightweight motorcycle.

scorch (skôrch) *vb.* to burn (something) slightly and leave a mark: *he scorched the cloth with the iron.* —*n.* a mark made by scorching: *the scorch ruined Mary's dress.*

score (skôr) *n.* 1. the record of points gained by competitors in a match, game, etc. 2. a groove or mark made by scratching or cutting. 3. twenty: *three score is sixty.* 4. a music copy showing each part and the instrument or voice performing it. 5. a debt; grudge: *he settled an old score.* —*vb.* **scor·ing, scored.** 1. to get points, goals, etc., in a game or match. 2. to record such points. 3. to make cuts or grooves in. 4. to cross out (writing, etc.). 5. (music) to write a score for. 6. to gain an advantage.

scorn (skôrn) *n.* an attitude of contempt or mockery; act of regarding people or things as inferior and unworthy of notice. —*vb.* to show scorn or contempt for. —'**scorn·ful** *adj.* —'**scorn·ful·ly** *adv.*

scor·pi·on ('skôrpēən) *n.* a creature related to the spider, having an armored body and a long tail ending in a poisonous sting.

scorpion

scour ('skouər) *vb.* to clean thoroughly by scrubbing, often with a rough cleaning pad.

scout (skout) *n.* 1. a person sent out to get information, esp. about an enemy before a battle. 2. **Scout** (also **Boy Scout** *or* **Girl Scout**) a member of an international organization that teaches boys and girls to look after themselves and to help others. *—vb.* to act as a scout or Boy or Girl Scout.

scowl (skoul) *vb.* to lower the eyebrows and pull them together in an angry frown. *—n.* the action of scowling; angry frown.

scrap (skrap) *n.* 1. a small piece broken off; fragment: *we gave the dog the leftover scraps of food.* 2. (informal) a fight. 3. old or leftover material. *—vb.* **scrap·ping, scrapped.** 1. to throw away something broken or old. 2. (informal) to fight or quarrel.

scrape (skrāp) *vb.* **scrap·ing, scraped.** 1. to rub or scratch (something) with a sharp or rough edge. 2. to remove (an outer layer) by scraping: *he scraped the mud off his shoes.* 3. (+ *up* or *together*) to collect or obtain (money, friends, etc.) with difficulty. **scrape through** to succeed at something with difficulty: *she scraped through her exams.* *—n.* 1. the act, the sound, or an instance of scraping. 2. (informal) a difficult situation; muddle: *she always got into scrapes because she was so naughty.*

scratch (skrach) *vb.* 1. to make a mark on (the surface of something) with a sharp object: *he scratched the desk with his knife.* 2. to wound or injure slightly: *the cat scratched him.* 3. to scrape with the fingernails to relieve itching. 4. to withdraw or cause to withdraw from a competition: *the horse was scratched from the race.* *—n.* 1. a mark made by scratching. 2. a cut or slight skin wound. *—adj.* for scribbling quick notes or calculations: *scratch paper.*

scream (skrēm) *vb.* to make a loud shrill cry or noise: *she screamed with terror.* *—n.* 1. a loud shrill cry. 2. (informal) a very amusing person or thing.

screech (skrēch) *vb.* to give a harsh shrill cry or yell; scream. *—n.* a shrill harsh cry or scream.

screen (skrēn) *n.* 1. a light and easily movable covered frame protecting things from light, heat, etc., dividing rooms, or concealing things. 2. a smooth white surface on which films are shown. 3. the front of a television set on which the picture is formed. 4. something that hides or conceals. *—vb.* 1. to protect, divide, or hide by means of a screen. 2. to project a movie film onto a screen. 3. to show on television.

screw (skrōō) *n.* 1. a piece of metal resembling and functioning as a nail with a special spiral form and a groove or other pattern in its head allowing it to be driven into wood or a metal hole by the turning action of a **screw·driv·er.** 2. anything similar to a screw in form or purpose. 3. the action or an instance of screwing. *—vb.* 1. to fit (a screw) or fasten with a screw. 2. to tighten by turning: *she screwed a cap on the bottle.* 3. (+ *up*) to twist out of shape; crumple: *Jane screwed up the newspaper.*

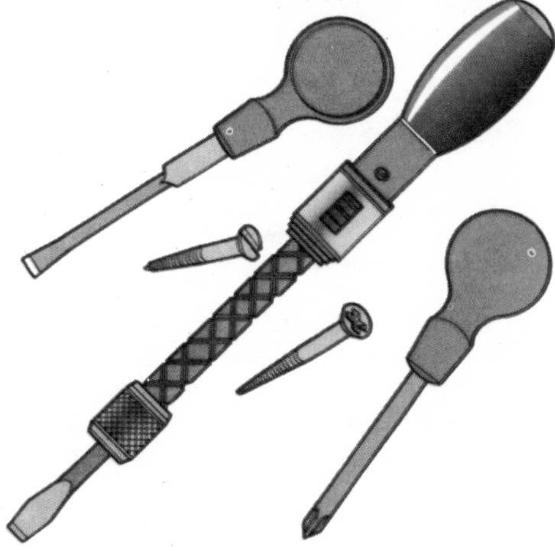

screwdriver

scrib·ble ('skribəl) *vb.* **scrib·bling, scrib·bled.** 1. to make meaningless marks with a pen, pencil, etc. 2. to write hurriedly: *David was scribbling notes.* *—n.* 1. meaningless marks. 2. hasty or poor handwriting.

script (skript) *n.* 1. handwriting, esp. when in a special or elegant style. 2. the text of a play, film, etc.

scroll (skrōl) *n.* 1. a roll of stiff paper or parchment bearing writing. 2. something shaped like a scroll, e.g. carved stonework.

scrub[1] (skrub) *vb.* **scrub·bing, scrubbed.** 1. to clean or wash (clothes, a floor, etc.) by means of very hard rubbing, usu. with a brush. 2. (informal) to cancel: *they scrubbed the idea.* *—n.* the action or an instance of scrubbing.

scrub[2] (skrub) *n.* 1. low-growing trees, shrubs, and bushes. 2. an area covered with this.

scru·ple ('skrōōpəl) *n.* a doubt or hesitation caused by an uneasy conscience: *I had scruples about borrowing his bicycle without asking him.* *—vb.* **scru·pling, scru·pled.** to feel such doubts. **scru·pu·lous** ('skrōōpyələs) *adj.* 1. avoiding doing anything morally wrong. 2. paying great attention to details: *he was scrupulous about checking every item on the list.* —'**scru·pu·lous·ly** *adv.*

scru·ti·ny ('skrōōtənē) *n.,pl.* **scru·ti·nies.** a very careful and close look, inspection, or examination. '**scru·ti·nize** *vb.* **scru·ti·niz·ing, scru·ti·nized.** to make such an examination.

sculp·ture ('skulpchər) *n.* 1. the art of creating figures and models of people, animals, etc., by carving stone or wood, or modeling clay. 2. the work of art created by sculpting. **sculpt** (skulpt) *vb.* to create or make as a sculpture. '**sculp·tor** *n.* a person who makes sculpture.

scum (skum) *n.* impure or filthy material floating on top of a liquid.

scur·ry ('skurē) *vb.* **scur·ry·ing, scur·ried.** to move with haste; run quickly: *the mouse scurried across the floor.* *—n.* the act or an instance of scurrying.

sea (sē) *n.* 1. an ocean or part of an ocean; extensive body of salt water. 2. a very large freshwater or saltwater lake such as the Dead Sea. 3. anything like a sea in appearance: *he saw the crowd as a sea of faces.* **at sea** 1. out on the sea in a ship, etc. 2. confused; not knowing what to do.

sea·gull ('sēgul) *n.* See GULL.

seal[1] (sēl) *n.* 1. a stamp or ring pressed into soft wax to produce a mark as an indication of authority or genuineness. 2. the mark made in this way. 3. a piece of wax placed over a letter, etc., in such a way that it must be broken before the letter can be opened. 4. anything that closes another thing tightly or keeps it secret. *—vb.* 1. to fix a seal to a paper, letter, etc. 2. to fasten or stick (something); close tightly: *she sealed the envelope.*

seal

seal² (sēl) *n.* 1. a flesh-eating sea MAMMAL having flippers instead of feet, a torpedo shaped body, and a thick layer of fat beneath the skin. 2. the fur or skin of this animal used to make clothes, etc.

seam (sēm) *n.* 1. the line where two pieces of material have been joined together. 2. a long thinnish layer of mineral, rock, etc.: *a coal seam.* —*vb.* to join two pieces of material by means of a seam.

search (sûrch) *vb.* to look for; examine carefully. —*n.* the action or an instance of searching.

sea·son ('sēzən) *n.* 1. one of the four main parts of the year that are each marked by their own weather conditions; spring, summer, fall, and winter. 2. the time when certain animals and birds may be hunted. 3. the appropriate time for a sport or other activity: *the baseball season.* **in season** 1. (of animals) ready for shooting. 2. (of vegetables, fruits, etc.) ready for picking and eating. **season ticket** a ticket that may be used any number of times over a stated time period. —*vb.* 1. to spice or flavor with herbs, etc. 2. to make more mature or tougher by exposing to weather, by drying, etc.: *to season wood.* **'sea·son·a·ble** *adj.* suitable for or characteristic of a particular time or season. —**'sea·son·a·bly** *adv.*

seat (sēt) *n.* 1. a chair, bench, stool, or other object upon which one may sit. 2. the buttocks or bottom. 3. a way of sitting, esp. on horses: *he has a good seat.* 4. a central point: *the seat of government.* —*vb.* 1. to cause to sit down. 2. to be able to provide seats for: *this car seats six people.*

sea·weed ('sēwēd) *n.* any plant growing in the sea.

se·clude (si'klo͞od) *vb.* **se·clud·ing, se·clud·ed.** to isolate; keep apart from. —**se·clud·ed** *adj.* shut off; solitary: *the secluded house was surrounded by a thickly wooded garden and a high fence.*

sec·ond¹ ('sekənd) *adj.* 1. following after the first. 2. another: *a second glass of milk.* 3. the same as; identical to in function, behavior, purpose, etc.: *a second Hitler.* —*adv.* after the first: *he came second in the competition.* —*n.* 1. someone or something that comes second in rank, position, quality, etc. 2. a person helping a boxer, etc. —*vb.* 1. to support or encourage (a boxer, etc.). 2. to support (an idea put forward by someone else) at a meeting.

sec·ond² ('sekənd) *n.* 1. a period of time lasting 1/60 of a minute. 2. (in geometry) an angle equal to 1/3600 of a degree.

sec·ond·ar·y ('sekənderē) *adj.* 1. second in rank, importance, authority, etc. 2. next after primary: *a high school is a secondary school.*

sec·ond·hand ('sekəndhand) *adj.* 1. not new; owned or used by one or more other people: *secondhand furniture.* 2. not fresh or original; not directly from the source: *he could only give us a secondhand report since he did not see it himself.* 3. dealing in used goods.

se·cret ('sēkrit) *adj.* kept hidden by the few people who know of it; not widely known: *a secret passage.* —*n.* something known to very few people. —**'se·cre·cy** *n.* —**'se·cret·ly** *adv.*

sec·re·tar·y ('sekriterē) *n.,pl.* **sec·re·tar·ies.** 1. a person who deals with the daily work of a business or other organization, typing letters and keeping records. 2. the head of a government department: *the Secretary of Agriculture.*

sect (sekt) *n.* a small group of people united by common religious views, esp. when different from the general beliefs of a larger group.

sec·tion ('sekshən) *n.* 1. a part; division: *a section of a book.* 2. a division of a township equaling one square mile. 3. a thin slice of something, put under a microscope for examination. 4. a diagram or drawing of an object or animal as if part of it had been cut away to show the inside of it. —*vb.* to cut or slice into sections. —**'sec·tion·al** *adj.* —**'sec·tion·al·ly** *adv.*

se·cure (si'kyo͝or) *adj.* 1. safe; protected from danger. 2. firmly in place; fixed. 3. preventing escape, failure, etc.; strong: *a secure prison.* —*vb.* **se·cur·ing, se·cured.** 1. to make secure. 2. to bring about; obtain for oneself: *Julie secured a good job.* —**se'cure·ly** *adv.* —**se'cur·i·ty** *n.*

see¹ (sē) *vb.* **see·ing, saw, seen.** 1. to view with one's eyes. 2. to understand: *he saw what they meant.* 3. to meet: *she saw her mother yesterday.* 4. to accompany (someone): *he saw her home.* 5. to make sure: *see that you do your homework.* **see about** to attend to; find out about. **see off** 1. to watch the departure of. 2. to send away roughly; drive off. **see through** 1. to help (a person) through a difficulty. 2. to be undeceived by: *he saw through the trick.* **see to** to deal with.

see² (sē) *n.* the area of influence of a pope, archbishop, or bishop or the area controlled.

seed (sēd) *n., pl.* **seed** *or* **seeds.** the tiny object from which a plant grows. —*vb.* 1. to sow or plant seeds. 2. to remove seeds from. 3. (sport) to put competitors in groups so that the best players do not meet each other until the later events. **'seed·y** *adj.* **seed·i·er, seed·i·est.** 1. gone to seed. 2. shabby; without freshness. 3. (informal) ill; unwell.

seek (sēk) *vb.* **seek·ing, sought.** 1. to look for; search for: *he sought his brother.* 2. to try to get: *he went to seek his fortune.* 3. to attempt: *they sought to escape.*

seem (sēm) *vb.* to appear to be; give the impression of being: *the salesman seems honest.*

seg·ment ('segmənt) *n. 1. a section or piece of something: he offered me a segment of orange.* 2. the part of a circle cut off by a CHORD (def. 2). 3. one of many similar pieces that form the bodies of certain animals, e.g. worms.

seize (sēz) **seiz·ing, seized.** *vb.* 1. to grab suddenly; grasp. 2. to attack or affect suddenly: *horror seized them.* 3. to capture: *the army seized the castle.* 4. to take away; confiscate. **sei·zure** ('sēzhər) *n.* 1. the act of seizing. 2. a sudden attack of illness.

sel·dom ('seldəm) *adv.* not often.

se·lect (si'lekt) *vb.* to choose; pick out. *he selected the best apple.* —*adj.* most desirable; best. —**se'lec·tive** *adj.* —**se'lec·tion** *n.*

self (self) *n.,pl.* **selves.** 1. the individual character or nature of a person or thing; identity. 2. personal interest: *you can't live for self alone, you must think of others.* —*pron.* (combined with *my-, your-, him-, her-, our-, them-*): *I myself did it; Bill hurt himself.*

self-cen·tered (self'sentərd) *adj.* concerned only with oneself and one's own interests; not caring about other people and their affairs.

self-con·trol (selfkən'trōl) *n.* the ability to keep one's temper, emotions, feelings, actions, etc., under control.

self-de·fense (selfdi'fens) *n.* 1. the act of defending oneself, esp. if unarmed: *I hit the mugger in self-defense.* 2. (law) the use of reasonable force against an attacker.

self·ish ('selfish) *adj.* caring only for oneself and one's own interests, comfort, pleasure, etc., without caring about anyone else. —**'self·ish·ly** *adv.* —**'self·ish·ness** *n.*

sell (sel) *vb.* **sell·ing, sold.** 1. to transfer (something) to someone else in return for money. 2. to offer for sale. 3. to betray or surrender (something) for a price: *Benedict Arnold tried to sell his country.* **sell off** to get rid of by selling cheaply. **sell out** 1. to have no more of a certain article for sale. 2. to desert one's friends in favor of an enemy. 3. to give up one's business by selling all one's goods.

sem·i·cir·cle ('semēsûrkəl) *n.* half a circle.

segment

sem·i·co·lon ('semēkōlən) *n.* a punctuation mark (;) indicating a longer pause than a comma, but a shorter pause than a period.

sem·i·fi·nal ('semēfīnəl) *n.* a sporting event coming immediately before the final one in a competition, which decides who shall compete in that final event. **sem·i'fi·nal·ist** *n.* a player or team in a semifinal.

sen·ate ('senit) *n.* 1. a political council, esp. the higher division of a legislative body in certain countries such as the U.S., where laws are proposed, and made into law or rejected. 2. the chief political body in ancient Rome. **'sen·a·tor** *n.* a member of a senate. —**sen·a·to·ri·al** (senə'tôrēəl) *adj.*

send (send) *vb.* **send·ing, sent.** 1. to cause (someone or something) to go or be carried somewhere: *he sent the parcel to his mother.* 2. to bring into a particular state or condition: *the flies sent the horses mad.* **send for** ask for (someone) to come or for (something) to be brought. **send packing** (informal) to get rid of (someone) very quickly and often roughly. **send up** (informal) to sentence to prison. **send out** to distribute, esp. by mail.

sen·ior ('sēnyər) *adj.* 1. higher in rank: *a senior officer.* 2. superior in age, experience, length of service, etc.: *Jones is senior to Lewis.* 3. the older of two people, esp. the father of a man who has the same name: *John Smith, Senior.* —*n.* someone who is senior. —**sen·ior·i·ty** (sēn'yôritē, sen'yoritē) *n.*

sen·sa·tion (sen'sāshən) *n.* 1. an impression of something received by any or all of the senses: *a sensation of warmth.* 2. something that creates great excitement, interest, curiosity, etc.: *the circus was a sensation.* **sen'sa·tion·al** *adj.* creating great excitement. —**sen'sa·tion·al·ly** *adv.*

sense (sens) *n.* 1. one of the five abilities connected with certain organs in the body by which external things are perceived; sight, smell, touch, hearing, or taste. 2. intelligence and good judgment; wisdom. 3. knowledge of something and of its proper use: *a sense of justice.* 4. the meaning of something: *I meant* bank *in the sense of* river bank *not* money bank. **sens·es** (*pl.*) intelligent or responsible behavior; awareness: *his father's warning brought him to his senses.* **common sense** practical ability or intelligence. **make sense** to have a meaning. **make sense of** to work out the meaning; understand. **'sense·less** *adj.* unreasonable; unthinking. —*vb.* **sens·ing, sensed.** to have a feeling or impression: *he sensed it would rain.*

sen·si·ble ('sensibəl) *adj.* having or showing good judgment, common sense, or understanding; reasonable. —**'sen·si·bly** *adv.*

sen·si·tive ('sensitiv) *adj.* 1. easily affected, stimulated, or stirred by something: *people's eyes are sensitive to light.* 2. showing gentleness or consideration: *the sick puppy needed sensitive treatment.* 3. sharp; keen: *sensitive hearing.* —**sen·si'tiv·i·ty** *n.*

sen·tence ('sentəns) *n.* 1. a word or group of words that makes sense if read alone and expresses a statement, command, question, etc. 2. a legal punishment given by a court or judge to a convicted criminal. —*vb.* **sen·tenc·ing, sen·tenced.** to condemn; pass sentences upon.

sen·ti·ment ('sentəmənt) *n.* 1. emotion or feeling, or an instance of this: *public sentiment was in favor of the new law.* 2. one of the finer emotions, such as joy, love, or pity. 3. often **sen·ti·ments** (*pl.*) opinion; feeling: *he expressed his sentiments in a letter.* **sen·ti'men·tal** (sentə'mentəl) *adj.* appealing to the emotions, esp. in an unnecessarily extreme way. —**sen·ti·men'tal·i·ty** *n.* —**sen·ti'men·tal·ly** *adv.*

sen·ti·nel ('sentənəl) *n.* a person who keeps guard over something or someone and alerts others to danger.

sen·try ('sentrē) *n.,pl.* **sen·tries.** a soldier acting as a guard or watchman.

sep·a·rate *vb.* ('sepərāt) **sep·a·rat·ing, sep·a·rat·ed.** 1. to divide or become divided; split up. 2. to stand between, often as a barrier: *a hedge separates the two gardens.* —*adj.* ('sepərit) separated; independent: *we couldn't find two seats together in the bar so we sat at separate tables.* —'**sep·a·rate·ly** *adv.* —**sep·a'ra·tion** *n.*

sep·tic ('septik) *adj.* (of a wound) poisoned or infected by germs.

se·rene (sə'rēn) *adj.* 1. calm; at peace and untroubled. 2. bright and clear. —**se'rene·ly** *adv.* —**se·ren·i·ty** (sə'renitē) *n.*

ser·geant ('sârjənt) *n.* 1. a policeman just below the rank of lieutenant. 2. a military officer one rank higher than a corporal.

se·ri·al ('sērēəl) *n.* a story published or broadcast in regular parts. —*adj.* relating to, arranged in, or belonging to a series. '**se·ri·al·ly** *adv.* one after the other.

se·ries ('sērēz) *n.,pl.* **se·ries.** a succession of people, events, things, etc., usu. arranged in a logical order; sequence: *he appeared in a series of television programs.*

se·ri·ous ('sērēəs) *adj.* 1. grave; thoughtful: *a serious boy.* 2. sincerely or earnestly meant: *a serious suggestion.* 3. not easily or lightly dealt with: *a serious problem.* 4. having important and often dangerous results: *a serious car crash.* —'**se·ri·ous·ly** *adv.* —'**se·ri·ous·ness** *n.*

ser·mon ('sûrmən) *n.* 1. a speech by a clergyman in a church service, usu. based on the Bible and making a moral or religious point. 2. any speech like a sermon.

ser·pent ('sûrpənt) *n.* 1. a snake. 2. the Devil. 3. any treacherous, cunning, or sly person.

se·rum ('sērəm) *n.* 1. the thin clear liquid forming part of the blood. 2. a dose of this fluid used to make another person or animal immune from a disease.

serv·ant ('sûrvənt) *n.* a person who serves, esp. a person employed to do domestic work in return for wages and a place to live.

serve (sûrv) *vb.* **serv·ing, served.** 1. to work for (someone): *he served the firm loyally for 35 years.* 2. to wait on table. 3. to obey and submit to: *to serve God.* 4. to be useful to; help: *to serve one's country.* 5. to carry out the duties of an office, membership of something, etc.: *he served as President.* 6. to go through (a prison sentence). 7. (in tennis, etc.) to put (the ball) into play: *it was my turn to serve.* —*n.* (tennis) the action or an instance of putting the ball into play.

serv·ice ('sûrvis) *n.* 1. the work or actions of a person who serves. 2. help, assistance, or use. 3. an action or piece of work carried out for someone in return for money, esp. such work done by an official organization: *the postal service.* 4. duty carried out as part of one's office, as a member of the armed forces, etc., or the time during which one occupies such a position. 5. a religious ceremony at a church. 6. the action or an instance of serving in tennis. 7. '**serv·ic·es** (*pl.*) the army, navy, and air force. —*vb.* **serv·ic·ing, serv·iced.** to repair or check (machinery, a car, etc.).

ses·sion ('seshən) *n.* 1. the period of time occupied by some activity, such as a meeting, game, school class, etc. 2. a meeting or series of meetings of any legislative body, e.g. Congress. 3. the part of the year during which a school, university, legislative body, or law court is in operation.

set·tee (se'tē) *n.* a long seat with a back and arms; couch.

settee

set·tle ('setəl) *vb.* **set·tling, set·tled.** 1. to make final: *they settled an agreement on prices.* 2. (often + *up*) to pay (a bill). 3. to go and live or cause to go and live in (a country, district, etc.): *the family finally settled in Ohio.* 4. to make or become calm. 5. to come to rest. **settle down** 1. to become less agitated. 2. to adopt regular habits. '**set·tle·ment** *n.* 1. the act of settling. 2. something settled. 3. a small colony or group of dwellings.

sev·er ('sevər) *vb.* to cut or be cut off; separate. —'**sev·er·ance** *n.*

sev·er·al ('sevərəl) *adj.* 1. two or more but less than many. 2. separate; distinct: *they went their several ways.* '**sev·er·al·ly** *adv.* separately; distinctly.

se·vere (si'vēr) *adj.* 1. strict; stern. 2. harsh; hard to bear. 3. serious; grave. —**se'vere·ly** *adv.* —**se·ver·i·ty** (si'veritē) *n.,pl.* **se·ver·i·ties.**

sew (sō) *vb.* **sew·ing, sewed, sewn.** 1. to use needle and thread to join one piece of material to another. 2. to make or repair by sewing. 3. (often + *up*) to fasten or close with stitches. **sew up** (informal) to finish or end (something) successfully: *we sewed up the match with two more goals.*

sew·age ('sōōij) *n.* waste material flowing through sewers.

sew·er ('sōōər) *n.* an underground pipe or passage through which waste material is carried away. '**sew·er·age** *n.* the system of sewers serving a town or city.

sex (seks) *n.* 1. the quality or character of being either male or female. 2. men or women considered collectively: *equality of the sexes.* 3. (also **sexual intercourse**) the act of making physical love. '**sex·y** *adj.* **sex·i·er, sex·i·est.** appearing or being physically attractive (to someone). —**sex·u·al** ('sekshōōəl) *adj.* **sex·u'al·i·ty** *n.* —'**sex·u·al·ly** *adv.*

shab·by ('shabē) *adj.* **shab·bi·er, shab·bi·est.** 1. worn out or faded. 2. (of a person) wearing worn-out clothes. 3. mean or unfair. —'**shab·bi·ly** *adv.* —'**shab·bi·ness** *n.*

shade (shād) *n.* 1. an area of relative darkness or coolness, esp. as produced by something standing in the way of the sun. 2. something that shields a source of light. 3. a variation in color: *a deep shade of pink.* 4. a tiny amount: *move it a shade more to the right.* —*vb.* **shad·ing, shad·ed.** 1. to protect from strong light and heat. 2. to make darker or add color to (a drawing, etc.). '**shad·y** *adj.* **shad·i·er, shad·i·est.** 1. producing or positioned in shade: *a shady tree.* 2. dishonest.

shad·ow ('shadō) *n.* 1. the dark image of an opaque object produced on a surface when the object stands between the surface and a light shining onto it. 2. shade. 3. a person following somebody closely. —*vb.* 1. to cast a shadow upon. 2. to follow closely, esp. secretly: *the detective was told to shadow the suspect.* '**shad·ow·box** *vb.* to pretend to box with an opponent as an exercise. '**shad·ow·y** *adj.* 1. full of shadow. 2. secret, often dishonest. 3. vague; not clear: *Tom and Mary had only a shadowy idea of how the game was played.*

shaft (shâft) *n.* 1. a long smooth rod forming the body of a spear or arrow. 2. the handle of an ax, etc. 3. a pole attached to the front of a cart, carriage, etc., to which the animal pulling the vehicle is harnessed. 4. a beam of light. 5. a long, narrow, vertical passage in a coal mine, etc.

shag·gy ('shagē) *adj.* **shag·gi·er, shag·gi·est.** 1. having long, untidy hair: *a shaggy dog.* 2. (of hair) long and untidy: *a shaggy beard.* **shaggy dog story** a long story with a silly or pointless joke at the end.

shake (shāk) *vb.* **shak·ing, shook, shak·en.** 1. to move or cause to move up and down or from side to side very quickly. 2. to startle or upset: *the bad news really shook me.* —*n.* the action or an instance of shaking or being shaken. '**shak·y** *adj.* **shak·i·er, shak·i·est.** 1. trembling. 2. unsteady; unsafe.

shal·low ('shalō) *adj.* 1. not deep. 2. superficial; lacking seriousness or thoughtfulness: *a shallow person.* '**shal·lows** *pl.n.* a shallow part of a body of water: *the children were swimming in the shallows.*

shame (shām) *n.* 1. an unpleasant emotion caused by the thought that one has done something wrong. 2. a disappointment: *it's a shame the weather is bad.* 3. disgrace: *his crimes brought shame upon his family.* —*vb.* **sham·ing, shamed.** to cause a feeling of shame or embarrassment in (someone). —'**shame·ful** *adj.* —'**shame·ful·ly** *adv.* —'**shame·ful·ness** *n.* '**shame·less** *adj.* feeling no shame. —'**shame·less·ly** *adv.* —'**shame·less·ness** *n.*

sham·poo (sham'pōō) *n.* 1. a soapy liquid or cream for washing the hair. 2. the process of washing hair with shampoo. —*vb.* to wash with shampoo.

shape (shāp) *n.* 1. a physical form or the outline of something. 2. a condition, state, or way of being: *his bank balance was in poor shape.* —*vb.* 1. to mold or give a particular shape to: *we began to shape our plans for the journey.* 2. to decide or determine. '**shape·ly** *adj.* well-proportioned; having a pleasing shape. —'**shape·less** *adj.*

share (sheər) *vb.* **shar·ing, shared.** 1. to divide up and give out the parts: *she shared the cake between the children.* 2. to have or use with another person or persons: *we shared a taxi to the station.* —*n.* 1. a portion; part. 2. one of the equal parts into which the ownership of a company is divided.

shark (shârk) *n.* 1. a large dangerous fish with several rows of sharp teeth and a tough skin. 2. a person who cheats; swindler.

sharp (shârp) *adj.* 1. suitable for cutting or piercing: *a sharp blade.* 2. having an acute angle; not gradual: *a sharp bend.* 3. sudden; unexpected: *a sharp rise in prices.* 4. (of a taste) acid; bitter. 5. (of a musical note) raised by half a TONE (def. 3) above its normal pitch: *E sharp.* 6. out of tune by being too high in pitch. 7. bright; keen; alert. —*n.* a note that is raised by half a tone above its normal pitch. —*adv.* precisely; exactly: *come at 10:30 sharp.* '**sharp·en** *vb.* to make or become sharp or sharper. —'**sharp·ly** *adv.* —'**sharp·ness** *n.*

shat·ter ('shatər) *vb.* 1. to break or cause to break suddenly into pieces. 2. to destroy suddenly: *he shattered her hopes.*

shave (shāv) *vb.* **shav·ing, shaved, shaved** *or* **shav·en.** 1. to remove (hair, bristles, etc.) with a razor or similar cutting implement. 2. to make the skin smooth in this way: *to shave one's face.* 3. to cut off thin slices of (wood, etc.). —*n.* the action or an instance of shaving. '**shav·er** *n.* an electric razor. '**shav·ings** *pl.n.* thin layers of wood, etc., cut away, e.g. by a chisel, plane, etc.

shawl (shôl) *n.* 1. a covering for the head, neck, and shoulders, worn by a woman. 2. a similar, usu. woolen, covering in which babies are wrapped.

sheaf (shēf) *n.,pl.* **sheaves** (shēvz). 1. a tied bundle of harvested wheat, rye, or other type of cereal. 2. a bundle of anything: *a sheaf of papers.*

shawl

shear (shēr) *vb.* **shear·ing, sheared, shorn.** to remove wool from (a sheep). **shears** *pl.n.* a large scissor-like tool for cutting garden hedges, clipping the wool from a sheep, etc.

sheath (shēth) *n.* 1. a protective covering for the blade of a knife or other sharp instrument. 2. anything that fits closely around something else. **sheathe** ('shēdh) *vb.* **sheath·ing, sheathed.** to put in a sheath; provide with a protective covering.

sheaves (shēvz) *n.* the plural of SHEAF.

shed[1] (shed) *n.* a small building, esp. one outside a house, used for storing wood, garden tools, etc.

shed[2] (shed) *vb.* **shed·ding, shed.** 1. to drop; let go of: *some trees shed their leaves every year.* 2. to throw off; repel: *a duck's oily feathers shed water.*

sheen (shēn) *n.* luster; gloss; shine: *Anna's hair had a lovely sheen when it was brushed.*

sheep (shēp) *n.,pl.* **sheep.** an animal related to the goat, most of whose species are bred for meat, milk, and wool. '**sheep·ish** *adj.* feeling foolish or embarrassed. '**sheep·skin** *n.* the skin of a sheep used for clothing, esp. a coat made of this.

sheer (shēr) *adj.* 1. steep: *a sheer drop from the top of a cliff.* 2. fine; almost transparent: *she wore sheer stockings.* 3. complete; total: *sheer stupidity.*

sheet[1] (shēt) *n.* 1. a large rectangular piece of cotton, linen, or other cloth that is spread on a bed. 2. a thin, flat, usu. rectangular piece of metal, paper, glass, etc.

sheet² (shēt) *n.* a rope or chain attached to the corner of a sail on a boat in order to control the sail.

sheikh *or* **sheik** (shēk) *n.* 1. the head of an Arab family or tribe. 2. an Arab political or religious leader. **'sheikh·dom** *or* **'sheik·dom** *n.* the area ruled by a sheikh.

shelf (shelf) *n.,pl.* **shelves** (shelvz). 1. a horizontal piece of wood, metal, etc., fixed to a wall or in a cupboard and used for storage. 2. anything resembling a shelf, e.g. a surface of rock or ice. **shelve** (shelv) *vb.* **shelv·ing, shelved.** 1. to place on a shelf. 2. to put off dealing with (something): *the plan to build a new school was shelved because of a shortage of funds.*

shell (shel) *n.* 1. the hard outer covering of some animals, eggs, seeds, or fruits, or the material of which this is made. 2. a metal case packed with explosives and fired from a cannon or large gun. 3. the frame of anything: *the shell of a building.* —*vb.* 1. to remove the shell (def. 1) from: *Lucy helped her mother prepare dinner by shelling the peas.* 2. to fire shells (def. 2) at.

shell·fish ('shelfish) *n.* any sea or river animal with a shell, e.g. a crab, lobster, oyster, etc.

shel·ter ('sheltər) *n.* something that gives protection against bad weather, danger, etc. —*vb.* to take or give shelter: *they sheltered in the basement during the typhoon.*

shelve (shelv) *vb.* See under SHELF.

shep·herd ('shepərd) *n.* a person employed to look after a flock of sheep. —*vb.* to guide in the manner of someone driving sheep: *the tourists spent the day being shepherded around the museum.*

sher·iff ('sherif) *n.* a law officer in a county or other administrative area in any of the states of the U.S.

sher·ry ('sherē) *n.,pl.* **sher·ries.** a type of wine with extra alcohol added, made mainly in Spain. It varies in colour from pale gold to dark brown.

shield (shēld) *n.* 1. a handheld piece of protective armor formerly carried in battle by soldiers. 2. anything that protects or looks like a shield: *the hedge was a shield for the sheep in the blizzard.* —*vb.* to protect; guard.

shells

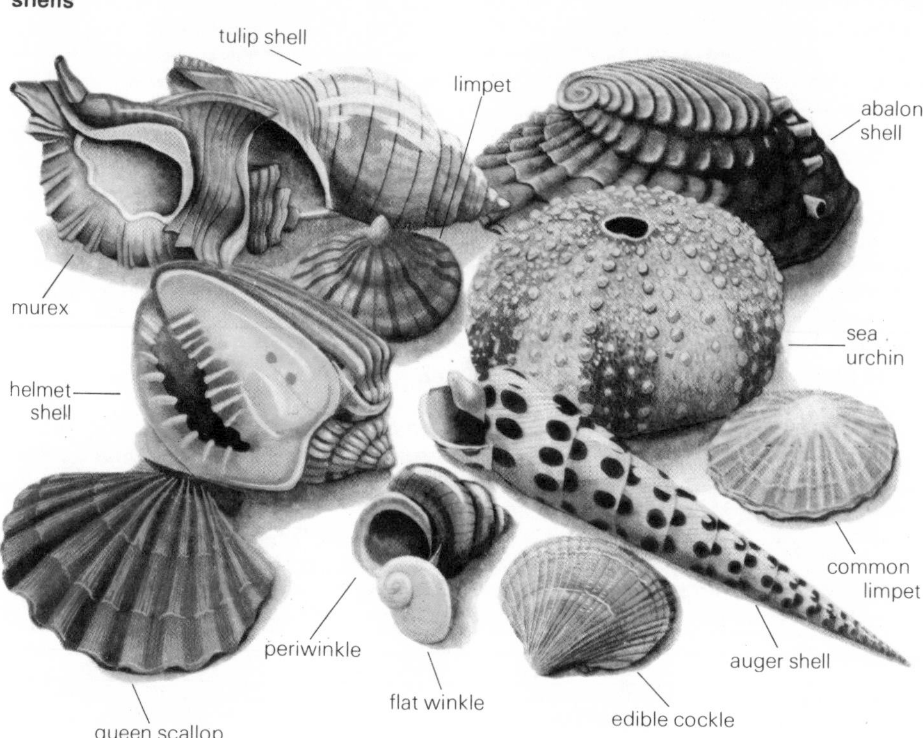

shift (shift) *vb.* to move or change or cause to move or change: *he shifted the furniture.* —*n.* 1. a change or movement. 2. a group of workers who work during a particular period of time each day: *the morning shift arrives just as the night shift is leaving the factory.* 3. the period worked by such a group: *the night shift is from 10 p.m. till 6 a.m.* 4. a woman's straight loose dress. **'shift·y** *adj.* **shift·i·er, shift·i·est.** sly; untrustworthy; evasive.

shin (shin) *n.* the front part of the leg between the knee and the ankle. —*vb.* **shin·ning, shinned.** to climb by gripping and pulling oneself up, using the hands and legs: *to shin up a tree.*

shield

shine (shīn) *vb.* **shin·ing, shone** (shōn) *or, esp. for def. 2,* **shined.** 1. to give out or reflect light. 2. to clean and polish (an object) so that it reflects light. 3. to do well: *he shines at swimming.* —*n.* the quality of a reflection: *the shine on the silverware.*

shirt (shûrt) *n.* a garment of light cloth covering the top half of the body, usu. having buttons down the front. **T–shirt** a long- or short-sleeved, shirt without buttons.

shiv·er ('shivər) *vb.* to shake or tremble, esp. because of cold or fright. —*n.* a shivering feeling: *a shiver ran down his spine.* **'shiv·er·y** *adj.* experiencing or producing shivers.

shoal¹ (shōl) *n.* a large group of fish swimming along close together in the same direction: *a shoal of herring.*

shoal² (shōl) *n.* a very shallow place in the sea or a river, esp. a bank of sand visible only at low tide.

shock (shok) *n.* 1. a sudden surprise. 2. a violent impact: *shock absorbers.* 3. the sensation caused when an electric current passes through one's body. 4. a medical condition produced as a reaction to fear, injury, etc.: *the driver was treated for shock after the crash.* —*vb.* 1. to cause a sudden great and usu. unpleasant surprise to somebody. 2. to cause to suffer an electric shock.

shoe (shoo) *n.* 1. a protective covering for the foot made of leather, wood, plastic, etc. 2. anything resembling a shoe in function or shape, e.g. a metal band on the runner of a sled. —*vb.* **shoe·ing, shod,** *or* **shoed.** to supply or fit with shoes.

shone (shōn) *vb.* a past tense and past participle of SHINE.

shook (shook) *vb.* the past tense of SHAKE.

shoot (shoot) *vb.* **shoot·ing, shot.** 1. to fire (a gun or similar weapon). 2. to fire (an arrow) from a bow. 3. to kill or wound with a gun, bow, etc. 4. to photograph and make a film of (a scene). 5. to hunt (game). —*n.* 1. a young plant or new part of a plant. 2. an area of land where game is kept for hunting: *a pheasant shoot.*

shop (shop) *n.* 1. a place where things are bought and sold; small store. 2. a workshop; place where things are made or repaired. —*vb.* **shop·ping, shopped.** 1. to visit a shop and buy things. 2. to compare various suppliers' prices for an item before buying it. **'shop·ping** *n.* 1. the activity of visiting a shop. 2. the things bought at a shop, esp. groceries.

shop·lift·er ('shopliftər) *n.* a person who steals goods from a store while pretending to be a customer.

shore (shôr) *n.* the land lying next to a large stretch of water such as a lake or sea.

shorn (shôrn) *vb.* the past participle of SHEAR.

short (shôrt) *adj.* 1. having little length, height, duration, etc. 2. having less than a usual or required length, height, amount, etc.: *our team cannot compete because it is two men short.* 4. impolitely abrupt in manner. **shorts** (*pl.*) 1. a pair of short trousers covering the thighs and sometimes extending to the knees. 2. men's underpants. **'short·age** *n.* a lack: *there's a shortage of paper.* **'short·en** *vb.* to make shorter; reduce. **'short·ly** *adv.* in a little space of time; soon. —**'short·ness** *n.*

short·com·ing ('shôrtkuming) *n.* a failure to come up to certain standards; defect.

shot (shot) *vb.* the past tense and past participle of SHOOT. —*n.* 1. the act of firing a gun, shooting an arrow, etc. 2. the sound made by this. 3. an attempt: *he had a shot at becoming president.* 4. the act or result of taking a photograph. 5. an injection. 6. tiny lead balls contained in a cartridge to be fired from a shotgun.

shot·gun ('shotgun) *n.* a short-range gun with a long barrel that fires cartridges filled with lead shot.

shoul·der ('shōldər) *n.* 1. the part of the body between the neck and the top of the arm; the joint that connects the arm to the body. 2. the part of a garment covering the shoulder. 3. the part of an animal where its foreleg joins the rest of its body. 4. a ridge or border at the side of some roads. —*vb.* 1. to take, carry on, or push with the shoulder: *she shouldered her way through the crowd.* 2. to accept (blame or responsibility).

shout (shout) *vb.* to speak loudly; yell. —*n.* a loud cry.

shove (shuv) *vb.* **shov·ing, shoved.** to push hard. —*n.* a hard push.

shov·el ('shuvəl) *n.* a tool with a broad blade at the end of a handle, used for moving loose material such as coal, soil, snow, sand, etc. —*vb.* to move by using a shovel.

show (shō) *vb.* **show·ing, showed, shown.** 1. to cause to be seen; display, esp. to the public. 2. to guide; conduct: *show him out.* 3. to explain; teach: *she showed me how to drive a car.* 4. to prove: *the evidence shows that you are right.* **show off** to act in a boastful way. **show up** 1. to embarrass. 2. to arrive or be present: *most of the guests showed up on time.* 3. to be seen. —*n.* 1. the act of showing. 2. a public entertainment, esp. one produced at a theater using much music and dancing. 3. an outdoor event, such as an aircraft display. 4. an appearance; pretense: *he made a show of being poor.* **'show·y** *adj.* **show·i·er, show·i·est.** 1. showing off. 2. visually attractive: *showy flowers.*

show·er ('shouər) *n.* 1. a sudden brief fall of rain, hail, or snow. 2. (also **shower bath**) a bath in which the bather stands under a spray of water. 3. the equipment or place used for this. —*vb.* 1. to cover in the manner of a shower: *he showered me with praise.* 2. to bathe by taking a shower.

shrank (shrangk) *vb.* the past tense of SHRINK.

shred (shred) *n.* 1. a small piece torn or cut from something. 2. a small amount: *if there had been a shred of proof, he would have been convicted.* —*vb.* **shred·ding, shred·ded** to tear or cut into shreds.

shrew (shroo) *n.* 1. a small mouselike animal with a long pointed nose. 2. a bad-tempered woman. **'shrew·ish** *adj.* bad-tempered; scolding or nagging. —**'shrew·ish·ly** *adv.* —**'shrew·ish·ness** *n.*

shrewd (shrood) *adj.* clever; intelligent; crafty. —**'shrewd·ly** *adv.* —**'shrewd·ness** *n.*

shriek (shrēk) *n.* a shrill cry or scream. —*vb.* to utter or say with such a cry: *the children shrieked as they jumped into the water.*

shrill (shril) *adj.* high-pitched and piercing: *a shrill cry.* —**'shrill·ness** *n.* —**shril·ly** *adv.*

shrimp (shrimp) *n., pl.* **shrimp** *or* **shrimps.** a type of small shellfish, having pale pink edible flesh. —*vb.* to catch shrimps.

shovel

shrine (shrīn) *n.* 1. a building, container, etc., holding a holy object. 2. a place that is devoted to a person, esp. a saint.

shrink (shringk) *vb.* **shrink·ing, shrank** *or* **shrunk, shrunk** *or* **shrunken.** 1. to make or become smaller: *my new sweater shrank in the washing machine.* 2. to draw back: *he shrank from the idea of hurting the dog.*

shriv·el ('shrivəl) *vb.* to make or become smaller, with the surface wrinkling in the process: *the flowers shriveled in the summer heat.*

shroud (shroud) *n.* 1. a cloth in which a dead body is wrapped. 2. something that covers and conceals: ***a shroud of fog.*** 3. **shrouds** (*pl.*) ropes bracing a ship's mast or linking a parachutist's harness to the parachute canopy. —*vb.* 1. to wrap (a dead body) in a shroud. 2. to cover and hide: ***darkness shrouded the scene.***

shrub (shrub) *n.* a bush or other small woody plant with no central stem.

shrug (shrug) *vb.* **shrug·ging, shrugged.** to raise (the shoulders) as an expression of indifference, doubt, ignorance, helplessness, etc. —*n.* the action or an instance of shrugging.

shrunk (shrungk) *vb.* a past tense and past participle of SHRINK.

shrunk·en (shrungkən) *vb.* a past participle of SHRINK. —*adj.* made or become less in size: ***during the drought the shrunken river could not supplyoenough water.***

shud·der ('shudər) *vb.* to shake or tremble; shiver. —*n.* the action or an instance of shuddering.

shuf·fle ('shufəl) *vb.* **shuf·fling, shuf·fled.** 1. to mix up (playing cards, etc.) randomly. 2. to drag or slide the feet along the ground while walking. 3. to fidget from one position to another. —*n.* the action or an instance of shuffling.

shut (shut) *vb.* **shut·ting, shut.** 1. to close or be closed. 2. to secure with a lock, catch, etc. 3. to confine: ***she shut the dog in the room.***

shutter

shut·ter (shutər) *n.* 1. a window cover, usu. of wood or metal, fixed on the outside to keep out sunlight and cold and prevent anyone from climbing in. 2. a device in a camera that opens and closes to allow light to pass through.

shy[1] (shī) *adj.* **shy·er, shy·est** *or* **shi·er, shi·est.** 1. nervous or uncomfortable when with other people: ***Paul was too shy to enjoy the party.*** 2. timid or embarrassed: ***a shy giggle.*** 3. (of animals) easily frightened. 4. lacking: ***the cash box is shy two dollars.*** —*vb.* **shy·ing, shied.** (esp. of horses) to move suddenly to one side or rear up when startled: ***the horse shied at the sight of the fence.***

shy[2] (shī) *vb.* **shy·ing, shied.** to throw (a stone, ball, etc.) fast and suddenly. —*n.,pl.* **shies.** a fast and sudden throw.

sick (sik) *adj.* 1. unwell; unhealthy. 2. having an attack of vomiting. 3. weary; tired: ***he was sick of work.*** 4. in bad taste: ***a sick joke.***

side (sīd) *n.* 1. any surface of an object that is not the front, back, top, or bottom. 2. any of the surfaces of a solid object: ***a cube has six sides.*** 3. any of the lines enclosing a square, triangle, etc. 4. either of the two surfaces of a piece of paper or cloth. 5. the area or part of something considered as being to the right or left, east or west, etc., of some central line or point: ***the south side of the city.*** 6. the right-hand or left-hand part of the body: ***he was shot in the side.*** 7. a group, team, or party in competition or disagreement with another one: ***our side won.*** 8. a line of descent: ***she has many cousins on her father's side.*** —*vb.* **sid·ing, sid·ed.** (+ ***with***) to support (one group or party) rather than another: ***he sided with the minority.*** **'sid·ing** *n.* a section of railroad track branching out from the main line, used for switching trains, storing freight trains, etc.

side·board ('sīdbôrd) *n.* 1. a piece of dining-room furniture, usu. with cupboards and drawers, used for storing crockery, cutlery, etc.

side·burns ('sīdbûrnz) *pl.n.* whiskers on the side of the face.

side·show ('sidshō) *n.* a small entertainment produced in addition to a larger show, esp. at a fair.

siege (sēj) *n.* a process used in war in which a fortified position, esp. a town, is surrounded and its supplies are cut off by enemy forces wishing to capture it.

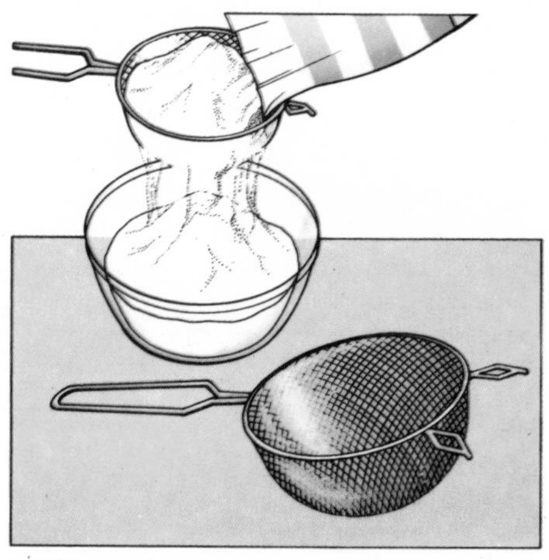

sieve

sieve (siv) *n.* a wire screen stretched within a frame for separating solids from liquids or large particles from small. —*vb.* **siev·ing, sieved.** to sift.

sift (sift) *vb.* 1. to separate by passing through a sieve. 2. to examine carefully and thoroughly: ***the police sifted the evidence.***

sigh (sī) *vb.* to take a deep breath and let it out slowly and with a sound expressing relief, weariness, sadness, etc. —*n.* the action or an instance of sighing.

sight (sīt) *n.* 1. the ability to see; the sense through which the world is observed by means of the eyes. 2. something seen or worth seeing; view: ***the snowy mountains were a fine sight.*** 3. also **sights** (*pl.*) a device on a gun to assist the user's aim. 5. an odd, unusual, or funny appearance: ***what a sight she looks in that dress.*** —*vb.* 1. to see: ***to sight land.*** 2. to aim (a gun) by means of a sight.

sign (sīn) *n.* 1. a gesture, symbol, or mark standing for something or pointing the way to some place. 2. an event indicating a present or future happening: ***a red sky at night may be a sign of good weather.*** 3. an indication; trace: ***there was not a sign of impurity in the metal.*** 4. a traffic notice, type of advertisement, etc.: ***an inn sign.*** —*vb.* 1. to write one's name by hand on (a paper). 2. to gesture; indicate. 3. (+ ***on*** or ***up***) to enter into employment, esp. in the army, navy, or air force. **sign off** to finish; conclude, esp. broadcasting.

sig·nal ('signəl) *n.* 1. a sign or message passed by signs. 2. a radio transmission. —*vb.* to indicate by means of a signal. —*adj.* noteworthy; outstanding: ***a signal achievement.***

si·lent ('sīlənt) *adj.* 1. making no sound; still. 2. not speaking; not mentioning a particular subject: ***he kept silent about the new plan.*** '**si·lence** *n.* complete stillness; absolute quiet. —'**si·lent·ly** *adv.*

sil·hou·ette (siloo'et) *n.* the shape of an object seen as dark against a bright background. —*vb.* **sil·hou·et·ting, sil·hou·et·ted.** to show as a silhouette.

silk (silk) *n.* a soft shiny fabric made from the thread produced by the caterpillar (**silkworm**) of a type of moth. —*adj.* made of silk. '**silk·y** *adj.* **silk·i·er, silk·i·est.** soft and smooth, like silk. —'**silk·i·ness** *n.*

sill (sil) *n.* a ledge made of timber or stone at the base of a window.

si·lo ('sīlō) *n.,pl.* **si·los.** 1. an airtight tower, pit, or other chamber where fodder or grain is stored. 2. a cylindrical pit in the earth from which ballistic missiles are fired. '**si·lage** *n.* the fodder kept in a silo.

silt (silt) *n.* a fine mass of earth or mud particles that settles to the bottom in water, as in a river. —*vb.* to block or be blocked up with silt.

sil·ver ('silvər) *n.* 1. a grayish-white shiny metal used for making coins, jewelry, spoons, etc. Chemical symbol: Ag. 2. coins, household articles, etc., made of silver. —*adj.* made of, producing, or having the color of silver.

sim·i·lar ('simələr) *adj.* (often + *to*) like; resembling: ***Bob's house is very similar to Jason's.*** **sim·i·lar·i·ty** (simə'laritē) *n.,pl.* **sim·i·lar·i·ties.** the condition of being similar or that element of something that is similar to an element in something else. —'**sim·i·lar·ly** *adv.*

sim·mer ('simər) *vb.* 1. to boil gently. 2. to be at a high pitch of emotion, anger, or excitement: ***she was simmering with rage all day.*** —*n.* the process of simmering.

sim·ple ('simpəl) *adj.* 1. easy to do or understand; not difficult: ***a simple problem.*** 2. ordinary; plain: ***simple food.*** 3. not clever; easily deceived or tricked. —**sim'plic·i·ty** *n.* —'**sim·ply** *adv.*

sim·pli·fy ('simpləfī) *vb.* **sim·pli·fy·ing, sim·pli·fied.** to make simple or less difficult. **sim·pli·fi'ca·tion** *n.* the action or an instance of simplifying.

sin (sin) *n.* 1. the action or an instance of breaking a moral or religious law, esp. one considered to have been given by God. 2. wickedness; immoral behavior. —*vb.* **sin·ning, sinned.** to commit a sin. —'**sin·ful** *adj.* —'**sin·ful·ly** *adv.* '**sin·ner** *n.* one who commits a sin.

sin·cere (sin'sēr) *adj.* 1. honest; true. 2. genuine; real. —**sin·cer·i·ty** (sin'seritē) *n.* —**sin'cere·ly** *adv.*

sinew ('sinyoo) *n.* 1. a strong cordlike part of the body that connects a muscle to a bone; TENDON. 2. (also **sinews**) strength; muscular power. '**sin·ew·y** *adj.* 1. of or like a sinew; stringy. 2. strong; powerful; vigorous.

singe (sinj) *vb.* **singe·ing, singed.** 1. to burn slightly; scorch. 2. to remove (hair) by singeing. —*n.* a slight superficial burn.

sin·gle ('singgəl) *adj.* 1. for, used by, or consisting of one only or one part only; not double or complex. 2. separate; individual: ***she looked at every single picture.*** 3. unmarried. —*n.* '**sin·gles** (*pl.*) a game of tennis, badminton, etc., between one pair of players only. '**sin·gle-'hand·ed** *adj., adv.* working alone; without help from anyone. '**sin·gle-'mind·ed** *adj.* having one aim or purpose in view.

sin·gu·lar ('singyələr) *adj.* unusual; odd; strange: ***she told us a singular story that was hard to believe.*** —*n.* a grammatical form indicating that a word refers to only one person or thing: ***the singular of children is child.*** —**sin·gu'lar·i·ty** *n.* —'**sin·gu·lar·ly** *adv.*

sin·is·ter ('sinistər) *adj.* indicating or threatening future evil; unlucky.

sink (singk) *vb.* **sink·ing, sank, sunk.** 1. to fall or move or cause to fall or move slowly downward, esp. below the surface of a liquid. 2. to go (into the mind); penetrate: ***the meaning of his words didn't sink in until later.*** 3. to pass to a lower or worse state: ***my spirits sank.*** 4. to put (money into something); invest: ***he sank his savings into the company.*** —*n.* a fixed basin with faucets for hot and cold water and a drain.

si·phon ('sīfən) *n.* 1. a bent tube or channel for transferring liquid from one level to a lower level. 2. a bottle containing a beverage under pressure. —*vb.* to draw off by means of a siphon.

site (sīt) *n.* 1. an area of ground on which a building is to be erected or where something is to be found or is being dug up. 3. a position; situation: ***the hill is a good site for a picnic.***

sit·u·ate ('sichooāt) *vb.* **sit·u·at·ing, sit·u·at·ed.** to put in a special area, position, or set of circumstances. **sit·u'a·tion** *n.* 1. a position; place. 2. a state, condition, or set circumstance. 3. position of employment; job.

size (sīz) *n.* 1. the largeness or smallness of a thing. 2. specific measurements of clothes, gloves, shoes, etc. —*vb.* **siz·ing, sized.** (+ *up*) to make a judgment about (a situation, person, etc.).

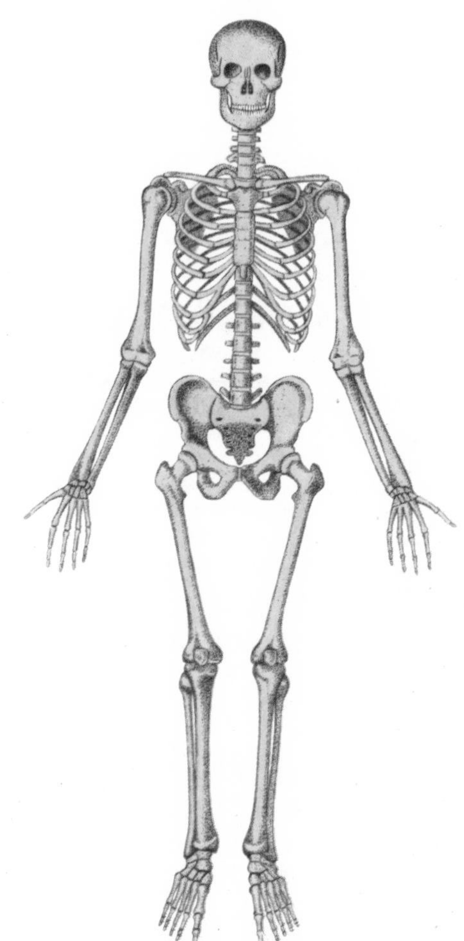

skeleton

skel·e·ton ('skelitən) *n.* 1. the bony frame supporting a person's or animal's body and covered by flesh and skin, hide, etc. 2. the basic part of something. —*adj.* consisting of the smallest number necessary for handling something: ***a skeleton crew.***

sketch (skech) *n.* 1. a rough or quickly done drawing. 2. an artistic drawing often intended to catch a temporary effect of light, movement, etc. 3. a short piece of writing giving an outline of something. 4. a short humorous stage entertainment or play. —*vb.* **sketch·ing, sketched.** (sometimes + *out*) to make a sketch of. **'sketch·y** *adj.* **sketch·i·er, sketch·i·est.** lacking detail.—**'sketch·i·ly** *adv.* —**'sketch·i·ness** *n.*

skew·er ('skyōōər) *n.* a long pointed metal or wooden pin for keeping meat together as it is being cooked. —*vb.* to stick a skewer through (meat).

ski (skē) *n.* 1. either of two long flat strips of wood or metal strapped to boots and used for moving over the surface of snow. 2. similar strips used for gliding over water. —*vb.* **ski·ing, skied.** to slide over snow or water on skis, esp. as a sport.

skid (skid) *vb.* **skid·ding, skid·ded.** to slide out of control: *the car skidded across the wet road.* —*n.* the action or an instance of skidding.

skies (skīz) *n.* the plural of SKY.

skill (skil) *n.* 1. the knowledge of or ability connected with an art, science, sport, etc.: *playing the piano is a skill.* 2. the ability needed to do something to a high standard. —**'skill·ful, skilled** *adj.* —**'skill·ful·ly** *adv.*

skim (skim) *vb.* **skim·ming, skimmed.** 1. to glide rapidly along or just above the surface of: *the seagull skims the waves.* 2. to remove floating matter from the surface of: *Ann skimmed the fat from the soup.* 3. (often + *through*) to read or examine quickly or hurriedly. **skimmed milk** *or* **skim milk** milk with the fat removed.

skin (skin) *n.* 1. the outer covering of the body. 2. the outer covering of an animal's body with or without the hair growing on it. 3. a water container, form of clothing, etc., made from an animal skin. 4. the outer covering of a banana and certain other fruit. —*vb.* **skin·ning, skinned.** to take the skin off. **'skin·ny** *adj.* **skin·ni·er, skin·ni·est.** very thin.

skip (skip) *vb.* **skip·ping, skipped.** 1. to make small jumps on one spot over a swinging rope. 2. to leave out (something), esp. when doing something hastily: *she skipped the third chapter.* 3. to move about quickly, esp. by small jumps. 4. (informal) to escape: *the thief skipped with the money.* —*n.* a small jump or leap.

skir·mish ('skurmish) *n.* a scrap or brief fight.

skirt (skûrt) *n.* 1. a woman's outer garment fitting around the waist and covering all or part of the legs. 2. the lower part of a dress. —*vb.* (often + *around*) to be on or move along or around the border or edge of: *he skirted around the subject of marriage.*

skull (skul) *n.* the bony framework of the head, enclosing the brain.

skunk (skungk) *n.* a small North American animal that gives out a foul-smelling odor when attacked.

skunk

sky (skī) *n.,pl.* **skies.** the apparently rooflike space above the earth, where the sun, moon, stars, and clouds are seen. **'sky·light** *n.* a glass window set into a roof to let in light. **'sky·line** *n.* 1. the apparent boundary between the earth and the sky; horizon. 2. the shape of buildings, trees, etc. on the horizon, silhouetted against the sky. **'sky·scrap·er** *n.* an extremely tall building, having many floors.

slab (slab) *n.* 1. a flat piece of stone or concrete. 2. a large heavy piece or chunk. 3. a large thick slice of bread, cake, etc.

slack (slak) *adj.* 1. not tight; loose; limp. 2. lazy; relaxed; inactive. 3. not strict. 4. not busy. —*n.* 1. the loose part of a rope, garment, etc. 2. **slacks** (*pl.*) loose pants for informal wear. —*vb.* 1. (also **'slack·en**) to make or become slack. 2. to be idle.

slam (slam) *vb.* **slam·ming, slammed.** 1. to shut noisily or violently. 2. to throw down or strike forcefully. 3. (informal) to blame or criticize very harshly. —*n.* 1. the action or an instance of slamming. 2. the sound of a slam.

slang (slang) *n.* a form of language different from standard speech, often thought to be unacceptable in more formal usage, e.g. *cop* is the slang word for *policeman.*

slant (slant) *vb.* 1. to slope or cause to slope. 2. to change (a discussion, report, etc.) slightly, usu. to prove a point: *the paper slanted the news story in favor of the criminal.* —*n.* 1. a sloping line, surface, or movement. 2. a point of view; way of looking at a thing.

slap (slap) *vb.* **slap·ping, slapped.** to strike with the palm of the hand. **slap down** 1. (informal) to speak sharply to (someone): *she slapped him down for his stupidity.* 2. to put (something) down sharply and noisily: *he slapped the papers down on the table.* —*n.* a blow of the open hand or the noise of this.

slap·stick ('slapstik) *n.* (also **slapstick comedy**) a noisy, crazy form of comedy gaining its humor from physical effects.

slash (slash) *vb.* 1. to make long cuts in with a knife, sword, whip, etc. 2. to reduce a great deal: *prices were slashed in the sale.* —*n.* 1. a long cut or gash. 2. the act of slashing. 3. a short diagonal stroke (/) used in writing fractions, etc.: *1/2 and/or 3/4.*

slate (slāt) *n.* 1. a dense gray rock easily split into thin plates. 2. a piece of this used in covering roofs or formerly as a writing tablet. 3. a dark gray-blue color. —*vb.* **slat·ing, slat·ed.** 1. to cover (a roof) with slates. 2. to plan or be planned or scheduled: *the play is slated to open on Broadway next week.*

slaugh·ter ('slôtər) *vb.* 1. to kill (animals) for meat. 2. to kill (large numbers of people). —*n.* the act or an instance of slaughtering, esp. large numbers of people.

slave (slāv) *n.* a person owned by and forced to work for and obey another. —*vb.* **slav·ing, slaved.** to work like a slave. **'slav·e·ry** *n.* 1. the condition of being a slave. 2. the owning of slaves.

sled

sled (sled) *or* **sledge** (slej) *n.* 1. a vehicle mounted on smooth strips of wood or metal and often drawn by horses or dogs, used for traveling or carrying goods over snow. 2. a toboggan. —*vb.* **sledd·ing, sledded.** to carry on or travel by sled.

sledge·ham·mer ('slejhamər) *n.* a large heavy hammer.

sleek (slēk) *adj.* 1. (of hair or an animal's coat) smooth; glossy. 2. having a neat well-groomed appearance or smooth manner: *John looked very sleek in his new suit.* —*vb.* to make sleek; smooth.

sleep (slēp) *n.* 1. a natural state of unconsciousness or complete rest with the eyes closed, usu. at night. 2. a period of this: *a sound sleep.* —*vb.* **sleep·ing, slept.** 1. to take rest; be in the state of sleep: *he slept for ten hours after a hard day.* 2. to provide sleeping accommodation for: *we can sleep five in our house.* **'sleep·er** *n.* 1. a person who sleeps. 2. a railroad car with sleeping accommodation. **'sleep·less** *adj.* without sleep: *we had a sleepless night.* —**'sleep·y** *adj.* **sleep·i·er, sleep·i·est.**

sleet (slēt) *n.* rain mixed with snow or hail. —*vb.* to send down sleet.

sleeve (slēv) *n.* 1. a part of a garment covering the arm. 2. an envelope-like cover for a record. —**'sleeve·less** *adj.*

sleigh (slā) *n.* a large sled often pulled by horses.

slen·der ('slendər) *adj.* 1. gracefully slim: *a slender girl.* 2. slight; insufficient: *I cannot afford it with my slender income.*

slept (slept) *vb.* the past tense and past participle of SLEEP.

slice (slīs) *n.* 1. a thin flat piece cut from something: *a slice of bread.* 2. a flat or broad-bladed type of knife for slicing cake, serving fish, etc. 3. a slash; slicing stroke. —*vb.* **slic·ing, sliced.** 1. to cut into thin flat pieces. 2. to cut a slice from. 3. to slash.

slick (slik) *adj.* 1. sleek; smooth. 2. smooth in speech or manner. 3. clever, esp. too clever: *he's a slick talker but I don't think he's sincere.* —*n.* (also **oil slick**) a patch of oil on the surface of the sea.

slide (slīd) *vb.* **slid·ing, slid** (slid). 1. to move or send in one smooth movement along a surface. 2. to slip, usu. by loss of footing: *my feet slid from under me.* —*n.* 1. the action or an instance of sliding. 2. a polished slippery track on an icy surface or a sloping apparatus used for sliding, e.g. at a playground. 3. a bed, groove, or rail on which a thing slides. 4. a piece of extra tubing in a trombone that can be extended or detached. 5. a picture for projecting on a screen. 6. a piece of glass for mounting objects to be examined under a microscope.

slight (slīt) *adj.* 1. of small size, amount, strength, power, importance, etc. —*vb.* 1. to treat as unimportant. 2. to insult. —*n.* an insult. **'slight·ly** *adv.* rather; somewhat: *he's slightly mad.*

slim (slim) *adj.* **slim·mer, slim·mest.** 1. gracefully thin; slender: *a slim waist.* 2. slight; small: *he had only a slim chance of winning.* —*vb.* (usu. + *down*) **slim·ming, slimmed.** to lose or cause to lose weight. **'slim·mer** *n.* a person on a diet trying to slim.

slime (slīm) *n.* a sticky, slippery, usu. unpleasant substance such as mud. **'slim·y** *adj.* **slim·i·er, slim·i·est.** 1. covered with slime. 2. (of a person) offensive. —**'slim·i·ness** *n.*

sling (sliŋ) *n.* 1. a device for throwing stones, often consisting of a loop of leather and cord from which the stone is hurled. 2. a rope or chain looped around something to lift or support it. 3. a strip of cloth or harness supporting an injured arm, etc. —*vb.* **sling·ing, slung.** 1. to throw. 2. to shoot or cast with a sling.

slip[1] (slip) *vb.* **slip·ping, slipped.** 1. to slide without meaning to; lose balance and fall. 2. to move or cause to move into or out of place. 3. to fall suddenly, usu. from the hand. 4. to slide: *the key slipped easily into the lock.* 5. (often + *away, by,* etc.) to move rapidly, quietly, or unnoticed: *Dave slipped away from the party early.* 6. to hand over, esp. secretly. 7. (sometimes + *up*) to make a mistake. —*n.* 1. the action or an instance of slipping; a sliding fall. 2. a mistake. 3. a woman's undergarment. 4. a pillowcase. **'slip·per·y** *adj.* 1. causing sliding because of being too smooth, wet, etc.: *slippery roads.* 2. cunning: *a slippery character.* —**'slip·per·i·ness** *n.*

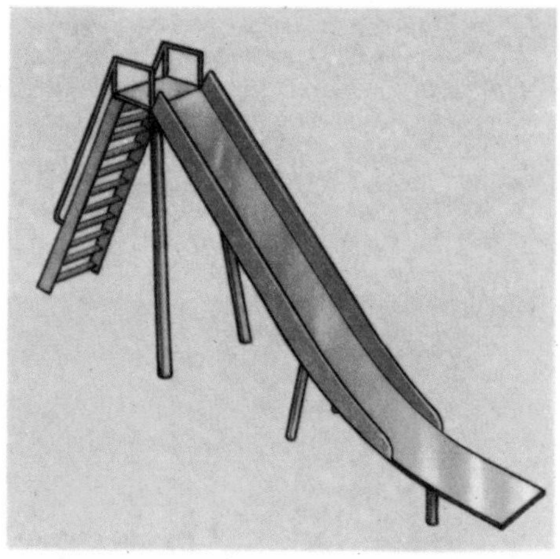

slide

slip[2] (slip) *n.* 1. a narrow strip of paper. 2. anything thin or narrow: *she was a slip of a girl.*

slip·per ('slipər) *n.* a loose soft shoe worn indoors.

slip·shod ('slipshod) *adj.* careless or untidy; rough: *the child was punished for his slipshod work.*

slit (slit) *vb.* **slit·ting, slit.** to make a long cut or tear; split. —*n.* a long narrow opening, tear, or split.

slo·gan ('slōgən) *n.* an easily remembered phrase or word used to advertise a product or arouse interest in and support for a political party, movement, or action.

slope (slōp) *n.* 1. a piece of ground or a surface rising or falling gradually from the horizontal. 2. the amount of this rise or fall: *the hill had a steep slope.* —*vb.* **slop·ing, sloped.** to place at an angle to the horizontal; be in an inclined position.

slot (slot) *n.* 1. a long narrow opening, esp. one able to take a coin in a vending machine. 2. a regularly placed position or time: *the new TV program appears in the eight o'clock time slot.* —*vb.* **slot·ting, slot·ted.** to make a slot in.

slow (slō) *adj.* 1. not quick; taking a long time. 2. moving at low speed. 3. (of a clock) showing a time earlier than the correct time. 4. stupid; unintelligent. 5. boring; uninteresting. —*vb.* (often + *down*) to cause to move more slowly. —'**slow·ly** *adv.* —'**slow·ness** *n.*

slug[1] (slug) *n.* 1. a small slow-moving often black or gray animal related to the snail but having no shell. 2. a lump of metal, esp. a bullet that has been fired. '**slug·gish** *adj.* slow-moving; not responding or acting quickly. —'**slug·gish·ly** *adv.* —'**slug·gish·ness** *n.*

slug[2] (slug) *vb.* **slug·ging, slugged.** (informal) to knock or hit violently. —*n.* a violent blow.

sluice

sluice (slōōs) *n.* 1. a manmade channel fitted with a gate for stopping or regulating the flow of water. 2. a trough for separating gold from sand. —*vb.* **sluic·ing, sluiced.** 1. to let out or drain by a sluice. 2. to wash thoroughly by means of or as if by means of a sluice.

slum (slum) *n.* 1. often **slums** (*pl.*) a street or district of overcrowded houses in poor condition. 2. a single house in bad condition. —*vb.* **slum·ming, slummed.** (informal) to visit a slum or other place considered to be of low or bad character.

slum·ber ('slumbər) *vb.* to sleep. —*n.* sleep.

slump (slump) *n.* a sudden fall in prices or demand; financial depression involving poor trade and causing much unemployment. —*vb.* 1. to collapse in a heap. 2. to sit down heavily and wearily. 3. (of prices) to fall suddenly.

slung (slung) *vb.* the past tense and past participle of SLING.

slur (slûr) *n.* 1. a statement or action having a bad effect on someone's reputation: *the rumor was a slur on his character.* 2. a blurred or unclear quality, as in speech when words are run together. 3. (music) a curved line joining notes to be played with a smooth gliding effect or sung to one syllable. —*vb.* **slur·ring, slurred.** 1. to pronounce indistinctly by running words together. 2. to sing or play (a number of notes) without a break.

slush (slush) *n.* 1. half-melted snow. 2. something sentimental and silly. —'**slush·y** *adj.* **slush·i·er, slush·i·est.**

sly (slī) *adj.* 1. cunning; crafty; dishonest. 2. mischievous; showing humor: *a sly wit.* —'**sly·ly** *adv.* —'**sly·ness** *n.*

smack (smak) *vb.* 1. to hit with the palm of the hand; slap. 2. to make a smacking noise. 3. to make a sound by pressing one's lips together and releasing quickly. —*n.* 1. a blow of the open hand. 2. a sharp noise; crack.

small (smôl) *adj.* not great in size, amount, value, power, or importance. **Small talk** casual or meaningless talk. **the small hours** the hours between midnight and dawn: *the book was so exciting that Mike read it into the small hours.*

small·pox (smôlpoks) *n.* a highly infectious disease characterized by fever and a violent rash that often leaves permanent marks and pits in the skin.

smart (smârt) *adj.* 1. clever; intelligent; quick-witted. 2. tidy, neat, and fashionable: *smart clothes.* —*vb.* 1. to feel a sharp stinging pain. 2. to feel resentful: *she was still smarting from the insult.* —*n.* a sharp pain, distress, or irritation. '**smart·en** *vb.* (often + *up*) to make or become smart. —'**smart·ly** *adv.* —'**smart·ness** *n.*

smash (smash) *vb.* 1. to shatter violently or fall into pieces. 2. to ruin or be ruined: *her plans for the future were smashed when she lost all her money.* 3. (often + *into*) to collide violently with; crash. —*n.* 1. the action or an instance of smashing; destruction or ruin.

smear (smēr) *n.* 1. a greasy or dirty stain or mark. 2. a slandering statement; insult; slur: *the scandal left a smear on his reputation.* —*vb.* 1. to stain, mark, or spread with dirt or grease. 2. to blur by rubbing. 3. to spread slander about (someone).

smell (smel) *n.* 1. the sense through which things are perceived by means of the nose. 2. an odor, stink, or scent: *a rose has a beautiful smell.* —*vb.* **smell·ing, smelled** *or* **smelt.** 1. to detect the smell of (something). 2. to give off a smell, often an unpleasant one: *rotten meat smells.* '**smell·y** *adj.* **smell·i·er, smell·i·est.** giving off an unpleasant smell.

smile (smīl) *n.* a facial expression in which the mouth is stretched sideways and the corners are turned upwards, usu. indicating pleasure, amusement, etc. —*vb.* **smil·ing, smiled.** to make a smile.

smock (smok) *n.* a loose outer garment, usu. worn over other clothes to protect them. —*vb.* to gather material in small folds and sew it in place with a decorative stitch.

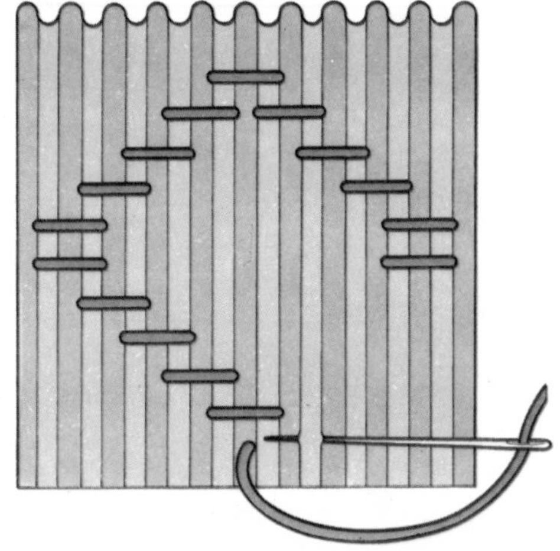

smock

smoke (smōk) *n.* 1. the visible gases and small particles given off by a fire. 2. anything resembling smoke. 3. the action or an instance of smoking a cigarette, cigar, or pipe. 4. (informal) a cigarette or cigar. —*vb.* **smok·ing, smoked.** 1. to give off smoke. 2. (of a house fire) to give off excessive smoke because of incomplete burning. 3. to preserve (meat or fish) by exposing it to smoke: *kippers are made by smoking herrings.* 4. to breathe in and blow out the fumes of tobacco, etc., from (a cigarette, pipe, cigar, etc.). 5. to do this regularly. '**smok·er** *n.* 1. a person who smokes. 2. a railroad car, etc., where smoking is allowed. —'**smoke·less** *adj.* —'**smok·y** *adj.* **smok·i·er, smok·i·est.**

smolder ('smōldər) *vb.* 1. to burn slowly with smoke but no flame. 2. to show strong emotion: *she smoldered with anger.*

smooth (smo͞odh) *adj.* 1. flat; even; without roughness or bumps. 2. without difficulty. 3. mild in taste. 4. too polite or persuasive; insincere. —*vb.* to make smooth. **smooth over** to settle (a quarrel, argument, etc.). —'**smooth·ly** *adv.* —'**smooth·ness** *n.*

smoth·er ('smudhər) *vb.* 1. to deprive of air; suffocate. 2. to put out (a fire). 3. to cover densely: *hamburgers smothered with relish.* 4. to crush or check: *the army smothered the rebellion.*

smudge (smuj) *vb.* **smudg·ing, smudged.** to blot; blur; smear. —*n.* a smear; blot.

smug (smug) *adj.* **smug·ger, smug·gest.** too satisfied with oneself. —'**smug·ly** *adv.* —'**smug·ness** *n.*

smug·gle ('smugəl) *vb.* **smug·gling, smug·gled.** 1. to bring or take (something) into or out of a country illegally or in secret, esp. without paying the required taxes. 2. to transport secretly.

snag (snag) *n.* 1. a difficulty or unexpected obstacle that holds up or endangers an action, plan, etc. 2. a hole or pulled thread in a garment. —*vb.* **snag·ging, snagged.** to tangle or tear on something sharp: *he snagged his sweater on a thorn.*

snail

snail (snāl) *n.* 1. a small slimy slow-moving animal carrying a spiral-shaped shell on its back into which it can withdraw. 2. a slow-moving or idle person: *Paul called his lazy sister a snail.*

snake (snāk) *n.* 1. a long-bodied slender scaly legless REPTILE, some species of which have a poisonous bite. 2. a treacherous deceitful person. —*vb.* **snak·ing, snaked.** 1. to move like a snake. 2. to wind along with many twists and turns: *the road snaked along the hills and valleys.*

snap (snap) *vb.* **snap·ping, snapped.** 1. to break with a sudden sharp movement. 2. to make or produce a sharp sound, as of something breaking. 3. to say or speak sharply or angrily. 4. to take an informal photograph of. **snap up** to take eagerly; grab. —*n.* 1. the sound or action of snapping or an instance of snapping. 2. (also '**snap·shot**) an informal photograph.

snatch (snach) *vb.* 1. to make a sudden grab for; seize suddenly or violently. 2. to take while one has the chance: *they snatched some sleep.* —*n.* 1. the act of snatching. 2. a short fragment of something: *a snatch of conversation.*

sneak (snēk) *vb.* 1. to creep secretly or unnoticed. 2. to take secretly: *he sneaked a bite of chocolate.* —*n.* a person who sneaks. '**sneak·y** *adj.* **sneak·i·er, sneak·i·est.** dishonest; sly; underhand. —'**sneak·i·ly** *adv.* —'**sneak·i·ness** *n.*

sneer (snēr) *vb.* to smile or speak in a contemptuous mocking way: *he sneered at my old dress.* —*n.* the action or an instance of sneering.

sneeze (snēz) *n.* a sudden uncontrollable release of air through the nose and mouth. —*vb.* **sneez·ing, sneezed.** to make a sneeze.

sniff (snif) *vb.* 1. to breathe in sharply and noisily through the nose, usu. to indicate contempt or because one has a cold. 2. to smell by sniffing: *the deer sniffed the air for danger.* —*n.* 1. the action or an instance of sniffing. 2. the sound produced by it.

snip (snip) *vb.* **snip·ping, snipped.** to cut out with scissors. —*n.* 1. a small piece of cloth snipped off. 2. a small cut made with scissors.

snipe (snīp) *vb.* **snip·ing, sniped.** 1. (often + *at*) to shoot at a person, usu. with a rifle, from a hiding place. 2. to criticize in an indirect way. '**snip·er** *n.* a person who shoots at people from a hiding place.

sniv·el ('snivəl) *vb.* to cry in a complaining or feeble way.

snob (snob) *n.* a person who shows contempt for people whom he considers inferior in social standing, wealth, ability, etc. —'**snob·ber·y** *n.* '**snob·bish** *adj.* —'**snob·bish·ly** —'**snob·bish·ness** *n.*

snoop (sno͞op) *vb.* to make secret, unwanted, or sly investigations into something; pry.

snore (snôr) *vb.* **snor·ing, snored.** to make a regular grunting sound while asleep by breathing through the mouth and nose. —*n.* the action or an instance of snoring: *his snores were so loud that the bed shook.*

snort (snôrt) *vb.* 1. to make an abrupt noise indicating contempt, etc., by vigorously forcing air out through the nose. 2. to say with a snort. —*n.* the noise made by a person or animal snorting: *he gave a snort of rage when the child broke the window.*

snout (snout) *n.* 1. the nose of certain animals, such as pigs and badgers. 2. anything resembling this.

snow (snō) *n.* frozen water vapor that falls from the air in white flakes and lies on the ground in cold weather. —*vb.* to fall as snow. —'**snow·y** *adj.* **snow·i·er, snow·i·est.**

snowflake

snow·ball ('snōbôl) *n.* a lump of snow pressed together into a ball. —*vb.* 1. to throw snowballs. 2. to increase quickly in size, force, etc.: *support for the new playground snowballed.*

snub (snub) *vb.* **snub·bing, snubbed.** to treat coldly or with contempt: *he snubbed our offer of help.* —*n.* snubbing behavior or words.

snuff[1] (snuf) *n.* powdered tobacco that is sniffed up the nose.

snuff[2] (snuf) *vb.* to put out (a flame).

snug (snug) *adj.* **snug·ger, snug·gest.** 1. cozy and warm. 2. closely fitting. —'snug·ly *adv.* —'**snug·ness** *n.*

snug·gle ('snugəl) *vb.* **snug·gling, snug·gled.** to settle down warmly and comfortably, esp. close to someone or something: *the kittens snuggled up to their mother.*

soak (sōk) *vb.* 1. to make completely wet: *the storm soaked my overcoat.* 2. to absorb; take in (liquid): *blotting paper soaks up ink.* 3. to submerge in liquid for some time: *she soaked the dirty shirts.* 4. to ooze through; penetrate: *the mud soaked through our shoes.* —*n.* the act of soaking.

soap (sōp) *n.* a substance for washing and cleaning, made in the form of blocks, powder, or liquid, —*vb.* to wash or cover with soap. —'**soap·y** *adj.* **soap·i·er, soap·i·est.**

soar (sôr) *vb.* 1. to rise into the air with apparent lack of effort: *the eagle soared over the cliffs.* 2. to rise sharply: *food prices soared last winter.*

so·ber ('sōbər) *adj.* 1. not drunk or under the influence of alcohol. 2. not bright or gay; subdued: *gray is a sober color.* —'**so·ber·ly** *adv.* —**so·bri·e·ty** (sə'briite) *or* '**so·ber·ness** *n.*

soc·cer ('sokər) *n.* a football game between two teams of eleven players each, in which a round ball is used and players kick the ball but are not allowed to touch it with their hands.

so·ci·e·ty (sə'siitē) *n.,pl.* **so·ci·e·ties.** 1. human beings as a group: *pollution is a threat to society.* 2. the traditions and culture associated with a particular way of organizing human beings as a group: *this country has a democratic society.* 3. a club or organization for people who share the same interest: *the amateur dramatic society.* 4. rich or fashionable people as a group.

sock (sok) *n.* a short knitted covering for the foot and lower leg.

sock·et ('sokit) *n.* a hollow opening into which something fits, e.g. an eye socket.

so·da ('sōdə) *n.* 1. a common white chemical substance that has many uses in industry, e.g. in making soap. 2. a carbonated soft drink.

so·di·um ('sōdēəm) *n.* a silvery white chemical element found in many compounds, e.g. ordinary table salt. Chemical symbol: Na.

soft (soft) *adj.* 1. not hard: *a soft bed.* 2. smooth; delicate to the touch: *a soft velvet curtain.* 3. not loud, harsh, or sharp: *a soft melody.* 4. feeble: *soft muscles.* **soft·en** ('sofən) *vb.* to make or become soft or softer. —'**soft·ly** *adv.* —'**soft·ness** *n.*

sog·gy ('sogē) *adj.* **sog·gi·er, sog·gi·est.** wet through; soaked: *it was hard work walking across the soggy ground.* —'**sog·gi·ness** *n.*

soil[1] (soil) *n.* the earth; the upper layers of the ground in which plants grow: *rice grows well in wet soil.*

soil[2] (soil) *vb.* to make or become dirty: *my hands are soiled with paint.*

so·lar ('sōlər) *adj.* of or from the sun: *solar energy is used to heat water in some parts of the world.*

sold (sōld) *vb.* the past tense and past participle of SELL.

sol·dier ('sōljər) *n.* a person who belongs to an army. —*vb.* to be or act as a soldier.

sole[1] (sōl) *adj.* 1. single; only one: *the boy was the sole heir.* 2. belonging to only one person or group: *the sole responsibility of the committee.* —'**sole·ly** *adv.*

sole[2] (sōl) *n.* the flat bottom or underside of a foot or shoe.

sole[3] (sōl) *n.* a dark brown flatfish found in the sea and much valued as food.

sol·emn ('soləm) *adj.* 1. impressive or dignified: *the solemn procession entered the church.* 2. serious: *a solemn face.* —'**sol·emn·ly** *adv.* —**so·lem·ni·ty** (sə'lemnitē) *n.*

sol·id ('solid) *adj.* 1. not hollow or covered or mixed with other material: *the table was made of solid oak.* 2. firm; hard. 3. not weak or unsettled: *a solid foundation.* 4. without a break: *the noise lasted five solid hours.* —*n.* a form of matter that is not a liquid or a gas and has a definite shape and hardness. **sol·i·dar·i·ty** (soli'daritē) *n.* unity or a feeling of sympathy caused by shared interests. **so·lid·i·fy** (sə'lidəfī) *vb.* **so·lid·i·fy·ing, so·lid·i·fied.** to make or become solid. **so'lid·i·ty** *n.* the state or quality of being solid. —'**sol·id·ly** *adv.*

sol·i·tar·y ('soliterē) *adj.* 1. lonely; without companions. 2. single: *there was only a solitary goat in sight.* **sol·i·tude** ('solitōōd, 'solityōōd) *n.* the state of being alone.

so·lo ('sōlō) *n.,pl.* **so·los.** 1. a piece of music or a dance written to be performed by one person. 2. a performance by one person. —*adj.* made for one person or instrument.

sol·stice ('solstis, 'sōlstis) *n.* the time of the year at which the sun is furthest from the equator, i.e. around 21 June and around 22 December.

so·lu·tion (sə'lōōshən) *n.* 1. the answer to a problem; means of dealing with a difficulty. 2. the mixture formed by dissolving a substance in a liquid. **sol·u·ble** ('solyəbəl) *adj.* able to be dissolved in a liquid.

solve (solv) *vb.* **solv·ing, solved.** to find the meaning of or the answer to (something): *she solved the problem.*

som·ber ('sombər) *adj.* dark and gloomy. —'**som·ber·ly** *adv.*

som·er·sault ('sumərsôlt) *n.* a movement in which one rolls one's body quickly forward or backward, heels over head. —*vb.* to perform this or a similar movement.

so·na·ta (sə'nâtə) *n.* a piece of music in three or four movements, written to be performed by one instrument, with or without the accompaniment of other instruments.

soot (sōōt) *n.* the black carbon powder left after burning. —'**soot·y** *adj.* **soot·i·er, soot·i·est.**

soothe (sōōdh) *vb.* **sooth·ing, soothed.** to calm; relieve or comfort.

sore (sôr) *adj.* **sor·er, sor·est.** 1. painful. 2. angry; resentful. —*n.* a cut, boil, abrasion, or other wound on the skin. '**sore·ly** *adv.* seriously; deeply: *he was sorely troubled by guilt.* —'**sore·ness** *n.*

sor·row ('sorō, 'sôrō) *n.* misery; regret. —*vb.* to feel grief or sadness; mourn. '**sor·row·ful** *adj.* —'**sor·row·ful·ly** *adv.*

sor·ry ('sorē, 'sôrē) *adj.* **sor·ri·er, sor·ri·est.** 1. apologetic; regretful. 2. miserable: *he was in a sorry state.*

sort (sôrt) *n.* a group of things that are alike; type or class: ***what sort of cookies do you like?***—*vb.* 1. to arrange by type; classify: ***letters are sorted at the post office.*** 2. (+ *out*) to tidy; arrange: ***I sorted out the drawers of my desk.***

sought (sôt) *vb.* the past tense and past participle of SEEK.

soul (sōl) *n.* 1. the spiritual part of a human being, believed to be able to survive after death. 2. sensitivity; sympathy: ***a brutal man with no soul.*** 3. a person: ***there wasn't a soul in sight.*** **'soul·ful** *adj.* appealing; emotional. —**'soul·ful·ly** *adv.*

sound[1] (sound) *n.* something that is heard by the ears; noise. —*vb.* 1. to make or cause to make a sound. 2. to seem to be: ***that price sounds fair.***

sound[2] (sound) *adj.* 1. healthy; in good condition: ***her injured leg is sound again.*** 2. sensible; useful. ***his advice is sound.*** 3. thorough; complete: ***a sound training in arithmetic.***

sound[3] (sound) *n.* a narrow stretch of water between two islands or an island and the mainland: ***Long Island Sound lies between Long Island and Connecticut.***

source (sôrs) *n.* 1. origin; starting point: ***Betty was the source of the rumor.*** 2. the spring or origin of a river. 3. original documents of other writings used as material by later authors: ***the statesman's diary was an important source for the history of his times.***

south (south) *n.* 1. the point on the compass that is on your left if you stand facing toward the sunset. 2. often **South** a region lying in this direction: ***the southern part of the U.S. is called the South.*** —*adj.* toward, from, or in the south. —*adv.* toward the south: ***they turned south.*** **south·ern** ('sudhərn) *adj.* of or in the south.

sou·ve·nir (sōōvə'nēr) *n.* a keepsake; something that is kept to remind one of a person, place, or event. —*adj.* intended as a keepsake.

sov·er·eign ('sovrin) *n.* 1. a monarch or supreme ruler. 2. a gold coin used in former times. —*adj.* 1. having supreme power. 2. effective. —**'sov·er·eign·ty** *n.*

sow[1] (sō) *vb.* **sow·ing, sowed, sown.** to plant (seeds).

sow

sow[2] (sou) *n.* an adult female pig.

space (spās) *n.* 1. the apparently limitless area in which the whole universe exists. 2. the zone beyond the earth's atmosphere; outer space. 3. unoccupied distance between objects: ***there is too little space between the houses.*** **spa·cious** ('spāshəs) *adj.* having a lot of space (def. 3); roomy. —*vb.* to separate by spaces (def. 3). —**'spa·cious·ly** *adv.*

spade (spād) *n.* 1. a garden tool with a long wooden handle and a broad, flat metal blade, used for digging. See IMPLEMENT 2. a playing card marked with one or more small black pointed leaf shapes.

span (span) *vb.* **span·ning, spanned.** to form an arch, link, bridge, etc., over time or space: ***the bridge spanned the valley.*** —*n.* 1. a stretch of time or space, esp. a lifetime. 2. the distance or part between the piers of a bridge, the pillars of an arch, etc. 3. the distance between the tips of the thumb and the little finger of an outstretched hand. **wing·span** the distance between the two wing-tips of a bird or aircraft.

spare (speər) *adj.* 1. extra; more than is needed; kept in reserve: ***a spare tire.*** 2. meager in quantity: ***a spare meal.*** —*n.* something extra. —*vb.* **spar·ing, spared.** 1. to be able to do without: ***can you spare some candy?*** 2. to give: ***he spared them only a few minutes.*** 3. to avoid hurting; show mercy to: ***she spared the boy's feelings by not scolding him in front of his friends.***

spark (spârk) *n.* 1. a tiny burning fragment of material. 2. a small flash of light caused by electricity. —*vb.* 1. to shoot out sparks. 2. to cause: ***his selfishness sparked a quarrel.***

spar·row ('sparō) *n.* one of many kinds of small gray or brown birds common in cities and the countryside all over the world.

spat (spat) *vb.* the past tense and past participle of SPIT[1].

spawn (spôn) *n.* the eggs of fish, frogs, etc., laid in water. —*vb.* to lay eggs in water.

spear (spēr) *n.* 1. a weapon, formerly widely used for hunting, fighting, etc., having a long handle with a sharp pointed head. 2. the thin straight stalk of a plant. —*vb.* to kill, pierce, etc., with a spear. **'spear·head** *n.* 1. the point of a spear. 2. the leaders of an attack, movement, etc.

spe·cial ('speshəl) *adj.* 1. exceptional; uncommon: ***a special treat.*** 2. particular to one person or thing: ***the queen traveled on a special train.*** —*n.* something special or out of the ordinary, e.g. a sale or a television show. **'spe·cial·ist** *n.* a person who knows a great deal about a particular science, skill, etc. **'spe·cial·ty** *n.,pl.* **spe·cial·ties.** 1. something in which one is particularly skilled or interested: ***knitting is her specialty.*** 2. a special product: ***chocolate cookies are the baker's specialty.*** **'spe·cial·ize** *vb.* **spe·cial·iz·ing, spe·cial·ized.** 1. to give particular time or attention to one branch of a science, skill, etc.: ***she specialized in surgery while at medical school,*** 2. to be or make fit for a special use. —**spe·cial·i'za·tion** *n.* —**'spe·cial·ly** *adv.*

spe·cies ('spēshēz, 'spēsēz) *n.,pl.* **spe·cies.** 1. a group of plants or animals with similar breeding habits and other qualities: ***dogs and cats are different species.*** 2. a type; kind.

sparrow

spec·i·men ('spesəmən) *n.* an example of a group that shows the characteristics of the whole group: *the bull was a fine specimen of its breed.*

speck (spek) *n.* a tiny particle: *there was a speck of dust in her eye.*

spectacles

spec·ta·cle ('spektəkəl) *n.* 1. a sight; something to be gazed at. 2. **spec·ta·cles** (*pl.*) glasses made of framed lenses worn in front of the eyes to correct faulty eyesight. **spec·tac·u·lar** (spek'takyələr) *adj.* 1. very impressive to a watcher. 2. amazing and praiseworthy.

spec·ta·tor ('spektātər) *n.* a watcher; onlooker.

spec·ter ('spektər) *n.* 1. a ghost. 2. a troublesome threat of something unpleasant: *the specter of illness.* —'**spec·tral** *adj.*

spec·trum ('spektrəm) *n.,pl.* **spec·tra** ('spektra) *or* '**spec·trums.** a band of colors formed by the breaking up of white light as it passes through a PRISM, raindrops, etc. A spectrum contains the colors red, orange, yellow, green, blue, indigo, and violet, arranged in that order.

speech (spēch) *n.* 1. the ability, act, or manner of speaking: *his speech is very quiet.* 2. a public talk. '**speech·less** *adj.* unable to speak, esp. because of strong emotion.

speed (spēd) *n.* 1. great quickness: *the speed of his thinking amazed them.* 2. rate of movement: *at what speed was the car going?* —*vb.* **speed·ing, sped** *or* **speed·ed.** 1. to go or cause to go fast or too fast. 2. (+ *up*) to increase the rate of progress, production, work etc. —'**speed·y** *adj.* **speed·i·er, speed·i·est.**

speed·om·e·ter (spi'domitər) *n.* the instrument on a train, car, etc., that measures and shows its speed.

spell[1] (spel) *vb.* **spell·ing, spelled** *or* **spelt.** 1. to say or write in their correct order the letters that form (a word). 2. to mean; be a sign of: *his carelessness spelt disaster.* '**spell·ing** *n.* 1. the act of spelling. 2. the way a word is spelt. **spell out** make completely clear.

spell[2] (spel) *n.* 1. a series of words, e.g. a charm or curse, that is thought to have a magical effect. 2. a fascination or attraction: *he was so in love that he fell completely under her spell.*

spell[3] (spel) *n.* 1. a period of time: *we are in for a cold spell.* 2. a period of activity, duty, etc.: *he took a spell at the lawn mower.*

spend (spend) *vb.* **spend·ing, spent.** 1. to pay out (money). 2. to pass (time): *he spent eleven years at school.* 3. to use up: *she spent her energy in caring for the sick.*

sphere (sfēr) *n.* 1. an object shaped like a ball; globe. 2. area of interest, influence, or activity; range of knowledge: *computers are outside his sphere.* —**spher·i·cal** ('sferikəl) *adj.*

sphinx

sphinx (sfiñgks) *n.,pl.* **sphinx·es.** an imaginary creature with the body of a lion and the head of a human being.

spice (spīs) *n.* a seed or other strongly tasting part of a plant used to add to the flavor of food. Pepper, nutmeg, and ginger are spices. —*vb.* **spic·ing, spiced.** to flavor with spice. —'**spic·i·ness** *n.* —'**spic·y** *adj.* **spic·i·er, spic·i·est.**

spi·der ('spīdər) *n.* a small creature with eight legs that often spins a web in which to trap insects for food. '**spi·der·y** *adj.* (of handwriting) thin and untidy.

spike (spīk) *n.* 1. a sharp pointed object. 2. a large heavy nail. —*vb.* **spik·ing, spiked.** 1. to pierce with a spike. 2. to add a strong alcoholic beverage to a mixed drink.

spill (spil) *vb.* **spill·ing, spilled** *or* **spilt.** 1. to cause or allow (liquid, powder, etc.) to pour out. 2. to flow out: *water was spilling over the dam wall.* —*n.* a fall, e.g. from a horse.

spin (spin) *vb.* **spin·ning, spun** *or* **span, spun.** 1. to twist (fibers of wool, cotton, etc.) into thread. 2. to make by means of threads: *the spider spun a web.* 3. to move or cause to move rapidly round and round: *Steve spun a coin.* 4. to feel dizzy or faint: *the noise made his head spin.* —*n.* 1. a rapid turning movement. 2. a short pleasure ride: *come for a spin in the car.*

spine (spīn) *n.* 1. the series of bones in the center of the back that supports the rest of the body. 2. a needle-like projection on an animal or plant. 3. the narrow back of a book. '**spine·less** *adj.* 1. having no spine or spines. 2. timid; unable to make decisions or act vigorously. —'**spin·y** *adj.* **spin·i·er, spin·i·est.**

spi·ral ('spīrəl) *n.* a continuous winding curve: *a chair spring is a spiral.* —*adj.* having the form of a spiral: *a spiral staircase.* —*vb.* to move in a spiral: *smoke spirals up from the bonfire.*

spire (spīər) *n.* a tall pointed structure in the shape of a cone or pyramid on top of a building, esp. a church.

spir·it ('spirit) *n.* 1. the part of a person that is thought to be able to exist independently of the body; soul. 2. a ghost or other supernatural being. 3. vigor; liveliness: *they sang with spirit.* 4. **spir·its** (*pl.*) state of one's feelings: *he was in low spirits after the accident.* 5. **spir·its** (*pl.*) strong alcoholic drink, e.g. gin. —*vb.* (usu. + *away*) to take away quickly and mysteriously. '**spir·i·tu·al** *adj.* 1. of the soul. 2. of religious matters. —*n.* a popular religious song, sung originally by the blacks of the southern U.S. '**spir·i·tu·al·ism** *n.* the belief that it is possible to receive messages from the spirits of the dead. '**spir·i·tu·al·ist** *n.* a believer in spiritualism. '**spir·i·tu·ous** *adj.* containing alcohol. —'**spir·i·tu·al·ly** *adv.*

spit[1] (spit) *vb.* **spit·ting, spat.** to force out (SALIVA, food, etc.) from the mouth; spurt out violently. —*n.* the liquid formed in the mouth; saliva.

spit[2] (spit) *n.* 1. a thin metal rod to which food is attached for cooking over or under a grill. 2. a narrow neck of land jutting out into the water.

spite (spīt) *n.* the desire to cause harm; malice. **'spite·ful** *adj.* showing or expressing spite. —**'spite·ful·ly** *adv.* —**'spite·ful·ness** *n.*

splash (splash) *vb.* 1. to cause (liquid) to fly about in drops. 2. to fly about and fall in drops. —*n.* 1. the act or sound of splashing. 2. a small mark: *a splash of red paint.*

splen·did ('splendid) *adj.* 1. very beautiful; impressive: *a splendid sunset.* 2. very good: *a splendid party.* **'splen·dor** *n.* great beauty; grandeur; magnificence. —**'splen·did·ly** *adv.*

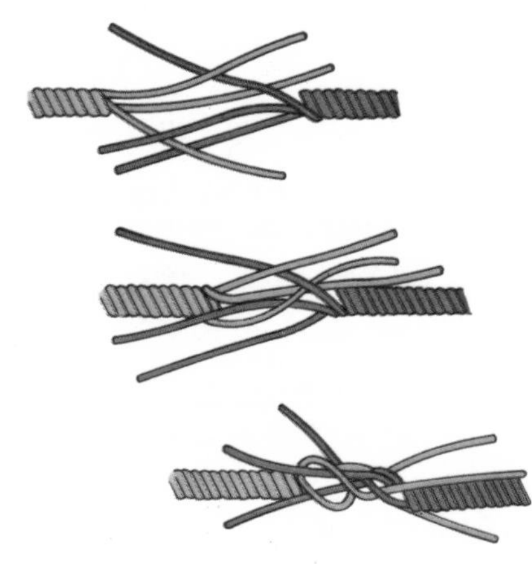
splice

splice (splīs) *vb.* **splic·ing, spliced.** to join (rope, wood, tape, etc.) by fastening the ends together.

splint (splint) *n.* a piece of wood, metal, etc., that is firmly tied to a broken bone or part of a plant to prevent it moving and so enable it to heal correctly.

splin·ter ('splintər) *n.* a thin sharp fragment that has broken off from a larger piece of material, esp. wood. —*vb.* to break or cause to break off in splinters: *the glass splintered when it fell to the floor.*

split (split) *vb.* **split·ting, split.** to break or cause to break apart; divide: *the old cushion split and its stuffing fell out.* —*n.* the act or result of splitting; division.

spoil (spoil) *vb.* **spoil·ing, spoiled** *or* **spoilt.** 1. to damage or make useless. 2. to become bad: *the cheese spoiled in the hot weather.* 3. to harm a person's character by being too kind. —*n.* (usu. **spoils**) advantages, money, and property gained as a result of the selling of favors by a public official.

spoke (spōk) *n.* one of the rods joining the outer rim to the center of a wheel.

spokes·man ('spōksmən) *n.,pl.* **spokes·men.** a man who speaks on behalf of another person or group of people. **spokes·wom·an,** *pl.* **spokes·wom·en.** a woman who speaks on behalf of others.

sponge (spunj) *n.* 1. a colony of sea animals that form together into an irregular mass interspersed with holes. 2. the absorbent skeleton of this used instead of a cloth for washing, cleaning, or mopping up. 3. a piece of manmade material similar in texture and uses to a natural sponge. 4. (also **sponge cake**) a light soft cake. —*vb.* **spong·ing, sponged.** 1. to clean with a damp sponge. 2. (informal) to live by taking advantage of the kindness or generosity of other people: *Bob avoided work and managed to sponge off his friends.*

spon·sor ('sponsər) *n.* 1. a person who provides financial or other support or takes responsibility for an enterprise. 2. a commercial advertiser on radio or TV. —*vb.* to act as sponsor.

spon·ta·ne·ous (spon'tānēəs) *adj.* 1. not planned beforehand; done on impulse: *the crowd broke into spontaneous applause before the act had finished.* 2. having no outside cause; self-acting: *we had no medicine but luckily she made a spontaneous recovery.* —**spon'ta·ne·ous·ly** *adv.*

spoon (spo͞on) *n.* a small utensil with a shallow bowl on the end of a handle, used for preparing and eating food. —*vb.* 1. to lift up with a spoon. 2. to scoop as if with a spoon.

sport (spôrt) *n.* 1. a game or games involving physical exercise. 2. fun: *the boys had great sport with their canoes.* 3. a person who plays fairly and does not mind losing. —*vb.* to play. **'sport·ing** *adj.* willing to play fairly and risk losing. **'sports·man** *n.,pl.* **sports·men** (**sports·wo·man,** *pl.* **sports·wo·men**). a person who frequently plays physical games. **'sports·man·ship** *n.* fair and generous behavior in sport.

spot (spot) *n.* 1. a small dirty mark. 2. a small area differing from its background. 3. a place: *we chose a good spot beneath a shady tree for our picnic.* —*vb.* **spot·ting, spot·ted.** 1. to see: *we spotted her in the distance.* 2. to mark with spots.

spout (spout) *vb.* to come or force out through a small opening. —*n.* a narrow tube or opening through which liquid comes or is forced.

sprain (sprān) *vb.* to twist or wrench a part of the body, causing injury. —*n.* an injury caused by spraining.

sponge

sprang (sprang) *vb.* the past tense of SPRING[1].

sprawl (sprôl) *vb.* 1. to lie or sit in an ungainly way. 2. to spread out untidily: *the housing development sprawled across the land.*

spray[1] (sprā) *n.* 1. a cloud or jet of liquid in the form of very small drops. 2. a device for applying liquid in this form. —*vb.* to make or apply a spray.

spray[2] (sprā) *n.* a small branch of a tree or plant with flowers or leaves, esp. one used as decoration.

spread (spred) *vb.* **spread·ing, spread.** 1. to stretch out; extend: *please spread the tablecloth.* 2. to make a thin layer of (something) on the surface of something else: *he spread jam on the toast.* 3. to become or cause to become widely distributed. —*n.* 1. the extent to which something is stretched out or open. 2. a type of soft food that is spread on bread or toast: *deviled ham spread.* 3. a cloth cover for a bed.

spring[1] (spring) *vb.* **spring·ing, sprang, sprung.** 1. to jump. 2. to snap or jerk quickly: *the car door sprang open.* 3. to appear or grow up suddenly: *grass sprang from the broken pavement.* 4. to cause to happen unexpectedly: *the teacher sprang a spelling test on us.* —*n.* 1. a jump. 2. a place where water appears from underground. 3. a coiled metal object that can be stretched or squashed and still return to its original shape: *a chair spring.* **'spring·y** *adj.* **spring·i·er, spring·i·est.** elastic. —**'spring·i·ness** *n.*

spring[2] (spriñg) *n.* the season of the year between winter and summer.

sprin·kle ('spriñgkəl) *vb.* **sprin·kling, sprin·kled.** to scatter in tiny drops or particles: *he sprinkled some pepper on the steaks.* **'sprin·kler** *n.* a device for casting a fine spray of water on plants and lawns.

sprint (sprint) *vb.* to run very fast for a short distance. —*n.* a short race run at high speed.

sprout (sprout) *vb.* to start growing. —*n.* a young growth or shoot of a plant. **Brussels sprout** a small round shoot of a cabbage-like plant, eaten as a vegetable.

sprung (spruñg) *vb.* the past participle of SPRING[1].

spun (spun) *vb.* the past tense and past participle of SPIN.

spur (spûr) *n.* a pointed metal object attached to the heel of a rider's boot and used to urge a horse to go faster. —*vb.* **spur·ring, spurred.** 1. to use spurs on a horse. 2. to urge on; encourage: *his sister's success spurred Ken to work harder.*

spurt (spûrt) *vb.* 1. to burst out suddenly in a stream. 2. to make a sudden intense effort. —*n.* 1. a sudden bursting or pouring out: *a spurt of flame.* 2. a sudden intense effort: *the horse's spurt in the last few yards enabled him to win the race.*

spy (spī) *n.,pl.* **spies.** a person who keeps watch secretly on the activities of other people, esp. someone used by a government to obtain secret information. —*vb.* **spy·ing, spied.** 1. to act as a spy. 2. to see; catch sight of: *I spied Tom in the crowd.*

squab·ble ('skwobəl) *vb.* **squab·bling, squab·bled.** to quarrel noisily about a small matter. —*n.* a noisy petty quarrel.

squadron

squad (skwod) *n.* a small group of people who train or work together: *a squad of soldiers.*

squad·ron ('skwodrən) *n.* a division of the army, navy, or air force containing a fairly small number of men, ships, or aircraft.

squall (skwôl) *n.* 1. a sudden violent wind. 2. a loud harsh cry, esp. of pain or fear. —*vb.* to cry loudly.

squan·der ('skwondər) *vb.* to waste money or time extravagantly.

square (skweər) *n.* 1. a shape that has four sides of equal length and four right angles. See GEOMETRY. 2. an area with the shape of a square: *we bought a square of carpet for the hall.* 3. an open area surrounded by buildings in a town. 4. the number that results when a number is multiplied by itself: *the square of 3 is 9* (3 × 3). —*adj.* 1. having the shape of a square (defs. 1 and 2). 2. having or forming a right angle: *the table has square corners.* 3. honest: *a square deal.* —*vb.* **squar·ing, squared.** 1. to bring into the form of a square or right angle. 2. (+ *off*) to mark off in squares. 3. to multiply (a number) by itself.

squash[1] (skwosh) *vb.* to press flat; crush. —*n.* a game played with rackets and a small rubber ball on a walled court.

squash[2] (skwosh) *n.* one of several types of fruits of various shapes that grow on vines and are eaten as vegetables.

squat (skwot) *vb.* **squat·ting, squat·ted.** 1. to crouch down with one's knees close to one's body. 2. to move in to live on land or in buildings that do not belong to one. —*adj.* short and thick. **'squat·ter** *n.* a person who occupies land or buildings without the owner's permission.

squeak (skwēk) *n.* a short shrill sound: *the squeak of a mouse.* —*vb.* to make such a sound.

squeeze (skwēz) *vb.* **squeez·ing, squeezed.** 1. to pinch or press hard: *Tim's fingers were squeezed in the door.* 2. to get by pressing hard: *can you squeeze any more juice from the lemon?* —*n.* the action or an instance of squeezing.

squid (skwid) *n.,pl.* **squid** *or* **squids.** a soft-bodied animal that lives in the sea and has ten long arms. Squid vary in size from a few inches to many feet in length.

squint (skwint) *vb.* 1. to peer through half-closed eyes: *the strong light made him squint.* 2. to look sideways: *the children tried to squint around the door to see what was happening at the party.*

squirm (skwûrm) *vb.* 1. to twist and wriggle. 2. to feel embarrassed or uncomfortable.

squir·rel ('skwûrəl, 'skwurəl) *n.* a small usu. tree-climbing animal that has a bushy tail and reddish-brown or gray fur. See RODENT.

squirt (skwûrt) *vb.* 1. to force out (liquid) in a thin stream. 2. to come out in a thin stream.

stab (stab) *vb.* **stab·bing, stabbed.** to wound or pierce with a weapon or pointed instrument. —*n.* 1. the act of stabbing. 2. a brief sharp sensation; pang. 3. (informal) an attempt: *Mike made a stab at mending the radio.*

sta·ble[1] ('stābəl) *adj.* steady; not easily upset or moved; firm. '**sta·bi·lize** *vb.* **sta·bi·liz·ing, sta·bi·lized.** to make steady. '**sta·bi·liz·er** *n.* a device that keeps a ship or aircraft steady.

sta·ble[2] ('stābəl) *n.* a building in which horses are kept and fed. —*vb.* **sta·bling, sta·bled.** to put or keep in a stable.

stack (stak) *n.* 1. a pile of objects: *a stack of books.* 2. a rack in which records or books are arranged. 3. (slang) a large amount: *I have a stack of homework to do.* —*vb.* to arrange in a pile.

sta·di·um ('stādēəm) *n., pl.* **sta·di·ums** or **sta·di·a** ('stādēa) a place in which sports contests are held, usu. consisting of a flat area surrounded by stands for large numbers of spectators.

staff (staf) *n.* 1. a strong stick or pole, esp. one used as a support. 2. a group of people who work together for an organization or individual. 3. *pl.* **staves** (stāvz) the set of five parallel lines on which musical notes are written.

stag (stag) *n.* an adult male of many types of deer.

stage (stāj) *n.* 1. a raised platform in a theater on which plays, etc., are performed. 2. the profession of acting in theaters. 3. the scene or setting for an event. 4. a step, section, or particular period in a process: *the last stage of the journey.* 5. (also '**stag·ing**) a temporary platform, e.g. for workmen to stand on. 6. a STAGECOACH. —*vb.* **stag·ing, staged.** 1. to present a play, etc., before an audience. 2. to arrange or organize in order to obtain a certain effect: *she staged a fainting fit.*

stagecoach

stage·coach ('stājkōch) *n.* (also **stage**) a large horse-drawn coach.

stag·ger ('stagər) *vb.* 1. to move or stand unsteadily. 2. to arrange at different times: *school lunch hours are staggered as the hall is too small for all the children to eat at once.* 3. to surprise greatly: *he was staggered by the shocking news.* —*n.* the act of walking or moving unsteadily.

stag·nant ('stagnənt) *adj.* 1. without a current; not flowing; still. *a stagnant pond soon becomes foul.* 2. inactive; sluggish. **stag·nate** ('stagnāt) *vb.* **stag·nat·ing, stag·nat·ed.** to be or become inactive.

stain (stān) *vb.* 1. to mark or make dirty. 2. to color with a dye. 3. to spoil or damage: *the lie stained his reputation for honesty.* —*n.* 1. a dirty mark. 2. a dye, esp. one used on wood. 3. a cause of shame or dishonor.

stair (steər) *n.* 1. usu. **stairs** (*pl.*) a series of fixed steps between different levels. 2. an individual step in such a series.

stake[1] (stāk) *n.* a post with one end sharpened to a point so that it can be hammered into the ground. —*vb.* **stak·ing, staked.** 1. to fasten or make secure by a stake or stakes. 2. to mark out by means of stakes. **stake a claim** to declare one's right to something.

stake[2] (stāk) *n.* 1. money, jewels, etc., which are put at risk in a gambling game or bet. 2. a share or interest: *he has a large stake in his father's business.* —*vb.* **stak·ing, staked.** to risk (something), esp. in gambling.

sta·lac·tite ('staləktīt, stə'ləktīt) *n.* a pillar of limestone that hangs from the roof of a cave and is formed by the continuous dripping of water.

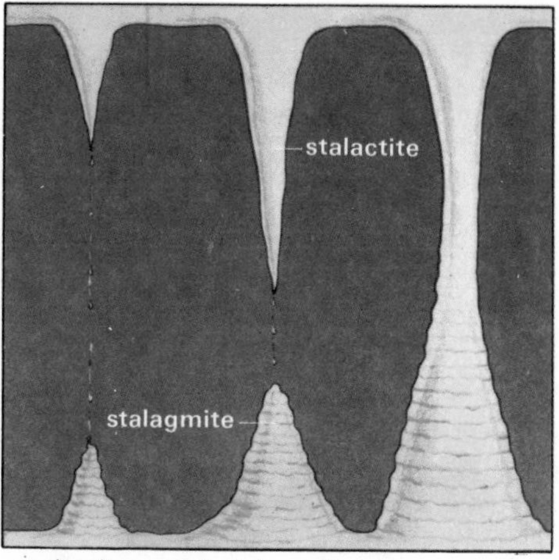

stalactites and stalagmites

sta·lag·mite ('staləgmīt, stə'ləgmīt) *n.* a pillar of limestone that grows upward from the floor of a cave, often directly under a STALACTITE.

stale (stāl) *adj.* **stal·er, stal·est.** 1. not fresh. 2. dull or uninteresting. 3. out of condition, esp. because of too little or too much practice.

stale·mate ('stālmāt) *n.* 1. a draw in chess, resulting when one player can only move his king into a position where it will be taken. 2. any position from which no further move seems possible.

stalk[1] (stôk) *n.* the fleshy or woody main stem of a plant that supports the leaves and flowers.

stalk[2] (stôk) *vb.* 1. to follow (someone or something) very quietly: *the cat stalked the sparrows.* 2. to walk in a very stiff and dignified way.

stall (stôl) *n.* 1. a space in a barn or stable in which one horse, cow, etc., is kept. 2. a stand, table, etc., in a street or market, on which goods are displayed for sale. 3. a theater seat near the stage or screen. —*vb.* 1. to come to a standstill: *the car's engine stalled as we drove through the water.* 2. to delay; fail to act for as long as possible: *he was always stalling to avoid making the decision.*

stal·lion ('stalyən) *n.* an adult male horse.

stam·i·na ('stamənə) *n.* toughness, strength, and energy necessary to overcome physical or mental trials.

stam·mer ('stamər) *n.* a speech habit in which sounds are often repeated several times at the beginnings of words. —*vb.* to speak with a stammer.

stamp (stamp) *n.* 1. a small piece of paper that is stuck on envelopes, post cards, etc., to indicate that postage has been paid. 2. a device that makes an imprint or mark. 3. the mark made by such a device. 4. the act of bringing down one's foot with force. —*vb.* 1. to bring one's foot or feet down forcefully. 2. (+ *out*) to destroy. 3. to mark (paper, etc.) with an inked block, pad, or other device. 4. to stick a postage stamp on (a letter, etc.).

stam·pede (stam'pēd) *n.* a sudden rush by many people or animals. —*vb.* **stam·ped·ing, stam·ped·ed.** to make a sudden rush in a group.

stanch (stanch, stônch) *or* **staunch** (stônch) *vb.* to stop (a flow of liquid), esp. of blood from a wound.

stand·ard ('standərd) *n.* 1. a person, practice, or thing set up as a good model for other people to copy: *he imposes very strict standards of behavior on his pupils.* 2. a flag or symbol. —*adj.* 1. normal; in accordance with accepted practices. 2. of recognized importance, authority, or value: *a standard school textbook.* **'stand·ard·ize** *vb.* **stand·ard·iz·ing, stand·ard·ized.** to make according to fixed rules or patterns.

stank (stangk) *vb.* the past tense of STINK.

sta·ple ('stāpəl) *n.* 1. a piece of bent metal wire that is driven through papers to fasten them together. 2. a U–shaped loop of metal driven into wood, etc. —*vb.* **sta·pling, sta·pled.** to fasten with staples.

star (stâr) *n.* 1. one of the many heavenly bodies like the sun, but so far away from the earth that they look like tiny dots of light in the night sky. 2. a shape with five or more points arranged around a center. 3. a person who is outstandingly successful in a particular activity, esp. a famous singer or actor. —*vb.* **star·ring, starred.** to play the leading part in a play, movie, etc. —**'star·ry** *adj.* **star·ri·er, star·ri·est.**

star·board ('stârbərd) *n.* the right-hand side of a ship or aircraft from the point of view of someone on board who is facing toward the front.

starch (stârch) *n.* 1. a white tasteless food substance produced and stored in many plants, e.g. potatoes, corn, etc. 2. a substance used to stiffen fabrics. —*vb.* to apply starch to (fabrics).

starfish

star·fish ('stârfish) *n.* a small animal that lives on the seabed and has a star-shaped flattish body.

star·ling ('stârling) *n.* a common bird with brown or shiny black lustrous feathers and a chattering voice, usu. found living in large flocks.

star·tle ('stârtəl) *vb.* **star·tling, star·tled.** to cause fright or surprise in: *the noisy car startled the horse.*

starve (stârv) *vb.* **starv·ing, starved.** 1. to die or suffer severely from lack of food: *the crops failed and the people starved.* 2. to cause to suffer or die from lack of food: *the cruel man starved his dog.* 3. to be very hungry: *the children were starving after the long walk.* —**star'va·tion** *n.*

state (stāt) *n.* 1. condition: *the stray cat was in a terrible state.* 2. a people or nation organized under one government. 3. a region or part of a country that is recognized as a separate part of the whole: *how many states are there in the U.S.?* 4. ceremony; grandeur: *the king rode in state through the streets.* —*vb.* **stat·ing, stat·ed.** to say clearly and plainly; declare: *she stated her objections to the plan.* **'state·ment** *n.* 1. the act of stating. 2. something that is declared or set out plainly.

states·man ('stātsmən) *n.,pl.* **states·men.** a man who has a high reputation for his skill and wisdom in governmental and international affairs.

sta·tion ('stāshən) *n.* 1. a building or other place at which trains, buses, etc., stop and pick up passengers and goods. 2. a building or other place where special tasks or services are performed or organized. 3. a place or position in which one stands for a particular purpose or duty: *the doorman was at his station near the main entrance.* 4. social position. 5. a radio or TV broadcasting channel. —*vb.* to place or be placed in a particular position: *the soldiers were stationed in Europe.*

sta·tion·ar·y ('stāshənerē) *adj.* 1. standing still: *a stationary line of cars.* 2. not able to be moved: *there was a large stationary crane on the building site.*

sta·tion·er·y ('stāshənerē) *n.* writing paper, envelopes, and other materials used for writing.

stat·ue ('stachōō) *n.* a large figure made of stone, bronze, etc., that has been carved or molded to represent something. **stat·u'ette** *n.* a small statue.

stay (stā) *vb.* 1. to remain or wait in a particular place: *stay here until I come back.* 2. to live for a short period away from one's home. 3. to continue; keep on being: *the weather stayed fine.* —*n.* a visit.

stead·fast ('stedfast) *adj.* unchanging; fixed; constant: *a steadfast companion.* —**'stead·fast·ly** *adv.*

stead·y ('stedē) *adj.* **stead·i·er, stead·i·est.** 1. not shaking or trembling: *he poured the wine with a steady hand.* 2. regular: *a steady stride.* 3. reliable; not easily upset: *steady nerves.* —*vb.* **stead·y·ing, stead·ied.** to make or become steady. —**'stead·i·ly** *adv.* —**'stead·i·ness** *n.*

steak (stāk) *n.* a slice of meat or fish that is usu. broiled or fried.

steal (stēl) *vb.* **steal·ing, stole, sto·len.** 1. to take (something belonging to someone else) without permission: *he stole the money.* 2. to do or move very quietly and secretly: *she stole downstairs without waking anyone.*

steam (stēm) *n.* the gas or vapor into which water is changed at boiling point. —*vb.* 1. to give off water vapor. 2. to treat or cook with steam. 3. to move by steam power: *the ship steamed away.* 4. (+ *up*) to be covered with moisture: *his spectacles steamed up in the sudden heat.* **'steam·er** *n.* 1. a ship powered by steam. 2. a kind of pan in which food is cooked by steam. **steam engine** an engine powered by steam.

steamroller

steam·roll·er ('stēmrōlər) *n.* a large vehicle with heavy rollers instead of wheels, used to smooth the surface of roads that are being paved. They were formerly driven by steam but are now motorized.

steel (stēl) *n.* a hard tough metal, usu. made of iron and carbon, used for making machinery, cars, and many other products.

steep (stēp) *adj.* sloping upward or downward at a very sharp angle: *the path to the top of the cliff was very steep.*

stee·ple ('stēpəl) *n.* a tall pointed structure in the shape of a cone or pyramid often built on top of church towers; spire.

steer[1] (stēr) *vb.* 1. to drive or guide a car, ship, etc., in a certain direction. 2. to guide: *he steered his son out of danger.*

steer[2] (stēr) *n.* a young altered bull reared for its meat.

stem (stem) *n.* 1. the main stalk of a plant or the smaller stalks supporting the flowers or leaves. 2. any slender support: *the stem of a wineglass.* 3. a branch of a family descended from the same ancestor. —*vb.* **stem·ming, stemmed.** (+ *from*) to descend or originate from: *the idea for the book stemmed from an old story he had heard.*

sten·cil ('stensəl) *n.* 1. a sheet of metal or card that has holes cut through it to form words, patterns, etc. The cut-out areas allow the penetration of ink or paint so that they can be used to print or mark surfaces. 2. the pattern or words produced by using a stencil. —*vb.* to use a stencil.

step (step) *n.* 1. the act of raising and putting down one foot when walking, running, or dancing; a stride. 2. a single stage in a series of stages: *he was a step nearer his aim.* 3. a ledge, rung, or stair on which one puts one's foot in moving from one level to another. 4. the sound made by putting down one's foot. —*vb.* **step·ping, stepped.** 1. to walk. 2. to put one's foot down: *he accidentally stepped on the beetle and crushed it.*

step·fa·ther ('stepfâdhər) *n.* the man whom one's mother marries but who is not one's real father.

step·lad·der ('stepladər) *n.* a small ladder having steps intead of rungs or bars, usu. one that can be folded away.

step·moth·er ('stepmudhər) *n.* the woman whom one's father marries but who is not one's real mother.

ster·ling ('stûrling) *n.* 1. British money. 2. (also **sterling silver**) a silver of standard purity, used to make jewelry, tableware, etc. —*adj.* 1. of or connected with British money. 2. having genuine moral worth: *he is a sterling character.*

stern[1] (stûrn) *adj.* 1. strict; severe: *she was such a stern teacher that no one dared misbehave in class.* 2. determined; ruthless: *he showed such stern courage that no enemy could stop him.* —'**stern·ly** *adv.* —'**stern·ness** *n.*

stern[2] (stûrn) *n.* the back end of a ship or aircraft.

steth·o·scope ('stethəskōp) *n.* a device used by doctors to enable them to listen to the sound of the heart, lungs, etc.

stew (stoo, styoo) *n.* a dish of meat and vegetables cooked slowly together. —*vb.* to cook (meat, vegetables, etc.) slowly and gently.

stew·ard ('stooərd, 'styooərd) *n.* 1. a man employed to attend a ship's or aircraft's passengers. 2. a man in charge of the day-to-day management of a large property or institution. 3. someone who helps organize meetings, entertainment, etc. '**stew·ard·ess** *n.* a woman employed to attend a ship's or aircraft's passengers.

stick[1] (stik) *n.* 1. a thin stiff rod, esp. of wood. 2. anything shaped like a stick of wood: *a stick of licorice.*

stick[2] (stik) *vb.* **stick·ing, stuck.** 1. to push (a pointed object) firmly into something; stab; pierce. 2. to fasten (paper, ribbon, tiles, etc.) to something else with glue, sticky tape, etc.: *he stuck a stamp on the envelope.* 3. to be unable to move or go on any further: *they were stuck in the heavy traffic.* 4. to hold or follow close to: *the dog stuck to the trail of the fox.* 5. to be or become fixed in place: *the nail stuck in the tire.* 6. to put in a particular place: *she stuck the clothes in the drawer.* 7. (+ *up* or *out*) to stand out from the surrounding area; project: *the nail was sticking out from the wood.* 8. to continue: *she stuck to her tennis classes for two years.* '**stick·er** *n.* a label that can be glued on. '**stick·y** *adj.* **stick·i·er, stick·i·est.** 1. able to stick (def. 2) to things. 2. feeling like damp glue to the touch. 3. (slang) difficult to manage or cope with: *a sticky problem.* —'**stick·i·ly** *adv.* —'**stick·i·ness** *n.*

stiff (stif) *adj.* 1. not easily bent or moved: *a stiff muscle.* 2. formal; not friendly or relaxed: *stiff manners.* 3. difficult; needing much effort, skill, etc.: *a stiff examination.* 4. strong; powerful: *a stiff breeze.* 5. harsh: *stiff penalties.* —*adv.* very much: *I was scared stiff.* '**stiff·en** *vb.* to make or become stiff or stiffer. —'**stiff·ly** *adv.* —'**stiff·ness** *n.*

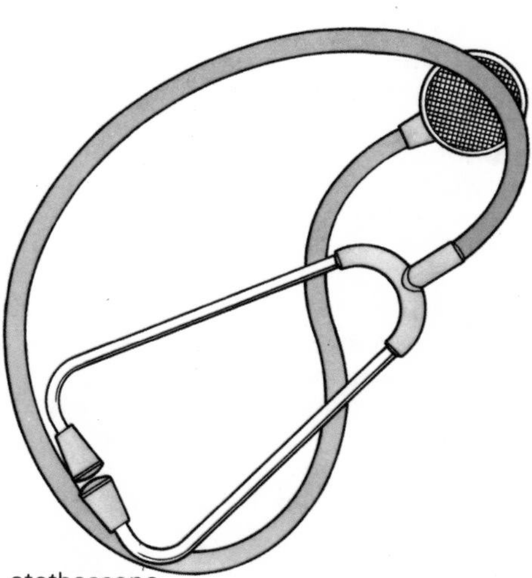
stethoscope

sti·fle ('stīfəl) *vb.* **sti·fling, sti·fled.** 1. to smother; choke by not allowing to breathe: *the thick smoke was stifling the firemen.* 2. to find it difficult to breathe, esp. because of heat, crowds, etc. 3. to hold back: *Jim stifled a laugh.*

stile (stīl) *n.* a part of a fence that has steps on either side so that people can climb over it.

still (stil) *adj.* 1. not moving. 2. quiet; silent. —*n.* one photograph from a series that together form a movie. —*vb.* to make calm and quiet. —*adv.* 1. without moving: *she stood still.* 2. up to and including a certain time: *he is still ill.* 3. even more; in a bigger degree or greater extent: *her plan was better still.* —*conj.* all the same; nevertheless: *although it was raining heavily, still she insisted on going.*

stilt

stilt (stilt) *n.* one of a pair of long poles with a block on which the foot is placed, used by people to raise themselves above the ground for walking.

stilt·ed ('stiltid) *adj.* stiff; not relaxed.

stim·u·late ('stimyəlāt) *vb.* **stim·u·lat·ing, stim·u·lat·ed.** to arouse (someone) to action: *we were stimulated to work harder by our teacher's praise.* —**stim·u'la·tion** *n.* '**stim·u·lus** *n.* something that stimulates.

sting (stiñg) *vb.* **sting·ing, stung.** 1. to pierce with a sharp point. 2. to cause or feel sharp burning pain: *the salt water stung her eyes.* 3. to make (someone or something) act by rousing sharply: *he was stung into action by her scorn.* 4. (slang) to overcharge: *the dealer stung him 80 dollars for that old carpet.* —*n.* 1. the organ of a bee, wasp, etc., that pierces the skin of its victim and leaves poison in the flesh. 2. the pain or wound caused by this. 3. a sharp mental or physical pain.

stin·gy ('stinjē) *adj.* **stin·gi·er, sting·i·est.** 1. miserly; unwilling to spend or give. 2. meager; not enough: *a stingy portion.*

stink (stiñgk) *vb.* **stink·ing, stank** *or* **stunk.** to give off a strong unpleasant smell. —*n.* 1. a strong unpleasant smell. 2. (slang) a fuss.

stir (stûr) *vb.* **stir·ring, stirred.** 1. to cause (a liquid, mixture, etc.) to be mixed up or set in motion by moving a spoon, etc., in it. 2. (often + *up*) to rouse (someone) into action; excite: *he stirred the crowd into a frenzy.* 3. to move slightly: *he stirred in his sleep.* —*n.* 1. the act of stirring. 2. excitement; disturbance: *his news caused quite a stir.*

stir·rup ('stirəp, 'stûrəp, 'sturəp) *n.* 1. one of two metal, leather, or wooden footrests hanging from either side of a saddle, used by the rider of a horse. 2. one of the three small bones in the middle ear that transmit sounds to the inner ear. See EAR.

stock (stok) *n.* 1. the supply of goods available for sale, distribution, etc.: *the shop had a good stock of new records.* 2. line of descent; ancestry: *she is of French stock.* 3. the handle or support of a gun, whip, etc. 4. shares in a business company. 5. a thin broth made from stewed bones, etc. —*vb.* to keep (goods) available for sale, distribution, etc.: *we stock every kind of toothpaste.*

stock·ade (sto'kād) *n.* 1. a protective fence made of tall upright posts, esp. around a fort. 2. the area enclosed by this fence.

stoke (stōk) *vb.* (often + *up*) to add fuel to (a fire, furnace, etc.). '**stok·er** *n.* a person whose job it is to put fuel into a furnace or boiler and keep it working.

stole[1] (stōl) *vb.* the past tense and past participle of STEAL.

stole[2] (stōl) *n.* a long scarf or shawl worn around a woman's shoulders.

stockade

sto·len ('stōlən) *vb.* the past participle of STEAL.

stom·ach ('stumək) *n.* 1. the organs of the body into which food passes when it is swallowed and where it is then partly digested. 2. the lower front part of the body below the chest. 3. inclination; desire: *I have no stomach for such violent films.* —*vb.* to endure or accept: *I can't stomach his rudeness any longer.*

stoop (stōōp) *vb.* to bend (the body) downward and forward. —*n.* a forward and downward curve of a person's head and shoulders.

stop·watch ('stopwoch) *n.* a watch with a hand that can be started and stopped as required, used esp. to time races.

store (stôr) *n.* 1. a supply of goods for future use. 2. a place where things are sold; a shop. —*vb.* **stor·ing, stored.** to keep (food, goods, etc.) for future use. '**stor·age** *n.* the storing of food, goods, information, etc.

stork (stôrk) *n.* a large long-legged bird with white, gray, or black feathers, often found near water. It sometimes builds nests on houses.

storm (stôrm) *n.* 1. a violent outbreak of bad weather with rain, hail, wind, or snow. 2. an outburst or upheaval: *the new road plans provoked a storm of protest from the townspeople.* —*vb.* 1. to show anger by shouting, etc. 2. to attack (a building, town, etc.) with violence in order to capture it.

sto·ry[1] ('stôrē) *n.,pl.* **sto·ries.** 1. an account of past or imaginary happenings. 2. (informal) lie: *he told stories to make his friends believe that his father was rich.*

sto·ry[2] ('stôrē) *n.,pl.* **sto·ries.** a floor or level in a building.

stout (stout) *adj.* 1. rather fat. 2. strong; not easily worn out: *stout shoes.* 3. (formerly) brave and determined: *a stout friend.*

stove (stōv) *n.* an apparatus with an enclosed source of heat, used for cooking food, heating a room, etc.

stow (stō) *vb.* (often + *away*) to pack (something) neatly and carefully: *Jonathan stowed his suitcases in the trunk of the car.*

stork

strag·gle ('stragəl) *vb.* **strag·gling, strag·gled.** 1. to be spread out or to grow in an untidy or irregular manner. 2. to wander away from or fall behind other people on the move. '**strag·gly** *adj.* **strag·gli·er, strag·gli·est.** scattered or growing in an untidy manner.

straight (strāt) *adj.* 1. not crooked or curved. 2. in good order: *nothing in the room was straight after the children had been there.* 3. (informal) honest. —*adv.* directly; without turning aside or delaying: *he looked straight ahead.* '**straight·en** *vb.* to make or become straight. —'**straight·ness** *n.*

straight·for·ward (strāt'fôrwərd) *adj.* 1. honest. 2. direct. 3. straight ahead. —**straight'for·ward·ly** *adv.* —**straight'for·ward·ness** *n.*

strain[1] (strān) *vb.* 1. to make a great effort: *he strained to hear the distant voice.* 2. to injure (a muscle, limb, etc.) by making too great an effort, e.g. when lifting something. 3. to stretch (a rope, etc.) tightly. 4. to pass (a liquid) through a cloth, strainer, etc., so as to separate the solids from it. —*n.* 1. pressure or force: *will the rope take the strain?* 2. conditions in a person's life that cause worry or tiredness; stress: *she was under great strain during her husband's illness.* 3. an injury caused by too great an effort. '**strain·er** *n.* a device with a fine mesh or many small holes used to strain (def. 4) liquids.

strain[2] (strān) *n.* 1. breed; stock: *the horse came from a pure strain.* 2. a quality in a person's character: *a strain of madness.* 3. a style of writing or speaking. 4. usu. **strains** (*pl.*) sounds, esp. of music, usu. heard only faintly.

strait (strāt) *n.* often **straits** (*pl.*) a narrow channel of water joining two seas: *the Bering Strait.*

strand[1] (strand) *n.* 1. a single thread, fiber, wire, etc., twisted with others into a rope or cable. 2. a lock of hair.

strand[2] (strand) *vb.* to leave (a person) in a difficult position, without money, transport, etc.: *the storm stranded us on the island without food or water.*

strange (strānj) *adj.* **strang·er, strang·est.** 1. unusual; unfamiliar. 2. shy; awkward: *he felt strange when he first went to school.* '**strang·er** *n.* 1. a person whom one does not know. 2. a person in a place he does not know: *I am a stranger in Rome.*

stran·gle ('stranggəl) *vb.* **stran·gling, stran·gled.** to kill a person by squeezing the throat to prevent him from breathing. —'**stran·gler** *n.* —**stran·gu·la·tion** (stranggyə'lāshən) *n.*

straw (strô) *n.* 1. the dry cut stalks of grain plants used as bedding for cattle. 2. a single such stalk. 3. (*also* **drinking straw**) a long thin paper or plastic tube for sucking up liquids.

straw·ber·ry ('strôberē) *n.,pl.* **straw·ber·ries.** 1. a small juicy red fruit. 2. the plant on which it grows.

stray (strā) *vb.* 1. to wander away (from a group, path, etc.). 2. (of thoughts) to wander idly over different subjects. —*n.* an animal that has strayed from its usual home, field, herd, etc. —*adj.* 1. unattended or lost; loose: *a stray dog.* 2. occasional or off course: *a stray bullet.*

streak (strēk) *n.* 1. a thin irregular line or mark different from the color or texture surrounding it. 2. (informal) a small amount: *a streak of good luck.* —*vb.* (informal) to move very quickly.

stream (strēm) *n.* 1. a small river. 2. an even flow (of air, people, liquid, etc.). —*vb.* 1. to flow. 2. to move steadily in a mass. '**stream·er** *n.* a long narrow flag, ribbon, etc.

strength (strength) *n.* 1. the quality or condition of being strong. 2. a strong point: *arithmetic is his strength.* '**strength·en** *vb.* to make or become strong or stronger.

stress (stres) *n.* 1. pressure or force. 2. conditions of hardship, trouble, etc. 3. particular weight or emphasis: *the stress on a word.* —*vb.* 1. to insist on the importance of: *I stressed this point in my speech because I thought it was vital.* 2. to put weight or emphasis on (a part of a word or sentence)

stretch (strech) *vb.* 1. to make tighter or bigger by pulling. 2. to make larger or extend (one's arm, abilities, etc.). —*n.* a period of time. '**stretch·er** *n.* a light folding bed for carrying a sick or injured person.

strict (strikt) *adj.* 1. stern; demanding obedience. 2. clearly limited and with no additions: *she told the strict truth.* —'**strict·ly** *adv.* —'**strict·ness** *n.*

strike[1] (strīk) *vb.* **strik·ing, struck.** 1. to hit. 2. (of a clock) to mark (the time) by making a striking sound. 3. to light (a match). 4. to arrive at; find: *we struck oil.* 5. (usu. + *off* or *from*) to cancel; to remove: *she struck his name off the list.* —*n.* an attack.

strike[2] (strīk) *vb.* **strik·ing, struck.** to withhold labor in order to obtain better pay, conditions, etc. —*n.* the refusal to work.

strawberry

stroke

string (striñg) *n.* 1. a fine cord. 2. the taut length of cord, wire, etc., that produces the sound in a musical instrument, e.g. a piano. 3. a series of objects threaded on a string or in a line: *a string of beads.* —*vb.* **string·ing, strung.** to thread (items) on a string.

strip (strip) *vb.* **strip·ping, stripped.** 1. to remove a covering, skin, paint, etc., from (something). 2. to remove one's clothes. 3. to remove furnishings from (a place). 4. (+ *of*) to take away the possessions, rights, etc., of (somebody): *the judge stripped him of the property he had stolen.* —*n.* a long narrow piece of land, paper, cloth, etc.

stroke[1] (strōk) *vb.* **strok·ing, stroked.** to move one's hand gently along or over (something). —*n.* the act of doing this.

stroke[2] (strōk) *n.* 1. a blow; the act of striking. 2. a sudden attack of illness that injures the brain and so causes part of the body to stop working. 3. one of a series of movements in swimming, e.g. the breaststroke. 4. a sudden unexpected happening: *a stroke of luck.*

strong (strôñg, stroñg) *adj.* **strong·er** ('strôñggər, 'stroñggər), **strong·est.** 1. having considerable physical strength, force, or power. 2. not easily broken or damaged: *a strong door.* 3. powerfully felt: *a strong desire.*

struck (struk) *vb.* the past tense and past participle of STRIKE.

strug·gle ('strugəl) *vb.* **strug·gling, strug·gled.** 1. to fight, usu. with a violent effort. 2. to try hard. —*n.* 1. a fight. 2. a great effort.

strung (struñg) *vb.* the past tense and past participle of STRING. **high-strung** (of a person or animal) nervous; likely to get excited.

strut[1] (strut) *vb.* **strut·ting, strut·ted.** to walk in a stiff or showy way. —*n.* a stiff or showy way of walking.

strut[2] (strut) *n.* a piece of wood or metal used to support or strengthen a framework or building.

stub (stub) *n.* 1. the short end of a pencil or cigarette left after the rest has been used. 2. part of a check, invoice, etc., kept as a record. —*vb.* **stub·bing, stubbed.** to hit (one's foot or toe) against something.

stub·ble ('stubəl) *n.* 1. the short stalks of grain left in the field after the harvest. 2. the short bristly growth of unshaven hair on the face.

stub·born ('stubərn) *adj.* determined not to alter one's own opinions, course of action, etc. —'**stub·born·ness** *n.* —'**stub·born·ly** *adv.*

stuck (stuk) *vb.* the past tense and past participle of STICK[2].

stud[1] (stud) *n.* 1. a small knob or button used on clothing, esp. collars and cuffs. 2. a large-headed nail sticking out from a surface: *studs in car tires help them to grip on ice.* —*vb.* **stud·ding, stud·ded.** to cover with studs or studlike objects for ornament or protection.

stud[2] (stud) *n.* 1. an animal, such as a horse, kept for breeding. 2. a farm for animal breeding.

stu·dent ('stōōdənt, 'styōōdənt) *n.* a person who studies, esp. in a school or university.

stu·di·o ('stōōdēō, 'styōōdēō) *n.,pl.* **stu·di·os.** 1. the room in which a painter, sculptor, or photographer works. 2. the place where movies are made. 3. the room from which TV and radio broadcasts are made. 4. the place where music is recorded for making phonograph records.

stud·y ('studē) *vb.* **stud·y·ing, stud·ied.** 1. to learn (something) by working steadily over a period of time. 2. to gaze at (something) closely and with interest. —*n.* a room used for studying. **stu·di·ous** ('stōōdēəs, 'styōōdēəs) *adj.* having the habit of studying. —'**stu·di·ous·ly** *adv.* —'**stu·di·ous·ness** *n.*

stuff (stuf) *n.* 1. the material or substance from which other articles are made. 2. (informal) a person's belongings: ***she left her stuff at my house while she looked for someplace to live.*** —*vb.* 1. to fill (something) tightly with something else. 2. to force (something) into a small space or container. '**stuff·ing** *n.* substance used for stuffing, e.g. feathers for pillows. '**stuff·y** *adj.* **stuff·i·er, stuff·i·est.** 1. (of a room) without fresh air. 2. (of a person) stiff in manner; formal.

stum·ble ('stumbəl) *vb.* **stum·bling, stum·bled.** to move jerkily or be almost falling, e.g. because one is ill or has tripped over something. —*n.* the act of stumbling.

stump (stump) *n.* 1. the part of a tree left just above the ground after the top and trunk have been removed. 2. anything left behind after the larger part has been removed or worn out: ***the stump of a pencil.*** —*vb.* 1. (often + *about*) to walk heavily and clumsily. 2. (informal) to be too difficult for: ***your question stumped him.*** '**stump·y** *adj.* **stump·i·er, stump·i·est.** short and thick.

stun (stun) *vb.* **stun·ning, stunned.** 1. to knock unconscious. 2. to amaze, astonish esp. unpleasantly: ***Lucy was stunned by the cost of the dress.***

stung (stung̃) *vb.* the past tense and past participle of STING.

stunk (stung̃k) *vb.* the past tense and past participle of STINK.

stunt[1] (stunt) *vb.* to halt or hamper the growth of (a child, plant, etc.). —'**stunt·ed·ness** *n.*

stunt[2] (stunt) *n.* an action done to gain publicity, e.g. to advertise something. '**stunt·man** a person who performs dangerous actions in movies, etc.

stu·pid ('stōōpid, 'styōōpid) *adj.* foolish, silly, and slow-witted. —**stu'pid·i·ty** *n.* —'**stu·pid·ly** *adv.*

stur·dy ('stûrdē) *adj.* strong and solid. —'**stur·di·ly** *adv.* —'**stur·di·ness** *n.*

stut·ter ('stutər) *vb.* to talk in jerks; to stammer: ***"p-p-please", stuttered Tom.*** —*n.* a jerky way of talking.

sty[1] (stī) *n.,pl.* **sties.** a place where pigs are kept.

sty[2] (stī) *n.,pl.* **sties.** a swollen sore on an eyelid.

style (stīl) *n.* 1. the manner in which something is done: ***he has a clumsy style of writing.*** 2. the particular quality that marks something out from other things: ***that dress was in the latest style.*** 3. the general form or design: ***a modern style of building.*** '**styl·ish** *adj.* fashionable; smart.

sub·ject *n.* ('subjikt) 1. any person who is not the ruler of a state; CITIZEN. 2. (in grammar) the word or words in a sentence that rule the verb, e.g. ***the dog*** is the subject in the sentence ***the dog ate the meat.*** 3. the thing to be studied or talked about: ***she talked on the subject of travel.*** —*adj.* 1. under the control of somebody else. 2. (+ *to*) likely to have: ***he is subject to fits.*** —*vb.* (səb'jekt) 1. to get (something) under one's control. 2. (+ *to*) to cause (someone or something) to undergo an experience: ***I was subjected to a terrible piercing noise.*** —**sub'jec·tion** *n.*

sub·ma·rine (submə'rēn) *n.* a ship able to travel under the surface of the water. —*adj.* of things below the surface of the sea.

sub·merge (səb'mûrj) *vb.* **sub·merg·ing, sub·merged.** to go or cause to go beneath the water. —**sub'mer·sion** *n.*

sub·mit (səb'mit) *vb.* **sub·mit·ting, sub·mit·ted.** 1. to put oneself under the control of another. 2. to put forward (a plan for discussion). —**sub'mis·sion** *n.*

sub·side (səb'sīd) *vb.* **sub·sid·ing, sub·sid·ed.** 1. (of water) to sink to a lower or more usual level. 2. (of land) to sink. 3. (of emotions or the wind) to become calm. —'**sub·si·dence** *n.*

sub·stance ('substəns) *n.* 1. material, particularly the material out of which something is made. 2. the most important part: ***the substance of a plan.*** 3. firmness; solidity. **sub·stan·tial** (səb'stanshəl) *adj.* 1. having importance. 2. having solidity.

sub·sti·tute ('substitōōt, 'substityōōt) *vb.* **sub·sti·tut·ing, sub·sti·tut·ed.** to put or use one thing in the place of another: ***they substituted an impostor for the real prince.*** —*n.* the person or thing substituted: ***the coach made Tom a substitute for John.*** —**sub·sti'tu·tion** *n.*

sub·tle ('sutəl) *adj.* 1. difficult to understand, explain, or sense because very delicate: ***a subtle perfume.*** 2. with the ability to understand subtle points: ***a subtle thinker.*** 3. cunning: ***a subtle thief.*** —'**sub·tle·ty** *n.,pl.* **sub·tle·ties.** —'**sub·tly** *adv.*

sub·tract (səb'trakt) *vb.* to take (something) away from some larger whole. —**sub'trac·tion** *n.*

sub·urb ('subûrb) *n.* an area on the edge of a town. **sub'ur·ban** *adj.* of or in the area between town and country. **sub'ur·bi·a** *n.* the suburbs.

submarine

sub·way ('subwā) *n.* an underground railroad.

suc·ceed (sək'sēd) *vb.* 1. to do what one has been trying to do. 2. to do well. 3. to follow next in order. **suc·cess** (sək'ses) *n.* 1. an achievement. 2. a person who does well. **suc'cess·ful** *adj.* of a person or activity that succeeds (defs. 1 and 2). **suc'ces·sion** *n.* the following of one thing after another in time or position. **suc'ces·sive** *adj.* following one after another. —**suc'ces·sor** *n.*

suck (suk) *vb.* 1. to draw (liquid) into the mouth by using the lip muscles. 2. to hold (something) in the mouth to melt it. '**suck·er** *n.* 1. a device that sticks to a surface by suction. 2. an offshoot from a plant. 3. (slang) a person who is easily cheated.

suc·tion ('sukshən) *n.* 1. the action of sucking (def. 1). 2. the force produced by a vacuum, causing something to stick to something else: *the rubber disk is attached to the wall by suction.*

suede (swād) *n.* leather with a soft unpolished surface, often used for jackets and shoes.

su·et ('sooit) *n.* the thick hard fat surrounding the kidneys of sheep and cattle. It is used in cooking.

suf·fer ('sufər) *vb.* 1. to feel or endure pain, injury, etc. 2. to be harmed: *his work suffered because of his illness.* 3. to allow. **on sufferance** allowed but not definitely wanted: *we let him come on sufferance.*

suf·fix ('sufiks) *n.* the letter(s) or syllable(s) added to the end of a word to make another word, e.g. in the word *strongly, -ly* is the suffix. —*vb.* to add a suffix to.

suf·fo·cate ('sufəkāt) *vb.* **suf·fo·cat·ing, suf·fo·cat·ed.** 1. to kill (someone) or die by stopping breathing. 2. to have or cause difficulty in breathing. —**suf·fo'ca·tion** *n.*

sug·ar ('shoogər) *n.* a sweet substance found in various plants, e.g. **sugarcane** and **sugarbeet,** and used to sweeten food. —*vb.* to make (something) sweet with sugar. —'**sug·ar·y** *adj.*

sug·gest (səg'jest) *vb.* 1. to put forward an idea, etc., as a possibility to be considered. 2. to bring an idea, etc., into the mind: *his suspicious behavior suggests that he is dishonest.* **sug'ges·tion** *n.* 1. an idea, etc., that is suggested. 2. a hint or trace: *there was a suggestion of a smile on her lips.* **sug'ges·tive** *adj.* tending to bring ideas, etc., into the mind.

suit (soot) *n.* 1. a set of clothing made of the same material. 2. a case in a law court; lawsuit. 3. one of the four sets in a pack of cards (spades, hearts, clubs, diamonds). —*vb.* 1. to satisfy: *if I meet you at eight, will that suit you?* 2. (of clothing) to look well when worn: *that shirt suits him.* '**suit·a·ble** *adj.* right for a purpose or occasion. '**suit·or** *n.* 1. a man who courts a woman. 2. a person who starts a lawsuit. —'**suit·a·bly** *adv.*

suit·case ('sootkās) *n.* an oblong box with a handle, used by travelers to carry their belongings.

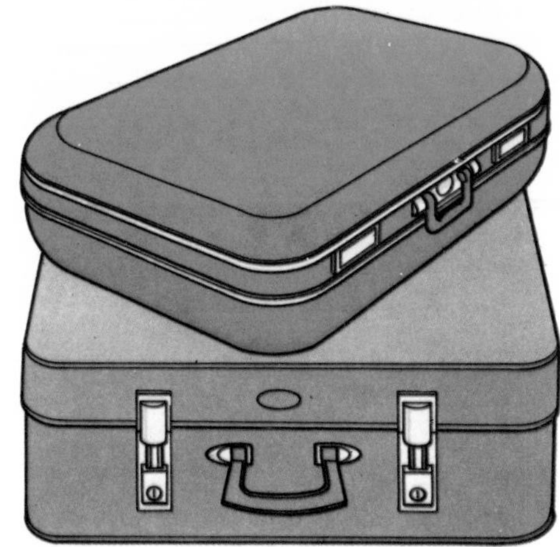

suitcase

sul·fur ('sulfər) *n.* a pale yellow chemical element that burns with a blue flame and smells strongly when mixed with other substances. Chemical symbol: S. '**sul·fur·ous** *adj.*

sulk (sulk) *vb.* to be in a bad temper, usu. showing this by refusing to talk. —'**sulk·y** *adj.* **sulk·i·er, sulk·i·est,** —'**sulk·i·ly** *adv.* —'**sulk·i·ness** *n.*

sulk·y (sul'kē) *n.* a light horse-drawn carriage having two wheels and only one seat.

sul·len ('sulən) *adj.* 1. (of a person) gloomy and bad-tempered. 2. (of the sky or weather) dark.

sul·tan ('sultən) *n.* a MUSLIM ruler. **sul·ta·na** (sul'tanə) *n.* the wife, daughter, or sister of a sultan.

sum·mer ('sumər) *n.* the warmest season of the year, between spring and fall. —'**sum·mer·y** *adj.*

sum·mit ('sumit) *n.* the top; highest level: *the climbers placed a flag on the summit of the mountain.*

sum·mon ('sumən) *vb.* 1. to send for or call. 2. (often + *up*) to gather together: *she summoned up her courage to jump off the high wall.* '**sum·mons** *sing.n.* a formal order or demand, esp. to attend a case in a law court.

sun (sun) *n.* the heavenly body that gives warmth and light to the earth. —'**sun·ny** *adj.* **sun·ni·er, sun·ni·est.** —'**sun·ni·ly** *adv.*

sun·bathe ('sunbādh) *vb.* **sun·bath·ing, sun·bathed.** to sit or lie in the sunlight for pleasure. —'**sun·bath·er** *n.*

sun·burn ('sunbûrn) *n.* the reddening and blistering of the skin caused by strong sunlight. —'**sun·burnt** *adj.*

sun·glass·es ('sunglasiz) *pl.n.* spectacles with darkened lenses, worn to protect the eyes against strong sunlight.

sunk (sungk) *vb.* the past participle of SINK.

sun·rise ('sunrīz) *n.* 1. the time of the sun's appearance above the horizon. 2. the sun's appearance in the morning.

sun·set ('sunset) *n.* 1. the time of the sun's disappearance below the horizon. 2. the sun's disappearance in the evening.

sun·stroke ('sunstrōk) *n.* illness caused by too much exposure to the sun's rays, esp. on the head.

sun·tan ('suntan) *n.* a brown or bronze coloring of the skin resulting from exposure to strong sunlight.

su·pe·ri·or (sə'pērēər) *adj.* 1. better. 2. higher in position: *the colonel was my superior officer.* 3. greater in number. —*n.* a person who is higher in rank or abilities than another. —**su·pe·ri·or·i·ty** (səpērē'ôritē) *n.*

su·per·la·tive (sə'pûrlətiv) *adj.* of the highest quality or degree. —*n.* (grammar) a form of an adjective, e.g. *biggest* is the superlative of *big.* —**su'per·la·tive·ly** *adv.*

su·per·mar·ket ('soopərmârkit) *n.* a big self-service store, usu. selling a wide range of merchandise.

su·per·son·ic (so͞opər'sonik) *adj.* faster than the speed of sound.

su·per·sti·tion (so͞opər'stishən) *n.* an unreasonable fear, esp. a belief that certain actions or things are unlucky: *there are many superstitions about black cats.* —**su·per'sti·tious** *adj.* —**su·per'sti·tious·ly** *adv.*

su·per·vise ('so͞opərvīz) *vb.* **su·per·vis·ing, su·per·vised.** to direct or oversee (work or workers); guide or keep an eye on: *the professor supervised my studies.* —**su·per·vi·sion** (so͞opər'vizhən) *n.* —**'su·per·vi·sor** *n.*

sup·per ('supər) *n.* the last meal of the day, often a light one.

sup·ple ('supəl) *adj.* easily bent; not stiff: *the ballerina's limbs were very supple.* —**'sup·ple·ness** *n.*

sup·ply (sə'plī) *vb.* **sup·ply·ing, sup·plied.** 1. to provide (someone or something) with necessary things; give (something) to somebody: *she supplied me with the answer I needed.* 2. produce some goods or services, usu. for sale. —*n.,pl.* **sup·plies.** the quantity of goods on hand or to be distributed: *the explorers drank their supplies of water.*

sup·port (sə'pôrt) *vb.* 1. to hold up (a weight, etc.). 2. to provide the money to enable (other people) to eat, be clothed, etc.: *the widow had to support her family on her own.* 3. to encourage or help (somebody). —*n.* 1. a person who supports (def. 2). 2. something that takes the weight of something else. **sup'port·er** *n.* a person who supports.

sup·pose (sə'pōz) *vb.* **sup·pos·ing, sup·posed.** 1. to take (something) as a fact: *let's suppose he is telling the truth.* 2. to guess or think: *we supposed he would do his share of the work, but we were mistaken.* **sup'pos·ing** *conj.* if. **sup'posed** *adj.* thought to be so: *the supposed prince was really a thief in disguise.* **sup·po·si·tion** (supə'zishən) *n.* 1. the act of supposing. 2. something supposed.

sure (sho͝or) *adj.* **sur·er, sur·est.** 1. positive that something is so: *are you sure of these figures?* 2. certain: *be sure to bring your swimsuit.* 3. trustworthy: *a high temperature is a sure sign of illness.* **'sure·ly** *adv.* 1. certainly. 2. if things work out as expected or probable: *surely, your parents will not forget your birthday.*

surfboard

surf (sûrf) *n.* large waves of the sea breaking on the seashore or on rocks. —*vb.* to ride such waves as a sport, usu. on a **surfboard.**

sur·face ('surfis) *n.* 1. the outside of something. 2. the upper layer of a liquid: *bubbles broke through the surface of the water.* —*adj.* appearing or happening on a surface, esp. of the land or sea: *he will never fly anywhere — he always goes by surface transport.* —*vb.* **sur·fac·ing, sur·faced.** to rise to the surface.

surge (sûrj) *vb.* **surg·ing, surged.** to move forward and upward with a movement like waves: *the crowd surged against the barrier.* —*n.* a forward rush like that of waves.

sur·geon ('sûrjən) *n.* a doctor who performs surgery. **'sur·ger·y** *n.,pl.* **sur·ger·ies.** treatment of disease or injury by repairing or removing parts of the body. **'sur·gi·cal** *adj.* of or by surgery.

sur·name ('sûrnām) *n.* the part of a person's name which he shares with all his family; family name: *Adams was the surname of two American presidents.*

sur·plus ('sûrpləs, 'sûrplus) *n.* an extra amount of goods, money, etc., over and above the basic or necessary amount: *the country produced a surplus of grain this year.*

sur·prise (sər'prīz) *n.* 1. something unexpected. 2. the feeling caused by an unexpected happening. —*vb.* **sur·pris·ing, sur·prised.** 1. to cause a feeling of surprise (def. 2) in. 2. to find or come upon (someone) unexpectedly: *we surprised the thief as he was breaking open the door.* **sur'pris·ing** *adj.* causing surprise.

sur·ren·der (sə'rendər) *vb.* 1. to give oneself up to an enemy, etc.: *the general surrendered when he realised the battle was lost.* 2. to give up possession of: *he surrendered his gun to the police.* 3. to give way to; yield: *he surrendered to despair.* —*n.* the action or an instance of surrendering.

sur·rep·ti·tious (sûrəp'tishəs) *adj.* done secretly or in a sly underhand way. —**sur·rep'ti·tious·ly** *adv.*

sur·round (sə'round) *vb.* to be or move around (something) on every side; encircle: *the army surrounded the fortress and cut it off from outside help.* **sur'round·ings.** *pl.n.* the conditions and objects around something: *the house was set in beautiful surroundings of trees and meadows.*

sur·vey *vb.* (sər'vā) 1. to take a general look at. 2. to measure (a piece of land, coastline, etc.) in order to make a map or chart. —*n.* ('sûrvā) 1. an overall or general view: *he made a rapid survey of the scene.* 2. the measuring and mapping of the earth. **sur'vey·or** *n.* a person whose occupation is surveying land.

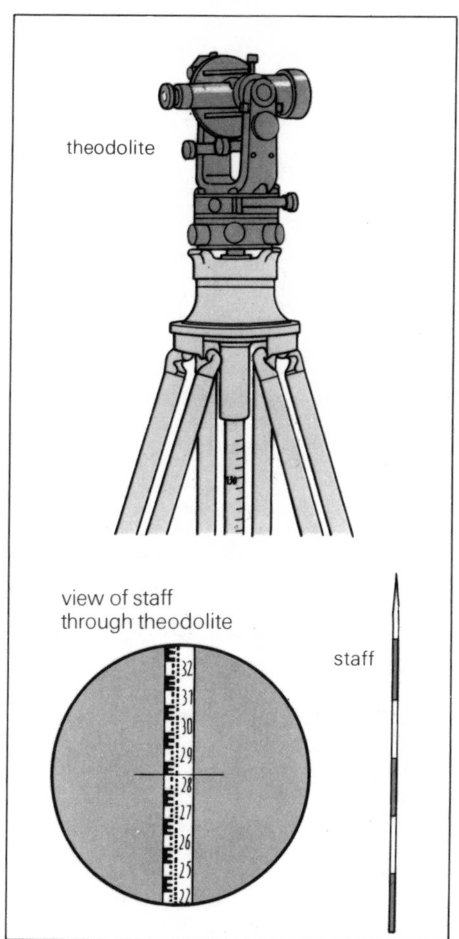

survey

sur·vive (sər'vīv) *vb.* **sur·viv·ing, sur·vived.** 1. to live longer than. 2. to remain alive, esp. after some accident, etc. **sur'vi·vor** *n.* a person who lives through a disaster.

sus·pect *vb.* (sə'spekt) 1. to have a feeling that something is so without being certain. 2. to be doubtful about: *I suspect his behavior.* 3. to believe (somebody) to be guilty of a crime, etc. —*n.* ('suspekt) a person who is thought to be guilty of a crime. —*adj.* ('suspekt) likely to cause suspicion.

sus·pend (sə'spend) *vb.* 1. to hang (something) from a support above. 2. to put off for a time: *the race was suspended because of rain.* 3. to shut out for a time: *they suspended him from the club.* **sus'pen·sion** *n.* 1. the state of being suspended. 2. the spring system of an automobile.

sus·pense (sə'spens) *n.* uncertainty about the outcome of an event, etc.

sus·pi·cion (sə'spishən) *n.* 1. the feeling that something is wrong or that someone is guilty without having definite proof of the fact. 2. a hint: *there was a suspicion of a smile on her face.* **sus'pi·cious** *adj.* having or causing suspicion. —**sus'pi·cious·ly** *adv.*

swal·low¹ ('swolō) *n.* a small fast-flying bird with long wings and a forked tail.

swal·low² ('swolō) *vb.* 1. to move food, drink, etc., from the mouth through the throat to the stomach. 2. to accept, usu. too easily: *he was so charming that I swallowed his lies.* 3. to suppress; retract: *he swallowed his pride.*

swam (swam) *vb.* the past tense of SWIM.

swamp (swomp) *n.* an area of soft ground with patches of water; marsh. —*vb.* 1. to flood with water. 2. to have too much of: *the teacher was swamped with work.* —'**swamp·y** *adj.* **swamp·i·er, swamp·i·est.**

swarm (swôrm) *n.* 1. a large gathering of insects, esp. honeybees. 2. a big crowd of people. —*vb.* 1. (of bees) to move in a swarm with the queen bee. 2. to move or be present in a crowd: *the children swarmed into the street.*

swear (sweər) *vb.* **swear·ing, swore, sworn.** 1. to say solemnly; promise. 2. to use bad language; curse.

sweat (swet) *n.* 1. the moisture that comes from the body through the skin, particularly if one is hot or worried. 2. (informal) an effort. —*vb.* 1. to produce sweat or something similar to sweat. 2. (informal) to work hard.

sweep (swēp) *vb.* **sweep·ing, swept.** 1. to clean (a room, floor, etc.) by brushing with a broom. 2. to move or cause to move swiftly: *the galloping horses swept past.* —*n.* a person whose job is sweeping chimneys. '**sweep·ing** *adj.* having a great effect: *sweeping changes.*

sweet (swēt) *adj.* 1. tasting like sugar. 2. pleasant; attractive. —*n.* something sweet to eat. '**sweet·en** *vb.* to make sweet. —'**sweet·ness** *n.*

swept (swept) *vb.* the past tense and past participle of SWEEP.

swift¹ (swift) *adj.* fast; speedy. —'**swift·ly** *adv.* —'**swift·ness** *n.*

swift² (swift) *n.* a small fast-flying insect-eating bird.

swim (swim) *vb.* **swim·ming, swam, swum.** to move through the water by using arms, fins, etc. —*n.* an instance of swimming.

swin·dle ('swindəl) *vb.* **swin·dling, swin·dled.** to cheat or get something by cheating, usu. in money matters. —*n.* something by which one is swindled. —'**swin·dler** *n.*

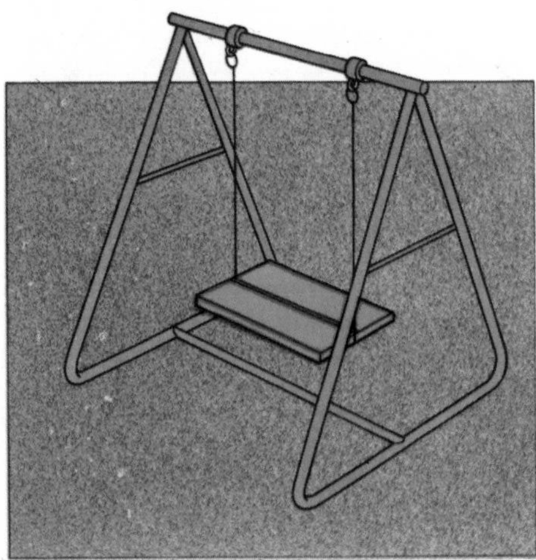
swing

swing (swing) *vb.* **swing·ing, swung.** 1. (esp. of an object with one fixed end) to move from side to side. 2. to turn or move along a curve: *the car swung around the corner.* —*n.* 1. a swinging movement. 2. a seat on which people swing backward and forward for pleasure.

switch (swich) *n.* a device for turning electric current on or off. —*vb.* (+ *on* or *off*) to use a switch to control electric current.

swol·len ('swōlən) *vb.* the past participle of SWELL.

sword (sôrd) *n.* a weapon with a long sharp-edged pointed steel blade.

swore (swôr) *vb.* the past tense of SWEAR.

sworn (swôrn) *vb.* the past participle of SWEAR.

swum (swum) *vb.* the past participle of SWIM.

swung (swung) *vb.* the past tense and past participle of SWING.

syl·la·ble ('siləbəl) *n.* the sound made by a single action of the voice. *sym·pa·thy* is a word with three syllables.

sym·bol ('simbəl) *n.* a sign, object, etc., used to stand for or represent something else. '**sym·bol·ize** *vb.* **sym·bol·iz·ing, sym·bol·ized.** to be or be used or regarded as a symbol of. —**sym·bol·ic** (sim'bolik) *adj.* —**sym'bol·i·cal·ly** *adv.*

sym·pa·thy ('simpəthē) *n.,pl.* **sym·pa·thies.** a feeling or ability by which a person is able to share in the feelings of others. **sym·pa·thet·ic** (simpə'thetik) *adj.* having or showing sympathy. '**sym·pa·thize** *vb.* **sym·pa·thiz·ing, sym·pa·thized.** to feel sympathy.

sym·pho·ny ('simfənē) *n.,pl.* **sym·pho·nies.** a piece of music, usu. in three or four sections, written to be played by a full orchestra. —**sym·phon·ic** (sim'fonik) *adj.*

symp·tom ('simptəm) *n.* 1. a change or outward sign in the body showing that it has an illness. 2. a sign that a certain condition exists: *overheating is a symptom of a faulty engine.*

syn·a·gogue ('sinəgog, 'sinəgôg) *n.* 1. the building where Jews gather to worship. 2. a Jewish religious meeting.

sys·tem ('sistəm) *n.* 1. a group of parts working together in an ordered way: *the solar system.* 2. an ordered set of ideas, methods, etc. **sys·tem·at·ic** (sistə'matik) *adj.* methodical. —**sys·tem'at·i·cal·ly** *adv.*

T

tab·let ('tablit) *n.* 1. a small hard lump of something. 2. a writing pad. 3. a flat block with words wriJten on it, e.g. one fixed to a wall in memory of somebody. 4. a hard flat pill: *take two tablets.*

tack (tak) *n.* 1. a small flat-headed nail. 2. a long loose temporary sewing stitch. —*vb.* 1. to nail down with tacks. 2. to stitch loosely. 3. to sail on a zig-zag course against the wind.

tack·le ('takəl) *n.* 1. a set of equipment for a certain task or activity: *fishing tackle.* 2. (sport) an attempt to get the ball away from an opponent. 3. a system of ropes and pulleys used for lifting loads. —*vb.* **tack·ling, tack·led.** 1. to seize. 2. to attempt to deal with: *to tackle a problem.*

tact (takt) *n.* the ability to understand other people and behave toward them in a manner that does not hurt their feelings. —**'tact·ful** *adj.* —**'tact·ful·ly** *adv.*

tac·tics ('taktiks) *pl.n.* 1. the art of moving soldiers, ships, etc., into a good position for fighting. 2. methods used in carrying out a plan: *she won the campaign by clever tactics.* —**'tac·ti·cal** *adj.* —**'tac·ti·cal·ly** *adv.*

tad·pole ('tadpōl) *n.* a young frog or toad after hatching from its egg and before it is fully developed. It lives in the water and uses its long tail in swimming.

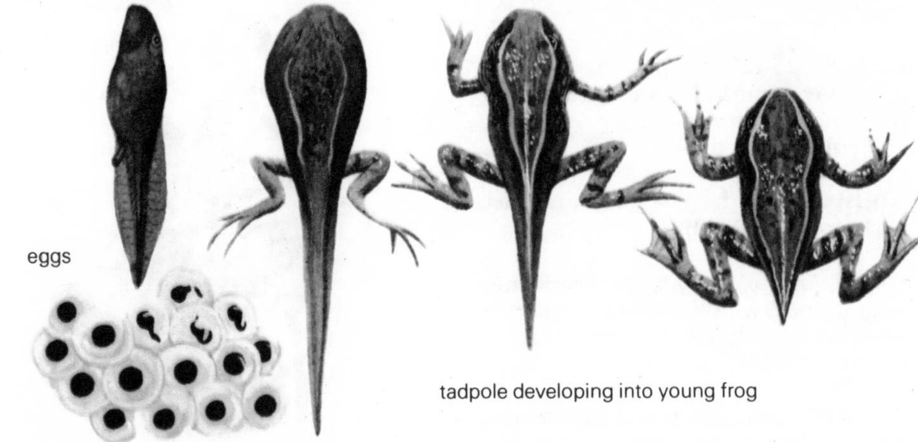

eggs

tadpole developing into young frog

tadpole

tag (tag) *n.* 1. a label, esp. one showing prices on goods in stores. 2. a metal or plastic tip, e.g. on a shoelace. 3. a game of running and catching people. —*vb.* **tag·ging, tag·ged.** 1. to put a label on (something). 2. to connect (something) to something else.

tail (tāl) *n.* 1. a bodily part, esp. a movable one, at the rear end of an animal. 2. something like a tail in position or function: *the tail of an airplane.* 3. usu. **tails** (*pl.*) the reverse side of a coin. —*vb.* (informal) to follow: *the police tailed the suspect.*

tai·lor ('tālər) *n.* a maker of outer clothing, esp. men's suits.

take-o·ver ('tākōvər) *n.* the act of taking control or power away from another and into one's own hands.

tale (tāl) *n.* a story or account, often an untrue or imaginary one.

tal·ent ('talənt) *n.* a special natural ability: *he has great talent as a singer.* —**'tal·ent·ed** *adj.*

talk (tôk) *vb.* 1. to speak or have a discussion. 2. to talk about: *they talked baseball all evening.* —*n.* 1. general discussion; conversation. 2. a formal speech. —**'talk·a·tive** *adj.*

tal·on ('talən) *n.* a long hooked claw of a bird of prey.

tambourine

tam·bou·rine (tambə'rēn) *n.* a musical instrument like a small flat drum with circles of metal loosely set in the rim that jingle when it is tapped or shaken.

tame (tām) *adj.* **tam·er, tam·est.** 1. (of animals) not wild. 2. dull; unexciting: *the plot of the movie was rather tame.* —*vb.* **tam·ing, tamed.** to make (a wild animal) tame or manageable.

tam·per ('tampər) *vb.* (+ *with*) 1. to meddle with. 2. to damage.

tan (tan) *adj.* light brown. —*n.* 1. a tan color. 2. a suntan. —*vb.* **tan·ning, tanned.** 1. to make or become tan, often in the sun. 2. to make (an animal's skin) into leather.

tang (tañg) *n.* a strong taste or smell: *the wind had the salt tang of the sea.*

tan·gle ('tañggəl) *n.* a confused untidy mass: *the kitten made the ball of wool into a tangle.* —*vb.* **tan·gling, tan·gled.** to make or become confused or untidy.

tank (tañgk) *n.* 1. a large storage container for liquid or gas. 2. a heavily armored vehicle moving on belt-like treads used in battle.

tanker

tank·er ('taŋgkər) *n.* 1. a ship with big tanks for carrying oil or other liquids in bulk. 2. a truck, plane or other vehicle with a large container for carrying liquids, esp. oil or gasoline.

tan·trum ('tantrəm) *n.* a fit of bad temper, usu. a sudden one about an unimportant matter.

tape (tāp) *n.* 1. a narrow piece of material used in dressmaking, for tying up parcels, etc. 2. a narrow gummed strip of material used for sticking things. 3. the magnetized strip used to record sound in a tape recorder. **tape recorder** an electric machine for recording sound, storing it on magnetic tape, and playing it back. —*vb.* **tap·ing, taped.** 1. to fasten with a tape. 2. to record (sound) on a tape recorder.

ta·per ('tāpər) *vb.* to make or become gradually narrower or thinner toward one end.

tap·es·try ('tapistrē) *n.,pl.* **tap·es·tries.** a cloth into which colored yarns are sewn or woven by hand to make designs.

tar (târ) *n.* a black sticky substance obtained from coal and used on road surfaces. —*vb.* **tar·ring, tarred.** to cover (something) with tar.

tar·get ('târgit) *n.* 1. the mark or object aimed at: *every arrow she shot hit the target.* 2. a person or thing being attacked.

tar·iff ('tarif) *n.* 1. a list of taxes on goods brought into a country. 2. a list of prices or charges, esp. at a hotel.

tar·pau·lin (târ'pôlin) *n.* a protective canvas sheet or covering made waterproof by being coated with tar.

tart[1] (târt) *n.* a saucer-shaped pastry base filled with jam, cooked fruit, etc., and usu. having no top crust.

tart[2] (târt) *adj.* sharp or sour in taste. —'**tart·ly** *adv.* —'**tart·ness** *n.*

tar·tan ('târtən) *n.* 1. Scottish woolen cloth with a criss-cross design of colored stripes. 2. a particular pattern of this cloth: *he wore a kilt of the Campbell tartan.*

task (task) *n.* a job of work.

taste (tāst) *n.* 1. the sense acting through the tongue and roof of the mouth that tells us the flavor of food. 2. the quality experienced by this sense: *lemons have a sour taste.* 3. a liking: *a taste for jazz.* 4. the ability to choose and enjoy good things in art, behavior, dress, etc. —*vb.* **tast·ing, tast·ed.** 1. to detect the taste of (something). 2. to have a taste of. '**tast·y** *adj.* **tast·i·er, tast·i·est.** having a nice taste. '**taste·ful** *adj.* showing good taste in art, etc.

tat·too[1] (ta'tōō) *n.,pl.* **tat·toos.** a continued tapping on a drum or other surface.

tat·too[2] (ta'tōō) *n.,pl.* **tat·toos.** a permanent marking or decoration on someone's skin, made by pricking it and rubbing on dyes.

taught (tôt) *vb.* the past tense and past participle of TEACH.

taunt (tônt) *vb.* to attack (someone) with unkind words: *they taunted him about his ragged clothes.* —*n.* a hurtful remark.

taut (tôt) *adj.* stretched tight; not slack; tense: *a taut rope.* —'**taut·ly** *adv.* —'**taut·ness** *n.*

tax (taks) *n.* money paid to a government for use on public services, national defense, etc. —*vb.* 1. to raise money by taxes. 2. to put a strain on: *having to work all day and study at night taxed his strength.* **tax'a·tion** *n.* system of collecting money by taxes.

tax·i ('taksē) *n.* a motorcar that can be hired, usu. for short journeys in a town; a taxicab. —*vb.* **tax·i·ing, tax·ied.** 1. to ride in a taxicab. 2. (of an aircraft) to move on wheels across the ground.

teach (tēch) *vb.* **teach·ing, taught.** 1. to give (someone) instruction in (a skill, subject, etc.). 2. to earn one's living by doing this, esp. in a school. —'**teach·er** *n.*

team (tēm) *n.* 1. a number of people joining together for work or play. 2. two or more animals, e.g. horses, pulling a plow, cart, etc., together.

tear[1] (teər) *vb.* **tear·ing, tore, torn.** 1. to damage or destroy by pulling sharply apart. 2. to become torn: *paper tears easily.* 3. to move excitedly or at speed: *he tore into the house with the news.* —*n.* a hole or split caused by tearing.

tear[2] (tēr) *n.* a drop of salty water produced from the eye. —'**tear·ful** *adj.*

tease (tēz) *vb.* **teas·ing, teased.** to make fun of (somebody) either unkindly or playfully. —*n.* a person who teases.

tech·ni·cal ('teknikəl) *adj.* 1. connected with one of the skills used in industry, e.g. printing. 2. connected with the methods used by experts: *technical knowledge.* —**tech'ni·cian** *n.*

tartan

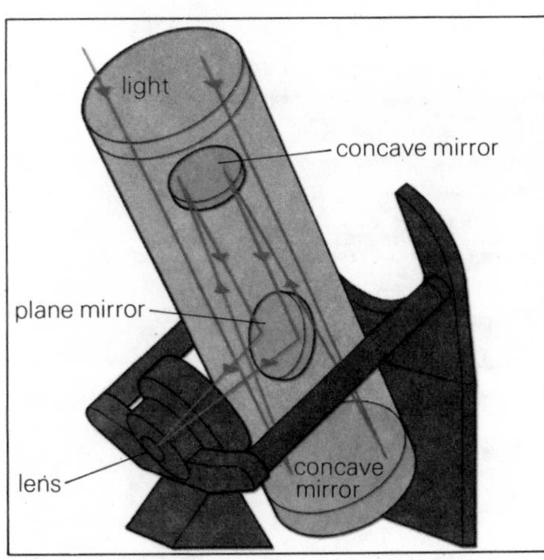

telescope

tech·nique (tek'nēk) *n.* the method or skill connected with doing something: *there are many new techniques in printing these days.*

teen·age ('tēnāj) *adj.* of or connected with a person between the ages of 13 and 19. —'**teen·ag·er** *n.*

teens (tēnz) *pl.n.* 1. the numbers 13 to 19. 2. the period of someone's life between the ages of 13 and 19: *the girls were in their teens.*

teeth (tēth) *n.* the plural of TOOTH.

tee·to·tal ('tētōtəl) *adj.* not drinking, or forbidding the drinking of, alcoholic liquor. —'**tee·to·tal·er** *n.*

tel·e·graph ('teləgraf) *n.* 1. an apparatus for sending messages quickly over long distances by means of a wire or by radio. 2. the system using this. —*vb.* to send a message by telegraph. '**tel·e·gram** *n.* a message sent by telegraph.

tel·e·phone ('teləfōn) *n.* an instrument used for talking to a person at a distance, using a system similar to a TELEGRAPH but adapted for speech. —*vb.* **tel·e·phon·ing, tel·e·phoned.** to make a telephone call.

tel·e·scope ('teliskōp) *n.* a tubelike instrument with a system of lenses and mirrors used to make distant objects appear closer. —**tel·e·scop·ic** (teli'skopik) *adj.*

tel·e·vis·ion ('televizhən) *n.* 1. a process of sending pictures and sound over a distance. 2. (also **television set** or TV set) a boxlike apparatus with a screen for receiving television broadcasts. **tel·e·vise** ('teləvīz) *vb.* **tel·e·vis·ing, tel·e·vised.** to send pictures by television.

tem·per ('tempər) *n.* 1. a mood or state of mind, esp. an unpleasant one: *in a bad temper.* 2. the degree of hardness, toughness, etc., of a substance. —*vb.* to alter the temper of a substance by heating, moistening, etc.

tem·per·a·ment ('tempərəmənt, 'temprəmənt) *n.* a person's natural condition of mind, feelings, and behavior: *we work happily together because we have similar temperaments.* **tem·per·a'men·tal** *adj.* given to rapid changes of mood; moody.

tem·per·ate ('tempərit) *adj.* 1. moderate or mild in speech, behavior, etc: *she discussed the issue in a very temperate manner.* 2. (of climate) neither too hot nor too cold. '**tem·per·ance** *n.* 1. self-control in speech, behavior, etc. 2. avoidance of alcoholic drinks.

tem·per·a·ture ('temprəchər) *n.* 1. the degree of heat of a thing. 2. a fever.

tem·pest ('tempist) *n.* a violent storm. —**tem·pes·tu·ous** (tem'peschōōəs) *adj.* —**tem'pes·tu·ous·ly** *adv.*

tem·ple[1] ('tempəl) *n.* a building used for religious worship.

tem·ple[2] ('tempəl) *n.* one of the two flat parts of the head on each side of the forehead.

tem·po ('tempō) *n.,pl.* **tem·pos** *or* **tem·pi** ('tempē). 1. the rate of activity or movement: *work continued at a faster tempo.* 2. the rate at which music is played: *a slow waltz tempo.*

tem·po·rar·y ('tempərerē) *adj.* lasting or designed to last for only a short time: *he made a temporary repair.* —**tem·po'rar·i·ly** *adv.*

tempt (tempt) *vb.* to encourage, persuade, or try to persuade (someone) to do something. **temp'ta·tion** *n.* 1. the action or an instance of tempting. 2. something that tempts: *the ripe peaches were a temptation to the hungry children.*

ten·ant ('tenənt) *n.* a person who pays rent for the use of land, rooms, etc., belonging to someone else. '**ten·an·cy** *n.,pl.* **ten·an·cies.** 1. the use of land, buildings, etc., by a tenant. 2. the length of time a tenant can use rented land, rooms, etc.

ten·der ('tendər) *adj.* 1. easily hurt or injured; sensitive or sore. 2. (of food) easily chewed; not tough. 3. loving.

ten·don ('tendən) *n.* a tough thick cordlike part of the body that joins a muscle to a bone: *the Achilles tendon runs from the back of the leg to the heel.*

ten·dril ('tendril) *n.* the threadlike part of a climbing plant by which the plant holds onto a support.

ten·e·ment ('tenəmənt) *n.* a large building, divided into many apartments, often providing poor living conditions.

ten·nis ('tenis) *n.* a game for two or four players, played with rackets and a ball on a marked court divided in half by a net.

tense[1] (tens) *n.* a form of a verb showing the time when an action happened, e.g. *went* is the past tense of *go.*

tense[2] (tens) *adj.* 1. (of things) tightly stretched. 2. (of people) feeling or showing strain. —*vb.* **tens·ing, tensed.** to make or become tense. '**ten·sion** *n.* 1. state of being tightly stretched. 2. a state of nervous strain or excitement: *the tension increased as we approached the enemy.*

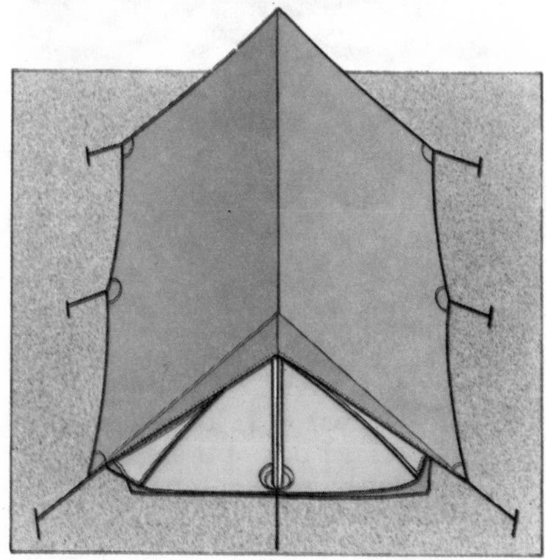
tent

tent (tent) *n.* a temporary shelter, usu. made of canvas sheets supported by poles and stretched by ropes.

ten·ta·cle ('tentəkəl) *n.* a long thin boneless outgrowth of certain soft-bodied animals, used for feeling, grasping, or moving: *an octopus has eight tentacles.*

tep·id ('tepid) *adj.* slightly warm; not quite cold. —**te'pid·i·ty** *n.*

term (tûrm) *n.* 1. a definite period of time: *the president's first term of office.* 2. a division of the year during which schools, colleges, etc., are open. 3. a word or phrase expressing a definite or special idea: *scientific terms.* 4. **terms** (*pl.*) the conditions under which something is done or agreed: *they came to terms over the disputed land.* —*vb.* to call or give a name to.

ter·mi·nal ('tûrminəl) *n.* 1. a place where bus routes, railroad lines, etc., end. 2. a piece of metal on electrical apparatus, a battery, wire, etc., to which a connection can be made. —*adj.* final: *a terminal illness.*

ter·mi·nus ('tûrminəs) *n.,pl.* **ter·mi·nus·es** *or* **ter·mi·ni** ('tûrmənī). the end of a railroad line or of a bus or air route.

ter·mite ('tûrmīt) *n.* an insect, sometimes called a white ant, which destroys timber, paper, fabrics, etc. Some tropical kinds build large nests or hills of hardened earth.

terrace

ter·race ('terəs) *n.* 1. a level area of ground formed out of a slope either naturally or by man, often in a series of such levels. 2. an outside balcony, esp. one connected with an apartment. —*vb.* **ter·rac·ing, ter·raced.** to cut terraces out of (a slope).

ter·ri·ble ('terəbəl) *adj.* bad, severe, or frightening. —'**ter·ri·bly** *adv.*

ter·ri·er ('terēər) *n.* a small lively type of dog, previously used for hunting.

ter·ri·fy ('terəfī) *vb.* **ter·ri·fy·ing, ter·ri·fied.** to fill with fear. **ter·rif·ic** (tə'rifik) *adj.* (informal) very large; excellent. **ter'rif·i·cal·ly** *adv.* (informal) very: *I am terrifically pleased that you won.*

ter·ri·to·ry ('teritôrē) *n.,pl.* **ter·ri·to·ries.** 1. land, esp. land under one government. 2. an area of land. **ter·ri'to·ri·al** *adj.* 1. of land. 2. belonging to a particular country: *fishing is restricted in most territorial waters.*

ter·ror ('terər) *n.* 1. great fear. 2. somebody or something that causes fear. '**ter·ror·ize** *vb.* **ter·ror·iz·ing, ter·ror·ized.** to cause terror to (someone). '**ter·ror·ism** *n.* the policy of causing terror by violence, murder, etc., to get what one wants in politics. —'**ter·ror·ist** *n.*

terse (tûrs) *adj.* short and concise: *he had very little time so he gave a terse answer to my question.* —'**terse·ly** *adv.* —'**terse·ness** *n.*

test (test) *n.* a trial or examination to discover qualities, abilities, etc.: *she came out top in the math test.* —*vb.* 1. to examine: *he tested the strength of the rope.* 2. to be a test of: *the child's crying tested his patience.*

tes·ta·ment ('testəmənt) *n.* 1. a formal written statement, esp. of a person's wishes as to what should be done with his belongings after his death. 2. **Testament** one of the two main parts of the Bible.

tes·ti·fy ('testəfī) *vb.* **tes·ti·fy·ing, tes·ti·fied.** to state solemnly, esp. when giving evidence in a law court.

teth·er ('tedhər) *n.* a rope or chain put on an animal to prevent it from wandering. —*vb.* to fasten or keep in one place with a tether.

text (tekst) *n.* 1. the main body of writing in a book, etc.: *I have only read part of the text of the play.* 2. a passage, esp. from the Bible, chosen as a subject for discussion. —'**tex·tu·al** *adj.* —'**tex·tu·al·ly** *adv.*

text·book ('tekstbŏŏk) *n.* a book used by pupils or students for study.

tex·tile ('tekstīl) *n.* 1. woven material. 2. material to be spun or woven. —*adj.* of the making of cloth.

tex·ture ('tekschər) *n.* 1. the way in which cloth is woven: *tweed has a coarse texture.* 2. the surface of a substance, esp. the way it looks or feels: *his skin has a rough texture.*

thank (thangk) *vb.* to say one is grateful to (someone). '**thank·ful** *adj.* grateful. '**thank·less** *adj.* (of actions) bringing no thanks or gratitude to the doer. —**thanks** *pl.n.*

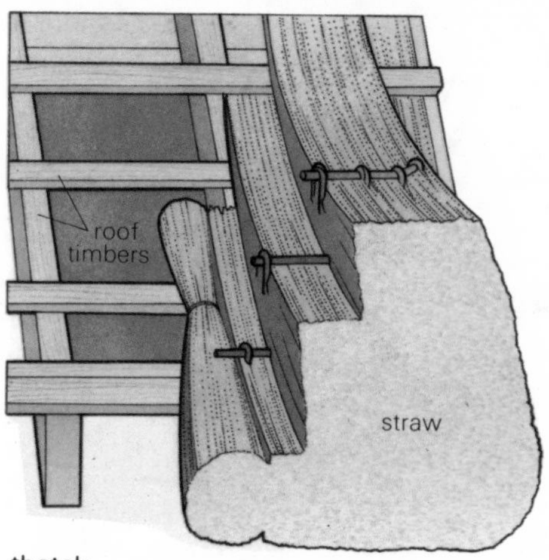

thatch

thatch (thach) *n.* dried straw, reeds, etc., made into a roof covering, esp. on old country cottages and houses. —*vb.* to put thatch on (a roof).

thaw (thô) *vb.* to become or cause to become soft or liquid again after being frozen. —*n.* a period of warmer weather causing ice, snow, etc., to melt.

the·a·ter ('thēətər) *n.* 1. a public building where stage plays are acted. 2. plays in general; drama. **the·at·ri·cal** (thē'atrikəl) *adj.* 1. of or for the theater. 2. behaving like an actor; showy or affected. —**the'at·ri·cal·ly** *adv.*

theft (theft) *n.* the action or an instance of stealing: *the boy's theft of the apples made the farmer very angry.*

theme (thēm) *n.* 1. the subject of a talk or piece of writing: *the theme of the novel was ambition.* 2. a tune that is often repeated in a longer piece of music. —**the'mat·ic** *adj.*

the·o·rem ('thēərəm) *n.* (mathematics) a statement that can be shown to be true by logical reasoning.

the·o·ry ('thēərē) *n.,pl.* **the·o·ries.** 1. a reason or explanation for something that has not yet been shown to be true: *the scientist had a theory about the causes of earthquakes.* 2. a general law or principle, or body of laws or principles: *economic theory.* **the·o·ret·i·cal** (thēə'retikəl) *adj.* based on theory, as opposed to practice. —**the·o'ret·i·cal·ly** *adv.* —'**the·o·rist** *n.*

ther·mom·e·ter (thər'momitər) *n.* an instrument for measuring temperature.

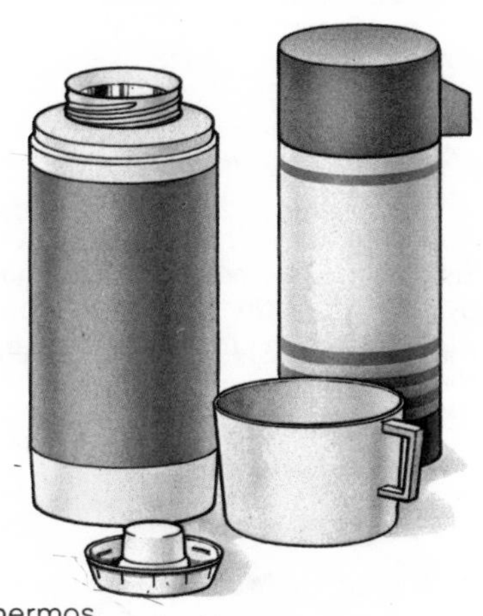
Thermos

Ther·mos ('thûrməs) *n.* (trademark) a small bottle, flask, or container used to keep liquids at a constant temperature.

ther·mo·stat ('thûrməstat) *n.* a device activated by temperature changes, used to control a heating or cooling apparatus to keep a room, refrigerator, etc., at a constant temperature.

thick (thik) *adj.* 1. big from side to side, back to front, or all round: *a thick plank.* 2. placed close together; dense: *a thick crowd.* 3. not flowing freely: *a thick syrup.* '**thick·en** *vb.* to make thick or thicker.

thick·et ('thikit) *n.* a group of trees or bushes growing close together.

thief (thēf) *n.,pl.* **thieves.** a person who steals, esp. in secret and without violence. **thieve** *vb.* **thiev·ing, thieved.** to steal. See also THEFT.

thigh (thī) *n.* the thick part of the leg above the knee.

thim·ble ('thimbəl) *n.* a small cap of metal or plastic used to protect the top of a finger when pushing a needle through cloth.

thin (thin) *adj.* **thin·ner, thin·nest.** 1. little in size from front to back, from side to side, or all round: *a thin wire.* 2. (of people) slender; not fat. 3. easily poured or watery: *a thin soup.* —*vb.* **thin·ning, thinned.** to become or cause to become sparser or more diluted. —'**thin·ly** *adv.* —'**thin·ness** *n.*

think (thingk) *vb.* **think·ing, thought.** 1. to use one's mind to deal with a problem or form an opinion. 2. to believe.

thirst (thûrst) *n.* 1. feeling of dryness in the mouth and throat caused by lack of moisture; a desire for drink. 2. a strong desire: *the thirst for power.* —*vb.* to feel thirst; desire to drink. —'**thirst·i·ly** *adv.* —'**thirst·i·ness** *n.* —'**thirst·y** *adj.* **thirst·i·er, thirst·i·est.**

this·tle ('thisəl) *n.* a wild plant with prickly leaves and purple, white, or yellow flowers.

thorn (thôrn) *n.* 1. a sharp spine or prickle on a plant's stem. 2. a tree or bush with many thorns. '**thorn·y** *adj.* **thorn·i·er, thorn·i·est.** 1. covered with thorns. 2. (of a problem, question, etc.) difficult; tricky.

thor·ough ('thûrō, 'thurō) *adj.* 1. complete: *the party was a thorough success.* 2. (of people) neglecting no detail: *Sally is always a thorough worker.* —'**thor·ough·ly** *adv.* —'**thor·ough·ness** *n.*

thought (thôt) *n.* 1. the process or act of thinking: *she was deep in thought.* 2. an idea, opinion, etc., formed by thinking. —*vb.* the past tense and past participle of THINK. '**thought·ful** *adj.* 1. thinking. 2. showing care for the needs of other people: *it was very thoughtful of you to visit her in the hospital.* —'**thought·ful·ly** *adv.* '**thought·less** *adj.* 1. selfish. 2. without thinking. —'**thought·less·ly** *adv.*

thread (thred) *n.* 1. a thin length of cotton, silk, etc., used for weaving and sewing. 2. a chain of thought or line in a story: *I lost the thread of my argument.* 3. the ridge or groove running around a bolt or screw. —*vb.* 1. to put thread through (a needle's eye). 2. to put (beads, etc.) on a string. 3. to make one's way in and out of a number of people or things: *she threaded her way through the crowd.*

threat (thret) *n.* 1. a statement expressing the intention of hurting or punishing. 2. a sign of coming trouble: *the threat of famine.* '**threat·en** *vb.* 1. to use threats against (someone). 2. to give warning of trouble. —'**threat·en·ing·ly** *adv.*

thresh (thresh) *vb.* to separate (grain) from the stalks or husks of a cereal plant. '**thresh·er** *n.* 1. a machine for threshing grain. 2. a person who threshes grain.

threw (throo) *vb.* the past tense of THROW.

thistle

thrift (thrift) *n.* care and economy in handling or using money or goods. —'**thrift·i·ness** *n.* —'**thrift·less** *adj.* —'**thrift·less·ness** *n.* —'**thrift·y** *adj.* **thrift·i·er, thrift·i·est.**

thrill (thril) *n.* 1. an experience causing an excited feeling. 2. an excited feeling caused by pleasure, horror, etc. —*vb.* to feel or cause to feel a thrill. '**thrill·er** *n.* something that causes thrills, esp. a story or movie.

thrive (thrīv) *vb.* **thriv·ing, thrived** *or* **throve.** 1. to grow strongly. 2. to succeed: *our business has thrived.*

throat (thrōt) *n.* 1. the front part of the neck. 2. the tube in the neck that carries food from the mouth to the stomach. '**throat·y** *adj.* **throat·i·er, throat·i·est.** (of a voice) deep.

throb (throb) *vb.* **throb·bing, throbbed.** (of the heart, pulse, etc.) to beat faster or harder than usual. —*n.* a throbbing feeling or sound.

throne (thrōn) *n.* the official ceremonial chair of a king, queen, or bishop.

throne

throng (thrông) *n.* a crowd. —*vb.* to move or be present in a crowd.

throt·tle ('throtəl) *vb.* **throt·tling, throt·tled.** to squeeze the throat of (a person or animal) to prevent breathing. —*n.* the control of an engine that regulates the flow of fuel.

throw (thrō) *vb.* **throw·ing, threw, thrown.** 1. to fling (something) through the air. 2. to put (clothing) on or off quickly: *she threw on her dress.* 3. to move violently: *he threw himself at the locked door.* 4. (of a horse) to unseat (a rider). —*n.* the action or an instance of throwing.

thrush (thrush) *n.* one of several kinds of small bird noted for their songs.

thrust (thrust) *vb.* **thrust·ing, thrust.** to push violently and unexpectedly: *he thrust his way through the jungle.* —*n.* a violent push or stab.

thud (thud) *n.* a dull heavy sound: *the book landed on the table with a thud.* —*vb.* **thud·ding, thud·ded.** to make a thud.

thumb (thum) *n.* the short thick digit of the human hand that is set apart from the four fingers. —*vb.* 1. (usu. + *through*) to turn over (the pages of a book) rapidly. 2. (of a hitchhiker) to ask (drivers of passing motor vehicles) for a lift, by signaling with the thumb.

thun·der ('thundər) *n.* 1. the loud crash or rumble from the sky accompanying lightning. 2. a loud noise like thunder. —*vb.* 1. to thunder (def.1). 2. to make a loud prolonged rumbling noise: *the heavy guns thundered all through the night.* '**thun·der·ous** *adj.* (of a noise) loud. '**thun·der·y** *adj.* (of the weather) likely to thunder.

thwart (thwôrt) *vb.* to prevent (somebody) from doing something; frustrate (intentions, plans, etc.): *the rain thwarted our plans for a picnic.*

tick[1] (tik) *n.* 1. the small regular sound made by a clock or watch. 2. any noise like this. —*vb.* (of a clock) to make a tick-tock sound.

tick[2] (tik) *n.* a small creature like a spider that fastens itself to an animal's skin and sucks its blood.

tick·et ('tikit) *n.* 1. a card or slip of paper giving the person who holds it the right to travel on a train, bus, etc., or attend an entertainment. 2. a small label showing the price of goods on sale. 3. a printed notice given to a motorist who has broken the traffic laws: *a speeding ticket.* 4. a list of candidates for election belonging to a political party.

tick·le ('tikəl) *vb.* **tick·ling, tick·led.** 1. to touch or rub (a person's skin) lightly, often causing him to laugh. 2. to have the feeling of being tickled. 3. to please or amuse. —*n.* the action or an instance of tickling. '**tick·lish** *adj.* 1. (of a person) sensitive to tickling. 2. (informal) touchy; requiring skill in handling: *a ticklish problem.*

tide (tīd) *n.* 1. the regular twice daily rise and fall in the level of the sea. 2. a trend or mass movement of opinion.

ti·dy ('tīdē) *adj.* **tid·i·er, tid·i·est.** neat; in order. —*vb.* **ti·dy·ing, ti·died.** (often + *up*) to put in order: *he tidied up his room.* —'**ti·di·ly** *adv.* —'**ti·di·ness** *n.*

tie (tī) *vb.* **ty·ing, tied.** 1. to fasten or secure (with string, wire, rope, etc.). 2. to make (a knot). 3. to make an equal score in a game: *the teams tied 2 – 2.* —*n.* 1. a necktie. 2. something that holds people together: *the ties of affection.* 3. one of the evenly spaced crosswise supports for railroad tracks. 4. an equal score.

tier (tēr) *n.* a row, usu. one of a number rising like steps, esp. of seats in an amphitheater or stadium: *there were empty seats in the upper tiers.*

ti·ger ('tīgər) *n.* a large fierce animal of the cat family, found in India and Asia, but is now becoming rare. It has a golden hide with black stripes. '**ti·gress** *n.* a female tiger.

tight (tīt) *adj.* 1. fixed or gripped closely: *the bottle was sealed with a tight cork.* 2. (of knots) difficult to unfasten. 3. stretched; taut: *a tight wire.* 4. (informal) stingy 5. difficult: *a tight situation.* '**tight·en** *vb.* to make or become tight or tighter. **tights** *pl.n.* closely-fitting garment for the feet, legs, and lower part of the body. —'**tight·ly** *adv.* —'**tight·ness** *n.*

tight·rope ('tītrōp) *n.* a rope on which acrobats balance and perform tricks.

tile (tīl) *n.* 1. a piece of baked clay used as one of several for a roof covering. 2. a flat usu. square or oblong piece of baked clay, cork, plastic, etc., used for covering floors or walls. —*vb.* **til·ing, tiled.** to cover (a roof, wall, etc.) with tiles.

till (til) *n.* the box or cash register in which money is kept in a shop.

tilt (tilt) *vb.* to have or cause to have a leaning position, neither flat nor upright: *he tilted the tray so that the cups slid off.* —*n.* a sloping or leaning position.

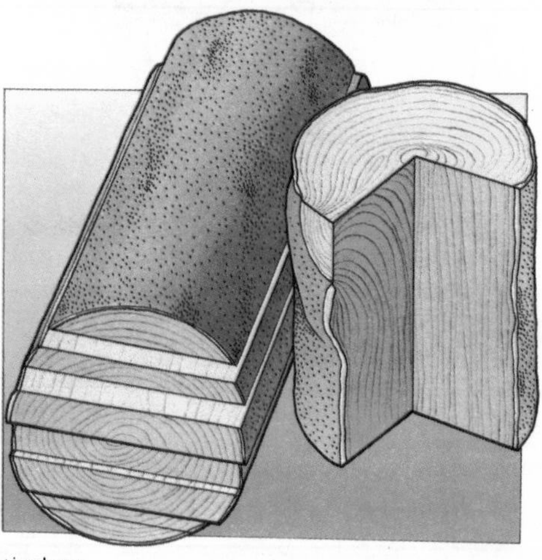

timber

tim·ber ('timbər) *n.* 1. standing trees as in a forest. 2. trees cut down and shaped, or ready to be shaped, into beams, planks, etc., for use in building and carpentry. 3. a large thick length of wood in a building.

time·ta·ble ('tīmtābəl) *n.* a list showing the times at which things are scheduled to happen, e.g. the arrival and departure of trains, etc.

tim·id ('timid) *adj.* easily frightened; lacking self-confidence or courage: *as timid as a mouse.* —**ti'mid·i·ty** *n.* —'**tim·id·ly** *adv.*

tin (tin) *n.* 1. a soft silvery-white metal. Chemical symbol: Sn. 2. anything made of tin: *a tobacco tin.* —*vb.* **tin·ning, tinned.** to cover or plate (another metal) with tin.

tin·gle ('tinggəl) *vb.* **tin·gling, tin·gled.** to have a slight stinging feeling in the skin: *Julie's skin tingled when she came in out of the cold.* —*n.* a stinging feeling.

tink·er ('tingkər) *vb.* (+ *with*) to try to repair or improve (something) without expert knowledge: *Stanley tinkers with his motorcycle almost every weekend.* —*n.* a person who travels around selling and mending pots and pans.

tint (tint) *n.* a shade or color, esp. a pale shade. —*vb.* to give a slight color to (something): *she tinted her hair red.*

tip[1] (tip) *n.* 1. the narrow or pointed end of something: *the tips of your fingers.* 2. a small piece put on the end of something else: *a filter tip on a cigarette.* —*vb.* **tip·ping, tipped.** to put a tip on (something).

tip[2] (tip) *vb.* **tip·ping, tipped.** (often + *up* or *over*) to tilt or cause to tilt, esp. to start a falling or sliding movement: *I tipped over the glass of wine and spilled it.*

tip[3] (tip) *n.* 1. a small gift of money to a waiter, taxi-driver, etc. 2. a piece of useful information often given as a secret: *she gave me some tips about how to cook.* —*vb.* **tip·ping, tipped.** 1. to give (somebody) a small sum of money, esp. as an extra reward for service, e.g. in a restaurant. 2. (often + *off*) to give a warning or advice to (somebody): *the police were tipped off about the robbery.*

tire[1] (tīər) *vb.* **tir·ing, tired.** 1. to make or become weary. 2. to make or become uninterested: *I'm tired of your chatter.* **'tire·some** *adj.* wearying —**'tired·ness** *n.* —**'tire·less** *adj.*

tire[2] (tiər) *n.* the outer ring of rubber, usu. hollow and filled with air, fitted around the outside of a wheel, e.g. of a car, bicycle, etc.

tis·sue ('tishoo) *n.* 1. a thin light cloth or fine delicate paper; a piece of this. 2. a group of CELLs (def. 2) of a particular nature forming part of an animal or plant, e.g. muscular tissue, nervous tissue.

ti·tle ('tītəl) *n.* 1. the name of a book, movie, etc. 2. a word put in front of a person's name to show rank, e.g. *Professor* or *Sir.*

toad

toad (tōd) *n.* an animal like a frog that spends most of its time on land and has a cold dry warty skin.

toad·stool ('tōdstōōl) *n.* an umbrella-shaped FUNGUS. Some kinds of toadstool look like mushrooms but are poisonous.

toast (tōst) *n.* 1. sliced bread browned by heat. 2. a public expression of good wishes confirmed by drinking a glass of wine, beer, etc.: *he proposed a toast to the winner.* —*vb.* 1. to heat (bread slices) until brown. 2. to wish (somebody) well by making a toast (def. 2).

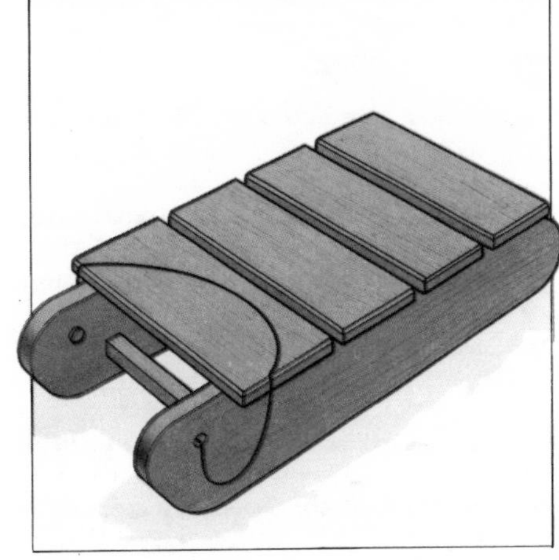

toboggan

to·bac·co (tə'bakō) *n.,pl.* **to·bac·cos** *or* **to·bac·coes.** dried leaves of the tobacco plant, smoked in cigarettes, cigars, and pipes. **to·bac·co·nist** (tə'bakənist) *n.* a person who sells tobacco, cigarettes, etc.

to·bog·gan (tə'bogən) *n.* a sled, sometimes with a curved forward end, used for sliding down snow-covered slopes, usu. as a sport. —*vb.* to slide over snow on a toboggan.

toe (tō) *n.* 1. one of the five digits at the front end of the foot. 2. the part of a sock, shoe, etc., covering the toes.

toil (toil) *vb.* to work very hard or make a great effort. —*n.* hard work.

toi·let ('toilit) *n.* a bowl, usu. of porcelain, provided with a seat and plumbing to flush away bodily wastes.

to·ken ('tōkən) *n.* 1. a proof or sign of something: *the orchid was a a token of his affection.* 2. a metal disk used instead of money: *bus tokens.*

tol·er·ate ('tolərāt) *vb.* **tol·er·at·ing, tol·er·at·ed.** to allow or put up with (something) without protest: *my parents tolerated the noise of the neighbor's radio.* **'tol·er·ance** *or* **tol·er'a·tion** *n.* ability to tolerate other people's behavior, opinions, etc. **'tol·er·ant** *adj.* possessing tolerance. **'tol·er·a·ble** *adj.* 1. bearable; able to be tolerated. 2. moderately good: *they gave a tolerable performance.* —**'tol·er·a·bly** *adv.* —**'tol·er·ant·ly** *adv.*

toll[1] (tōl) *vb.* (of a bell) to ring or cause to ring slowly and steadily. —*n.* the sound of a bell rung in this way.

toll[2] (tōl) *n.* 1. a payment for the use of a road, bridge, etc. 2. cost in loss or damage: *colds take a heavy toll of workers in winter.*

to·ma·to (tə'mātō) *n.,pl.* **to·ma·toes.** 1. a soft juicy red fruit used in salads. 2. the plant on which this fruit grows.

tomb (tōōm) *n.* the place dug in the ground or built to house a dead person's body.

ton (tun) *n.* a measure of weight equal to 2000 pounds.

tone (tōn) *n.* 1. a sound, esp. referring to its quality. 2. a degree or shade of color, light, etc. 3. the interval between one note of the musical scale and the next. —*vb.* **ton·ing, toned.** 1. to give a particular tone of color or sound to. 2. (+ *in with* or *with*) (of colors) to blend or be in harmony.

tongs (tongz) *pl.n.* a scissor-like household device for gripping and lifting a lump of sugar, a piece of coal, etc.

tongue (tung) *n.* 1. the muscular movable piece of flesh attached to the bottom of the mouth and used for tasting, licking, and, by humans, also for speaking. 2. a language: *the French tongue.* 3. anything shaped like a tongue: *the tongue of a bell.*

ton·ic ('tonik) *n.* 1. a medicine to restore one's strength. 2. anything that encourages and gives strength: *the vacation was a real tonic after her illness.* 3. an effervescent, slightly bitter drink.

ton·sil ('tonsəl) *n.* one of two lumps of spongy flesh on either side of the inner wall of the throat. **ton·sil·li·tis** (tonsi'lītis) *n.* a painful inflammation of the tonsils.

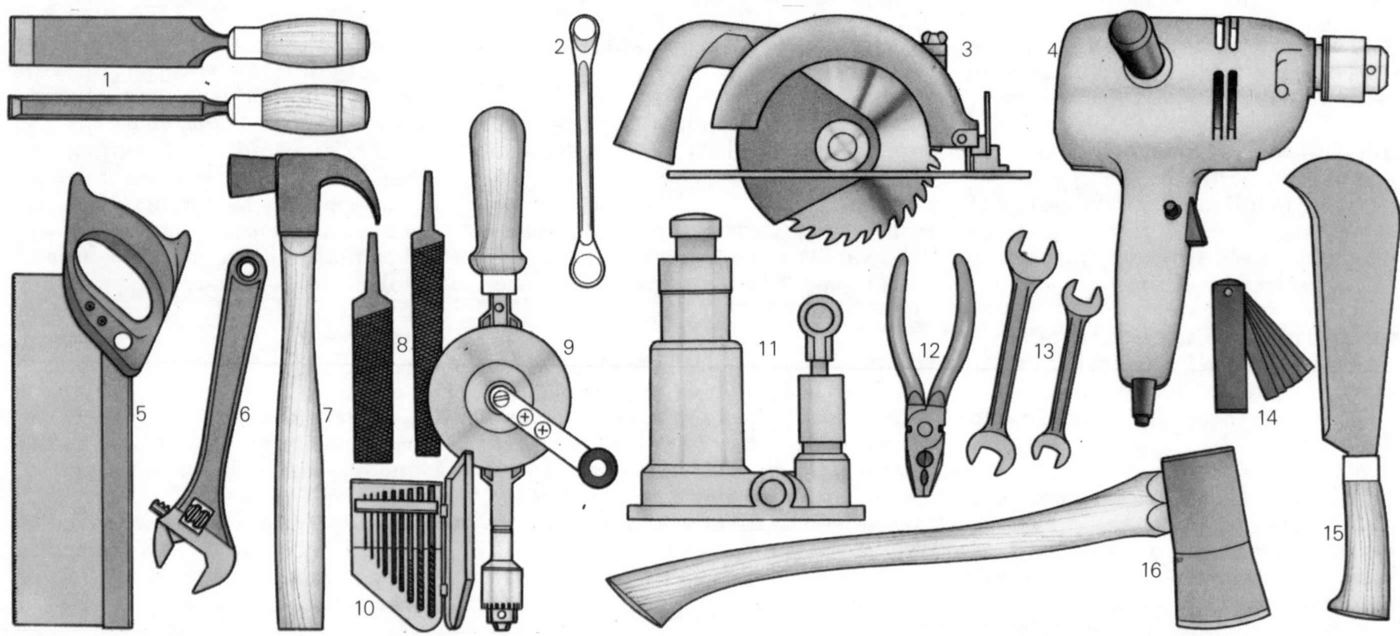

tools 1 chisels; 2 long-box wrench; 3 circular saw; 4 electric drill; 5 tenon saw; 6 monkey wrench; 7 claw hammer; 8 files; 9 hand drill; 10 drill bits; 11 hydraulic jack; 12 pliers; 13 open-ended wrenches; 14 feeler gauge; 15 billhook; 16 ax.

tool (to͞ol) *n.* an instrument used by people to do a job of work.

tooth (to͞oth) *n.,pl.* **teeth.** 1. one of the small hard white structures in the jaws used for biting and chewing food. 2. any small sharp object jutting out like a tooth: *the teeth of a comb.*

top·ic ('topik) *n.* a subject for discussion, an essay, a speech, etc. '**top·i·cal** *adj.* having interest because connected with current affairs.

torch (tôrch) *n.* a piece of wood or other material with one end soaked in oil and set on fire to give a light.

tore (tôr) *vb.* the past tense of TEAR[1].

torn (tôrn) *vb.* the past participle of TEAR[1].

tor·na·do (tôr'nādō) *n.,pl.* **tor·na·does.** a violent destructive whirling wind in the form of a narrow funnel, usu. traveling at high speeds.

tor·pe·do (tôr'pēdō) *n.,pl.* **tor·pe·does.** a self-propelled long metal shell packed with explosives and released at ships to blow them up. —*vb.* to attack with a torpedo.

tor·rent ('tôrənt, 'torənt) *n.* 1. a violent rush of water. 2. any violent flow: *a torrent of complaints.* —**tor·ren·tial** (tə'renshəl) *adj.*

tor·toise ('tôrtəs) *n.* a four-legged slow-moving REPTILE that lives on land and has a hard shell on its back.

tor·ture ('tôrchər) *vb.* **tor·tur·ing, tor·tured.** to cause (somebody) great pain, esp. in order to get information. —*n.* 1. the action of causing great pain. 2. something that causes great pain.

to·tal ('tōtəl) *n.* the complete sum or amount. —*adj.* complete. —*vb.* to add up to; amount to. '**to·tal·ly** *adv.* completely.

touch (tuch) *vb.* 1. to put one's hand lightly on. 2. to be in contact with: *the curtains touch the floor.* 3. to affect (somebody's feelings): *his story touched me.* —*n.* 1. an act of touching. 2. the sensation given by touching.

tough (tuf) *adj.* 1. not easily damaged or worn out. 2. (of meat) not easily chewed. 3. (of people) strong; having great endurance. 4. (of work) difficult. '**tough·en** *vb.* to make tough or tougher.

tour (to͝or) *n.* a journey during which one visits several places. —*vb.* to make a tour. —'**tour·ist** *n.*

tour·na·ment ('to͝ornəmənt) *n.* an organized series of games between different players.

tow (tō) *vb.* to pull (a boat, car, trailer, etc.) along, esp. by a rope or chain. —*n.* the act of towing.

tow·el ('touəl) *n.* a piece of cloth or paper used for drying something.

tow·er ('touər) *n.* 1. a tall building. 2. a part of a building that is much taller than the rest. —*vb.* to be very tall.

town (toun) *n.* 1. a group of houses and

torpedo

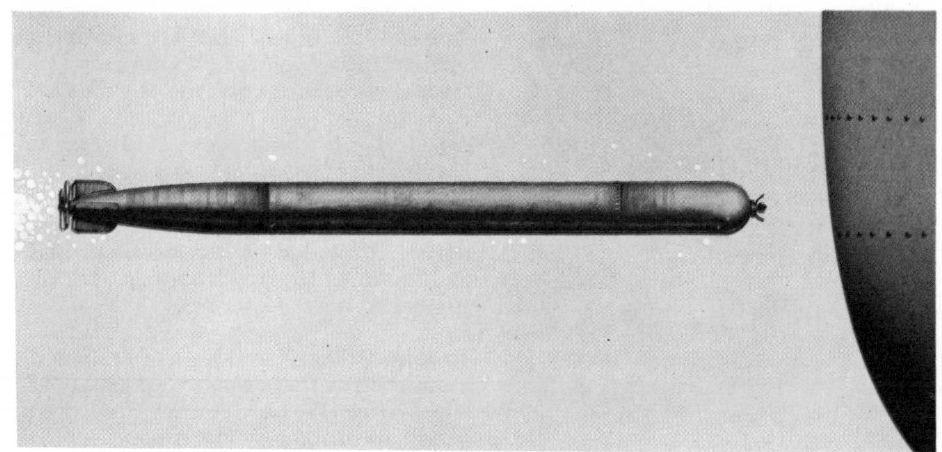

other buildings larger than a village with many people living in it. 2. the people of a town.

tox·ic ('toksik) *adj.* poisonous.

trace (trās) *vb.* **trac·ing, traced.** 1. to copy (a drawing, map, etc.) by marking the outline on transparent paper. 2. to follow or discover (somebody or something) by following small bits of evidence: *the police eventually traced him to Paris.* —*n.* 1. a mark or sign made by something that has been present. 2. a very small amount: *there was a slight trace of garlic in the casserole.*

track (trak) *n.* 1. a series of marks left by somebody or something moving along. 2. a path made by constant use. 3. a set of rails or a specially prepared course: *a railroad track.* —*vb.* to pursue (somebody or something) by following the marks or traces left.

tractor

trac·tor ('traktər) *n.* a powerful motor vehicle used esp. by farmers for pulling heavy loads, plows, etc.

trade (trād) *n.* 1. the business of buying and selling goods. 2. a way of earning a living, esp. by skilled work in industry. 3. the people involved in a particular trade (def. 2). —*vb.* **trad·ing, trad·ed.** to buy, sell, or exchange (goods). **'trad·er** *n.* a person who trades. **'trades·man** *n.,pl.* **trades·men.** a storekeeper.

trade·mark ('trādmârk) *n.* a special design or name that a company puts on its goods to identify them.

traf·fic ('trafik) *n.* 1. movement of people and vehicles along roads and railroads; movement of aircraft in and out of airports. 2. trading, often illegally: *the traffic in drugs.* —*vb.* **traf·fick·ing, traf·ficked.** to trade.

trag·e·dy ('trajidē) *n.,pl.* **trag·e·dies.** 1. a serious stage play with a sad ending. 2. a sad event in real life. **'trag·ic** *adj.* 1. of a sad play or plays. 2. of a sad event. —**'trag·i·cal·ly** *adv.*

trail (trāl) *n.* 1. a line of marks, footprints, etc., left by a person or animal. 2. a path, usu. through rough country. —*vb.* 1. to pull or be pulled along after. 2. to walk wearily. 3. (of plants, hair, etc.) to grow along the ground or over a surface. **'trail·er** *n.* 1. a boxlike vehicle pulled along by another, esp. a house on wheels designed to be pulled by a motor vehicle. 2. a series of extracts from a movie shown in advance to advertise it.

train[1] (trān) *n.* 1. a line of railroad cars connected to an engine. 2. a number of people, animals, etc., moving along in a line. 3. several connected ideas or events. 4. the part of a long formal dress or cloak that trails on the ground behind the wearer.

train[2] (trān) *vb.* 1. to prepare (a child, soldier, animal, etc.) for a particular purpose by instruction and practice. 2. to make a plant grow in a particular direction. **'train·er** *n.* a person who trains sportsmen, animals, etc.

trai·tor ('trātər) *n.* a person who is disloyal to a friend, his country, etc.

tramp (tramp) *vb.* 1. to walk heavily. 2. to walk a long way, esp. over rough ground. —*n.* 1. a person who walks from place to place and has no home or regular job; a bum. 2. the sound of heavy footsteps. 3. a long walk.

tram·po·line ('trampəlēn) *n.* a sheet of strong canvas supported in a frame by strong springs, used to enable acrobats, gymnasts, etc., to jump high into the air.

trampoline

trance (trans) *n.* a half-conscious state in which a person seems to be asleep but is able to carry out some actions.

tran·quil ('trangkwil) *adj.* peaceful; quiet. **'tran·quil·ize** *vb.* **tran·quil·iz·ing, tran·quil·ized.** to make calm or calmer. —**tran'quil·li·ty** *n.*

trans·fer *vb.* (trans'fûr, 'transfər) **trans·fer·ring, trans·ferred.** 1. to take (something) from one place to another. 2. to hand over (property) to someone else, esp. in a legal sense. —*n.* ('transfər) 1. a move from one place to another. 2. a person or thing transferred.

trans·form (trans'fôrm) *vb.* to alter completely (the appearance or nature of something). **trans'form·er** *n.* an electrical apparatus for changing electric current from one voltage to another. —**trans·for'ma·tion** *n.*

trans·fu·sion (trans'fyo͞ozhən) *n.* the transfer of blood given by a donor into another person.

tran·sis·tor (tran'zistər) *n.* 1. a very small device for controlling the power of an electric current. 2. a small radio using such devices.

trans·late (tranz'lāt) *vb.* **trans·lat·ing, trans·lat·ed.** to change words in one language into words of another. —**trans'la·tion** *n.*

trans·mit (tranz'mit) *vb.* **trans·mit·ting, trans·mit·ted.** 1. to send or pass on: *many diseases are transmitted by flies.* 2. to broadcast by radio or television. **trans'mit·ter** *n.* 1. something that sends or passes something on. 2. a device for sending out radio or TV broadcasts. —**trans'mis·sion** *n.*

trans·par·ent (trans'peərənt, trans'parənt) *adj.* 1. able to be seen through. 2. clear. **trans'par·en·cy** *n.,pl.* **trans·par·en·cies.** a transparent photograph or piece of photographic film.

trans·plant *vb.* (trans'plant) 1. to take (a living plant) from one place and plant it in another. 2. to replace a diseased part of the body with a healthy one. —*n.* ('transplant) an operation to remove and replace a diseased part of the body.

trans·port *vb.* (trans'pôrt) to carry (people, goods, etc.) from one place to another. —*n.* ('transpôrt) a vehicle, ship, or aircraft used for transporting.

trap (trap) *n.* 1. a device for catching (something). 2. a trick to put somebody in a difficult position or to force him to do something against his wishes. —*vb.* **trap·ping, trapped.** to catch (something) in a trap.

trav·el ('travəl) *vb.* 1. to make journeys, esp. long ones. 2. to move over a distance: *news travels fast.* —*n.* the experience of making long journeys: *they say that travel broadens the mind.* —**'trav·el·er** *n.*

trawl·er ('trôlər) *n.* a fishing boat that tows a trawl net. **trawl** *vb.* to fish with a trawl. —*n.* 1. *also* **trawl net.** a large baglike net used for fishing. 2. *also* **trawl line.** a long fishing line having many shorter lines with baited hooks attached to them.

treach·er·ous ('trechərəs) *adj.* 1. disloyal; not to be trusted; liable to betray. 2. dangerous; having concealed hazards.

tread (tred) *vb.* **tread·ing, trod, trod·den.** 1. to walk. 2. to crush down or push in with the feet. —*n.* 1. the manner or sound of walking. 2. the level part or step of a stair. 3. the patterned part of a rubber tire that runs on the road.

trea·son ('trēzən) *n.* the betrayal of one's country or ruler; disloyalty. **'trea·son·a·ble** *adj.* disloyal.

treas·ure ('trezhər) *n.* 1. a store of precious things, e.g. jewels, gold; wealth. 2. any highly valued person or thing: *an efficient secretary is a treasure.* —*vb.* **treas·ur·ing, treas·ured.** 1. to value highly. 2. (+ *up*) to store for future use. **'treas·ur·er** *n.* a person in charge of money for a society, company, etc. **'treas·ur·y** *n.,pl.* **treas·ur·ies.** 1. the government department handling a country's money. 2. any building where treasures are kept.

treat (trēt) *vb.* 1. to behave toward (someone or something) in a particular way: *she treated him kindly.* 2. to give medical attention to. 3. to supply (someone) with food, drink, or entertainment at one's own expense. 4. to put something through a process, esp. in industry: *the metal was treated with polish to give it a shine.* —*n.* an enjoyable event, esp. one that is unexpected or not often experienced. —**'treat·ment** *n.*

trea·ty ('trētē) *n.,pl.* **trea·ties.** a formal agreement made between nations.

tre·ble ('trebəl) *vb.* **tre·bling, tre·bled.** to make or become three times as much. —*n., adj.* three times as much or as many; three-fold.

trem·ble ('trembəl) *vb.* **trem·bling, trem·bled.** to shake or shiver, esp. because of cold, excitement, anger, etc. —*n.* a shaking or shivering.

tre·men·dous (tri'mendəs) *adj.* 1. very great; powerful: *a tremendous gust of wind blew the tree over.* 2. (informal) excellent; first rate. —**tre'men·dous·ly** *adv.*

trem·or ('tremər) *n.* a slight shaking movement lasting only a short time.

trend (trend) *n.* a particular direction or inclination: *there has been an upward trend in prices recently.*

tres·pass ('trespəs) *vb.* (often + *on* or *upon*) 1. to go or be upon private land without right or permission. 2. to intrude: *business trespasses upon my leisure time.*

trawler

trestle

tres·tle ('tresəl) *n.* 1. a bar with four legs used as a support. 2. a horizontal beam used to support a bridge or other structure.

tri·al ('trīəl) *vb.* 1. a test to find out whether something is suitable, useful, etc. 2. an examination of facts in a court of law. 3. a nuisance: *working on Saturdays is a great trial.*

tri·an·gle ('trīanggəl) *n.* 1. a plane figure having three sides and three angles. See GEOMETRY. 2. a musical instrument made of a metal rod bent into the shape of a triangle. —**tri·an·gu·lar** (trī'anggyələr) *adj.*

tribe (trīb) *n.* a group of people made up of many families that share the same language and customs, esp. in a primitive society. —**'trib·al** *adj.*

trib·u·tar·y ('tribyəterē) *n.,pl.* **trib·u·tar·ies.** a river that flows into a larger river.

trib·ute ('tribyo͞ot) *n.* 1. (in history) a regular payment made by a tribe or small state to its ruler: *many tribes paid tribute to Rome.* 2. something done or said to show respect, gratitude, etc.

trick (trik) *n.* 1. something done to cheat or fool somebody: *he escaped from prison by a trick.* 2. a skillful or clever act: *the magician performs tricks.* 3. a piece of mischief; joke. —*vb.* to cheat or fool. **'trick·y** *adj.* **trick·i·er, trick·i·est.** full of problems; needing careful handling. —**'trick·er·y** *n.* —**'trick·ster** *n.*

trick·le ('trikəl) *vb.* **trick·ling, trick·led.** to flow or cause to flow slowly or drop by drop: *tears trickled down the child's cheeks.* —*n.* a slow-flowing thin stream.

tri·cy·cle ('trīsikəl) *n.* a vehicle like a BICYCLE but with one wheel in front and two behind, often used by little children before they learn to ride a bicycle.

tri·fle ('trīfəl) *n.* 1. a thing or happening of little importance or value. 2. (informal) a small amount, esp. of money. —*vb.* **tri·fling, tri·fled.** 1. to act or talk idly. 2. (+ *with*) to play with. '**tri·fling** *adj.* unimportant.

trig·ger ('trigər) *n.* the small lever that works on a spring and is pulled to fire a gun, pistol, etc. —*vb.* to start (something) suddenly and violently: *the news of the disaster triggered a panic.*

trig·o·nom·e·try (trigə'nomitrē) *n.* the branch of mathematics that deals with triangles, and the relationship between their angles and sides.

trim (trim) *vb.* **trim·ming, trimmed.** 1. to make (something) tidy by cutting away uneven or overgrown parts: *he trimmed the hedge.* 2. to decorate (a hat, a cake, etc.). —*adj.* **trim·mer, trim·mest.** neat. —*n.* 1. (informal) a haircut. 2. an ornament or decoration.

tri·o ('trēō) *n.,pl.* **tri·os.** 1. a group of three. 2. a piece of music to be played by three players.

tri·ple ('tripəl) *adj.* made up of three parts. —*vb.* **tri·pling, tri·pled.** to make or become three times as much or many.

tri·plet ('triplit) *n.* one of a set of three, esp. one of three babies born to one mother at the same time.

tri·pod ('trīpod) *n.* a three-legged support, esp. for a camera.

tri·umph ('trīumf) *n.* 1. a great success or victory. 2. the joy caused by a success: *a feeling of triumph.* —*vb.* to win or succeed.

trod (trod) *vb.* the past tense of TREAD.

trol·ley ('trolē) *n.* a bus-like vehicle, powered by electricity and running on rails, used as a form of transportation, esp. in cities; a trolley car.

trom·bone (trom'bōn) *n.* a brass musical instrument, having a movable U-shaped tube that the player moves to produce different notes.

troop (trōōp) *n.* 1. a group of people or animals usu. moving or doing something together: *a troop of baboons.* 2. **troops** (*pl.*) soldiers. —*vb.* to move in a troop. '**troop·er** *n.* 1. a soldier in a CAVALRY regiment. 2. a policeman who rides a horse or motorcycle. 3. a policeman who is part of a statewide police force (**state trooper**).

tro·phy ('trōfē) *n.,pl.* **tro·phies.** something given as an award, esp. in sport.

trop·ic ('tropik) *n.* the line of latitude 23°27′ north (**Tropic of Cancer**) or south (**Tropic of Capricorn**) of the Equator. See GLOBE. **the tropics** the hot part of the world between these lines. —'**trop·i·cal** *adj.*

trot (trot) *vb.* **trot·ting, trot·ted.** 1. (of animals) to move at a pace faster than a walk but slower than a canter. 2. (of people) to move briskly or run, usu. with short steps. —*n.* the pace of an animal faster than a walk.

trou·ble ('trubəl) *vb.* **trou·bling, trou·bled.** 1. to have or cause to have worry, pain, inconvenience, etc.: *his headache was troubling him.* 2. to cause (someone) to make a particular effort: *may I trouble you for the jam?* —*n.* 1. a difficult or worrying person or situation. 2. an extra effort.

trough (trôf, trof) *n.* a long narrow open box-like container, esp. one from which animals eat or drink.

trout (trout) *n.,pl.* **trout.** a freshwater fish prized for food and for the sport it provides for those who try to catch it with a rod and line.

trow·el ('trouəl) *n.* 1. a small flat-bladed tool used by builders for spreading mortar, plaster, etc. 2. a tool with a scoop-shaped blade used by gardeners. See IMPLEMENT.

trombone

truce (trōōs) *n.* 1. an agreed pause in fighting. 2. the agreement made between enemies to stop fighting for a stated period.

truck (truk) *n.* 1. a large motor vehicle for transporting goods. 2. a small wheeled vehicle used for moving light loads (**hand truck**). —*vb.* to move (goods) by truck.

true (trōō) *adj.* **tru·er, tru·est.** 1. agreeing with facts; not false 2. real; genuine: *she is a true friend.* 3. correct: *a true portrait.* '**tru·ly** *adv.* 1. truthfully. 2. sincerely. 3. certainly: *her visit was truly a great surprise.*

trum·pet ('trumpit) *n.* 1. a brass musical instrument consisting of a tube with a mouthpiece at one end and a bell-like flare at the other. 2. a sound like that of a trumpet.

trunk (trungk) *n.* 1. the main woody stem of a tree. 2. the main part of a body excluding the head and limbs. 3. a large box for holding one's belongings, esp. when traveling. 4. an elephant's nose. 5. the compartment for baggage in an automobile.

trust (trust) *vb.* 1. to believe or have faith in: *I trusted his promises.* 2. to give (something) to someone to be kept safely; entrust. —*n.* 1. belief; confidence: *he put his trust in the doctor.* 2. an arrangement under which property or money is looked after for someone else's benefit.

truth (trōōth) *n.,pl.* **truths** (trōōdhz). 1. the quality of being true or honest. 2. something that is true: *are you telling the truth?* '**truth·ful** *adj.* 1. (of persons) always telling the truth. 2. giving a true account of the facts.

try (trī) *vb.* **try·ing, tried.** 1. to make an attempt to do something. 2. to test: *he tried the car's brakes.* 3. to examine in a court of law. 4. to put a strain on: *the noise tried her nerves.* '**try·ing** *adj.* causing strain or annoyance.

tube (tōōb, tyōōb) *n.* a hollow piece of rubber, metal, plastic, etc.

tuck (tuk) *vb.* 1. (+ *in*) to fold or put the edges of (something) in place: *he tucked in his shirt.* 2. (+ *away* or *under*) to put (something) in a safe or covered place. 3. (+ *in*) to put to bed.

tug (tug) *vb.* **tug·ging, tugged.** to pull hard. —*n.* 1. a sudden hard pull. 2. a small powerful boat used to help move other boats, esp. in a harbor.

tulip

tu·lip ('to͞olip, 'tyo͞olip) *n.* a cup-shaped flower, often brightly colored, that grows from a bulb.

tum·ble ('tumbəl) *vb.* **tum·bling, tum·bled.** 1. to fall in a clumsy way. 2. to do acrobatic tricks. —*n.* a fall. '**tum·bler** *n.* 1. a large cylindrical drinking glass. 2. an acrobat.

tu·mor ('to͞omər, 'tyo͞omər) *n.* a diseased swelling or lump growing in a part of the body.

tu·mult ('to͞omult, 'tyo͞omult) *n.* 1. an uproar: *the appearance of the rock band caused a tumult in the crowded hall.* 2. agitation; very great excitement. **tu'mul·tu·ous** *adj.* violently disturbed or noisy.

tune (to͞on, tyo͞on) *n.* a series of notes that make up the melody in a piece of music. **in tune** (music) in correct pitch. —*vb.* **tun·ing, tuned.** to put or bring into tune. '**tune·ful** *adj.* having an attractive tune.

tun·nel ('tunəl) *n.* an underground passage. —*vb.* to make an underground passage.

tur·ban ('tûrbən) *n.* a headdress made of a long strip of cloth wound around the head, worn esp. by men in India and Arab countries.

tur·bine ('tûrbīn) *n.* an engine that is driven by a stream of water, steam, etc., hitting against the blades of a wheel and forcing it to go around.

tur·bu·lent ('tûrbyələnt) *adj.* rough or violent. —'**tur·bu·lence** *n.* —'**tur·bu·lent·ly** *adj.*

turf (tûrf) *n.* 1. the surface of the soil with grass growing on it. 2. a piece of this used to make a lawn.

tur·key ('tûrkē) *n.* a large white or brown bird that is raised for food. Turkeys make a gobbling noise and the male birds have fan-shaped tails.

tur·moil ('tûrmoil) *n.* great confusion; uproar.

tur·nip ('tûrnip) *n.* a plant with a round white or yellow root that is used for food.

turn·stile ('tûrnstīl) *n.* a gate or bar fixed at an entrance or an exit, e.g. to a football stadium, in such a way as to let only one person through at a time.

tur·pen·tine ('tûrpəntīn) *n.* an oily, strong-smelling liquid used to mix oil-base paints.

tur·quoise ('tûrkwoiz) *n.* a greenish-blue precious stone. —*adj., n.* (having) the color of a turquoise.

tur·ret ('tûrit, 'turit) *n.* 1. a small tower on a building, usu. at a corner. 2. a structure on which guns are placed in a warship, tank, etc.

tur·tle ('tûrtəl) *n.* a REPTILE with a flat body protected by a hard shell. Turtles live in the sea, in fresh water, and on land.

tusk (tusk) *n.* a long pointed tooth sticking out of the mouth of certain animals, e.g. walrus, elephant.

tu·tor ('to͞otər, 'tyo͞otər) *n.* a teacher, esp. one who gives private lessons. —*vb.* to teach privately. —**tu·to·ri·al** (to͞o'tôrēəl, tyo͞o'tôrēəl) *adj.*

tweed (twēd) *n.* a heavy woolen cloth, usu. woven with several colors of wool.

tweez·ers ('twēzərz) *pl.n.* a small pair of pincers used to pick up or grasp very small things: *eyebrow tweezers.*

typewriter

twi·light ('twīlīt) *n.* 1. the dim hazy light from the sun soon after sunset or just before sunrise. 2. the time of the day when this light is in the sky, esp. early evening.

twin (twin) *n.* one of a set of two, esp. one of two children born to one mother at the same time. —*adj.* of, concerning, or being a a twin.

twine (twīn) *vb.* **twin·ing, twined.** to twist or wind: *the rambling rose twined around the old tree.* —*n.* strong string made of strands twisted together.

twinge (twinj) *n.* a sudden sharp pain: *a twinge of toothache.*

twin·kle ('twiṅgkəl) *vb.* **twin·kling, twin·kled.** to shine with a flickering light: *the stars seem to twinkle.* —*n.* 1. an unsteady light. 2. a sparkle.

twirl (twûrl) *vb.* to turn or cause to turn around quickly; spin.

twist (twist) *vb.* 1. to wind or turn (something) around another object: *they twisted the rope around the post.* 2. to turn (something) sharply: *I twisted my ankle.* 3. to curve or turn in different directions: *the path twisted through the hills.* 4. to change the meaning of (something): *she twisted my words to make Tom believe that I was angry with him.* —*n.* 1. the act of twisting. 2. something made by twisting: *a twist of tobacco.* 3. an injury caused by twisting.

twitch (twich) *n.* 1. a quick nervous movement. 2. a sudden pull or jerk. —*vb.* to make a quick or nervous movement.

type (tīp) *n.* 1. a class or group of things that are in some ways the same: *what type of music do you like?* 2. raised letters made on small metal blocks and used for printing. —*vb.* **typ·ing, typed.** to use a typewriter.

type·writ·er ('tīprītər) *n.* a machine for printing letters on paper.

ty·phoon (tī'fo͞on) *n.* a violent storm with strong winds, occurring particularly over the western Pacific Ocean.

typ·i·cal ('tipikəl) *adj.* having the qualities or characteristics of a certain type: *a typical cat hates water.* —'**typ·i·cal·ly** *adv.*

typ·ist ('tīpist) *n.* a person who uses a typewriter, esp. in an office.

U

ud·der ('udər) *n.* the baglike part of the body of certain female animals, e.g. cow, goat, in which milk is produced.

ug·ly ('uglē) *adj.* **ug·li·er, ug·li·est.** 1. unpleasant in appearance. 2. troublesome, rough, or threatening: *ugly weather.* —'**ug·li·ness** *n.*

ul·cer ('ulsər) *n.* an open sore, esp. in the stomach or mouth or on the skin.

ul·ti·mate ('ultəmit) *adj.* 1. being or coming at the end; latest or last: *the ultimate result.* 2. unable to be bettered: *the ultimate weapon.*

ul·ti·ma·tum (ultə'mātəm) *n.* a final demand or order that must be agreed to or obeyed.

ul·tra·vi·o·let (ultrə'vīələt) *adj.* (of light waves) too short to be seen by the human eye; found below violet in the visible color SPECTRUM.

um·brel·la (um'brelə) *n.* a circular or dome-shaped shade made of cloth, etc., stretched over a light collapsible frame, and used for shelter from the rain or sun.

um·pire ('umpīər) *n.* 1. a referee or judge in a game, esp. baseball or tennis. 2. a judge in an argument, dispute, etc. —*vb.* **um·pir·ing, um·pir·ed.** to act as an umpire.

umbrella

u·nan·i·mous (yo͞o'nanəməs) *adj.* agreed to or accepted by everyone: *the vote against his idea was unanimous.* **u·na·nim·i·ty** (yo͞onə'nimitē) *n.* full agreement. —**u'nan·i·mous·ly** *adv.*

un·a·ware (unə'weər) *adj.* not knowing or realizing. **un·a'wares** *adv.* unexpectedly; by surprise: *he crept up behind her and caught her unawares.*

un·can·ny (un'kanē) *adj.* strange or odd; unusually good: *Tom has an uncanny talent as a detective.* —**un'can·ni·ly** *adv.*

un·con·scious (un'konshəs) *adj.* 1. not conscious; not aware of any sensations, etc.: *the blow knocked him unconscious.* 2. done or said without full awareness: *Mary had an unconscious habit of scratching her head when thinking.* —**un'con·scious·ly** *adv.* —**un'con·scious·ness** *n.*

un·couth (un'ko͞oth) *adj.* clumsy or awkward in manners or behavior.

un·der·dog ('undərdôg, 'undərdog) *n.* 1. the weaker person or side in a competition, fight, etc., that is expected to lose. 2. a person who is ignored or continually ill-treated by others.

un·der·go (undər'gō) *vb.* **un·der·go·ing, un·der·went, un·der·gone.** to experience, endure, or be put through (a test, difficulties, etc.).

un·der·grad·u·ate (undər'grajo͞oit) *n.* a college or university student studying for his or her first degree.

un·der·ground ('undərground) *adv.* 1. beneath the ground. 2. in or into hiding or secrecy. —*adj.* 1. used or situated underground. 2. secret; not public because unlawful or against established custom. —*n.* a secret group or organization, esp. a revolutionary one.

un·der·growth ('undərgrōth) *n.* small bushes or trees growing among larger trees, as in a jungle.

un·der·hand ('undərhand) *adj.* sly, cunning, or secretive. —*adv.* slyly; secretly.

un·der·line ('undərlīn) *vb.* **un·der·lin·ing, un·der·lined.** 1. to draw or mark a line underneath (a word, sentence, etc.). 2. to emphasize or indicate the importance of (a point in an argument): *the President banged on the table to underline the most important points of his speech.*

un·der·mine (undər'mīn) *vb.* **un·der·min·ing, un·der·mined.** 1. to weaken (a building, wall, etc.) by digging tunnels underneath it. 2. to weaken (a person's authority, spirit, etc.), esp. by secret methods.

un·der·neath (undər'nēth) *prep.* beneath; in a lower position than; under. —*adv.* in a lower position; beneath. —*n.* the lowest part of something; base.

un·der·stand (undər'stand) *vb.* **un·der·stand·ing, un·der·stood.** 1. to know or realize the meaning of: *I understand German.* 2. to learn or accept (something)as a fact: *I understand that he arrives tomorrow morning.* **un·der'stand·ing** *n.* the ability to realize the meaning of something. —**un·der'stand·a·ble** *adj.* —**un·der'stand·a·bly** *adv.*

un·der·stud·y ('undərstudē) *n.,pl.* **un·der·stud·ies.** an actor or actress who learns another's part in order to take over if the other is unable to perform.

un·der·take (undər'tāk) *vb.* **un·der·tak·ing, un·der·took, un·der·tak·en.** 1. to agree or promise (something or to do something): *we undertake to get you there on time.* 2. to take on (a job, etc.): *why did you undertake such a difficult duty?* '**un·der·tak·er** *n.* a person who prepares dead bodies for burial, makes coffins, etc. '**un·der·tak·ing** *n.* a job; task.

un·der·tone ('undərtōn) *n.* 1. a quiet voice: *he spoke to her in an undertone.* 2. a hint or suspicion: *there was an* *intense undertone of sadness in her words*

un·der·world ('undərwûrld) *n.* 1. (in many ancient beliefs) the place to which the souls of the dead are taken. 2. the world of criminals: *the police used their contacts in the underworld to help them solve a big crime.* —*adj.* connected with the world of criminals.

un·der·writ·er ('undərrītər) *n.* a person who insures ships, cars, houses, etc., and pays out money if there is a loss.

un·do (un'doo) *vb.* **un·do·ing, un·did, un·done.** 1. to untie or unfasten (clothing, shoelaces, etc.). 2. to spoil or ruin (what has already been done): *this mistake has undone all my good work.* **un'do·ing** *n.* the cause of one's ruin or misery: *drink was his undoing.* **un'done** *adj.* ruined; finished.

un·doubt·ed (un'doutid) *adj.* accepted or undisputed: *Carolyn is the undoubted champion at table tennis.* —**un'doubt·ed·ly** *adj.*

un·due ('undoo, 'undyoo) *adj.* more than is usual, suitable, or necessary: *he had no undue worries about his exams as he had worked hard all year.* —**un'du·ly** *adv.*

un·du·late ('unjəlāt) *vb.* **un·du·lat·ing, un·du·lat·ed.** to go up and down like waves on the sea; to move in waves: *the snake undulated across the floor.* —**un·du'la·tion** *n.*

un·earth (un'ûrth) *vb.* 1. to dig up, out of the ground: *he unearthed a Roman vase.* 2. to discover: *he unearthed a valuable picture amongst the junk in his attic.*

un·earth·ly (un'ûrthlē) *adj.* unnatural; frightening: *the dog gave an unearthly howl in the night.*

un·eas·y (un'ēzē) *adj.* worried or disturbed in one's mind. —**un'eas·i·ly** *adv.* —**un'eas·i·ness** *n.*

un·e·ven (un'ēvən) *adj.* not even; not level, balanced, or smooth: *the game was uneven as one team was a man short.* —**un'e·ven·ly** *adv.*

un·fit (un'fit) *adj.* not fit; not suitable or healthy.

un·fold (un'fōld) *vb.* 1. to open something (cloth, paper, etc.) that has been folded up. 2. to make or become known; tell or be told: *he unfolded his story to the police.*

un·for·tu·nate (un'fôrchənit) *adj.* 1. not successful or lucky: *it was unfortunate that he lost the race.* 2. in misery or poverty. 3. ill-timed; not properly thought about: *John's unfortunate comment upset his mother.*

un·found·ed (un'foundid) *adj.* without foundation in fact: *the reports of his intention to leave town were completely unfounded.*

un·gain·ly (un'gānlē) *adj.* awkward or clumsy; not graceful: *Mary has an ungainly way of walking.*

un·gu·late ('unggyəlit) *n.* an animal that has hooves, such as a horse.

u·ni·corn ('yoonəkôrn) *n.* a legendary animal resembling a horse and having a single horn growing out of the middle of its forehead.

unicorn

u·ni·form ('yoonəfôrm) *adj.* never different; unchanging, equal, etc. —*n.* official clothing worn by policemen, soldiers, nurses, etc.

u·ni·fy ('yoonəfī) *vb.* **u·ni·fy·ing, u·ni·fied.** unite; make into a single whole or unit.

un·ion ('yoonyən) *n.* 1. the state or result of being joined. 2. a group or association organized for a particular purpose, esp. a labor union. —**'un·ion·ism** *n.* —**'un·ion·ist** *n.*

u·nique (yoo'nēk) *adj.* completely unlike anything else; being the only one of its kind: *an elephant's trunk is unique among animals.* —**u'nique·ly** *adv.* —**u'nique·ness** *n.*

u·ni·son ('yoonisən) *n.* harmony agreement. **in unison** 1. together; in agreement. 2. (of two musical parts) using or performing the same notes.

u·nit ('yoonit) *n.* 1. a single person or thing or a number of people or things considered as a single group: *an army unit.* 2. a fixed quantity used as the basis of measuring length, weight, etc.: *the meter is a unit of length.* 3. piece of equipment: *a kitchen unit.* 4. the number one (1).

u·nite (yoo'nīt) *vb.* **u·nit·ing, u·nit·ed.** to join or be joined together; make into or become a unit. —**u·ni·ty** ('yoonitē) *n.* the state of being one or in agreement.

u·ni·verse ('yoonəvûrs) *n.* all that exists; the entire total of all things. **u·ni'vers·al** *adj.* existing or occurring everywhere.

u·ni·ver·si·ty (yoonə'vûrsitē) *n.,pl.* **u·ni·ver·si·ties.** a place of education to which students go after leaving secondary school in order to obtain a degree.

un·kempt (un'kempt) *adj.* rough or dirty; having untidy hair and an unshaven face.

un·rav·el (un'ravəl) *vb.* 1. to cause (threads of cloth, etc.) to separate, or (of cloth threads) to be separated. 2. to solve or work out (a difficult problem): *he unraveled the mystery.*

un·known (un'nōn) *adj.* not known; strange or unfamiliar. —*n.* something or somewhere that is not familiar.

un·rest (un'rest) *n.* discontentment, esp. when it leads to violence or other disturbance.

un·rul·y (un'roolē) *adj.* badly behaved; rowdy.

un·told (un'tōld) *adj.* 1. not told or made known. 2. uncounted or uncountable: *there were untold numbers of bison in the herd.*

un·wield·y (un'wēldē) *adj.* difficult to handle, use, etc.; awkward; clumsy. —**un'wield·i·ness** *n.*

up·bring·ing ('upbringing) *n.* the care and education of a child as he or she is growing up.

up·heav·al (up'hēvəl) *n.* a complete, often violent, change or disturbance.

urn

up·hold (up'hōld) *vb.* **up·hold·ing, up·held.** to support; keep; preserve: *the job of the police is to uphold the law.*

up·hol·ster·y (up'hōlstərē) *n.* the cushions, padding, and coverings used in sofas, armchairs, car seats, etc. **up'hol·ster** *vb.* to provide (furniture) with upholstery.

up·keep ('upkēp) *n.* 1. the act of keeping a house, car, etc., in good order. 2. the cost of doing this.

up·right ('uprīt) *adj.* 1. vertical. 2. morally correct; honest: *an upright person.* —*adv.* vertically: *stand upright.* —*n.* something standing vertically, e.g. a pillar.

up·ris·ing ('uprīziŋ) *n.* an armed rebellion; revolution: *many people were killed in the Hungarian uprising.*

up·roar ('uprôr) *n.* noisy shouting, as of a crowd of people. **up'roar·i·ous** *adj.* noisily happy: *we had an uproarious time at John's party last night.* —**up'roar·i·ous·ly** *adv.* —**up'roar·i·ous·ness** *n.*

up·set *vb.* (up'set) **up·set·ting, up·set.** 1. knock over; spill. 2. to make (someone) sad or angry. —*n.* ('upset) a surprise, esp. an unpleasant one; shock: *her arrival caused an upset.*

up·shot ('upshot) *n.* the result (of something): *the upshot of his stopping to eat on the journey was that he arrived late.*

u·ra·ni·um (yə'rānēəm) *n.* a heavy metallic radioactive chemical element used in producing NUCLEAR power. Chemical symbol: U.

ur·chin ('ûrchin) *n.* a naughty child, esp. a ragged little boy. **sea urchin** a small sea animal with a round spiked shell.

urge (ûrj) *vb.* **urg·ing, urged.** to encourage someone to do something: *he was urged to continue his studies by his parents.* —*n.* 1. a strong form of encouragement. 2. an instinct or compulsion: *he felt an urge to run away.*

ur·gent ('ûrjənt) *adj.* requiring haste; pressing; needing immediate attention. —**'ur·gen·cy** *n., pl.* **ur·gen·cies.**

u·rine (yə'rin) *n.* the liquid waste matter excreted from the BLADDER. See also KIDNEY.

urn (ûrn) *n.* 1. a large container for plants. 2. a tall narrow-necked container in which the ashes of a dead person are placed. 3. a tall metal container for hot tea or coffee.

use *vb.* (yōōz) **us·ing, used.** 1. to apply; employ; utilize. 2. (often + *up*) finish; exhaust the supply of: *I've used all of the sugar.* 3. to treat (a person) in a certain way, esp. to take advantage of him. —*n.* (yōōs) 1. service or employment. 2. purpose; point: *there's no use worrying.* 3. function: *of what use is a black window?* 4. the act of using or state of being used. **use·ful** ('yōōsfəl) *adj.* helpful; having value: *a nail is useful for hanging a picture.* **use·less** ('yōōslis) *adj.* worthless; having no purpose, value, or effect.

ush·er ('ushər) *n.* a person who shows people to their seats in a theater or church. **ush·er'ette** *n.* a woman who acts as an usher in a theater. —*vb.* to act as an usher.

u·su·al ('yōōzhōōəl) *adj.* normal; typical; common. —*n.* something that is normal or customary. —**'u·su·al·ly** *adv.*

u·surp (yōō'sûrp) *vb.* to take over (a throne, kingdom, etc.) unlawfully, esp. by force: *Tim usurped the form captain's authority.* —**u·sur'pa·tion** *n.*

u·ten·sil (yōō'tensəl) *n.* a useful object, esp. an article used in the kitchen.

utensils: 1 mixing bowl; 2 whisk; 3 kitchen tools; 4 can opener; 5 scales; 6 roasting pan; 7 bun tin.

u·til·i·ty (yōō'tilitē) *n.,pl.* **u·til·i·ties.** 1. usefulness. 2. something employed by many people; a public service: *the water supply is a public utility.* **u·ti·lize** ('yōōtəlīz) *vb.* **u·ti·liz·ing, u·ti·lized.** to use.

ut·most ('utmōst) *adj.* 1. the greatest, highest, most serious, etc.: *handle those glasses with the utmost care.* 2. the furthest: *from the utmost regions of the north.* —*n.* the most, greatest, best, furthest, etc.

ut·ter[1] ('utər) *vb.* 1. to make (a sound): *she uttered a fearful cry.* 2. to speak: *never utter her name again.* **'ut·ter·ance** *n.* something spoken.

ut·ter[2] ('utər) *adj.* complete; absolute: *you utter fool!* —**'ut·ter·ly** *adv.*

V

va·cant ('vākənt) *adj.* 1. not occupied; empty. 2. (of a job, etc.) waiting to be filled or taken on: *the secretary's job is vacant.* 3. uninterested or stupid: *a vacant stare.* **'va·can·cy** *n.,pl.* **va·can·cies.** 1. the state of being vacant. 2. a vacant job, room, etc. —**'va·cant·ly** *adv.*

va·ca·tion (vā'kāshən) *n.* 1. a period of rest or freedom, e.g. from work or school. 2. a period during which universities, courts of law, etc., are closed.

vac·ci·nate ('vaksənāt) *vb.* **vac·ci·nat·ing, vac·ci·nat·ed.** to inject into (a patient) the modified form of a virus in order to build up his resistance against a disease. **vac·cine** (vak'sēn) *n.* the modified form of a virus injected in this way. —**vac·ci'na·tion** *n.*

vac·u·um ('vakyooəm) *n.* a complete absence of air or any other gas; emptiness: *outer space is almost a vacuum.* **vacuum cleaner** a household appliance for removing dust from carpets, etc., by suction.

vag·a·bond ('vagəbond) *n.* a person, e.g. a tramp or a tinker, who wanders from place to place without a settled home.

va·grant ('vāgrənt) *n.* a beggar or tramp with no settled home; vagabond. —*adj.* of, like, or living as a vagrant.

vague (vāg) *adj.* 1. uncertain; indefinite. 2. unclear in one's thoughts or words: *his instructions were so vague that we couldn't follow them.*

vain (vān) *adj.* 1. conceited or proud, esp. about one's appearance, character, etc. 2. having no value, use, or success: *John made a vain attempt to roller-skate, but he could never keep his balance.* —**'vain·ly** *adv.*

val·id ('valid) *adj.* 1. lawful: *a valid document.* 2. strong or convincing: *valid reasons.* —**va·lid·i·ty** (və'liditē) *n.* —**'val·id·ly** *adv.*

val·ley ('valē) *n.* 1. a long narrow piece of low-lying land running between hills or mountains. 2. anything resembling a valley.

val·or ('valər) *n.* bravery or courage. —**'val·or·ous** *adj.*

val·ue ('valyoo) *n.* 1. usefulness or importance: *the value of travel is that it broadens the mind.* 2. the worth of something, as measured in money, etc.: *the value of this painting is* $500. —*vb.* **val·u·ing, val·ued.** 1. to think highly of. 2. to work out the value of (something) in money. **'val·u·a·ble** *adj.* of great value, esp. worth a lot of money: *this painting is valuable.*

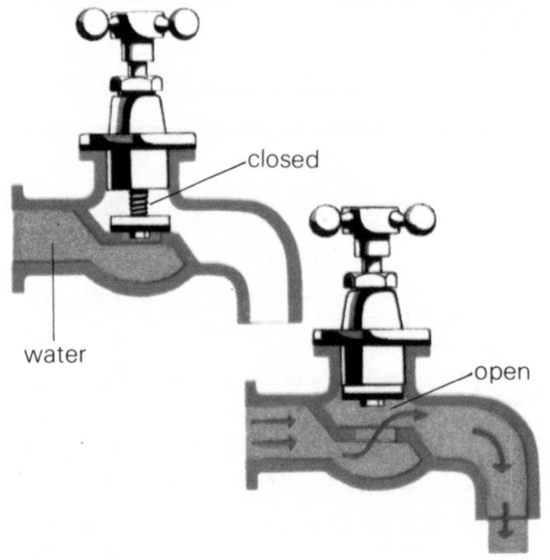

valve

valve (valv) *n.* 1. a piece of equipment that can be opened or closed to control the flow of a liquid or gas. 2. an organ, esp. in the HEART, controlling the flow of blood.

vam·pire ('vampīər) *n.* 1. (in legend) a corpse that comes to life at night and sucks the blood of sleeping persons. 2. any of several different species of bat, some of which feed on blood.

van·dal ('vandəl) *n.* a person who willfully destroys something, esp. for no reason.

vane (vān) *n.* 1. one of the blades of a propeller or other machine. 2. (also **weather vane**) a movable flat metal object mounted on the roof of a building in such a way as to show the direction of the wind.

va·nil·la (və'nilə) *n.* a substance used in food-flavoring, perfume, etc., obtained from the beanlike fruit (**vanilla beans**) of a tropical orchid.

van·ish ('vanish) *vb.* to become invisible; disappear.

van·i·ty ('vanitē) *n.,pl.* **van·i·ties.** 1. the quality of being vain about oneself; conceit or excessive pride. 2. something that one is conceited about.

van·quish ('vangkwish) *vb.* to conquer; be victorious over.

va·por ('vāpər) *n.* matter in a cloudlike, misty, or gaseous form. **'va·por·ize** *vb.* **va·por·iz·ing, va·por·ized.** to become or cause to become vapor. —**'va·por·ous** *adj.*

va·ri·e·ty (və'rīitē) *n.,pl.* **va·ri·e·ties.** 1. the quality of not always being the same; variation. 2. a type or kind: *there are several varieties of pony in this country.* 3. a varying collection: *we sell a variety of cars.* **var·i·ous** ('veərēəs) *adj.* several or different: *we have various animals for sale.*

var·nish ('vârnish) *n.* a liquid substance that, when dry, produces a hard shiny transparent surface upon wood, metal, etc. —*vb.* to put varnish on.

var·y ('veərē) *vb.* **var·y·ing, var·ied.** to be or cause to be different; change or alter. **var·i'a·tion** *n.* a change or the result of a change. **'var·ied** *adj.* not equally or always the same; showing change or variation.

vase (vāz, vâz) *n.* a container made of glass or pottery, usu. a tall one used for holding flowers.

vast (vast) *adj.* of enormous size, proportions, degree, etc.; huge: *a vast amount of money.*

vehicles

vault[1] (vôlt) *n.* 1. a great curved arch forming a roof over a hall, etc. 2. an underground or strongly protected room in which money or other valuable things are stored. 3. a room sometimes attached to a church where coffins containing the dead are kept.

vault[2] (vôlt) *vb.* to leap or jump, esp. to spring over (a high fence, bar, etc.) with one's hands resting on something or with the aid of a long pole. —*n.* the action or an instance of vaulting.

veer (vēr) *vb.* 1. (esp. of the wind) to change direction. 2. to turn suddenly off course: *the car veered off the road into a ditch.*

veg·e·ta·ble ('vejtəbəl) *n.* any of numerous plants whose fruits, leaves, seeds, etc., are used for food. —*adj.* of or like a plant or vegetable.

veg·e·tar·i·an (veji'teərēən) *n.* a person who does not eat meat or fish.

veg·e·ta·tion (veji'tāshən) *n.* plants collectively, esp. the plants of a certain area.

ve·hi·cle ('vēikəl) *n.* 1. a cart, car, bus, or other wheeled object used for transport on land. 2. any means for carrying people or goods: *a space vehicle.*

veil (vāl) *n.* a piece of material, usu. thin or delicate, used esp. by women as a covering for the face. —*vb.* to cover with or put on a veil.

vein (vān) *n.* 1. one of the vessels in the body through which blood flows back to the HEART. 2. a layer, streak of color, etc., appearing in something and resembling a vein: *a vein of silver in rock.* 3. a mood: *music in a sad vein.*

ve·loc·i·ty (və'lositē) *n., pl.* **ve·loc·i·ties.** 1. the speed or rate of motion of an object. 2. rapidity or swiftness.

vel·vet ('velvit) *n.* a type of cloth, usu. cotton or silk, having a thick soft pile.

ve·neer (və'nēr) *n.* 1. a thin layer of fine quality wood glued onto a surface to give it a pleasant appearance. 2. an outwardly pleasant appearance: *his veneer of charm hid an unpleasant personality.* —*vb.* to put a veneer on.

ven·geance ('venjəns) *n.* injury or suffering caused to someone as a punishment for a past wrong.

ven·om ('venəm) *n.* 1. poison, esp. the poison of a snake or other animal. 2. something having an effect resembling that of poison; malice: *he spoke of his enemy with venom.*

vent (vent) *n.* 1. an opening in something allowing the escape of air, smoke, etc. 2. an opening in the back of a coat or jacket. —*vb.* to express (an emotion): *to vent one's anger.*

ven·ti·late ('ventəlāt) *vb.* **ven·ti·lat·ing, ven·ti·lat·ed.** to pass fresh air through (a room, etc.). —**ven·ti'la·tion** *n.* —**'ven·ti·la·tor** *n.*

ven·tril·o·quist (ven'triləkwist) *n.* an entertainer able to speak without moving his lips, thus making his voice appear to come from somewhere else, usu. through the mouth of a dummy. —**ven'tril·o·quism** *n.*

ven·ture ('venchər) *n.* a job or task involving risk or uncertainty. —*vb.* **ven·tur·ing, ven·tured.** 1. to put at risk; endanger. 2. to go forward without worrying about possible dangers: *the explorer ventured into the jungle.*

ve·ran·da *or* **ve·ran·dah** (və'randə) *n.* a roofed, partially enclosed section built onto a house; porch.

verb (vûrb) *n.* a word belonging to a certain class of words in a language that express an action, e.g. *run* and *hit.*

ver·bal ('vûrbəl) *adj.* 1. of or connected with words, esp. the spoken rather than the written word; oral: *a verbal agreement.* 2. of or concerning verbs.

ver·bose (vûr'bōs) *adj.* containing or using too many words; wordy. —**ver·bos·i·ty** (vûr'bositē) *n.*

ver·dict ('vûrdikt) *n.* 1. a decision about the correct way to treat someone, made on the basis of evidence, as by a jury in a law court. 2. a judgment about something.

verge (vûrj) *n.* the edge of something. —*vb.* **verg·ing, verged.** (usu. + *on* or *upon*) to border on; touch or come close to.

ver·mil·ion (vər'milyən) *n.* a bright scarlet or red color. —*adj.* of or having this color.

ver·min ('vûrmin) *pl.n.* rats, mice, and other small animals regarded as a nuisance to man or a danger to his health.

verse (vûrs) *n.* 1. a poem or poetry in general. 2. a line or group of lines in a poem. 3. a numbered section in a chapter from the Bible.

ver·sion ('vûrzhən) *n.* 1. an account of an event or situation given from a particular point of view: *we only heard his version of the story.* 2. a form of something different from the original form: *the film version of* Treasure Island.

ver·sus ('vûrsəs) *prep.* (esp. used in competitions) against: *John Brown versus Bill Smith.* Abbreviation: **v.,vs.**

ver·te·bra ('vûrtəbrə) *n.,pl.* **ver·te·brae** ('vûrtəbrā). any of the several bones that make up the backbone. **'ver·te·brate** *n.* an animal having a backbone. *adj.* of vertebrae or of an animal that has vertebrae.

ver·ti·cal ('vûrtikəl) *n.* extending upward in a straight line. —*n.* something vertical, such as a pillar.

ves·sel ('vesəl) *n.* 1. a container for liquid. 2. something resembling this: *a blood vessel.* 3. a boat or ship.

vestment

vest·ment ('vestmənt) *n.* one of the official garments worn by someone at a ceremony, esp. a priest in a church service.

ves·try ('vestrē) *n.,pl.* **ves·tries.** a room in a church in which a priest, members of the choir, etc., dress for a service or ceremony.

vet·er·an ('vetərən) *n.* 1. an experienced person. 2. a person who has served for a long time in the army, navy, or air force. —*adj.* having been in service or use for a long time: *a veteran car.*

vet·er·i·nar·y ('vetərənerē) *adj.* connected with the medical and surgical treatment of animals. **vet** *or* **veterinary surgeon** *n.* a person qualified to provide such treatment.

vex (veks) *vb.* to make angry or distressed; annoy or worry.

vi·a·duct ('vīədukt) *n.* a bridge supported by high arches and carrying a road or railway over a valley.

vi·brate ('vībrāt) *vb.* **vi·brat·ing, vi·brat·ed.** to move rapidly back and forth or up and down; shake: *the heavy traffic on the freeway caused the whole apartment to vibrate.* —**vi'bra·tion** *n.*

vic·ar ('vikər) *n.* a clergyman who acts as priest to a parish.

vice (vīs) *n.* 1. wickedness: *a life of vice.* 2. a bad habit: *drinking too much alcohol is a vice.*

vi·ce ver·sa ('vīsə 'vûrsə) the other way around: *Tony dislikes Mary and vice versa.*

vi·cin·i·ty (vi'sinitē) *n.,pl.* **vi·cin·i·ties.** the region near or surrounding a particular place; neighbourhood: *there are no theaters in the vicinity of our home.*

vi·cious ('vishəs) *adj.* cruel, spiteful, or wicked: *he has a vicious temper.*

vic·tim ('viktim) *n.* a person or animal who is killed, injured, or made to suffer by someone or something else: *he became a victim of a crippling disease.*

vic·to·ry ('viktərē) *n.,pl.* **vic·to·ries.** 1. the act or fact of conquering an opponent or enemy; conquest. 2. any triumph or success: *this is a victory for common sense.* **vic·tor** ('viktər) *n.* the winner of a victory; conqueror. —**vic·to·ri·ous** (vik'tôrēəs) *adj.*

view (vyōō) *n.* 1. the action of seeing or the ability to see: *our view was blocked by a car.* 2. the appearance to the eye of a landscape or other scene: *the view from my window was wonderful.* 3. an opinion: *what is your view on education?* —*vb.* 1. to look at or run the eye over. 2. to watch (a television program). 3. to consider, esp. in a particular way.

vig·il ('vijəl) *n.* an act of keeping watch or of staying awake, often done for religious or political reasons. **'vig·i·lance** *n.* watchfulness; awareness. —**'vig·i·lant** *adj.*

vig·or ('vigər) *n.* strength; force; energy: *the old man swam with surprising vigor.* —**'vig·or·ous** *adj.* —**'vig·or·ous·ly** *adv.*

vile (vīl) *adj.* **vil·er, vil·est.** 1. offensive or disgusting: *a vile smell.* 2. morally bad; worthless: *he's a vile fellow.* 3. thoroughly bad or unpleasant: *vile weather.* —**'vile·ly** *adv.* —**'vile·ness** *n.*

vil·lage ('vilij) *n.* a very small group of houses, stores, etc., usu. in a country area.

vil·lain ('vilən) *n.* an evil, cruel, or criminal person. —**'vil·lain·ous** *adj.* —**'vil·lain·ous·ly** *adv.* —**'vil·lain·y** *n.*

vine (vīn) *n.* 1. a creeping or climbing plant on which grapes grow. 2. a long branch or stem of such a plant.

vin·e·gar ('vinigər) *n.* a sour liquid, consisting of dilute acetic acid, made from wine, etc., and used to flavor or pickle food.

vin·tage ('vintij) *n.* 1. the time when grapes are picked for wine-making. 2. the wine made in a particular year: *the 1960 vintage.* —*adj.* 1. especially fine: *1960 was a vintage year.* 2. made in a good year or belonging to a good period in the past: *a vintage wine.*

vi·nyl ('vīnəl) *n.* a tough plastic used esp. in phonograph records and furnishings. —*adj.* made of vinyl.

vi·o·la (vē'ōlə) *n.* a stringed musical instrument of the violin family. It is slightly larger and deeper in pitch than the violin.

vi·o·late ('vīəlāt) *vb.* **vi·o·lat·ing, vi·o·lat·ed.** 1. to break (a treaty, rule, etc.). 2. to disturb or shatter (peace, a pleasant situation): *our quiet afternoon was violated by the noise of a drill.* —**vi·o'la·tion** *n.*

vi·o·lence ('vīələns) *n.* power or force, esp. that which causes destruction or injury. **'vi·o·lent** *adj.* using or involving violence.

vi·o·let ('vīəlit) *n.* 1. a little round-leaved creeping plant that grows wild and produces small purple, blue, or white flowers. 2. a purplish-blue color. —*adj.* having the color violet.

violin

vi·o·lin (vīə'lin) *n.* a four-stringed musical instrument usu. played with a bow. **vi·o'lin·ist** *n.* a person who plays the violin.

vine

vi·per ('vīpər) *n.* a poisonous snake found in Europe, Africa, and Asia.

vir·tue ('vûrchōō) *n.* 1. moral worth or quality; merit: *patience is a virtue.* 2. profit or advantage. **'vir·tu·ous** *adj.* morally good.

vi·rus ('vīrəs) *n.,pl.* **vi·rus·es.** a germ that is smaller than a bacterium and causes such diseases as influenza, chickenpox, mumps, and measles.

vi·sa ('vēzə) *n.* a stamp placed on someone's passport by an official from a certain country allowing the passport-holder free passage through the country, usu. for a limited period.

vise (vīs) *n.* a device consisting of two adjustable jawlike parts in which an object may be held steady while work is being done on it.

vis·i·ble ('vizəbəl) *adj.* able to be seen: *stars are visible at night.* **vis·i'bil·i·ty** *n.* 1. the ability to see. 2. the distance over which one can see: *fog cut visibility to forty yards.*

vi·sion ('vizhən) *n.* 1. sight. 2. a vivid dreamlike experience. 3. imagination: *a man of vision.*

vis·it ('vizit) *vb.* 1. to go to see or stay with someone for a short time, esp. to call upon (a friend). 2. to go to (a place) on business or vacation. —*n.* the act or an instance of visiting. —**'vis·i·tor** *n.*

vis·u·al ('vizhōōəl) *adj.* of, connected with, or involving vision. **'vis·u·al·ize** *vb.* **vis·u·al·iz·ing, vis·u·al·ized.** to create a picture of (someone or something) in one's mind. —**'vis·u·al·ly** *adv.*

vi·tal ('vītəl) *adj.* 1. connected with or necessary for life. 2. very important or urgent. **vi'tal·i·ty** *n.* freshness or liveliness. —**'vi·tal·ly** *adv.*

vi·ta·min ('vītəmin) *n.* any of a number of chemical substances present in various foods and necessary in small amounts for keeping a person alive and healthy.

vi·va·cious (vi'vāshəs) *adj.* lively and animated: *Bill and Carolyn were engaged in vivacious conversation.*

viv·id ('vivid) *adj.* 1. very bright: *scarlet is a vivid color.* 2. full of life; lively: *a vivid character.* 3. lifelike; believable: *a vivid dream.* 4. strong: *vivid feelings.*

vix·en ('viksən) *n.* a female FOX.

vo·cab·u·lar·y (vō'kabyəlerē) *n.,pl.* **vo·cab·u·lar·ies.** 1. the collection of all the words used in a language, sometimes arranged in alphabetical order to form a dictionary. 2. the number of words in a language known to and used by any person: *Mike's French vocabulary is very limited.*

vo·cal ('vōkəl) *adj.* of, connected with, or using the voice. —*n.* (informal) the part of a piece of music written to be sung. —**'vo·cal·ly** *adv.*

vo·cal·ize ('vōkəlīz) *vb.* **vo·cal·iz·ing, vo·cal·ized.** to express using the voice; make sounds with the voice. **vo·cal·i·za·tion** *n.* a sound or utterance produced by the voice.

vo·ca·tion (vō'kāshən) *n.* a type of work to which a person feels that he is called, esp. to serve others: *nursing was her vocation.* —**vo'ca·tion·al** *adj.*

vogue (vōg) *n.* 1. a fashion. 2. something that is popular for a short time.

voice (vois) *n.* 1. the sound or sounds made by a person in speaking, singing, shouting, etc.: *she has a beautiful singing voice.* 2. something similar to a voice in its effect or function: *the voice of reason.* 3. the right to express an opinion: *everyone should have a voice in the government.* —*vb.* **voic·ing, voiced.** to put (something) into words.

void (void) *adj.* having no force; not effective: *the law was declared void.* —*n.* space; emptiness.

vol·a·tile ('volətil, 'volətəl) *adj.* 1. (of a liquid) giving off a vapor. 2. behaving in a changeable way.

volcano

vol·ca·no (vol'kānō) *n.,pl.* **vol·ca·noes.** a mountain with a hole or crater in its top through which hot ash and melted rock (LAVA) are released from inside the earth.

vole (vōl) *n.* a small RODENT with a rounded head, usu. found in fields.

vol·ley ('volē) *n.* 1. a number of shots, arrows, etc., fired at the same moment. 2. (tennis) several exchanges of a ball across the net without it bouncing. 3. the act of striking a ball that has not bounced. —*vb.* (tennis) to engage in a volley.

volt (vōlt) *n.* a unit of electrical force; the electrical force needed to cause a current of one ampere to flow through a resistance of one ohm.

vol·ume ('volyo͞om) *n.* 1. the space taken up by something, measured in cubic units. 2. a book, esp. one of a series. 3. the strength of a sound; loudness. 4. an amount or quantity, esp. a large one.

vol·un·tar·y ('volənterē) *adj.* 1. willing; not forced or compelled: *diving into a pool is a voluntary action; accidently falling in is not.* 2. not controlled by the state; private: *a voluntary organization.* 3. controlled by one's own mind; deliberate: *a voluntary movement of the body.* **vol·un'teer** *n.* someone who does something without being asked. *adj.* of or connected with a volunteer. —**'vol·un·tar·i·ly** *adv.*

vom·it ('vomit) *vb.* to throw out (food, etc.) from the stomach through the mouth; throw up.

vote (vōt) *vb.* **vot·ing, vot·ed.** (often + *for*) to indicate one's opinion or choice, as at an election, etc. —*n.* 1. the act or a result of voting. 2. choice.

vouch (vouch) *vb.* (+ *for*) to declare or guarantee the truth, correctness, honesty, etc., of (someone or something). **'vouch·er** *n.* a paper showing that something is in order or guaranteeing a person's right to something.

vow (vou) *n.* a serious promise, often made to God or in God's name. —*vb.* to make a vow; promise.

vow·el ('vouəl) *n.* 1. a continuous speech sound in which the passage of breath through the mouth is not blocked. 2. a letter representing such a sound, e.g. *a, e, i, o, u,* or *y.* Compare CONSONANT.

voy·age ('voiij) *n.* a journey, esp. a long one, by ship. —*vb.* **voy·ag·ing, voy·aged.** to travel over the sea in a ship.

vul·gar ('vulgər) *adj.* 1. rude; offensive: *vulgar language.* 2. (old-fashioned) common; used by the public. —**vul'gar·i·ty** *n.*

vul·ner·a·ble ('vulnərəbəl) *adj.* helpless; unprotected from injury, attack, etc.: *Mary is very vulnerable to criticism.* —**vul·ner·a'bil·i·ty** *n.*

vul·ture ('vulchər) *n.* a large bird that feeds on dead animals.

vulture

W

wad (wod) *n.* 1. (also **wad·ding**) small mass of soft material used for plugging a hole or for packing. 2. a bundle of folded banknotes or papers. 3. (of money) a large amount.

wade (wād) *vb.* **wad·ing, wad·ed.** to walk through (water, snow, mud, etc.). **'wad·er** *n.* 1. a bird that wades in water. 2. a tall waterproof boot.

wa·fer ('wāfər) *n.* a very thin crisp cookie often sweetened and eaten with ice cream.

waft (woft) *vb.* to float or carry along upon or as if upon the air or water: *pleasant smells wafted in from the kitchen.* —*n.* something floating along on the air.

wag (wag) *vb.* **wag·ging, wagged.** to move or cause to move up and down or from side to side; shake or wave.

wage (wāj) *n.* often **wag·es** (*pl.*) the sum of money that a person receives in return for his work. —*vb.* **wag·ing, waged.** to fight (a war, battle, etc.).

wag·on ('wagən) *n.* 1. a large four-wheeled cart pulled by horses or oxen and now usu. used for carrying goods. 2. a small fourwheeled cart with a long handle used by children as a toy. **'wag·on·er** *n.* a person who drives a wagon.

wagon

wail (wāl) *n.* a long loud cry of sadness. —*vb.* to cry out sadly.

waist (wāst) *n.* 1. the middle part of the body, just above the hips. 2. the central narrowest part of something, such as a violin.

wait (wāt) *vb.* 1. (usu. + *for*) to keep oneself or be kept ready for (something expected or hoped for): *there's a message waiting for you.* 2. to do nothing until something expected happens: *we waited all day.* **'wait·er** *n.* a man who serves at a restaurant. **'wait·ress** *n.* a female waiter.

wake (wāk) *vb.* **wak·ing, woke, wok·en.** (often + *up*) 1. to come or bring out of a state of sleep. 2. to become or cause to become excited or aware.

walk (wôk) *vb.* (of people or certain animals) to move over land by means of the feet.

wal·la·by ('woləbē) *n., pl.* **wal·la·bies.** an Australian animal that is similar to a small kangaroo.

wal·let ('wolit) *n.* a small folding case used for carrying paper money, identification, etc.

wal·low ('wolō) *vb.* to roll or play around in mud, water, etc. —*n.* 1. the action or an instance of wallowing. 2. a place for wallowing.

wal·rus ('wôlrəs) *n.,pl.* **wal·rus·es.** a sea animal related to the seal and living in northern regions. It has flippers and a pair of long tusks.

walrus

waltz (wôlts) *n.* 1. a piece of dance music, having three beats in each bar. 2. the ballroom dance performed to this music. —*vb.* to dance a waltz.

wand (wond) *n.* a rod or stick used by a magician or, supposedly, by fairies.

wan·der ('wondər) *vb.* 1. to travel about with no real purpose. 2. to move away from the correct course, etc.: *we seem to have wandered away from the subject.*

wane (wān) *vb.* **wan·ing, waned.** (esp. of the moon) to get smaller or less: *his courage waned as the monster came nearer.* —*n.* the action of becoming smaller or less. Compare WAX².

war (wôr) *n.* 1. a fight or struggle using weapons, waged between two or more countries or groups within a country. 2. any fight: *the war against poverty.* —*vb.* **war·ring, warred.** to carry on a war.

war·ble ('wôrbəl) *vb.* **war·bling, war·bled.** (esp. of birds) to sing sweetly with a trill or fluttering sound. —*n.* 1. a song produced in this way. 2. the act of warbling.

war·bler ('wôblər) *n.* any of numerous small birds that sing with a warbling voice and often have bright colored plumage.

ward (wôrd) *n.* 1. a room in a hospital containing beds for a number of patients. 2. an administrative or political division of a town or city. 3. a person under the protection of someone else: *a ward of court.* —*vb.* (+ *off*) to drive or keep away; prevent from doing injury, etc. '**war·den** *n.* an official or person in charge of something: *a prison warden; a game warden.*

ward·robe ('wôrdrōb) *n.* 1. a tall cupboard for storing clothes. 2. all the clothes belonging to a person or a theatrical company.

ware·house ('weərhous) *n.* a building used for storing goods, material, etc.

warn (wôrn) *vb.* (often + *of*) to advise or inform (someone) that something is about to happen, esp. something dangerous, important, etc.

war·ren ('wôrən, 'worən) *n.* a system of tunnels and burrows occupied by a number of rabbits.

war·ri·or ('wôrēər, 'worēər) *n.* a person experienced in fighting, esp. in wars.

war·ship ('wôrship) *n.* a ship equipped with weapons and used in war.

wart (wôrt) *n.* a small fleshy lump on the skin.

war·y ('weərē) *adj.* **war·i·er, war·i·est.** on one's guard, alert, or cautious.

waterfall

wasp (wosp) *n.* a stinging insect having a very narrow waist and transparent wings.

waste (wāst) *vb.* **wast·ing, wast·ed.** 1. to use (something) unnecessarily, inefficiently, or carelessly, or to lose (something) by using too much of it: *they waste money on luxuries when they should be saving it.* 2. (often + *away*) to become or cause to become weak or thin: *his body was wasting away through lack of food.* 3. to destroy (land, homes, etc.). —*n.* 1. the action or an instance of wasting: *it's a waste of money.* 2. rubbish; garbage. —*adj.* of no more use: *waste paper.*

watch (woch) *vb.* 1. to look at. 2. to keep guard over. 3. to keep awake or vigilant. —*n.* 1. the action or an instance of watching. 2. a period of watching. 3. someone who watches, such as a guard. 4. a small device for measuring time, worn on the wrist or carried in a pocket. —'**watch·man** *n.,pl.* **watch·men.**

wa·ter ('wôtər, 'wotər) *n.* 1. the liquid that forms the seas, rivers, and lakes on the earth. Pure water is a colorless liquid having no smell or taste. 2. a body of water: *a boat was floating on the water.* 3. **wa·ters** (*pl.*) area of the sea: *the boat was in home waters.* —*vb.* 1. to put water on (flowers, plants, etc.). 2. to give water to (animals). '**wa·ter·y** *adj.* 1. of or containing water. 2. (of color) pale.

wa·ter·col·or ('wôtərkulər, 'wotərkulər) *n.* 1. paint that is soluble in water. 2. a picture painted in watercolors. —*adj.* of or connected with watercolors.

wa·ter·fall ('wôtərfôl, 'wotərfôl) *n.* a place in a river where there is a steep dip in the riverbed forming a cliff over which the flowing river pours.

wa·ter·logged ('wôtərlôgd, 'wôtərlogd, 'wotərlôgd, 'wotərlogd) *adj.* soaked through by water: *waterlogged earth.*

wa·ter·proof ('wôtərpro͞of, 'wotərpro͞of) *adj.* specially treated to allow no water to pass through: *a waterproof raincoat.* —*n.* a garment, etc., that is waterproof. —*vb.* to make (a coat, etc.) waterproof.

wa·ter·shed ('wôtərshed, 'wotərshed) *n.* 1. an area from which water is drained into a river, stream, etc. 2. a ridge dividing a drainage area.

watt (wot) *n.* a unit of electrical power; the amount of power produced by a current of one ampere flowing with the force of one VOLT.

wave (wāv) *n.* 1. a curving movement or ridge seen on the surface of a liquid, such as a lake or the sea. 2. anything resembling a wave in movement or shape: *her hair had beautiful waves in it.* 3. an up-and-down or sideways movement of the hand, a flag, etc. 4. a sudden rush: *a wave of fear overtook her.* 5. a short period: *a heat wave.* —*vb.* **wav·ing, waved.** to move or cause to move in waves or wavelike motions. —'**wav·y** *adj.* **wav·i·er, wav·i·est.**

wax[1] (waks) *n.* 1. (also **beeswax**) a substance produced by bees for building their honeycombs. 2. a similar substance produced from other things that is easy to shape and is used for candles, model-making, polishes, etc. 3. the yellow substance that collects in the ears. —*vb.* to cover with wax polish. —*adj.* made of or from wax: *a wax figure.* —'**wax·y** *adj.* **wax·i·er, wax·i·est.**

wax[2] (waks) *vb.* 1. (esp. of the moon) to get bigger or brighter. 2. to increase; become: *he waxed enthusiastic about the new idea.* Compare WANE.

weak (wēk) *adj.* 1. not strong; faint; feeble. 2. not good: *he needs extra teaching as his English is weak.* '**weak·en** *vb.* to make or become weak or weaker. '**weak·ling** *n.* a weak person. '**weak·ness** *n.* 1. the state of being weak. 2. some failure or defect: *a weakness in the glass caused the window to break.*

wealth (welth) *n.* 1. a great deal of money or valuable things; riches. 2. a large number or amount of something: *he had a wealth of reasons for not coming.*

weap·on ('wepən) *n.* an instrument or method used in fighting: *his sword was his most trusted weapon.*

wear (weər) *vb.* **wear·ing, wore, worn.** 1. to carry (clothes, etc.) on one's body. 2. to have or show: *he wore a frown.* 3. to damage or be damaged by continual use: *he wore a hole in his shoe.* 4. to last a long time despite being in continual use: *this carpet has worn well.* —*n.* 1. the act of wearing: *this shirt is suitable for casual wear.* 2. clothes: *children's wear.* 3. damage caused by continual use: *the furniture shows signs of wear.* 4. usefulness: *there's plenty of wear left in this old suit of mine.*

wea·ry ('wērē) *adj.* **wea·ri·er, wea·ri·est.** 1. tired; exhausted: *weary after a hard day's work.* 2. impatient: *I'm weary of your excuses.* —*vb.* **wea·ry·ing, wea·ried.** (often + *of*) to make or become weary.

wea·sel ('wēzəl) *n.* a small warm-blooded slim-bodied animal with short legs that feeds mainly on rabbits and other small animals.

weath·er ('wed͟hər) *n.* atmospheric conditions in a certain area and at a particular time: *the weather is warm.* —*vb.* 1. to be affected, changed, or worn by being left in the open air. 2. to come through safely: *we have weathered the crisis.*

weathervane

weath·er·vane ('wed͟hərvān) *n.* a device mounted to spin freely on a vertical axis to indicate the direction of the wind.

weave (wēv) *vb.* **weav·ing, wove, wo·ven.** 1. to make (cloth, etc.) by twisting or interlacing threads together. 2. to follow a winding course or path. —*n.* a pattern of weaving.

web (web) *n.* the netlike object of sticky thread spun by a spider to catch the insects on which it feeds.

wed (wed) *vb.* **wed·ding, wed·ded** *or* **wed.** 1. to marry. 2. to combine: *the composer wed beautiful music and beautiful words.* '**wed·ding** *n.* a ceremony at which a man and woman marry.

weed (wēd) *n.* a plant that is useless or unwanted. —*vb.* 1. to remove the weeds from (a garden). 2. (+ *out*) to remove unnecessary or harmful people or things: *the class soon settled down after he had weeded out the troublemakers.*

weep (wēp) *vb.* **weep·ing, wept.** to cry; shed tears.

weigh (wā) *vb.* 1. to measure the heaviness of (something). 2. to have a particular measurable heaviness: *the meat weighs two pounds.* 3. to consider carefully: *she weighed the advantages of his plan.* **weight** (wāt) *n.* 1. the heaviness of a person or thing, resulting from the pull of gravity upon him or it: *your weight is 100 pounds.* 2. a heavy object: *he used a stone as a weight to keep his papers from blowing about.* 3. a load or burden: *solving that problem has taken a weight off my mind.* 4. importance: *the chairman's opinions carry weight.* —'**weight·y** *adj.* '**weight·less** *adj.* having no apparent weight, e.g. a feather or an object or man in outer space. —'**weight·less·ly** *adv.* —'**weight·less·ness** *n.*

wel·come ('welkəm) *vb.* **wel·com·ing, wel·comed.** 1. to greet someone in a friendly manner. 2. to receive happily: *he welcomed the news of his son.* —*n.* the action of welcoming: *our friends gave us a marvelous welcome when we visited.*

wel·fare ('welfeər) *n.* 1. a person's state of health or happiness: *your parents are concerned about your welfare.* 2. money provided by the government to people who are ill, out of work, etc. 3. the department looking after this fund.

well[1] (wel) *adv.* **bet·ter, best.** 1. in a good way; satisfactorily: *he sings well.* 2. thoroughly; completely: *stir the mixture well.* 3. very much; considerably: *she looks well over 40.* —*adj.* healthy: *I hope you are well.* —*interj.* (used to begin a sentence or express surprise): *well, I haven't seen you for ages.*

well

well[2] (wel) *n.* a hole dug in the ground in order to obtain water, gas, or oil from beneath the earth.

wept (wept) *vb.* the past tense and past participle of WEEP.

west (west) *n.* 1. the direction in which one turns to see the sunset. 2. the 3art of a country lying in this direction. **the West** *n.* the part of the U.S. lying west of the Mississippi River. —*adj.* lying in or toward the west: *the west side of the street.* —*adv.* toward the west: *moving west.* '**west·ern** *adj.* of or in the west. *n.* a film, book, etc., dealing with cowboys, Indians, and early settlers in the western U.S.

whale (wāl, hwāl) *n.* a very large MAMMAL that lives in the sea and resembles a fish.

wheat (wēt, hwēt) *n.* a type of grass that produces grains from which flour is made.

wheel (wēl, hwēl) *n.* a circular disk that revolves on an axle fitted to a car, cart, etc., to allow it to move.

wheel

wheel·chair ('wēlcheər, 'hwēlcheər) *n.* a chair fitted with wheels for use by people who cannot walk.

whimper ('wimpər, 'hwimpər) *vb.* to cry with soft sobbing or weak sounds: *the dog whimpered because he wanted to go out.* —*n.* the sound of whimpering: *the child gave a whimper.*

whine (wīn, hwīn) *vb.* **whin·ing, whined.** to make complaining or miserable sounds; moan: *the dog was whining for its food.*

whip (wip, hwip) *n.* a flexible rod or leather strap with a handle used for punishment, for making horses go faster, etc. —*vb.* **whip·ping, whipped.** 1. to hit with a whip or rod. 2. to beat or stir (eggs, cream, etc.).

whirl (wûrl, hwûrl) *vb.* to spin or cause to spin rapidly: *the dancer whirled his partner around the room.* —*n.* a rapid spin or something like it, e.g. a confused state: *I'm in a whirl because of all the excitement.*

whirl·pool ('wûrlpōōl, 'hwûrlpōōl) *n.* a water current that spins quickly and sucks down to its center anything caught in it.

whirl·wind ('wûrlwind, 'hwûrlwind) *n.* a wind that causes a rapid circular motion in the air; hurricane or tornado.

whisk (wisk, hwisk) *n.* an instrument for beating eggs, cream, etc. —*vb.* to beat with a whisk.

whisk·er ('wiskər, 'hwiskər) *n.* usu. **whiskers** (*pl.*) 1. hair growing on a man's face as part of his mustache or beard. 2. one of the long hairs on the face of a cat or other animal.

whis·key ('wiskē, 'hwiskē) *n.* a very strong alcoholic drink made from corn or other grain.

whis·per ('wispər, 'hwispər) *vb.* to speak or talk very quietly. —*n.* a very quiet sound: *the whisper of the breeze.*

whis·tle ('wisəl, 'hwisəl) *vb.* **whis·tling, whis·tled.** to make a high, piercing sound, usu. by blowing air through puckered lips. —*n.* 1. a high-pitched sound made by or as if by whistling. 2. a device that produces such a sound when blown through.

white·wash ('wītwosh, 'wītwôsh, 'hwītwosh, 'hwītwôsh) *n.* a watery white paint used on walls, fences, etc. —*vb.* 1. to paint with whitewash. 2. (informal) to make (something or someone) appear in a favorable way: *the manager had whitewashed the job to impress the new employee.*

whole (hōl) *adj.* complete; total: *the whole bill comes to two dollars, although my share was only 95 cents.* —*n.* the complete or entire amount of something: *I offered him only a slice but he ate the whole cake.* —*adv.* in one; without being broken up: *the snake swallowed the egg whole.* '**whol·ly** *adv.* completely; totally: *she can't be wholly bad if she did a kind act.*

whole·heart·ed ('hōl'hârtid) *adj.* without holding anything back; complete: *you have our wholehearted agreement.* —'**whole'heart·ed·ly** *adv.*

whole·sale ('hōlsāl) *n.* the selling of goods in large quantities to shopkeepers who then sell (RETAIL) them to individual customers. —*adj.* in large amounts; considerable: *the earthquake caused wholesale destruction.* —*adv.* 1. by wholesale. 2. completely: *because he doesn't like me he dismissed my ideas wholesale.*

wick (wik) *n.* a piece of cotton, etc., in a candle, oil lamp, etc., through which the melted or liquid fuel is drawn up to be burnt.

wick·ed ('wikid) *adj.* 1. evil; not good in character: *the devil is wicked.* 2. naughty: *you wicked child!* 3. showing evil or naughtiness: *a wicked smile.* —'**wick·ed·ness** *n.*

wick·et ('wikit) *n.* a small door or gate.

wide (wīd) *adj.* **wid·er, wid·est.** 1. extending over a large area. 2. having a certain distance from one side to the other: *six feet wide.* 3. great; considerable: *a wide variety of articles.* —*adv.* 1. (also **far and wide**) over a large area. 2. as much as possible: *open your mouth wide.*

wid·ow ('widō) *n.* a woman whose husband has died. —*vb.* to make (someone) a widow. '**wid·ow·er** *n.* a man whose wife has died.

width (width) *n.* the distance of something measured from one side of it to the other; breadth.

wife (wīf) *n.,pl.* **wives.** a married woman.

wild (wīld) *adj.* 1. living or existing outside human control; natural: *wild animals.* 2. out of control; disorderly, untidy, etc.: *it was such a wild party that most of the glasses were broken.* —*adv.* without being controlled: *flowers growing wild.*

wil·der·ness ('wildərnis) *n.* an area of land showing no trace of human existence or control.

will (wil) *n.* 1. a person's wish, intention, or command, esp. as expressed in the legal document left by someone who has died. 2. control over one's own mind: *Luke has a strong will to win.* —*vb.* (used with infinitive to express intention or the future tense in English): *I will come tomorrow.* '**will·ful** *adj.* 1. obstinate or unmanageable. 2. intentional. —'**will·ful·ly** *adv.* —'**will·ful·ness** *n.*

will·ing ('wiliŋ) *adj.* agreeable; prepared: *I'm willing to come.* —'**will·ing·ly** *adv.* —'**will·ing·ness** *n.*

wil·low ('wilō) *n.* a tree with long, easily bent branches that are used for making wickerwork, etc.

willow

wind[1] (wind) *n.* 1. a current of moving air caused by temperature changes in the earth's atmosphere. 2. one's breath or energy: *the race took all the wind out of him.*

wind[2] (wīnd) *vb.* **wind·ing, wound** (wound). 1. to turn: *the boy winds the handle of the musical box.* 2. to wrap or roll up with a circular motion: *she wound the bandage around his finger.* 3. to twist along or follow a curving path: *the road wound up the hill.* 4. (often + *up*) to tighten the spring of (a clock or watch).

wind·fall ('windfôl) *n.* 1. a fruit or fruits blown from a tree by the wind. 2. something good, esp. a sum of money, that one obtains by chance, e.g. as an inheritance.

wind·mill ('windmil) *n.* a mill powered by the wind pushing against large blades or sails.

wind·pipe ('windpīp) *n.* the tubelike air passage in the body leading down from the throat to the lungs.

wind·shield ('windshēld) *n.* a protective pane of glass or clear plastic in the front of a car, etc., through which the driver views the road ahead.

wine (wīn) *n.* any of several different kinds of alcoholic drink made from the juice of grapes or other fruit, flowers, etc.

wing (wing) *n.* 1. any of the movable limbs of a bird, bat, or insect specially adapted for flying. 2. one of two structures situated on either side of an aircraft. 3. a side section of a house, stage, etc. —*vb.* to move by using wings; fly. '**wing·span** *n.* the distance between the two wing-tips of a bird or aircraft.

win·ter ('wintər) *n.* the coldest season of the year in the northern hemisphere, officially between December 22 and March 21. —*vb.* to spend the winter in a place.

wire (wīər) *n.* 1. a long thin strand of metal. 2. a telegram or cablegram. —*vb.* **wir·ing, wired.** 1. (often + *up*) to fit out with wires for carrying electricity: *my brother wired the house.* 2. to send a telegram. —*adj.* made of wire.

wise (wīz) *adj.* **wis·er, wis·est.** clever or sensible. **wis·dom** ('wizdəm) —*n.* 1. the condition of being wise. 2. cleverness or good sense.

wish (wish) *vb.* 1. (+ *for* or *to*) to need or desire greatly; want: *I wish to go out.* 2. to hope strongly for (something): *I wish I had more money.* —*n.* a need, hope, or desire: *what is your wish?*

wisp (wisp) *n.* a tiny or thin bit of something, usu. fragile or slight: *a wisp of smoke.*

wit (wit) *n.* 1. the ability to make clever or humorous remarks about something. 2. a person who does this. 3. often **wits** (*pl.*) sense or intelligence. —'**wit·ty** *adj.* **wit·ti·er, wit·ti·est.**

witch (wich) *n.* a woman supposed to have magic powers, esp. evil ones.

with·draw (with'drô) *vb.* **with·draw·ing, with·drew, with·drawn.** 1. to take or be taken away: *the commander withdrew his men from the battle.* 2. to leave: *I had to withdraw from the room while they discussed my case.* 3. to take back: *he withdrew his offer.*

with·er ('widhər) *vb.* to become less, die off, or shrivel up.

with·hold (with'hōld) *vb.* **with·hold·ing, with·held.** to keep (something) back; refuse to give: *Mr. Jones withheld his permission for his son to get married.*

with·stand (with'stand) *vb.* **with·stand·ing, with·stood.** to stand up to; refuse to give in under: *he can withstand a lot of pain.*

wit·ness ('witnis) *n.* a person who has seen or heard an event, esp. a crime or accident. —*vb.* to act as a witness to (something).

wives (wīvz) *n.* the plural of WIFE.

wiz·ard ('wizərd) *n.* 1. a man supposed to have magic powers. 2. someone who is very clever at something: *John is a wizard at model-making.*

woke (wōk) *vb.* the past tense of WAKE.

wo·ken ('wōkən) *vb.* the past participle of WAKE.

wolf (woolf) *n.,pl.* **wolves.** a large wild animal of the dog family living in cold regions and hunting in large groups called packs. —*vb.* to eat quickly: *don't wolf your food.*

won·der ('wundər) *vb.* 1. to be curious to know: *I wonder where my mother has gone.* 2. to be or feel amazed or surprised at something: *I wonder how you can be so silly.* —*n.* 1. something strange, unusual, or surprising. 2. a feeling of awe or admiration. '**won·der·ful** *adj.* excellent: *we had a wonderful time.*

wood (wood) *n.* 1. the hard, dense material that makes up most of a tree. 2. (often **woods**) a place where there are large numbers of trees. '**wood·en** *adj.* made of wood. '**wood·ed** *adj.* (of land) covered by trees.

wood·peck·er ('woodpekər) *n.* a bird with a strong pointed beak. It feeds on insects which it catches by hammering its beak into the tree trunks where they live.

woodpecker

wood·wind ('woodwind) *n.* any of a group of musical wind instruments originally made of wood, including FLUTEs, OBOEs, and CLARINETs.

wool (wool) *n.* the outer covering of soft curly hair on a sheep's body, spun into yarn and made into cloth. —'**wool·en** *adj.* —'**wool·ly** *adj.*

wore (wôr) *vb.* the past tense of WEAR.

work (wûrk) *n.* 1. something done or to be done, esp. as a job in return for wages. 2. a great effort: *running up the hill was hard work.* 3. a piece of writing, painting, or music: *Shakespeare's works.* —*vb.* 1. to do a job: *I work for the government.* 2. to make a great effort: *work hard and you will pass your test.* 3. to operate: *can you work the machine?*

world (wûrld) *n.* 1. the whole of the earth; our planet. 2. a part of this: *the western world.* 3. everyone on the earth: *the whole world knows his name.* 4. a field of activity or interest: *the business world.*

worm (wûrm) *n.* an animal having a long thin soft body and no legs. —*vb.* (esp. **worm one's way into**) to crawl or get into (something) unnoticed or by underhanded means.

worn (wôrn) *adj.* damaged through long use. —*vb.* the past participle of WEAR.

wor·ry ('wûrē, 'wurē) *vb.* **wor·ry·ing, wor·ried.** to be or cause to be anxious or distressed about (something). —*n.,pl.* **wor·ries.** something that makes a person worry.

worth (wûrth) *n.* value: *it costs a dollar but that is not its true worth.* —*prep.* 1. having the value of: *this painting is worth a lot of money.* 2. good enough for: *this party was certainly worth coming to.* —**worth·i·ness** ('wûrdhinis) *n.* —'**worth·y** *adj.* **worth·i·er, worth·i·est.**

wound[1] (wōōnd) *n.* an injury; cut or other hurt. —*vb.* to hurt; injure.

wound[2] (wound) *vb.* the past tense and past participle of WIND[2]

wove (wōv) *vb.* the past tense of WEAVE.

wo·ven ('wōvən) *vb.* the past participle of WEAVE.

wrap (rap) *vb.* **wrap·ping, wrapped.** 1. (often + *up*) to cover, pack, or enclose (something): *she wrapped the presents in paper.* 2. to place or wind (something) around another object.

wreath

wreath (rēth) *n.,pl.* **wreaths** (rēdhz). a bunch of leaves or flowers woven together to form a circle. **wreathe** (rēdh) *vb.* **wreath·ing, wreathed.** to bind or wrap round with or as if with a wreath: *fog wreathed the tree tops.*

wreck (rek) *vb.* to destroy or ruin, esp. to destroy a ship at sea. —*n.* something that is wrecked.

wrench (rench) *n.* 1. a sudden sharp strong twist. 2. a tool with an opening for loosening or tightening nuts and bolts. —*vb.* to give (something) a sudden sharp twist.

wres·tle ('resəl) *vb.* **wres·tling, wres·tled.** 1. to struggle with (an opponent) and try to force him to the ground. 2. to struggle with something. '**wres·tler** *n.* a person who takes part in the sport of wrestling.

wrig·gle ('rigəl) *vb.* **wrig·gling, wrig·gled.** to twist and turn like a snake or worm.

wring (ring) *vb.* **wring·ing, wrung.** 1. to remove (liquid) from something by twisting it. 2. to dry (something) by squeezing water out. 3. to get (information) from someone by using force. 4. to press and twist (the hands) together.

wrin·kle ('ringkəl) *vb.* **wrin·kling, wrin·kled.** to form or cause to form creases: *her face wrinkled into a smile.* —*n.* a small fold or crease in a surface: *the old lady's face is full of wrinkles.*

wrist (rist) *n.* the joint between the arm and the hand.

wrist·watch ('rist wach) *n., pl.* **wrist·watch·es.** a WATCH (*n.* def. 4) that is attached to a strap made of leather, metal, plastic, etc., and worn around the wrist.

write (rīt) *vb.* **writ·ing, wrote, writ·ten.** 1. to form letters, words, or other marks on paper. 2. to send a letter to someone. 3. to put down (stories, articles, etc.) on paper. '**writ·er** *n.* a person who writes books stories, articles, etc.

writhe (rīdh) *vb.* **writh·ing, writhed.** to twist or turn: *he was writhing in pain.*

wrong (rông, rong) *adj.* 1. not right; not true, correct, morally good, or suitable. 2. out of order: *something is wrong with my car.*

wrote (rōt) *vb.* the past tense of WRITE.

wrought (rôt) *adj.* 1. produced or formed; made. 2. produced by beating with a hammer: *wrought iron.*

XYZ

xe·non (zē'non) *n.* a rare gas, which makes up a tiny proportion of air. Chemical symbol: Xe.

xe·ro·phyte (zē'rəfit) *n.* a plant that grows in dry conditions.

Xerox (zēr'oks) *n.* a trade name for a machine that copies documents without touching the originals.

Xmas ('eksməs) *n.* a short way of writing CHRISTMAS.

x-ray ('eksrā) *n.* 1. an apparatus that uses a special type of ray that can pass through substances that ordinary light rays cannot. 2. a photograph taken with this apparatus: *the x-ray of her arm showed a small break in the bone.* —*vb.* to take a photograph of (a person, part of the body, etc.) using x-rays.

xylophone

xy·lo·phone ('zīləfōn) *n.* a musical instrument that is made of a row or rows of wooden bars of different lengths on a frame. The player hits these bars with wooden hammers to make a tune.

yacht

yacht (yot) *n.* 1. a ship, usu. with space on board for people to eat and sleep, used for pleasure cruising. 2. a small light sailing vessel for racing, pleasure sailing, etc.

yak (yak) *n.* a long-haired ox found in central Asia. Tame yaks are used to carry loads and also for their milk and meat.

yard[1] (yârd) *n.* 1. a unit of length 3 feet or 36 inches long. 2. a rod fixed to a ship's mast and used to support a sail.

yard[2] (yârd) *n.* a small enclosed area of ground near or around buildings.

yarn (yârn) *n.* 1. a thread, esp. a woolen thread, prepared for weaving or knitting. 2. (informal) a story.

yawn (yôn) *vb.* 1. to open the mouth wide and draw in breath involuntarily because one is sleepy or bored. 2. to be wide open: *the pit yawned in front of them.* —*n.* the act of yawning.

year (yēr) *n.* the period of time that it takes the earth to revolve once around the sun; 365¹/₄ days.

yeast (yēst) *n.* a substance made of tiny FUNGUS plants and used in making bread, brewing beer, etc.

yew

yew (yo͞o) *n.* an evergreen tree with small dark leaves and red berries.

yield (yēld) *vb.* 1. to produce or give forth: *the orchard yields a heavy crop* *of apples.* 2. to give way, esp. as a result of pressure or force: *the door yielded to their push.* —*n.* the amount produced: *the farm's yield of wheat has improved this year.*

yo·del ('yōdəl) *vb.* to sing or shout in a musical way, in the manner of Swiss mountain-dwellers, making one's voice travel over a great distance. —*n.* a yodeled song or cry.

yo·ga ('yōgə) *n.* a religious practice that originated in India and involving breathing control, body postures, and mental training.

yo·gi ('yōgi) *n.* a person who practices yoga.

yo·gurt ('yōgərt) *n.* clotted liquid food made from sour milk and often flavored with fruit or other flavoring.

yoke (yōk) *n.* 1. a wooden frame placed across the necks of oxen or other working animals. 2. a pair of animals joined together by a yoke. 3. the part of a dress, coat, shirt, etc., that fits across the shoulders. —*vb.* **yok·ing, yoked.** to put (animals) in a yoke.

yolk (yōk) *n.* the yellow part of an egg.

young (yuñg) *adj.* **young·er** ('yuñggər), **young·est** ('yuñggist). not old; having existed for only a short time. —*n.* young offspring.

youth (yo͞oth) *n.,pl.* **youths** (yo͞oths, yo͞odhz). 1. the condition of being young. 2. the time of life between being a child and being grown up. 3. a young man. —'**youth·ful** *adj.*

yo-yo ('yōyō) *n.,pl.* **yo-yos.** (trademark) a toy made of two disks held together by a pin with a string wound around it so that it runs up and down the string when released.

zeal (zēl) *n.* enthusiasm.

zeal·ot ('zelət) *n.* a person who shows great enthusiasm for a religion, a cause, etc. **zeal·ous** ('zeləs) *adj.* full of enthusiasm.

ze·bra ('zēbrə) *n.* a wild animal from Africa that looks like a donkey but has a black and white striped skin.

ze·ro ('zērō) *n.,pl.* **ze·ros.** 1. the figure 0; nought. 2. the point between + and - on a scale, e.g. that of a thermometer, from which something is measured: *the temperature was eight degrees below zero.*

zest (zest) *n.* enthusiasm, pleasure and interest: *he worked with zest at his model railway.*

zig·zag ('zigzag) *n.* a pattern, line, path, etc., that goes in a series of short sharp turns from one side to another. —*vb.* **zig·zag·ging, zig·zagged.** to move in a zigzag: *lightning zigzagged across the sky.*

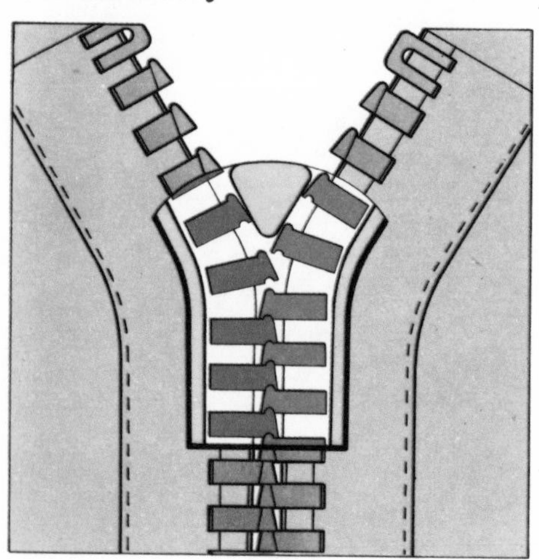

zip

zoo

zinc (ziñgk) *n.* a grayish white metallic chemical element used in electric batteries and for coating steel used in roofing, buckets, etc. Chemical symbol: Zn.

zip·per ('zipər) *n.* a device made of two rows of interlocking metal or plastic teeth, used for fastening clothes, suitcases, etc. —*vb.* **zip, zip·ping, zipped.** (often + *up*) to close (something) with a zipper.

zir·con ('zurkon) *n.* a mineral that occurs in various colors. Transparent varieties are used in jewelry.

zo·di·ac ('zōdēak) *n.* an area of the night sky divided on an imaginary plan into twelve parts known as the signs of the zodiac.

zone (zōn) *n.* 1. one of the five regions of the earth's surface, called after the type of climate found there, e.g. the arctic zone. 2. any region or area that has some special quality, feature, or purpose: *there is a new factory zone in our town.*

zoo (zo͞o) *n.* a park or area where animals are exhibited to the public and rare species are bred.

zo·ol·ogy (zō'oləjē) *n.* the scientific study of animals. —**zo·o·log·i·cal** (zōə'lojikəl) *adj.* —**zo'ol·o·gist** *n.*

zoom (zo͞om) *vb.* to move suddenly and at speed, often noisily: *the motorcyclist zoomed past the cars.*

zy·gote ('zīgōt) *n.* a fertilized egg cell.